CW00525372

Peugeot 407
Owners Workshop Manual

Peter T. Gill

Models covered

Peugeot 407 Saloon & Estate (SW) with 1.6 litre (1560cc) & 2.0 litre (1997cc) turbo-diesel engines

Also covers most features of Coupe
Does NOT cover 2.2, 2.7 or 3.0 litre diesel engines, petrol models or 'Bioflex' models

(5550 - 352 - 6AT1)

© Haynes Publishing 2014

ABCDE
FGHIJ
KLMNO
PQR

A book in the **Haynes Owners Workshop Manual Series**

All rights reserved. No part of this book may be reproduced or transmitted in any form or by any means, electronic or mechanical, including photocopying, recording or by any information storage or retrieval system, without permission in writing from the copyright holder.

ISBN **978 0 85733 982 9**

British Library Cataloguing in Publication Data
A catalogue record for this book is available from the British Library.

Printed in the USA

Haynes Publishing
Sparkford, Yeovil, Somerset BA22 7JJ, England

Haynes North America, Inc
861 Lawrence Drive, Newbury Park, California 91320, USA

Haynes Publishing Nordiska AB
Box 1504, 751 45 UPPSALA, Sverige

Contents

Illegal Copying

It is the policy of Haynes Publishing to actively protect its Copyrights and Trade Marks. Legal action will be taken against anyone who unlawfully copies the cover or contents of this Manual. This includes all forms of unauthorised copying including digital, mechanical, and electronic in any form. Authorisation from Haynes Publishing will only be provided expressly and in writing. Illegal copying will also be reported to the appropriate statutory authorities.

Contents

REPAIRS AND OVERHAUL

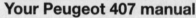

The Peugeot 407 was introduced into the UK in February 2004. At its launch, the 407 was offered with a choice of 1.8 litre, 2.0 litre, 2.2 litre and 3.0 litre petrol engines, or 1.6 litre and 2.0 litre turbo-diesel engines. It was available in two body styles – saloon or estate (SW), and in October 2005 the coupe model was released.

The engines fitted to the 407 range are all versions of the well-proven units which have appeared in many Peugeot/Citroën vehicles over the years, including the 1.6 litre HDi engine, which was developed in a joint venture with the Ford Motor Co.

The engine is mounted transversely at the front of vehicle, with the transmission mounted on its left-hand end. All engines are fitted with a manual transmission as standard (an automatic transmission is available on certain engines).

The front suspension is fitted with double wishbones, with a drop-linked alloy support for the hub carrier and incorporating shock absorbers, coil springs and an anti-roll bar. The rear suspension is a 5-point multi-link suspension with anti-roll bar and shock absorbers, which are angled to enhance stability.

A wide range of standard and optional equipment is available within the range to suit most tastes, including central locking, electric windows and front, side and curtain airbags. An air conditioning system is available on all models.

Provided that regular servicing is carried out in accordance with the manufacturer's recommendations, the vehicle should prove reliable and very economical. The engine compartment is well designed, and most of the items requiring frequent attention are easily accessible.

Your Peugeot 407 manual

The aim of this manual is to help you get the best value from your vehicle. It can do so in several ways. It can help you decide what work must be done (even should you choose to get it done by a garage). It will also provide information on routine maintenance and servicing, and give a logical course of action and diagnosis when random faults occur. However, it is hoped that you will use the manual by tackling the work yourself. On simpler jobs it may even be quicker than booking the car into a garage and going there twice, to leave and collect it. Perhaps most important, a lot of money can be saved by avoiding the costs a garage must charge to cover its labour and overheads.

The manual has drawings and descriptions to show the function of the various components so that their layout can be understood. Tasks are described and photographed in a clear step-by-step sequence.

References to the 'left' and 'right' of the vehicle are in the sense of a person in the driver's seat facing forward.

Acknowledgements

Thanks are due to Draper tools Limited, who provided some of the workshop tools, and to all those people at Sparkford who helped in the production of this manual.

We take great pride in the accuracy of information given in this manual, but vehicle manufacturers make alterations and design changes during the production run of a particular vehicle of which they do not inform us. No liability can be accepted by the authors or publishers for loss, damage or injury caused by any errors in, or omissions from, the information given.

Working on your car can be dangerous. This page shows just some of the potential risks and hazards, with the aim of creating a safety-conscious attitude.

General hazards

Scalding

• Don't remove the radiator or expansion tank cap while the engine is hot.
• Engine oil, transmission fluid or power steering fluid may also be dangerously hot if the engine has recently been running.

Burning

• Beware of burns from the exhaust system and from any part of the engine. Brake discs and drums can also be extremely hot immediately after use.

Crushing

• When working under or near a raised vehicle, always supplement the jack with axle stands, or use drive-on ramps.
Never venture under a car which is only supported by a jack.

• Take care if loosening or tightening high-torque nuts when the vehicle is on stands. Initial loosening and final tightening should be done with the wheels on the ground.

Fire

• Fuel is highly flammable; fuel vapour is explosive.
• Don't let fuel spill onto a hot engine.
• Do not smoke or allow naked lights (including pilot lights) anywhere near a vehicle being worked on. Also beware of creating sparks (electrically or by use of tools).
• Fuel vapour is heavier than air, so don't work on the fuel system with the vehicle over an inspection pit.
• Another cause of fire is an electrical overload or short-circuit. Take care when repairing or modifying the vehicle wiring.
• Keep a fire extinguisher handy, of a type suitable for use on fuel and electrical fires.

Electric shock

• Ignition HT and Xenon headlight voltages can be dangerous, especially to people with heart problems or a pacemaker. Don't work on or near these systems with the engine running or the ignition switched on.

• Mains voltage is also dangerous. Make sure that any mains-operated equipment is correctly earthed. Mains power points should be protected by a residual current device (RCD) circuit breaker.

Fume or gas intoxication

• Exhaust fumes are poisonous; they can contain carbon monoxide, which is rapidly fatal if inhaled. Never run the engine in a confined space such as a garage with the doors shut.

• Fuel vapour is also poisonous, as are the vapours from some cleaning solvents and paint thinners.

Poisonous or irritant substances

• Avoid skin contact with battery acid and with any fuel, fluid or lubricant, especially antifreeze, brake hydraulic fluid and Diesel fuel. Don't syphon them by mouth. If such a substance is swallowed or gets into the eyes, seek medical advice.
• Prolonged contact with used engine oil can cause skin cancer. Wear gloves or use a barrier cream if necessary. Change out of oil-soaked clothes and do not keep oily rags in your pocket.
• Air conditioning refrigerant forms a poisonous gas if exposed to a naked flame (including a cigarette). It can also cause skin burns on contact.

Asbestos

• Asbestos dust can cause cancer if inhaled or swallowed. Asbestos may be found in gaskets and in brake and clutch linings. When dealing with such components it is safest to assume that they contain asbestos.

Special hazards

Hydrofluoric acid

• This extremely corrosive acid is formed when certain types of synthetic rubber, found in some O-rings, oil seals, fuel hoses etc, are exposed to temperatures above 4000C. The rubber changes into a charred or sticky substance containing the acid. *Once formed, the acid remains dangerous for years. If it gets onto the skin, it may be necessary to amputate the limb concerned.*
• When dealing with a vehicle which has suffered a fire, or with components salvaged from such a vehicle, wear protective gloves and discard them after use.

The battery

• Batteries contain sulphuric acid, which attacks clothing, eyes and skin. Take care when topping-up or carrying the battery.
• The hydrogen gas given off by the battery is highly explosive. Never cause a spark or allow a naked light nearby. Be careful when connecting and disconnecting battery chargers or jump leads.

Air bags

• Air bags can cause injury if they go off accidentally. Take care when removing the steering wheel and trim panels. Special storage instructions may apply.

Diesel injection equipment

• Diesel injection pumps supply fuel at very high pressure. Take care when working on the fuel injectors and fuel pipes.

 Warning: Never expose the hands, face or any other part of the body to injector spray; the fuel can penetrate the skin with potentially fatal results.

Remember...

DO

• Do use eye protection when using power tools, and when working under the vehicle.

• Do wear gloves or use barrier cream to protect your hands when necessary.

• Do get someone to check periodically that all is well when working alone on the vehicle.

• Do keep loose clothing and long hair well out of the way of moving mechanical parts.

• Do remove rings, wristwatch etc, before working on the vehicle – especially the electrical system.

• Do ensure that any lifting or jacking equipment has a safe working load rating adequate for the job.

DON'T

• Don't attempt to lift a heavy component which may be beyond your capability – get assistance.

• Don't rush to finish a job, or take unverified short cuts.

• Don't use ill-fitting tools which may slip and cause injury.

• Don't leave tools or parts lying around where someone can trip over them. Mop up oil and fuel spills at once.

• Don't allow children or pets to play in or near a vehicle being worked on.

The following pages are intended to help in dealing with common roadside emergencies and breakdowns. You will find more detailed fault finding information at the back of the manual, and repair information in the main chapters.

If your car won't start and the starter motor doesn't turn

☐ If it's a model with automatic transmission, make sure the selector is in the P or N position.
☐ Open the bonnet and make sure that the battery terminals are clean and tight.
☐ Switch on the headlights and try to start the engine. If the headlights go very dim when you're trying to start, the battery is probably flat. Try jump starting (see next page) using another car.

If your car won't start even though the starter motor turns as normal

☐ Is there fuel in the tank?
☐ Is there moisture on electrical components under the bonnet? Switch off the ignition, and then wipe off any obvious dampness with a dry cloth. Spray a water-repellent aerosol product (WD-40 or equivalent) on fuel system electrical connectors like those shown in the photos.

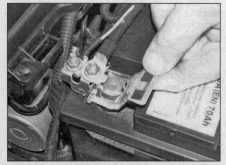

A Remove the plastic cover and check the condition and security of the battery connections.

B Check that the fuel system wiring connectors are securely connected.

C Check that the alternator wiring connectors are securely connected.

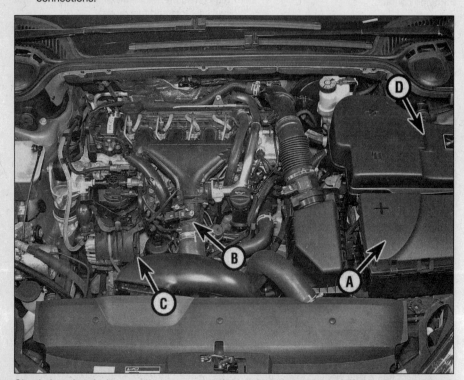

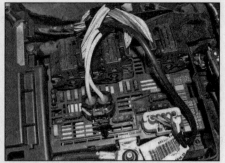

D Check that all fuses are still in good condition and none have blown.

Check that electrical connections are secure (with the ignition switched off) and spray them with a water dispersant spray like WD-40 if you suspect a problem due to damp.

Jump starting

HAYNES HiNT *Jump starting will get you out of trouble, but you must correct whatever made the battery go flat in the first place. There are three possibilities:*

1 *The battery has been drained by repeated attempts to start, or by leaving the lights on.*

2 *The charging system is not working properly (alternator drivebelt slack or broken, alternator wiring fault or alternator itself faulty).*

3 *The battery itself is at fault (electrolyte low, or battery worn out).*

When jump-starting a car, observe the following precautions:

✓ Before connecting the booster battery, make sure that the ignition is switched off.

Caution: Remove the key in case the central locking engages when the jump leads are connected

✓ Ensure that all electrical equipment (lights, heater, wipers, etc) is switched off.

✓ Take note of any special precautions printed on the battery case.

✓ Make sure that the booster battery is the same voltage as the discharged one in the vehicle.

✓ If the battery is being jump-started from the battery in another vehicle, the two vehicles MUST NOT TOUCH each other.

✓ Make sure that the transmission is in neutral (or PARK, in the case of automatic transmission).

HAYNES HiNT *Budget jump leads can be a false economy, as they often do not pass enough current to start large capacity or diesel engines. They can also get hot.*

1 Connect one end of the red jump lead to the positive (+) terminal of the flat battery

2 Connect the other end of the red lead to the positive (+) terminal of the booster battery.

3 Connect one end of the black jump lead to the negative (-) terminal of the booster battery

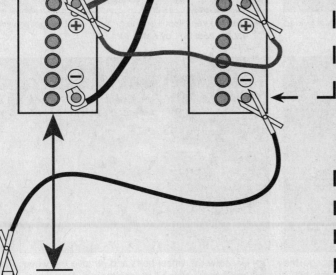

4 Connect the other end of the black jump lead to a bolt or bracket on the engine block, well away from the battery, on the vehicle to be started.

5 Make sure that the jump leads will not come into contact with the fan, drive-belts or other moving parts of the engine.

6 Start the engine using the booster battery and run it at idle speed. Switch on the lights, rear window demister and heater blower motor, then disconnect the jump leads in the reverse order of connection. Turn off the lights etc.

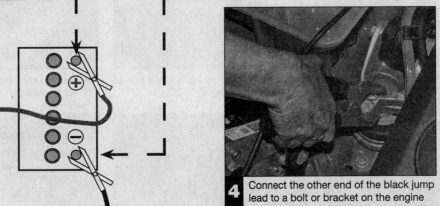

Wheel changing

⚠️ **Warning: Do not change a wheel in a situation where you risk being hit by another vehicle. On busy roads, try to stop in a lay-by or a gateway. Be wary of passing traffic while changing the wheel – it is easy to become distracted by the job in hand.**

Preparation

☐ When a puncture occurs, stop as soon as it is safe to do so.

☐ Park on firm level ground, if possible, and well out of the way of other traffic.

☐ Use hazard warning lights if necessary.

☐ If you have one, use a warning triangle to alert other drivers of your presence.

☐ Apply the handbrake and engage first or reverse gear (or Park on models with automatic transmission).

☐ If the ground is soft, use a flat piece of wood to spread the load under the foot of the jack.

Changing the wheel

1 The spare wheel and tools are stored in the luggage compartment, lift up the floor panel/carpet. Release the retaining strap and remove the tool kit and jack from the centre of the spare wheel. Remove the spare wheel.

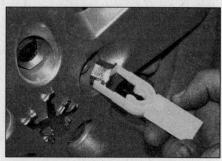

2 On models with steel wheels, remove the wheel trim/hub cap. On models with alloy wheels remove the plastic cover using the yellow plastic tool in the tool kit . . .

3 . . . then unscrew the anti-theft bolt using the special tool provided – normally stored in the passenger glovebox or toolkit.

4 With the vehicle still on the ground, use the tool provided to slacken each wheel bolt by half a turn.

5 Make sure the jack is located on firm ground, and engage the jack head correctly with the sill. Then raise the jack until the wheel is raised clear of the ground. Use a stone to chock the wheel diagonally opposite the wheel to be removed to prevent the car from rolling.

6 Unscrew the wheel bolts and remove the wheel. Place the wheel under the vehicle sill in case the jack fails.

7 Fit the spare wheel and screw in the bolts. Lightly tighten the bolts with the wheel brace then lower the car to the ground.

8 Securely tighten the wheel bolts in a diagonal sequence then refit the wheel trim/hub cap/wheel bolt covers (as applicable). Stow the punctured wheel and tools back in the boot, and secure them in position.

Finally . . .

☐ Remove the wheel chock.

☐ Check the tyre pressure on the wheel just fitted. If it is low, or if you don't have a pressure gauge with you, drive slowly to the next garage and inflate the tyre to the correct pressure.

☐ On models with a space-saver spare wheel, a higher pressure is given for the spare tyre and note that this spare is for temporary use only; whilst the spare is fitted, the vehicle should not be driven at speeds in excess of 50 mph.

☐ The wheel bolts should be slackened and retightened to the specified torque at the earliest possible opportunity (see Chapter 1).

☐ Have the damaged tyre or wheel repaired as soon as possible, or another puncture will leave you stranded.

Towing

When all else fails, you may find yourself having to get a tow home – or of course you may be helping somebody else. Long-distance recovery should only be done by a garage or breakdown service. For shorter distances, DIY towing using another car is easy enough, but observe the following points:

☐ Use a proper tow-rope – they are not expensive. The vehicle being towed must display an ON TOW sign in its rear window.

☐ The towing eye is kept inside the spare wheel (see *Wheel changing*). To fit the eye, unclip the access cover from the relevant bumper and screw the eye firmly into position **(see illustrations)**.

☐ Always turn the ignition key to the 'on' position when the vehicle is being towed, so that the steering lock is released, and that the direction indicator and brake lights work.

☐ Before being towed, release the handbrake and select neutral on the transmission.

Caution: On models with automatic transmission, do not tow the car at speeds in excess of 30 mph or for a distance greater than 30 miles. If towing speeds/ distances are to exceed these limits, then the car must be towed with its front wheels off the ground.

☐ Note that greater-than-usual pedal pressure will be required to operate the brakes, since the vacuum servo unit is only operational with the engine running.

☐ The driver of the car being towed must keep the tow-rope taut at all times to avoid snatching.

☐ Make sure that both drivers know the route before setting off.

☐ Only drive at moderate speeds and keep the distance towed to a minimum. Drive smoothly and allow plenty of time for slowing down at junctions.

Unclip the cover from the rear bumper . . .

. . . then use the wheel brace to screw the towing eye in securely

Use the towing eye to unclip the cover in the front bumper . . .

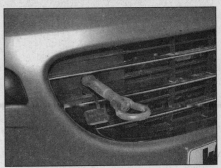

. . . and then screw the towing eye firmly into position

Identifying leaks

Puddles on the garage floor or drive, or obvious wetness under the bonnet or underneath the car, suggest a leak that needs investigating. It can sometimes be difficult to decide where the leak is coming from, especially if an engine undershield is fitted. Leaking oil or fluid can also be blown rearwards by the passage of air under the car, giving a false impression of where the problem lies.

 Warning: Most automotive oils and fluids are poisonous. Wash them off skin, and change out of contaminated clothing, without delay.

 The smell of a fluid leaking from the car may provide a clue to what's leaking. Some fluids are distinctively coloured. It may help to remove the engine undershield, clean the car carefully and to park it over some clean paper overnight as an aid to locating the source of the leak. Remember that some leaks may only occur while the engine is running.

Sump oil

Engine oil may leak from the drain plug...

Oil from filter

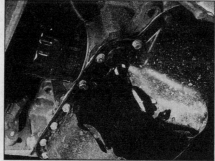

...or from the base of the oil filter.

Gearbox oil

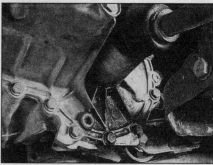

Gearbox oil can leak from the seals at the inboard ends of the driveshafts.

Antifreeze

Leaking antifreeze often leaves a crystalline deposit like this.

Brake fluid

A leak occurring at a wheel is almost certainly brake fluid.

Power steering fluid

Power steering fluid may leak from the pipe connectors on the steering rack.

Introduction

There are some very simple checks which need only take a few minutes to carry out, but which could save you a lot of inconvenience and expense.

These *Weekly checks* require no great skill or special tools, and the small amount of time they take to perform could prove to be very well spent, for example:

☐ Keeping an eye on tyre condition and pressures, will not only help to stop them wearing out prematurely, but could also save your life.

☐ Many breakdowns are caused by electrical problems. Battery-related faults are particularly common, and a quick check on a regular basis will often prevent the majority of these.

☐ If your car develops a brake fluid leak, the first time you might know about it is when your brakes don't work properly. Checking the level regularly will give advance warning of this kind of problem.

☐ If the oil or coolant levels run low, the cost of repairing any engine damage will be far greater than fixing the leak, for example.

Underbonnet check points

◄ 1.6 litre engine

A *Engine oil level dipstick*

B *Engine oil filler cap*

C *Coolant expansion tank*

D *Brake (and clutch) fluid reservoir*

E *Screen washer fluid reservoir*

F *Power steering fluid reservoir*

G *Battery*

◄2.0 litre engine

A *Engine oil level dipstick*

B *Engine oil filler cap*

C *Coolant expansion tank*

D *Brake (and clutch) fluid reservoir*

E *Screen washer fluid reservoir*

F *Power steering fluid reservoir*

G *Battery*

Engine oil level

Before you start

✔ Make sure that your car is on level ground.
✔ Check the oil level before the car is driven, or at least 5 minutes after the engine has been switched off.

The correct oil

Modern engines place great demands on their oil. It is very important that the correct oil for your car is used (see *Lubricants and fluids*).

Car care

● If you have to add oil frequently, you should check whether you have any oil leaks. Place some clean paper under the car overnight, and check for stains in the morning. If there are no leaks, the engine may be burning oil.
● Always maintain the level between the upper and lower dipstick marks (see photo 2). If the level is too low severe engine damage may occur. Oil seal failure may result if the engine is overfilled by adding too much oil.

1 The dipstick is located at the front of the engine on 1.6 litre engines and next to the oil filler cap on 2.0 litre engines (see *Underbonnet check points*). The dipstick is often brightly-coloured or has a picture of an oil can on the top for identification. Withdraw the dipstick, and wipe it clean.

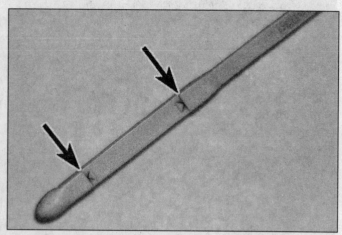

2 Insert the clean dipstick into the tube as far as it will go, then withdraw it again. Note the oil level on the end of the dipstick, which should be between the upper (MAX) mark and lower (MIN) mark.

3 Oil is added through the filler cap on top of the engine. Unscrew the cap and top-up the level; a funnel may help to reduce spillage.

4 Add the oil slowly, checking the level on the dipstick often. Don't overfill (see *Car care*). Approximately 1.5 litre of oil will raise the level from the lower mark to the upper mark.

Coolant level

 Warning: *DO NOT attempt to remove the expansion tank pressure cap when the engine is hot, as there is a very great risk of scalding. Do not leave open containers of coolant about, as it is poisonous.*

Car care

● Adding coolant should not be necessary on a regular basis. If frequent topping-up is required, it is likely there is a leak. Check the radiator, all hoses and joint faces for signs of staining or wetness, and rectify as necessary.

● It is important that antifreeze is used in the cooling system all year round, not just during the winter months. Don't top-up with water alone, as the antifreeze will become too diluted.

1 The coolant level must be checked with the engine cold. Remove the pressure cap (see *Warning*) from the expansion tank, which is located on the right-hand side of the engine compartment.

2 The coolant level should be between the MAX and MIN marks on the expansion tank.

3 If topping-up is necessary, add a mixture of water and antifreeze to the expansion tank until the coolant level is between the level marks. Once the level is correct, securely refit the cap.

Brake and clutch fluid level

 Warning: *Brake fluid can harm your eyes and damage painted surfaces, so use extreme caution when handling and pouring it. Do not use fluid that has been standing open for some time, as it absorbs moisture from the air, which can cause a dangerous loss of braking effectiveness.*

Before you start

✔ Make sure that your car is on level ground.
✔ Cleanliness is of great importance when dealing with the braking system, so take care to clean around the reservoir cap before topping-up. Use only clean brake fluid.

Safety first!

● If the reservoir requires repeated topping-up this is an indication of a fluid leak somewhere in the system, which should be investigated immediately.
● If a leak is suspected, the car should not be driven until the braking system has been checked. Never take any risks where brakes are concerned.

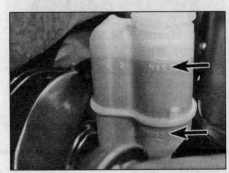

1 The upper (MAX) and lower (DANGER) fluid level marking are on the side of the reservoir, which is located in the left-hand rear corner of the engine compartment.

2 If topping-up is necessary, first wipe clean the area around the filler cap with a clean cloth, and then unscrew the cap from the top of the reservoir.

3 Carefully add fluid, avoiding spilling it on the surrounding paintwork. Use only the specified hydraulic fluid. After filling to the correct level, refit the cap and diaphragm and tighten it securely. Wipe off any spilt fluid.

Tyre condition and pressure

It is very important that tyres are in good condition, and at the correct pressure - having a tyre failure at any speed is highly dangerous. Tyre wear is influenced by driving style - harsh braking and acceleration, or fast cornering, will all produce more rapid tyre wear. As a general rule, the front tyres wear out faster than the rears. Interchanging the tyres from front to rear ("rotating" the tyres) may result in more even wear. However, if this is completely effective, you may have the expense of replacing all four tyres at once! Remove any nails or stones embedded in the tread before they penetrate the tyre to cause deflation. If removal of a nail does reveal that the tyre has been punctured, refit the nail so that its point of penetration is marked. Then immediately change the wheel, and have the tyre repaired by a tyre dealer.

Regularly check the tyres for damage in the form of cuts or bulges, especially in the sidewalls. Periodically remove the wheels, and clean any dirt or mud from the inside and outside surfaces. Examine the wheel rims for signs of rusting, corrosion or other damage. Light alloy wheels are easily damaged by "kerbing" whilst parking; steel wheels may also become dented or buckled. A new wheel is very often the only way to overcome severe damage.

New tyres should be balanced when they are fitted, but it may become necessary to re-balance them as they wear, or if the balance weights fitted to the wheel rim should fall off. Unbalanced tyres will wear more quickly, as will the steering and suspension components. Wheel imbalance is normally signified by vibration, particularly at a certain speed (typically around 50 mph). If this vibration is felt only through the steering, then it is likely that just the front wheels need balancing. If, however, the vibration is felt through the whole car, the rear wheels could be out of balance. Wheel balancing should be carried out by a tyre dealer or garage.

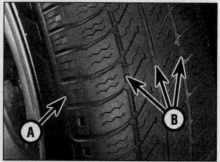

1 Tread Depth - visual check
The original tyres have tread wear safety bands (B), which will appear when the tread depth reaches approximately 1.6 mm. The band positions are indicated by a triangular mark on the tyre sidewall (A).

2 Tread Depth - manual check
Alternatively, tread wear can be monitored with a simple, inexpensive device known as a tread depth indicator gauge.

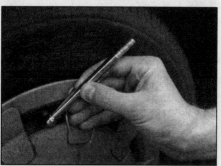

3 Tyre Pressure Check
Check the tyre pressures regularly with the tyres cold. Do not adjust the tyre pressures immediately after the vehicle has been used, or an inaccurate setting will result.

Tyre tread wear patterns

Shoulder Wear

Underinflation (wear on both sides)
Under-inflation will cause overheating of the tyre, because the tyre will flex too much, and the tread will not sit correctly on the road surface. This will cause a loss of grip and excessive wear, not to mention the danger of sudden tyre failure due to heat build-up.
Check and adjust pressures
Incorrect wheel camber (wear on one side)
Repair or renew suspension parts
Hard cornering
Reduce speed!

Centre Wear

Overinflation
Over-inflation will cause rapid wear of the centre part of the tyre tread, coupled with reduced grip, harsher ride, and the danger of shock damage occurring in the tyre casing.
Check and adjust pressures

If you sometimes have to inflate your car's tyres to the higher pressures specified for maximum load or sustained high speed, don't forget to reduce the pressures to normal afterwards.

Uneven Wear

Front tyres may wear unevenly as a result of wheel misalignment. Most tyre dealers and garages can check and adjust the wheel alignment (or "tracking") for a modest charge.
Incorrect camber or castor
Repair or renew suspension parts
Malfunctioning suspension
Repair or renew suspension parts
Unbalanced wheel
Balance tyres
Incorrect toe setting
Adjust front wheel alignment
Note: *The feathered edge of the tread which typifies toe wear is best checked by feel.*

Power steering fluid level

Before you start
✔ Park the vehicle on level ground.
✔ Set the steering wheel straight-ahead.
✔ The engine should be cold and turned off.

Safety first!
● The need for frequent topping-up indicates a leak, which should be investigated immediately.

1 The fluid reservoir is on the right-hand side of the engine compartment. On 1.6 litre models, it is a traditional system with the power steering pump being driven by the auxiliary belt. Clean the area around the reservoir cap before removal.

2 On 2.0 litre models, the fluid reservoir is also on the right-hand side of the engine compartment. It is an electrohydraulic system, where there is an electric motor attached to the side of the power steering reservoir. Clean the area around the reservoir cap before removal.

3 On 1.6 litre models remove the reservoir cap and check the level (arrowed) inside the fluid reservoir neck.

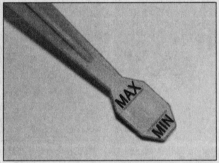

4 On 2.0 litre models, check the markings on the dipstick. Unscrew the reservoir cap, and check the fluid level is up to the upper (MAX) level indicator.

5 Top-up the reservoir with the specified type of the fluid, using a funnel, if necessary. Once the level is between the level marks, securely refit the reservoir cap. Do not overfill the reservoir.

Screen washer fluid level

● Screenwash additives not only keep the windscreen clean during foul weather, they also prevent the washer system freezing in cold weather – which is when you are likely to need it most. Don't top-up using plain water as the screenwash will become too diluted, and will freeze during cold weather.

 Warning: On no account use coolant antifreeze in the washer system – this could discolour or damage paintwork.

1 The washer fluid reservoir is located in the right-hand front corner of the engine compartment. To check the fluid level, open the cap and look down the filler neck.

2 If topping-up is necessary, add water and a screenwash additive in the quantities recommended on the bottle.

Battery

Caution: Before carrying out any work on the vehicle battery, read the precautions given in 'Safety first!' at the start of this manual.

✔ Make sure that the battery tray is in good condition, and that the clamp is tight. Corrosion on the tray, retaining clamp and the battery itself can be removed with a solution of water and baking soda. Thoroughly rinse all cleaned areas with water. Any metal parts damaged by corrosion should be covered with a zinc-based primer, and then painted.

✔ Periodically (approximately every three months), check the charge condition of the battery, as described in Chapter 5A.

✔ If the battery is flat, and you need to jump start your vehicle, see *Jump starting*.

Battery corrosion can be kept to a minimum by applying a layer of petroleum jelly to the clamps and terminals after they are reconnected.

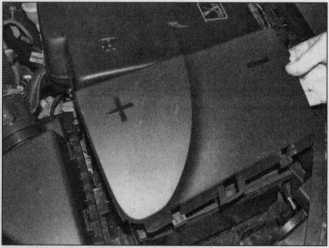

1 Lift the plastic cover to gain access to the battery positive terminal, which is located on the left-hand side of the engine compartment. The exterior of the battery should be inspected periodically for damage such as a cracked case or cover.

2 Check the battery lead clamps for tightness to ensure good electrical connections, and check the leads for signs of damage.

3 If corrosion (white, fluffy deposits) is evident, remove the cables from the battery terminals, clean them with a small wire brush, then refit them. Automotive stores sell a tool for cleaning the battery post . . .

4 . . . as well as the battery cable clamps.

Bulbs and fuses

✔ Check all external lights and the horn. Refer to the appropriate Sections of Chapter 12 for details if any of the circuits are found to be inoperative.
✔ Visually check all accessible wiring connectors, harnesses and retaining clips for security, and for signs of chafing or damage.

 HAYNES HiNT *If you need to check your brake lights and indicators unaided, back up to a wall or garage door and operate the lights. The reflected light should show if they are working properly.*

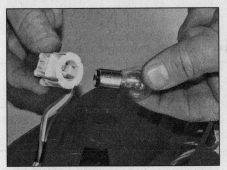

1 If a single indicator light, brake light, sidelight or headlight has failed, it is likely that a bulb has blown, and will need to be renewed. Refer to Chapter 12 for details. If both brake lights have failed, it is possible that the switch has failed (see Chapter 9).

2 If more than one indicator or tail light has failed, it is likely that either a fuse has blown or that there is a fault in the circuit. Fuses are located behind a cover in the glovebox. Open the glovebox, release the upper clips and remove the cover.

3 Spare fuses are located in the fusebox cover, along with a pair of tweezers for removal of fuses. Additional fuses and relays are located in the left-hand side of the engine compartment fusebox (see *If your car won't start* at the beginning of this Chapter).

4 To renew a blown fuse, simply pull it out, using the tweezers provided, and then fit a new fuse of the correct rating (see Chapter 12). If the fuse blows again, it is important that you find out why – a complete checking procedure is given in Chapter 12.

Wiper blades

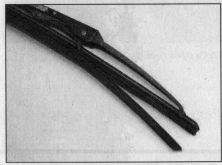

1 Check the condition of the wiper blades: if they are cracked or show signs of deterioration, or if the glass swept area is smeared, renew them. For maximum clarity of vision, wiper blades should be renewed annually.

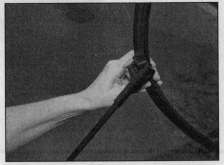

2 To remove a windscreen wiper blade, turn the ignition on, then turn the ignition off and press the wiper switch stalk down once. This places the arms in the 'service' position. Lift the wiper arm and twist the blade at 90° degrees to the arm.

3 Pull the wiper blade and release it from the end of the arm, taking care not to allow the arm to spring back and damage the windscreen. When wiper blade has been refitted, return the blades to the park position by pressing the wiper switch stalk again.

Lubricants and fluids

Engine . . . . Fully-synthetic multigrade engine oil 5W30 to 10W40 to ACEA B3 or API CFB3 specification
Esso Ultron diesel or Total Activa/Quartz 9000

Cooling system . . . . Glysantin G33 or Revkogel 2000

Manual transmission . . . . Esso 75W80 EZL 848 or Total 75W80 H 6965

Automatic transmission

  AL4 transmission. . . . . Esso LT 71141 Automatic Transmission Fluid

  AM6 transmission . . . . Esso JWS 3309 Automatic Transmission Fluid

Braking and clutch system . . . . Hydraulic fluid to DOT 4

Power steering . . . . Total Fluide DA

Tyre pressures

Note 1: *The make of tyres, the sizes and the pressures for each specific vehicle are given on a label attached to the driver's door A-pillar **(see illustration)**. On models with a space-saver spare wheel, a separate pressure is given for the spare tyre, note that the spare is for temporary use only; whilst the spare is fitted, the vehicle should not be driven at speeds in excess of 50 mph.*
Note 2: *Pressures on the label apply to original-equipment tyres listed, and may vary if any other make or type of tyre is fitted; check with the tyre manufacturer or supplier for correct pressures if necessary.*
Note 3: *Tyre pressures must always be checked with the tyres cold to ensure accuracy.*

Driver's door A-pillar label

Chapter 1
Routine maintenance and servicing

Contents

Degrees of difficulty

Easy, suitable for novice with little experience | **Fairly easy,** suitable for beginner with some experience | **Fairly difficult,** suitable for competent DIY mechanic | **Difficult,** suitable for experienced DIY mechanic | **Very difficult,** suitable for expert DIY or professional

Specifications

Engine identification

1.6 litre:
   Designation DV6TED4
   Engine codes . . . . 9HY or 9HZ
2.0 litre:
   Designation . . . . DW10BTED4 or DW10CTED4
   Engine codes:
      DW10BTED4 . . . . RHF, RHL or RHR
      DW10CTED4 . . . . RHH

Lubricants and fluids . . . . See end of *Weekly checks* on page 0•18

Capacities
Note: *All values are approximate.*

Engine oil
Drain and refill, with filter change:
   1.6 litre engines . . . . 3.75 litres
   2.0 litre engines . . . . 5.25 litres
Between dipstick MAX and MIN markings:
   1.6 litre engines . . . . 1.5 litres
   2.0 litre engines . . . . 2.0 litres

Cooling system
1.6 litre engines . . . . 7.2 litres
2.0 litre engines:
   Manual transmission . . . . 9.0 litres
   Automatic transmission . . . . 10.0 litres

Transmission
Manual:
   Drain and refill:
     BE4R . . . . 1.9 litres
     ML6C:
       Without cooling fins on the gearbox casing . . . . 2.6 litres
       With cooling fins on the gearbox casing . . . . 1.9 litres
Automatic:
   Drain and refill:
     AL4 . . . . 4.5 litres
     AM6 . . . . 3.0 litres
   Total capacity, including torque converter:
     AL4 . . . . 6.0 litres
     AM6 . . . . 7.0 litres
Fuel tank . . . . 67.0 litres

Cooling system
Antifreeze mixture:*
   50% antifreeze . . . . Protection down to -37°C
   55% antifreeze . . . . Protection down to -45°C
* **Note:** *Refer to antifreeze manufacturer for latest recommendations.*

Brakes
	Front	Rear
Brake pad friction material minimum thickness	2.5 mm	3.0 mm
Disc minimum thickness	24.0 mm	12.0 mm

Remote control battery
Type CR1620
Volts 3V

Torque wrench settings
	Nm	lbf ft
Automatic transmission:		
AL4:		
Fluid drain plug	33	24
Fluid filler plug	24	18
Fluid level plug:		
To RPO 9855 (hexagonal)	24	18
From RPO 9856 (socket key)	9	7
AM6:		
Drain/overflow plug	48	35
Level plug (centre of drain/overflow plug)	7	5
Filler plug	40	30
Engine oil sump drain plug:		
1.6 litre engines	25	18
2.0 litre engines	34	25
Manual transmission:		
BE4R:		
Filler/level plug	22	16
Drain plug	35	26
ML6C:		
Drain plug	30	22
Oil filter cap	25	18
Wheel bolts	90	66

The maintenance intervals in this manual are provided with the assumption that you will be carrying out the work yourself. These are the minimum maintenance intervals recommended by ourselves for vehicles driven daily, based on the schedule produced by the manufacturer. If you wish to keep your vehicle in peak condition at all times, you may wish to perform some of these procedures more often. We encourage frequent maintenance, because it enhances the efficiency, performance and resale value of your vehicle.

If the vehicle is driven in dusty areas, used to tow a trailer, or driven frequently at slow speeds (idling in traffic) or on short journeys, more frequent maintenance intervals are recommended.

When the vehicle is new, it should be serviced by a dealer service department (or other workshop recognised by the vehicle manufacturer as providing the same standard of service) in order to preserve the warranty. The vehicle manufacturer may reject warranty claims if you are unable to prove that servicing has been carried out as and when specified, using only original equipment parts or parts certified to be of equivalent quality.

All Peugeot models are equipped with a service indicator function incorporated into the mileage recorder, which will indicate the mileage until the next service is due. However, Peugeot point out that, 'due to the relationship between time and mileage, some operating conditions will make annual service more suitable'.

Every 250 miles or weekly
☐ Refer to *Weekly checks*

Every 12 000 miles or 12 months – whichever comes first
☐ Engine oil and filter renewal (Section 3)
☐ Service indicator resetting (Section 4)
☐ Hoses and fluids leak check (Section 5)
☐ Steering and suspension components check (Section 6)
☐ Brake pad wear and disc check (Section 7)
☐ Handbrake check and adjustment (Section 8)
☐ Seat belt condition check (Section 9)
☐ Airbag system check (Section 10)
☐ Headlight beam alignment check (Section 11)
☐ Road test (Section 12)
☐ Coolant antifreeze concentration check (Section 13)
☐ Driveshaft joints and gaiters check (Section 14)
☐ Exhaust system check (Section 15)
☐ Hinges and locks lubrication (Section 16)
☐ Fuel filter draining (Section 17)
☐ Auxiliary drivebelt condition check (Section 18)

Every 24 000 miles or 2 years – whichever comes first
☐ Pollen filter renewal (Section 19)

Every 2 years
☐ Brake fluid renewal (Section 20)
☐ Remote control battery renewal (Section 21)
☐ Coolant renewal (Section 22)
Note: *This work is not included in the Peugeot schedule, and should not be required if the recommended Peugeot antifreeze/inhibitor is used.*

Every 36 000 miles or 3 years – whichever comes first
☐ Air filter element renewal (Section 23)
☐ Manual transmission oil level check (Section 24)
☐ Automatic transmission fluid level check (Section 25)
☐ Fuel filter renewal (Section 17)

Every 60 000 miles or 5 years – whichever comes first
☐ Particulate filter renewal (Section 26)
Note: *1.6 litre engines*

Every 72 000 miles or 6 years – whichever comes first
☐ Eolys 176 fluid check (Section 27)

Every 96 000 miles or 8 years – whichever comes first
☐ Particulate filter renewal (Section 28)
Note: *2.0 litre engines*
☐ Timing belt renewal (Section 29)
Note: *The interval recommended by Peugeot is 150 000 miles or 10 years. However, It is strongly recommended that the interval be reduced on vehicles that are subjected to intensive use, ie, mainly short journeys or a lot of stop-start driving. The actual belt renewal interval is very much up to the individual owner, but bear in mind that severe engine damage will result if the belt breaks*

Every 15 years
☐ Airbags renewal (Section 30)

Underbonnet view – 1.6 litre model

1 Engine oil dipstick
2 Engine oil filler cap
3 Power steering reservoir filler cap
4 Washer fluid reservoir
5 Coolant expansion tank filler cap
6 Brake/clutch cylinders fluid reservoir
7 Engine compartment electrical box
8 Battery cover
9 Air cleaner housing
10 Fuel filter

Underbonnet view – 2.0 litre model

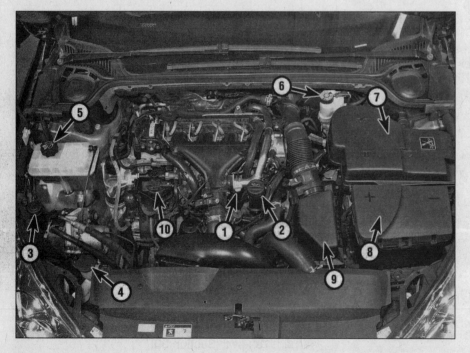

1 Engine oil dipstick
2 Engine oil filler cap
3 Power steering reservoir filler cap
4 Washer fluid reservoir
5 Coolant expansion tank filler cap
6 Brake/clutch cylinders fluid reservoir
7 Engine compartment electrical box
8 Battery cover
9 Air cleaner housing
10 Fuel filter

Front underbody view – 1.6 litre model

1 Engine oil drain plug
2 Transmission drain plug
3 Air conditioning compressor
4 Catalytic converter/particulate filter
5 Brake caliper
6 Lower suspension arm
7 Track rod
8 Anti-roll bar
9 Radiator
10 Intercooler

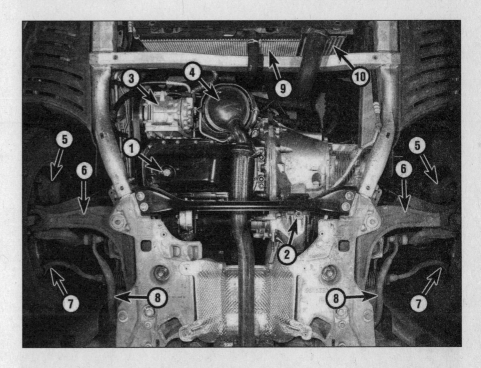

Front underbody view – 2.0 litre model

1 Engine oil drain plug
2 Transmission drain plug
3 Air conditioning compressor
4 Pre-catalytic converter
5 Brake caliper
6 Lower suspension arm
7 Track rod
8 Anti-roll bar
9 Radiator
10 Intercooler

Rear underbody view

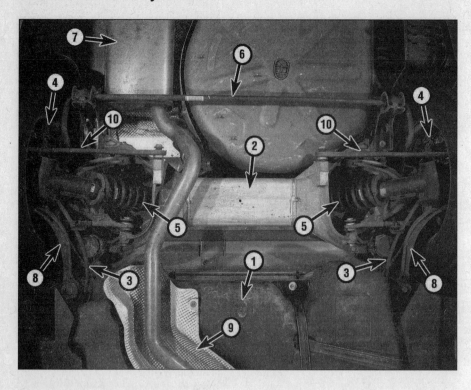

1 Fuel tank
2 Rear axle
3 Handbrake cable
4 Brake caliper
5 Shock absorber/coil spring assembly
6 Anti-roll bar
7 Exhaust rear silencer
8 Rear longitudinal arms
9 Heat shield
10 Lower suspension arm

1 General information

This Chapter is designed to help the home mechanic maintain his/her vehicle for safety, economy, long life and peak performance.

The Chapter contains a master maintenance schedule, followed by Sections dealing specifically with each task in the schedule. Visual checks, adjustments, component renewal and other helpful items are included. Refer to the accompanying illustrations of the engine compartment and the underside of the vehicle for the locations of the various components.

Servicing your vehicle in accordance with the mileage/time maintenance schedule and the following Sections will provide a planned maintenance programme, which should result in a long and reliable service life. This is a comprehensive plan, so maintaining some items, but not others, at the specified service intervals will not produce the same results.

As you service your vehicle, you will discover that many of the procedures can – and should – be grouped together, because of the particular procedure being performed, or because of the close proximity of two otherwise-unrelated components to one another. For example, if the vehicle is raised for any reason, the exhaust system could be inspected at the same time as the suspension and steering components.

The first step in this maintenance programme is to prepare yourself before the actual work begins. Read through all the Sections relevant to the work to be carried out, then make a list and gather together all the parts and tools required. If a problem is encountered, seek advice from a parts specialist, or a dealer service department.

2 Regular maintenance

If, from the time the vehicle is new, the routine maintenance schedule is followed closely, and frequent checks are made of fluid levels and high-wear items, as suggested throughout this manual, the engine will be kept in relatively good running condition, and the need for additional work will be minimised.

It is possible that there will be times when the engine is running poorly due to the lack of regular maintenance. This is even more likely if a used vehicle, which has not received regular and frequent maintenance checks, is purchased. In such cases, additional work may need to be carried out, outside of the regular maintenance intervals.

If engine wear is suspected, a compression test (refer to Chapter 2A or 2B) will provide valuable information regarding the overall performance of the main internal components. Such a test can be used as a basis to decide on the extent of the work to be carried out. If, for example, a compression test indicates serious internal engine wear, conventional maintenance as described in this Chapter will not greatly improve the performance of the engine, and may prove a waste of time and money, unless extensive overhaul work (Chapter 2C) is carried out first.

The following series of operations are those most often required to improve the performance of a generally poor-running engine:

Primary operations

a) Clean, inspect and test the battery ('Weekly checks' and Chapter 5A)
b) Check all the engine-related fluids ('Weekly checks').
c) Check the condition and tension of the auxiliary drivebelt (Section 18).
d) Check the condition of the air filter element, and renew if necessary (Section 23).
e) Check the condition of all hoses, and check for fluid leaks (Section 5).

If the above operations do not prove fully effective, carry out the following secondary operations:

Secondary operations

a) Check the charging system (Chapter 5A).
b) Check the fuel system (Chapter 4B).

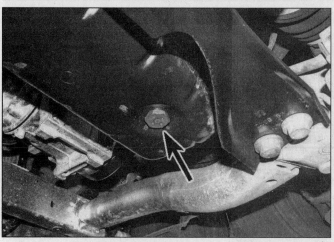

3.5a Engine sump drain plug – 1.6 litre

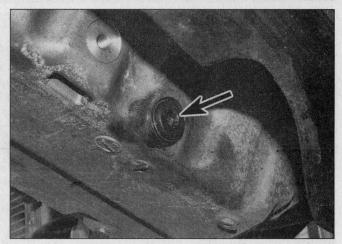

3.5b Engine sump drain plug – 2.0 litre

Every 12 000 miles or 12 months

3 Engine oil and filter renewal

1 Frequent oil changes are the most important preventative maintenance the DIY home mechanic can give the engine, because ageing oil becomes diluted and contaminated, which leads to premature engine wear.

2 Before starting this procedure, gather together all the necessary tools and materials. Also make sure that you have plenty of clean rags and newspapers handy, to mop-up any spills. Ideally, the engine oil should be warm, as it will drain better, and more built-up sludge will be removed with it. Take care, however, not to touch the exhaust or any other hot parts of the engine when working under the vehicle. To avoid any possibility of scalding, and to protect yourself from possible skin irritants and other harmful contaminants in used engine oils, it is advisable to wear gloves when carrying out this work.

3 Access to the filter and drain plug will be greatly improved if the front of the vehicle is raised and support securely on axle stands (see *Jacking and vehicle support*).

4 Undo the fasteners and remove the engine undershield.

5 Slacken the plug about half a turn **(see illustrations)**. Position the draining container under the drain plug, then remove the plug completely – recover the sealing washer **(see Haynes Hint)**.

6 Allow some time for the old oil to drain, noting that it may be necessary to reposition the container as the oil flow slows to a trickle.

7 The oil filter is of a separate disposable paper element contained under a plastic cap, which is screwed into a housing on the front of the cylinder block. Using a socket or spanner, slacken the oil filter plastic cap a couple of turns to allow the oil in the filter housing to drain into the sump **(see illustrations)**. Do not completely remove at this stage.

8 After all the oil has drained, wipe off the drain plug with a clean rag. Clean the area around

the drain plug opening, and refit the plug with a new sealing washer **(see illustration)**. Tighten the plug to the specified torque.

HAYNES HiNT

As the drain plug releases from the threads, move it away sharply so the stream of oil issuing from the sump runs into the container, not up your sleeve.

3.7a Slacken the engine oil filter cover . . .

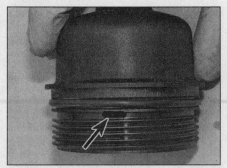

3.7b . . . until the vent hole (arrowed) is uncovered

3.8 Fit a new sealing washer to the drain plug

3.9 Unscrew the oil filter plastic cover

3.10a Remove the inlet ducting . . .

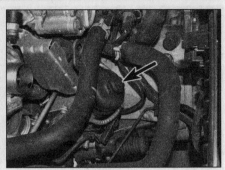

3.10b . . . to access the oil filter cover

9 The oil filter plastic cap can now be unscrewed the rest of the way off by hand **(see illustration)**. Use a rag to catch any oil spillage as the filter is removed.
10 On 1.6 litre engines, undo the screw and manoeuvre the air inlet ducting from the air filter housing to access the oil filter cap **(see illustrations)**.
11 Lift the oil filter plastic cap away, depending on model the paper filter element may stay in the lower part of the housing or will stay in the cap as it is removed. Remove the paper element from the filter housing, if required.
12 Use a clean rag to remove all oil and dirt from inside the filter cap and housing, and then remove the O-ring seal from the cap **(see illustration)**. A new seal should be supplied with the new filter.
13 Fit a new O-ring seal to the cap, and fit the new paper element to the cap. On 1.6 litre engines, fit the element to the housing, ensuring the lug on the base of the element locates correctly in the corresponding hole in the housing. Lightly lubricate the O-ring seal with clean engine oil **(see illustrations)**.
14 Screw the cap into place by hand, and then tighten it to the specified torque.
15 Lower the vehicle to the ground, then remove the oil filler cap and withdraw the level dipstick from the tube **(see illustrations)**.
16 Fill the engine, using the correct oil (see *Lubricants and fluids*). An oil can spout or funnel may help to reduce spillage. Pour in half the specified quantity of oil first (see Specifications), and then wait a few minutes for the oil to run to the sump. Continue adding oil a small quantity at a time until the level is up to the lower mark on the dipstick. Adding a further 1.5 litres will bring the level up to the upper mark on the dipstick **(see illustration)**. Insert the dipstick, and refit the filler cap when completed.
17 Refit the engine undershield.
18 Start the engine and run it for a few minutes; check for leaks around the oil filter seal and the sump drain plug. Note that there may be a delay of a few seconds before the oil pressure warning light goes out when the

3.12 Renew the O-ring seal . . .

3.13a . . . insert the new filter into the cap . . .

3.13b . . . then apply a little clean oil to the seal

3.13c Ensure the filter locating peg (arrowed) locates into the corresponding hole in the housing (arrowed)

3.15a Oil level dipstick – 2.0 litre engine

3.15b Oil level dipstick – 1.6 litre engine

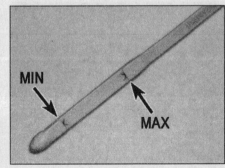

3.16 Upper and lower dipstick markings (arrowed)

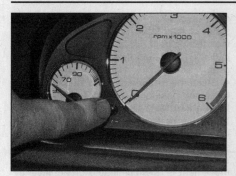

4.2 Press the reset button on the instrument panel

engine is first started, as the oil circulates through the engine oil galleries and the new oil filter before the pressure builds-up.

19 Switch off the engine, and wait a few minutes for the oil to settle in the sump once more. With the new oil circulated and the filter completely full, recheck the level on the dipstick, and add more oil as necessary.

20 Dispose of the used engine oil safely, in accordance with the guidance given in *General repair procedures*.

4 Service indicator resetting

1 The instrument cluster mileage recorder incorporates a service interval indicator. When the vehicle is started, the unit displays the mileage until the next service, or the mileage covered since the service was due. The service indicator is manually reset to zero after the vehicle has been serviced. The indicator can also be reset at any time using the Peugeot diagnostic tool.

2 Switch off the ignition then, on the instrument panel, press and hold down the reset button **(see illustration)**.

3 Switch on the ignition – the distance remaining until (or covered since) the next service is due will flash in the display. Keep the button pressed until the display resets to zero and the maintenance 'spanner' disappears. Release the knob.

5 Hoses and fluids leak check

Cooling system

 Warning: Refer to the safety information given in 'Safety first!' and Chapter 0 before disturbing any of the cooling system components.

1 Carefully check the radiator and heater coolant hoses along their entire length. Renew any hose that is cracked, swollen or which shows signs of deterioration. Cracks will show up better if the hose is squeezed. Pay close

A leak in the cooling system will usually show up as white- or antifreeze-coloured deposits on the area adjoining the leak.

attention to the clips that secure the hoses to the cooling system components. Hose clips that have been overtightened can pinch and puncture hoses, resulting in cooling system leaks.

2 Inspect all the cooling system components (hoses, joint faces, etc) for leaks. Where any problems of this nature are found on system components, renew the component or gasket with reference to Chapter 3 **(see Haynes hint)**.

Fuel system

 Warning: Refer to the safety information given in 'Safety first!' and Chapter 4A before disturbing any of the fuel system components.

3 Diesel leaks are easier to spot than petrol, but can be difficult to pinpoint unless the leakage is significant and hence easily visible. Fuel tends to spread, especially in a hot engine bay. Small drips can spread before you get a chance to identify the point of leakage. If you suspect that there is a fuel leak from the area of the engine bay, leave the vehicle overnight then start the engine from cold, with the bonnet open. Metal components tend to shrink when they are cold, and rubber seals and hoses tend to harden, so any leaks will be more apparent whilst the engine is warming-up from a cold start.

4 Check all fuel lines at their connections to the fuel rail, fuel pressure regulator, fuel filter, fuel cooler and especially the return hoses on top of the injectors. Examine each rubber fuel hose along its length for splits or cracks. Check for leakage from the crimped joints between rubber and metal fuel lines. Examine the unions between the metal fuel lines and the fuel filter housing. Also check the area around the fuel injectors for signs of O-ring leakage.

5 To identify fuel leaks between the fuel tank and the engine bay, the vehicle should be raised and securely supported on axle stands (see *Jacking and vehicle support*). Inspect the fuel tank and filler neck for punctures, cracks and other damage. The connection between

the filler neck and tank is especially critical. Sometimes a rubber filler neck or connecting hose will leak due to loose retaining clamps or deteriorated rubber.

6 Carefully check all rubber hoses and metal fuel lines leading away from the fuel tank. Check for loose connections, deteriorated hoses, kinked lines, and other damage. Pay particular attention to the vent pipes and hoses, which often loop up around the filler neck and can become blocked or kinked, making tank filling difficult. Follow the fuel supply and return lines to the front of the vehicle, carefully inspecting them all the way for signs of damage or corrosion. Renew damaged sections as necessary.

Engine oil

7 Inspect the area around the camshaft cover, cylinder head, oil filter and sump joint faces. Bear in mind that, over a period of time, some very slight seepage from these areas is to be expected – what you are really looking for is any indication of a serious leak caused by gasket failure. Engine oil seeping from the base of the timing belt cover or the transmission bellhousing may be an indication of crankshaft or transmission input shaft oil seal failure. Should a leak be found, renew the failed gasket or oil seal by referring to the appropriate Chapters in this manual.

Automatic transmission fluid

8 Where applicable, check the hoses leading to the transmission fluid cooler at the front of the engine bay for leakage. Look for deterioration caused by corrosion and damage from grounding, or debris thrown up from the road surface. Automatic transmission fluid is a thin oil and is usually red in colour.

Air conditioning refrigerant

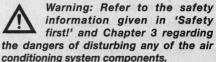 *Warning: Refer to the safety information given in 'Safety first!' and Chapter 3 regarding the dangers of disturbing any of the air conditioning system components.*

9 The air conditioning system is filled with a liquid refrigerant, which is retained under high pressure. If the air conditioning system is opened and depressurised without the aid of specialised equipment the refrigerant will immediately turn into gas and escape into the atmosphere. If the liquid comes into contact with your skin, it can cause severe frostbite. In addition, the refrigerant contains substances which are environmentally damaging; for this reason, it should not be allowed to escape into the atmosphere in an uncontrolled fashion.

10 Any suspected air conditioning system leaks should be immediately referred to a Peugeot dealer or air conditioning specialist. Leakage will be shown up as a steady drop in the level of refrigerant in the system.

11 Note that water may drip from the condenser drain pipe, underneath the car, immediately after the air conditioning system has been in use. This is normal, and should not be cause for concern.

Brake/clutch fluid

Warning: Refer to the safety information given in 'Safety first!' and Chapter 9 regarding the dangers of handling brake fluid.

12 With reference to Chapter 9, examine the area surrounding the brake/clutch pipe unions at the master cylinder for signs of leakage. Check the area around the base of fluid reservoir, for signs of leakage caused by seal failure. Also examine the brake pipe unions at the ABS hydraulic unit.

13 If fluid loss is evident, but the leak cannot be pinpointed in the engine bay, the brake calipers and underbody brake lines should be carefully checked with the vehicle raised and supported on axle stands (see *Jacking and vehicle support*). Leakage of fluid from the braking system is a serious fault that must be rectified immediately.

14 Brake/clutch hydraulic fluid is a toxic substance with a watery consistency. New fluid is almost colourless, but it becomes darker with age and use.

Unidentified fluid leaks

15 If there are signs that a fluid of some description is leaking from the vehicle, but you cannot identify the type of fluid or its exact origin, park the vehicle overnight and slide a large piece of card underneath it. Providing that the card is positioned in roughly the right location, even the smallest leak will show up on the card. Not only will this help you to pinpoint the exact location of the leak, it should be easier to identify the fluid from its colour. Bear in mind, though, that the leak may only be occurring when the engine is running!

Vacuum hoses

16 Although the braking system is hydraulically-operated, the brake servo unit amplifies the effort applied at the brake pedal by making use of the vacuum supplied by the vacuum pump, driven by the engine. Vacuum is ported to the servo by means of a large-bore hose. Any leaks that develop in this hose will reduce the effectiveness of the braking system, and may affect the running of the engine.

17 In addition, a number of the underbonnet components, particularly the turbocharger control components, are driven by vacuum supplied from the vacuum pump via narrow-bore hoses. A leak in a vacuum hose means that air is being drawn into the hose (rather than escaping from it) and this makes leakage very difficult to detect. One method is to use an old length of vacuum hose as a kind of stethoscope – hold one end close to (but not in) your ear and use the other end to probe the area around the suspected leak. When the end of the hose is directly over a vacuum leak, a hissing sound will be heard clearly through the hose. Care must be taken to avoid contacting hot or moving components, as the engine must be running, when testing in this manner. Renew any vacuum hoses that are found to be defective.

6 Steering and suspension components check

Front suspension and steering

1 Raise the front of the vehicle, and securely support it on axle stands (see *Jacking and vehicle support*).

2 Visually inspect the balljoint dust covers and the steering rack-and-pinion gaiters for splits **(see illustration)**, chafing or deterioration. Any wear of these components will cause loss of lubricant, together with dirt and water entry, resulting in rapid deterioration of the balljoints or steering gear.

3 Check the power steering fluid hoses for chafing or deterioration, and the pipe and hose unions for fluid leaks. Also check for signs of fluid leakage under pressure from the steering gear rubber gaiters, which would indicate failed fluid seals within the steering gear.

4 Grasp the roadwheel at the 12 o'clock and 6 o'clock positions, and try to rock it **(see illustration)**. Very slight free play may be felt, but if the movement is appreciable, further investigation is necessary to determine the source. Continue rocking the wheel while an assistant depresses the footbrake. If the movement is now eliminated or significantly reduced, it is likely that the hub bearings are at fault. If the free play is still evident with the footbrake depressed, then there is wear in the suspension joints or mountings.

5 Now grasp the wheel at the 9 o'clock and 3 o'clock positions, and try to rock it as before. Any movement felt now may again be caused by wear in the hub bearings or the steering track rod balljoints. If the outer balljoint is worn, the visual movement will be obvious. If the inner joint is suspect, it can be felt by placing a hand over the rack-and-pinion rubber gaiter and gripping the track rod. If the wheel is now rocked, movement will be felt at the inner joint if wear has taken place.

6 Using a large screwdriver or flat bar, check for wear in the suspension mounting bushes by levering between the relevant suspension component and its attachment point. Some movement is to be expected, as the mountings are made of rubber, but excessive wear should be obvious. Also check the condition of any visible rubber bushes, looking for splits, cracks or contamination of the rubber.

7 With the car standing on its wheels, have an assistant turn the steering wheel back-and-forth, about an eighth of a turn each way. There should be very little, if any, lost movement between the steering wheel and roadwheels. If this is not the case, closely observe the joints and mountings previously described. In addition, check the steering column universal

6.2 Check the steering rack gaiters for damage

6.4 Check for wear in the hub bearings by grasping the wheel and trying to rock it

joints for wear, and also check the rack-and-pinion steering gear itself.

8 The front suspension mountings should be checked for tightness.

Rear suspension

9 Chock the front wheels, then jack up the rear of the vehicle and support securely on axle stands (see *Jacking and vehicle support*).
10 Working as described previously for the front suspension, check the rear hub bearings, the suspension bushes and the strut or shock absorber mountings (as applicable) for wear.
11 The rear suspension mountings should be checked for tightness.

Shock absorber

12 Check for any signs of fluid leakage around the shock absorber bodies, or from the rubber gaiters around the piston rods. Should any fluid be noticed, the shock absorber is defective internally, or the rubber gaiter is split, and may need renewing. **Note:** *Shock absorbers should always be renewed in pairs on the same axle.*

7 Brake pad wear and disc check

1 The work described in this Section should be carried out at the specified intervals, or whenever a defect is suspected in the braking system. Any of the following symptoms could indicate a potential brake system defect:

a) *The vehicle pulls to one side when the brake pedal is depressed.*
b) *The brakes make squealing, scraping or dragging noises when applied.*
c) *Brake pedal travel is excessive, or pedal feel is poor.*
d) *The brake fluid requires repeated topping-up. Note that, because the hydraulic clutch shares the same fluid as the braking system (see Chapter 6), this problem could be due to a leak in the clutch system.*

Front disc brakes

2 Chock the rear wheels then loosen the front wheel bolts. Jack up the front of the vehicle, and support it on axle stands (see *Jacking and vehicle support*).
3 For better access to the brake calipers, remove the wheels.
4 Look through the inspection window in the caliper, and check that the thickness of the friction lining material on each of the pads is not less than the recommended minimum thickness given in the Specifications **(see Haynes hint).** Bear in mind that the lining material is normally bonded to a metal backing plate. To differentiate between the metal and the lining material, it is helpful to turn the disc slowly at first – the edge of the disc can then be identified, with the lining material on each pad either side of it, and the backing plates behind.

For a quick check, the thickness of the friction material on each brake pad can be measured through the aperture in the caliper body.

5 If it is difficult to determine the exact thickness of the pad linings, or if you are at all concerned about the condition of the pads, then remove them from the calipers for further inspection (refer to Chapter 9).
6 Check the other caliper in the same way.
7 If any one of the brake pads has worn down to, or below, the specified limit, *all four* pads at that end of the car must be renewed as a set **(see illustration).** If the pads on one side are significantly more worn than the other, this may indicate that the caliper pistons have partially seized – refer to the brake pad renewal procedure in Chapter 9, and push the pistons back into the caliper to free them.
8 Measure the thickness of the discs with a micrometer, if available, to make sure that they still have service life remaining. Do not be fooled by the lip of rust which often forms on the outer edge of the disc, which may make the disc appear thicker than it really is – scrape off the loose rust if necessary, without scoring the disc friction (shiny) surface.
9 If any disc is thinner than the specified minimum thickness, renew both (refer to Chapter 9).
10 Check the general condition of the discs. Look for excessive scoring and discolouration caused by overheating. If these conditions exist, remove the relevant disc and have it resurfaced or renewed (refer to Chapter 9).
11 Make sure that the transmission is in neutral. Spin the wheel, and check that the brake is not binding. Some drag is normal with a disc brake, but it should not require any great effort to turn the wheel – also, do not confuse brake drag with resistance from the transmission.
12 Before refitting the wheels, check all brake lines and hoses (refer to Chapter 9). In particular, check the flexible hoses in the vicinity of the calipers, where they are subjected to most movement. Bend them between the fingers (but do not actually bend them double, or the casing may be damaged) and check that this does not reveal previously hidden cracks, cuts or splits.
13 On completion, refit the wheels and lower the car to the ground. Tighten the wheel bolts

7.7 Check the thickness of the brake pad friction material

to the specified torque.

Rear disc brakes

14 Loosen the rear wheel bolts then chock the front wheels. Jack up the rear of the car, and support it on axle stands. Release the handbrake and remove the rear wheels.
15 The procedure for checking the rear brakes is much the same as described in paragraphs 2 to 13 above. Check that the rear brakes are not binding, noting that transmission resistance is not a factor on the rear wheels. Abnormal effort may indicate that the handbrake needs adjusting – see Chapter 9.

8 Handbrake check and adjustment

1 To check the handbrake adjustment, apply normal moderate pressure and pull the handbrake lever to the fully applied position, counting the number of clicks emitted from the handbrake ratchet mechanism. If adjustment is correct, there should be 1 notch before the brakes begin to apply, and no more than 4 notches before the handbrake is fully-applied. If this is not the case, adjust as described in Chapter 9, Section 14.

9 Seat belt condition check

1 Working on each seat belt in turn, carefully examine the seat belt webbing for cuts, or for any signs of serious fraying or deterioration. Pull the belt all the way out, and examine the full extent of the webbing.
2 Fasten and unfasten the belt, ensuring that the locking mechanism holds securely, and releases properly when intended. Check also that the retracting mechanism operates correctly when the belt is released.
3 Check the security of all seat belt mountings and attachments which are accessible from inside the vehicle without removing any trim or other components.
4 Check the function of the seat belt reminder lamp.

10 Airbag system check

1 The following work can be carried out by the home mechanic, however, if an electronic fault is apparent, it will be necessary to take the car to a Peugeot dealer or specialist, who will have the necessary diagnostic equipment to extract fault codes from the system.
2 Turn the ignition switch to the drive position (ignition warning lights on), and check that the airbag warning light is illuminated for approximately 6 seconds. After this period the light should go out, indicating that the system has been checked and is functioning correctly.
3 If the warning light remains on or refuses to light, have the system checked by a Peugeot dealer or specialist.
4 Visually examine the steering wheel centre pad, knee airbag and the passenger airbag modules for external damage. Also check the exterior of the front seats around the side airbag locations. If damage is evident, consult a Peugeot dealer or specialist.
5 In the interests of safety, make sure that there are no loose items inside the car, which could be thrown onto the airbag modules in the event of an accident.

11 Headlight beam alignment check

Refer to Chapter 12 for details.

12 Road test

Instruments and electrical equipment

1 Check the operation of all instruments and electrical equipment.
2 Make sure that all instruments read correctly, and switch on all electrical equipment in turn to check that it functions properly. Check the function of the heating, air conditioning and automatic climate control systems.

Steering and suspension

3 Check for any abnormalities in the steering, suspension, handling or road 'feel'.
4 Drive the vehicle, and check that there are no unusual vibrations or noises.
5 Check that the steering feels positive, with no excessive 'sloppiness', or roughness, and check for any suspension noises when cornering, or when driving over bumps. Check that the power steering system operates correctly.

Drivetrain

6 Check the performance of the engine, clutch (manual transmission), transmission and driveshafts.

7 Listen for any unusual noises from the engine, clutch (manual transmission) and transmission.
8 Make sure that the engine runs smoothly when idling, and that there is no hesitation when accelerating.
9 On manual transmission models, check that the clutch action is smooth and progressive, that the drive is taken up smoothly, and that the pedal travel is correct. Also listen for any noises when the clutch pedal is depressed. Check that all gears can be engaged smoothly, without noise, and that the gear lever action is smooth and not abnormally vague or 'notchy'.
10 On automatic transmission models, make sure that all gearchanges occur smoothly without snatching, and without an increase in engine speed between changes. Check that all the gear positions can be selected with the vehicle at rest. If any problems are found, they should be referred to a Peugeot dealer.
11 Listen for a metallic clicking sound from the front of the vehicle, as the vehicle is driven slowly in a circle with the steering on full lock. Carry out this check in both directions. If a clicking noise is heard, this indicates wear in a driveshaft joint, in which case, refer to Chapter 8.

Braking system

12 Make sure that the vehicle does not pull to one side when braking, and that the wheels do not lock when braking hard.
13 Check that there is no vibration through the steering when braking.
14 Check that the handbrake operates correctly, without excessive movement of the lever, and that it holds the vehicle stationary on a slope.
15 Test the operation of the brake servo unit as follows. With the engine off, depress the footbrake four or five times to exhaust the vacuum, and then start the engine while holding the brake pedal depressed. As the engine starts, there should be a noticeable 'give' in the brake pedal as vacuum builds-up. Allow the engine to run for at least two minutes, and then switch it off. If the brake pedal is now depressed again, it should be possible to detect a 'hiss' from the servo as the pedal is depressed. After about four or five applications, no further sound should be heard, and the pedal should feel considerably harder.

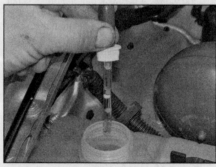
13.3 Check the antifreeze concentration using a hydrometer

13 Coolant antifreeze concentration check

1 The cooling system should be filled with the recommended antifreeze and corrosion protection fluid. Over a period of time, the concentration of fluid may be reduced due to topping-up (this can be avoided by topping-up with the correct antifreeze mixture) or fluid loss. If loss of coolant has been evident, it is important to make the necessary repair before adding fresh fluid. The exact mixture of antifreeze-to-water that you should use depends on the relative weather conditions. The mixture should contain at least 40% antifreeze, but not more than 70%. Consult the mixture ratio chart on the antifreeze container before adding coolant. Hydrometers are available at most automotive accessory shops to test the coolant. Use antifreeze which meets the vehicle manufacturer's specifications.
2 With the engine cold, carefully remove the cap from the expansion tank. If the engine is not completely cold, place a cloth rag over the cap before removing it, and remove it slowly to allow any pressure to escape.
3 Antifreeze checkers are available from car accessory shops. Draw some coolant from the expansion tank and observe how many plastic balls are floating in the checker **(see illustration)**. Usually, 2 or 3 balls must be floating for the correct concentration of antifreeze, but follow the manufacturer's instructions.
4 If the concentration is incorrect, it will be necessary to either withdraw some coolant and add antifreeze, or alternatively drain the old coolant and add fresh coolant of the correct concentration.

14 Driveshaft joints and gaiters check

1 With the front of the vehicle raised and securely supported on stands, turn the steering onto full lock then slowly rotate the roadwheel. Inspect the condition of the outer constant velocity (CV) joint rubber gaiters while squeezing the gaiters to open out the folds **(see illustration)**. Check for signs

14.1 Check the driveshaft gaiter for damage

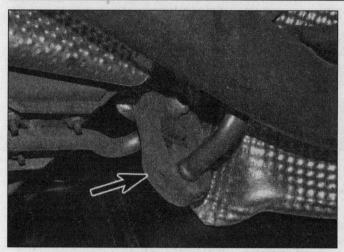

15.2a Check the condition of the exhaust rubber mountings (arrowed) . . .

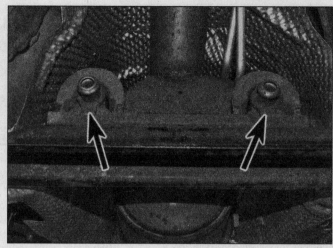

15.2b . . . and the front exhaust rubber mountings at the front (arrowed)

of cracking, splits or deterioration of the rubber, which may allow the grease to escape and lead to water and grit entry into the joint. Also check the security and condition of the retaining clips. Repeat these checks on the inner CV joints. If any damage or deterioration is found, the gaiters should be renewed as described in Chapter 8.

2 At the same time check the general condition of the CV joints themselves by first holding the driveshaft and attempting to rotate the wheel. Repeat this check by holding the inner joint and attempting to rotate the driveshaft. Any appreciable movement indicates wear in the joints, wear in the driveshaft splines or a loose driveshaft retaining nut.

15 Exhaust system check

1 With the engine cold, check the complete exhaust system, from its starting point at the engine to the end of the tailpipe. If necessary, raise the front and rear of the vehicle and support it on axle stands (see *Jacking and vehicle support*). Remove any engine undershields as necessary for full access to the exhaust system.

2 Check the exhaust pipes and connections for evidence of leaks, severe corrosion, and damage. Make sure that all brackets and mountings are in good condition and that all relevant nuts and bolts are tight **(see illustrations)**. Leakage at any of the joints or in other parts of the system will usually show up as a black sooty stain in the vicinity of the leak.

3 Rattles and other noises can often be traced to the exhaust system, especially the brackets and rubber mountings. Try to move the pipes and silencers. If the components are able to come into contact with the body or suspension parts, secure the system with new mountings. Otherwise separate the joints

(if possible) and twist the pipes as necessary to provide additional clearance.

16 Hinges and locks lubrication

1 Work around the vehicle and lubricate the hinges of the bonnet, doors and tailgate with a light machine oil.

2 Lightly lubricate the two bonnet release locks with a smear of grease.

3 Check carefully the security and operation of all hinges, latches and locks. Check that the central locking system operates correctly.

4 Check the condition and operation of the bonnet and tailgate/boot lid struts, renewing them if either is leaking or no longer able to support the bonnet/tailgate/boot lid.

17 Fuel filter draining and renewal

Draining

1 The purpose of this operation is to purge the filter assembly of any accumulated water.

17.2 Fuel filter drain screw (arrowed) – 2.0 litre engine

Remove the plastic cover on the top of the engine. On 1.6 litre engines, undo the screw and remove the inlet air ducting from the front of the engine compartment to the air cleaner housing **(see illustration 3.10a)**.

2 Place a container underneath the filter, then slacken the fuel filter drain screw, and operate the hand priming pump a few times until all water or impurities cease to run out **(see illustration)**. Tighten the drain screw.

3 Start the engine and run it at a fast idle speed (less than 2000 rpm) for 30 seconds. Refit the engine cover.

Renewal

1.6 litre engines

4 Disconnect the battery negative lead (see Chapter 5A), then remove the plastic cover from the top of the engine.

5 Undo the screw and remove the inlet air ducting from the front of the engine compartment to the air cleaner housing **(see illustration 3.10a)**.

6 Undo the screws securing the air filter cover, disconnect the mass airflow sensor wiring plug, then slacken the clamp securing the inlet pipe to the turbocharger, and manoeuvre the cover/ducting assembly from place **(see illustrations)**.

17.6a Undo the two retaining screws (arrowed) . . .

17.6b ... disconnect the hose from the turbo ...

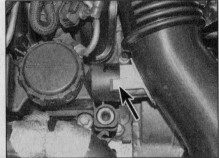

17.6c ... then disengage it from the breather ...

17.6d ... and remove it from the engine compartment

7 Note their fitted positions and disconnect the pipes and wiring plug from the fuel filter assembly **(see illustrations)**. Plug the openings to prevent contamination.

8 Release the retaining clip and lift the filter from place **(see illustration)**.
9 Release the clip and detach the fuel heater from the side of the filter assembly **(see illustrations)**.

10 Clip the fuel heater into place on the new filter. Fit the new filter into place, remove the plugs and reconnect the pipes, and the wiring plug.
11 Refit the air pipes.

2.0 litre engines

12 Disconnect the battery negative lead (see Chapter 5A), then remove the plastic cover from the top of the engine.
13 Undo the fasteners and remove the engine undershield.
14 Slacken the drain screw at the base of the filter and allow the filter to drain **(see illustration)**.
15 Thoroughly clean the area around the fuel pipe connectors, then disconnect the pipes and wiring connector (where applicable) at the top of the filter assembly **(see illustrations)**. Plug the openings to prevent contamination.

17.7a Depress the release button (arrowed) ...

17.7b ... then disconnect the pipes from the fuel filter

17.8 Release the clip and slide the filter upwards

17.9a Release the clip (arrowed) ...

17.9b ... and slide the heater from the filter body

17.14 Slacken the drain screw at the base of the filter

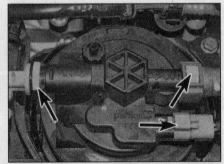

17.15a Depress the release buttons, disconnect the fuel pipes and the wiring plug (arrowed)

7.15b Plug the ends to prevent contamination

17.16 Use a socket to unscrew the filter head . . .

17.17 . . . then lift out the filter element

17.19a Renew the O-ring seal . . .

17.19b . . . insert the new filter element into the filter head . . .

18 Auxiliary drivebelt condition check

16 Using a 27 mm socket, unscrew the filter head **(see illustration)**.

17 Lift the filter head, and extract the filter element **(see illustration)**. Discard the seal on the filter head – a new one must be fitted.

18 Thoroughly clean the filter housing chamber using clean, lint-free rags.

19 Fit the new seal and filter element into the filter head, and then lubricate the new seal using clean fuel, and fit it in place on the filter head **(see illustrations)**.

20 Refit the filter head and tighten it until the filter head touches the stop **(see illustrations)**.

21 Remove the protective plugs, reconnect the fuel pipes/wiring plug, and refit the engine undershield.

All engines

22 Reconnect the battery negative lead as described in Chapter 5A.

23 Bleed the fuel system as described in Chapter 4A, Section 3.

1 On all engines, a single, multi-grooved auxiliary drivebelt is used to transmit drive from the crankshaft pulley to the alternator and the refrigerant compressor. The drivebelt is tensioned automatically by a spring-loaded tensioner pulley.

2 For better access to the drivebelt, chock the rear wheels then jack up the front of the car and support it on axle stands (see *Jacking and vehicle support*). Remove the right-hand front roadwheel, and then remove the plastic liner from under the right-hand wheel arch to expose the crankshaft pulley **(see illustrations)**.

3 Using a suitable socket and extension bar fitted to the crankshaft pulley bolt, rotate the crankshaft so that the entire length of the drivebelt(s) can be examined. Examine the drivebelt for cracks, splitting, fraying, or other damage **(see illustration)**. Check also for signs of glazing (shiny patches) and for separation of the belt plies. Renew the belt if worn or damaged, as described in Chapter 5A.

17.20a . . . and then refit to fuel filter housing . . .

17.20b . . . tighten filter head until it reaches the stop (arrowed)

18.3 Check the condition of the auxiliary belt

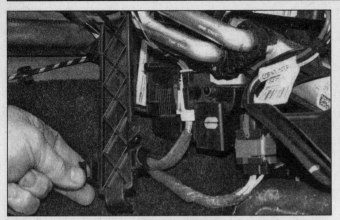

19.2a Unclip the filter cover . . .

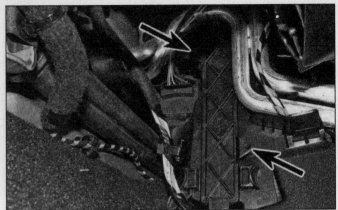

19.2b . . . remove the retaining screws (arrowed) – where fitted . . .

Every 24 000 miles or 2 years

19 Pollen filter renewal

1 Undo the fasteners and remove the trim panel from below the glovebox, above the passenger's footwell.

2 Release the securing clips and remove the plastic cover from the side of the heater unit housing (see illustrations). Note: *There maybe two screws used to secure the cover in place.*
3 Note which way around it's fitted, then pull the filter from the housing (see illustration).
4 Fit the new element using a reversal of the removal procedure.

19.3 . . . then slide the pollen filter out

Every 2 years

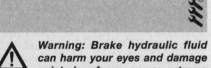

20 Brake fluid renewal

⚠ *Warning: Brake hydraulic fluid can harm your eyes and damage painted surfaces, so use extreme caution when handling and pouring it. Do not use fluid that has been standing open for some time, as it absorbs moisture from the air. Excess moisture can cause a dangerous loss of braking effectiveness.*

1 The procedure is similar to that for the bleeding of the hydraulic system as described in Chapter 9.

2 Working as described in Chapter 9, open the first bleed screw in the sequence, and pump the brake pedal gently until nearly all the old fluid has been emptied from the master cylinder reservoir. Top-up to the MAX level with new fluid, and continue pumping until only the new fluid remains in the reservoir, and new fluid can be seen emerging from the bleed screw. Tighten the screw, and top the reservoir level up to the MAX level line.
3 Work through all the remaining bleed screws in the sequence until new fluid can be seen at all of them. Be careful to keep the master cylinder reservoir topped-up to above the DANGER level at all times, or air may enter the system and greatly increase the length of the task.

4 When the operation is complete, check that all bleed screws are securely tightened, and that their dust caps are refitted (see illustration). Wash off all traces of spilt fluid, and recheck the master cylinder reservoir fluid level.
5 Check the operation of the brakes before taking the car on the road.

21 Remote control battery renewal

1 Insert a small screwdriver or coin, then twist it to separate the 2 halves of the control (see illustrations).

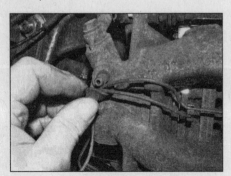

20.4 Make sure the dust caps are fitted to the bleed screws

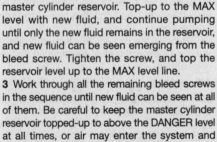

21.1a Twist the coin in the slot provided . . .

21.1b . . . and unclip the cover from the key

2 Unclip the circuit board and slide out the battery from its place on the circuit board (see illustration). Note: *Avoid touching the battery contacts or remote control circuitry with bare fingers.*

3 Insert the new battery as shown, and clip together the two halves of the control (see illustration).

4 It is now necessary to synchronise the control with the receiver, by inserting the key into the ignition switch, turning the ignition on, then immediately pressing the 'locking' button, and holding it down until the locks actuate.

21.2 Remove the circuit board from the cover

21.3 Slide the new battery into its location on the circuit board

22 Coolant renewal

Note: *This work is not included in the Peugeot schedule, and should not be required if the recommended Peugeot antifreeze/inhibitor is used.*

⚠ *Warning: Do not allow antifreeze to come in contact with your skin or painted surfaces of the vehicle. Flush contaminated areas immediately with plenty of water. Don't store new coolant, or leave old coolant lying around, where it's accessible to children or pets – they're attracted by its sweet smell. Ingestion of even a small amount of coolant can be fatal. Wipe up garage-floor and drip pan spills immediately. Keep antifreeze containers covered, and repair cooling system leaks as soon as they're noticed.*

⚠ *Warning: Never remove the expansion tank filler cap when the engine is running, or has just been switched off, as the cooling system will be hot, and the consequent escaping steam and scalding coolant could cause serious injury.*

⚠ *Warning: Wait until the engine is cold before starting these procedures.*

Cooling system draining

1 With the engine completely cold, remove the expansion tank filler cap. Turn the cap anti-clockwise, wait until any pressure remaining in

the system is released, then unscrew it and lift it off.

2 Chock the rear wheels, and then raise the front of the vehicle and support it on axle stands (see *Jacking and vehicle support*). Undo the retaining screws and remove the engine undershield.

1.6 litre engines

3 Position a suitable container beneath the radiator lower hose outlet at the lower centre of the radiator.

4 Release the retaining clip and disconnect the radiator lower hose (see illustration). Be prepared for coolant spillage.

5 Open the bleed screws; there are two bleed screws, one on the heater hose at the bulkhead connection and one on the top of

the thermostat housing at the left-hand side of the cylinder head (see illustrations).

6 To drain the engine, pull out the clip and remove the plug located in the coolant housing at the rear of the engine (see illustration). The plug must be refitted with a new clip and O-ring.

7 Once the coolant has finished draining, refit the plug, and reconnect the bottom hose. If the coolant has been drained for a reason other than renewal, then provided it is clean and less than two years old, it can be re-used, though this is not always recommended.

2.0 litre engine

8 Detach the bottom hose from the radiator, and drain the coolant into a container (see illustration).

9 Although a cylinder block drain plug is

22.4 Release the hose clip (arrowed) and disconnect the hose

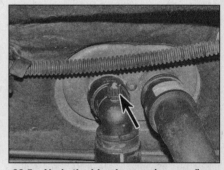

22.5a Undo the bleed screw (arrowed) on the heater hose . . .

22.5b . . . and the bleed screw (arrowed) on the thermostat housing

22.6 Prise out the retaining clip (arrowed) and pull out the coolant drain plug

22.8 Release the hose clip (arrowed) and disconnect the hose

22.9 Access to the cylinder block drain plug (arrowed) is extremely limited

22.10a Undo the bleed screw (arrowed) on the heater hose . . .

22.10b . . . and the bleed screw (arrowed) on the thermostat housing

fitted to the rear of the cylinder block, access to the plug is extremely limited. We found it impossible to undo the plug with the engine fitted **(see illustration)**.

10 Open the bleed screws; there are two bleed screws, one on the EGR cooler hose at the rear of the cylinder head and one on the top of the thermostat housing at the left-hand side of the cylinder head **(see illustrations)**.

11 When the flow of coolant stops, refit the coolant hose, and refit the undershield. Lower the vehicle to the ground.

12 If the coolant has been drained for a reason other than renewal, then provided it is clean and less than two years old, it can be re-used, though this is not always recommended.

Cooling system flushing

13 If coolant renewal has been neglected, or if the antifreeze mixture has become diluted, then in time the cooling system may gradually lose efficiency, as the coolant passages become restricted due to rust, scale deposits and other sediment. The cooling system efficiency can be restored by flushing the system clean.

14 The radiator should be flushed independently of the engine, to avoid unnecessary contamination.

Radiator flushing

15 Disconnect the top and bottom hoses and any other relevant hoses from the radiator, with reference to Chapter 3.

16 Insert a garden hose into the radiator top inlet. Direct a flow of clean water through the radiator, and continue flushing until clean water emerges from the radiator bottom outlet.

17 If after a reasonable period, the water still does not run clear, the radiator can be flushed with a good proprietary cleaning agent. It is important that the manufacturer's instructions are followed carefully. If the contamination is particularly bad, remove the radiator and insert the hose in the bottom outlet, and reverse-flush the radiator, then refit it.

Engine flushing

18 Remove the thermostat as described in Chapter 3. If the radiator top hose has been

disconnected, temporarily reconnect the hose.

19 With the top and bottom hoses disconnected from the radiator, insert a garden hose into the radiator top hose. Direct a clean flow of water through the engine, and continue flushing until clean water emerges from the radiator bottom hose.

20 On completion of flushing, refit the thermostat and reconnect the hoses with reference to Chapter 3.

Cooling system filling

21 Before attempting to fill the cooling system, make sure that all hoses and clips are in good condition, and that the clips are tight. Note that an antifreeze mixture must be used all year round, to prevent corrosion of the engine components.

22 Make sure that the air conditioning (A/C) or automatic climate control (ACC) is switched off. This is to prevent the air conditioning system starting the radiator cooling fan before the engine is at normal temperature when refilling the system.

23 Ensure the bleed screws are open (see paragraphs 5 or 10 as applicable).

24 To provide the required 'head' of coolant

HAYNES HINT

Cut the bottom off an old antifreeze container to make a 'header tank' for use when refilling the cooling system. The seal at the point arrowed should be as tight as possible – use an O-ring if available, or seal the joint by some other means.

necessary to force all trapped air from the system, a 'header tank' must be used by refitting. Although Peugeot dealers use a special header tank, the same effect can be achieved by using a suitable bottle, with a seal between the bottle and the expansion tank **(see Haynes hint)**.

25 Fit the 'header tank' to the expansion tank, and slowly fill the system. Coolant will emerge from the bleed screws, starting with the lowest screw. As soon as coolant free from air bubbles emerges from the bleed screw, tighten it, and watch the next bleed screw in the system. Repeat the procedure until the coolant is emerging from the highest bleed screw in the cooling system and all bleed screws are securely tightened.

26 Ensure the header tank is full (at least 0.5 litres of coolant). Start the engine, and run it at a fast idle speed (do not exceed 2000 rpm) until the cooling fan cuts in, and then cuts out 3 times. Stop the engine.

27 Stop the engine, and allow it to cool, and then remove the 'header tank'. Recheck the coolant level with reference to *Weekly checks*. Top-up the level if necessary and refit the expansion tank filler cap.

Antifreeze mixture

28 Always use an ethylene-glycol based antifreeze which is suitable for use in mixed-metal cooling systems. The quantity of antifreeze and levels of protection are given in the Specifications.

29 Before adding antifreeze, the cooling system should be completely drained, preferably flushed, and all hoses checked for condition and security.

30 After filling with antifreeze, a label should be attached to the expansion tank, stating the type and concentration of antifreeze used, and the date installed. Any subsequent topping-up should be made with the same type and concentration of antifreeze.

Caution: Do not use engine antifreeze in the windscreen/tailgate washer system, as it will cause damage to the vehicle paintwork. A screen wash additive should be added to the washer system in the quantities stated on the bottle.

Every 36 000 miles or 3 years

23 Air filter element renewal

1.6 litre engines

1 Pull the plastic cover upwards from the top of the engine (see illustration).
2 Undo the retaining screw and manoeuvre the air inlet ducting from the air filter housing (see illustration).
3 Slacken the securing clips from each end of the air inlet ducting to the turbocharger, release the breather tube clips and remove the air ducting (see illustrations).
4 Disconnect the wiring plug connector from the mass airflow sensor (see illustration).
5 Undo the air filter cleaner cover retaining screws, and lift the cover from air filter housing (see illustrations).
6 Note which way round the air filter element is fitted, and then lift it out from the housing (see illustration).
7 Wipe clean the inner surfaces of the cover and main housing, then locate the new element in the housing, making sure that the sealing lip is correctly engaged with the edge of the housing.
8 Refit the filter cover/inlet ducting assembly, ensuring the rear edge of the cover engages correctly with the rear of the filter housing.
9 Connect the wiring plug to the airflow sensor, and then refit the plastic cover to the top of the engine.

2.0 litre engines

10 Disconnect the mass airflow sensor wiring plug (see illustration).

23.1 Unclip the engine cover . . .

23.2 . . . remove the air inlet pipe . . .

23.3a . . . then slacken the retaining clips (arrowed) . . .

23.3b . . . and remove the turbo inlet hose from the breather (arrowed)

23.4 Disconnect the mass airflow sensor wiring plug

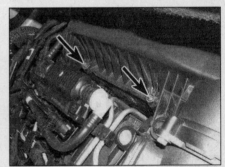

23.5a Undo the two retaining screws (arrowed) . . .

23.5b . . . remove the filter upper housing . . .

23.6 . . . and lift out the filter element

23.10 Disconnect the mass air flow sensor wiring plug

23.11 Undo the four retaining screws (arrowed) . . .

23.12 . . . and slacken the retaining clip

11 Undo the 4 retaining screws, and lift the cover from place (see illustration).
12 Slacken the securing clip from the air inlet ducting and remove the upper part of the air filter housing (see illustration).
13 Lift the air filter element from place, noting which way around it's fitted (see illustration).
14 Wipe clean the inner surfaces of the cover and main housing, then locate the new element in the housing, making sure that the sealing lip is correctly engaged with the edge of the housing.
15 Refit the cover, and secure it with the screws.
16 Reconnect the mass airflow sensor wiring plug.

23.13 Lift the filter element out from the lower housing

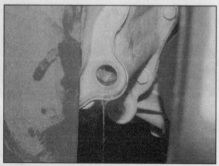

24.3 Add oil until a trickle emerges from the plug hole

24 Manual transmission oil level check

Note: *There is no recommendation in the manufacturer's schedule to check the oil level on ML6C transmissions. They are described as 'Lubricated for life' and there is no level plug. If it is suspected the oil level is low, drain and refill the transmission as described in Chapter 7A. The following information applies only to the BE4R transmission.*

1 Take the car on a short journey to warm the transmission up to normal operating

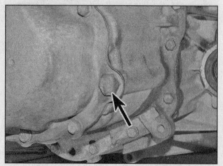

24.2 Fluid level plug (arrowed) – BE4R transmission

25.2 Unscrew the transmission filler plug (arrowed)

temperature. Position the car over an inspection pit, or alternatively jack up the front and rear of the car and support on axle stands (see *Jacking and vehicle support*). Whichever method is used, make sure that the car is level for checking the fluid level later.
2 Position a suitable container beneath the transmission, and then unscrew the filler/level plug located on the left-hand side of the transmission casing (see illustration).
3 The fluid level should be up to the bottom of the filler/level plug hole. If necessary, add the specified fluid until it begins to run out of the hole (see illustration).
4 Refit the filler/level plug and tighten it to the specified torque.
5 Lower the vehicle to the ground.

25 Automatic transmission fluid level check

Note: *There is no recommendation in the manufacturer's schedule to check the oil level on automatic transmissions fitted to the 407. They are described as 'Lubricated for life'. However, we consider it prudent to check the fluid level, as a leak from a driveshaft oil seal or sealing washer could cause expensive damage.*

1 Take the vehicle on a short journey, to warm the transmission up to normal operating temperature, and then park the vehicle on level ground. Firmly apply the handbrake and place the selector lever in the P position.
2 Wipe clean the area around the filler plug, which is situated on the top of the transmission, directly beneath the air cleaner assembly. Remove the air cleaner assembly as described in Chapter 4A, then unscrew the filler plug from the transmission and recover the sealing washer (see illustration).
3 Carefully add 0.5 litre of the specified type of fluid to the transmission via the filler plug aperture. Fit a new sealing washer to the filler

plug then refit the plug, tightening it to the specified torque.

4 Undo the screws and remove the engine undershield – where fitted.

5 Position a suitable container under the drain/level plug arrangement, situated on the base of the transmission. The level plug is the smaller plug fitted to the centre of the larger drain plug **(see illustration)**.

Caution: Do not remove the drain plug by mistake.

6 Refit the air cleaner then start the engine and allow it to idle. With the engine running, retain the drain plug then slacken and remove the level plug and sealing washer.

 Warning: The fluid will be hot, take precautions against scalding.

7 If there is sufficient fluid in the transmission unit, fluid should trickle out the centre of the drain plug before slowing to a drip. **Note:** *If no fluid trickles out, or just a few drips appear when the plug is removed, the fluid level is too low. Refit the level plug then switch off the engine. Add a further 0.5 litre of fluid to the transmission then refit the filler plug and repeat the check.*

8 Once the flow of fluid stops, the level is correct. Fit a new sealing washer to the level plug then refit the plug and tighten it to the specified torque. Switch off the engine.

25.5 Unscrew the level plug (arrowed) from the centre of the drain plug

Every 60 000 miles or 5 years

26 Particulate filter (1.6 litre engines) renewal

Renewal of the particulate filter is described in Chapter 4A, Section 18.

Every 72 000 miles or 6 years

27 Eolys 176 fluid check

1 Eolys 176 fluid is an additive used on vehicles equipped with a particulate filter incorporated into the exhaust system. Over a period of time, the soot produced by the engine will clog the filter. When the filter requires cleaning, the engine management system injects a small quantity of fuel into the combustion chamber after combustion has taken place. The unburnt fuel enters the exhaust system, where it ignites, and burns the soot deposits from the particulate filter. In order to lower the temperature at which the soot is burnt, Eolys 176 fluid is added to the fuel in the tank. The fluid is stored in a separate tank adjacent to the fuel tank, and added to the main fuel tank. Every time the fuel tank is filled, the system computes how much Eolys 176 fluid to add. Eventually the level of fluid will fall below a minimum level and a warning light will illuminate on the instrument cluster. If the system runs out of fluid, the particulate filter will be unable to purge, causing its blockage, and premature failure. Unfortunately, the process of checking the level, replenishing the Eolys fluid tank and resetting the engine management values requires access to Peugeot diagnostic equipment, and therefore must be entrusted to a Peugeot dealer or suitably-equipped specialist. Failure to reset the ECM values will prevent the filter cleaning process from occurring.

Every 96 000 miles or 8 years

28 Particulate filter (2.0 litre engines) renewal

Renewal of the particulate filter is described in Chapter 4A, Section 18.

29 Timing belt renewal

Refer to Chapter 2A or 2B, as applicable.

Every 10 years

30 Airbags renewal

Renewal of the airbags is described in Chapter 12.

Chapter 2 Part A:
1.6 litre engine in-car repair procedures

Contents

Degrees of difficulty

Easy, suitable for novice with little experience	**Fairly easy,** suitable for beginner with some experience	**Fairly difficult,** suitable for competent DIY mechanic	**Difficult,** suitable for experienced DIY mechanic	**Very difficult,** suitable for expert DIY or professional

Specifications

General

Designation	DV6TED4
Engine codes:*	
Without particulate filter	9HY
With particulate filter	9HZ
Capacity	1560 cc
Bore	75.0 mm
Stroke	88.3 mm
Direction of crankshaft rotation	Clockwise (viewed from the right-hand side of vehicle)
No 1 cylinder location	At the transmission end of block
Maximum power output	80 kW @ 4000 rpm
Maximum torque output	240 Nm @ 1750 rpm
Compression ratio	18.0 :1

* The engine code is stamped on a plate attached to the front of the cylinder block

Compression pressures (engine hot, at cranking speed)

Normal	20 ± 5 bar
Minimum	15 bar
Maximum difference between any two cylinders	5 bar

Camshaft

Drive:	
Inlet camshaft	Toothed belt from crankshaft
Exhaust camshaft	Chain-drive from inlet camshaft

Lubrication system

Oil pump type	Gear-type, driven directly by the right-hand end of the crankshaft by two flats machined along the crankshaft journal
Minimum oil pressure at 110°C:	
1000 rpm	1.2 bar
2000 rpm	2.0 bar
3000 rpm	2.7 bar
4000 rpm	2.9 bar

Torque wrench settings

	Nm	lbf ft
Ancillary drivebelt tensioner roller	20	15
Big-end bolts:*		
Stage 1	10	7
Stage 2	Slacken 180°	
Stage 3	30	22
Stage 4	Angle-tighten a further 140°	
Camshaft bearing caps	10	7
Camshaft cover/bearing ladder:		
Studs	10	7
Bolts	10	7
Camshaft position sensor bolt	5	4
Camshaft sprocket:		
Stage 1	20	15
Stage 2	Angle-tighten a further 50°	
Coolant outlet housing bolts	7	5
Crankshaft position/speed sensor bolt	5	4
Crankshaft pulley/sprocket bolt:*		
Stage 1	35	26
Stage 2	Angle-tighten a further 190 °	
Cylinder head bolts:		
Stage 1	20	15
Stage 2	40	30
Stage 3	Angle-tighten a further 260°	
Cylinder head cover/manifold	10	7
EGR valve	10	7
Engine mountings:		
Left-hand engine/transmission mounting:		
Mounting bracket to transmission	55	41
Mounting to bracket	60	44
Rear engine/transmission mounting:		
Connecting link to mounting assembly	60	44
Connecting link-to-subframe nut/bolt	60	44
Mounting to engine	60	44
Right-hand engine mounting:		
Mounting to body	60	44
Mounting to support bracket	60	44
Support bracket to engine	55	41
Engine-to-transmission fixing bolts	60	44
Flywheel bolt:*		
Dual mass flywheel:		
Stage 1	25	18
Stage 2	Fully slacken	
Stage 3	8	6
Stage 4	30	22
Stage 5	Angle-tighten a further 90°	
Traditional flywheel:		
Stage 1	25	18
Stage 2	Fully slacken	
Stage 3	8	6
Stage 4	17	13
Stage 5	Angle-tighten a further 75°	
Fuel pump sprocket	50	37
Main bearing ladder outer seam bolts:		
Stage 1	5	4
Stage 2	10	7
Main bearing ladder to cylinder block:		
Stage 1	10	7
Stage 2	Slacken 180°	
Stage 3	30	22
Stage 4	Angle-tighten a further 140°	
Piston oil jet spray tube bolt	20	15
Oil filter cover	25	18
Oil pick-up pipe	10	7
Oil pressure switch	20	15
Oil pump to cylinder block	10	7
Sump bolts/nuts	12	9
Sump drain plug	25	18

Torque wrench settings (continued)

	Nm	lbf ft
Timing belt idler pulley	35	26
Timing belt tensioner pulley	25	18
Timing chain tensioner	10	7
Vacuum pump (brakes):		
Stage 1	3	2
Stage 2	5	4
Stage 3	18	13
Stage 4	Angle-tighten a further 5°	

Do not re-use

1 General information

How to use this Chapter

This Part of Chapter 2 describes the repair procedures that can reasonably be carried out on the engine while it remains in the vehicle. If the engine has been removed from the vehicle and is being dismantled as described in Part C, any preliminary dismantling procedures can be ignored.

Note that, while it may be possible physically to overhaul items such as the piston/connecting rod assemblies while the engine is in the car, such tasks are not usually carried out as separate operations. Usually, several additional procedures are required (not to mention the cleaning of components and oilways); for this reason, all such tasks are classed as major overhaul procedures, and are described in Part C of this Chapter.

Part C describes the removal of the engine/transmission from the car, and the full overhaul procedures that can then be carried out.

DV series engines

The 1.6 litre DV series engine is the result of development collaboration between Citroën/Peugeot and Ford. The engine is of double overhead camshaft (DOHC) 16-valve design. The direct injection, turbocharged, four-cylinder engine is mounted transversely, with the transmission mounted on the left-hand side.

A toothed timing belt drives the inlet camshaft, high-pressure fuel pump and coolant pump. The inlet camshaft drives the exhaust camshaft via a chain. The camshafts operate the inlet and exhaust valves via rocker arms, which are supported at their pivot ends by hydraulic self-adjusting tappets. The camshafts are supported by bearings machined directly in the cylinder head and camshaft bearing housing.

The high-pressure fuel pump supplies fuel to the fuel rail, and subsequently to the electronically-controlled injectors that inject the fuel directly into the combustion chambers. This design differs from the previous type where an injection pump supplies the fuel at high pressure to each injector. The earlier, conventional type injection pump required fine calibration and timing, and these functions are now completed by the high-pressure pump, electronic injectors and engine management ECM.

The crankshaft runs in five main bearings of the usual shell type. Endfloat is controlled by thrustwashers either side of No 2 main bearing.

The pistons are selected to be of matching weight, and incorporate fully-floating gudgeon pins retained by circlips.

Repair operations precaution

The engine is a complex unit with numerous accessories and ancillary components. The design of the engine compartment is such that every conceivable space has been utilised, and access to virtually all of the engine components is extremely limited. In many cases, ancillary components will have to be removed, or moved to one side, and wiring, pipes and hoses will have to be disconnected or removed from various cable clips and support brackets.

When working on this engine, read through the entire procedure first, look at the car and engine at the same time, and establish whether you have the necessary tools, equipment, skill and patience to proceed. Allow considerable time for any operation, and be prepared for the unexpected.

Because of the limited access, many of the engine photographs appearing in this Chapter were, by necessity, taken with the engine removed from the vehicle.

⚠️ **Warning: It is essential to observe strict precautions when working on the fuel system components of the engine, particularly the high-pressure side of the system. Before carrying out any engine operations that entail working on, or near, any part of the fuel system, refer to the special information given in Chapter 4A.**

Operations with engine in car

a) Compression pressure – testing.
b) Cylinder head cover – removal and refitting.
c) Crankshaft pulley – removal and refitting.
d) Timing belt covers – removal and refitting.
e) Timing belt – removal, refitting and adjustment.
f) Timing belt tensioner and sprockets – removal and refitting.
g) Camshaft oil seal – renewal.
h) Camshaft, rocker arms and hydraulic tappets – removal, inspection and refitting.
i) Sump – removal and refitting.
j) Oil pump – removal and refitting.
k) Crankshaft oil seals – renewal.
l) Engine/transmission mountings – inspection and renewal.
m) Flywheel – removal, inspection and refitting.

2 Compression and leakdown tests – description and interpretation

Compression test

Note: *A compression tester specifically designed for diesel engines must be used for this test.*

1 When engine performance is down, or if misfiring occurs which cannot be attributed to the fuel system, a compression test can provide diagnostic clues as to the engine's condition. If the test is performed regularly, it can give warning of trouble before any other symptoms become apparent.

2 A compression tester specifically intended for diesel engines must be used, because of the higher pressures involved. The tester is connected to an adapter that screws into the glow plug or injector hole. On this engine, an adapter suitable for use in the glow plug holes will be required, so as not to disturb the fuel system components. It is unlikely to be worthwhile buying such a tester for occasional use, but it may be possible to borrow or hire one – if not, have the test performed by a garage.

3 Unless specific instructions to the contrary are supplied with the tester, observe the following points:

a) The battery must be in a good state of charge, the air filter must be clean, and the engine should be at normal operating temperature.
b) All the glow plugs should be removed as described in Chapter 5B before starting the test.
c) The wiring connectors on the engine management system ECM (located in the plastic box behind the battery) must be disconnected.

4 The compression pressures measured are not so important as the balance

between cylinders. Values are given in the Specifications.

5 The cause of poor compression is less easy to establish on a diesel engine than on a petrol one. The effect of introducing oil into the cylinders ('wet' testing) is not conclusive, because there is a risk that the oil will sit in the swirl chamber or in the recess on the piston crown instead of passing to the rings. However, the following can be used as a rough guide to diagnosis.

6 All cylinders should produce very similar pressures; any difference greater than that specified indicates the existence of a fault. Note that the compression should build-up quickly in a healthy engine; low compression on the first stroke, followed by gradually increasing pressure on successive strokes, indicates worn piston rings. A low compression reading on the first stroke, which does not build-up during successive strokes, indicates leaking valves or a blown head gasket (a cracked head could also be the cause). Deposits on the undersides of the valve heads can also cause low compression.

7 A low reading from two adjacent cylinders is almost certainly due to the head gasket having blown between them; the presence of coolant in the engine oil will confirm this.

8 If the compression reading is unusually high, the cylinder head surfaces, valves and pistons are probably coated with carbon deposits. If this is the case, the cylinder head should be removed and decarbonised (see Part C).

Leakdown test

9 A leakdown test measures the rate at which compressed air fed into the cylinder is lost. It is an alternative to a compression test, and in many ways it is better, since the escaping air provides easy identification of where pressure loss is occurring (piston rings, valves or head gasket).

10 The equipment needed for leakdown testing is unlikely to be available to the home mechanic. If poor compression is suspected, have the test performed by a suitably-equipped garage.

3 Engine assembly/valve timing holes – general information and usage

Note: *Do not attempt to rotate the engine whilst the crankshaft and camshaft are locked in position. If the engine is to be left in this state for a long period of time, it is a good idea to place suitable warning notices inside the vehicle, and in the engine compartment. This will reduce the possibility of the engine being accidentally cranked on the starter motor, which is likely to cause damage with the locking pins in place.*

1 Timing holes or slots are located only in the crankshaft pulley flange and camshaft sprocket hub. The holes/slots are used to

position the pistons halfway up the cylinder bores. This will ensure that the valve timing is maintained during operations that require removal and refitting of the timing belt. When the holes/slots are aligned with their corresponding holes in the cylinder block and cylinder head, suitable diameter bolts/pins can be inserted to lock the crankshaft and camshaft in position, preventing rotation.

2 Note that the HDi type fuel system used on these engines does not have a conventional diesel injection pump, but instead uses a high-pressure fuel pump that does not have to be timed. The alignment of the fuel pump sprocket (and hence the fuel pump itself) with respect to crankshaft and camshaft position is therefore irrelevant.

3 To align the engine assembly/valve timing holes, proceed as follows.

4 Chock the rear wheels then jack up the front of the vehicle and support it on axle stands (see *Jacking and vehicle support*). Remove the right-hand front roadwheel.

5 To gain access to the crankshaft pulley, to enable the engine to be turned, the wheel arch plastic liner must be removed. The liner is secured by several plastic expanding rivets/nut/screws. To remove the rivets, push in the centre pins a little, and then prise the clips from place. Remove the liner from under the front wing. The crankshaft can then be turned

using a suitable socket and extension bar fitted to the pulley bolt.

6 Remove the upper and lower timing belt covers as described in Section 6.

7 Temporarily refit the crankshaft pulley bolt, remove the crankshaft locking tool, then turn the crankshaft until the timing hole in the camshaft sprocket hub is aligned with the corresponding hole in the cylinder head. Note that the crankshaft must always be turned in a clockwise direction (viewed from the right-hand side of vehicle). Use a small mirror so that the position of the sprocket hub timing slot can be observed. When the slot is aligned with the corresponding hole in the cylinder head, the camshaft is positioned correctly.

8 Remove the crankshaft drivebelt pulley as described in Section 5.

9 Insert a 5 mm diameter bolt, rod or drill through the hole in crankshaft sprocket flange and into the corresponding hole in the oil pump **(see illustration)**, if necessary, carefully turn the crankshaft either way until the rod enters the timing hole in the block.

10 Insert an 8 mm bolt, rod or drill through the hole in the camshaft sprocket hub and into engagement with the cylinder head **(see illustrations)**. Note that a modified 3-segment camshaft sprocket is fitted to later models.

11 The crankshaft and camshaft are now locked in position, preventing unnecessary rotation.

3.9 Insert a 5.0 mm drill bit/bolt through the round hole in the sprocket flange into the hole in the oil pump housing (lower timing belt cover removed for clarity)

3.10a Insert an 8.0 mm drill bit/bolt through the hole in the camshaft sprocket into the corresponding hole in the cylinder head

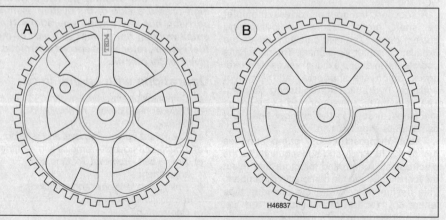

3.10b Early models (A) and later models (B) camshaft sprocket

4.1 Pull the plastic cover upwards to release the rubber mountings

4.2a Undo the screw (arrowed) . . .

4.2b . . . and remove the air inlet ducting

4 Cylinder head cover/ manifold – removal and refitting

Removal

1 Pull the plastic cover upwards from the top of the engine (see illustration)

2 Remove the inlet and outlet air ducting from the air filter housing (see illustrations).

3 Disconnect the mass airflow meter wiring plug (see illustration).

4 Unscrew the air filter housing cover bolts, then remove the cover and filter element – refer to Chapter 4A (see illustrations). Pull the air filter housing from its mountings.

5 Disconnect the wiring plugs from the top of each injector, undo the guide bolts, then make sure all wiring harnesses are freed from any retaining brackets on the cylinder head cover/ inlet manifold (see illustration). Disconnect any vacuum pipes as necessary, having first noted their fitted positions.

6 Remove the EGR cooler as described in Chapter 4B.

7 Depress the release buttons and disconnect the fuel feed and return hoses at the right-hand end of the cylinder head, then disconnect the

4.2c Disconnect the hose to the turbocharger . . .

4.2d . . . and release the clips (arrowed) and disconnect the breather pipe

4.3 Release the clip and disconnect the mass airflow meter wiring plug

4.4a Undo the cover screws (arrowed) . . .

4.4b . . . and remove the ducting/cover assembly

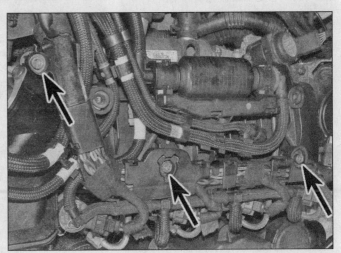

4.5 Undo the bolts (arrowed) and position the wiring harness/ guide to one side

4.7a Depress the release buttons (arrowed) and disconnect the fuel feed and return hoses

4.7b Disconnect the fuel temperature sensor wiring plug (arrowed) . . .

4.7c . . . then unclip the fuel priming bulb/ pipes (arrowed)

fuel temperature sensor wiring plug and move the pipe/priming bulb assembly to the rear **(see illustrations)**.

8 Release the clamps, undo the bolts and remove the inlet ducting between the turbocharger and the inlet manifold. Make

a note of their fitted positions, and then disconnect the various wiring plugs as the assembly is withdrawn **(see illustrations)**.

9 Undo the retaining bolts and remove the oil separator from the top of the cylinder head **(see illustration)**. Recover the rubber seal.

10 Prise out the retaining clips and disconnect the fuel return pipes from the injectors, then undo the unions and remove the high-pressure fuel pipes from the injectors and the common fuel rail at the rear of the cylinder head – counterhold the unions with a second spanner **(see illustrations)**. Plug the openings to prevent dirt ingress.

11 Undo the 2 bolts securing the cylinder head cover/inlet manifold. Lift the assembly away **(see illustration)**. Recover the manifold rubber seals.

4.8a Slacken the left-hand turbocharger outlet hose bolt, undo the right-hand bolt (arrowed) . . .

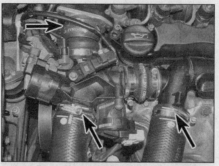

4.8b . . . then slacken the hose clamps (arrowed), disconnect the wiring plugs . . .

4.8c . . . undo the bolt on the end (arrowed) . . .

4.8d . . . and the 2 at the front (arrowed), then remove the assembly

4.9 Undo the bolts and remove the oil separator (arrowed)

4.10a Prise out the clip and pull the return hose from the top of each injector

4.10b Use a second spanner to hold the injector port whilst slackening the fuel pipe unions

4.11 Undo the 2 remaining bolts (arrowed) and pull the cover/manifold upwards

Refitting

12 Refitting is a reversal of removal, bearing in mind the following points:
a) Examine the seals for signs of damage and deterioration, and renew if necessary. Smear a little clean engine oil on the manifold seals.
b) Renew the fuel injector high-pressure pipes – see Chapter 4A.

5 Crankshaft pulley – removal and refitting

5.2 The locking pin/bolt (arrowed) must locate in the hole in the flywheel (arrowed) to prevent rotation

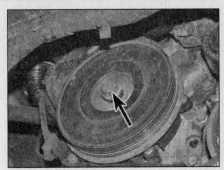

5.3 Undo the crankshaft pulley retaining bolt (arrowed)

Removal

1 Remove the auxiliary drivebelt as described in Chapter 5A.
2 To lock the crankshaft, working underneath the engine, insert Peugeot tool No 0194-C into the hole in the right-hand face of the engine block casting over the lower section of the flywheel. Rotate the crankshaft until the tool engages in the corresponding hole in the flywheel. In the absence of the Peugeot tool, insert a 12 mm rod or drill into the hole **(see illustration)**. *Note: The hole in the casting and the hole in the flywheel are provided purely to lock the crankshaft whilst the pulley bolt is undone, it does **not** position the crankshaft at TDC.*
3 Using a suitable socket and extension bar, unscrew the retaining bolt, remove the

washer, then slide the pulley off the end of the crankshaft **(see illustration)**. If the pulley is tight fit, it can be drawn off the crankshaft using a suitable puller. If a puller is being used, refit the pulley retaining bolt without the washer to avoid damaging the crankshaft as the puller is tightened.

Caution: Do not touch the outer magnetic sensor ring of the sprocket with your fingers, or allow metallic particles to come into contact with it.

Refitting

4 Refit the pulley to the end of the crankshaft.
5 Thoroughly clean the threads of the pulley retaining bolt, then apply a coat of locking compound to the bolt threads. Peugeot

recommend the use of Loctite (available from your Peugeot dealer); in the absence of this, any good-quality locking compound may be used.
6 Refit the crankshaft pulley retaining bolt and washer. Tighten the bolt to the specified torque, then through the specified angle, preventing the crankshaft from turning using the method employed on removal.
7 Refit and tension the auxiliary drivebelt as described in Chapter 5A.

6 Timing belt covers – removal and refitting

⚠️ **Warning: Refer to the precautionary information contained in Section 1 before proceeding.**

Removal

Upper cover

1 Remove the plastic cover from the top of the engine.
2 Release the wiring harness and fuel pipes from the upper cover **(see illustrations)**.
3 Undo the five screws and remove the timing belt upper cover **(see illustration)**.

Lower cover

4 Remove the upper cover as described previously.

6.2a Unclip the fuel pipes (arrowed) . . .

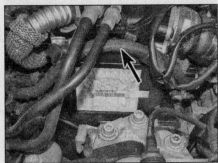

6.2b . . . and the wiring harness (arrowed) from the timing belt upper cover

6.3 Upper timing belt cover screws (arrowed)

6.6 Lower timing belt cover screws (arrowed)

5 Remove the crankshaft pulley as described in Section 5.

6 Remove the auxiliary drivebelt tensioner locking tool (where applicable), then undo the five bolts and remove the lower cover **(see illustration)**.

Refitting

7 Refitting of all the covers is a reversal of the relevant removal procedure, ensuring that each cover section is correctly located, and that the cover retaining bolts are securely tightened. Ensure that all disturbed hoses are reconnected and retained by their relevant clips.

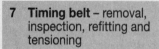

7 Timing belt – removal, inspection, refitting and tensioning

General

1 The timing belt drives the inlet camshaft, high-pressure fuel pump, and coolant pump from a toothed sprocket on the end of the crankshaft. If the belt breaks or slips in service, the pistons are likely to hit the valve heads, resulting in expensive damage.

2 The timing belt should be renewed at the specified intervals, or earlier if it is contaminated with oil or at all noisy in operation (a 'scraping' noise due to uneven wear).

3 If the timing belt is being removed, it is a wise precaution to check the condition of the coolant pump at the same time (check for signs of coolant leakage). This may avoid the need to remove the timing belt again at a later stage should the coolant pump fail.

Removal

4 Chock the rear wheels then jack up the front of the vehicle and support it on axle stands (see *Jacking and vehicle support*). Remove the front right-hand roadwheel, wheel arch liner (to expose the crankshaft pulley), and the engine undershield. The wheel arch liner is secured

7.10 Undo the bolt (arrowed) and remove the crankshaft position sensor

by several plastic expanding rivets/nuts/plastic clips or screws. Push the centre pins in a little then prise the rivets from place. The engine undershield is retained by several screws.

5 Remove the auxiliary drivebelt as described in Chapter 5A.

6 Remove the upper and lower timing belt covers, as described in Section 6.

7 Refer to Chapter 4A and disconnect the front exhaust pipe at the flexible section.

8 Position a trolley jack under the engine, and using a block of wood on the jack head, take the weight of the engine.

9 Undo the bolts/nut and remove the right-hand engine mounting and support bracket – see Section 17.

10 Undo the screw and remove the crankshaft position sensor adjacent to the crankshaft sprocket flange, and move it to one side **(see illustration)**.

11 Undo the retaining screw and remove the timing belt protection bracket, again adjacent to the crankshaft sprocket flange **(see illustration)**.

12 Lock the crankshaft and camshaft in the correct position as described in Section 3. If necessary, temporarily refit the crankshaft pulley bolt to enable the crankshaft to be rotated.

13 Insert a hexagon key into the belt tensioner pulley centre, slacken the pulley bolt, and

7.11 Remove the timing belt protection bracket

allow the tensioner to rotate, relieving the belt tension **(see illustration)**. With belt slack, temporarily tighten the pulley bolt.

14 Note its routing, then remove the timing belt from the sprockets.

Inspection

15 Renew the belt as a matter of course, regardless of its apparent condition. The cost of a new belt is nothing compared with the cost of repairs should the belt break in service. If signs of oil contamination are found, trace the source of the oil leak and rectify it. Wash down the engine timing belt area and all related components, to remove all traces of oil. Check that the tensioner and idler pulleys rotate freely without any sign of roughness, and also check that the coolant pump pulley rotates freely. If necessary, renew these items.

Refitting and tensioning

16 Commence refitting by ensuring that the crankshaft and camshaft timing pins are still in position correctly.

17 Locate the timing belt on the crankshaft sprocket, then keeping it taut, locate it around the idler pulley, camshaft sprocket, high-pressure pump sprocket, coolant pump sprocket, and the tensioner pulley **(see illustration)**.

7.13 Slacken the bolt and allow the tensioner to rotate, relieving the tension on the belt

7.17 Timing belt routing

7.19 The index arm must align with the lug (arrowed)

18 Refit the timing belt protection bracket and tighten the retaining bolt securely.
19 Slacken the tensioner pulley bolt, and using a hexagonal key, rotate the tensioner anti-clockwise, which moves the index arm clockwise, until the index arm is aligned as shown (**see illustration**).
20 Remove the camshaft and crankshaft timing pins and, using a socket on the crankshaft pulley bolt, turn the crankshaft clockwise 10 complete revolutions. Refit the crankshaft and camshaft locking pins.
21 Check that the tensioner index arm is still aligned between the edges of the area shown (**see illustration 7.19**). If it is not, remove and belt and begin the refitting process again, starting at Paragraph 17.
22 The remainder of refitting is a reversal of removal. Tighten all fasteners to the specified torque where given.

8 Timing belt sprockets and tensioner – removal and refitting

Camshaft sprocket

Removal

1 Remove the timing belt as described in Section 7.
2 Remove the locking tool from the camshaft sprocket/hub. Slacken the sprocket hub retaining bolt. To prevent the camshaft rotating as the bolt is slackened, a sprocket

8.11a Slide the sprocket from the crankshaft . . .

A sprocket holding tool can be made from two lengths of steel strip bolted together to form a forked end. Drill holes and insert bolts in the ends of the fork to engage with the sprocket spokes.

holding tool will be required. In the absence of the special Peugeot tool, an acceptable substitute can be fabricated at home (**see Tool Tip 1**). *Do not* attempt to use the engine assembly/valve timing locking tool to prevent the sprocket from rotating whilst the bolt is slackened.
3 Remove the sprocket hub retaining bolt, and slide the sprocket and hub off the end of the camshaft.
4 Clean the camshaft sprocket thoroughly, and renew it if there are any signs of wear, damage or cracks.

Refitting

5 Refit the camshaft sprocket to the camshaft (**see illustration**).
6 Refit the sprocket hub retaining bolt. Tighten the bolt to the specified torque, preventing the camshaft from turning as during removal.
7 Align the engine assembly/valve timing slot in the camshaft sprocket hub with the hole in the cylinder head and refit the timing pin to lock the camshaft in position.
8 Fit the timing belt around the pump sprocket and camshaft sprocket, and tension the timing belt as described in Section 7.

Crankshaft sprocket

Removal

9 Remove the timing belt as described in Section 7.

8.11b . . . and recover the Woodruff key

8.5 Ensure the lug on the sprocket hub engages with the slot on the end of the camshaft (arrowed)

10 Check that the engine assembly/valve timing holes are still aligned as described in Section 3, and the camshaft sprocket and flywheel are locked in position.
11 Slide the sprocket off the end of the crankshaft and collect the Woodruff key (**see illustrations**).
12 Examine the crankshaft oil seal for signs of oil leakage and, if necessary, renew it as described in Section 14.
13 Clean the crankshaft sprocket thoroughly, and renew it if there are any signs of wear, damage or cracks. Recover the crankshaft locating key.

Refitting

14 Refit the key to the end of the crankshaft, then refit the crankshaft sprocket (with the flange facing the crankshaft pulley).
15 Fit the timing belt around the crankshaft sprocket, and tension the timing belt as described in Section 7.

Fuel pump sprocket

Removal

16 Remove the timing belt as described in Section 7.
17 Using a suitable socket, undo the pump sprocket retaining nut. The sprocket can be held stationary by inserting a suitably-sized locking pin, drill or rod through the hole in the sprocket, and into the corresponding hole in the backplate (**see illustration**), or by using a suitable forked tool engaged with the holes in the sprocket (**see Tool Tip 1**).

8.17 Insert a suitable drill bit through the sprocket into the hole in the backplate

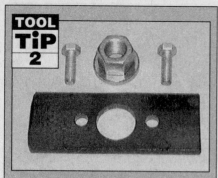

TOOL TiP 2

Make a sprocket releasing tool from a short strip of steel. Drill two holes in the strip to correspond with the two holes in the sprocket. Drill a third hole just large enough to accept the flats of the sprocket retaining nut.

18 The pump sprocket is a taper fit on the pump shaft and it will be necessary to make up another tool to release it from the taper (see Tool Tip 2).

19 Partially unscrew the sprocket retaining nut, fit the home-made tool, and secure it to the sprocket with two suitable bolts. Prevent the sprocket from rotating as before, and unscrew the sprocket retaining nut. The nut will bear against the tool, as it is undone, forcing the sprocket off the shaft taper. Once the taper is released, remove the tool, unscrew the nut fully, and remove the sprocket from the pump shaft.

20 Clean the sprocket thoroughly, and renew it if there are any signs of wear, damage or cracks.

Refitting

21 Refit the pump sprocket and retaining nut, and tighten the nut to the specified torque. Prevent the sprocket rotating as the nut is tightened using the sprocket holding tool.

22 Fit the timing belt around the pump

8.31 Timing belt idler pulley retaining nut (arrowed)

sprocket, and tension the timing belt as described in Section 7.

Coolant pump sprocket

23 The coolant pump sprocket is integral with the pump, and cannot be removed. Coolant pump removal is described in Chapter 3.

Tensioner pulley

Removal

24 Remove the timing belt as described in Section 7.

25 Remove the tensioner pulley retaining bolt, and slide the pulley off its mounting stud.

26 Clean the tensioner pulley, but do not use any strong solvent that may enter the pulley bearings. Check that the pulley rotates freely, with no sign of stiffness or free play. Renew the pulley if there is any doubt about its condition, or if there are any obvious signs of wear or damage.

27 Examine the pulley mounting stud for signs of damage and if necessary, renew it.

Refitting

28 Refit the tensioner pulley to its mounting stud, and fit the retaining bolt.

29 Refit the timing belt as described in Section 7.

Idler pulley

Removal

30 Remove the timing belt as described in Section 7.

31 Undo the retaining bolt/nut and withdraw the idler pulley from the engine (see illustration).

32 Clean the idler pulley, but do not use any strong solvent that may enter the bearings. Check that the pulley rotates freely, with no sign of stiffness or free play. Renew the idler pulley if there is any doubt about its condition, or if there are any obvious signs of wear or damage.

Refitting

33 Locate the idler pulley on the engine, and fit the retaining bolt/nut. Tighten the bolt/nut to the specified torque.

34 Refit the timing belt (see Section 7).

9 Camshafts, rocker arms and hydraulic tappets – removal, inspection and refitting

Removal

1 Remove the cylinder head cover/manifold as described in Section 4.

2 Remove the injectors as described in Chapter 4A.

3 Remove the camshaft sprocket as described in Section 8.

4 Refit the right-hand engine mounting, but only tighten the bolts moderately; this will keep the engine supported during the camshaft removal.

5 Undo the bolts and remove the vacuum pump. Recover the pump O-ring seals (see illustration).

6 Remove the fuel filter (see Chapter 1), then undo the bolts and remove the fuel filter mounting bracket.

7 Release the wiring harness clips, then undo the 3 bolts and remove the timing belt inner, upper cover (see illustration).

9.5 Vacuum pump bolts (arrowed)

9.7 Timing belt inner, upper cover bolts (arrowed)

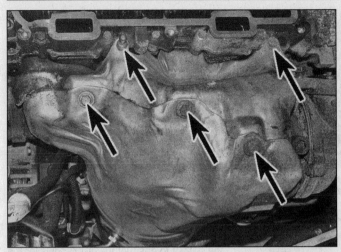

9.9a Undo the bolts (arrowed) and remove the rear section of the heat shield

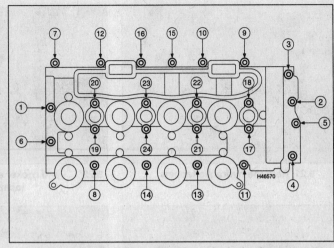

9.9b Camshaft cover/bearing ladder bolt slackening sequence

8 Disconnect the wiring plug, unscrew the retaining bolt, and remove the camshaft position sensor from the camshaft cover/bearing ladder.

9 Undo the 5 bolts and remove the upper rear section of the turbocharger heat shield, then working gradually and evenly, slacken and remove the bolts securing the camshaft cover/bearing ladder to the cylinder head in sequence **(see illustrations)**. Lift the cover/ladder from position complete with the camshafts.

10 Undo the retaining bolts and remove the bearing caps. Note their fitted positions, as they must be refitted into their original positions **(see illustration)**. Note that the bearing caps are marked A for inlet, and E for exhaust, and 1 to 4 from the flywheel end of the cylinder head.

11 Undo the bolts securing the chain tensioner assembly to the camshaft cover/bearing ladder, and then lift the camshafts, chain and tensioner from place **(see illustrations)**. Discard the camshaft oil seal.

12 Obtain 16 small, clean plastic containers, and number them 1 to 8 inlet and 1 to 8

exhaust; alternatively, divide a larger container into 16 compartments.

13 Lift out each rocker arm. Place the rocker arms in their respective positions in the box or containers.

14 A compartmentalised container filled with engine oil is now required to retain the hydraulic tappets while they are removed from the cylinder head. Withdraw each hydraulic tappet and place it in the container, keeping them each identified for correct refitting. The tappets must be totally submerged in the oil to prevent air entering them.

Inspection

15 Inspect the cam lobes and the camshaft bearing journals for scoring or other visible evidence of wear. Once the surface hardening of the cam lobes has been eroded, wear will occur at an accelerated rate. **Note:** *If these symptoms are visible on the tips of the camshaft lobes, check the corresponding rocker arm, as it will probably be worn as well.*

16 Examine the condition of the bearing surfaces in the cylinder head and camshaft bearing housing. If wear is evident, the cylinder head and bearing housing will both have to be renewed, as they are a matched assembly.

17 Inspect the rocker arms and tappets for scuffing, cracking or other damage and renew any components as necessary. Also check the condition of the tappet bores in the cylinder head. As with the camshafts, any wear in this area will necessitate cylinder head renewal.

Refitting

18 Thoroughly clean the sealant from the mating surfaces of the cylinder head and camshaft bearing housing. Use a suitable liquid gasket dissolving agent (available from Peugeot dealers) together with a soft putty knife; do not use a metal scraper or the faces will be damaged. As there is no conventional gasket used, the cleanliness of the mating faces is of the utmost importance. Prise out the oil injector oil seals from the camshaft bearing housing.

19 Clean off any oil, dirt or grease from both components and dry with a clean lint-free cloth. Ensure that all the oilways are completely clean.

20 Liberally lubricate the hydraulic tappet bores in the cylinder head with clean engine oil.

21 Insert the hydraulic tappets into their

9.10 The camshaft bearing caps are numbered 1 to 4 from the flywheel end – A for inlet, and E for exhaust (arrowed)

9.11a Undo the tensioner bolts (arrowed) . . .

9.11b . . . then lift the camshafts, chain and tensioner from place

9.21 Refit the hydraulic tappets . . .

9.22 . . . and rocker arms to their original locations

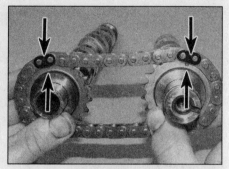

9.23 Align the marks on the sprockets with the centre of the black-coloured chain links (arrowed). There must be 12 link pins between the sprocket marks

9.24a Assemble the chain tensioner between the upper and lower runs of the chain . . .

9.24b . . . and lower the camshafts, chain and tensioner into position

the sealant to obstruct the oil channels for the hydraulic chain tensioner.

26 Check that the black-coloured links on the chain are still aligned with the marks on the camshaft sprockets, then refit the camshaft cover/bearing ladder, and gradually and evenly tighten the retaining bolts until the cover/ladder is in contact with the cylinder head, then tighten the bolts to the specified torque in sequence **(see illustration)**. **Note:** *Ensure the cover/ladder is correctly located by checking the bores of the vacuum pump and camshaft oil seal at each end of the cover/ladder.*

27 Fit a new camshaft oil seal as described in Section 14.

28 Refit the camshaft sprocket, and tighten the retaining bolt finger-tight.

29 Using a spanner on the camshaft sprocket bolt, rotate the camshafts approximately 40 complete revolutions clockwise. Check the black-coloured links on the chain still align with the marks on the camshaft sprockets.

30 If the marks still align, refit the camshaft sprocket as described in Section 8.

31 Refit and adjust the camshaft position sensor as described in Chapter 4A.

original bores in the cylinder head unless they have been renewed **(see illustration)**.

22 Lubricate the rocker arms and place them over their respective tappets and valve stems **(see illustration)**.

23 Engage the timing chain around the camshaft sprockets, aligning the black-coloured links with the marked teeth on the camshaft sprockets **(see illustration)**. If the black colouring has been lost, there must be 12 chain link pins between the marks on the sprockets.

24 Fit the chain tensioner between the upper

and lower runs of the chain, then lubricate the bearing surfaces with clean engine oil, and fit the camshafts into position on the underside of the camshaft cover/bearing ladder. Refit the bearing caps to their original positions and tighten the retaining bolts to the specified torque **(see illustrations)**. Tighten the tensioner retaining bolts to the specified torque.

25 Apply a thin bead of sealant to the mating surface of the camshaft cover/bearing ladder as shown. Peugeot recommend the use of Autojoint Noir **(see illustration)**. Do not allow

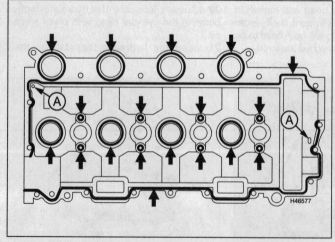

9.25 Apply sealant to the camshaft cover/bearing ladder as indicated by the heavy black lines. Ensure sealant does not enter the tensioner oil holes – marked A

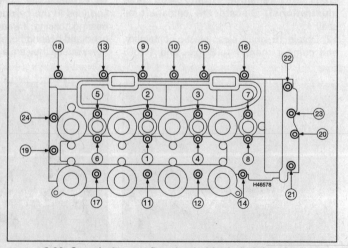

9.26 Camshaft cover/bearing ladder bolt tightening sequence

32 Press the new oil seals into the bearing housing, using a tube/socket of approximately 20 mm outside diameter, ensuring the inner lip of the seal fits around the injector guide tube **(see illustrations)**. Refit the injectors as described in Chapter 4A.

33 Refit the cylinder head cover/manifold as described in Section 4.

10 Cylinder head –
removal and refitting

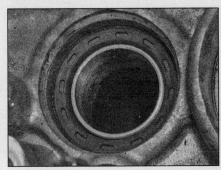

9.32a Fit the new seal around a 20 mm outside diameter socket . . .

9.32b . . . and push it into place

Removal

1 Chock the rear wheels then jack up the front of the vehicle and support it on axle stands (see *Jacking and vehicle support*). Remove the front right-hand roadwheel, the engine undershield, and the front wheel arch liner. The undershield is secured by several screws, and the wheel arch liner is secured by several plastic expanding rivets/nuts/plastic clips. Push the centre pins in a little, then prise the rivet from place.

2 Disconnect the battery negative lead as described in Chapter 5A.

3 Drain the cooling system as described in Chapter 1.

4 Remove the camshafts, rocker arms and hydraulic tappets as described in Section 9.

5 Remove the turbocharger as described in Chapter 4A.

6 Remove the glow plugs as described in Chapter 5B.

7 Undo the 3 mounting bolts and move the power steering pump to one side (there's no need to disconnect the hoses).

8 Undo the upper mounting bolts, and pivot the alternator away from the engine, undo the oil dipstick guide tube bolt, then undo the bolts securing the alternator/power steering pump mounting bracket to the cylinder head/block **(see illustration)**.

9 Undo the coolant outlet housing (left-hand end of the cylinder head) retaining bolts, slacken the two bolts securing the housing support bracket to the top of the transmission bellhousing, and move the outlet housing away from the cylinder head a little **(see illustration)**. There is no need to disconnect the hoses.

10 Disconnect the high-pressure fuel pipe from the common rail to the pump, and disconnect the fuel supply and return hoses.

Remove the bracket at the rear of the pump, then undo the bolt/nut and remove the pump and mounting bracket as an assembly **(see illustrations)**. Note that a new high-pressure pipe must be fitted – see Chapter 4A.

11 Working in the **reverse** of the sequence shown **(see illustration 10.32)** undo the cylinder head bolts.

12 Release the cylinder head from the cylinder block and location dowels by rocking it. The Peugeot tool for doing this consists simply of two metal rods with 90-degree angled ends **(see illustration)**. Do not prise between the mating faces of the cylinder head and block, as this may damage the gasket faces.

13 Lift the cylinder head from the block, and recover the gasket.

14 If necessary, remove the exhaust manifold with reference to Chapter 4A.

10.8 The engine oil level dipstick is secured to the alternator bracket by a Torx bolt (arrowed)

10.9 Undo the bolts (arrowed) and pull the coolant outlet housing from the left-hand end of the cylinder head

10.10a Remove the high-pressure pipe (arrowed) . . .

10.10b . . . and the bracket (arrowed)

10.10c Pump mounting bracket upper nut and lower mounting bolt (arrowed)

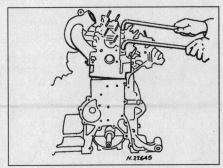

10.12 Free the cylinder head using angled rods

10.17a Pull the non-return valve from the cylinder head . . .

10.17b . . . and push a new one into place

10.21 Measure the piston protrusion using a DTI gauge

Preparation for refitting

15 The mating faces of the cylinder head and cylinder block must be perfectly clean before refitting the head. Peugeot recommend the use of a scouring agent for this purpose, but acceptable results can be achieved by using a hard plastic or wood scraper to remove all traces of gasket and carbon. The same method can be used to clean the piston crowns. Take particular care to avoid scoring or gouging the cylinder head/cylinder block mating surfaces during the cleaning operations, as aluminium alloy is easily damaged. Make sure that the carbon is not allowed to enter the oil and water passages – this is particularly important for the lubrication system, as carbon could block the oil supply to the engine's components. Using adhesive tape and paper, seal the water, oil and bolt holes in the cylinder block. To prevent carbon entering the gap between the pistons and bores, smear a little grease in the gap. After cleaning each piston, use a small brush to remove all traces of grease and carbon from the gap, and then wipe away the remainder with a clean rag.

16 Check the mating surfaces of the cylinder block and the cylinder head for nicks, deep scratches and other damage. If slight, they may be removed carefully with a file, but if excessive, machining may be the only alternative to renewal. If warpage of the cylinder head gasket surface is suspected, use a straight-edge to check it for distortion. Refer to Part C of this Chapter if necessary.

17 Thoroughly clean the threads of the cylinder head bolt holes in the cylinder block. Ensure that the bolts run freely in their threads,

and that all traces of oil and water are removed from each bolt hole. If required, pull the oil feed non-return valve from the cylinder head, and check the ball moves freely. Push a new valve into place if necessary **(see illustrations)**.

Gasket selection

18 Remove the crankshaft timing pin, then turn the crankshaft until pistons 1 and 4 are at TDC (Top Dead Centre). Position a dial test indicator (dial gauge) on the cylinder block adjacent to the rear of No 1 piston, and zero it on the block face. Transfer the probe to the crown of No 1 piston (10.0 mm in from the rear edge), and then slowly turn the crankshaft back-and-forth past TDC, noting the highest reading on the indicator. Record this reading as protrusion A.

19 Repeat the check described in paragraph 18, this time 10.0 mm in from the front edge of the No 1 piston crown. Record this reading as protrusion B.

20 Add protrusion A to protrusion B, then divide the result by 2 to obtain an average reading for piston No 1.

21 Repeat the procedure described in paragraphs 18 to 20 on piston 4, then turn the crankshaft through 180° and carry out the procedure on the piston Nos 2 and 3 **(see illustration)**. Check that there is a maximum difference of 0.07 mm protrusion between any two pistons.

22 If a dial test indicator is not available, piston protrusion may be measured using a straight-edge and feeler blades or Vernier calipers. However, this is much less accurate, and cannot therefore be recommended.

23 Note the greatest piston protrusion measurement, and use this to determine the correct cylinder head gasket from the following table. The series of notches/holes on the side of the gasket are used for thickness identification **(see illustration)**.

Piston protrusion	Gasket identification
0.6115 to 0.720 mm	2 notches
0.721 to 0.770 mm	3 notches
0.771 to 0.820 mm	1 notches
0.821 to 0.870 mm	4 notches
0.871 to 0.977 mm	5 notches

Head bolt examination

24 Carefully examine the cylinder head bolts for signs of damage to the threads or head, and for any sign of corrosion. If the bolts are in a satisfactory condition, measure the length of each bolt from the underside of the head to the end of the shank. The bolts may be re-used providing that the measured length does not exceed 149.0 mm **(see illustration)**. **Note:** *Considering the stress to which the cylinder head bolts are subjected, it is highly recommended that they be all renewed, regardless of their apparent condition.*

Refitting

25 Turn the crankshaft and position Nos 1 and 4 pistons at TDC, then turn the crankshaft a quarter turn (90°) anti-clockwise.

26 Thoroughly clean the surfaces of the cylinder head and block.

27 Make sure that the locating dowels are in place, then fit the correct gasket the right way round on the cylinder block **(see illustration)**.

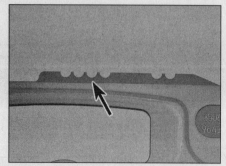

10.23 Cylinder head gasket thickness identification notches (arrowed)

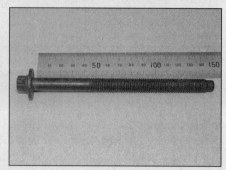

10.24 Measure the length from under the bolt head to its end

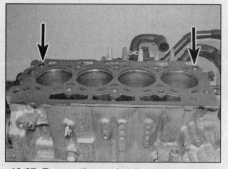

10.27 Ensure the gasket locates over the dowels (arrowed)

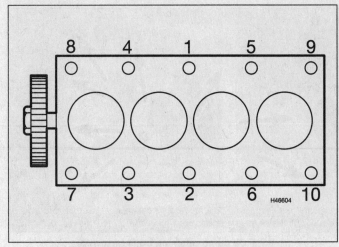

10.32 Cylinder head bolt tightening sequence

11.8 Apply a bead of sealant to the sump or crankcase mating surface. Ensure the sealant is applied on the inside of the retaining bolt holes

28 If necessary, refit the exhaust manifold to the cylinder head as described in Chapter 4A.

29 Carefully lower the cylinder head onto the gasket and block, making sure that it locates correctly onto the dowels.

30 Apply a smear of grease to the threads, and to the underside of the heads, of the cylinder head bolts. Peugeot recommend the use of Molykote G Rapid Plus (available from your Peugeot dealer); in the absence of the specified grease, any good-quality high melting-point grease may be used.

31 Carefully insert the cylinder head bolts into their holes (do not drop them in) and initially finger-tighten them.

32 Working progressively and in sequence, tighten the cylinder head bolts to their Stage 1 torque setting, using a torque wrench and suitable socket (see illustration).

33 Once all the bolts have been tightened to their Stage 1 torque setting, working again in the specified sequence, tighten each bolt to the specified Stage 2 setting. Finally, angle-tighten the bolts through the specified Stage 3 angle. It is recommended that an angle-measuring gauge be used during this stage of tightening, to ensure accuracy. **Note:** *Retightening of the cylinder head bolts after running the engine is not required.*

34 Refit the hydraulic tappets, rocker arms, and camshaft housing (complete with camshafts) as described in Section 9.

35 Refit the timing belt as described in Section 7.

36 The remainder of refitting is a reversal of removal, noting the following points.

a) *Use a new seal when refitting the coolant outlet housing.*

b) *When refitting a cylinder head, it is good practice to renew the thermostat.*

c) *Refit the camshaft position sensor and set the air gap with reference to Chapter 4A.*

d) *Tighten all fasteners to the specified torque where given.*

e) *Refill the cooling system as described in Chapter 1.*

f) *The engine may run erratically for the first few miles, until the engine management ECM relearns its stored values.*

11 Sump – removal and refitting

Removal

1 Drain the engine oil, then clean and refit the engine oil drain plug, tightening it securely. If the engine is nearing the service interval when the oil and filter are due for renewal, it is recommended that the filter is also removed, and a new one fitted. After reassembly, the engine can then be refilled with fresh oil. Refer to Chapter 1 for further information.

2 Chock the rear wheels then jack up the front of the vehicle and support it on axle stands (see *Jacking and vehicle support*). Undo the screws and remove the engine undershield.

3 Remove the exhaust front pipe as described in Chapter 4A.

4 Where necessary, disconnect the wiring connector from the oil temperature sender unit, which is screwed into the sump.

5 Progressively slacken and remove all the sump retaining bolts/nuts. Since the sump bolts vary in length, remove each bolt in turn, and store it in its correct fitted order by pushing it through a clearly marked cardboard template. This will avoid the possibility of installing the bolts in the wrong locations on refitting.

6 Try to break the joint by striking the sump with the palm of your hand, then lower and withdraw the sump from under the car. If the sump is stuck (which is quite likely) use a putty knife or similar carefully inserted between the sump and block. Ease the knife along the joint until the sump is released. While the sump is removed, take the opportunity to check the oil pump pick-up/strainer for signs of clogging or splitting. If necessary, remove the pump as described in Section 12, and clean or renew the strainer.

Refitting

7 Clean all traces of sealant from the mating surfaces of the cylinder block/crankcase and sump, and then use a clean rag to wipe out the sump and the engine's interior.

8 On engines where the sump was fitted without a gasket, ensure that the sump mating surfaces are clean and dry, then apply a thin coating of suitable sealant to the sump or crankcase mating surface (see illustration).

9 Offer up the sump to the cylinder block/ crankcase. Refit its retaining bolts/nuts, ensuring that each bolt is screwed into its original location. Tighten the bolts evenly and progressively to the specified torque setting (see illustration).

10 Where necessary, align the air conditioning compressor with its mountings on the sump, and insert the retaining bolts. Securely tighten the compressor retaining bolts, then refit the drivebelt as described in Chapter 5A.

11 Reconnect the wiring connector to the oil temperature sensor (where fitted).

12 Lower the vehicle to the ground, then refill the engine with oil as described in Chapter 1.

11.9 Refit the sump and tighten the bolts

12.4 Oil pick-up tube Allen screws (arrowed)

12.5 Oil pump retaining bolts (arrowed)

12 Oil pump – removal, inspection and refitting

Removal

1 Remove the sump as described in Section 11.
2 Remove the crankshaft sprocket as described in Section 8. Recover the locating key from the crankshaft.
3 Disconnect the wiring plug, undo the bolts and remove the crankshaft position sensor, located on the right-hand end of the cylinder block.
4 Undo the three Allen screws and remove the oil pump pick-up tube from the pump/block (see illustration). Discard the oil seal; a new one must be fitted.
5 Undo the 8 bolts, and remove the oil pump (see illustration).

Inspection

6 Undo and remove the Torx bolts securing the cover to the oil pump (see illustration). Examine the pump rotors and body for signs of wear and damage. If worn, the complete pump must be renewed.
7 Remove the circlip, and extract the cap, valve piston and spring, noting which way around they are fitted (see illustrations). The condition of the relief valve spring can only be measured by comparing it with a new one; if there is any doubt about its condition, it should also be renewed.
8 Refit the relief valve piston and spring, and then secure them in place with the circlip.
9 Refit the cover to the oil pump, and tighten the Torx bolts securely.

Refitting

10 Remove all traces of sealant, and thoroughly clean the mating surfaces of the oil pump and cylinder block.
11 Apply a 4 mm wide bead of silicone sealant to the mating face of the cylinder block (see illustration). Ensure that no sealant enters any of the holes in the block.

12.6 Undo the Torx bolts and remove the pump cover

12.7a Remove the circlip . . .

12.7b . . . cap . . .

12.7c . . . spring . . .

12.7d . . . and piston

12.11 Apply a bead of sealant to the cylinder block mating surface

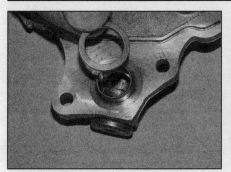

12.12a Fit a new seal . . .

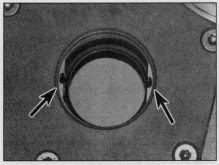

12.12b . . . align the pump gear flats (arrowed) . . .

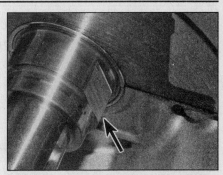

12.12c . . . with those of the crankshaft (arrowed)

12 With a new oil seal fitted, refit the oil pump over the end of the crankshaft, aligning the flats in the pump drivegear with the flats machined in the crankshaft **(see illustrations)**. Note that new oil pumps are supplied with the oil seal already fitted, and a seal protector sleeve. The sleeve fits over the end of the crankshaft to protect the seal as the pump is fitted.

13 Install the oil pump bolts and tighten them to the specified torque.

14 Refit the oil pick-up tube to the pump/ cylinder block using a new O-ring seal. Ensure the oil dipstick guide tube is correctly refitted.

15 Refit the woodruff key to the crankshaft, and slide the crankshaft sprocket into place.

16 The remainder of refitting is a reversal of removal.

13 Oil cooler – removal and refitting

Removal

1 Chock the rear wheels then jack up the front of the vehicle and support it on axle stands (see *Jacking and vehicle support*). Undo the screws and remove the engine undershield.

2 The oil cooler is fitted to the front of the oil filter housing. Drain the coolant as described in Chapter 1.

3 Drain the engine oil as described in Chapter 1, or be prepared for fluid spillage.

4 Undo the 5 bolts/stud and remove the oil cooler. Recover the O-ring seals **(see illustrations)**.

Refitting

5 Fit new O-ring seals into the recesses in the oil filter housing, and refit the cooler. Tighten the bolts securely.

6 Refill or top-up the cooling system and engine oil level as described in Chapter 1 or *Weekly Checks* (as applicable). Start the engine, and check the oil cooler for signs of leakage.

14 Oil seals – renewal

Crankshaft

Right-hand oil seal

1 Remove the crankshaft sprocket and Woodruff key as described in Section 8.

2 Measure and note the fitted depth of the oil seal.

3 Pull the oil seal from the housing using a screwdriver. Alternatively, drill a small hole in the oil seal, and use a self-tapping screw and a pair of pliers to remove it **(see illustration)**.

4 Clean the oil seal housing and the crankshaft sealing surface.

5 The seal has a Teflon lip and must not be oiled or marked. The new seal should be supplied with a protector sleeve, which fits over the end of the crankshaft to prevent any damage to the seal lip. With the sleeve in place, press the seal (open end first) into the pump to the previously-noted depth, using a suitable tube or socket **(see illustrations)**.

13.4a Undo the oil cooler bolts/stud (arrowed)

13.4b Renew the O-ring seals (arrowed)

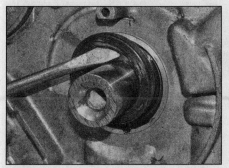

14.3 Take great care not to mark the crankshaft whilst levering out the oil seal

14.5a Slide the seal and protective sleeve over the end of the crankshaft . . .

14.5b . . . and press the seal into place

14.12 Slide the seal and protective sleeve over the left-hand end of the crankshaft

14.16 Drill a hole, insert a self-tapping screw, and pull the seal from place using pliers

14.18 Fit the protective sleeve and seal over the end of the camshaft

6 Where applicable, remove the plastic sleeve from the end of the crankshaft.

7 Refit the timing belt crankshaft sprocket as described in Section 8.

Left-hand oil seal

8 Remove the flywheel, as described in Section 16.

9 Measure and note the fitted depth of the oil seal.

10 Pull the oil seal from the housing using a screwdriver. Alternatively, drill a small hole in the oil seal, and use a self-tapping screw and a pair of pliers to remove it **(see illustration 14.3)**.

11 Clean the oil seal housing and the crankshaft sealing surface.

12 The seal has a Teflon lip and must not be oiled or marked. The new seal should be supplied with a protector sleeve, which fits over the end of the crankshaft to prevent any damage to the seal lip **(see illustration)**. With the sleeve in place, press the seal (open end first) into the housing to the previously-noted depth, using a suitable tube or socket.

13 Where applicable, remove the plastic sleeve from the end of the crankshaft.

14 Refit the flywheel, as described in Section 16.

Camshaft

15 Remove the camshaft sprocket as described in Section 8. In principle there is no need to remove the timing belt completely, but remember that if the belt has been contaminated with oil, it must be renewed.

16 Pull the oil seal from the housing using a hooked instrument. Alternatively, drill a small hole in the oil seal and use a self-tapping screw and a pair of pliers to remove it (see illustration).

17 Clean the oil seal housing and the camshaft sealing surface.

18 The seal has a Teflon lip and must not be oiled or marked. The new seal should be supplied with a protector sleeve, which fits over

the end of the camshaft to prevent any damage to the seal lip (see illustration). With the sleeve in place, press the seal (open end first) into the housing, using a suitable tube or socket that bears only on the outer edge of the seal.

19 Refit the camshaft sprocket as described in Section 8.

20 Where necessary, fit a new timing belt with reference to Section 7.

15 Oil pressure switch and level sensor – removal and refitting

Removal

Oil pressure switch

1 The oil pressure switch is located at the front of the cylinder block, adjacent to the oil dipstick guide tube. Note that on some models, access to the switch may be improved if the vehicle is jacked up and supported on axle stands, then undo the screws and remove the engine undershield so that the switch can be reached from underneath (see *Jacking and vehicle support*).

2 Remove the protective sleeve from the wiring plug (where applicable), and then disconnect the wiring from the switch.

3 Unscrew the switch from the cylinder block, and recover the sealing washer **(see illustration)**. Be prepared for oil spillage, and if the switch is to be left removed from the engine for any length of time, plug the hole in the cylinder block.

Oil level sensor

4 The oil level sensor is located at the rear of the cylinder block. Jack up the front of the vehicle and support it securely on axle stands (see *Jacking and vehicle support*). Undo the screws and remove the engine undershield.

5 Reach up between the driveshaft and the cylinder block and disconnect the sensor wiring plug **(see illustration)**.

15.3 The oil pressure switch is located on the front face of the cylinder block (arrowed)

15.5 The oil level sensor is located on the rear face of the cylinder block (arrowed)

16.8 Flywheel retaining Torx bolts

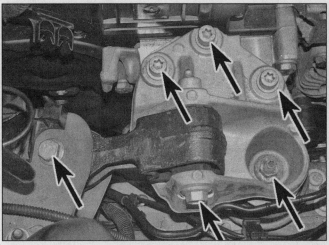

17.7 Undo the right-hand engine mounting bolts/nut (arrowed)

6 Using an open-ended spanner, unscrew the sensor and withdraw it from position.

Refitting

Oil pressure switch

7 Examine the sealing washer for any signs of damage or deterioration, and if necessary renew.
8 Refit the switch, complete with washer, and tighten it to the specified torque.
9 Refit the engine undershield, and lower the vehicle to the ground.

Oil level sensor

10 Smear a little silicone sealant on the threads and refit the sensor to the cylinder block, tightening it securely.
11 Reconnect the sensor wiring plug.
12 Refit the engine undershield, and lower the vehicle to the ground.

16 Flywheel – removal, inspection and refitting

Removal

1 Remove the transmission as described in Chapter 7A, then remove the clutch assembly as described in Chapter 6.
2 Prevent the flywheel from turning by locking the ring gear teeth **(see illustration 5.2)**. Alternatively, bolt a strap between the flywheel and the cylinder block/crankcase. *Do not* attempt to lock the flywheel in position using the crankshaft pulley locking tool described in Section 3. Insert a 12 mm diameter rod or drill bit through the hole in the flywheel cover casting, and into a slot in the flywheel.
3 Make alignment marks between the flywheel and crankshaft to aid refitment. Slacken and remove the flywheel retaining

bolts, and remove the flywheel from the end of the crankshaft. Be careful not to drop it; it is heavy. If the flywheel locating dowel (where fitted) is a loose fit in the crankshaft end, remove it and store it with the flywheel for safe-keeping. Discard the flywheel bolts; new ones must be used on refitting.

Inspection

4 Examine the flywheel for scoring of the clutch face, and for wear or chipping of the ring gear teeth. If the clutch face is scored, the flywheel may be surface-ground, but renewal is preferable. Seek the advice of a Peugeot dealer or engine reconditioning specialist to see if machining is possible. If the ring gear is worn or damaged, the flywheel must be renewed, as it is not possible to renew the ring gear separately.

Refitting

5 Clean the mating surfaces of the flywheel and crankshaft. Remove any remaining locking compound from the threads of the crankshaft holes, using the correct size of tap, if available.
6 If the new flywheel retaining bolts are not supplied with their threads already pre-coated, apply a suitable thread-locking compound to the threads of each bolt.
7 Ensure that the locating dowel is in position. Offer up the flywheel, locating it on the dowel (where fitted), and fit the new retaining bolts. Where no locating dowel is fitted, align the previously-made marks to ensure the flywheel is refitted in its original position.
8 Lock the flywheel using the method employed on dismantling, and tighten the retaining bolts to the specified torque **(see illustration)**.
9 Refit the clutch as described in Chapter 6. Remove the flywheel locking tool, and refit the transmission as described in Chapter 7A.

17 Engine/transmission mountings – inspection and renewal

Inspection

1 If improved access is required, chock the rear wheels then jack up the front of the car and support it on axle stands (see *Jacking and vehicle support*). Undo the screws and remove the engine undershield.
2 Check the mounting rubbers to see if they are cracked, hardened or separated from the metal at any point; renew the mounting if any such damage or deterioration is evident.
3 Check that all the mountings' fasteners are securely tightened; use a torque wrench to check if possible.
4 Using a large screwdriver or a crowbar, check for wear in each mounting by carefully levering against it to check for free play. Where this is not possible, enlist the aid of an assistant to move the engine/transmission back-and-forth, or from side-to-side, while you watch the mounting. While some free play is to be expected even from new components, excessive wear should be obvious. If excessive free play is found, check first that the fasteners are correctly secured, and then renew any worn components as described below.

Renewal

Right-hand mounting

5 Release all the relevant hoses and wiring from their retaining clips. Place the hoses/wiring clear of the mounting so that the removal procedure is not hindered. Undo the screws and remove the engine undershield.
6 Place a jack beneath the engine, with a block of wood on the jack head. Raise the jack until it is supporting the weight of the engine.
7 Undo the bolts/nut securing the engine mounting to the body and the support bracket **(see illustration)**.

17.15 Left-hand engine/transmission mounting bolts (arrowed)

17.20 Undo the lower engine torque rod mounting bolt (arrowed)

8 If required, undo the bolts/nuts securing the support bracket to the cylinder head/cylinder block.

9 Check all components carefully for signs of wear or damage, and renew as necessary.

10 Where removed, refit the support bracket to the cylinder head, and tighten the bolts securely.

11 Refit the mount to the body and support bracket, and then tighten the bolts to the specified torque.

12 Remove the jack from underneath the engine.

Left-hand mounting

13 Remove the engine management ECM and module box as described in Chapter 4A.

14 Undo the screws and remove the engine undershield, then place a jack beneath the transmission, with a block of wood on the jack head. Raise the jack until it is supporting the weight of the transmission.

15 Slacken and remove the bolts securing the mounting to the support bracket and vehicle body. If required, undo the bolts/nut and remove the support bracket (see illustration).

16 Check all components carefully for signs of wear or damage, and renew as necessary.

17 Refit the mounting, tighten the bolts to the specified torque settings, and remove the jack from underneath the transmission.

18 Refit the module box and ECM as described in Chapter 4A.

Lower engine torque link

19 If not already done, chock the rear wheels, then jack up the front of the vehicle and support it securely on axle stands (see *Jacking and vehicle support*). Undo the screws and remove the engine undershield.

20 Unscrew and remove the bolt securing the movement limiter link to the driveshaft intermediate bearing housing (see illustration).

21 Remove the bolt securing the link to the subframe. Withdraw the engine torque link.

22 To remove the intermediate bearing housing assembly it will first be necessary to remove the right-hand driveshaft as described in Chapter 8.

23 With the driveshaft removed, undo the retaining bolts and remove the bearing housing from the rear of the cylinder block.

24 Check carefully for signs of wear or damage on all components, and renew them where necessary. The rubber bush fitted to the bearing housing is available as a separate item (at the time of writing), and can be pressed out of, and back into place.

25 On reassembly, fit the bearing housing assembly to the rear of the cylinder block, and tighten its retaining bolts securely. Refit the driveshaft as described in Chapter 8.

26 Refit the movement limiter link, and tighten both its bolts to their specified torque settings. Refit the engine undershield.

27 Lower the vehicle to the ground.

Chapter 2 Part B:
2.0 litre engine in-car repair procedures

Contents

Degrees of difficulty

Easy, suitable for novice with little experience	**Fairly easy,** suitable for beginner with some experience	**Fairly difficult,** suitable for competent DIY mechanic	**Difficult,** suitable for experienced DIY mechanic	**Very difficult,** suitable for expert DIY or professional

Specifications

General

Designation	DW10BTED4 or DW10CTED4
Engine code:*	
DW10BTED4	RHF, RHL or RHR
DW10CTED4	RHH
Capacity	1997 cc
Bore	85.00 mm
Stroke	88.00 mm
Direction of crankshaft rotation	Clockwise (viewed from the right-hand side of vehicle)
No 1 cylinder location.......................................	At the transmission end of block
Maximum power output :	
RHL, RHF or RHR...	100 kW @ 4000 rpm
RHH	120 kW @ 3750 rpm
Maximum torque output:	
RHL, RHF or RHR...	320 Nm @ 2000 rpm
RHH	340 Nm @ 2000 rpm
Compression ratio	18.0 : 1

* The engine code is stamped on a plate attached to the front of the cylinder block.

Compression pressures (engine hot, at cranking speed)
Normal . . . .   20 ± 5 bar
Maximum difference between any two cylinders . . . .   5 bar

Camshaft
Drive . . . .   Toothed belt

Lubrication system
Oil pump type . . . .   Gear-type, chain-driven off the crankshaft right-hand end
Minimum oil pressure @ 110°C:
  2000 rpm . . . .   2.0 bar
  4000 rpm . . . .   4.0 bar
Oil pressure warning switch operating pressure . . . .   0.8 bar

Torque wrench settings

	Nm	lbf ft
Big-end bearing cap nuts:*		
Stage 1	20	15
Stage 2	Angle-tighten a further 70°	
Camshaft bearing housing bolts	10	7
Camshaft position sensor bolt	6	4
Camshaft sprocket bolt:		
Stage 1	20	15
Stage 2	Angle-tighten a further 60°	
Clutch bellhousing closure plate	18	13
Coolant outlet housing	18	13
Crankshaft pulley bolt:		
Stage 1	70	52
Stage 2	Angle-tighten a further 60°	
Crankshaft right-hand oil seal housing bolts	14	10
Crankshaft sensor bolt	7	5
Cylinder head bolts:		
Stage 1	15	11
Stage 2	60	44
Stage 3	Angle-tighten a further 220° ± 5°	
Cylinder head cover bolts	10	7
Driveplate bolts:*		
Stage 1	20	15
Stage 2	66	49
Engine mountings:		
Left-hand engine/transmission mounting:		
Bracket-to-transmission bolts	60	44
Bracket-to-transmission nut	55	41
Mounting to body/bracket	60	44
Rear engine mounting/torque rod bolts/nuts	60	44
Right-hand engine mounting bolts/nuts	60	44
Engine-to-transmission fixing bolts	55	41
Exhaust manifold nuts	25	18
Flywheel bolts*	50	37
High-pressure fuel pump bolts	20	15
Main bearing cap bolts:		
Stage 1	25	18
Stage 2	Angle-tighten a further 60°	
Oil filter cap	25	18
Oil pressure switch	32	24
Oil level sensor	27	20
Oil pump mounting bolts	16	12
Piston oil jet spray tube bolt	10	7
Sump bolts	16	12
Sump drain plug	34	25
Timing belt idler pulley bolt	56	41
Timing belt tensioner	21	15
Timing chain tensioner bolts	6	4
Vacuum pump (brakes)	9	7

* Do not re-use.

1 General information

How to use this Chapter

This Part of Chapter 2 describes the repair procedures that can reasonably be carried out on the engine while it remains in the vehicle. If the engine has been removed from the vehicle and is being dismantled as described in Part C, any preliminary dismantling procedures can be ignored.

Note that, while it may be possible physically to overhaul items such as the piston/connecting rod assemblies while the engine is in the car, such tasks are not usually carried out as separate operations. Usually, several additional procedures are required (not to mention the cleaning of components and oilways); for this reason, all such tasks are classed as major overhaul procedures, and are described in Part C of this Chapter.

Part C describes the removal of the engine/transmission from the car, and the full overhaul procedures that can then be carried out.

DW engines

This engine is based on the well-proven DW10 SOHC direct injection engine, which has appeared in many Peugeot and Citroën vehicles. In particular, the cylinder block components are very similar but the remainder of the engine has been completely redesigned. The engine is of double overhead camshaft (DOHC) 16-valve design. The turbocharged, four-cylinder engine is mounted transversely, with the transmission mounted on the left-hand side.

A toothed timing belt drives the exhaust camshaft, and coolant pump. The exhaust camshaft drives the inlet camshaft via a chain at the timing belt end. The camshafts operate the inlet and exhaust valves via rocker arms, which are supported at their pivot ends by hydraulic self-adjusting tappets. The camshafts are supported by bearings machined directly in the cylinder head and camshaft bearing housing.

The high-pressure fuel pump is driven from the left-hand end of the exhaust camshaft. The high-pressure fuel pump supplies fuel to the fuel rail, and subsequently to the electronically-controlled injectors that inject the fuel directly into the combustion chambers. This design differs from the previous type where an injection pump supplies the fuel at high pressure to each injector. The earlier conventional type injection pump required fine calibration and timing, and these functions are now completed by the high-pressure pump, electronic injectors and engine management ECM.

The crankshaft runs in five main bearings of the usual shell type. Endfloat is controlled by thrustwashers either side of No 2 main bearing.

The pistons are selected to be of matching weight, and incorporate fully-floating gudgeon pins retained by circlips.

The oil pump is chain-driven from the right-hand end of the crankshaft.

Throughout the manual it is often necessary to identify the engines not only by their cubic capacity, but also by their engine code. The engine code consists of three letters (eg, RHR). The code is stamped on a plate attached to the front of the cylinder block.

Repair operations precaution

The engine is a complex unit with numerous accessories and ancillary components. The design of the engine compartment is such that every conceivable space has been utilised, and access to virtually all of the engine components is extremely limited. In many cases, ancillary components will have to be removed, or moved to one side, and wiring, pipes and hoses will have to be disconnected or removed from various cable clips and support brackets.

When working on this engine, read through the entire procedure first, look at the car and engine at the same time, and establish whether you have the necessary tools, equipment, skill and patience to proceed. Allow considerable time for any operation, and be prepared for the unexpected. Any major work on these engines is not for the faint-hearted!

Because of the limited access, many of the engine photographs appearing in this Chapter were, by necessity, taken with the engine removed from the vehicle.

⚠ **Warning: It is essential to observe strict precautions when working on the fuel system components of the engine, particularly the high-pressure side of the system. Before carrying out any engine operations that entail working on, or near, any part of the fuel system, refer to the special information given in Chapter 4A, Section 2.**

Operations with engine in vehicle

a) Compression pressure – testing.
b) Cylinder head cover(s) – removal and refitting.
c) Crankshaft pulley – removal and refitting.
d) Timing belt covers – removal and refitting.
e) Timing belt/chain – removal, refitting and adjustment.
f) Timing belt tensioner and sprockets – removal and refitting.
g) Camshaft oil seal – renewal.
h) Camshafts, rocker arms and hydraulic tappets – removal, inspection and refitting.
i) Sump – removal and refitting.
j) Oil pump – removal and refitting.
k) Crankshaft oil seals – renewal.
l) Engine/transmission mountings – inspection and renewal.
m) Flywheel/driveplate – removal, inspection and refitting.

2 Compression and leakdown tests – description and interpretation

Compression test

Note: A compression tester specifically designed for diesel engines must be used for this test.

1 When engine performance is down, or if misfiring occurs which cannot be attributed to the fuel system, a compression test can provide diagnostic clues as to the engine's condition. If the test is performed regularly, it can give warning of trouble before any other symptoms become apparent.

2 A compression tester specifically intended for diesel engines must be used, because of the higher pressures involved. The tester is connected to an adapter that screws into the glow plug or injector hole. On these engines, an adapter suitable for use in the glow plug holes will be required, so as not to disturb the fuel system components. It is unlikely to be worthwhile buying such a tester for occasional use, but it may be possible to borrow or hire one – if not, have the test performed by a garage.

3 Unless specific instructions to the contrary are supplied with the tester, observe the following points:

a) The battery must be in a good state of charge, the air filter must be clean, and the engine should be at normal operating temperature.
b) All the glow plugs should be removed as described in Chapter 5B before starting the test.
c) The wiring connector on the engine management system ECM (see Chapter 4A) must be disconnected.

4 The compression pressures measured are not so important as the balance between cylinders. Values are given in the Specifications.

5 The cause of poor compression is less easy to establish on a diesel engine than on a petrol one. The effect of introducing oil into the cylinders ('wet' testing) is not conclusive, because there is a risk that the oil will sit in the swirl chamber or in the recess on the piston crown instead of passing to the rings. However, the following can be used as a rough guide to diagnosis.

6 All cylinders should produce very similar pressures; any difference greater than that specified indicates the existence of a fault. Note that the compression should build-up quickly in a healthy engine; low compression on the first stroke, followed by gradually increasing pressure on successive strokes, indicates worn piston rings. A low compression reading on the first stroke, which does not build-up during successive strokes, indicates leaking valves or a blown head gasket (a cracked head could also be the cause). Deposits on the undersides of the valve heads can also cause low compression.

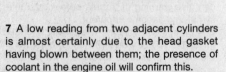

3.7a The tool fits through the hole in the cylinder block flange . . .

3.7b . . . and into a hole in the rear of the flywheel

3.8 Fit the tool through the hole in the exhaust camshaft sprocket, into the timing hole in the cylinder head

7 A low reading from two adjacent cylinders is almost certainly due to the head gasket having blown between them; the presence of coolant in the engine oil will confirm this.

8 If the compression reading is unusually high, the cylinder head surfaces, valves and pistons are probably coated with carbon deposits. If this is the case, the cylinder head should be removed and decarbonised (see Part C).

Leakdown test

9 A leakdown test measures the rate at which compressed air fed into the cylinder is lost. It is an alternative to a compression test, and in many ways it is better, since the escaping air provides easy identification of where pressure loss is occurring (piston rings, valves or head gasket).

10 The equipment needed for leakdown testing is unlikely to be available to the home mechanic. If poor compression is suspected, have the test performed by a suitably-equipped garage.

3 Engine assembly/valve timing holes – general information and usage

Note: *Do not attempt to rotate the engine whilst the crankshaft and camshaft are locked in position. If the engine is to be left in this state for a long period of time, it is a good idea to place suitable warning notices inside the vehicle, and in the engine compartment. This will reduce the possibility of the engine being accidentally cranked on the starter motor, which is likely to cause damage with the locking pins in place.*

1 Timing holes or slots are located only in the flywheel/driveplate and camshaft sprocket hub. The holes/slots are used to align the crankshaft and camshaft at the TDC position for Nos 1 and 4. This will ensure that the valve timing is maintained during operations that require removal and refitting of the timing belt. When the holes/slots are aligned with their corresponding holes in the cylinder block and cylinder head, suitable diameter bolts/pins can be inserted to lock the crankshaft and camshaft in position, preventing rotation. Note

that with the timing holes aligned, No 4 piston is at TDC on its compression stroke.

2 To align the engine assembly/valve timing holes, proceed as follows.

3 Chock the rear wheels then jack up the front of the vehicle and support it on axle stands (see *Jacking and vehicle support*). Remove the right-hand front roadwheel.

4 To gain access to the crankshaft pulley, to enable the engine to be turned, the wheel arch plastic liner must be removed. The liner is secured by several plastic expanding rivets. To remove the rivets, push in the centre pins a little, and then prise the clips from place. Remove the liner from under the front wing. Where necessary, unclip the coolant hoses from under the wing to improve access further. The crankshaft can then be turned using a suitable socket and extension bar fitted to the pulley bolt.

5 Remove the upper timing belt cover as described in Section 6.

6 Turn the crankshaft until the timing hole in the camshaft sprocket is aligned with the corresponding hole in the cylinder head. Note that the crankshaft must always be turned in a clockwise direction (viewed from the right-hand side of vehicle). Use a small mirror so that the position of the sprocket timing slot can be observed. When the slot is aligned with the corresponding hole in the cylinder head, the camshaft is positioned correctly.

7 Insert Peugeot tool No (-).0188.X or an 8 mm diameter bolt, rod or drill through the hole in the left-hand flange of the cylinder block by the starter motor; if necessary, carefully turn

the crankshaft either way until the rod enters the timing hole in the flywheel/driveplate (see illustrations). Note that if a bolt/rod/drill bit is used, it must be flat (not tapered at all) at the end. If improved access is required, remove the starter motor as described in Chapter 5A.

8 Insert the 8 mm bolt, rod or drill through the hole in the camshaft sprocket hub and into engagement with the cylinder head (see illustration).

9 The crankshaft and camshaft are now locked in position, preventing unnecessary rotation.

4 Cylinder head cover/ manifold – removal and refitting

Removal

1 Remove the plastic cover from the top of the engine. The cover simply pulls up from its rubber mountings.

2 The cylinder head cover is integral with the inlet manifold. Begin by disconnecting any wiring connectors and releasing the wiring harness from the timing belt upper cover.

3 Disconnect the wiring plug, and then unscrew the camshaft position sensor from the cover (see illustration).

4 Undo the bolts securing the upper timing belt cover to the cylinder head cover/inlet manifold (see illustration).

5 Disconnect the wiring connectors and

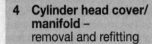

4.3 Undo the bolt and remove the camshaft position sensor (arrowed)

4.4 Undo the upper cover bolt

4.5a Disconnect the wiring connectors . . .

4.5b . . . and disconnect the air inlet hoses

4.6 Release the clips (arrowed) and detach the injector wiring harness duct

disconnect the air inlet hose(s) from the front of the inlet manifold **(see illustrations)**.

Siemens fuel system

6 Disconnect the injectors' wiring plugs, and then detach the harness duct from the inlet manifold/cover and position it to one side **(see illustration)**.
7 Disconnect the crankcase ventilation hoses from the inlet manifold/cover, then release the clamp and disconnect the EGR pipe from the inlet manifold **(see illustrations)**.
8 Release the glow plugs' wiring harness from the 2 clips on the rear of the cover.
9 Slacken the clamps and disconnect the inlet hoses from the manifold.
10 Unclip the fuel temperature sensor from the underside of the manifold.
11 Undo the manifold/cover retaining bolts in the **reverse** of the sequence shown in illustration 4.22. Check around the manifold/cover for any wiring or hoses, and then remove the manifold/cover and discard the gaskets. New gaskets must be used on refitting.

Delphi fuel system

12 Disconnect the breather hose from across the rear of the inlet manifold/cover **(see illustration)**.
13 Disconnect the breather hose from left-hand rear of the inlet manifold/cover **(see illustration)**.
14 Release the retaining clip and disconnect the EGR pipe **(see illustration)**.
15 Unclip the fuel pipes from under the side of the inlet manifold **(see illustration)**.

4.7a Release the clamps and disconnect the breather hose (arrowed) from the cylinder head cover . . .

4.7b . . . the EGR pipe from the inlet manifold . . .

4.7c . . . then slide out the locking clip and disconnect the breather hose from the rear of the cylinder head cover

4.12 Disconnect the breather hose

4.13 Disconnect the breather hose from the cover

4.14 Release the EGR pipe securing clip (arrowed)

4.15 Unclip the fuel pipes (arrowed) from under the manifold

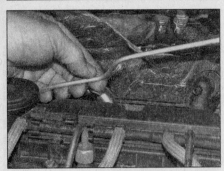

4.16 Unclip the vacuum pipe from the rear of the cover

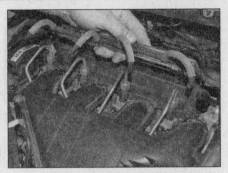

4.17 Remove the fuel return hoses

4.18 Unbolt the mounting bracket from the cover

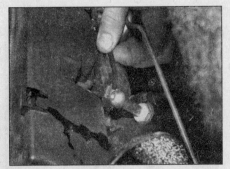

4.19 Unclip the glow plug wiring from the rear of the cover

4.20 Remove the inlet manifold/cover from the engine

16 Disconnect the vacuum hose and unclip the vacuum pipe from the rear of the cylinder head cover **(see illustration)**.

17 Disconnect the fuel return pipes from the injectors and the fuel pump, and then detach the harness duct from the inlet manifold/cover and position it to one side **(see illustration)**.

18 Unbolt the mounting bracket from the right-hand rear of the cylinder head **(see illustration)** to access the cylinder head cover retaining bolt.

19 Release the glow plugs' wiring harness from the 2 clips on the rear of the cover **(see illustration)**.

20 Undo the manifold/cover retaining bolts in the **reverse** of the sequence shown in illustration 4.22. Check around the manifold/cover for any wiring or hoses, and then remove the manifold/cover and discard the gaskets. New gaskets must be used on refitting **(see illustration)**.

Refitting

21 Clean the sealing surfaces of the manifold/cover and the cylinder head.

22 Fit the new seals to the inlet manifold/cover, and then fit it to the cylinder head. Use a little petroleum jelly on the manifold O-rings to ease reassembly. Tighten the bolts to the specified torque in sequence **(see illustration)**.

23 The remainder of refitting is a reversal of removal, noting the following points:
a) Tighten all fasteners to their specified torque.
b) Before refitting the timing belt upper cover, adjust the camshaft position sensor air gap as described in Chapter 4A, Section 12.

5 Crankshaft pulley – removal and refitting

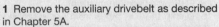

Removal

1 Remove the auxiliary drivebelt as described in Chapter 5A.

2 Position the camshaft and crankshaft as described in Section 3. **Note:** *It is essential that the crankshaft and camshaft timing pins are in place as described in Section 3. This is because on these engines, the crankshaft sprocket has a wider keyway to allow it to rotate a little independently of the crankshaft during the belt tensioning procedure. Failure to lock the crankshaft and camshaft could result in the timing being lost.*

3 To prevent crankshaft turning whilst the pulley retaining bolt is being slackened the flywheel/driveplate ring gear can be locked using (Peugeot tool No (-).0188.F) or a suitable tool made from steel angle. Remove the starter motor as described in Chapter 5A, and bolt the tool to the bellhousing flange

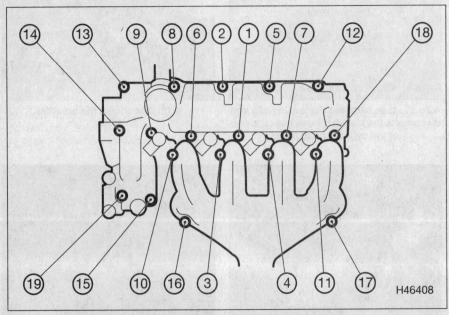

4.22 Inlet manifold/cylinder head cover bolt tightening sequence

Note that the 55 mm bolt is fitted in position 14, and the 70 mm bolts are fitted in positions 16 and 17

H46408

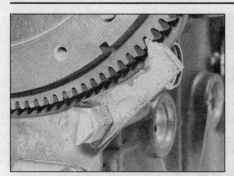

5.3 Use a fabricated tool similar to this to lock the flywheel ring gear and prevent crankshaft rotation

5.4 Undo the bolt and remove the crankshaft pulley

6.4 Depress the clips and disconnect the fuel pipes (arrowed)

so it engages with the ring gear teeth **(see illustration)**. *Do not* attempt to lock the pulley by only inserting a bolt/drill through the timing hole.

4 Using a suitable socket and extension bar, unscrew the retaining bolt, remove the washer, then slide the pulley off the end of the crankshaft **(see illustration)**. If the pulley is a tight fit, it can be drawn off the crankshaft using a suitable puller. If a puller is being used, refit the pulley retaining bolt without the washer, to avoid damaging the crankshaft as the puller is tightened.

Refitting

5 Ensure the camshaft and crankshaft are positioned at TDC as described previously, and the flywheel/driveplate ring gear is locked in position, as described in paragraph 3.

6 Thoroughly clean the threads of the pulley retaining bolt, then apply a coat of locking compound to the bolt threads. Peugeot recommend the use of Loctite (available from your Peugeot dealer); in the absence of this, any good-quality locking compound may be used.

7 Refit the crankshaft pulley retaining bolt and washer. Tighten the bolt to the specified torque, then through the specified angle.

8 Remove the crankshaft, camshaft and flywheel/driveplate locking tools.

9 Refit and tension the auxiliary drivebelt as described in Chapter 5A.

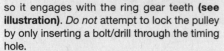

6 Timing belt covers – removal and refitting

⚠ *Warning: Refer to the precautionary information contained in Section 1 before proceeding.*

Removal

Upper cover

1 Pull up the plastic cover from the top of the engine, then undo the screws and remove the engine undershield.

2 Position a trolley jack under the engine, and using a piece of wood on the jack head, support the weight of the engine.

3 Undo the bolts and remove the right-hand engine mounting and support bracket – see Section 17.

4 At the connections at the right-hand end of the cylinder head, disconnect the fuel supply and return hose quick-release fittings using a small screwdriver to press down and release the locking clip **(see illustration)**. Cover the open unions to prevent dirt entry, using small plastic bags, or fingers cut from clean rubber gloves.

5 Release the two fuel hoses from the retaining clips at the right-hand end of cylinder head.

6 Move the electrical harness to one side, then undo the screws/nut and remove the upper timing belt cover **(see illustration)**.

Lower cover

7 Remove the upper cover as described previously.

8 Remove the crankshaft pulley as described in Section 5.

9 Undo the bolt and position the crankshaft sensor to one side **(see illustration)**.

10 Carefully pull the crankshaft sensor signal disc from the crankshaft **(see illustration)**. If the disc is reluctant to move, screw in two 6.0 mm bolts into the threaded holes in the disc and force it from place.

11 Undo the bolts and remove the lower timing belt cover.

Refitting

12 Refitting of all the covers is a reversal of the relevant removal procedure, ensuring that each cover section is correctly located, and that the cover retaining bolts are securely tightened. Ensure that all disturbed hoses are reconnected and retained by their relevant clips.

7 Timing belt – removal, inspection, refitting and tensioning

General

1 The timing belt drives the camshaft and coolant pump from a toothed sprocket on the end of the crankshaft. If the belt breaks or

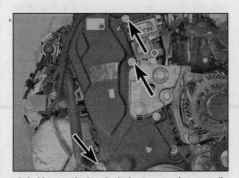

6.6 Upper timing belt fasteners (arrowed)

6.9 Crankshaft position sensor bolt (arrowed)

6.10 Sensor signal disc

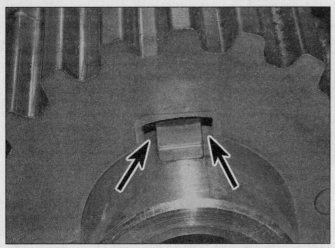

7.12 Position the crankshaft sprocket so that equal gaps exists each side of the key (arrowed)

7.14 Timing belt routing

slips in service, the pistons are likely to hit the valve heads, resulting in expensive damage.

2 The timing belt should be renewed at the specified intervals, or earlier if it is contaminated with oil or at all noisy in operation (a 'scraping' noise due to uneven wear).

3 If the timing belt is being removed, it is a wise precaution to check the condition of the coolant pump at the same time (check for signs of coolant leakage). This may avoid the need to remove the timing belt again at a later stage should the coolant pump fail.

Removal

4 Chock the rear wheels then jack up the front of the vehicle and support it on axle stands (see *Jacking and vehicle support*). Remove the front right-hand roadwheel, wheel arch liner (to expose the crankshaft pulley), and the engine undershield. The wheel arch liner is secured by several plastic expanding rivets, or push-in clips. Push the centre pins in a little then prise the rivet from place. Undo the retaining screws and remove the engine undershield.

5 Remove the crankshaft pulley as described in Section 5, then use 6.0 mm bolts to draw the sensor disc from the end of the crankshaft **(see illustration 6.10)**.

6 Remove the upper and lower timing belt covers as described in the previous Section.

7 Ensure the engine is positioned at TDC as described in Section 3, with the camshaft and crankshaft locking tools described in place.

8 Loosen the bolt on the tensioner pulley, and turn the tensioner clockwise to release the tension on the timing belt. Use an Allen key in the hole provided, to turn the tensioner bracket against the spring tension. Retighten the bolt sufficiently to hold the tensioner in its released position; do not fully-tighten the bolt in this position.

9 Mark the timing belt with an arrow to indicate its running direction as a reference for refitting. Remove the belt from the sprockets.

Inspection

10 Renew the belt as a matter of course, regardless of its apparent condition. The cost of a new belt is nothing compared with the cost of repairs should the belt break in service. If signs of oil contamination are found, trace the source of the oil leak and rectify it. Wash down the engine timing belt area and all related components, to remove all traces of oil. Check that the tensioner and idler pulleys rotate freely without any sign of roughness,

and also check that the coolant pump rotates freely. If necessary, renew these items.

Refitting and tensioning

11 Commence refitting by ensuring that the TDC timing pins are still in position correctly.

12 Centre the crankshaft sprocket by inserting Peugeot tool (-).0188.AH either side of the crankshaft key, and into the keyway in the sprocket. In the absence of the tool, position the sprocket centrally, ensuring a gap exists each side of the key **(see illustration)**.

13 Fit the timing belt to the camshaft sprocket. Peugeot technicians use a clip to retain the belt on the sprocket; if necessary, use a plastic cable-tie to hold it.

14 Continue to fit the belt in the following order, keeping the belt taut as it's fitted around the idler pulley and the crankshaft sprocket **(see illustration)**:

a) Idler pulley.
b) Crankshaft sprocket.
c) Coolant pump sprocket.
d) Tensioner pulley.

15 Remove the tool/cable-tie securing the belt to the camshaft sprocket, and the crankshaft sprocket centring tool.

16 Slacken the tensioner pulley retaining bolt, then using an Allen key, rotate the tensioner anti-clockwise until the index pointer is aligned with the lower, outside edge of the reference plate **(see illustrations)**. Tighten the tensioner pulley retaining bolt to the specified torque.

17 Ensure the crankshaft/flywheel ring gear locking tool is still in place, then refit the lower timing belt cover, sensor disc and crankshaft pulley, and tighten the retaining bolt to 70 Nm (52 lbf ft).

18 Remove the camshaft sprocket and crankshaft locking/timing tools.

19 Rotate the crankshaft 10 times in the normal direction of rotation, and refit the camshaft sprocket and crankshaft locking/timing tools.

20 With the flywheel ring gear locked, slacken the crankshaft pulley bolt.

21 Slacken the timing belt tensioner retaining

7.16a Use an Allen key in the tensioner (arrowed)

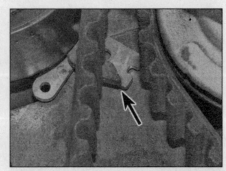

7.16b Rotate the tensioner anti-clockwise until the index pointer is aligned with the lower edge of the reference plate (arrowed)

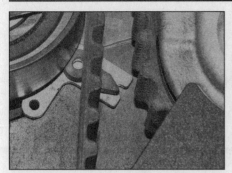

7.21 Align the index pointer with the notch in the reference plate

bolt, then use an Allen key to rotate the tensioner clockwise until the index pointer aligns with the notch in the reference plate **(see illustration)**. Tighten the tensioner pulley bolt to the specified torque.

22 Tighten the crankshaft pulley bolt to 70 Nm (52 lbf ft), at this stage.

23 Remove the camshaft sprocket, and crankshaft/flywheel ring gear locking/aligning tools, and rotate the crankshaft 2 complete revolutions in the normal direction of rotation (clockwise).

24 Check that the camshaft sprocket and crankshaft/flywheel aligning tools can still be inserted, and that the tensioner index pointer is still aligned with the notch in the reference plate. If necessary, repeat the tensioning procedure until the pointer and notch align.

25 Lock the flywheel ring gear using the previously described tool and undo the crankshaft pulley bolt.

26 Refit the crankshaft sensor. Tighten the retaining bolt securely.

27 Apply a little thread-locking compound to the threads, then tighten the crankshaft pulley retaining bolt to the specified torque.

28 Remove the camshaft sprocket, and crankshaft/flywheel ring gear locking/aligning tools.

29 The remainder of refitting is a reversal of removal.

8 Timing belt sprockets and tensioner – removal and refitting

Camshaft sprocket

Removal

1 Remove the timing belt as described in Section 7.

2 Remove the locking tool from the camshaft sprocket, then slacken the sprocket retaining bolt. To prevent the camshaft rotating as the bolt is slackened, Peugeot technicians use tool No 6016-T. In the absence of this tool, fabricate a substitute as described **(see Tool Tip)**. *Do not* attempt to use the camshaft sprocket locking tool to prevent the sprocket from rotating whilst the bolt is slackened.

To make a sprocket holding tool, obtain two lengths of steel strip about 6.0 mm thick by about 30 mm wide or similar, one 600 mm long, the other 200 mm long (all dimensions approximate). Bolt the two strips together to form a forked end, leaving the bolt slack so that the shorter strip can pivot freely. At the other end of each 'prong' of the fork, drill a suitable hole and fit a nut and bolt to engage with the spokes or holes in the sprocket. It may be necessary to cut-off or grind the side slightly to allow them to fit in the sprocket holes.

Note: *Take care not to damage the sensor signal disc integral with the sprocket.*

3 Remove the bolt, and slide the sprocket from the camshaft. If the Woodruff key is a loose fit in the camshaft, remove it for safekeeping. Examine the camshaft oil seal for signs of oil leakage and, if necessary, renew it as described in Section 14.

4 Clean the camshaft sprocket thoroughly, and renew it if there are any signs of wear, damage or cracks.

Refitting

5 Where applicable, refit the Woodruff key to the end of the camshaft, and then refit the camshaft sprocket and hub.

6 Refit the sprocket retaining bolt and washer. Tighten the bolt to the specified torque, preventing the camshaft from turning as during removal.

7 Align the timing slot in the camshaft sprocket with the hole in the cylinder head and refit the tool locking the camshaft in position.

8.10a Slide off the crankshaft pulley . . .

8 Refit the timing belt as described in Section 7.

Crankshaft sprocket

Removal

9 Remove the timing belt as described in Section 7.

10 Slide the sprocket off the end of the crankshaft and collect the Woodruff key **(see illustrations)**.

11 Examine the crankshaft oil seal for signs of oil leakage and, if necessary, renew it as described in Section 14.

12 Clean the crankshaft sprocket thoroughly, and renew it if there are any signs of wear, damage or cracks.

Refitting

13 Refit the Woodruff key to the end of the crankshaft, and then refit the crankshaft sprocket (with the flange nearest the cylinder block).

14 Refit the timing belt as described in Section 7.

Coolant pump sprocket

15 The coolant pump sprocket is integral with the pump, and cannot be removed.

Tensioner pulley

Removal

16 Remove the timing belt as described in Section 7.

17 Remove the tensioner pulley retaining bolt, and slide the pulley off its mounting stud.

18 Clean the tensioner pulley, but do not use any strong solvent that may enter the pulley bearings. Check that the pulley rotates freely, with no sign of stiffness or free play. Renew the pulley if there is any doubt about its condition, or if there are any obvious signs of wear or damage.

Refitting

19 Refit the tensioner pulley, and insert the retaining bolt.

20 Refit the timing belt as described in Section 7.

Idler pulley

Removal

21 Remove the timing belt as described in Section 7.

8.10b . . . and recover the Woodruff key

22 Undo the retaining bolt and withdraw the idler pulley from the engine.

23 Clean the idler pulley, but do not use any strong solvent, which may enter the bearings. Check that the pulley rotates freely, with no sign of stiffness or free play. Renew the idler pulley if there is any doubt about its condition, or if there are any obvious signs of wear or damage.

Refitting

24 Locate the idler pulley on the engine, and fit the retaining bolt. Tighten the bolt to the specified torque.

25 Fit the timing belt around the idler pulley, and tension the timing belt as described in Section 7.

9.8 Lift up the upper chain guide rail and insert a 2.0 mm diameter rod/drill bit into the hole in the tensioner body

9.9 Undo the tensioner retaining bolts (arrowed)

---

9 Camshafts, rocker arms and hydraulic tappets – removal, inspection and refitting

Removal

1 Remove the cylinder head cover as described in Section 4.

2 Remove the camshaft sprocket as described in Section 8.

3 Slacken the retaining clamps and disconnect the air inlet hose from the left-hand end of the cylinder head. Remove the intercooler air duct from the left-hand end of the cylinder head.

4 Remove the air cleaner assembly, high-pressure fuel pump, and fuel injectors as described in Chapter 4A.

5 Refit the right-hand engine mounting, but only tighten the bolts moderately; this will keep the engine supported during the camshaft removal.

6 Disconnect the vacuum pipe from the brake vacuum pump on the left-hand end of the cylinder head.

7 Remove the vacuum pump from the cylinder head with reference to Chapter 9.

8 Compress the timing chain tensioner and insert a 2.0 mm drill bit into the tensioner body to lock the piston in the compressed state **(see illustration)**.

9 Undo the bolts and remove the timing chain tensioner **(see illustration)**.

10 Working in a spiral pattern from the outside to the inside, progressively loosen the camshaft bearing cap housing bolts until they can be removed.

11 Withdraw the bearing cap housing from the cylinder head. The housing is likely to be initially tight to release, as it is located by two dowels on the forward facing side of the cylinder head. If necessary, very carefully prise up the housing using a screwdriver inserted in the slotted lug adjacent to each dowel location. Once the bearing housing is free, lift it squarely from the cylinder head. The camshaft will rise up slightly under the pressure of the valve springs – be careful it doesn't tilt and jam in the cylinder head or bearing housing section.

12 Check that the camshafts and chain are marked in relation to each other – the chain should have two black or copper links that align with marks on the teeth. If necessary, mark the chain and teeth with dabs of paint. The marks on the teeth are the most important as they determine the valve timing, however the chain links can be marked as they are 7 links (inclusive) apart **(see illustrations)**.

13 Simultaneously, lift the camshafts and chain from the cylinder head. Release the camshafts from the chain.

14 Either get sixteen small, clean plastic containers, and number them 1 to 16, or divide a larger container into sixteen compartments.

15 Lift out each rocker arm and release it from the spring clip on the tappet **(see illustration)**. Place the rocker arms in their respective positions in the box or containers.

16 A compartmentalised container filled with engine oil is now required to retain the hydraulic tappets while they are removed from the cylinder head. Using a rubber sucker, withdraw each hydraulic tappet and place it in the container, keeping them each identified for correct refitting. The tappets must be totally submerged in the oil to prevent air entering them.

Inspection

17 Inspect the cam lobes and the camshaft bearing journals for scoring or other visible evidence of wear. Once the surface hardening of the cam lobes has been eroded, wear will occur at an accelerated rate. **Note:** *If these symptoms are visible on the tips of the camshaft lobes, check the corresponding rocker arm, as it will probably be worn as well.*

18 Examine the condition of the bearing surfaces in the cylinder head and camshaft bearing housing. If wear is evident, the cylinder head and bearing housing will both have to be renewed, as they are a matched assembly.

19 Inspect the rocker arms and tappets for scuffing, cracking or other damage and renew any components as necessary. Also check the condition of the tappet bores in the cylinder head. As with the camshafts, any wear in this area will necessitate cylinder head renewal.

Refitting

20 Thoroughly clean the sealant from the mating surfaces of the cylinder head and camshaft bearing housing. Use a suitable

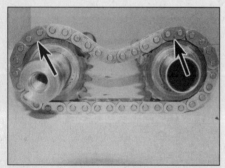

9.12a The coloured links on the chain (arrowed) align with the marks on the camshaft sprockets . . .

9.12b . . . the mark on the sprockets is a dot and a line

9.15 Lift out the rocker arms with the hydraulic tappets

liquid gasket dissolving agent (available from Peugeot dealers) together with a soft putty knife; do not use a metal scraper or the faces will be damaged. As there is no conventional gasket used, the cleanliness of the mating faces is of the utmost importance.

21 Clean off any oil, dirt or grease from both components and dry with a clean lint-free cloth. Ensure that all the oilways are completely clean.

22 To prevent any possibility of the valves contacting the pistons as the camshaft is refitted, remove the locking pin/drill from the flywheel/driveplate and turn the crankshaft a quarter turn in the *opposite* direction to normal rotation (ie, anti-clockwise), to position all the pistons at mid-stroke.

23 Liberally lubricate the hydraulic tappet bores in the cylinder head with clean engine oil.

24 Insert the hydraulic tappets into their original bores in the cylinder head unless they have been renewed **(see illustration)**.

25 Lubricate the rocker arms and place them over their respective tappets and valve stems. Ensure that the ends of the rocker arms engage with the spring clips on the tappets.

26 Lubricate the camshaft bearing journals in the cylinder head sparingly with oil, taking care not to allow the oil to spill over onto the camshaft bearing housing contact areas.

27 Engage the camshafts with the chain, making sure that the coloured links are aligned with the marked teeth, fit the tensioner between the chain runs, and then lower them into position. The longer exhaust camshaft must go at the rear of the cylinder head. Rotate the camshaft so the mark on the inlet camshaft is in the 12 o'clock position **(see illustration)**.

28 Fit a new camshaft oil seal as described in Section 14.

29 Refit the camshaft sprocket, lightly tighten the retaining bolt, and then fit the camshaft sprocket locking tool.

30 Check the marks on the camshaft sprockets still align with the coloured links on the chain.

31 Ensure that the mating faces of the cylinder head and camshaft bearing housing are clean and free of any oil or grease.

9.24 Insert the tappets and rocker arms into their original locations

9.27 Position the camshafts so the mark on the inlet camshaft (arrowed) is in the 12 o'clock position

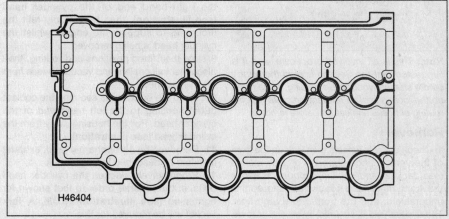

9.32a Apply a thin bead of sealant as indicated by the heavy black line

32 Sparingly apply a bead of sealant (Loctite 518) to the mating face of the camshaft bearing housing, taking care not to allow the product to contaminate the camshaft bearing journal areas **(see illustrations)**.

33 Lower the housing into place, then insert and tighten the camshaft bearing housing bolts to the specified torque, in sequence **(see illustration)**.

34 Refit the chain tensioner, tighten the retaining bolts to the specified torque, then pull out the locking pin and allow the tensioner to act upon the chain.

35 The remainder of refitting is a reversal of removal.

9.32b We inserted a tapered rod (arrowed) into the tensioner oil supply hole to prevent any sealant from entering

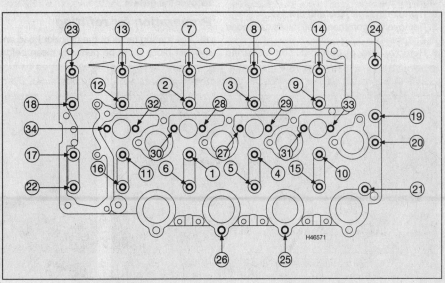

9.33 Camshaft bearing cap housing bolts tightening sequence

10.5 Remove the timing chain pad from the cylinder head

10.8 Undo the bracket upper bolt (arrowed)

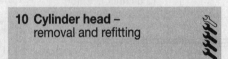

10 Cylinder head –
removal and refitting

Note: *This is an involved procedure, and it is suggested that the Section is read thoroughly before starting work. To aid refitting, make notes on the locations of all relevant brackets and the routing of hoses and cables before removal.*

Removal

1 Chock the rear wheels then jack up the front of the vehicle and support it on axle stands (see *Jacking and vehicle support*). Remove the front right-hand roadwheel, the engine undershield, and the front wheel arch liner. The undershield is secured by several screws, and the wheel arch liner is secured by several plastic expanding rivets. Push the centre pins in a little, and then prise the rivet from place.
2 Remove the battery (see Chapter 5A).
3 Drain the cooling system as described in Chapter 1.
4 Remove the camshafts, rocker arms and hydraulic tappets as described in Section 9.
5 Remove the timing chain pad at the right-hand side of the cylinder head (see illustration).
6 Remove the fuel filter and bracket.
7 Remove the common (fuel) rail as described in Chapter 4A.
8 Remove the uppermost bolt securing the engine mounting support bracket to the right-hand end of the cylinder head (see illustration), then temporarily refit the mounting to support the engine whilst the cylinder head is being removed.
9 Note their fitted positions and routing, then disconnect all coolant and vacuum hoses from the cylinder head.
10 Undo the bolts/studs securing the coolant outlet housing to the left-hand end of the cylinder head. Pull the housing away from the cylinder head (see illustration).
11 Remove the turbocharger and exhaust manifold as described in Chapter 4A.
12 Progressively slacken the cylinder head bolts, in the **reverse** order to that shown for tightening (see illustration 10.33). A Torx socket will be required for this.
13 When all the bolts are loose, unscrew them fully and remove them from the cylinder head.
14 Release the cylinder head from the cylinder block and location dowels by rocking it. The Peugeot tool for doing this consists simply of two metal rods with 90-degree angled ends. Do not prise between the mating faces of the cylinder head and block, as this may damage the gasket faces.
15 Lift the cylinder head from the block, and recover the gasket.

Preparation for refitting

16 The mating faces of the cylinder head and cylinder block must be perfectly clean before refitting the head. Peugeot recommend the use of a scouring agent for this purpose, but acceptable results can be achieved by using a hard plastic or wood scraper to remove all traces of gasket and carbon. The same method can be used to clean the piston crowns. Take particular care to avoid scoring or gouging the cylinder head/cylinder block mating surfaces during the cleaning operations, as aluminium alloy is easily damaged. Make sure that the carbon is not allowed to enter the oil and water passages – this is particularly important for the lubrication system, as carbon could block the oil supply to the engine's components. Using adhesive tape and paper, seal the water, oil and bolt holes in the cylinder block. To prevent carbon entering the gap between the pistons and bores, smear a little grease in the gap. After cleaning each piston, use a small brush to remove all traces of grease and carbon from the gap, and then wipe away the remainder with a clean rag.
17 Check the mating surfaces of the cylinder block and the cylinder head for nicks, deep scratches and other damage. If slight, they may be removed carefully with a file, but if excessive, machining may be the only alternative to renewal. If warpage of the cylinder head gasket surface is suspected, use a straight-edge to check it for distortion. Refer to Part C of this Chapter if necessary.
18 Thoroughly clean the threads of the cylinder head bolt holes in the cylinder block. Ensure that the bolts run freely in their threads, and that all traces of oil and water are removed from each bolt hole. If possible, use a M12 x 150 tap to clean out the threads.

Gasket selection

19 Turn the crankshaft until pistons 1 and 4 are at TDC (Top Dead Centre). Position a dial test indicator (dial gauge) on the cylinder block adjacent to the rear of No 1 piston, and zero it on the block face (see illustration). Transfer the probe to the crown of No 1 piston (10.0 mm in from the rear edge), and then slowly turn the crankshaft back-and-forth past TDC, noting the highest reading on the indicator. Record this reading as protrusion A.

10.10 Undo the nuts (arrowed) and remove the coolant outlet housing

10.19 Zero the DTI on the gasket face

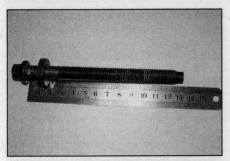

10.25 Measure the length of the cylinder head bolts from under the bolt head, not the washer

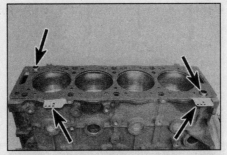

10.28 Fit the new gasket over the dowels, with the thickness identification holes at the front (arrowed)

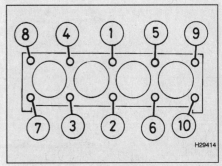

10.33 Cylinder head bolt tightening sequence

20 Repeat the check described in paragraph 19, this time 10.0 mm in from the front edge of the No 1 piston crown. Record this reading as protrusion B.

21 Add protrusion A to protrusion B, then divide the result by 2 to obtain an average reading for piston No 1.

22 Repeat the procedure described in paragraphs 19 to 21 on piston 4, then turn the crankshaft through 180° and carry out the procedure on the piston Nos 2 and 3. Check that there is a maximum difference of 0.07 mm protrusion between any two pistons.

23 If a dial test indicator is not available, piston protrusion may be measured using a straight-edge and feeler blades or Vernier calipers. However, this is much less accurate, and cannot therefore be recommended.

24 Note the greatest piston protrusion measurement, and use this to determine the correct cylinder head gasket from the following table. The series of holes on the front side of the gasket are used for thickness identification.

Piston protrusion	Gasket identification
0.55 to 0.60 mm	1 hole
0.61 to 0.65 mm	2 holes
0.66 to 0.70 mm	3 holes
0.71 to 0.75 mm	4 holes

Head bolt examination

25 Carefully examine the cylinder head bolts for signs of damage to the threads or head, and for any sign of corrosion. If the bolts are in a satisfactory condition, measure the length of each bolt from the underside of the head to the end of the shank. Two different types of bolts may be fitted. The older type do not have integral, captive washers; on these bolts, they may be re-used providing that the measured length from beneath the head to the very end of the bolt, does not exceed 129.0 mm ± 0.5 mm **(see illustration)**. On the later type of bolt, there is a washer which is captive under the head of the bolt; on these bolts, they may be re-used providing the measured length from beneath head (not the washer) to the end of the bolt, does not exceed 134.5 mm ± 0.05 mm. **Note:** *Considering the stress to which the cylinder head bolts are subjected, it is highly recommended that they are all renewed, regardless of their apparent condition.*

Refitting

26 Turn the crankshaft and position Nos 1 and 4 pistons at TDC, then turn the crankshaft a quarter turn (90°) anti-clockwise.

27 Thoroughly clean the surfaces of the cylinder head and block.

28 Make sure that the locating dowels are in place, then fit the correct gasket the right way round on the cylinder block **(see illustration)**.

29 If necessary, refit the exhaust manifold with reference to Chapter 4A.

30 Carefully lower the cylinder head onto the gasket and block, making sure that it locates correctly onto the dowels.

31 Apply a light smear of grease to the threads, and to the underside of the heads, of the cylinder head bolts. Peugeot recommend the use of Molykote G Rapid Plus (available from your Peugeot dealer); in the absence of the specified grease, any good-quality high melting-point grease may be used.

32 Carefully insert the cylinder head bolts into their holes *(do not drop them in)* and initially finger-tighten them.

33 Working progressively and in sequence, tighten the cylinder head bolts to their Stage 1 torque setting, using a torque wrench and suitable socket **(see illustration)**.

34 Once all the bolts have been tightened to their Stage 1 torque setting, working again in the specified sequence, tighten each bolt to the specified Stage 2 setting. Finally, angle-tighten the bolts through the specified Stage 3 angle. It is recommended that an angle-measuring gauge be used during this stage of tightening, to ensure accuracy. **Note:** *Retightening of the cylinder head bolts after running the engine is not required.*

35 The remainder of refitting is a reversal of removal, noting the following points.

a) Use a new seal when refitting the coolant outlet housing.

b) Refit the camshaft position sensor and set the air gap with reference to Chapter 4A.

c) Tighten all fasteners to the specified torque where given.

d) Refill the cooling system as described in Chapter 1.

e) The engine may run erratically for the first few miles, until the engine management ECM relearns its stored values.

11 Sump – removal and refitting

Removal

1 Drain the engine oil, then clean and refit the engine oil drain plug, tightening it securely. If the engine is nearing its service interval when the oil and filter are due for renewal, it is recommended that the filter is also removed, and a new one fitted. After reassembly, the engine can then be refilled with fresh oil. Refer to Chapter 1 for further information.

2 Chock the rear wheels then jack up the front of the vehicle and support it on axle stands (see *Jacking and vehicle support*). Undo the screws and remove the engine undershield.

3 On models with air conditioning, where the compressor is mounted onto the side of the sump, remove the drivebelt as described in Chapter 5A. Unbolt the compressor, and position it clear of the sump. Support the weight of the compressor by tying it to the vehicle, to prevent any excess strain being placed on the compressor lines. Do not disconnect the refrigerant lines from the compressor (refer to the warnings given in Chapter 3).

4 Where fitted. undo the 4 Torx bolts, release the retaining clips and remove the sump shield.

5 Slacken the clamps, undo the bolts and remove the charge air pipe from under the sump **(see illustration)**.

6 Where necessary, disconnect the wiring

11.5 Remove the charge air pipe securing bolts (arrowed)

11.7a Undo the 2 bolts securing the sump to the transmission (arrowed) . . .

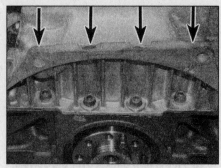

11.7b . . . access to the sump end bolts is through the holes (arrowed)

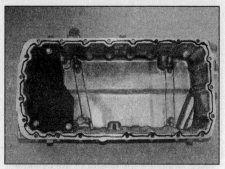

11.10 Apply a bead of sealant around the inside of the bolt holes

connector from the oil temperature sender unit, which is screwed into the sump.

7 Progressively slacken and remove all of the sump retaining bolts **(see illustrations)**. Since the sump bolts vary in length, remove each bolt in turn, and store it in its correct fitted order by pushing it through a clearly marked cardboard template. This will avoid the possibility of installing the bolts in the wrong locations on refitting.

8 Try to break the joint by striking the sump with the palm of your hand, then lower and withdraw the sump from under the car. If the sump is stuck (which is quite likely) use a putty knife or similar carefully inserted between the sump and block. Ease the knife along the joint until the sump is released. While the sump is removed, take the opportunity to check the oil pump pick-up/strainer for signs of clogging or splitting. If necessary, remove the pump as described in Section 12, and clean or renew the strainer.

Refitting

9 Clean all traces of sealant/gasket from the mating surfaces of the cylinder block/crankcase and sump, and then use a clean rag to wipe out the sump and the engine's interior.

10 Ensure that the sump mating surfaces are clean and dry, then apply a thin coating of suitable sealant (E10 – available from Peugeot dealers) to the sump or crankcase mating surface **(see illustration)**.

11 Offer up the sump to the cylinder block/crankcase. Refit its retaining bolts, ensuring that each bolt is screwed into its original location. Tighten the bolts evenly and progressively to the specified torque setting.

12 The remainder of refitting is a reversal of removal, remembering to refill the engine with oil as described in Chapter 1.

12 Oil pump – removal, inspection and refitting

Removal

1 Remove the timing belt as described in Section 7, then slide off the crankshaft sprocket. Recover the Woodruff key from the end of the crankshaft.

2 Remove the sump as described in Section 11.

3 Undo the retaining bolts and remove the front cover and crankshaft seal. Note the original locations of the cover screws – they are different lengths.

4 Undo the bolt securing the oil level pipe **(see illustration)**.

5 Pull out the key from the end of the crankshaft sprocket, then undo the pump mounting bolts, slide the pump, chain and crankshaft sprocket from the end of the engine **(see illustrations)**. Recover the O-ring between the sprocket and crankshaft.

Inspection

6 Examine the oil pump sprocket for signs of damage and wear, such as chipped or missing teeth. If the sprocket is worn, the pump assembly must be renewed, since the sprocket is not available separately. It is also recommended that the chain and drive sprocket, fitted to the crankshaft, be renewed at the same time.

7 Undo the retaining screws and remove the cover from the oil pump **(see illustration)**.

12.4 Oil level pipe bracket bolt (arrowed)

12.5a Remove the sprocket key . . .

12.5b . . . undo the pump mounting bolts (arrowed), slide the assembly from the crankshaft . . .

12.5c . . . and recover the O-ring between the sprocket and the crankshaft (arrowed)

12.7 Oil pump cover screws

Note the location of any identification marks on the inner and outer rotors for refitting.

8 Unscrew the plug and remove the pressure relief valve, spring and plunger, clean out and check the condition of the components **(see illustration)**.

9 Examine the pump rotors and body for signs of wear ridges or scoring. If worn, the complete pump assembly must be renewed.

10 Examine the relief valve piston for signs of wear or damage, and renew if necessary. The condition of the relief valve spring can only be measured by comparing it with a new one; if there is any doubt about its condition, it should also be renewed. Both the piston and spring are available individually.

11 Thoroughly clean the oil pump strainer with a suitable solvent, and check it for signs of clogging or splitting. If the strainer is damaged, the strainer and cover assembly must be renewed.

12 Locate the relief valve spring and piston in the strainer cover. Refit the cover to the pump body, aligning the relief valve plunger with its bore in the pump. Refit the baffle plate (where fitted) and the cover retaining bolts, and tighten them securely.

13 Prime the pump by filling it with clean engine oil before refitting.

Refitting

14 Before refitting the oil pump, ensure the mating faces of the pump and engine block are completely clean.

15 Fit the O-ring to the end of the crankshaft **(see illustration)**.

16 Engage the drive chain with the oil pump and crankshaft sprockets, then slide the crankshaft sprocket into place (aligning the slot in the sprocket with the keyway in the crankshaft) as the pump is refitted. Refit the crankshaft key.

17 Refit the mounting bolts and tighten them to the specified torque. Note that the front, left-hand bolt is slightly longer than the others.

18 Apply a 3 mm bead of sealant to the oil seal housing flange. Refit the housing and tighten the bolts to the specified torque.

12.8 Oil pressure relief valve plug

19 Fit a new oil seal to the carrier as described in Section 14.

20 Refit the bolt securing the oil level pipe.

21 The remainder of refitting is a reversal of removal.

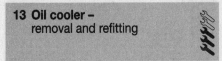

13 Oil cooler – removal and refitting

Note: *New sealing rings will be required on refitting – check for availability prior to commencing work.*

Removal

1 The cooler is fitted to the oil filter housing on the front of the cylinder block. Access is from under the vehicle. Undo the fasteners and remove the engine undershield. To further improve access, undo the mounting bolts and move the air conditioning compressor to one side. Suspend the compressor using wire or straps. There is no need to disconnect the refrigerant pipes.

2 Undo the 4 retaining bolts and detach the cooler from the housing **(see illustration)**. Recover the sealing rings and be prepared for coolant/oil spillage.

Refitting

3 Refitting is a reversal of removal, bearing in mind the following points:
 a) Use new sealing rings.

12.15 Fit the O-ring to the end of the crankshaft

 b) Tighten the cooler mounting bolts securely.
 c) On completion lower the car to the ground. Check and if necessary top-up the oil and coolant levels, then start the engine and check for signs of oil or coolant leakage.

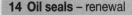

14 Oil seals – renewal

Crankshaft

Right-hand oil seal

1 Remove the crankshaft sprocket as described in Section 8.

2 Measure and note the fitted depth of the oil seal.

3 Pull the oil seal from the housing using a hooked instrument. Alternatively, drill a small hole in the oil seal, and use a self-tapping screw and a pair of pliers to remove it **(see illustrations)**.

4 Clean the oil seal housing and the crankshaft sealing surface.

5 Press the new seal into the housing (open end first) to the previously-noted depth, using a suitable tube or socket. A piece of thin plastic or tape wound around the front of the crankshaft is useful to prevent damage to the oil seal as it is fitted. Note that special tools to guide the seal onto the crankshaft and drive it

13.2 Oil cooler retaining bolts (arrowed)

14.3a Drill a small hole in the seal . . .

14.3b . . . insert a self-tapping screw and pull out the seal

14.5a Locate the new seal and guide over the end of the crankshaft . . .

14.5b . . . then drive the seal home until it's flush with housing

14.10a Drill a hole in the seal . . .

14.10b . . . then insert a self-tapping screw and pull out the seal

14.19a Use a socket or similar to drive the seal into place . . .

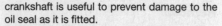

14.19b . . . until it's flush with the casing surface

into place may be available from Peugeot **(see illustrations)**.

6 Where applicable, remove the plastic or tape from the end of the crankshaft.

7 Refit the crankshaft sprocket as described in Section 8.

Left-hand oil seal

8 Remove the flywheel/driveplate, as described in Section 16.

9 Measure and note the fitted depth of the oil seal.

10 Pull the oil seal from the housing using a hooked instrument. Alternatively, drill a small hole in the oil seal, and use a self-tapping screw and a pair of pliers to remove it **(see illustrations)**.

11 Clean the oil seal housing and the crankshaft sealing surface.

12 Press the new seal into the housing (open end first) to the previously-noted depth, using a suitable tube or socket. A piece of thin plastic or tape wound around the end of the

crankshaft is useful to prevent damage to the oil seal as it is fitted.

13 Where applicable, remove the plastic or tape from the end of the crankshaft.

14 Refit the flywheel/driveplate, as described in Section 16.

Camshaft

Right-hand oil seal

15 Remove the camshaft sprocket as described in Section 8. In principle there is no need to remove the timing belt completely, but remember that if the belt has been contaminated with oil, it must be renewed.

16 Pull the oil seal from the housing using a hooked instrument. Alternatively, drill a small hole in the oil seal and use a self-tapping screw and a pair of pliers to remove it **(see illustration 14.3b)**.

17 Clean the oil seal housing and the camshaft sealing surface.

18 Fit it over the end of the camshaft, open end first. Note that the seal must not be oiled prior to fitting. A piece of thin plastic or tape wound around the end of the camshaft is useful to prevent damage to the oil seal as it is fitted.

19 Press the seal into the housing until it is flush with the end face of the cylinder head. Use an M10 bolt (screwed into the end of the camshaft), washers and a suitable tube or socket that bears only on the outer edge of the seal to press it into position **(see illustrations)**.

20 Refit the camshaft sprocket as described in Section 8.

21 Where necessary, fit a new timing belt with reference to Section 7.

15 Oil pressure switch – removal and refitting

Removal

1 The switch is screwed into the oil filter housing **(see illustration)**. Access is from under the vehicle. Undo the fasteners and remove the engine undershield.

2 Remove the protective sleeve from the wiring plug (where applicable), and then disconnect the wiring from the switch **(see illustration)**.

3 Unscrew the switch from the filter housing, and recover the sealing washer. Be prepared for oil spillage, and if the switch is to be left removed from the engine for any length of time, plug the hole in the cylinder block.

15.1 Oil pressure warning light switch (arrowed)

15.2 Disconnect the wiring plug from the switch

Refitting

4 Examine the sealing washer for any signs of damage or deterioration, and if necessary renew.

5 Refit the switch, complete with washer, and tighten it to the specified torque.

6 Where applicable, refit any components removed for access to the switch.

7 Check the engine oil level, and top-up as required (see *Weekly checks*).

8 Check for correct operation of the warning light, and for signs of oil leaks once the engine has been started and warmed-up to normal operating temperature.

16 Flywheel/driveplate – removal, inspection and refitting

Removal

Flywheel

1 Remove the transmission as described in Chapter 7A, then remove the clutch assembly as described in Chapter 6.

2 Prevent the flywheel from turning by locking the ring gear teeth **(see illustration 5.3)**. Alternatively, bolt a strap between the flywheel and the cylinder block/crankcase. *Do not* attempt to lock the flywheel in position using the crankshaft pulley locking tool described in Section 3.

3 Slacken and remove the flywheel retaining bolts, and remove the flywheel from the end of the crankshaft **(see illustration)**. Be careful not to drop it; it is heavy. If the flywheel locating dowel is a loose fit in the crankshaft end, remove it and store it with the flywheel for safe-keeping. Discard the flywheel bolts; new ones must be used on refitting.

Driveplate

4 Remove the transmission as described in Chapter 7B. Lock the driveplate as described in paragraph 2 of this Section. Mark the relationship between the torque converter plate and the driveplate, and slacken all the driveplate retaining bolts.

5 Remove the retaining bolts, along with the torque converter plate and the two shims (one fitted on each side of the torque converter

plate). Note that the shims are of different thickness, the thicker one being on the outside of the torque converter plate. Discard the driveplate retaining bolts; new ones must be used on refitting.

6 Remove the driveplate from the end of the crankshaft. If the locating dowel is a loose fit in the crankshaft end, remove it and store it with the driveplate for safekeeping.

Inspection

7 On models with manual transmission, examine the flywheel for scoring of the clutch face, and for wear or chipping of the ring gear teeth. If the clutch face is scored, the flywheel may be surface-ground, but renewal is preferable. Seek the advice of a Peugeot dealer or engine reconditioning specialist to see if machining is possible. If the ring gear is worn or damaged, the flywheel must be renewed, as it is not possible to renew the ring gear separately.

8 On models with automatic transmission, check the torque converter driveplate carefully for signs of distortion. Look for any hairline cracks around the bolt holes or radiating outwards from the centre, and inspect the ring gear teeth for signs of wear or chipping. If any sign of wear or damage is found, the driveplate must be renewed.

Refitting

Flywheel

9 Clean the mating surfaces of the flywheel and crankshaft. Remove any remaining locking compound from the threads of the crankshaft holes, using the correct size of tap, if available.

10 If the new flywheel retaining bolts are not supplied with their threads already pre-coated, apply a suitable thread-locking compound to the threads of each bolt.

11 Ensure that the locating dowel is in position. Offer up the flywheel, locating it on the dowel, and fit the new retaining bolts **(see illustration)**.

12 Lock the flywheel using the method employed on dismantling, and tighten the retaining bolts to the specified torque.

13 Refit the clutch as described in Chapter 6. Remove the flywheel locking tool, and refit the transmission as described in Chapter 7A.

Driveplate

14 Carry out the operations described above in paragraphs 9 and 10, substituting 'driveplate' for all references to the flywheel.

15 Locate the driveplate on its locating dowel.

16 Offer up the torque converter plate, with the thinner shim positioned behind the plate and the thicker shim on the outside, and align the marks made prior to removal.

17 Fit the new retaining bolts, then lock the driveplate using the method employed on dismantling. Tighten the retaining bolts to the specified torque wrench setting.

18 Remove the driveplate locking tool, and refit the transmission (see Chapter 7B).

17 Engine/transmission mountings – inspection and renewal

Inspection

1 If improved access is required, chock the rear wheels then jack up the front of the car and support it on axle stands (see *Jacking and vehicle support*). Undo the screws and remove the engine undershield.

2 Check the mounting rubbers to see if they are cracked, hardened or separated from the metal at any point; renew the mounting if any such damage or deterioration is evident.

3 Check that all the mountings' fasteners are securely tightened; use a torque wrench to check if possible.

4 Using a large screwdriver or a crowbar, check for wear in each mounting by carefully levering against it to check for free play. Where this is not possible, enlist the aid of an assistant to move the engine/transmission back-and-forth, or from side-to-side, while you watch the mounting. While some free play is to be expected even from new components, excessive wear should be obvious. If excessive free play is found, check first that the fasteners are correctly secured, and then renew any worn components as described below.

Renewal

Right-hand mounting

5 Release all the relevant hoses and wiring from their retaining clips **(see illustration)**.

16.3 Flywheel retaining bolts

16.11 Note the locating dowel and the corresponding hole (arrowed)

17.5 Unclip the pipes from across the top of the mounting

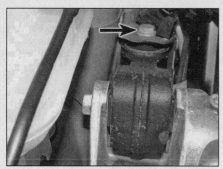

17.7a Upper torque arm mounting bolt (arrowed)

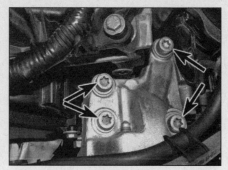

17.7b Right-hand engine mounting bolts (arrowed)

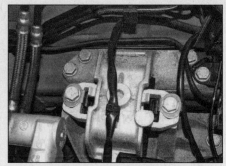

17.16 Left-hand engine/transmission mounting assembly

Place the hoses/wiring clear of the mounting so that the removal procedure is not hindered. Undo the screws and remove the engine undershield.

6 Place a jack beneath the engine, with a block of wood on the jack head. Raise the jack until it is supporting the weight of the engine.

7 Undo the bolts/nuts securing the engine mounting to the body and the support bracket **(see illustrations)**.

8 If required, undo the bolts/nuts securing the support bracket to the cylinder head/cylinder block.

9 Check all components carefully for signs of wear or damage, and renew as necessary.

10 Where removed, refit the support bracket to the cylinder head, and tighten the bolts securely.

11 Refit the mount to the body and support bracket, and then tighten the bolts to the specified torque.

12 Remove the jack from underneath the engine.

Left-hand mounting

13 Remove the battery (see Chapter 5A). Undo the screws and remove the engine undershield.

14 Remove the diesel engine management ECM and module box as described in Chapter 4A.

15 Place a jack beneath the transmission, with a block of wood on the jack head. Raise the jack until it is supporting the weight of the transmission.

16 Undo the nuts securing the mounting in position and remove it from the engine compartment **(see illustration)**.

17 If required, undo the bolts/nut and remove the support bracket.

18 Check all components carefully for signs of wear or damage, and renew as necessary.

19 Clean the threads of the mounting stud (where applicable), and apply a coat of thread-locking compound to its threads.

20 Refit the support bracket and mounting,

tightening the bolts/nuts to the specified torque.

21 The remainder of refitting is a reversal of removal.

Rear engine torque rod

22 If not already done, chock the rear wheels, then jack up the front of the vehicle and support it securely on axle stands (see *Jacking and vehicle support*). Undo the screws and remove the engine undershield.

23 Unscrew and remove the bolt securing the torque rod to the driveshaft intermediate bearing housing **(see illustration)**.

24 Remove the bolt securing the torque rod to the subframe. Withdraw the torque rod **(see illustration)**.

25 To remove the intermediate bearing housing assembly it will first be necessary to remove the right-hand driveshaft as described in Chapter 8.

26 With the driveshaft removed, undo the retaining bolts and remove the bearing housing from the rear of the cylinder block.

27 Check carefully for signs of wear or damage on all components, and renew them where necessary. The rubber bush fitted to the bearing housing is available as a separate item (at the time of writing), and can be pressed out of, and back into place.

28 On reassembly, fit the bearing housing assembly to the rear of the cylinder block, and tighten its retaining bolts securely. Refit the driveshaft as described in Chapter 8.

29 Refit the torque rod, and tighten both its bolts to their specified torque settings. Refit the engine undershield.

30 Lower the vehicle to the ground.

17.23 Undo the mounting bolts (arrowed) . . .

17.24 . . . and remove the rear engine torque rod

Chapter 2 Part C:
Engine removal and overhaul procedures

Contents

Degrees of difficulty

Easy, suitable for novice with little experience   **Fairly easy,** suitable for beginner with some experience   **Fairly difficult,** suitable for competent DIY mechanic   **Difficult,** suitable for experienced DIY mechanic   **Very difficult,** suitable for expert DIY or professional

Specifications

Engine identification
1.6 litre:
  Designation DV6TED4
  Engine codes . . . . 9HY or 9HZ
2.0 litre:
  Designation . . . . DW10BTED4 or DW10CTED4
  Engine codes:
    DW10BTED4 . . . . RHF, RHL or RHR
    DW10CTED4 . . . . RHH

Cylinder block
Cylinder bore diameter:
  1.6 litre (reboring not possible) . . . . 75.00 mm (nominal)
  2.0 litre . . . . 85.00 mm (nominal)

Cylinder head
Maximum gasket face distortion . . . . 0.03 mm
New cylinder head height:
  1.6 litre . . . . 124.0 ± 0.05 mm
  2.0 litre . . . . 133.0 ± 0.05 mm
Minimum cylinder head height after machining:
  1.6 litre . . . . N/A
  2.0 litre . . . . 132.60 mm
Valve head-to-cylinder head measurement:
  1.6 litre . . . . N/A
  2.0 litre . . . . 0.20 mm maximum

Valves

Valve head diameter:
1.6 litre . . . .   N/A
2.0 litre:
   Inlet . . . .   35.6 mm
   Exhaust. . . . .   33.8 mm
Valve stem diameter:
1.6 litre
   Inlet . . . .   5.485 +0.0, -0.015 mm
   Exhaust . . . .   5.475 +0.0, -0.015 mm
2.0 litre:
   Inlet . . . .   5.978 ± 0.009 mm
   Exhaust . . . .   5.968 ± 0.009 mm

Piston rings

End gaps:
1.6 litre:
   Top compression ring. . . . .   0.15 to 0.25 mm
   Second compression ring. . . . .   0.30 to 0.50 mm
   Oil control ring . . . .   0.35 to 0.55 mm
2.0 litre:
   Top compression ring. . . . .   0.20 to 0.35 mm
   Second compression ring. . . . .   0.80 to 1.00 mm
   Oil control ring . . . .   0.25 to 0.50 mm

Crankshaft

Endfloat:
1.6 litre . . . .   0.10 to 0.30 mm (thrustwasher thickness 2.40 ± 0.05 mm)
2.0 litre . . . .   0.07 to 0.32 mm
Maximum bearing journal out-of-round (all engines) . . . .   0.007 mm

Torque wrench settings

1.6 litre engines

Refer to Chapter 2A Specifications

2.0 litre engines

Refer to Chapter 2B Specifications

1 General information

Included in this Part of Chapter 2 are details of removing the engine/transmission from the car and general overhaul procedures for the cylinder head, cylinder block/crankcase and all other engine internal components.

The information given ranges from advice concerning preparation for an overhaul and the purchase of parts, to detailed step-by-step procedures covering removal, inspection, renovation and refitting of engine internal components.

After Section 5, all instructions are based on the assumption that the engine has been removed from the car. For information concerning in-car engine repair, as well as the removal and refitting of those external components necessary for full overhaul, refer to Part A or B of this Chapter, as applicable and to Section 5. Ignore any preliminary dismantling operations that are no longer relevant once the engine has been removed from the car.

Apart from torque wrench settings, which are given at the beginning of Parts A or B, all specifications relating to engine overhaul are at the beginning of this Part of Chapter 2.

2 Engine overhaul – general information

1 It is not always easy to determine when, or if, an engine should be completely overhauled, as a number of factors must be considered.
2 High mileage is not necessarily an indication that an overhaul is needed, while low mileage does not preclude the need for an overhaul. Frequency of servicing is probably the most important consideration. An engine which has had regular and frequent oil and filter changes, as well as other required maintenance, should give many thousands of miles of reliable service. Conversely, a neglected engine may require an overhaul very early in its life.
3 Excessive oil consumption is an indication that piston rings, valve seals and/or valve guides are in need of attention. Make sure that oil leaks are not responsible before deciding that the rings and/or guides are worn. Perform a compression test, as described in Part A or B of this Chapter (as applicable), to determine the likely cause of the problem.
4 Check the oil pressure with a gauge fitted in place of the oil pressure switch, and compare it with that specified. If it is extremely low, the main and big-end bearings, and/or the oil pump, are probably worn out.
5 Loss of power, rough running, knocking or metallic engine noises, excessive valve gear noise, and high fuel consumption may also point to the need for an overhaul, especially if they are all present at the same time. If a complete service does not remedy the situation, major mechanical work is the only solution.
6 A full engine overhaul involves restoring all internal parts to the specification of a new engine. During a complete overhaul, the pistons and the piston rings are normally renewed, although this is a specialist task on these engines as the pistons and bore liners are matched. New main and big-end bearings are generally fitted; if necessary, the crankshaft may be reground, to compensate for wear in the journals. The valves are also serviced as well, since they are usually in less-than-perfect condition at this point. While the engine is being overhauled, other components, such as

the starter and alternator, can be overhauled as well. Always pay careful attention to the condition of the oil pump when overhauling the engine, and renew it if there is any doubt as to its serviceability. The end result should be an as-new engine that will give many trouble-free miles.

7 Critical cooling system components such as the hoses, thermostat and water pump should be renewed when an engine is overhauled. The radiator should be checked carefully, to ensure that it is not clogged or leaking. Also, it is a good idea to renew the oil pump whenever the engine is overhauled.

8 Before beginning the engine overhaul, read through the entire procedure, to familiarise yourself with the scope and requirements of the job. Overhauling an engine is not difficult if you carefully follow all of the instructions, have the necessary tools and equipment, and pay close attention to all specifications. It can, however, be time-consuming. Plan on the car being off the road for a minimum of two weeks, especially if parts must be taken to an engineering works for repair or reconditioning. Check on the availability of parts and make sure that any necessary special tools and equipment are obtained in advance. Most work can be done with typical hand tools, although a number of precision measuring tools are required for inspecting parts to determine if they must be renewed. Often the engineering works will handle the inspection of parts and offer advice concerning reconditioning and renewal.

9 Always wait until the engine has been completely dismantled, and until all components (especially the cylinder block/crankcase and the crankshaft) have been inspected, before deciding what service and repair operations must be performed by an engineering works. The condition of these components will be the major factor to consider when determining whether to overhaul the original engine, or to buy a reconditioned unit. Do not, therefore, purchase parts or have overhaul work done on other components until they have been thoroughly inspected. As a general rule, time is the primary cost of an overhaul, so it does not pay to fit worn or sub-standard parts.

10 As a final note, to ensure maximum life and minimum trouble from a reconditioned engine, everything must be assembled with care, in a spotlessly clean environment.

3 Engine removal – methods and precautions

1 If you have decided that the engine must be removed for overhaul or major repair work, several preliminary steps should be taken.

2 Locating a suitable place to work is extremely important. Adequate work space, along with storage space for the car, will be needed. Engine/transmission removal is extremely complicated and involved on these vehicles. It must be stated, that unless the vehicle can be positioned on a ramp, or raised and supported on axle stands over an inspection pit, it will be very difficult to carry out the work involved.

3 Cleaning the engine compartment and engine/transmission before beginning the removal procedure will help keep tools clean and organised.

4 An engine hoist or A-frame will also be necessary. Make sure the equipment is rated in excess of the weight of the engine. Safety is of primary importance, considering the potential hazards involved in lifting the engine/transmission out of the car.

5 The help of an assistant is essential. Apart from the safety aspects involved, there are many instances when one person cannot simultaneously perform all of the operations required during engine/transmission removal.

6 Plan the operation ahead of time. Before starting work, arrange for the hire or obtain all of the tools and equipment you will need. Some of the equipment necessary to perform engine/transmission removal and installation safely and with relative ease (in addition to an engine hoist) is as follows: a heavy duty trolley jack, complete sets of spanners and sockets (see Tools and working facilities), wooden blocks, and plenty of rags and cleaning solvent for mopping-up spilled oil, coolant and fuel. If the hoist must be hired, make sure that you arrange for it in advance, and perform all of the operations possible without it beforehand. This will save you money and time.

7 Plan for the car to be out of use for quite a while. An engineering machine shop or engine reconditioning specialist will be required to perform some of the work that cannot be accomplished without special equipment. These places often have a busy schedule, so it would be a good idea to consult them before removing the engine, in order to accurately estimate the amount of time required to rebuild or repair components that may need work.

8 During the engine/transmission removal procedure, it is advisable to make notes of the locations of all brackets, cable-ties, earthing points, etc, as well as how the wiring harnesses, hoses and electrical connections are attached and routed around the engine and engine compartment. An effective way of doing this is to take a series of photographs of the various components before they are disconnected or removed; the resulting photographs will prove invaluable when the engine/transmission is refitted.

9 On all models, the engine must be removed complete with the transmission as an assembly. There is insufficient clearance in the engine compartment to remove the engine leaving the transmission in the vehicle. The assembly is removed by raising the front of the vehicle, and lowering the assembly out from the engine compartment.

10 Always be extremely careful when removing and refitting the engine/transmission. Serious injury can result from careless actions. Plan ahead and take your time, and a job of this nature, although major, can be accomplished successfully.

4 Engine – removal and refitting

Note: *Such is the complexity of the power unit arrangement on these vehicles, and the variations that may be encountered according to model and optional equipment fitted, the following should be regarded as a guide to the work involved, rather than a step-by-step procedure. Where differences are encountered, or additional component disconnection or removal is necessary, make notes of the work involved as an aid to refitting.*

Removal

1 Remove the battery and battery support tray (see Chapter 5A).

2 Apply the handbrake, then jack up the front of the vehicle and support it on axle stands (see *Jacking and vehicle support*). Remove both front roadwheels. Undo the screws and remove the engine undershield.

3 Unclip the plastic cover from the top of the engine.

4 Drain the cooling system with reference to Chapter 1.

5 Drain the transmission oil/fluid as described in Chapter 7A or 7B. Refit the drain and filler plugs, and tighten them to their specified torque settings.

6 If the engine is to be dismantled, drain the engine oil and remove the oil filter as described in Chapter 1. Clean and refit the drain plug, tightening it securely.

7 Remove the front bumper and bumper bar as described in Chapter 11.

8 Remove the air cleaner housing and ducting, with reference to Chapter 4A.

9 Remove the intercooler as described in Chapter 4A.

10 Remove the radiator, cooling fan and front panel assembly as described in Chapter 3. On air conditioned models, tie the condenser to one side **(see illustration)**. **Do not** disconnect the refrigerant pipes.

11 Refer to Chapter 8 and remove both front driveshafts.

4.10 Using a piece of cardboard to protect the condenser

4.12a Disconnect the power steering pipe brackets (arrowed) . . . .

4.12b . . . from the front subframe

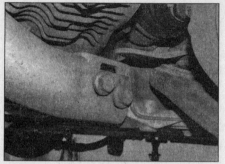

4.13 Front subframe mounting bolts (one side shown)

4.14a Undo the front mounting bolts . . .

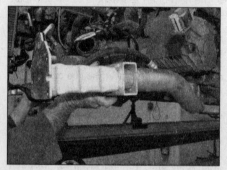

4.14b . . . and withdraw the front subframe from the vehicle

12 Undo the retaining bolts and disconnect the power steering pipe brackets from the front subframe **(see illustrations)**.
13 Undo the four bolts (two each side) securing the front subframe to the main subframe **(see illustration)**.
14 Undo the two bolts on the front securing brackets, and then remove the front subframe from the vehicle **(see illustrations)**.
15 Refer to Chapter 1 and remove the auxiliary drivebelt.
16 On 1.6 litre models with an engine mounted power steering pump, remove the pump as described in Chapter 10.
17 Disconnect the engine/transmission wiring harness plugs at the fusebox/ECM on the left-hand side of the engine compartment **(see illustration)**. The wiring connections will vary depending on model, follow the wiring loom to the engine/transmission unit and disconnect

the relevant wiring connectors, noting their fitted position. Refer to Chapter 12 for wiring diagrams.
18 Disconnect the earth cable from the top of the transmission housing **(see illustration)**.
19 Disconnect the exhaust system from the manifold with reference to Chapter 4A.
20 Disconnect the hose from the vacuum pump on the left-hand end of the cylinder head – see Chapter 9.
21 Disconnect the fuel feed and return hoses. Plug the end of the hoses to prevent dirt ingress, refer to Chapter 1 or 4A, for further information.
22 Disconnect the selector cable(s) from the transmission as described in Chapter 7A or 7B.
23 On manual transmission models, unbolt the clutch slave cylinder, then tie it to one side, without disconnecting the fluid pipe (refer to

Chapter 6). Use an elastic band around the cylinder to prevent the piston from coming out.
24 From underneath the vehicle, slacken and remove the nuts and bolts securing the lower rear engine mounting connecting link to the subframe, and remove the connecting link. Refer to Chapter 2A or 2B.
25 On models with air conditioning, refer to Chapter 3 and unbolt the compressor from the engine. **Do not** disconnect the refrigerant lines. Support or tie the compressor to one side.
26 Completely pull out the wire retaining clips and disconnect the heater hoses at the engine compartment bulkhead **(see illustration)**.
27 Using a hoist attached to the lifting eyes on the cylinder head, take the weight of the engine and transmission.
28 Remove the right-hand and left-hand engine mountings and support brackets as described in Chapter 2A or 2B.
29 Make a final check to ensure all wiring; hoses and brackets that would prevent the removal of the assembly have been disconnected.
30 Move the engine/transmission forwards and lower it out from the front of the vehicle. Enlist the help of an assistant during this procedure, as it may be necessary to tilt and twist the assembly slightly to clear the body panels and adjacent components. Taking care not to damage any of the air conditioning components, move the unit clear of the car and lower it to the ground.

4.17 Note the position of the wiring before disconnecting

4.18 Earth cable securing bolt (arrowed) on top of the transmission

4.26 Heater hose retaining clips (arrowed)

4.36 On 1.6 litre engines, the stud must be removed to access the front transmission-to-engine bolt

Separation

31 With the engine/transmission assembly removed, support the assembly on suitable blocks of wood on a workbench (or failing that, on a clean area of the workshop floor).

32 Undo the retaining bolts, and remove the flywheel lower cover plate (where fitted) from the transmission.

33 Slacken and remove the retaining bolts, and remove the starter motor from the transmission.

34 Disconnect any remaining wiring connectors at the transmission, then move the main engine wiring harness to one side.

35 On automatic transmission models, locate the access hole at the lower rear of the cylinder block, then turn the crankshaft by means of a socket on the crankshaft pulley bolt, until one of the three torque converter retaining nuts is accessible through the access hole. Undo the accessible torque converter bolt, then turn the crankshaft as necessary and undo the remaining two bolts.

36 Ensure that both engine and transmission are adequately supported, then slacken and remove the remaining bolts securing the transmission housing to the engine. Note the correct fitted positions of each bolt (and the relevant brackets) as they are removed, to use as a reference on refitting. On 1.6 litre models, the left-hand catalytic converter mounting stud must be removed to access the front transmission-to-engine bolt **(see illustration)**.

37 Carefully withdraw the transmission from the engine, ensuring that the weight of the transmission is not allowed to hang on the input shaft while it is engaged with the clutch friction disc (manual transmission models) or that the torque converter does not slip from the input shaft (automatic transmission models).

38 If they are loose, remove the locating dowels from the engine or transmission, and keep them in a safe place.

Refitting

39 If the engine and transmission have not been separated, perform the operations described below from paragraph 46 onwards.

40 Apply a smear of high melting-point grease (Peugeot recommend the use of Molykote BR2 plus – available from your Peugeot dealer) to the splines of the transmission input shaft. Do not apply too much; otherwise there is a possibility of the grease contaminating the clutch friction disc. **Note:** *On late models, Peugeot recommend* **no** *grease be applied.*

41 On automatic transmission models, prior to reconnection it is necessary to make a simple tool to align the torque converter with the driveplate as the transmission is refitted. To make the tool, carry out the following:

a) *Obtain a bolt of the same size as the torque converter retaining bolts, but long enough to extend through the access hole in the cylinder block when the transmission is refitted.*

b) *Cut the head off the bolt and cut a slot (to enable it to be unscrewed) in the plain end. Check that the tool will slide easily through the torque converter retaining bolt hole in the driveplate.*

c) *Turn the engine crankshaft so that one of the torque converter retaining bolt holes in the driveplate, is aligned with the access hole in the cylinder block. Screw the alignment tool (finger-tight only) into one of the retaining bolt holes in the torque converter. Turn the torque converter so that the alignment tool is in approximately the correct position, relative to the cylinder block access hole. As the transmission is refitted, the alignment tool will pass through the retaining bolt hole in the driveplate and through the access hole. It can then be unscrewed with a screwdriver and the first torque converter retaining bolt fitted in its place.*

d) *Check that the torque converter support bush fitted to the centre of the crankshaft is in good condition, and in place.*

42 Ensure that the locating dowels are correctly positioned in the engine or transmission, and then carefully offer the transmission to the engine until the locating dowels are engaged. On manual transmission models, ensure that the weight of the transmission is not allowed to hang on the input shaft as it is engaged with the clutch friction disc. On automatic transmission models, ensure the torque converter studs engage correctly with the corresponding holes in the driveplate.

43 Refit the transmission housing-to-engine bolts, ensuring that all the necessary brackets are correctly positioned, and tighten them securely.

44 Refit the starter motor, and securely tighten its retaining bolts.

45 Refit the lower flywheel cover plate (where fitted) to the transmission, and securely tighten the bolts.

46 Reconnect the hoist and lifting tackle to the engine lifting brackets. With the aid of an assistant, lift the assembly into the engine compartment, taking care not to damage surrounding components.

47 Refit the right-hand engine mounting and support bracket, but leave the bolts finger-tight at this stage.

48 Working on the left-hand mounting, refit the rubber mounting to the body over the stud, and tighten the bolts, then refit the centre nut and washer and finger-tighten.

49 Remove the hoist.

50 From underneath the vehicle, refit the rear mounting connecting link and finger-tighten the bolts.

51 Rock the engine to settle it on its mountings, then go around and tighten all the mounting nuts and bolts to their specified torque settings.

52 The remainder of the refitting procedure is a direct reversal of the removal sequence, with reference to the relevant chapters and noting the following points:

a) *Ensure that the wiring loom is correctly routed and retained by all the relevant retaining clips; all connectors should be correctly and securely reconnected.*

b) *Prior to refitting the driveshafts to the transmission, renew the driveshaft oil seals as described in Chapter 7A or 7B.*

c) *Ensure that all coolant hoses are correctly reconnected, and securely retained by their retaining clips.*

d) *Refill the engine and transmission with the correct quantity and type of lubricant, as described in Chapters 1, and 7A or 7B.*

e) *Refill the cooling system as described in Chapter 1.*

f) *Initialise the engine management ECM as follows. Start the engine and run to normal temperature. Carry out a road test during which the following procedure should be made. Engage third gear and stabilise the engine at 1000 rpm. Now accelerate fully to 3500 rpm.*

5 Engine overhaul – dismantling sequence

1 It is much easier to dismantle and work on the engine if it is mounted on a portable engine stand. These stands can often be hired from a tool hire shop. Before the engine is mounted on a stand, the flywheel/driveplate should be removed, so that the stand bolts can be tightened into the end of the cylinder block/crankcase.

2 If a stand is not available, it is possible to dismantle the engine with it blocked up on a sturdy workbench, or on the floor. Be extra careful not to tip or drop the engine when working without a stand.

3 If you are going to obtain a reconditioned engine, all the external components must be removed first, to be transferred to the new engine (just as they will if you are doing a complete engine overhaul yourself). These components include the following:

a) *Ancillary unit mounting brackets (oil filter, starter, alternator, power steering pump, etc).*

b) *Thermostat and housing (Chapter 3).*

c) *Dipstick tube/level sensor.*

d) *All electrical switches and sensors.*

e) *Inlet and exhaust manifolds (Chapter 4A).*

f) *Flywheel/driveplate (Part A or B of this Chapter).*

Note: *When removing the external components from the engine, pay close attention to details that may be helpful or important during refitting. Note the fitted position of gaskets, seals, spacers, pins, washers, bolts, and other small items.*

4 If you are obtaining a 'short' engine (which consists of the engine cylinder block/crankcase, crankshaft, pistons and connecting rods all assembled), then the cylinder head, sump, oil pump, and timing belt will have to be removed also.

5 If you are planning a complete overhaul, the engine can be dismantled, and the internal components removed, in the order given below, referring to Part A or B of this Chapter unless otherwise stated.

a) *Inlet and exhaust manifolds – where applicable (Chapter 4A).*

b) *Timing belts, sprockets and tensioner(s).*

c) *Cylinder head.*

d) *Flywheel/driveplate.*

e) *Sump.*

f) *Oil pump.*

g) *Piston/connecting rod assemblies (Section 9).*

h) *Crankshaft (Section 10).*

6 Before beginning the dismantling and overhaul procedures, make sure that you have all of the correct tools necessary. Refer to *Tools and working facilities* for further information.

6 Cylinder head – dismantling

Note: *New and reconditioned cylinder heads are available from the manufacturer, and from engine overhaul specialists. Be aware that some specialist tools are required for the dismantling and inspection procedures, and new components may not be readily available. It may therefore be more practical and economical for the home mechanic to purchase a reconditioned head, rather than dismantle, inspect and recondition the original head.*

1 Remove the cylinder head as described in Part A or B of this Chapter (as applicable).

2 If not already done, remove the inlet and exhaust manifolds with reference to Chapter 4A. Remove any remaining brackets or housings as required.

3 Remove the camshafts, hydraulic tappets and rockers, as described in Part A or B of this Chapter.

4 On the 2.0 litre engines, remove the camshaft drive chain guide from the cylinder head **(see illustration)**.

5 If not already done, remove the glow plugs as described in Chapter 5B.

6 On all models, using a valve spring compressor, compress each valve spring in turn until the split collets can be removed. Release the compressor, and lift off the spring retainer and spring. Note access to the valves is limited, and it may be necessary to make up an adapter out of metal tube – cut out a

6.4 Remove the camshaft drive chain guide – 2.0 litre engine

'window' so that the valve collets can be removed

7 If, when the valve spring compressor is screwed down, the spring retainer refuses to free and expose the split collets, gently tap the top of the tool, directly over the retainer, with a light hammer. This will free the retainer.

8 Withdraw the valve from the combustion chamber, and then remove the valve stem oil seal from the top of the guide. The valve stem oil seal also forms the spring seat and is deeply recessed in the cylinder head. It is also a tight fit on the valve guide making it difficult to remove with pliers or a conventional valve stem oil seal removal tool. It can be easily removed, however, using a self-locking nut of suitable diameter screwed onto the end of a bolt and locked with a second nut. Push the nut down onto the top of the seal; the locking portion of the nut will grip the seal allowing it to be withdrawn from the top of the valve guide **(see illustrations)**.

6.8a Compress the valve spring using a spring compressor . . .

6.8b . . . then extract the collets and release the spring compressor

6.8c Using a metal tube adapter for access to the valve collets

6.8d Remove the spring retainer . . .

6.8e . . . followed by the valve spring . . .

6.8f . . . and the spring seat (not all models)

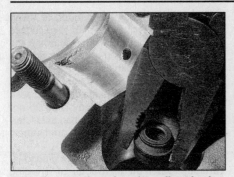

6.8g Remove the valve stem oil seal using a pair of pliers

6.8h Secure a self-locking nut of suitable diameter to a long bolt, then use the tool to remove the valve stem oil seal

6.9 Place each valve and its associated components in a labelled bag

9 It is essential that each valve is stored together with its collets, retainer and spring. The valves should also be kept in their correct sequence, unless they are so badly worn that they are to be renewed. If they are going to be kept and used again, place each valve assembly in a labelled polythene bag or similar small container **(see illustration)**. Note that No 1 valve is nearest to the transmission (flywheel/driveplate) end of the engine.

<table>
<tr><td>7</td><td>**Cylinder head and valves –** cleaning and inspection</td></tr>
</table>

1 Thorough cleaning of the cylinder head and valve components, followed by a detailed inspection, will enable you to decide how much valve service work must be carried out during the engine overhaul. **Note:** *If the engine has been severely overheated, it is best to assume that the cylinder head is warped – check carefully for signs of this.*

Cleaning

2 Scrape away all traces of old gasket material from the cylinder head.
3 Scrape away the carbon from the combustion chambers and ports, then wash the cylinder head thoroughly with paraffin or a suitable solvent.
4 Scrape off any heavy carbon deposits that may have formed on the valves, then

use a power-operated wire brush to remove deposits from the valve heads and stems.

Inspection

Note: *Be sure to perform all the following inspection procedures before concluding that the services of a machine shop or engine overhaul specialist are required. Make a list of all items that require attention.*

Cylinder head

5 Inspect the head very carefully for cracks, evidence of coolant leakage, and other damage. If cracks are found, a new cylinder head should be obtained. Use a straight-edge and feeler blade to check that the cylinder head gasket surface is not distorted **(see illustration)**. If it is, it may be possible to have it machined, provided that the cylinder head height is not significantly reduced.
6 Examine the valve seats in each of the combustion chambers. If they are severely pitted, cracked, or burned, they will need to be renewed or recut by an engine overhaul specialist. If they are only slightly pitted, this can be removed by grinding-in the valve heads and seats with fine valve grinding compound, as described below. If in any doubt, have the cylinder head inspected by an engine overhaul specialist.
7 Check the valve guides for wear by inserting the relevant valve, and checking for side-to-side motion of the valve. A very small amount of movement is acceptable. If the movement seems excessive, remove the valve. Measure the valve stem diameter (see

below), and renew the valve if it is worn. If the valve stem is not worn, the wear must be in the valve guide, and the guide must be renewed. The renewal of valve guides is best carried out by a Peugeot dealer or engine overhaul specialist, who will have the necessary tools available.
8 If renewing the valve guides, the valve seats should be recut or reground only *after* the guides have been fitted.
9 Where applicable, examine the camshaft oil supply non-return valve in the oil feed bore at the timing belt end of the cylinder head. Check that the valve is not loose in the cylinder head and that the ball is free to move within the valve body. If the valve is a loose fit in its bore, or if there is any doubt about its condition, it should be renewed. The non-return valve can be removed (assuming it is not loose), using compressed air, such as that generated by a tyre foot pump. Place the pump nozzle over the oil feed bore of the camshaft bearing journal and seal the corresponding oil feed bore with a rag. Apply the compressed air and the valve will be forced out of its location in the underside of the cylinder head **(see illustrations)**. Fit the new non-return valve to its bore on the underside of the head ensuring it is fitted the correct way. Oil should be able to pass upwards through the valve to the camshafts, but the ball in the valve should prevent the oil from returning back to the cylinder block. Use a thin socket or similar to push the valve fully into position.

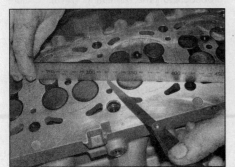

7.5 Check the cylinder head gasket surface for distortion

7.9a Apply compressed air to the oil feed bore of the inlet camshaft, seal the bore in the exhaust camshaft with a rag . . .

7.9b . . . and the camshaft oil supply non-return valve will be ejected from the underside of the cylinder head

7.11 Measure the valve stem diameter with a micrometer

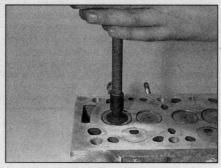

7.14 Grinding-in a valve

Valves

10 Examine the head of each valve for pitting, burning, cracks, and general wear. Check the valve stem for scoring and wear ridges. Rotate the valve, and check for any obvious indication that it is bent. Look for pits or excessive wear on the tip of each valve stem. Renew any valve that shows any such signs of wear or damage.

11 If the valve appears satisfactory at this stage, measure the valve stem diameter at several points using a micrometer **(see illustration)**. Any significant difference in the readings obtained indicates wear of the valve stem. Should any of these conditions be apparent, the valve must be renewed.

12 If the valves are in satisfactory condition, they should be ground (lapped) into their respective seats, to ensure a smooth, gas-tight seal. If the seat is only lightly pitted, or if it

has been recut, use fine grinding compound *only* to produce the required finish. Coarse valve-grinding compound should *not* be used, unless a seat is badly burned or deeply pitted. If this is the case, the cylinder head and valves should be inspected by an expert, to decide whether seat recutting, or even the renewal of the valve or seat insert (where possible) is required.

13 Valve grinding is carried out as follows. Place the cylinder head upside-down on a bench.

14 Smear a trace of (the appropriate grade of) valve-grinding compound on the seat face, and press a suction grinding tool onto the valve head **(see illustration)**. With a semi-rotary action, grind the valve head to its seat, lifting the valve occasionally to redistribute the grinding compound. A light spring placed under the valve head will greatly ease this operation.

15 If coarse grinding compound is being used, work only until a dull, matt even surface is produced on both the valve seat and the valve, then wipe off the used compound, and repeat the process with fine compound. When a smooth unbroken ring of light grey matt finish is produced on both the valve and seat, the grinding operation is complete. *Do not* grind-in the valves any further than absolutely necessary, or the seat will be prematurely sunk into the cylinder head.

16 When all the valves have been ground-in, carefully wash off *all* traces of grinding compound using paraffin or a suitable solvent, before reassembling the cylinder head.

Valve components

17 Examine the valve springs for signs of damage and discoloration. No minimum free length is specified by Peugeot, so the only way of judging valve spring wear is by comparison with a new component.

18 Stand each spring on a flat surface, and check it for squareness. If any of the springs are damaged, distorted or have lost their tension, obtain a complete new set of springs. It is normal to renew the valve springs as a matter of course if a major overhaul is being carried out.

19 Renew the valve stem oil seals regardless of their apparent condition.

8.1a Locate the valve stem oil seal (arrowed) on the valve guide ...

8.1b ... and press the seal firmly onto the guide using a suitable socket

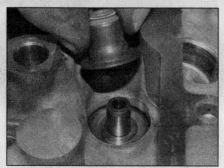

8.1c On some engines, the valve stem oil seal is integral with the spring seat

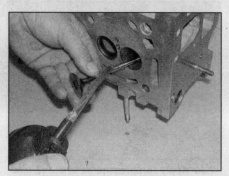

8.2 Lubricate the stem of the valve and insert it into the guide

8 Cylinder head – reassembly

1 Working on the first valve assembly, refit the spring seat then dip the new valve stem oil seal in fresh engine oil. Locate the seal on the valve guide and press the seal firmly onto the guide using a suitable socket **(see illustrations)**.

2 Lubricate the stem of the first valve, and insert it in the guide **(see illustration)**.

3 Locate the valve spring on top of its seat, and then refit the spring retainer.

4 Compress the valve spring, and locate the split collets in the recess in the valve stem. Release the compressor, then repeat the procedure on the remaining valves. Ensure that each valve is inserted into its original location. If new valves are being fitted, insert them into the locations to which they have been ground.

5 With all the valves installed, support the cylinder head and, using a hammer and interposed block of wood, tap the end of each valve stem to settle the components.

6 Refit the camshafts, hydraulic tappets and rocker arms, as described in Part A or B of this Chapter.

7 Refit any remaining components using the reverse of the removal sequence and with new seals or gaskets as necessary.

8 The cylinder head can then be refitted as described in Part A or B of this Chapter.

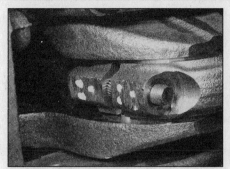

9.3 Connecting rod and big-end bearing cap identification marks (No 3 shown)

9.5 Remove the big-end bearing shell and cap

9.6 To protect the crankshaft journals, tape over the connecting rod stud threads

9 Piston/connecting rod assembly – removal

1 Remove the cylinder head, sump and oil pump as described in Part A or B of this Chapter.
2 If there is a pronounced wear ridge at the top of any bore, it may be necessary to remove it with a scraper or ridge reamer, to avoid piston damage during removal. Such a ridge indicates excessive wear of the cylinder bore.
3 Using quick-drying paint, mark each connecting rod and big-end bearing cap with its respective cylinder number on the flat machined surface provided; if the engine has been dismantled before, note carefully any identifying marks made previously (see illustration). Note that No 1 cylinder is at the transmission (flywheel) end of the engine.
4 Turn the crankshaft to bring pistons 1 and 4 to BDC (bottom dead centre). On 1.6 litre engines, remove the main bearing ladder as described in Section 10 of this Chapter.
5 Unscrew the nuts or bolts, as applicable, from No 1 piston big-end bearing cap. Take off the cap, and recover the bottom half bearing shell (see illustration). If the bearing shells are to be re-used, tape the cap and the shell together.
6 Where applicable, to prevent the possibility of damage to the crankshaft bearing journals, tape over the connecting rod stud threads (see illustration).
7 Using a hammer handle, push the piston up

through the bore, and remove it from the top of the cylinder block. Recover the bearing shell, and tape it to the connecting rod for safekeeping.
8 Loosely refit the big-end cap to the connecting rod, and secure with the nuts/bolts – this will help to keep the components in their correct order.
9 Remove No 4 piston assembly in the same way.
10 Turn the crankshaft through 180° to bring pistons 2 and 3 to BDC (bottom dead centre), and remove them in the same way.

10 Crankshaft – removal

1 Remove the crankshaft sprocket and the oil pump as described in Part A or B of this Chapter (as applicable).
2 Remove the pistons and connecting rods, as described in Section 9. If no work is to be done on the pistons and connecting rods, there is no need to remove the cylinder head, or to push the pistons out of the cylinder bores. The pistons should just be pushed far enough up the bores so that they are positioned clear of the crankshaft journals. Note: On 1.6 litre engines, the main bearing ladder must be removed before the piston/connecting rods.
3 Check the crankshaft endfloat as described in Section 13, then proceed as follows.

1.6 litre engine

4 Work around the outside of the cylinder

block, and unscrew all the small bolts securing the main bearing ladder to the base of the cylinder block. Note the correct fitted depth of the left-hand crankshaft oil seal in the cylinder block/main bearing ladder.
5 Working in a diagonal sequence, evenly and progressively slacken the large main bearing ladder retaining bolts by a turn at a time. Once all the bolts are loose, remove them from the ladder. Note: Prise up the two caps at the flywheel end of the ladder to expose the two end main bearing bolts (see illustration).
6 With all the retaining bolts removed, carefully lift the main bearing ladder casting away from the base of the cylinder block (see illustration). Recover the lower main bearing shells, and tape them to their respective locations in the casting. If the two locating dowels are a loose fit, remove them and store them with the casting for safekeeping. Undo the big-end bolts and remove the pistons/connecting rods as described in Section 9.
7 Lift out the crankshaft, and discard both the oil seals.
8 Recover the upper main bearing shells, and store them along with the relevant lower bearing shell. Also recover the two thrustwashers (one fitted either side of No 2 main bearing) from the cylinder block.

2.0 litre engine

9 Slacken and remove the retaining bolts, and remove the oil seal housing from the right-hand (timing belt) end of the cylinder block (see illustration).

10.5 On 1.6 litre engines, prise up the two caps to expose the main bearing bolts at the flywheel end

10.6 Remove the crankshaft bearing cap housing

10.9 Remove the oil seal housing from the right-hand end of the cylinder block

10.10a Remove the oil pump drive chain . . .

10.10b . . . then slide off the drive sprocket . . .

10.10c . . . and remove the Woodruff key from the crankshaft

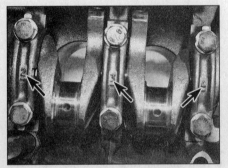

10.11 Main bearing cap Identification markings (arrowed)

10.12 Note the thrustwasher fitted to the No 2 main bearing cap (arrowed)

10.13 Lift out the crankshaft

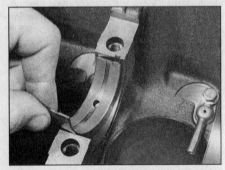

10.14 Remove the upper main bearing shells

10 Remove the oil pump drive chain, and slide the drive sprocket and spacer (where fitted) off from the crankshaft. Remove the Woodruff key, and store it with the sprocket for safekeeping **(see illustrations)**.

11 The main bearing caps should be numbered 1 to 5, starting from the transmission (flywheel) end of the engine **(see illustration)**. If not, mark them accordingly using a centre-punch. Also note the correct fitted depth of the crankshaft oil seal in the bearing cap.

12 Slacken and remove the main bearing cap retaining bolts, and lift off each bearing cap. Recover the lower bearing shells, and tape them to their respective caps for safekeeping. Also recover the lower thrustwasher halves from the side of No 2 main bearing cap **(see illustration)**. Remove the sealing strips from the sides of No 1 main bearing cap, and discard them.

13 Lift out the crankshaft, and discard the left-hand (flywheel end) oil seal **(see illustration)**.

14 Recover the upper bearing shells from the cylinder block, and tape them to

their respective caps for safekeeping **(see illustration)**. Remove the upper thrustwasher halves from the side of No 2 main bearing, and store them with the lower halves.

11 Cylinder block/crankcase – cleaning and inspection

Cleaning

1 Remove all external components and electrical switches/sensors from the block.

2 For complete cleaning, the core plugs should ideally be removed **(see illustrations))**. Drill a small hole in the plugs, and then insert a self-tapping screw into the hole. Pull out the plugs by pulling on the screw with a pair of grips, or by using a slide hammer.

3 Where applicable, undo the retaining bolts

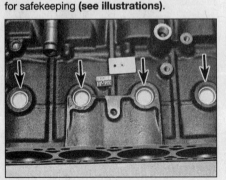

11.2a Cylinder block core plugs (arrowed)

11.2b Remove the air conditioning compressor bracket

11.2c Remove the crankcase ventilation/oil separator box

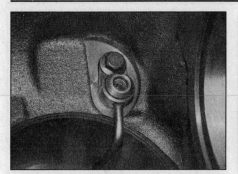

11.3 Piston cooling jets may be fitted to the base of each cylinder bore

11.9 Use a suitable tap to clean out the cylinder block threads

12.2 Remove the piston rings with the aid of feeler gauges

and remove the piston oil jet spray tubes (there is one for each piston) from inside the cylinder block **(see illustration)**.

4 Scrape all traces of gasket from the cylinder block/crankcase, and from the main bearing ladder/caps (as applicable), taking care not to damage the gasket/sealing surfaces.

5 Remove all oil gallery plugs (where fitted). The plugs are usually very tight – they may have to be drilled out, and the holes retapped. Use new plugs when the engine is reassembled.

6 If any of the castings are extremely dirty, all should be steam-cleaned.

7 After the castings are returned, clean all oil holes and oil galleries one more time. Flush all internal passages with warm water until the water runs clear. Dry thoroughly, and apply a light film of oil to all mating surfaces, to prevent rusting. If you have access to compressed air, use it to speed up the drying process, and to blow out all the oil holes and galleries.

 Warning: Wear eye protection when using compressed air.

8 If the castings are not very dirty, you can do an adequate cleaning job with hot (as hot as you can stand), soapy water and a stiff brush. Take plenty of time, and do a thorough job. Regardless of the cleaning method used, be sure to clean all oil holes and galleries very thoroughly, and to dry all components well.

9 All threaded holes must be clean, to ensure accurate torque readings during reassembly. To clean the threads, run the correct-size tap into each of the holes to remove rust, corrosion, thread sealant or sludge, and to restore damaged threads **(see illustration)**. If possible, use compressed air to clear the holes of debris produced by this operation.

10 Apply suitable sealant to the new oil gallery plugs, and insert them into the holes in the block. Tighten them securely. Also apply suitable sealant to new core plugs, and drive them into the block using a tube or socket.

11 Where applicable, clean the threads of the piston oil jet retaining bolts, and apply a drop of thread-locking compound (Peugeot recommend Loctite Frenetanch) to each bolt threads. Refit the piston oil jet spray tubes to the cylinder block, and tighten the retaining bolts to the specified torque setting.

12 If the engine is not going to be reassembled right away, cover it with a large plastic bag to keep it clean; protect all mating surfaces and the cylinder bores as described above, to prevent rusting.

Inspection

13 Visually check the castings for cracks and corrosion. Look for stripped threads in the threaded holes. If there has been any history of internal water leakage, it may be worthwhile having an engine overhaul specialist check the cylinder block/crankcase with special equipment. If defects are found, have them repaired if possible, or renew the assembly.

14 Check each cylinder bore for scuffing and scoring. Check for signs of a wear ridge at the top of the cylinder, indicating that the bore is excessively worn.

15 If the necessary measuring equipment is available, measure the bore diameter of each cylinder at the top (just under the wear ridge), centre, and bottom of the cylinder bore, parallel to the crankshaft axis.

16 Next, measure the bore diameter at the same three locations, at right angles to the crankshaft axis. Compare the results with the figures given in the Specifications. If there is any doubt about the condition of the cylinder bores, seek the advice of a Peugeot dealer or suitable engine-reconditioning specialist.

17 At the time of writing, it was not clear whether oversize pistons were available for all models. Consult your Peugeot dealer or engine specialist for the latest information on piston availability. If oversize pistons are available, then it may be possible to have the cylinder bores rebored and fit the oversize pistons. If oversize pistons are not available, and the bores are worn, renewal of the block seems to be the only option.

12 Piston/connecting rod assembly – inspection

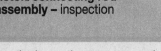

1 Before the inspection process can begin, the piston/connecting rod assemblies must be cleaned, and the original piston rings removed from the pistons.

2 Carefully expand the old rings over the top of the pistons. The use of two or three old feeler blades will be helpful in preventing the rings dropping into empty grooves **(see illustration)**. Be careful not to scratch the piston with the ends of the ring. The rings are brittle, and will snap if they are spread too far. They are also very sharp – protect your hands and fingers. Note that the third ring incorporates an expander. Always remove the rings from the top of the piston. Keep each set of rings with its piston if the old rings are to be re-used.

3 Scrape away all traces of carbon from the top of the piston. A hand-held wire brush (or a piece of fine emery cloth) can be used, once the majority of the deposits have been scraped away.

4 Remove the carbon from the ring grooves in the piston, using an old ring. Break the ring in half to do this (be careful not to cut your fingers – piston rings are sharp). Be careful to remove only the carbon deposits – do not remove any metal, and do not nick or scratch the sides of the ring grooves.

5 Once the deposits have been removed, clean the piston/connecting rod assembly with paraffin or a suitable solvent, and dry thoroughly. Make sure that the oil return holes in the ring grooves are clear.

6 If the pistons and cylinder bores are not damaged or worn excessively, and if the cylinder block does not need to be rebored (where possible), the original pistons can be refitted. Normal piston wear shows up as even vertical wear on the piston thrust surfaces, and slight looseness of the top ring in its groove. New piston rings should always be used when the engine is reassembled.

7 Carefully inspect each piston for cracks around the skirt, around the gudgeon pin holes, and at the piston ring 'lands' (between the ring grooves).

8 Look for scoring and scuffing on the piston skirt, holes in the piston crown, and burned areas at the edge of the crown. If the skirt is scored or scuffed, the engine may have been suffering from overheating, and/or abnormal combustion, which caused excessively high operating temperatures. The cooling and lubrication systems should be checked thoroughly. Scorch marks on the sides of the pistons show that blow-by has occurred. A hole in the piston crown, or burned areas at the edge of the piston crown, indicates that

12.14a Prise out the circlip . . .

12.14b . . . and withdraw the gudgeon pin

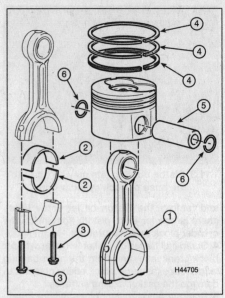

12.18 Piston and connecting rod assembly
– 1.6 litre engine

1 Connecting rod   4 Piston rings
2 Big-end shells   5 Gudgeon pin
3 Big-end bolt   6 Circlips

abnormal combustion (pre-ignition, knocking, or detonation) has been occurring. If any of the above problems exist, the causes must be investigated and corrected, or the damage will occur again. The causes may include incorrect ignition/injection pump timing, or a faulty injector (as applicable).

9 Corrosion of the piston, in the form of pitting, indicates that coolant has been leaking into the combustion chamber and/or the crankcase. Again, the cause must be corrected, or the problem may persist in the rebuilt engine.

10 On aluminium block engines, it is not possible to renew the pistons separately; pistons are only supplied with piston rings and a liner as a part of a matched assembly.

11 Examine each connecting rod carefully for signs of damage, such as cracks around the big-end and small-end bearings. Check that the rod is not bent or distorted. Damage is highly unlikely, unless the engine has been seized or badly overheated. Detailed checking of the connecting rod assembly can only be carried out by a Peugeot dealer or engine specialist with the necessary equipment.

12 The connecting rod big-end cap bolts/nuts must be renewed whenever they are disturbed. Although Peugeot do not specify that the bolts must also be renewed, it is recommended that the nuts and bolts are renewed as a complete set.

13 The gudgeon pins are of the floating type, secured in position by two circlips. The pistons and connecting rods can be separated as described in the following paragraphs.

14 Using a small flat-bladed screwdriver, prise out the circlips, and push out the gudgeon pin (see illustrations). Hand pressure should be sufficient to remove the pin. Identify the piston and rod to ensure correct reassembly. Discard the circlips – new ones *must* be used on refitting.

15 Examine the gudgeon pin and connecting rod small-end bearing for signs of wear or damage. Wear can be cured by renewing both the pin and bush (where possible) or connecting rod. Bush renewal, however, is a specialist job – press facilities are required, and the new bush must be reamed accurately.

16 The connecting rods themselves should not be in need of renewal, unless seizure or some other major mechanical failure has occurred. Check the alignment of the connecting rods visually, and if the rods are not straight, take them to an engine overhaul specialist for a more detailed check.

17 Examine all components, and obtain any new parts from your Peugeot dealer. If new pistons are purchased, they will be supplied complete with gudgeon pins and circlips. Circlips can also be purchased individually.

18 On 1.6 litre engines, position the piston as shown (see illustration).

19 On 2.0 litre engines, position the piston so that the valve recesses on the piston crown are on the opposite side to the connecting rod big-end bearing shell cut-outs.

20 Ensure the piston and connecting rod are correctly positioned then apply a smear of clean engine oil to the gudgeon pin. Slide it into the piston and through the connecting

rod small-end. Check that the piston pivots freely on the rod, then secure the gudgeon pin in position with two new circlips. Ensure that each circlip is correctly located in its groove in the piston.

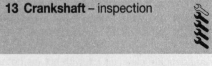

13 Crankshaft – inspection

Checking endfloat

1 If the crankshaft endfloat is to be checked, this must be done when the crankshaft is still installed in the cylinder block/crankcase, but is free to move (see Section 10).

2 Check the endfloat using a dial gauge in contact with the end of the crankshaft. Push the crankshaft fully one way, and then zero the gauge. Push the crankshaft fully the other way, and check the endfloat. The result can be compared with the specified amount, and will give an indication as to whether new thrustwashers are required (see illustration).

3 If a dial gauge is not available, feeler blades can be used. First push the crankshaft fully towards the flywheel end of the engine, and then use feeler blades to measure the gap between the web of No 2 crankpin and the thrustwasher (see illustration).

Inspection

4 Clean the crankshaft using paraffin or a suitable solvent, and dry it, preferably with compressed air if available. Be sure to clean the oil holes with a pipe cleaner or similar probe, to ensure that they are not obstructed.

13.2 Check the crankshaft endfloat using
a DTI gauge . . .

13.3 . . . or with feeler gauges

Warning: Wear eye protection when using compressed air.

5 Check the main and big-end bearing journals for uneven wear, scoring, pitting and cracking.

6 Big-end bearing wear is accompanied by distinct metallic knocking when the engine is running (particularly noticeable when the engine is pulling from low speed) and some loss of oil pressure.

7 Main bearing wear is accompanied by severe engine vibration and rumble – getting progressively worse as engine speed increases – and again by loss of oil pressure.

8 Check the bearing journal for roughness by running a finger lightly over the bearing surface. Any roughness (which will be accompanied by obvious bearing wear) indicates that the crankshaft requires regrinding (where possible) or renewal.

9 Check the oil seal contact surfaces at each end of the crankshaft for wear and damage. If the seal has worn a deep groove in the surface of the crankshaft, consult an engine overhaul specialist; repair may be possible, but otherwise a new crankshaft will be required.

10 Take the crankshaft to a Peugeot dealer or engine-reconditioning specialist to have it measured for journal wear. If excessive wear is evident, they will be able to advise you with regard to regrinding the crankshaft and supplying new bearing shells.

11 If the crankshaft has been reground, check for burrs around the crankshaft oil holes (the holes are usually chamfered, so burrs should not be a problem unless regrinding has been carried out carelessly). Remove any burrs with a fine file or scraper, and thoroughly clean the oil holes as described previously.

12 At the time of writing, it was not clear whether Peugeot produce undersize bearing shells for all of these engines. On some engines, if the crankshaft journals have not already been reground, it may be possible to have the crankshaft reconditioned, and to fit undersize shells. If no undersize shells are available and the crankshaft has worn beyond the specified limits, it will have to be renewed. Consult your Peugeot dealer or engine specialist for further information on parts availability.

14 Main and big-end bearings – inspection

1 Even though the main and big-end bearings should be renewed during the engine overhaul, the old bearings should be retained for close examination, as they may reveal valuable information about the condition of the engine. The bearing shells are graded by thickness, the grade of each shell being indicated by the colour code marked on it.

2 Bearing failure can occur due to lack of lubrication, the presence of dirt or other foreign particles, overloading the engine, or corrosion

(see illustration). Regardless of the cause of bearing failure, the cause must be corrected (where applicable) before the engine is reassembled, to prevent it from happening again.

3 When examining the bearing shells, remove them from the cylinder block/crankcase, the main bearing ladder/caps (as appropriate), the connecting rods and the connecting rod big-end bearing caps. Lay them out on a clean surface in the same general position as their location in the engine. This will enable you to match any bearing problems with the corresponding crankshaft journal. *Do not* touch any shell's bearing surface with your fingers while checking it, or the delicate surface may be scratched.

4 Dirt and other foreign matter may get into the engine in a variety of different ways. It may be left in the engine during assembly, or it may pass through filters or the crankcase ventilation system. It may get into the oil, and from there into the bearings. Metal chips from machining operations and normal engine wear are often present. Abrasives are sometimes left in engine components after reconditioning, especially when parts are not thoroughly cleaned using the proper cleaning methods. Whatever the source, these foreign objects often end up embedded in the soft bearing material, and are easily recognised. Large particles will not embed in the bearing, and will score or gouge the bearing and journal. The best prevention for this cause of bearing failure is to clean all parts thoroughly, and keep everything spotlessly clean during engine assembly. Frequent and regular engine oil and filter changes are also recommended.

5 Lack of lubrication (or lubrication breakdown) has a number of interrelated causes. Excessive heat (which thins the oil), overloading (which squeezes the oil from the bearing face) and oil leakage (from excessive bearing clearances, worn oil pump or high engine speeds) all contribute to lubrication breakdown. Blocked

FATIGUE FAILURE

CRATERS OR POCKETS

IMPROPER SEATING

BRIGHT (POLISHED) SECTIONS

SCRATCHED BY DIRT

DIRT EMBEDDED INTO BEARING MATERIAL

LACK OF OIL

OVERLAY WIPED OUT

EXCESSIVE WEAR

OVERLAY WIPED OUT

TAPERED JOURNAL

RADIUS RIDE

H 28395

14.2 Typical bearing failures

oil passages, which usually are the result of misaligned oil holes in a bearing shell, will also oil-starve a bearing, and destroy it. When lack of lubrication is the cause of bearing failure, the bearing material is wiped or extruded from the steel backing of the bearing. Temperatures may increase to the point where the steel backing turns blue from overheating.

6 Driving habits can have a definite effect on bearing life. Full-throttle, low-speed operation (labouring the engine) puts very high loads on bearings, tending to squeeze out the oil film. These loads cause the bearings to flex, which produces fine cracks in the bearing face (fatigue failure). Eventually, the bearing material will loosen in pieces, and tear away from the steel backing.

7 Short-distance driving leads to corrosion of bearings, because insufficient engine heat is produced to drive off the condensed water and corrosive gases. These products collect in the engine oil, forming acid and sludge. As the oil is carried to the engine bearings, the acid attacks and corrodes the bearing material.

8 Incorrect bearing installation during engine assembly will lead to bearing failure as well. Tight-fitting bearings leave insufficient bearing running clearance, and will result in oil starvation. Dirt or foreign particles trapped behind a bearing shell result in high spots on the bearing, which lead to failure.

9 *Do not* touch any shell's bearing surface with your fingers during reassembly; there is a risk of scratching the delicate surface, or of depositing particles of dirt on it.

10 As mentioned at the beginning of this Section, the bearing shells should be renewed as a matter of course during engine overhaul; to do otherwise is false economy.

15 Engine overhaul – reassembly sequence

1 Before reassembly begins, ensure that all new parts have been obtained, and that all necessary tools are available. Read through the entire procedure to familiarise yourself with the work involved, and to ensure that all items necessary for reassembly of the engine are at hand. In addition to all normal tools and materials, thread-locking compound will be needed. A tube of suitable liquid sealant will also be required for the joint faces that are fitted without gaskets. It is recommended that Peugeot's own product(s) be used, which are specially formulated for this purpose; the relevant product names are quoted in the text of each Section where they are required.

2 In order to save time and avoid problems, engine reassembly can be carried out in the following order, referring to Part A or B of this Chapter unless otherwise stated:

a) *Crankshaft (See Section 17).*
b) *Piston/connecting rod assemblies (See Section 18).*
c) *Oil pump.*

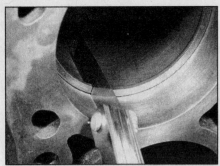

16.5 Measure the piston ring end gap with feeler gauges

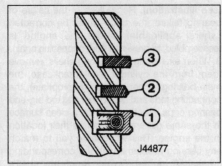

16.9a Piston ring fitting diagram (typical)

1 *Oil control ring*
2 *Second compression ring*
3 *Top compression ring*

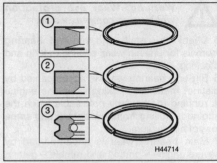

16.9b Piston rings (1.6 litre engine)

1 *Top compression ring*
2 *Second compression ring*
3 *Oil control ring*

d) *Sump.*
e) *Flywheel/driveplate.*
f) *Cylinder head.*
g) *Injection pump and mounting bracket (Chapter 4A).*
h) *Timing belt tensioner pulley(s) and sprockets, and timing belt.*
i) *Engine external components.*

3 At this stage, all engine components should be absolutely clean and dry, with all faults repaired. The components should be laid out (or in individual containers) on a completely clean work surface.

16 Piston rings – refitting

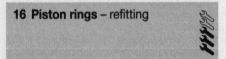

1 Before fitting new piston rings, the ring end gaps must be checked as follows.
2 Lay out the piston/connecting rod assemblies and the new piston ring sets, so that the ring sets will be matched with the same piston and cylinder during the end gap measurement and subsequent engine reassembly.
3 Insert the top ring into the first cylinder, and push it down the bore using the top of the piston. This will ensure that the ring remains square with the cylinder walls. Position the ring near the bottom of the cylinder bore, at the lower limit of ring travel. Note that the top and second compression rings are different. The second ring can be identified by its taper. On 1.6 litre engines, the top ring has a chamfer on its upper/outer edge.
4 Measure the end gap using feeler blades.
5 Repeat the procedure with the ring at the top of the cylinder bore, at the upper limit of its travel **(see illustration)**, and compare the measurements with the figures given in the Specifications. If the end gaps are incorrect, check that you have the correct rings for your engine and for the cylinder bore size.
6 Repeat the checking procedure for each ring in the first cylinder, and then for the rings in the remaining cylinders. Remember to keep rings, pistons and cylinders matched up.
7 Once the ring end gaps have been checked

and if necessary corrected, the rings can be fitted to the pistons.
8 Fit the oil control ring expander (where fitted) then install the ring. The ring gap should be positioned 180° from the expander gap.
9 The second and top rings are different and can be identified from their cross-sections; the top ring is symmetrical whilst the second ring is tapered. Fit the second ring, ensuring its identification (TOP) marking is facing upwards, and then install the top ring **(see illustrations)**. Arrange the second and top ring end gaps so they are equally spaced 120° apart. **Note:** *Always follow any instructions supplied with the new piston ring sets – different manufacturers may specify different procedures. Do not mix up the top and second compression rings, as they have different cross-sections.*

17 Crankshaft – refitting

Selection of bearing shells

1 Have the crankshaft inspected and measured by a Peugeot dealer or engine reconditioning

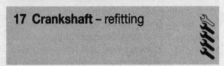

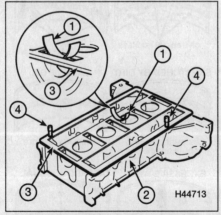

17.3 Main bearing shell refitment (1.6 litre engine)

1 *Bearing shell*   3 *Peugeot tool*
2 *Main bearing ladder*   4 *Aligning pins*

specialist. They will be able to carry out any regrinding/repairs, and supply suitable main and big-end bearing shells.

Crankshaft refitting

Note: *New main bearing cap/lower crankcase bolts must be used when refitting the crankshaft.*
2 Where applicable, ensure that the oil spray jets are fitted to the bearing locations in the cylinder block.

1.6 litre engine

3 Place the bearing shells in their locations. If new shells are being fitted, ensure that all traces of protective grease are cleaned off using paraffin. Wipe dry the shells with a lint-free cloth. The upper bearing shells all have a grooved surface, whereas the lower shells have a plain surface. On these engines, it's essential that the lower bearing shells are centrally located in the bearing cap housing/ladder. To ensure this use Peugeot tool No 0194-QZ positioned over the housing/ladder, and insert the bearing shells through the slots in the tool **(see illustration)**.
4 Liberally lubricate each bearing shell in the cylinder block with clean engine oil then lower the crankshaft into position.
5 Insert the thrustwashers to either side of No 2 main bearing upper location and push them around the bearing journal until their edges are horizontal **(see illustration)**. Ensure that the oilway grooves on each thrustwasher face outwards (away from the bearing journal).

17.5 Ensure the oil grooves on each thrustwasher are facing outwards from the No 2 main bearing location

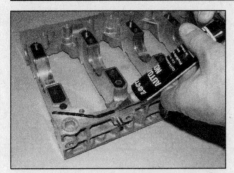

17.7 Apply a thin bead of RTV sealant to the bearing cap housing mating surface

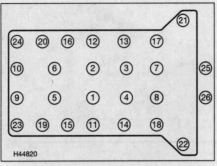

17.10 Main bearing cap housing/ladder retaining bolt tightening sequence – 1.6 litre engine

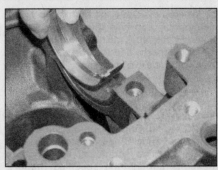

17.16a Ensure the grooved main bearing shells are fitted to the cylinder block . . .

6 Refit the piston/connecting rod assemblies to the crankshaft as described in Section 18.
7 Thoroughly degrease the mating surfaces of the cylinder block and the crankshaft bearing cap housing. Apply a thin bead of RTV sealant to the bearing cap housing mating surface **(see illustration)**. Peugeot recommend the use of Loctite Autojoint Noir for this purpose.
8 Lubricate the lower bearing shells with clean engine oil, then refit the bearing cap housing, ensuring that the shells are not displaced, and that the locating dowels engage correctly.
9 Install the ten large diameter and sixteen smaller diameter crankshaft bearing cap housing retaining bolts, and screw them in until they are just making contact with the housing.
10 Working in sequence, tighten the bolts to the torque settings given in the Specifications **(see illustration)**.
11 With the bearing cap housing in place, check that the crankshaft rotates freely.
12 Refit the oil pump and sump.
13 Fit a new crankshaft left-hand oil seal, then refit the flywheel.
14 Where removed, refit the cylinder head, crankshaft sprocket and timing belt.

2.0 litre engine

15 Using a little grease, stick the thrustwashers to each side of No 2 main bearing upper location and bearing cap **(see illustration 17.5)**. Ensure that the oilway grooves on each thrustwasher face outwards (away from the cylinder block).
16 Place the bearing shells in their locations **(see illustrations)**. If new shells are being

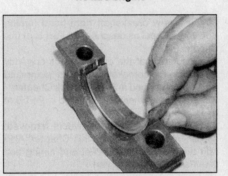

17.16b . . . and the plain bearing shells to the bearing caps

fitted, ensure that all traces of protective grease are cleaned off using paraffin. Wipe dry the shells and connecting rods with a lint-free cloth. Liberally lubricate each bearing shell in the cylinder block/crankcase and cap with clean engine oil.
17 Lower the crankshaft into position so that Nos 2 and 3 cylinder crankpins are at TDC; Nos 1 and 4 cylinder crankpins will be at BDC, ready for fitting No 1 piston. Check the crankshaft endfloat, referring to Section 13.
18 Lubricate the lower bearing shells in the main bearing caps with clean engine oil. Make sure that the locating lugs on the shells engage with the corresponding recesses in the caps.
19 Fit main bearing caps Nos 2 to 5 to their correct locations, ensuring that they are fitted the correct way round (the bearing shell tab recesses in the block and caps must be on

17.19 Fit the No 2 to 5 bearing caps and install the bearing cap bolts

the same side) **(see illustration)**. Ensure the thrustwashers remain correctly fitted to No 2 bearing cap then refit the bearing cap bolts, tightening them only lightly at this stage.
20 Apply a small amount of sealant to the No 1 main bearing cap mating face on the cylinder block, around the sealing strip holes **(see illustration)**.
21 Locate the tab of each sealing strip over the pins on the base of No 1 bearing cap, and press the strips into the bearing cap grooves. It is now necessary to obtain two thin metal strips, of 0.25 mm thickness or less, in order to prevent the strips moving when the cap is being fitted. Peugeot garages use the tool shown, which acts as a clamp. Metal strips (such as old feeler blades) can be used, provided all burrs that may damage the sealing strips are first removed **(see illustrations)**.

17.20 Apply sealant to the No 1 main bearing cap mating face on the cylinder block, around the sealing strip holes and in the corners

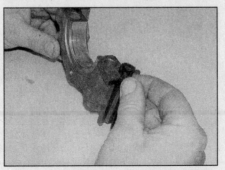

17.21a Fit the sealing strips to each side of No 1 main bearing cap, ensuring they are correctly engaged

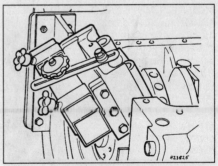

17.21b Using the Peugeot tool to fit the No 1 main bearing cap

22 Where applicable, oil both sides of the metal strips, and hold them on the sealing strips. Fit the No 1 main bearing cap, insert the bolts loosely, and then carefully pull out the metal strips in a horizontal direction, using a pair of pliers **(see illustration)**.

23 Working in sequence **(see illustration)**, tighten the main bearing cap bolts evenly and progressively to the specified Stage 1 torque wrench setting. Once all the bolts have been tightened to the Stage 1 setting, working in the specified sequence, angle-tighten the bolts through the specified Stage 2 angle, using a socket and extension bar. It is recommended that an angle-measuring gauge be used during this stage of the tightening, to ensure accuracy. If a gauge is not available, use a dab of white paint to make alignment marks between the bolt head and casting prior to tightening; the marks can then be used to check that the bolt has been rotated sufficiently during tightening.

24 Check that the sealing strips protrude slightly from above the cylinder block/crankcase mating surface by approximately 1 mm. If not, remove the bearing cap again and refit; the seals are supplied the correct length and should not be cut. Also check that the crankshaft rotates freely.

25 Fit a new crankshaft left-hand (flywheel end) oil seal as described in Part B of this Chapter.

26 Refit the piston/connecting rod assemblies to the crankshaft as described in Section 18.

27 Fit a new sealing ring (where fitted) the crankshaft then refit the Woodruff key and slide on the oil pump drive sprocket and spacer. Locate the drive chain on the sprocket.

28 Ensure that the mating surfaces of the right-hand (timing belt end) oil seal housing and cylinder block are clean and dry. Note the correct fitted depth of the oil seal then, using a large flat-bladed screwdriver, lever the old seal out of the housing.

29 Apply a smear of suitable sealant to the oil seal housing mating surface. Ensure that the locating dowels are in position, and then slide the housing over the end of the crankshaft and into position on the cylinder block. Tighten the housing retaining bolts to the specified torque.

17.22 Using 2 metal strips to hold the sealing strips in place as the bearing cap is fitted

30 Fit a new crankshaft right-hand (timing belt end) oil seal as described in Part B of this Chapter.

31 Ensuring that the drive chain is correctly located on the sprocket, refit the oil pump and sump as described in Part B of this Chapter.

32 Refit the flywheel as described in Part B of this Chapter.

33 Refit the cylinder head (where removed) as described in Part B of this Chapter. Also refit the crankshaft sprocket and timing belt (see Part B of this Chapter).

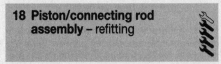

18 Piston/connecting rod assembly – refitting

Note: *New big-end cap nuts/bolts must be used on refitting.*

1 Note that the following procedure assumes that the crankshaft and main bearing ladder/caps are in place.

2 Clean the backs of the bearing shells, and the bearing locations in both the connecting rod and bearing cap.

2.0 litre engine

3 Press the bearing shells into their locations, ensuring that the tab on each shell engages in the notch in the connecting rod and cap. Take care not to touch any shell's bearing surface with your fingers **(see illustration)**.

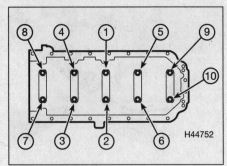

17.23 Main bearing cap bolt tightening sequence – 2.0 litre engine

All engines

4 Lubricate the cylinder bores, the pistons, and piston rings, then lay out each piston/connecting rod assembly in its respective position.

5 Start with assembly No 1. Make sure that the piston rings are still spaced as described in Section 16, and then clamp them in position with a piston ring compressor.

6 Insert the piston/connecting rod assembly into the top of cylinder No 1; ensuring the piston is correctly positioned as follows.

  a) On 1.6 litre engines, ensure that the DIST mark or arrow on the piston crown is towards the timing belt end of the engine.

  b) On 2.0 litre engines, ensure that the valve recesses on the piston crown are towards the rear of the cylinder block.

7 Once the piston is correctly positioned, using a block of wood or hammer handle against the piston crown, tap the assembly into the cylinder until the piston crown is flush with the top of the cylinder **(see illustration)**.

2.0 litre engine

8 Ensure that the bearing shell is still correctly installed. Liberally lubricate the crankpin and both bearing shells. Taking care not to mark the cylinder bores, pull the piston/connecting rod assembly down the bore and onto the crankpin. Refit the big-end bearing cap and fit the new nuts, tightening them finger-tight at first **(see illustration)**. Note that the faces with

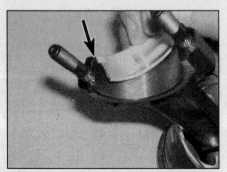

18.3 Ensure the bearing shell tab (arrowed) locates correctly in the cut-out

18.7 Tap the piston into the bore using hammer handle

18.8 Fit the big-end bearing cap, ensuring it is fitted the right-way around, and screw on the new nuts

the identification marks must match (which means that the bearing shell locating tabs abut each other).

9 Tighten the bearing cap retaining nuts evenly and progressively to the Stage 1 torque setting. Once both nuts have been tightened to the Stage 1 setting, angle-tighten them through the specified Stage 2 angle, using a socket and extension bar. It is recommended that an angle-measuring gauge be used during this stage of the tightening, to ensure accuracy.

10 If an angle gauge is not available, use a dab of white paint to make alignment marks between the nut and bearing cap prior to tightening; the marks can then be used to check that the nut has been rotated sufficiently during tightening.

1.6 litre engine

11 On these engines, the connecting rod is made in one piece, and the big-end bearing cap is 'cracked' off. This ensures that the cap fits onto the connecting rod only in one position, and with maximum rigidity. Consequently, there are no locating notches for the bearing shells to fit into.

12 To ensure that the big-end bearing shells are centrally located in the connecting rod and cap, two special tools are available from Peugeot. These half-moon shaped tools are pressed in from either side of the rod/cap and locate the shell exactly in the centre **(see illustration)**. Fit the shells into the connecting rods and big-end caps and lubricate them with plenty of clean engine oil.

13 Pull the connecting rods and pistons down the bores and onto the crankshaft journals. Fit the big-end caps – they will only fit properly one way round (see paragraph 11), and insert the new bolts.

14 Tighten the bolts to the Stage 1 torque setting, then slacken them 180° (Stage 2). Tighten the bolts to the Stage 3 setting,

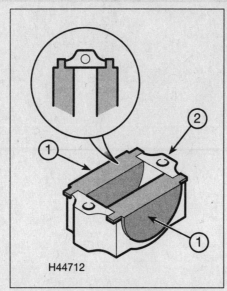

H44712

18.12 Big-end bearing shell positioning – 1.6 litre diesel engine

1 Peugeot tool No 0194-P
2 Bearing shell in the cap

followed by the Stage 4 angle-tightening setting.

15 Continue refitting the main bearing shells and ladder as described in Section 17.

All engines

16 Once the bearing cap retaining nuts have been correctly tightened, rotate the crankshaft. Check that it turns freely; some stiffness is to be expected if new components have been fitted, but there should be no signs of binding or tight spots.

17 Refit the cylinder head and oil pump as described in Part A or B of this Chapter (as applicable).

19 Engine – initial start-up after overhaul

1 With the engine refitted in the vehicle, double-check the engine oil and coolant levels. Make a final check that everything has been reconnected, and that there are no tools or rags left in the engine compartment.

2 On the models covered in this Manual, the oil pressure warning light is linked to the STOP warning light, and is not illuminated when the ignition is initially switched on. Therefore it is not possible to check the oil pressure warning light when turning the engine on the starter motor.

3 Prime the fuel system (refer to Chapter 4A).

4 Fully depress the accelerator pedal, turn the ignition key to position M, and wait for the preheating warning light to go out.

5 Start the engine, noting that this may take a little longer than usual, due to the fuel system components having been disturbed.

6 While the engine is idling, check for fuel, water and oil leaks. Don't be alarmed if there are some odd smells and smoke from parts getting hot and burning off oil deposits.

7 Assuming all is well; keep the engine idling until hot water is felt circulating through the top hose, and then switch off the engine.

8 After a few minutes recheck the oil and coolant levels as described in Weekly checks, and top-up as necessary.

9 Note that there is no need to retighten the cylinder head bolts once the engine has first run after reassembly.

10 If new pistons, rings or crankshaft bearings have been fitted, the engine must be treated as new, and run-in for the first 500 miles. Do not operate the engine at full-throttle, or allow it to labour at low engine speeds in any gear. It is recommended that the oil and filter be changed at the end of this period.

Chapter 3
Cooling, heating and ventilation systems

Contents

Degrees of difficulty

Easy, suitable for novice with little experience	Fairly easy, suitable for beginner with some experience	Fairly difficult, suitable for competent DIY mechanic	Difficult, suitable for experienced DIY mechanic	Very difficult, suitable for expert DIY or professional

Specifications

General
Coolant type	Glysantin G33 or Revkogel 2000
Expansion bottle volume	1.6 litres
Maximum system pressure	1.4 bars

Engine coolant temperature sensor resistance (approx):
1.6 litre engine:	
60°C	1266 Ω
80°C	642 Ω
2.0 litre engine:	
20°C	6200 Ω

Cooling fan
Electric fan power:
1.6 litre engine	150 W
2.0 litre engine:	
Manual transmission	150 W
Automatic transmission	160 W

Electric fan operation temperature:
Level 1	98° C
Level 2	105° C

Thermostat
Start of opening temperature	83° C
Completely open temperature	95° C

Refrigerant
Quantity	625 ± 25 g
Type	R134a

Torque wrench settings
	Nm	lbf ft
Air conditioning compressor mounting bolts:		
1.6 litre engine	25	18
2.0 litre engine	35	26
Air conditioning pipes	7	5
Air conditioning pressostat switch in condenser	6	4
Air conditioning pressure relief valve to heater unit	7	5
Coolant outlet housing	10	7
Coolant pump:		
1.6 litre engine	10	7
2.0 litre engine	16	12

1 General information and precautions

1 The cooling system is of pressurised type, comprising a coolant pump driven by the timing belt, an aluminium radiator, an expansion tank, an electric cooling fan, a thermostat, a heater matrix, and all associated hoses and switches.

2 The system functions as follows. Cold coolant in the bottom of the radiator passes through the bottom hose to the coolant pump, where it is pumped around the cylinder block and head passages. After cooling the cylinder bores, combustion surfaces and valve seats, the coolant reaches the underside of the thermostat, which is initially closed. The coolant passes through the heater, and is returned via the cylinder block to the coolant pump.

3 When the engine is cold, the coolant circulates only through the cylinder block, cylinder head, and heater. When the coolant reaches a predetermined temperature, the thermostat opens, and the coolant passes through the top hose to the radiator. As the coolant passes down through the radiator, it is cooled by the inrush of air when the car is in forward motion. The airflow is supplemented by the action of the electric cooling fan when necessary. Upon reaching the bottom of the radiator, the coolant has now cooled, and the cycle is repeated.

4 On models with automatic transmission, a proportion of the coolant is recirculated through the transmission fluid cooler mounted on the transmission. On models fitted with an engine oil cooler, the coolant is also passed through the oil cooler.

5 The operation of the electric cooling fan(s) is controlled by the engine management control module.

 Warning: Do not attempt to remove the expansion tank filler cap, or to disturb any part of the cooling system, while the engine is hot, as there is a high risk of scalding. If the expansion tank filler cap must be removed before the engine and radiator have fully cooled (even though this is not recommended), the pressure in the cooling system must first be relieved. Cover the cap with a thick layer of cloth to avoid scalding, and slowly unscrew the filler cap until a hissing sound is heard. When the hissing has stopped, indicating that the pressure has reduced, slowly unscrew the filler cap until it can be removed; if more hissing sounds are heard, wait until they have stopped before unscrewing the cap. At all times keep well away from the filler cap opening, and protect your hands.

 Warning: Do not allow antifreeze to come into contact with your skin, or with the painted surfaces of the vehicle. Rinse off spills immediately, with plenty of water. Never leave antifreeze lying around in an open container, or in a puddle in the driveway or on the garage floor. Children and pets are attracted by its sweet smell, but antifreeze can be fatal if ingested.

 Warning: If the engine is hot, the electric cooling fan(s) may start rotating even if the engine is not running. Be careful to keep your hands, hair, and any loose clothing well clear when working in the engine compartment.

Warning: Refer to Section 11 for precautions to be observed when working on models equipped with air conditioning.

2 Cooling system hoses – disconnection and renewal

Note: Refer to the warnings given in Section 1 of this Chapter before proceeding. Hoses should only be disconnected once the engine has cooled sufficiently to avoid scalding.

1 If the checks described in the *Hose and fluid leak check* Section in Chapter 1 reveal a faulty hose, it must be renewed as follows.

2 First drain the cooling system (see Chapter 1). If the coolant is not due for renewal, it may be re-used, providing it is collected in a clean container.

3 To disconnect a hose, proceed as follows, according to the type of hose connection.

Conventional connections

4 On conventional connections, the clips used to secure the hoses in position may be standard worm-drive clips, spring clips or disposable crimped types. The crimped type of clip is not designed to be re-used and should be renewed with a worm-drive type on reassembly.

5 To disconnect a hose, release the retaining clips and move them along the hose, clear of the relevant inlet/outlet. Carefully work the hose free. The hoses can be removed with relative ease when new – on an older car; they may have stuck **(see illustration)**.

6 If a hose proves to be difficult to remove, try to release it by rotating its ends before attempting to free it. Gently prise the end of the hose with a blunt instrument (such as a flat-bladed screwdriver), but do not apply too much force, and take care not to damage the pipe stubs or hoses. Note in particular that the radiator inlet stub is fragile; do not use excessive force when attempting to remove the hose. If all else fails, cut the hose with a sharp knife, then slit it so that it can be peeled off in two pieces. Although this may prove expensive if the hose is otherwise undamaged, it is preferable to buying a new radiator. Check first, however, that a new hose is readily available.

7 When fitting a hose, first slide the clips onto the hose, and then work the hose into position. If crimped-type clips were originally fitted, use standard worm-drive clips when refitting the hose.

8 Work the hose into position, checking that it is correctly routed, and then slide each clip back along the hose until it passes over the flared end of the relevant inlet/outlet, before tightening the clip securely.

9 Refill the cooling system (see Chapter 1).

10 Check thoroughly for leaks as soon as possible after disturbing any part of the cooling system.

Click-fit connections

Note: New sealing ring should be used when reconnecting the hose.

11 On certain models, some cooling system hoses are secured in position with click-fit connectors where the hose is retained by a large circlip.

12 To disconnect this type of hose fitting, carefully prise the wire clip out of position then disconnect the hose connection **(see illustration)**. Once the hose has been disconnected, refit the wire clip to the hose union. Inspect the hose unit sealing ring for signs of damage or deterioration and renew if necessary.

13 On refitting, ensure that the sealing ring is in position and wire clip is correctly located

2.5 Release the retaining clip and move it along the hose

2.12 Prise out the circlip then disconnect the hose

2.13 Ensure the sealing ring and circlip are correctly fitted to the hose union before reconnecting a connector

3.3 Slide out the retaining clip (arrowed)

3.4 Squeeze the collar (arrowed) to release the coolant pipe

in the groove in the union **(see illustration)**. Lubricate the sealing ring with a smear of soapy water, to ease installation, and then push the hose into its union until it is heard to click into position.

14 Ensure the hose is securely retained by the wire clip then refill the cooling system as described in Chapter 1.

15 Check thoroughly for leaks as soon as possible after disturbing any part of the cooling system.

3 Coolant expansion tank – removal and refitting

Removal

1 Referring to Chapter 1, drain the cooling

system sufficiently to empty the contents of the expansion tank. Do not drain any more coolant than is necessary.

2 Where fitted, disconnect the wiring connector from the level sensor in the top of the expansion tank.

3 Slide out the retaining clip, and disconnect the hose from the bottom of the expansion tank **(see illustration)**.

4 Squeeze together the collar, and then pull the plastic hose from the top of the expansion tank **(see illustration)**.

5 Unscrew the mounting bolt and lift the expansion tank upwards to release it from the rubber mounts in the inner wing panel **(see illustration)**. Take care not to lose the mounting rubber.

6 Check around the expansion tank as it is being removed to check for any other hoses that may be still connected.

3.5 Expansion tank mounting bolt (arrowed)

Refitting

7 Refitting is the reverse of removal, ensuring the hoses are securely reconnected. On completion, top-up the coolant level as described in *Weekly checks*.

4 Radiator – removal, inspection and refitting

Note: *If leakage is the reason for removing the radiator, bear in mind that minor leaks can often be cured using a radiator sealant with the radiator in its fitted position.*

Removal

1 Drain the cooling system (see Chapter 1).
2 Remove the front bumper as described in Chapter 11.

1.6 litre models

3 Undo the bolt and move the pressure differential sensor and bracket rearwards a little (located at the upper right-hand corner of the radiator) **(see illustration)**.
4 Release the retaining clips and disconnect the upper and lower coolant hoses from the radiator **(see illustration)**. Note the bottom hose may have been removed already, to drain the cooling system.
5 Slacken the clamps and disconnect the air hoses from the intercooler, inlet manifold and turbocharger.
6 Undo the retaining nut and bolt, and then detach the air hose support bracket from the top of the radiator **(see illustrations)**.

4.3 Undo the bolt (arrowed) and move the sensor bracket rearwards

4.4 Release the retaining clip (arrowed) and move it along the hose

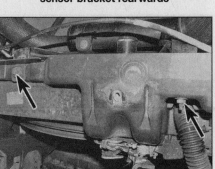
4.6a Undo the nut and bolt (arrowed) . . .

4.6b . . . then remove the air hose support bracket (arrowed)

4.7a Prise out the retaining clip . . .

4.7b . . . and remove the air inlet ducting

4.8 Release the retaining clip and disconnect the coolant hose

2.0 litre models

7 Release the securing clip and remove the air inlet ducting from the engine compartment **(see illustrations)**.
8 Release the retaining clips and disconnect the upper and lower coolant hoses from the radiator **(see illustration)**. Note the bottom hose may have been removed already, to drain the cooling system.
9 Release the retaining clips and disconnect the air inlet hoses from the inlet manifold and the intercooler and remove them from the engine compartment **(see illustration)**.
10 Where applicable (depending on model), disconnect the cooling fan wiring harness connections from across the rear of the intercooler at the top.

All models

11 Squeeze together the collar, and then pull the plastic hose from the top of the radiator **(see illustration)**.
12 Using a thin screwdriver, release the retaining clips securing the radiator upper mounting brackets to the front panel. Unclip both brackets and carefully pull the top of the radiator towards the engine to release it from the front panel **(see illustrations)**.
13 Lift the radiator upwards to release it from the rubber mountings in the front lower crossmember **(see illustration)**. Take care not to damage the radiator fins, as it is being withdrawn from the engine compartment.
14 If required, recover the radiator lower mounting rubbers and check their condition **(see illustration)**.

Inspection

15 If the radiator has been removed due to suspected blockage, reverse-flush it as described in Chapter 1. Clean dirt and debris from the radiator fins, using an airline (in which case, wear eye protection) or a soft brush. Be careful, as the fins are sharp, and easily damaged.
16 If necessary, a radiator specialist can perform a 'flow test' on the radiator, to establish whether an internal blockage exists.
17 A leaking radiator must be referred to a specialist for permanent repair. Do not attempt to weld or solder a leaking radiator, as damage to the plastic components may result.
18 Inspect the condition of the radiator mounting rubbers, and renew them if necessary.

Refitting

19 Refitting is a reversal of removal, bearing in mind the following points:
  a) Ensure that the lower lugs on the radiator

4.9 Release the retaining clips and disconnect the air inlet hose

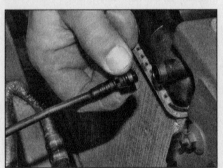

4.11 Squeeze the collar to release the coolant pipe from the radiator

4.12a Release the upper retaining clips (arrowed) . . .

4.12b . . . and withdraw the radiator from the upper crossmember

4.13 Lift the radiator out from the engine compartment

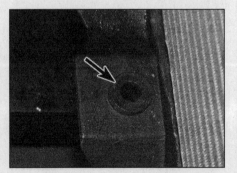

4.14 Recover the radiator lower mounting rubbers (one side arrowed)

5.2 Remove the air inlet ducting from the engine compartment – 1.6 litre engine

5.3 Disconnect the wiring connector (arrowed)

5.6 Remove the air inlet ducting from the engine compartment – 2.0 litre engine

are correctly engaged with the mounting rubbers in the front crossmember.
b) Reconnect the hoses with reference to Section 2, using new sealing rings where applicable.
c) On completion, refill the cooling system as described in Chapter 1.

5 Thermostat – removal, testing and refitting

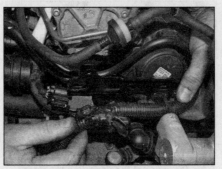

5.7 Unclip the wiring loom from the bracket

5.8 Thermostat housing retaining nuts (arrowed)

Note: *The thermostat is located in the coolant outlet housing on the left-hand end of the cylinder head. The thermostat is integral with the housing, which will require complete removal of the outlet housing.*

Removal

1 Drain the cooling system (see Chapter 1).

1.6 litre models

2 Undo the retaining bolt, release the air inlet ducting and remove it from the engine compartment **(see illustration)**.
3 Disconnect the wiring connector from the temperature sensor, and then disconnect all hoses having noted their fitted locations **(see illustration)**. Unscrew the four retaining bolts and remove the housing from the cylinder head. Discard the gasket, as a new one will be required for refitting.

2.0 litre models

4 Unclip the engine cover from the top of the engine.
5 Remove the air cleaner housing and air ducting as described in Chapter 4A.
6 Undo the retaining bolt, release the air inlet ducting and remove it from the engine compartment **(see illustration)**.
7 Unclip the wiring loom from the mounting bracket and remove the mounting bracket to access the coolant housing **(see illustration)**.
8 Disconnect the wiring from the temperature sensor (and solenoid valve, on models up to RPO No 10310), and then disconnect all hoses having noted their fitted locations **(see illustration)**. Unscrew the retaining bolts and remove the housing from the cylinder head. Discard the gasket, as a new one will be required for refitting.

Testing

9 A rough test of the thermostat may be made by suspending it with a piece of string in a container full of water. Heat the water to bring it to the boil – the thermostat must open by the time the water boils. If not, renew it.
10 If a thermometer is available, the precise opening temperature of the thermostat may be determined; compare with the figures given in the Specifications. The opening temperature is also marked on the thermostat.
11 A thermostat which fails to close as the water cools must also be renewed.

Refitting

12 Refitting is a reversal of removal, bearing in mind the following points.
a) Renew the coolant housing gasket where removed.

6.2a Unclip the plastic cover . . .

b) Examine any sealing rings for damage or deterioration, and if necessary, renew.
c) On completion, refill the cooling system as described in Chapter 1.

6 Electric cooling fan – removal and refitting

Removal

1 Remove the front bumper as described in Chapter 11.

Cooling fan assembly

2 Unclip the plastic cover from the cooling fan wiring and disconnect the wiring to the fan **(see illustration)**.

6.2b . . . and disconnect the wiring connectors

6.3 Undo the mounting bolts (arrowed) . . .

6.4 . . . and withdraw the cooling fan from the front panel

6.5 Power steering cooler mounting bracket (one side arrowed)

6.7 Undo the retaining screw – left-hand thread

6.9a Disconnect the wiring connectors . . .

6.9b . . . and undo the retaining screws (arrowed)

3 Slacken and remove the four bolts and washers securing the cooling fan to the front panel **(see illustration)**.

4 Withdraw the cooling fan assembly out from the front panel, release the wiring harness from the retaining clips as the fan is manoeuvred out of position **(see illustration)**.

5 If required, slacken the power steering cooler mounting bracket bolts to allow for more room for the cooling fan assembly to be removed **(see illustration)**.

Cooling fan blades

6 Remove the cooling fan assembly, as described previously in this Section.

7 Undo the screw (left-hand thread) from the centre of the plastic fan blades, and then remove the fan blades from the motor **(see illustration)**. Note this screw has a **left-hand**

thread, use thread-lock on the screw when refitting.

Cooling fan motor/resistor

8 Remove the fan blades as described in paragraphs 6 and 7.

9 Disconnect the wiring connectors from the rear of the fan motor/resistor, and then undo the three retaining screws to remove the motor/resistor from the plastic housing **(see illustrations)**.

Cooling fan relays

10 The relays are fitted to the front panel and are located behind the cover on the left-hand side of the cooling fan **(see illustration 6.2a)**.

11 Release the clips and remove the cover from the front panel. Disconnect the wiring connector and remove the relay(s) **(see illustration)**.

Refitting

12 Refitting is a reversal of removal.

7 Coolant temperature sensors – general information, removal and refitting

General information

1 There is only one coolant temperature sensor on most models, which is fitted to the coolant outlet housing on the left-hand end of the cylinder head **(see illustrations)**. The coolant temperature gauge and the cooling fan are all operated by the engine management ECM using the signal supplied by this sensor.

6.11 Disconnect the wiring connector from the relay

7.1a Coolant temperature sensor (arrowed) – 1.6 litre engine

7.1b Coolant temperature sensor (arrowed) – 2.0 litre engine

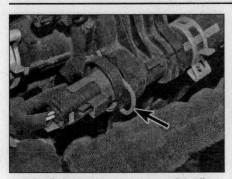

7.9a Release the sensor securing clip (arrowed) – 1.6 litre engine

7.9b Release the sensor securing clip (arrowed) – 2.0 litre engine

Removal

Note: *Ensure the engine is cold before removing a temperature sensor.*

2 Partially drain the cooling system to just below the level of the sensor (as described in Chapter 1).

1.6 litre models

3 On 1.6 litre engines, undo the retaining bolt, release the air inlet ducting and remove it from the engine compartment **(see illustration 5.2)**.

2.0 litre models

4 Unclip the engine cover from the top of the engine.

5 Remove the air cleaner housing and air ducting as described in Chapter 4A.

6 Undo the retaining bolt, release the air inlet ducting and remove it from the engine compartment **(see illustration 5.6)**.

7 Unclip the wiring loom from the mounting bracket and remove the mounting bracket to access the coolant housing **(see illustration 5.7)**.

All models

8 Disconnect the wiring connector from the sensor.

9 Prise out the sensor retaining circlip, and then remove the sensor and sealing ring from the housing **(see illustrations)**. If the system is to be left for any amount of time, plug the sensor aperture to prevent further coolant loss or dirt ingress.

Refitting

10 Fit a new sealing ring to the sensor, push the sensor firmly into the housing and secure it in position with the circlip, ensuring it is correctly located in the housing groove.

11 Reconnect the wiring connector then refit any components that have been removed for access.

12 Top-up the cooling system as described in *Weekly checks*.

8 Coolant pump – removal and refitting

Removal

1 Drain the cooling system (see Chapter 1).

2 Remove the timing belt as described in Chapter 2A or 2B as applicable.

3 Slacken and remove the retaining bolts and withdraw the pump assembly from the engine. Recover the pump gasket and discard it; a new one must be used on refitting **(see illustrations)**.

Refitting

4 Ensure that the pump and cylinder block/housing mating surfaces are clean and dry.

5 Fit the new gasket to the pump, then refit the pump assembly, tightening its retaining bolts securely. **Note:** *On 2.0 litre engines the retaining bolt with a threaded stud is fitted to*

the rear of the engine for securing the timing cover (see illustration 8.3b).

6 Refit the timing belt as described in Chapter 2A or 2B (as applicable).

7 Refill the cooling system as described in Chapter 1 (as applicable).

9 Heating and ventilation system – general information

Note: *Refer to Section 11 for information on the air conditioning side of the system.*

Manually-controlled system

1 The heating/ventilation system consists of a multi-speed blower motor (housed behind the facia), face level vents in the centre and at each end of the facia, and air ducts to the front footwells.

2 The control module is located in the facia, and the controls operate flap valves to deflect and mix the air flowing through the various parts of the heating/ventilation system. The flap valves are contained in the air distribution housing, which acts as a central distribution unit, passing air to the various ducts and vents.

3 Cold air enters the system through the grille in the scuttle. If required, the airflow is boosted by the blower, and then flows through the various ducts, according to the settings of the controls. Stale air is expelled through ducts at the rear of the vehicle. If warm air is required, the cold air is passed over the heater matrix, which is heated by the engine coolant.

4 A recirculation lever enables the outside air supply to be closed off, while the air inside the vehicle is recirculated. This can be useful to prevent unpleasant odours entering from outside the vehicle, but should only be used briefly, as the recirculated air inside the vehicle will soon become stale.

5 On some models an electric heater is fitted into the heater housing. When the coolant is cold, the heater warms the air before it enters the heater matrix. This quickly increases the temperature of the heater matrix on cold starts, resulting in warm air being available to heat the vehicle interior soon after start-up.

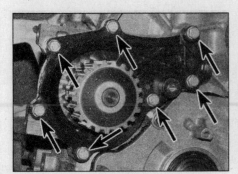

8.3a Undo the coolant pump bolts (arrowed) – 1.6 litre engine

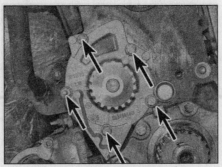

8.3b Undo the coolant pump bolts (arrowed) – 2.0 litre engine

8.3c Renew the coolant pump gasket

Automatic climate control

6 A fully-automatic electronic climate control system was offered as an option on most models. The main components of the system are exactly the same as those described for the manual system, the only major difference being that the temperature and distribution flaps in the heating/ventilation housing are operated by electric motors rather than cables.

7 The operation of the system is controlled by the electronic control module (which is incorporated in the blower motor assembly) along with the following sensors.

a) *The passenger compartment sensor – informs the control module of the temperature of the air inside the passenger compartment.*

b) *Evaporator temperature sensor – informs the control module of the evaporator temperature.*

c) *Heater matrix air temperature sensor(s) – informs the control module of the heater matrix temperature.*

8 Using the information from the above sensors, the control module determines the appropriate settings for the heating/ventilation system housing flaps to maintain the passenger compartment at the desired setting on the control panel.

9 If the system develops a fault, the vehicle should be taken to a Peugeot dealer. A complete test of the system can then be carried out using a special electronic

10.2 Unclip the upper part of the control panel from the facia

diagnostic test unit, which is simply plugged into the system's diagnostic connector (located inside the centre console armrest).

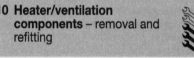

10 Heater/ventilation components – removal and refitting

Control panel

1 Remove the audio unit (see Chapter 12).

2 Starting at the top, carefully unclip the heater control panel from the facia **(see illustration)**.

3 Disconnect the wiring connectors from the rear of the control panel and remove it from the vehicle **(see illustration)**.

10.3 Disconnect the wiring connectors from the rear of the panel

4 Refitting is the reverse of removal, making sure all connections are fitted correctly.

Heater matrix

Note: *Peugeot recommend that the complete dash facia panel should be removed to access the heater matrix. We found that by removing the glovebox and slackening the left-hand side of the facia panel we were able to withdraw the heater matrix from the heater housing.*

5 Disconnect the battery earth connection (refer to Chapter 5A).

6 To improve access to the matrix unions on the bulkhead, remove the air cleaner housing inlet ducting (see Chapter 4A).

7 Drain the cooling system (see Chapter 1). Alternatively, clamp the heater matrix coolant hoses to minimise coolant loss.

8 Release the retaining clips and disconnect the coolant hoses from the heater matrix pipe unions on the engine compartment bulkhead **(see illustrations)**.

9 Slacken and remove the screw securing the heater matrix pipes to the bulkhead and remove the retaining plate and seal **(see illustrations)**.

10 Working inside the passenger compartment, remove the glovebox (refer to Chapter 11). Undo the retaining screw, and then unclip the kick panel from the front of the centre console and remove it from the front footwell **(see illustration)**.

11 Undo the retaining screw and remove the

10.8a Prise out the wire retaining clips . . .

10.8b . . . and disconnect the heater hoses

10.9a Undo the retaining screw (arrowed) . . .

10.9b . . . and remove the retaining plate (arrowed)

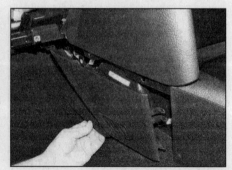

10.10 Remove the trim panel . . .

10.11 . . . and remove the heater ducting

10.12a Undo the retaining screw . . .

10.12b . . . and move the wiring bracket to one side

air duct from the side of the heater housing **(see illustration)**.

12 Undo the retaining screw and move the wiring and plastic mounting bracket to one side **(see illustrations)**.

13 Position a container or some rags beneath the heater matrix pipe unions on the left-hand side of the heating/ventilation housing to catch any coolant.

Models from RPO No 11438

14 Release the retaining clip and remove the clamps securing the coolant pipes to the heater matrix **(see illustrations)**.

15 Free the pipes from the matrix, catching the coolant in the container, and then (if required) free them from the bulkhead and remove them from the vehicle. Recover the sealing rings fitted to the pipe unions and discard them; new ones should be used on refitting.

16 Slide the matrix out from the housing, keeping the matrix unions uppermost as the matrix is removed to prevent coolant spillage **(see illustration)**.

Models up to RPO No 11437

17 On earlier models (before RPO No 11437), the two coolant pipes will need to be cut, as they are part of the heater matrix. With the pipes cut the heater matrix can then be withdrawn from the heater/ventilation housing. On this type, a new heater matrix will need to be fitted, complete with coolant pipes and retaining clamps.

All models

18 Ease the matrix into the housing, making sure it is fitted all the way into the housing.

19 Manoeuvre the coolant pipes into position and refit the retaining clamps, securing the pipes to the matrix. Use new seals when refitting.

20 Refit the plastic mounting bracket across the heater matrix and secure the wiring back in place **(see illustration)**.

21 Refit the air duct to the side of the heater/ ventilating housing.

22 Refit the glovebox and the kick panel to the front of the centre console (refer to Chapter 11).

23 Working in the engine compartment, refit the seal and retaining plate to the heater matrix pipes and securely tighten the retaining screw. Remove the clamps (where fitted) then

reconnect the coolant hoses, securing them in position with the retaining clips.

24 Refit the battery (see Chapter 5A).

25 Refill the cooling system (see Chapter 1).

Heater blower motor

26 The blower motor is fitted to the top of the heating/ventilation housing, on the left-hand side.

27 On right-hand drive models, remove the glovebox (see Section 27 of Chapter 11). Access to the motor can then be gained through the glovebox aperture.

28 On left-hand drive models, remove the steering column as described in Chapter 10 to gain access to the motor.

29 Where necessary, slacken and remove the retaining screw securing the motor to the housing, this screw may not always be fitted **(see illustration)**.

10.14a Release the securing clamp . . .

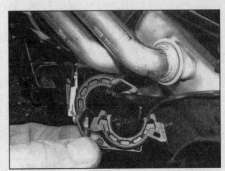

10.14b . . . and remove it from the heater pipe

10.16 Slide the heater matrix from the housing

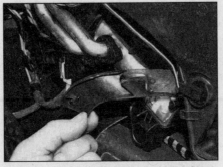

10.20 Refit the wiring bracket back into place

10.29 Undo the retaining screw (arrowed) – where fitted

10.30 Disconnect the wiring connector

10.31a Release the locking clip . . .

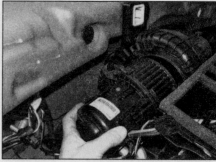

10.31b . . . and rotate the motor cover clockwise to remove

30 Disconnect the wiring connector(s) from the blower motor (see illustration).

31 Press down on the locking clip and rotate the motor clockwise to free it from the housing, then manoeuvre it out of position (see illustrations). Note: *The blower motor locking clip is located at the top on models from RPO No 11438, as seen in the illustrations provided. On models up to RPO No 11437 the blower motor locking clip is at the lower front edge of the motor.*

32 Refitting is the reverse of removal. If the motor is not a secure fit in the housing, fix it in position by fitting a self-tapping screw to the hole provided (see paragraph 29).

Heater blower motor resistor

33 Undo the fasteners and remove the trim panel from below the glovebox, above the passenger's footwell.

34 Reach up behind the glovebox and disconnect the wiring connector from the resistor (see illustration).

35 Turn the resistor anti-clockwise and withdraw it from the heater housing, below the blower motor (see illustrations).

36 Manoeuvre the resistor into position and turn it clockwise to lock it in position. Connect the wiring connector and refit any components that where removed for access.

Heater housing assembly

⚠ Warning: Refer to Section 11 for precautions to be observed when working on models equipped with air conditioning. Do not attempt the following procedure unless the system has been professionally discharged.

37 Have the air conditioning system discharged by an air conditioning specialist and obtain some plugs to seal the air conditioning pipe unions whilst the system is disconnected.

38 To improve access to the matrix unions on the bulkhead, remove the air cleaner housing inlet ducting (see Chapter 4A).

39 Drain the cooling system (see Chapter 1). Alternatively, working in the engine compartment, clamp the heater matrix coolant hoses to minimise coolant loss.

40 Release the retaining clips and disconnect the coolant hoses from the heater matrix pipe unions on the engine compartment bulkhead (see illustrations 10.8a and 10.8b).

41 Slacken and remove the screw securing the heater matrix pipes to the bulkhead and remove the retaining plate and seal (see illustrations 10.9a and 10.9b).

42 Unscrew the two nuts securing the air conditioning pipe union to the bulkhead (see illustrations). Separate the pipes from the evaporator and quickly seal the pipe and evaporator unions to prevent the entry of moisture into the refrigerant circuit. Discard the sealing rings, new ones must be used on refitting.

⚠ Warning: Failure to seal the refrigerant pipe unions will result in the dehydrator reservoir become saturated, necessitating its renewal.

43 Slacken and remove the bolt securing the

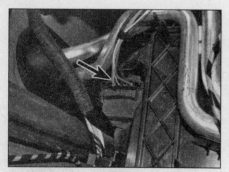

10.34 Disconnect the wiring connector

10.35a Rotate the blower motor resistor . . .

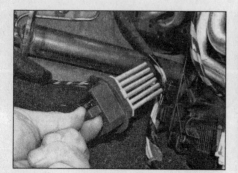

10.35b . . . and withdraw it from the heater housing

10.42a Remove the bulkhead heat shield – where fitted . . .

10.42b . . . then undo the two nuts securing the refrigerant pipes

heating/ventilation housing to the bulkhead **(see illustration).**

44 Working inside the vehicle, remove the facia assembly as described in Chapter 11.

45 Disconnect the wiring connectors from the heating/ventilation housing components. Disconnect the earth cable from the left-hand side of the housing and the drain hose from the right-hand side of the housing **(see illustration)**. Note the routing of the wiring loom and connections for refitting.

46 Undo the retaining nut at the right-hand rear of the housing **(see illustration)**, and then withdraw the heater housing assembly from the vehicle, keeping the heater matrix pipe unions uppermost as the assembly is removed to prevent coolant spillage.

47 Recover the rubber seal from the bulkhead and heater matrix pipes, and the seal from the air conditioning pipes. Renew the rubber seals if they show signs of damage or deterioration.

48 Ensure the bulkhead seals are correctly fitted to the evaporator, matrix pipes and housing mounting. Manoeuvre the housing assembly into position, locating the housing drain hose correctly in its hole in the floor.

49 Loosely refit the housing mounting bolt then refit the retaining plate to the heater matrix pipe and loosely install the retaining screw.

50 Lubricate the new evaporator union sealing rings with compressor oil. Remove the plugs and install the sealing rings then quickly fit the refrigerant pipe union to the evaporator.

51 Ensure the refrigerant pipes and evaporator are correctly joined then refit the retaining nuts, and tighten them securely.

52 Tighten the matrix pipe retaining screw securely and tighten the housing mounting bolt.

53 The remainder of refitting is the reverse of removal. On completion, refill the cooling system (see Chapter 1).

Blown air sensors

Note: *There are two blown air sensors, one at each side of the heater housing. The removal*

10.43 Undo the nut (arrowed) securing the heater housing to the bulkhead

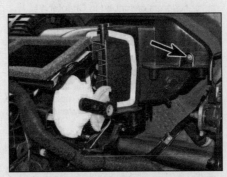

10.46 Undo the nut (arrowed) securing the heater housing to the bulkhead

and refitting procedure is the same for both sensors.

54 Undo the retaining screw, and then unclip the kick panel from the front of the centre console and remove it from the front footwell **(see illustration 10.10).**

55 To make access easier, undo the retaining screw and remove the air ducting to access the sensor **(see illustration).**

56 Disconnect the wiring connector from the sensor, then turn the sensor clockwise (on the left-hand side) or anti-clockwise (on the right-hand side), a quarter of a turn to release it from the housing **(see illustrations).**

57 Refitting is a reversal of removal. **Note:** *Turn the sensor clockwise (on the right-hand side) or anti-clockwise (on the left-hand side),*

10.45 Disconnect the drain hose from the heater housing

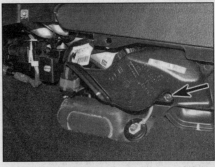

10.55 Undo the heater ducting retaining screw (arrowed)

a quarter of a turn to refit the sensor. See direction arrow on housing for refitting.

Cabin air heating element

58 On right-hand drive models, remove the glovebox and passenger side central kick panel as described in Chapter 11.

59 On left-hand drive models, remove the trim panel above the pedals, undo the two fasteners and remove the kick panel at the front of the centre console, adjacent to the pedals.

60 Undo the bolt securing the heater earth connection **(see illustration)**

61 Disconnect the heater wiring plug, then undo the screw, release the retaining clip,

10.56a Disconnect the wiring connector . . .

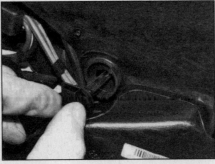

10.56b . . . and remove the air sensor

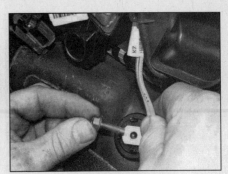

10.60 Disconnect the earth cable from the floor panel

10.61a Disconnect the wiring connector . . .

10.61b . . . undo the retaining screw . . .

10.61c . . . and withdraw the heating element

and slide the heater from the housing **(see illustrations)**.

62 Refitting is the reverse of removal.

Air control motors

63 There are a number of control motors fitted to the heater housing assembly, depending on model. To access the motors remove the glovebox and facia lower trim panels as described in Chapter 11.

64 Disconnect the motor wiring plug, undo the retaining screws, and remove the motor from the housing **(see illustrations)**.

65 Refitting is a reversal of removal.

Ambient temperature sensor

66 The ambient temperature sensor is located on the underside of the driver's side exterior door mirror. To remove the sensor, remove the

mirror cover as described in Chapter 11.

67 Unclip the sensor from the mirror housing **(see illustrations)**. To remove the sensor completely, the two wires going to the sensor will need to be cut, as they go into the door wiring harness. The wires must be cut more than 30mm away from the sensor.

68 When refitting the sensor, make sure the connections are made correctly, and insulated using a heat-shrink sleeve.

Interior air temperature sensor

69 The sensor is located in the silver long thin trim panel across the top of the glovebox. Unclip the trim from the facia panel.

70 Unclip the sensor from the trim panel, and disconnect the wiring plug.

71 Refitting is a reversal of removal.

Sunlight/rain sensor

Mirror base-mounted sensor

72 Unclip the plastic trim from the windscreen **(see illustration)**.

73 Disconnect the wiring plug connector and then unclip the sensor from the mounting base **(see illustration)**.

74 Refitting is a reversal of removal.

Facia-mounted sensor

75 Remove the multifunction display unit from the centre of the facia as described in Chapter 12.

76 Undo the retaining screws and remove the heater vent panel from the top of the facia **(see illustrations)**.

77 Undo the retaining screws and remove the grille panel from the top of the facia **(see**

10.64a Air control motors (arrowed) on the right-hand side . . .

10.64b . . . and left-hand side of the heater housing

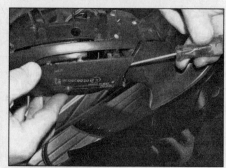

10.67a Unclip the mirror lower panel . . .

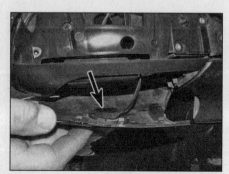

10.67b . . . to access the ambient air temperature sensor (arrowed)

10.72 Unclip the trim panel . . .

10.73 . . . and disconnect the wiring connector from the sensor

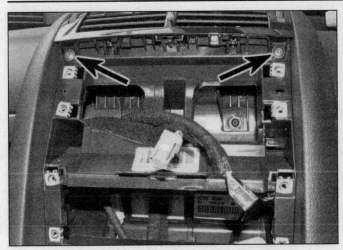

10.76a Undo the two retaining screws (arrowed) . . .

10.76b . . . and remove the centre air vent panel

illustrations). Disconnect the wiring plug as the sensor is withdrawn.
78 Refitting is a reversal of removal.

11 Air conditioning system – general information and precautions

General information

1 An air conditioning system is available on most models. It enables the temperature of incoming air to be lowered, and also dehumidifies the air, which makes for rapid demisting and increased comfort.
2 The cooling side of the system works in the same way as a domestic refrigerator. Refrigerant gas is drawn into a belt-driven compressor, and passes into a condenser mounted on the front of the radiator, where it loses heat and becomes liquid. The liquid passes through an expansion valve to an evaporator, where it changes from liquid under high pressure to gas under low pressure. This change is accompanied by a drop in temperature, which cools the evaporator. The refrigerant returns to the compressor, and the cycle begins again.

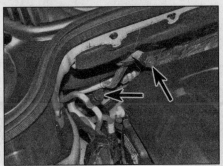

11.5 Air conditioning high- and low-pressure circuits' service ports (arrowed)

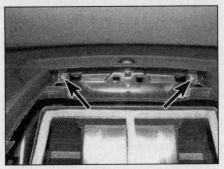

10.77a Undo the two retaining screws (arrowed) . . .

3 Air blown through the evaporator passes to the heating/ventilation housing, where it is mixed with hot air blown through the heater matrix to achieve the desired temperature in the passenger compartment.
4 The heating side of the system works in the same way as on models without air conditioning (see Section 9).
5 The operation of the system is controlled electronically by the ECM integral with the control panel. Any problems with the system should be referred to a Peugeot dealer, or suitably-equipped specialist **(see illustration)**.

Precautions

6 When an air conditioning system is fitted, it is necessary to observe special precautions whenever dealing with any part of the system, or its associated components. The refrigerant is potentially dangerous, and should only be handled by qualified persons. Uncontrolled discharging of the refrigerant is dangerous and damaging to the environment for the following reasons.
a) *If it is splashed onto the skin, it can cause frostbite.*
b) *The refrigerant is heavier then air and so displaces oxygen. In a confined space,*

10.77b . . . and disconnect the wiring connector (arrowed) from the sensor

which is not adequately ventilated, this could lead to a risk of suffocation. The gas is odourless and colourless so there is no warning of its presence in the atmosphere.
c) *Although not poisonous, in the presence of a naked flame (including a cigarette) it forms a noxious gas that causes headaches, nausea, etc.*

⚠ *Warning: Never attempt to open any air conditioning system refrigerant pipe/hose union without first having the system fully discharged by an air conditioning specialist. On completion of work, have the system recharged with the correct type and amount of fresh refrigerant.*

⚠ *Warning: Always seal disconnected refrigerant pipe/hose unions as soon as they are disconnected. Failure to form an air-tight seal on any union will result in the dehydrator reservoir become saturated, necessitating its renewal. Also renew all sealing rings disturbed.*

Caution: Do not operate the air conditioning system if it is known to be short of refrigerant as this could damage the compressor.

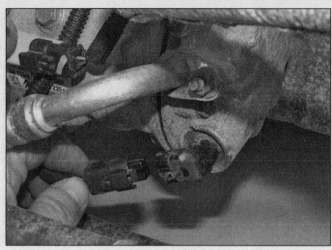

12.3a Disconnect the two . . .

12.3b . . . wiring connectors from the compressor

12 Air conditioning system components – removal and refitting

⚠ **Warning: Refer to the precautions given in Section 11 and have the system discharged by an air conditioning specialist before carrying out any work on the air conditioning system**

Compressor

Removal

1 Have the air conditioning system fully discharged and evacuated by an air conditioning specialist.

2 Remove the auxiliary drivebelt as described in Chapter 1.

3 Disconnect the wiring connectors from the compressor and unclip the engine wiring harness **(see illustrations)**.

4 Unscrew the nuts securing the refrigerant pipe retaining plates to the compressor **(see illustration)**. Separate the pipes from the compressor and quickly seal the pipe and compressor unions to prevent the entry of moisture into the refrigerant circuit. Discard the sealing rings, new ones must be used on refitting.

⚠ **Warning: Failure to seal the refrigerant pipe unions will result in the dehydrator reservoir become saturated, necessitating its renewal.**

5 Unscrew the compressor mounting bolts, and then free the compressor from its mounting bracket and remove it from the engine **(see illustration)**.

6 If the compressor is to be renewed, drain the refrigerant oil from the old compressor. The specialist who recharges the refrigerant system will need to add this amount of oil to the system.

Refitting

7 If a new compressor is being fitted, drain the refrigerant oil.

8 Manoeuvre the compressor into position and fit the mounting bolts. Tighten the compressor mounting bolts to the specified torque.

9 Lubricate the new refrigerant pipe sealing rings with compressor oil. Remove the blanking plugs and install the sealing rings then quickly fit the refrigerant pipes to the compressor. Ensure the refrigerant pipes are correctly joined, and then refit the retaining nuts to the specified torque.

10 Reconnect the wiring connectors then refit the auxiliary drivebelt (see Chapter 1).

11 Have the air conditioning system recharged with the correct type and amount of refrigerant by a specialist before using the system. Remember to inform the specialist which components have been renewed, so they can add the correct amount of oil.

Condenser

Removal

12 Have the air conditioning system fully discharged by an air conditioning specialist.

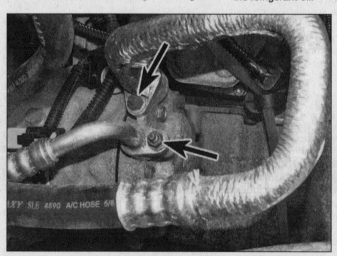

12.4 Unscrew the refrigerant pipes retaining nuts (arrowed)

12.5 Remove the compressor mounting bolts (arrowed)

12.14 Disconnect the switch (arrowed) wiring connector

12.15a Unscrew the refrigerant pipe upper retaining nut (arrowed) . . .

13 Remove the radiator as described in Section 4.

14 Disconnect the wiring connector from the pressostat switch at the bottom right-hand corner of the condenser (see illustration).

15 Undo the retaining nuts and disconnect the refrigerant pipes from the right-hand side of the condenser and quickly seal the pipe and condenser unions to prevent the entry of moisture into the refrigerant circuit. Recover the O-ring seals (see illustrations). Note it may be necessary to withdraw the condenser slightly to access the lower refrigerant pipe.

 Warning: Failure to seal the refrigerant pipe unions will result in the dehydrator reservoir become saturated, necessitating its renewal.

16 Move the top of the condenser towards the engine and then withdraw it from the front panel.

Refitting

17 Refitting is a reversal of removal. Noting the following points:

a) Ensure the upper and lower mounting rubbers are correctly fitted then seat the condenser in position in the front panel (see illustrations).

b) Lubricate the sealing rings with compressor oil. Remove the plugs and install the sealing rings then quickly fit the refrigerant pipes to the condenser. Securely tighten the dehydrator pipe union nut and ensure the compressor pipe is correctly joined.

c) Have the air conditioning system recharged with the correct type and amount of refrigerant by a specialist before using the system.

Receiver/drier

18 The receiver/drier is located on the left-hand side of the condenser (see illustration). See paragraphs 12 to 16 to remove the condenser. The receiver/drier is not available separately; see your local dealer for further information.

Pressostat switch

Removal

19 The switch is located at the bottom right-hand corner of the condenser (see illustration 12.14).

20 Have the air conditioning system fully discharged by an air conditioning specialist.

21 Remove the condenser, as described

12.15b . . . and lower refrigerant pipe retaining nut (arrowed)

in paragraphs 12 to 16. It is not necessary to completely remove the condenser, just withdraw the condenser away from the front panel to access the switch.

22 Disconnect the wiring connector, and then unscrew the switch from the condenser. Quickly seal the condenser union to prevent the entry of moisture into the refrigerant circuit.

 Warning: Failure to seal the refrigerant pipe unions will result in the dehydrator reservoir become saturated, necessitating its renewal.

12.17a Ensure the condenser lower (arrowed) . . .

12.17b . . . and upper (arrowed) mountings are correctly fitted

12.18 Receiver/drier (arrowed) fitted to the side of the condenser

12.27a Undo the various screws and clips around the housing (arrowed) ...

12.27b ... including the ones hidden at the sides (arrowed) ...

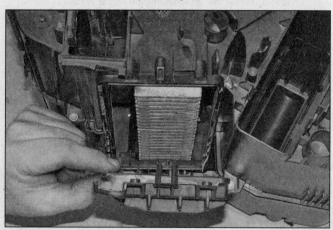

12.27c ... remove the base cover ...

12.27d ... and separate the 2 halves of the housing

Refitting

23 Refitting is a reversal of removal noting the following points:

a) *Lubricate the switch seal with compressor oil.*

b) *Have the air conditioning system recharged with the correct type and amount of refrigerant by a specialist prior to using the system.*

Evaporator

Removal

24 Have the air conditioning system fully discharged and evacuated by an air conditioning specialist.

25 Remove the heating/ventilation housing as described in Section 10.

26 Note their fitted positions, and then disconnect the wiring plugs and harness from the housing.

27 Release the retaining clips, undo the screws and separate the two halves of the heater housing **(see illustrations)**. Note the position of the screws may vary depending on model, check around the housing to make

sure all screws are removed before splitting the two halves of the housing.

28 With the two halves of the housing separated, undo the 2 screws, remove the pipe cover, and then slide the evaporator from the housing **(see illustrations)**.

Refitting

29 Refitting is a reversal of removal but have the air conditioning system recharged with the correct type and amount of refrigerant by a specialist prior to using the system.

12.28a Undo the screws (arrowed), remove the pipe cover ...

12.28b ... then slide the evaporator from the housing

12.28c Ensure the nut plate is in place when refitting the evaporator

12.32a Disconnect the wiring connector . . .

12.32b . . . and remove the air flap motor

Evaporator sensor

Removal

30 The evaporator sensor is located in the left-hand side of the heater housing.

31 Undo the retaining screw, and then unclip the kick panel from the front of the centre console and remove it from the front footwell **(see illustration 10.10)**.

32 On models after RPO No 11438, disconnect the wiring connector and remove the air mixing flap motor from the side of the heater housing **(see illustrations)**.

33 Unclip the sensor from the housing and disconnect the wiring connector **(see illustrations)**.

Refitting

34 Refitting is a reversal of removal.

Expansion valve

Removal

35 Have the air conditioning system fully discharged and evacuated by an air conditioning specialist.

36 To improve access to the matrix unions on the bulkhead, remove the air cleaner housing inlet ducting (see Chapter 4A).

37 Remove the sound insulation material/heat shield from the engine compartment bulkhead.

38 Undo the nuts securing the refrigerant pipes to the connection at the engine compartment bulkhead **(see illustration)**. Plug/cover the openings to prevent contamination/saturation. Recover and discard the O-ring seals – new ones must be fitted.

> ⚠ **Warning: Failure to seal the refrigerant pipe unions will result in the receiver/drier becoming saturated, necessitating its renewal**

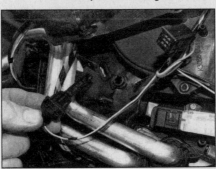

12.33a Unclip the evaporator sensor from the housing . . .

39 Pull the seal from around the pipes connection at the bulkhead, then undo the 2 studs using a Torx socket, and remove the expansion valve **(see illustrations)**. Recover and discard the O-ring seals – new ones must be fitted.

Refitting

40 Refitting is a reversal of removal but have the air conditioning system recharged with the correct type and amount of refrigerant by a specialist prior to using the system.

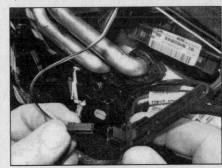

12.33b . . . and disconnect the wiring connector

12.38 Undo the two nuts securing the refrigerant pipes to the bulkhead

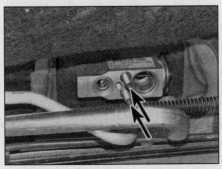

12.39a Undo the 2 studs (arrowed) using a Torx socket

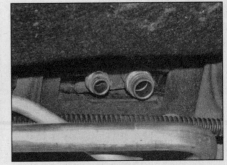

12.39b Renew the expansion valve seals on the pipes

Chapter 4 Part A:
Fuel and exhaust systems

Contents

Degrees of difficulty

Easy, suitable for novice with little experience	Fairly easy, suitable for beginner with some experience	Fairly difficult, suitable for competent DIY mechanic	Difficult, suitable for experienced DIY mechanic	Very difficult, suitable for expert DIY or professional

Specifications

Engine identification
1.6 litre:
Designation.. DV6TED4
Engine codes .... 9HY or 9HZ
2.0 litre:
Designation.. DW10BTED4 or DW10CTED4
Engine codes:
  DW10BTED4.. RHF, RHL or RHR
  DW10CTED4.. RHH

General
System type .... HDi (High-pressure Diesel injection) with full electronic control, direct injection and turbocharger
Designation:
  1.6 litre engines .... Bosch EDC 16 C3
  2.0 litre engines:
    RHF .... Delphi DCM 3,4
    RHH .... Delphi DCM 3,5
    RHL .... Siemens SID 803 or Delphi DCM 3,4
    RHR .... Siemens SID 803
Firing order.. 1-3-4-2 (No 1 at flywheel end)
Fuel system operating pressure............................ 200 to 1800 bars (according to engine speed)

Injectors
Type .... Electromagnetic or Piezo

Turbocharger
Type:
  1.6 litre engines .... Garrett GT1544V
  2.0 litre engines .... Garrett GT1749V
Boost pressure (approximate):
  1.6 litre engines .... 0.9 bar @ 3500 rpm
  2.0 litre engines .... 1.0 bar @ 4000 rpm

Torque wrench settings

	Nm	lbf ft
Camshaft position sensor bolt	6	4
Common rail mounting bolts	23	17
Engine knock sensor	20	15
Exhaust manifold nuts:		
1.6 litre engines	20	15
2.0 litre engines:		
DW10BTED4	25	18
DW10CTED4:		
Stage 1	10	7
Stage 1	20	15
Exhaust system fasteners:		
Catalytic converter-to-manifold nuts	40	30
Clamping ring nuts	20	15
Fuel filter water sensor	25	18
Fuel injector clamp bolts/nuts:		
1.6 litre engines		
Stage 1	4	3
Stage 2	Angle-tighten a further 65°	
2.0 litre engines (Siemens):		
Stage 1	4	3
Stage 2	Angle-tighten a further 45°	
2.0 litre engines (Delphi):		
DW10BTED4:		
Stage 1	4	3
Stage 2	Angle-tighten a further 77°	
DW10CTED4:		
Stage 1	7	5
Stage 2	Angle-tighten a further 55°	
Fuel pipe unions:		
1.6 litre engines	25	18
2.0 litre engines:		
DW10BTED4):		
Stage 1	23	17
Stage 2	30	22
DW10CTED4:		
Stage 1	18	13
Stage 2	27	20
Fuel pressure regulator:		
Screw-in type	28	20
With retaining screws:		
Stage 1	3	2
Stage 2	Slacken 180°	
Stage 3	2	1
Stage 4	3	2
Stage 5	6	4
Fuel temperature sensor (Delphi systems)	15	11
High-pressure fuel pump mounting bolts:		
1.6 litre engines	25	18
2.0 litre engines (Siemens)	20	15
2.0 litre engines (Delphi)		
DW10BTED4:		
2 lower bolts	20	15
1 upper bolt (from engine side)	8	6
DW10CTED4	20	15
High-pressure fuel pump rear mounting bolts/nut (8 mm)	17	13
High-pressure fuel pump sprocket nut	50	37
Inlet manifold bolts	10	7
Turbocharger mounting bolts/nuts	25	18
Turbocharger oil feed pipe banjo bolts:		
1.6 litre engines	30	20
2.0 litre engines:		
Engine pipe to cylinder block	40	30
All other connections	25	18
Turbocharger oil return pipe bolts:		
1.6 litre engines	30	20
2.0 litre engines	10	7

1 General information and system operation

The fuel system consists of a rear-mounted fuel tank with an immersed level sensor, a fuel pump, a fuel filter with integral water separator, a fuel cooler mounted under the car (depending on model), and an electronically-controlled High-pressure Diesel injection (HDi) system, together with a single turbocharger.

The exhaust system is conventional, but to meet the latest emission levels an unregulated catalytic converter and an exhaust gas recirculation system are fitted to all models. On some 2.0 litre models, there is also a pre-cat, which is fitted directly to the exhaust manifold. Also, an exhaust emission particulate filter may be fitted – refer to Chapter 4B for further details.

The HDi system (generally known as a 'common rail' system) derives its name from the fact that a common rail, or fuel reservoir, is used to supply fuel to all the fuel injectors. Instead of an in-line or distributor type injection pump, which distributes the fuel directly to each injector, a high-pressure pump is used, which generates a very high fuel pressure (up to 1800 bar at high engine speed) in the common rail. The common rail stores fuel, and maintains a constant fuel pressure with the aid of a pressure control valve. Each injector is supplied with high-pressure fuel from the common rail, and the injectors are individually controlled via signals from the system electronic control module (ECM). The injectors are electronically-operated.

In addition to the various sensors used on models with a conventional fuel injection pump; common rail systems also have a fuel pressure sensor. The fuel pressure sensor allows the ECM to maintain the required fuel pressure, via the pressure control valve.

System operation

For the purposes of describing the operation of a common rail injection system, the components can be divided into three sub-systems; the low-pressure fuel system, the high-pressure fuel system and the electronic control system.

Low-pressure fuel system

The low-pressure fuel system consists of the following components:
a) Fuel tank.
b) Fuel pump.
c) Fuel cooler.
d) Fuel heater (not all models).
e) Fuel filter/water trap.
f) Low-pressure fuel lines.

The low-pressure system (fuel supply system) is responsible for supplying clean fuel to the high-pressure fuel system.

High-pressure fuel system

The high-pressure fuel system consists of the following components:

a) High-pressure fuel pump with pressure control valve.
b) High-pressure fuel common rail.
c) Fuel injectors.
d) High-pressure fuel lines.

After passing through the fuel filter, the fuel reaches the high-pressure pump, which forces it into the common rail. As diesel fuel has a certain elasticity, the pressure in the common rail remains constant, even though fuel leaves the rail each time one of the injectors operates. Additionally, a pressure control valve mounted on the high-pressure pump ensures that the fuel pressure is maintained within preset limits.

The pressure control valve is operated by the ECM. When the valve is opened, fuel is returned from the high-pressure pump to the tank, via the fuel return lines, and the pressure in the common rail falls. To enable the ECM to trigger the pressure control valve correctly, the pressure in the common rail is measured by a fuel pressure sensor.

The electronically controlled fuel injectors are operated individually, via signals from the ECM, and each injector injects fuel directly into the relevant combustion chamber. The fact that high fuel pressure is always available allows very precise and highly flexible injection in comparison to a conventional injection pump: for example combustion during the main injection process can be improved considerably by the pre-injection of a very small quantity of fuel.

Electronic control system

The electronic control system consists of the following components:
a) Electronic control module (ECM).
b) Crankshaft speed/position sensor.
c) Camshaft position sensor.
d) Accelerator pedal position sensor.
e) Coolant temperature sensor.
f) Fuel temperature sensor.
g) Airflow meter.
h) Fuel pressure sensor.
i) Fuel injectors.
j) Fuel pressure control valve.
k) Preheating control module.
l) EGR solenoid valve.
m) Air temperature sensor
n) Atmospheric pressure sensor – integral with the ECM.
o) Inlet manifold pressure sensor.

The information from the various sensors is passed to the ECM, which evaluates the signals. The ECM contains electronic 'maps' which enable it to calculate the optimum quantity of fuel to inject, the appropriate start of injection, and even pre- and post-injection fuel quantities, for each individual engine cylinder under any given condition of engine operation.

Additionally, the ECM carries out monitoring and self-diagnostic functions. Any faults in the system are stored in the ECM memory, which enables quick and accurate fault diagnosis using appropriate diagnostic equipment (such as a suitable fault code reader).

2 High-pressure diesel injection system – special information

Warnings and precautions

1 It is essential to observe strict precautions when working on the fuel system components, particularly the high-pressure side of the system. Before carrying out any operations on the fuel system, refer to the precautions given in *Safety first!* at the beginning of this manual, and to the following additional information.

- Do not carry out any repair work on the high-pressure fuel system unless you are competent to do so, have all the necessary tools and equipment required, and are aware of the safety implications involved.
- Before starting any repair work on the fuel system, wait at least 30 seconds after switching off the engine to allow the fuel circuit pressure to reduce.
- Never work on the high-pressure fuel system with the engine running.
- Keep well clear of any possible source of fuel leakage, particularly when starting the engine after carrying out repair work. A leak in the system could cause an extremely high pressure jet of fuel to escape, which could result in severe personal injury.
- Never place your hands or any part of your body near to a leak in the high-pressure fuel system.
- Do not use steam cleaning equipment or compressed air to clean the engine or any of the fuel system components.

Procedures and information

2 Strict cleanliness must be observed at all times when working on any part of the fuel system. This applies to the working area in general, the person doing the work, and the components being worked on.

3 Before working on the fuel system components, they must be thoroughly cleaned with a suitable degreasing fluid. Specific cleaning products may be obtained from Peugeot dealers. Alternatively, a suitable brake cleaning fluid may be used. Cleanliness is particularly important when working on the fuel system connections at the following components:
a) Fuel filter.
b) High-pressure fuel pump.
c) Common rail.
d) Fuel injectors.
e) High-pressure fuel pipes.

4 After disconnecting any fuel pipes or components, the open union or orifice must be immediately sealed to prevent the entry of dirt or foreign material. Plastic plugs and caps in various sizes are available in packs from motor factors and accessory outlets, and are particularly suitable for this application (see

2.4 Typical plastic plug and cap set for sealing disconnected fuel pipes and components

2.7 Two crow-foot adapters will be necessary for tightening the fuel pipe unions

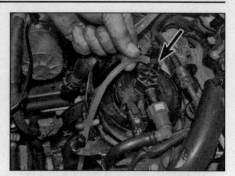

3.1 Attach a hose to the filter bleed screw (arrowed) and bleed the fuel into a container

illustration). Fingers cut from disposable rubber gloves should be used to protect components such as fuel pipes, fuel injectors and wiring connectors, and can be secured in place using elastic bands. Suitable gloves of this type are available at no cost from most petrol station forecourts.

5 Whenever any of the high-pressure fuel pipes are disconnected or removed, new pipes must be obtained for refitting.

6 On the completion of any repair on the high-pressure fuel system, Peugeot recommend the use of a leak-detecting compound. This is a powder which is applied to the fuel pipe unions and connections and turns white when dry. Any leak in the system will cause the product to darken indicating the source of the leak.

7 The torque wrench settings given in the Specifications must be strictly observed when tightening component mountings and

connections. This is particularly important when tightening the high-pressure fuel pipe unions. To enable a torque wrench to be used on the fuel pipe unions, two Peugeot crow-foot adapters are required. Suitable alternatives are available from motor factors and accessory outlets **(see illustration).**

3 Fuel system – priming and bleeding

1 Should the fuel supply system be disconnected between the fuel tank and high-pressure pump, it is necessary to prime the fuel system. This is achieved by connecting a suitable hose (if necessary, a special Peugeot hose No 444-T may be available) from the fuel filter outlet pipe to

the fuel return pipe and forcing fuel through the filter into the return system. If the suitable hose is not available, it will suffice to connect a length of hose to the filter outlet, with the other end of the hose in a suitable container **(see illustration).** The method of forcing the fuel through differs according to engine type:

1.6 litre engines
Operate the hand priming pump for approximately 2 minutes.

2.0 litre engines
Operate the hand priming pump for approximately 1 minute.

2 Operate the starter until the engine starts.

4 Air cleaner assembly – removal and refitting

Removal

1 Pull the plastic engine cover up and remove it.

1.6 litre engines

2 Undo the screw and remove the air inlet ducting from the front of the engine compartment to the air filter housing **(see illustration).**

3 Undo the two screws securing the air filter cover to the housing, disconnect the mass airflow sensor wiring plug, slacken the clamp securing the air inlet ducting to the turbocharger, release the clips securing the breather tube to the cylinder head cover, then manoeuvre the inlet ducting/filter cover assembly from position **(see illustrations).**

4.2 Undo the bolt (arrowed) and remove the inlet duct

4.3a Undo the air filter cover screws (arrowed) . . .

4.3b . . . disconnect the turbocharger inlet duct . . .

4.3c . . . release the clip (arrowed) and disconnect the breather . . .

4.3d . . . then remove the cover/duct assembly

4.4a Withdraw the lower part of the housing . . .

4.4b . . . noting the rubber mountings (arrowed) are still in place

4.5 Disconnect the wiring connector . . .

4.6 . . . slacken the air ducting securing clamp . . .

4.7 . . . and release the locating clip to remove

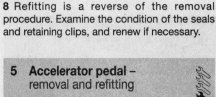

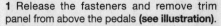

4 Pull the air filter lower housing upwards from the rubber mounting grommets (see illustrations).

2.0 litre engines

5 Disconnect the airflow meter wiring plug (see illustration).

6 Slacken the clamps and disconnect the air outlet hose from the airflow meter, and pull the air inlet hose upwards from the front of the air cleaner assembly (see illustration).

7 Depress the retaining clip and lift the air

cleaner upwards to release the mountings (see illustration).

Refitting

8 Refitting is a reverse of the removal procedure. Examine the condition of the seals and retaining clips, and renew if necessary.

5 Accelerator pedal – removal and refitting

Removal

1 Release the fasteners and remove trim panel from above the pedals (see illustration).
2 Disconnect the accelerator pedal position sensor wiring plug from the top of the pedal (see illustration).
3 Undo the three nuts and remove the pedal assembly (see illustration).

Refitting

4 Refitting is a reversal of the removal procedure.

6 Fuel lift pump – removal and refitting

The fuel lift pump is located in the fuel gauge sender unit, and the removal and refitting procedures are the same. Refer to Section 7 of this Chapter.

7 Fuel gauge sender unit – removal and refitting

Removal

1 For access to the fuel gauge sender unit, tilt or remove the right-hand rear seat cushion forward and lift up the access flap in the carpet (see illustration).
2 Using a flat blade, carefully release the three plastic access cover retaining clips at the points indicated by the small arrows, and

5.1 Unclip the trim panel

5.2 Disconnect the wiring connector . . .

5.3 . . . and undo the pedal assembly securing nuts (arrowed)

7.1 Lift up the flap in the carpet . . .

7.2 . . . and release the plastic access cover

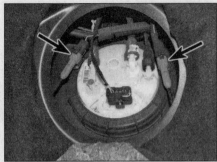

7.3 ABS rear sensor wiring connectors (arrowed)

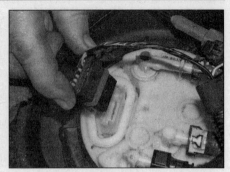

7.4 Disconnect the wiring connector . . .

remove the cover from the floor to expose the sender unit **(see illustration)**.
3 Unclip the two ABS sensor wiring connectors from the outer ring of the fuel sender unit **(see illustration)**. Move the wires to one side, while removing the sender unit.
4 Disconnect the wiring connector from the sender unit, and tape the connector to the vehicle body, to prevent it from disappearing behind the tank **(see illustration)**.
5 Release the retaining clip(s) and detach the fuel pipe(s) from the top of the sender unit **(see illustrations)**. See information given in Section 2 on warnings and precautions of the fuel system before disconnecting. Plug the pipe end(s) to minimise fuel loss and prevent the entry of dirt. Note the fitted position of the fuel pipes for refitting.
6 Noting the alignment marks on the fuel tank and the locking ring, unscrew the ring and remove it from the tank. Although Peugeot recommend the use of a special tool to unscrew the locking ring, this can be accomplished by making a home-made tool, fabricated out of a couple of pieces of metal bar and threaded rod, to locate on the raised ribs of the outer ring **(see illustrations)**
7 Carefully lift the sender unit assembly out of the fuel tank, taking great care not to damage the fuel gauge sender unit float arm, or to spill fuel onto the interior of the vehicle **(see illustrations)**. Recover the rubber sealing ring and discard it – a new one must be used on refitting.
8 Note that the sender unit (at the time of writing) is only available as a complete assembly – no components are available separately. Check with your local dealer for availability of parts.

Refitting

9 Fit the new sealing ring to the top of the fuel tank.

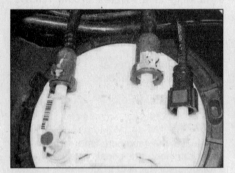

7.5a . . . note the position of the fuel pipes . . .

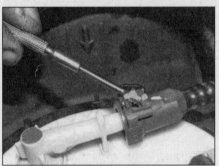

7.5b . . . and release the locking clips to disconnect pipes

7.6a Note the fuel tank and collar alignment marks (arrowed)

7.6b Using a home-made tool to slacken the collar

7.6c Remove the collar from the top of the fuel tank

7.7a Withdraw the sender unit . . .

7.7b . . . and remove the seal – discard as a new one is required

7.10 Make sure the sender unit is aligned with the cut-away (arrowed)

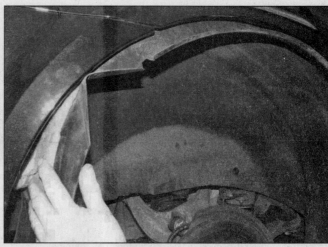

8.5 Remove the inner wheel arch liner

10 Carefully manoeuvre the sender unit into the fuel tank, making sure that it is located correctly in the cut-away in the fuel tank **(see illustration)**. Take care not to damage the float arm as the sender unit is fitted.

11 Refit the locking ring and tighten it securely until its alignment mark aligns with the arrow on the fuel tank, as noted on removal **(see illustration 7.6a)**.

12 Securely reconnect the fuel pipes to the sender unit, and then reconnect the wiring connector.

13 Secure the two ABS sensor wiring connectors to the outer ring.

14 Prime the fuel system (see Section 3). Start the engine and check the fuel pump feed and return hoses unions for signs of leakage.

15 If all is well, refit the plastic access cover ensuring it's locating correctly; this is to make sure that no fuel vapours will come into the vehicle.

16 Refit the rear seat cushion (see Chapter 11).

---

8 Fuel tank and cooler – removal and refitting

Fuel tank

Note: *Refer to the warnings and precautions in Section 2 before proceeding.*

1 Before removing the fuel tank, all fuel must be drained from the tank. Since a fuel tank drain plug is not provided, it is therefore preferable to carry out the removal operation when the tank is nearly empty. Before proceeding, disconnect the battery (see Chapter 5A) and siphon or hand-pump the remaining fuel from the tank.

2 Remove the rear seat cushion and, using a flat blade, carefully release the three access cover retaining clips at the points indicated by the small arrows, and remove the cover

from the floor to expose the fuel pump **(see illustration 7.2)**.

3 Disconnect the wiring connectors and fuel pipes from the top of the fuel sender/pump assembly, with reference to Section 7 of this Chapter. Plug the pipe end(s) to minimise fuel loss and prevent the entry of dirt. Note the fitted position of the fuel pipes for refitting.

4 Chock the front wheels then jack up the rear of the vehicle and support it on axle stands (*see Jacking and vehicle support*). Remove the right-hand rear roadwheel

5 Remove the fasteners and remove the right-hand rear wheel arch liner **(see illustration)**.

8.7 Unbolt the heat shield

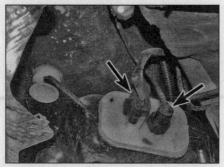

8.9 Disconnect the wiring connector and the fuel pipe (arrowed)

6 Remove the rear section of the exhaust system as described in Section 18.

7 Unscrew the fasteners and remove the heat shield from the tank underside **(see illustration)**.

Models with particulate filter

8 Undo the fasteners, and remove the plastic undershield(s) from below the additive tank on the left-hand side of the fuel tank **(see illustration)**.

9 Disconnect the wiring connector and fuel pipe from the front of the additive tank **(see illustration)**.

10 Disconnect the fuel pipe from the left-hand side of the additive tank **(see illustration)**.

8.8 Remove the plastic undershield

8.10 Release the fuel pipe (arrowed) from the side of the tank

8.12a Undo the mounting bolt (arrowed) . . .

8.12b . . . the two securing strap mounting bolts (arrowed) . . .

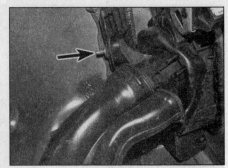

8.12c . . . and the fuel filler neck securing bolt (arrowed)

8.17 Fuel cooler (arrowed) located under the vehicle

8.18 Unclip the plastic shield from under the vehicle

as described in Section 3. Check for signs of leakage prior to taking the vehicle out on the road.

Fuel cooler

Note: *The fuel cooler is not fitted to all models.*
17 The fuel cooler is located under the right-hand side of the vehicle **(see illustration)**. Jack up the rear of the vehicle, and support it on axle stands (see *Jacking and vehicle support*).
18 Undo the fasteners and remove the undershield from the right-hand underside of the vehicle **(see illustration)**.
19 Working underneath the vehicle, undo the retaining nut, and release the cooler bracket from the locating holes **(see illustrations)**.
20 Release the pipes from the clips on the vehicle underside, then depress the release buttons and disconnect the fuel feed and return hoses from each end of the cooler. Be prepared for fuel spillage, and plug the hose and cooler openings to prevent dirt ingress **(see illustration)**.
21 Refitting is a reversal of removal,

All models

11 Place a trolley jack with an interposed block of wood beneath the tank, then raise the jack until it is supporting the weight of the tank.
12 Slacken and remove the bolts securing the fuel tank to the body, and the bolts securing the filler neck **(see illustrations)**. Release the filler neck seal from the body at the filler cap aperture.
13 Slowly lower the fuel tank; ensuring the filler neck assembly is guided out of position without placing any stress on it. Reach above the fuel tank as it is being lowered to release the rear ABS sensor wiring loom from the top of the fuel tank.
14 If the tank is contaminated with sediment or water, remove the fuel sender unit (Section 7), and swill the tank out with clean fuel. The tank is injection-moulded from a synthetic material – if seriously damaged, it should be

renewed. However, in certain cases, it may be possible to have small leaks or minor damage repaired. Seek the advice of a specialist before attempting to repair the fuel tank.
15 It is not possible to separate the filler neck from the tank. If damaged, the complete assembly must be renewed.
16 Refitting is the reverse of the removal procedure, noting the following points:
a) Ensure the wiring connectors and fuel pipes are securely reconnected and retained by all the relevant clips. When lifting the tank back into position, take care to ensure that the pipes/wiring do not become trapped between the tank and vehicle body.
b) As the fuel tank is raised, make sure the ABS sensor wiring loom is located correctly.
c) Refit the rear section of the exhaust, as described in Section 18.
d) On completion, refill the tank with a small amount of fuel and prime the fuel system

---

9 High-pressure fuel pump – removal and refitting

⚠️ **Warning: Refer to the information contained in Section 2 before proceeding.**
Note: *A new fuel pump-to-common rail high-pressure fuel pipe will be required for refitting.*

8.19a Undo the retaining nut (arrowed) . . .

8.19b . . . and unclip the locating pegs from the vehicle chassis

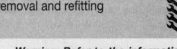

8.20 Release the fuel pipes (one side arrowed) from the cooler

Removal

1.6 litre engines

1 Disconnect the battery (see Chapter 5A) and remove the timing belt as described in Chapter 2A. After removal of the timing belt, temporarily refit the right-hand engine mounting but do not fully-tighten the bolts.

2 Remove the air cleaner assembly as described in Section 4.

3 Remove the EGR cooler as described in Chapter 4B.

4 Undo the bolts/nuts and remove the 3 support brackets above the fuel common rail and the high-pressure pump **(see illustrations)**.

5 Undo the union nuts and remove the high-pressure fuel pipe between the fuel common rail and the high-pressure pump. Plug the openings to prevent contamination.

6 Disconnect the wiring plug from the high-pressure fuel pump.

7 Depress the release buttons and disconnect the fuel supply and return hoses from the pump. Note that the hoses may have a release button on each side of the fitting. Plug the openings to prevent contamination.

8 Hold the pump sprocket stationary, and loosen the centre nut securing it to the pump shaft **(see Tool Tip 1)**.

9 The fuel pump sprocket is a taper fit on the pump shaft and it will be necessary to make up a tool to release it from the taper **(see Tool Tip 2)**. Partially unscrew the sprocket retaining nut, fit the home-made tool, and secure it to the sprocket with two 7.0 mm bolts and nuts. Prevent the sprocket from rotating as before, and screw down the nuts, forcing the sprocket off the shaft taper. Once the taper is released, remove the tool, unscrew the nut fully, and remove the sprocket from the pump shaft.

10 Undo the three bolts, and remove the pump from the mounting bracket.

Caution: The high-pressure fuel pump is manufactured to extremely close tolerances and must not be dismantled in any way. Do not unscrew the fuel pipe male union on the rear of the pump, or attempt to remove the sensor, piston de-activator switch, or the seal on the pump shaft. No parts for the pump are available separately and if the unit is in any way suspect, it must be renewed.

11 Undo the bolts securing the bracket to the rear of the pump (where fitted), then undo the 3 bolts and pull the pump from the inner timing cover.

2.0 litre engines

12 Disconnect the battery negative lead as described in Chapter 5A.

13 Remove the plastic cover from the top of the engine.

14 Undo the retaining bolts and securing clip and remove the turbocharger inlet duct from the engine compartment **(see illustrations)**.

15 Release the retaining clips and unclip the wiring loom from the mounting bracket at the end of the cylinder head, and then remove the mounting bracket **(see illustrations)**.

9.4a Remove the air filter support bracket (arrowed) ...

9.4b ... and the brackets around the fuel pump (arrowed)

A sprocket holding tool can be made from two lengths of steel strip bolted together to form a forked end. Bend the ends of the strip through 90° to form the fork 'prongs'.

Make a sprocket releasing tool from a short strip of steel. Drill two holes in the strip to correspond with the two holes in the sprocket. Drill a third hole just large enough to accept the flats of the sprocket retaining nut.

9.14a Undo the turbo inlet duct securing bolt (arrowed) ...

9.14b ... and withdraw the ducting from the engine compartment

9.15a Unclip the wiring loom ...

9.15b ... and then undo the bracket retaining nuts (arrowed)

9.16 Unscrew the high-pressure fuel pipe (arrowed)

9.17 Disconnect the fuel hoses (arrowed) from the pump

9.19a Unscrew the three bolts (arrowed) and remove the pump

9.19b Delphi fuel pumps have a mounting bolt (arrowed) on the cylinder head side of the pump

16 Thoroughly clean the high-pressure fuel pipe unions on the fuel pump and common rail. Using an open-ended spanner, unscrew the union nuts securing the high-pressure fuel pipe to the fuel pump and common rail. Counterhold the unions on the pump and common rail with a second spanner, while unscrewing the union nuts. Withdraw the high-pressure fuel pipe and plug or cover the open unions to prevent dirt entry **(see illustration)**. Note that a new high-pressure fuel pipe will be required for refitting. **Note:** *The fuel lines must be renewed every time they are removed, as it is possible for minute metal particles to enter them as a result of tightening the union nuts. If these particles enter the fuel injectors, fuel at high pressure can enter the combustion chambers unrestricted.*

17 Disconnect the fuel supply and return hoses from the high-pressure pump **(see illustration)**. Plug the openings to prevent contamination.

18 Note their fitted positions, and disconnect the wiring plugs from the pump. Move the wiring harness to one side.

19 Undo the 3 bolts and withdraw the fuel pump from the cylinder head **(see illustrations)**. Note on Delphi fuel pumps the upper bolt is accessed from the cylinder head side of the fuel pump.

Caution: The high-pressure fuel pump is manufactured to extremely close tolerances and must not be dismantled in any way. Do not unscrew the fuel pipe male union on the rear of the pump, or attempt to remove the pressure control valve, piston de-activator switch, or the seal on the pump shaft. No parts for the pump are available separately and if the unit is in any way suspect, it must be renewed.

Refitting

20 Refitting is a reversal of removal, noting the following points:

a) *Always renew the pump-to-common rail high-pressure pipe.*

b) *Renew the fuel pump drive seal.*

c) *With everything reassembled and reconnected, and observing the precautions listed in Section 2, start the engine and allow it to idle. Check for leaks at the high-pressure fuel pipe unions with the engine idling. If satisfactory, increase the engine speed to 3000 rpm and check again for leaks.*

d) *Take the car for a short road test and check for leaks once again on return. If any leaks are detected, obtain and fit another new high-pressure fuel pipe. **Do not** attempt to cure even the slightest leak by further tightening of the pipe unions.*

10 Common rail – removal and refitting

⚠ *Warning: Refer to the information contained in Section 2 before proceeding.*

Note: *A complete new set of high-pressure fuel pipes will be required for refitting.*

Removal

1 Disconnect the battery (refer to Chapter 5A).

2 Remove the plastic cover from the top of the engine.

1.6 litre engines

3 Remove the cylinder head cover/inlet manifold as described in Chapter 2A.

4 Drain the cooling system as described in Chapter 1.

5 Remove the EGR cooler as described in Chapter 4B.

6 Undo the 2 mounting bolts, slacken the clamps, and move the coolant pump outlet assembly aside **(see illustration)**.

7 Clean around the pipe, then undo the unions and remove the high-pressure pipe from the common rail to the high-pressure pump. Plug the openings to prevent contamination.

8 Disconnect the pressure sensor wiring plug from the common rail **(see illustration)**.

9 Unscrew the two rail mounting bolts and manoeuvre it from place **(see illustration)**.

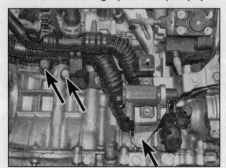

10.6 Undo the bolts (arrowed) and move the coolant pump outlet assembly to one side

10.8 The pressure sensor is located at the end of the common rail (arrowed)

10.9 Common rail mounting bolt/stud (arrowed)

10.14a Unscrew the unions from the rail . . .

10.14b . . . and plug the ends to prevent contamination

10.15 Counterhold the injector with a second spanner whilst slackening the pipe union

Note: *Peugeot insist that the fuel pressure sensor on the common rail must not be removed.*
Caution: Do not attempt to remove the four high-pressure fuel pipe male unions from the common rail. These parts are not available separately and if disturbed are likely to result in fuel leakage on reassembly.

2.0 litre engines

10 Disconnect the engine breather hose from the cylinder head cover.
11 Remove the air filter as described in Section 4.
12 Remove the inlet manifold/cylinder head cover as described in Section 13.
13 Move the oil filler neck to one side.
14 Thoroughly clean all the high-pressure fuel pipe unions on the common rail, fuel pump and injectors. Using an open-ended spanner, unscrew the union nuts securing the high-pressure fuel pipe to the fuel pump and common rail. Counterhold the unions on the pump and common rail (where applicable) with a second spanner, while unscrewing the union nuts. Withdraw the high-pressure fuel pipe and plug or cover the open unions to prevent dirt entry **(see illustrations)**.
15 Again using two spanners, hold the unions and unscrew the union nuts securing the high-pressure fuel pipes to the fuel injectors

and common rail **(see illustration)**. Withdraw the high-pressure fuel pipes and plug or cover the open unions to prevent dirt entry.
16 Undo the 2 mounting nuts and manoeuvre the common rail from position. Recover the mounting spacers. Disconnect the sensor wiring plug(s) as the common rail is withdrawn. **Note:** *Peugeot insist that the fuel pressure sensor on the common rail must not be removed.*

Refitting

17 Locate the common rail in position, refit and finger-tighten the mounting bolts/nuts.
18 Reconnect the common rail wiring plug(s).
19 Fit the new pump-to-rail high-pressure pipe, and only finger-tighten the unions at first, then tighten the unions to the specified torque setting. Use a second spanner to counterhold the union screwed into the pump body.
20 Fit the new set of rail-to-injector high pressure pipes, and finger-tighten the unions. If it's not possible to fit the new pipes to the injector unions, remove and refit the injectors as described in Section 11, and then try again.
21 Tighten the common rail mounting bolts/nuts to the specified torque.
22 Tighten the rail-to-injector pipe unions to the specified torque setting. Use a second spanner to counterhold the injector unions.
23 The remainder of refitting is a reversal of removal, noting the following points:

a) Ensure all wiring connectors and harnesses are correctly refitting and secured.
b) Reconnect the battery as described in Chapter 5A.
c) Observing the precautions listed in Section 2, start the engine and allow it to idle. Check for leaks at the high-pressure fuel pipe unions with the engine idling. If satisfactory, increase the engine speed to 3000 rpm and check again for leaks. Take the car for a short road test and check for leaks once again on return. If any leaks are detected, obtain and fit additional new high-pressure fuel pipes as required. **Do not** attempt to cure even the slightest leak by further tightening of the pipe unions.

11 Fuel injectors –
removal and refitting

⚠️ **Warning: Refer to the information contained in Section 2 before proceeding.**

Removal

1 Remove the plastic cover from the top of the engine, and disconnect the battery negative lead as described in Chapter 5A.

1.6 litre engines

Note: *The following procedure describes the removal and refitting of the injectors as a complete set, however each injector may be removed individually if required. New copper washers, upper seals, and a high-pressure fuel pipe will be required for each disturbed injector when refitting.*
2 Remove the EGR cooler as described in Chapter 4B.
3 Undo the bolts, slacken the clamps and remove the air inlet ducting assembly from between the turbocharger and the inlet manifold. Note their fitted positions, and disconnect the various wiring plugs as the assembly is withdrawn **(see illustrations)**.
4 Disconnect the injector wiring plugs.

11.3a Unscrew the inlet ducting clamps (arrowed) . . .

11.3b . . . and the ducting securing bolts (arrowed)

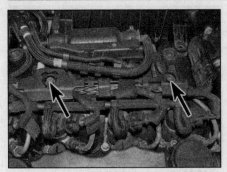

11.5 Wiring harness support bracket bolts (arrowed)

11.7 Prise out the clip and pull the return pipe from each injector

11.8 Use a second spanner to counterhold the high-pressure pipe union nuts

5 Undo the bolts and move aside the wiring harness support bracket **(see illustration)**.
6 Release the manual fuel priming pump and its support.
7 Extract the retaining circlip and disconnect the leak-off pipe from each fuel injector **(see illustration)**.
8 Clean the area around the high-pressure fuel pipes between the injectors and the common rail, then unscrew the pipe unions. Use a second spanner to counterhold the union screwed into the injector body **(see illustration)**. The injectors' screwed-in unions must not be allowed to move. Remove the bracket above the common rail unions, and then remove the pipes. Plug the openings in the common rail and injectors to prevent dirt ingress.
9 Unscrew the injector retaining nuts, and carefully pull or lever the injector from place.

If necessary, use an open-ended spanner and twist the injector to free it from position **(see illustrations)**. Do not lever against or pull on the solenoid housing at the top of the injector. Note down the injectors position – if the injectors are to be re-used, they must be refitted to their original locations. If improved access is required, undo the bolts and remove the oil separator housing from the front of the cylinder head cover.
10 Remove the copper washer and the upper seal from each injector, or from the cylinder head if they remained in place during injector removal. New copper washers and upper seals will be required for refitting. Cover the injector hole in the cylinder head to prevent dirt ingress.
11 Examine each injector visually for any signs of obvious damage or deterioration. If any defects are apparent, renew the

injector(s). Note down the 8-digit injector classification number – this may be needed during the refitting procedure if the ECM has been renewed **(see illustration 11.19a)**.
Caution: The injectors are manufactured to extremely close tolerances and must not be dismantled in any way. Do not unscrew the fuel pipe union on the side of the injector, or separate any parts of the injector body. Do not attempt to clean carbon deposits from the injector nozzle or carry out any form of ultrasonic or pressure testing.

2.0 litre engines

Note: *New copper washers, upper seals, studs and a high-pressure fuel pipe will be required for each disturbed injector when refitting.*
12 Remove the inlet manifold/cylinder head cover as described in Section 13.
13 Disconnect the wiring plugs from the injectors **(see illustration)**.
14 Thoroughly clean all the high-pressure fuel pipe unions on the fuel injectors and common rail. Using two open-ended spanners, unscrew the union nuts securing the high-pressure fuel pipes to the fuel injectors and common rail **(see illustration 10.15)**. Withdraw the high-pressure fuel pipes and plug or cover the open unions on the injectors and common rail to prevent dirt entry. Note that a new high-pressure fuel pipe will be required for each removed injector when refitting.
15 On Siemens systems, release the retaining clip and disconnect the leak-off pipe from each fuel injector **(see illustrations)**.

11.9a Injector retaining nuts (arrowed)

11.9b Use a spanner to twist the injector and free it from position

11.13 Disconnect the injector wiring plugs

11.15a Prise down the lower edge of the retaining clip (shown with the hose disconnected for clarity) . . .

11.15b . . . then pull the hose from the injector

11.16a Cover the inlet ports to prevent anything being dropped inside

11.16b Undo the injector retaining nuts

16 Cover the inlet ports in the cylinder head, and then progressively and evenly slacken and remove the injector retaining nuts (see illustrations).

17 Carefully pull the injectors upwards from the cylinder head (see illustrations). Note down the injectors' position – if the injectors are to be re-used, they must be refitting to their original locations.

18 Remove the lower copper washer and upper seal from each injector.

19 Examine each injector visually for any signs of obvious damage or deterioration. If any defects are apparent, renew the injector(s). Note down the injector classification number – this may be needed during the refitting procedure if the ECM has been renewed (see illustrations).

Caution: The injectors are manufactured to extremely close tolerances and must not be dismantled in any way. Do not unscrew the fuel pipe union on the side of the injector, or separate any parts of the injector body. Do not attempt to clean carbon deposits from the injector nozzle or carry out any form of ultrasonic or pressure testing.

20 If the injectors are in a satisfactory condition, plug the fuel pipe union (if not already done) and suitably cover the electrical element and the injector nozzle.

Refitting

21 Unscrew the injector retaining studs from the cylinder head and renew (see illustrations).

22 Clean out the injector recess in the cylinder

head and make sure it is free from any dirt see illustration)

23 Locate a new upper seal in the cylinder

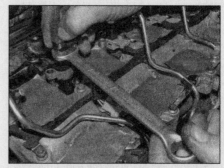

11.17a Use a spanner to slightly twist the injector . . .

11.17b . . . and then free it from its position in the head

11.19a Note the Bosch injector classification number . . .

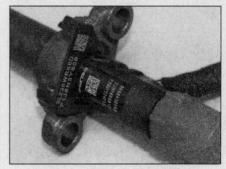

11.19b . . . and the Delphi injector classification number

11.21a Unscrew the old injector retaining studs . . .

11.21b . . . and fit new studs

11.22 Make sure the injector recess (arrowed) is clean

11.23a Fit a new upper seal ...

11.23b ... and use a length of wire to guide the new sealing washer into place

head, and place a new copper washer down the injector recess in the cylinder head **(see illustrations)**.

24 Where fitted, refit the injector clamp locating dowels to the cylinder head.

25 Ensure the injector clamps are in place over their respective circlips on the injector bodies, and then fit the injectors into place in the cylinder head. If the original injectors are being refitted, ensure they are fitted into their original positions **(see illustrations)**.

26 Fit the injector retaining bolts/nuts, but only finger-tighten them at this stage **(see illustration)**. When tightening the nuts/bolts, ensure the clamps stay horizontal.

27 Working on one fuel injector at a time, remove the blanking plugs from the fuel pipe unions on the common rail and the relevant injector. Locate a new high-pressure fuel pipe over the unions and screw on the union

nuts **(see illustration)**. Take care not to cross-thread the nuts or strain the fuel pipes as they are fitted. Once the union nut threads have started, finger-tighten the nuts to the ends of the threads.

28 When all the fuel pipes are in place, tighten the injector clamp retaining nuts/bolts to the specified torque and angle **(see illustration)**.

29 Using an open-ended spanner, hold each fuel pipe union in turn and tighten the union nut to the specified torque using a torque wrench and crow-foot adapter **(see illustration)**. Tighten all the disturbed union nuts in the same way.

30 If new injectors have been fitted, their classification numbers must be programmed into the engine management ECM using dedicated diagnostic equipment/scanner. If this equipment is not available, entrust this task to a Peugeot dealer or suitably-equipped

repairer. Note that it should be possible to drive the vehicle, albeit with reduced performance/increased emissions, to a repairer for the numbers to be programmed.

31 The remainder of refitting is a reversal of removal, noting the following points:

a) *Ensure all wiring connectors and harnesses are correctly refitting and secured.*

b) *Reconnect the battery as described in Chapter 5A.*

c) *Observing the precautions listed in Section 2, start the engine and allow it to idle. Check for leaks at the high-pressure fuel pipe unions with the engine idling. If satisfactory, increase the engine speed to 3000 rpm and check again for leaks. Take the car for a short road test and check for leaks once again on return. If any leaks are detected, obtain and fit additional new high-pressure fuel pipes as required.* **Do not** *attempt to cure even the slightest leak by further tightening of the pipe unions.*

12 Electronic control system components – testing, removal and refitting

Testing

1 If a fault is suspected in the electronic control side of the system, first ensure that all the wiring connectors are securely connected and free of corrosion. Ensure that the suspected problem is not of a mechanical nature, or due to poor maintenance; ie, check that the

11.25a Ensure the circlip (arrowed) is in place (where applicable) ...

11.25b ... then fit the injectors into their original locations

11.26 Fit new injector securing nuts

11.27 Screw the high-pressure fuel pipes to the fuel rail

11.28 Using an angle gauge to tighten the injector securing nuts

11.29 Using a crow-foot adapter to tighten the injector pipes

air cleaner filter element is clean, the engine breather hoses are clear and undamaged, and that the cylinder compression pressures are correct, referring to Chapters 1 and 2A or 2B for further information.

2 If these checks fail to reveal the cause of the problem, the vehicle should be taken to a Peugeot dealer or suitably-equipped garage for testing. A diagnostic socket is located in the centre console inside the armrest storage compartment **(see illustration)** to which a fault code reader or other suitable test equipment can be connected. By using the code reader or test equipment, the engine management ECM (and the various other vehicle system ECMs) can be interrogated, and any stored fault codes can be retrieved. This will allow the fault to be quickly and simply traced, alleviating the need to test all the system components individually, which is a time-consuming operation that carries a risk of damaging the ECM.

Removal and refitting

3 Before carrying out any of the following procedures, disconnect the battery (refer to Chapter 5A). Reconnect the battery on completion of refitting.

Electronic control module (ECM)

Note: *If a new ECM is to be fitted, this work must be entrusted to a Peugeot dealer or suitably-equipped specialist. It is necessary to initialise the new ECM after installation, which requires the use of dedicated Peugeot diagnostic equipment.*

4 The ECM is located in a plastic box, which

12.2 On board diagnostic (OBD) socket location (arrowed)

is mounted on the left-hand inner wing in front of the battery.

5 Undo the four fasteners and lift off the ECM box lid **(see illustration)**.

6 Undo the 2 Torx bolts and lift the ECM upwards and remove it from its location **(see illustrations)**.

7 Release the wiring connector(s) by depressing the tab and moving the locking lever on top of the connector. Carefully withdraw the connectors from the ECM pins **(see illustration)**

8 To remove the ECM box, release the clips, disconnect the positive feed connection, and lift the fusebox from place. Note the location of the wiring connectors and then disconnect them, undo the mounting bolts, and remove the module box **(see illustrations)**. Release any wiring harness retaining clips as the box is withdrawn.

9 Refitting is a reversal of removal.

12.5 Undo the four retaining screws and remove the cover

Crankshaft speed/position sensor

10 The crankshaft position sensor is located adjacent to the crankshaft pulley on the right-hand end of the engine. Slacken the right-hand front roadwheel bolts, and then jack the front of the vehicle up and support it on axle stands (see *Jacking and vehicle support*). Remove the right-hand front roadwheel.

11 Push in the centre pins a little, then prise out the rivets and remove the wheel arch liner.

12 Disconnect the sensor wiring plug **(see illustration)**.

13 Undo the bolt and remove the sensor.

14 Refitting is a reversal of removal, tightening the sensor retaining bolt securely.

Camshaft position sensor – 1.6 litre engines

15 The camshaft position sensor is mounted

12.6a Undo the two retaining screws (arrowed) . . .

12.6b . . . and remove the electronic control module (ECM)

12.7 Release the locking clips and disconnect the wiring plugs

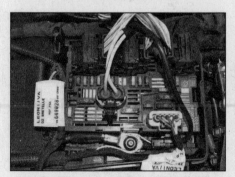

12.8a Note the location of the wiring connectors before removal

12.8b Extra fuses are located under the fusebox

12.12 Crankshaft position sensor (arrowed)

12.18 Undo the camshaft sensor retaining bolt (arrowed) – 1.6 litre engine

12.19a The gap between the used sensor and the signal wheel (arrowed) . . .

12.19b . . . must be 1.2 mm measured with a feeler gauge

on the right-hand end of the cylinder head cover, directly behind the camshaft sprocket.
16 Remove the upper timing belt cover, as described in Chapter 2A.
17 Unplug the sensor wiring connector.
18 Undo the bolt and pull the sensor from position **(see illustration)**.
19 Upon refitting, position the sensor so that the air gap between the sensor end and the webs of the signal wheel is 1.2 mm, measured with feeler gauges **(see illustrations)**. If a new sensor is being fitted, position it so the nipple of the sensor is just in contact with the camshaft signal wheel. Tighten the sensor retaining bolt to the specified torque.
20 The remainder of refitting is a reversal of removal.

Camshaft position sensor – 2.0 litre engines

Note: *The camshaft position sensor is mounted on the right-hand end of the cylinder head cover, directly behind the camshaft sprocket.*
21 Remove the plastic cover from the top of the engine.
22 Disconnect the sensor wiring plug **(see illustration)**.
23 Undo the retaining bolt and remove the sensor **(see illustration)**.
24 To refit and adjust the sensor position, locate the sensor on the cylinder head cover and loosely refit the retaining bolt.
25 When refitting a used sensor, insert a 8.5 mm drill bit in between the sensor and the timing belt cover to get the sensor in position **(see illustration)**. Tighten the retaining bolt securely.
26 When fitting a new sensor, slide the sensor into position until the plastic nipple on the tip of the sensor just comes into contact with the spoke on the camshaft sprocket. Tighten the retaining bolt securely. Note that, depending on the position of the camshaft sprocket, it may need to be rotated slightly to get one of the spokes on sprocket to align with the hole for the sensor.

Accelerator pedal position sensor

27 The pedal sensor is integral with the accelerator pedal assembly. Refer to Section 5 of this Chapter for the pedal removal procedure.

Coolant temperature sensor

28 Refer to Chapter 3.

Fuel temperature sensor – 1.6 litre engines

⚠️ *Warning: Refer to the information contained in Section 2 before proceeding.*

29 The sensor is clipped in to the plastic fuel manifold at the right-hand rear end of the cylinder head. To remove the sensor, disconnect the wiring plug, and then unclip the sensor from the manifold. Be prepared for fuel spillage **(see illustration)**.
30 Refitting is a reversal of removal. Observing the precautions listed in Section 2, start the engine and allow it to idle. Check for leaks at the fuel temperature sensor with the engine idling. If satisfactory, increase the engine speed to 4000 rpm and check again for leaks. Take

the car for a short road test and check for leaks once again on return. If any leaks are detected, obtain and fit a new sensor.

Fuel temperature sensor – 2.0 litre engines (Siemens)

⚠️ *Warning: Refer to the information contained in Section 2 before proceeding.*

31 The fuel temperature sensor (where fitted) is located in the fuel supply pipe between the fuel filter and the high-pressure pump, in the vicinity of the common rail.
32 Disconnect the fuel temperature sensor wiring connector.
33 Thoroughly clean the area around the sensor and its location.
34 Suitably protect the components below the sensor and have plenty of clean rags handy. Be prepared for considerable fuel spillage.

12.22 Disconnect the wiring connector

12.23 Withdraw the sensor from the cover

12.25 Using a 8.5 mm drill bit to measure the position of the sensor

12.29 Fuel temperature sensor (arrowed) – 1.6 litre engine

12.39 Delphi fuel temperature sensor (arrowed) – 2.0 litre engine

12.47a Disconnect the airflow meter wiring plug – 1.6 litre engines

35 Release the retaining clips and detach the sensor from the fuel pipes.
36 Refit the sensor to the fuel pipes, ensuring the clips fully engage.
37 Reconnect the sensor wiring plug.
38 Observing the precautions listed in Section 2, start the engine and allow it to idle. Check for leaks at the fuel temperature sensor with the engine idling. If satisfactory, increase the engine speed to 4000 rpm and check again for leaks. Take the car for a short road test and check for leaks once again on return. If any leaks are detected, obtain and fit a new sensor.

Fuel temperature sensor – 2.0 litre engines (Delphi)

39 The fuel temperature sensor is located in the high-pressure fuel pump **(see illustration)**.
40 Disconnect the fuel temperature sensor wiring connector.
41 Thoroughly clean the area around the sensor and its location.
42 Suitably protect the components below the sensor and have plenty of clean rags handy. Be prepared for considerable fuel spillage.
43 Undo the sensor and remove it from the fuel pump.
44 Refitting is a reversal of removal, tightening the sensor to the specified torque.
45 Observing the precautions listed in Section 2, start the engine and allow it to idle. Check for leaks at the fuel temperature sensor with the engine idling. If satisfactory, increase the engine speed to 4000 rpm and check again for leaks. Take the car for a short road test and check for leaks once again on return. If any leaks are detected, obtain and fit a new sensor.

Airflow meter

46 The airflow meter is located in the inlet ducting from the air cleaner housing.
47 Disconnect the meter wiring plug **(see illustrations)**.

12.47b Disconnect the airflow meter wiring plug – 2.0 litre engines

48 Slacken the retaining clips and disconnect the air inlet ducting from either side of the airflow meter. Suitably plug or cover the turbocharger inlet duct, using clean rag to prevent any dirt or foreign material from entering.
49 Undo the retaining screws and disconnect the airflow meter from the air cleaner cover.
50 Refitting is reverse of the removal procedure.

Fuel pressure sensor

51 The fuel pressure sensor is integral with the common rail, and is not available separately. Peugeot insist that the sensor is not removed from the rail.

Fuel pressure regulator

52 The fuel pressure regulator is located in the high-pressure fuel pump **(see illustration)**. Depending on fuel system, the regulator may be screwed into the fuel pump or it may have two retaining screws securing it to the fuel pump.
53 Disconnect the wiring connector from the fuel pressure regulator.
54 Thoroughly clean the area around the sensor and its location.
55 Suitably protect the components below the sensor and have plenty of clean rags handy. Be prepared for considerable fuel spillage.
56 Depending on type fitted, either unscrew the regulator and remove it from the fuel pump

12.52 Delphi fuel pressure regulator (arrowed) – 2.0 litre engine

or undo the two retaining screws and remove the regulator from the pump.
57 Refitting is a reversal of removal, tightening the sensor to the specified torque.
58 Observing the precautions listed in Section 2, start the engine and allow it to idle. Check for leaks at the fuel temperature sensor with the engine idling. If satisfactory, increase the engine speed to 4000 rpm and check again for leaks. Take the car for a short road test and check for leaks once again on return. If any leaks are detected, obtain and fit a new sensor.

EGR solenoid valve

59 Refer to Chapter 4B, Section 2.

Vehicle speed sensor

60 The engine management ECM receives the vehicle speed signal from the wheel speed sensors via the ABS ECM. Refer to Chapter 9 for wheel speed sensor removal.

13 Inlet manifold – removal and refitting

1 The inlet manifold is integral with the cylinder head cover. Refer to the relevant part of Chapter 2A or 2B for the removal and refitting procedure.

14.2a Exhaust manifold – 1.6 litre engines

14.2b Exhaust manifold – 2.0 litre engines

- Always allow the engine to return to idle speed before switching it off – do not blip the throttle and switch off, as this will leave the turbo spinning without lubrication.
- Allow the engine to idle for several minutes before switching off after a high-speed run.
- Observe the recommended intervals for oil and filter changing, and use a reputable oil of the specified quality. Neglect of oil changing, or use of inferior oil, can cause carbon formation on the turbo shaft, leading to subsequent failure.

14 Exhaust manifold – removal and refitting

Removal

1 Remove the turbocharger as described in Section 16.
2 Undo the retaining nuts, recover the spacers (where fitted), and remove the manifold. Recover the gasket **(see illustrations)**.

Refitting

3 Refitting is a reverse of the removal procedure, bearing in mind the following points:
a) *Ensure that the manifold and cylinder head mating faces are clean, with all traces of old gasket removed.*
b) *Use new gaskets when refitting the manifold to the cylinder head.*
c) *Tighten the exhaust manifold retaining nuts to the specified torque, starting with the ones at the centre and then working your way to the outer ones.*

15 Turbocharger – description and precautions

Description

1 A turbocharger is fitted to increase engine efficiency by raising the pressure in the inlet manifold above atmospheric pressure.

Instead of the air simply being sucked into the cylinders, it is forced in.
2 Energy for the operation of the turbocharger comes from the exhaust gas. The gas flows through a specially shaped housing (the turbine housing) and, in so doing, spins the turbine wheel. The turbine wheel is attached to a shaft, at the end of which is another vaned wheel known as the compressor wheel. The compressor wheel spins in its own housing, and compresses the inlet air on the way to the inlet manifold.
3 Boost pressure (the pressure in the inlet manifold) is limited by a wastegate, which diverts the exhaust gas away from the turbine wheel in response to a pressure-sensitive actuator. The turbocharger incorporates a variable inlet nozzle to improve boost pressure at low engine speeds.
4 The turbo shaft is pressure-lubricated by an oil feed pipe from the main oil gallery. The shaft 'floats' on a cushion of oil. A drain pipe returns the oil to the sump.

Precautions

The turbocharger operates at extremely high speeds and temperatures. Certain precautions must be observed, to avoid premature failure of the turbo, or injury to the operator.
- Do not operate the turbo with any of its parts exposed, or with any of its hoses removed. Foreign objects falling onto the rotating vanes could cause excessive damage, and (if ejected) personal injury.
- Do not race the engine immediately after start-up, especially if it is cold. Give the oil a few seconds to circulate.

16 Turbocharger – removal, inspection and refitting

Removal

1 Chock the rear wheels then jack up the front of the vehicle and support it on axle stands (see *Jacking and vehicle support*). Undo the screws and remove the engine undershield.
2 Disconnect the battery negative lead as described in Chapter 5A.

1.6 litre engines

3 Place a sheet of thick cardboard over the rear of the radiator to protect it from accidental damage.
4 Slacken the clamps, undo the bolts, and remove the air ducts to and from the turbocharger and inlet manifold **(see illustrations 11.3a and 11.3b)**. Note their fitted positions and disconnect the various wiring plugs, as the assembly is withdrawn.
5 Disconnect the vacuum hose from the turbocharger wastegate control assembly **(see illustration)**.
6 Undo the mounting bolts **(see illustration)**, and remove the heat shield from above turbocharger.
7 Remove the catalytic converter/particulate filter (where applicable) as described in Section 18.
8 Undo the oil supply pipe banjo bolts and recover the sealing washers **(see illustration)**.
9 Slacken the retaining clip and disconnect the oil return pipe from the turbocharger and cylinder block.
10 Unscrew the four nuts, and the nut securing the support bracket, then remove the

16.5 Disconnect the vacuum pipe from the wastegate control assembly (arrowed)

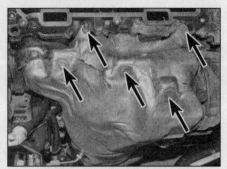

16.6 Undo the bolts (arrowed) and remove the turbocharger heat shield

16.8 Turbocharger oil supply and return pipes (arrowed)

16.10 Undo the 3 nuts (arrowed – one hidden) and remove the support bracket (arrowed)

16.12a Undo the crossbar retaining bolts (one side arrowed)

16.12b Remove the rear torque arm from the mounting bracket

turbocharger from the exhaust manifold **(see illustration)**.

2.0 litre engines

11 Remove the air cleaner assembly as described in Section 4.

12 Working underneath the vehicle, undo the retaining bolts and remove the crossbar that is bolted to the front subframe. Then undo the rear lower engine torque link bolts and remove the torque link mounting from under the vehicle. Move the lower part of the engine forwards and wedge a block of wood (approx 75 mm thick) between the transmission and the subframe **(see illustrations)**.

13 Undo the retaining clamp and disconnect the exhaust front pipe from the pre-catalyser **(see illustration)**.

14 Where applicable undo the retaining bolts and remove the heat shield from over the pre-catalyser **(see illustration)**. Note on some models the heat shield is removed with the pre-catalyser.

15 Undo the pre-catalyser mounting bolts/nuts, remove the pre-catalyst support bracket at the right-hand upper end, undo the mounting bolt at the left-hand end **(see illustrations)**.

16 Slacken the clamp securing the pre-catalyst to the turbocharger, and remove the pre-catalyst **(see illustrations)**. Note the clamp is self-slackening; as the bolt is slackened it will open up to release from the flange, discard as a new one will be required for refitting.

16.13 Exhaust pipe to pre-catalyst securing clamp (arrowed)

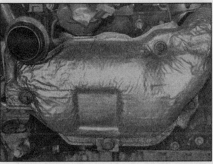

16.14 Pre-catalyst heat shield can be removed on some models

16.15a Undo the upper mounting bracket (arrowed) . . .

16.15b . . . and the mounting bolt (arrowed) on the left-hand side

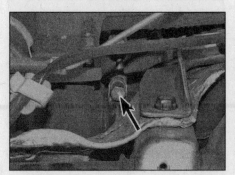

16.16a Slacken the clamp (arrowed) securing the pre-cat to the turbo . . .

16.16b . . . and then withdraw the pre-cat from under the vehicle

16.16c The clamp is self-slackening

16.18 Remove the air inlet and outlet ducts (arrowed)

16.19 Disconnect the wiring connector and the vacuum pipe (arrowed)

16.20a Disconnect the turbocharger oil supply pipe (arrowed) . . .

16.20b . . . and the return pipe (arrowed)

16.21 Turbocharger lower mounting bracket bolt (arrowed)

Refitting

27 Refitting is a reverse of the removal procedure, bearing in mind the following points:
  a) Renew the turbocharger retaining nuts and gaskets.
  b) When fitting the new clamp to the pre-catalyser, align the clamp on the flange **(see illustrations)**.
  c) If a new turbocharger is being fitted, change the engine oil and filter. Also renew the filter in the oil feed pipe.
  d) Prime the turbocharger by injecting clean engine oil through the oil feed pipe union before reconnecting the union.

17 Depending on model, it may be necessary to disconnect the wiring connector from the gas temperature sensor fitted in the top of the pre-catalyser.
18 Undo the retaining bolts and disconnect the turbocharger air inlet and outlet ducts **(see illustration)**.
19 Disconnect the vacuum pipe and wiring plug from the turbocharger control valve **(see illustration)**.
20 Disconnect the oil supply and return pipes from the engine cylinder block **(see illustrations)**. Tape over the openings.
21 Remove the support bracket beneath the turbocharger **(see illustration)**.
22 Undo the nuts/bolt securing the turbocharger to the exhaust manifold, lift the assembly slightly, then lower the turbocharger downwards from position **(see illustration)**.

Inspection

23 With the turbocharger removed, inspect the housing for cracks or other visible damage.
24 Spin the turbine or the compressor wheel to verify that the shaft is intact and to feel for excessive shake or roughness. Some play is normal, since in use the shaft is 'floating' on a film of oil. Check that the wheel vanes are undamaged.
25 If oil contamination of the exhaust or induction passages is apparent, it is likely that turbo shaft oil seals have failed.
26 No DIY repair of the turbo is possible and none of the internal or external parts are available separately. If the turbocharger is suspect in any way a complete new unit must be obtained. Do not attempt to dismantle the turbocharger control assemblies.

17 Intercooler – removal and refitting

Removal

1 The intercooler is located at the front of the engine compartment, on the left-hand side of the radiator. Chock the rear wheels then jack up the front of the vehicle and support it on axle stands (see *Jacking and vehicle support*). Undo the screws and remove the engine undershield.
2 Remove the front bumper as described in Chapter 11.
3 On 2.0 litre models, remove the air cleaner assembly as described in Section 4. On 1.6 litre

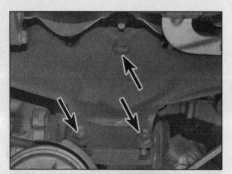

16.22 Turbocharger upper mounting nuts and bolt (arrowed)

16.27a Unclip the old inner sealing washer from the old clamp

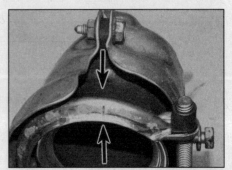

16.27b Fit the alignment mark on the new clamp (arrowed) with the upper flange of the pre-cat

models, remove the air inlet ducting from the front of the engine compartment to the air filter housing.

4 Loosen the clip and disconnect the outlet air duct from the intercooler (see illustration).

5 Working under the car, loosen the clip and disconnect the inlet air duct from the intercooler (see illustration).

6 Using a thin screwdriver, release the clips in the upper cross panel and pull the top mounting from the crossmember (see illustrations).

7 Lift the intercooler from its lower mountings and remove from the vehicle.

Refitting

8 Refitting is a reversal of removal.

18 Exhaust system – general information and component renewal

General information

1 According to model, the exhaust system consists of either three or four sections. Three-section systems consist of a catalytic converter, an intermediate pipe, and a tailpipe. Four-section systems consist of a pre-catalyst after the turbocharger, followed by a catalytic converter, particulate filter (not all models), intermediate pipe, and tailpipe.

2 The exhaust joints are of either the spring-loaded ball type (to allow for movement in the exhaust system) or clamp-ring type.

3 The system is suspended throughout its entire length by rubber mountings.

Removal

4 Each exhaust section can be removed individually, or alternatively, the complete system can be removed as a unit.

5 To remove the system or part of the system, first jack up the front or rear of the car, and support it on axle stands (see *Jacking and vehicle support*). Alternatively, position the car over an inspection pit, or on car ramps.

Catalytic converter/particulate filter – 1.6 litre engines

6 Undo the screws and remove the engine undershield.

7 Unscrew the pressure take-off unions from the side and base of the assembly (see illustrations).

8 Disconnect the sensor wiring plug on the side of the catalytic converter.

9 Undo the bolts and remove the heat shield from the catalytic converter/particulate filter.

10 Slacken the retaining clamps joining the catalytic converter to the turbocharger, and exhaust pipe. Take care not to damage the

17.4 Disconnect the upper hose from the intercooler

17.6a Release the upper securing clips . . .

flexible section of the front exhaust pipe (see illustration).

11 Slacken the clamp securing the catalytic converter to the turbocharger.

12 Undo the 2 nuts securing the catalytic

18.7a Unscrew the pressure take-off union from the side of the catalyst/filter . . .

17.5 Lower hose securing clamp (arrowed)

17.6b . . . and withdraw the intercooler from the front panel

converter to the cylinder block and manoeuvre it down and out of the engine compartment (see illustration).

13 If required, note its fitted position, then slacken the clamp and detach the particulate

18.7b . . . and the one at the base

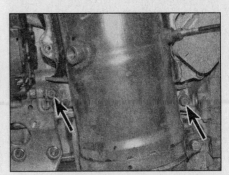

18.10 Exhaust pipe-to-catalyst/filter clamp (arrowed)

18.12 Catalytic converter/particulate filter mounting nuts (arrowed)

18.13 Undo the clamp (arrowed) and slide the particulate filter from the catalytic converter

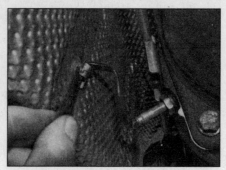

18.14 Unclip the wiring from the heat shield

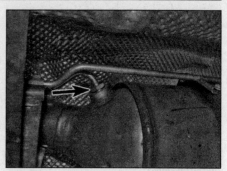

18.15a Unscrew the pressure take-off union from the front of the catalyst/particulate filter

18.15b ... and the one at rear of the catalyst/particulate filter

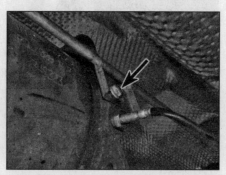

18.15c Undo the pipe retaining bracket bolt (arrowed)

filter from the base of the catalytic converter (see illustration).

Catalytic converter/particulate filter – 2.0 litre engines

14 Trace the wire back and disconnect the temperature sensor wiring connector from the particulate filter (see illustration).

15 Carefully unscrew the pressure pipes and disconnect them from the catalytic converter (see illustrations). Undo the securing bolt on the side of the catalytic converter, and then fasten the pipes to one side to prevent any damage.

16 Undo the front pipe retaining clamp on the pre-catalyser (see illustration).

17 Undo the rear clamp bolt and pull the exhaust apart, slide the catalytic converter/particulate filter from the rubber mountings as it is removed from under the vehicle (see illustrations).

18 It is possible to separate the particulate filter from the catalytic converter. With the assembly on a bench, undo the four bolts/nuts and separate the two halves. Discard the gasket, as a new one will be required for refitting (see illustration).

Pre-catalytic converter – 2.0 litre engines

19 The pre-catalyst removal procedure is described within the turbocharger removal procedure – see Section 16.

18.16 Exhaust pipe-to-pre-catalyst clamp (arrowed)

18.17a Undo the exhaust securing clamp ...

18.17b ... and slide the catalyst/particulate filter from the intermediate pipe ...

18.17c ... releasing it from the front rubber mountings (arrowed)

18.18 Fit a new gasket between the catalyst and the particulate filter

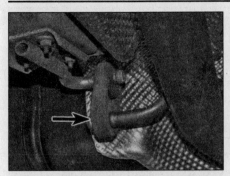

18.21 Unclip the exhaust from the rubber mounting (arrowed)

18.23 Rear silencer rubber mounting (arrowed)

18.24 Unclip the plastic undershields to remove the heat shields from under the vehicle

Intermediate pipe

20 Slacken the clamping ring bolts, and disengage both clamps from the flange joints.
21 Release the pipe from its mounting rubber and remove it from underneath the vehicle **(see illustration)**. Alternatively, undo the nuts securing the mounting bracket to the vehicle body.

Tailpipe

22 Slacken the tailpipe clamping ring bolts, and disengage the clamp from the flange joint.
23 Unhook the tailpipe from its mounting rubbers, and remove it from the vehicle **(see illustration)**. Alternatively, undo the nuts/bolts securing the mounting bracket to the vehicle body.

Heat shield(s)

24 The heat shields are secured to the underside of the body by various fasteners. Each shield can be removed once the relevant exhaust section has been removed **(see illustration)**. If a shield is being removed to gain access to a component located behind it, it may prove sufficient in some cases to remove the fasteners and simply lower the shield, without disturbing the exhaust system.

Refitting

25 Each section is refitted by reversing the removal sequence, noting the following points:
 a) Ensure that all traces of corrosion have been removed from the flanges, and renew all necessary gaskets.
 b) Inspect the rubber mountings for signs of damage or deterioration, and renew as necessary.
 c) On joints secured together by a clamping ring, apply a smear of exhaust system jointing paste to the flange joint, to ensure a gas-tight seal. Tighten the clamping ring nuts evenly and progressively, so that the clearance between the clamp halves remains equal on either side.
 d) Prior to tightening the exhaust system fasteners, ensure that all rubber mountings are correctly located, and that there is adequate clearance between the exhaust system and vehicle underbody.

Notes

Chapter 4 Part B:
Emission control systems

Contents

Degrees of difficulty

Easy, suitable for novice with little experience	**Fairly easy,** suitable for beginner with some experience	**Fairly difficult,** suitable for competent DIY mechanic	**Difficult,** suitable for experienced DIY mechanic	**Very difficult,** suitable for expert DIY or professional

1 General information

All engines are also designed to meet strict emission requirements, and are equipped with a crankcase emission control system and a catalytic converter. To further reduce exhaust emissions, all engines are also fitted with an exhaust gas recirculation (EGR) system. Additionally, some models may be equipped with a particulate emission filter, which uses porous silicon carbide substrate to trap particulates of carbon as the exhaust gases pass through.

The emission control systems function as follows.

Crankcase emission control

To reduce the emission of unburned hydrocarbons from the crankcase into the atmosphere, the engine is sealed and the blow-by gases and oil vapour are drawn from inside the crankcase, through a wire mesh oil separator, into the inlet tract to be burned by the engine during normal combustion.

Under all conditions the gases are forced out of the crankcase by the (relatively) higher crankcase pressure; if the engine is worn, the raised crankcase pressure (due to increased blow-by) will cause some of the flow to return under all manifold conditions.

Exhaust emission control

To minimise the level of exhaust pollutants released into the atmosphere, a catalytic converter is fitted in the exhaust system of all models.

The catalytic converter consists of a canister containing a fine mesh impregnated with a catalyst material, over which the hot exhaust gases pass. The catalyst speeds up the oxidation of harmful carbon monoxide, unburnt hydrocarbons and soot, effectively reducing the quantity of harmful products released into the atmosphere via the exhaust gases.

Exhaust gas recirculation

This system is designed to recirculate small quantities of exhaust gas into the inlet tract, and therefore into the combustion process. This process reduces the level of oxides of nitrogen present in the final exhaust gas, which is released into the atmosphere.

The volume of exhaust gas recirculated is controlled by the system electronic control module.

A vacuum-operated valve is fitted to the exhaust manifold, to regulate the quantity of exhaust gas recirculated. The valve is operated by the vacuum supplied by the solenoid valve.

Particulate filter

The particulate filter is combined with the catalytic converter in the exhaust system, and its purpose it to trap particulates of carbon (soot) as the exhaust gases pass through, in order to comply with latest emission regulations.

The filter can be automatically regenerated (cleaned) by the system's ECM on-board the vehicle. The engine's high-pressure injection system is utilised to inject fuel into the exhaust gases during the post-injection period; this causes the filter temperature to increase

sufficiently to oxidise the particulates, leaving an ash residue. The regeneration period is automatically controlled by the on-board ECM. Subsequently, at the correct service interval the filter must be removed from the exhaust system, and renewed.

To assist the combustion of the trapped carbon (soot) during the regeneration process, a fuel additive (cerium-based Eolys) is automatically mixed with the diesel fuel in the fuel tank. The additive is stored in a 5-litre container attached to the bottom left-hand side of the fuel tank, and the ECM regulates the amount of additive to send to the fuel tank by means of an additive injector located on the top of the fuel tank.

2 Emission control systems – testing and component renewal

Crankcase emission control

1 The components of this system require no attention other than to check that the hose(s) are clear and undamaged at regular intervals.

Exhaust emission control

2 The performance of the catalytic converter can be checked only by measuring the exhaust gases using a good-quality, carefully calibrated exhaust gas analyser.

3 If the catalytic converter is thought to be faulty, before assuming the catalytic converter is faulty, it is worth checking the problem is not due to a faulty injector(s). Refer to your Peugeot dealer for further information.

2.9a EGR cooler-to-valve clamp (arrowed) . . .

2.9b . . . EGR cooler-to-pipe clamp (arrowed)

2.11 EGR valve mounting bolts (arrowed –
one hidden)

Catalytic converter

4 Refer to Chapter 4A.

Exhaust gas recirculation system

5 Testing of the system should ideally be
entrusted to a Peugeot dealer since a vacuum
pump and vacuum gauge are required.

EGR valve

1.6 litre engine

6 The EGR valve is located on the left-hand
rear of the cylinder head.
7 Disconnect the battery negative lead (refer
to Chapter 5A).

8 Remove the air cleaner housing as
described in Chapter 4A.
9 Release the clamps securing the EGR pipe
to the EGR cooler, and the EGR cooler to the
EGR valve (see illustrations).
10 Disconnect the EGR valve wiring plug.
11 Undo the 2 EGR valve mounting bolts, move
the EGR cooler to one side, and manoeuvre
the valve from position (see illustration).
Recover the gasket/seal. If required, the CLIC
type clamps can be replaced with normal
worm-drive clips.
12 Refitting is a reversal of removal.

2.0 litre engine

13 Unclip the plastic cover from the top of the
engine.
14 Disconnect the battery negative lead (refer
to Chapter 5A).
15 Release the retaining clips and remove
the breather pipe from across the rear of the
cylinder head cover (see illustration).
16 Drain the cooling system as described in
Chapter 1, and then disconnect the coolant
hoses from the EGR cooler at the rear of the
cylinder head (see illustrations)
17 Working down the right-hand rear of the
engine, disconnect the wiring connectors and
unbolt the mounting bracket from the rear of
the cylinder head (see illustrations). Move
the mounting bracket and valve to one side.
18 Unclip the coolant hose from the retaining

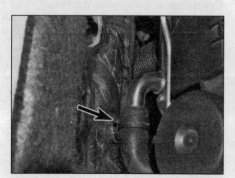

2.15 Remove the breather hose

2.16a Release the retaining clip and
remove the hose

2.16b Release the hose clamp (arrowed)

2.17a Disconnect the wiring connector . . .

2.17b . . . and undo the bracket securing
bolts

2.18a Unclip the hose from the heat shield . . .

2.18b . . . and undo the securing nut (arrowed)

2.19 Remove the cooler pipe elbow

clip on the side of the heat shield, and then undo the retaining nut and remove the heat shield from above the manifold (see illustrations).

19 Undo the retaining bolts and then release the cooler pipe collar, and remove the elbow from the right-hand rear of the exhaust manifold (see illustration).

20 Disconnect the wiring connector from the top of the EGR valve (and vacuum pipe where fitted) (see illustration).

21 Undo the retaining bolts and release the EGR pipe from the top of the valve housing (see illustration).

22 Undo the retaining nut from the EGR cooler lower mounting bracket (see illustration).

23 Undo the retaining bolt from the EGR valve housing lower mounting bracket (see illustration).

24 Undo the two retaining bolts from the top of the EGR valve housing and then lift out the EGR valve complete with cooler from the rear of the engine (see illustrations).

25 To remove the EGR solenoid valve and housing from the cooler, undo the two retaining bolts (see illustration).

26 Refitting is a reversal of removal.

EGR heat exchanger

Note: For 2.0 litre models, see EGR valve.

27 Drain the cooling system (see Chapter 1). Alternatively, fit hose clamps to the hoses connected to the EGR heat exchanger.

2.20 Disconnect the wiring connector from the EGR valve (arrowed)

2.21 Undo the EGR pipe retaining bolts (arrowed)

2.22 Undo the EGR cooler lower mounting bracket nut (arrowed)

2.23 EGR valve housing lower mounting bolt (arrowed)

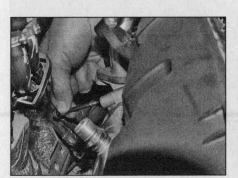

2.24a Remove the EGR valve housing mounting bolts . . .

2.24b . . . and remove the EGR cooler

2.25 Cooler-to-EGR valve housing securing bolts (arrowed)

2.32 Release the two hose securing clamps (arrowed)

2.36 Remove the plastic undershield

28 Remove the battery as described in Chapter 5A.
29 Remove the air cleaner housing as described in Chapter 4A.
30 Remove the heat shield over the EGR pipe, where fitted.
31 Undo the 2 bolts securing the EGR pipe, and release the clamp securing the pipe to the EGR cooler.
32 Release the clamps and disconnect the coolant hoses from the cooler **(see illustration)**, then undo the mounting bolts/nuts, remove the bracket, and manoeuvre it from place. Undo the 2 bolts and remove the EGR valve along with the cooler.
33 Refitting is a reversal of removal.

Particulate filter fuel additive system pressure

34 It is possible to check the fuel additive pump delivery pressure, however, this should be made by a Peugeot dealer or specialist.

Fuel additive reservoir

Note: *Ideally, the additive reservoir should be empty before removing it, otherwise take precautions against spillage.*

2.37 Unbolt the heat shield . . .

⚠ *Warning: Wear protective gloves and eye protection when handling the reservoir.*

35 To remove the fuel additive reservoir, chock the front wheels then jack up the rear of the vehicle and support on axle stands (see *Jacking and vehicle support*). The reservoir is attached to the left-hand side of the fuel tank.
36 Remove the plastic undershield from beneath the fuel additive tank **(see illustration)**

2.38 . . . disconnect the wiring connector . . .

37 Undo the retaining nuts and remove the heat shield from beneath the front of the additive reservoir **(see illustration)**.
38 Disconnect the wiring from the level sensor on the rear of the reservoir **(see illustration)**.
39 Note the location of the additive pipes on the reservoir, then depress the release buttons and disconnect them **(see illustrations)**. Tape over or plug the openings to prevent dirt ingress.
40 Undo the fuel tank retaining bolt, and

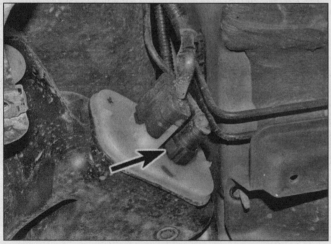

2.39a . . . then disconnect the fuel pipe (arrowed) . . .

2.39b . . . and the fuel pipe (arrowed) from the side of the tank

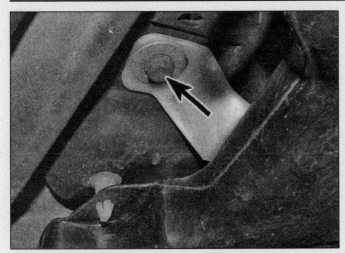

2.40a Undo the retaining bolt (arrowed) . . .

2.40b . . . release the securing clips . . .

release the retaining clips to lower the additive tank from under the vehicle **(see illustrations)**. Have a suitable container available to catch spilled additive.
41 Refitting is a reversal of removal.
42 Have the reservoir refilled by a Peugeot dealer or specialist.

Particulate filter

43 Renewal of the particulate filter is described in Chapter 4A, Section 18.

Pressure differential sensor

44 This sensor measures the pressure at the entrance and exit of the particulate filter, and is located in the engine compartment **(see illustrations)**. It is fitted to the top right-hand corner of the radiator on 1.6 litre engines, and on the rear engine bulkhead on 2.0 litre engines.
45 Note their fitted positions, and then disconnect the rubber hoses and wiring plug from the sensor.

46 Undo the mounting bolts and remove the sensor.

3 Catalytic converter – general information and precautions

1 The catalytic converter is a reliable and simple device which needs no maintenance in itself, but there are some facts of which an owner should be aware if the converter is to function properly for its full service life.
a) DO NOT use fuel or engine oil additives – these may contain substances harmful to the catalytic converter.
b) DO NOT continue to use the car if the engine burns oil to the extent of leaving a visible trail of blue smoke.
c) Remember that the catalytic converter operates at very high temperatures.

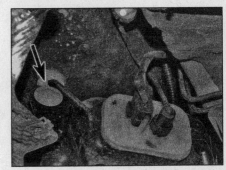

2.40c . . . and release the tank from the locating pegs (arrowed)

DO NOT, therefore, park the car in dry undergrowth, over long grass or piles of dead leaves after a long run.
d) Remember that the catalytic converter is FRAGILE – do not strike it with tools.

2.44a Pressure differential sensor location – 1.6 litre engines

2.44b Pressure differential sensor location – 2.0 litre engines

Chapter 5 Part A:
Starting and charging systems

Contents

Degrees of difficulty

Easy, suitable for novice with little experience	**Fairly easy,** suitable for beginner with some experience	**Fairly difficult,** suitable for competent DIY mechanic	**Difficult,** suitable for experienced DIY mechanic	**Very difficult,** suitable for expert DIY or professional

Specifications

System type. . . . . 12 volt, negative earth

Battery

Type . . . . Low maintenance or 'maintenance-free' sealed for life
Charge condition:
  Poor . . . . 12.5 volts
  Normal . . . . 12.6 volts
  Good . . . . 12.7 volts

Alternator

Type . . . . Bosch, Valeo, Denso, Magneti Marelli, or Mitsubishi (depending on model)
Rating . . . . 150 or 180 amp

Starter motor

Type . . . . Denso, Mitsubishi, Valeo or Bosch (depending on model)

Torque wrench settings

	Nm	lbf ft
Alternator mounting bolts:		
1.6 litre models:		
Front upper bolt	40	30
Rear bolts	49	36
2.0 litre models:		
Front bolts.	40	30
Rear upper bolt.	49	36
Rear lower bolt	40	30
Alternator mounting bracket-to-cylinder block bolts:		
1.6 litre models.	25	18
2.0 litre models.	20	15
Auxiliary belt idler roller to mounting bracket (1.6 litre models)	45	33
Auxiliary belt tensioner-to-cylinder block bolt:		
1.6 litre models.	20	15
2.0 litre models.	43	32
Oil level sensor	27	20
Oil pressure switch:		
1.6litre	20	15
2.0 litre	32	24
Starter motor:		
1.6 litre models.	20	15
2.0 litre models.	35	26

1 General information and precautions

The engine electrical system consists mainly of the charging and starting systems. Because of their engine-related functions, these components are covered separately from the body electrical devices such as the lights, instruments, etc (which are covered in Chapter 12). Refer to Part B for information on the preheating system.

The electrical system is of the 12 volt negative earth type.

The battery is of the low maintenance or 'maintenance-free' (sealed for life) type and is charged by the alternator, which is belt-driven from the crankshaft pulley.

The starter motor is of the pre-engaged type incorporating an integral solenoid. On starting, the solenoid moves the drive pinion into engagement with the flywheel ring gear before the starter motor is energised. Once the engine has started, a one-way clutch prevents the motor armature being driven by the engine until the pinion disengages from the flywheel.

Precautions

Further details of the various systems are given in the relevant Sections of this Chapter. While some repair procedures are given, the usual course of action is to renew the component concerned.

It is necessary to take extra care when working on the electrical system to avoid damage to semi-conductor devices (diodes and transistors), and to avoid the risk of personal injury. In addition to the precautions given in *Safety first!* at the beginning of this manual, observe the following when working on the system:

- Always remove rings, watches, etc, before working on the electrical system. Even with the battery disconnected, capacitive discharge could occur if a component's live terminal is earthed through a metal object. This could cause a shock or nasty burn.
- Do not reverse the battery connections. Components such as the alternator, electronic control modules, or any other components having semi-conductor circuitry could be irreparably damaged.
- If the engine is being started using jump leads and a slave battery, connect the batteries positive-to-positive and negative-to-negative (see *Jump starting*). This also applies when connecting a battery charger.
- Never disconnect the battery terminals, the alternator, any electrical wiring or any test instruments when the engine is running.
- Do not allow the engine to turn the alternator when the alternator is not connected.
- Never 'test' for alternator output by 'flashing' the output lead to earth.
- Never use an ohmmeter of the type incorporating a hand-cranked generator for circuit or continuity testing.
- Always ensure that the battery negative lead is disconnected when working on the electrical system.
- Before using electric-arc welding equipment on the car, disconnect the battery, alternator and components such as the fuel injection/ignition electronic control module to protect them from the risk of damage.

2 Electrical fault finding – general information

Refer to Chapter 12.

3 Battery – testing and charging

Testing

Standard and low maintenance battery

1 If the vehicle covers a small annual mileage, it is worthwhile checking the specific gravity of the electrolyte every three months to determine the state of charge of the battery. Use a hydrometer to make the check and compare the results with the following table. Note that the specific gravity readings assume an electrolyte temperature of 15°C; for every 10°C below 15°C subtract 0.007. For every 10°C above 15°C add 0.007.

	Above 25°C	Below 25°C
Fully-charged	1.210 to 1.230	1.270 to 1.290
70% charged	1.170 to 1.190	1.230 to 1.250
Discharged	1.050 to 1.070	1.110 to 1.130

2 If the battery condition is suspect, first check the specific gravity of electrolyte in each cell. A variation of 0.040 or more between any cells indicates loss of electrolyte or deterioration of the internal plates.

3 If the specific gravity variation is 0.040 or more, the battery should be renewed. If the cell variation is satisfactory but the battery is discharged, it should be charged as described later in this Section.

Maintenance-free battery

4 In cases where a 'sealed for life' maintenance-free battery is fitted, topping-up and testing of the electrolyte in each cell is not possible. The condition of the battery can therefore only be tested using a battery condition indicator or a voltmeter.

5 Certain models may be fitted with a 'Delco' type maintenance-free battery, with a built-in charge condition indicator. The indicator is located in the top of the battery casing, and indicates the condition of the battery from its colour (see illustration). If the indicator shows green, then the battery is in a good state of charge. If the indicator shows black, then the battery requires charging, as described later in this Section. If the indicator shows blue, then the electrolyte level in the battery is too low to allow further use, and the battery should be renewed.

Caution: Do not attempt to charge, load or jump start a battery when the indicator shows clear/yellow.

All battery types

6 If testing the battery using a voltmeter, connect the voltmeter across the battery and compare the result with those given in the Specifications under 'charge condition'. The test is only accurate if the battery has not been subjected to any kind of charge for the previous six hours. If this is not the case, switch on the headlights for 30 seconds, then wait four to five minutes before testing the battery after switching off the headlights. All other electrical circuits must be switched off, so check that the doors and tailgate/boot lid are fully shut when making the test.

7 If the voltage reading is less than 12.2 volts, then the battery is discharged, whilst a reading of 12.2 to 12.4 volts indicates a partially-discharged condition.

8 If the battery is to be charged, remove it

from the vehicle (Section 4) and charge it as described later in this Section.

Charging

Note: *The following is intended as a guide only. Always refer to the manufacturer's recommendations (often printed on a label attached to the battery) before charging a battery.*

Standard and low maintenance battery

9 Charge the battery at a rate of 3.5 to 4 amps and continue to charge the battery at this rate until no further rise in specific gravity is noted over a four hour period.

10 Alternatively, a trickle charger charging at the rate of 1.5 amps can safely be used overnight.

11 Specially rapid 'boost' charges, which are claimed to restore the power of the battery in 1 to 2 hours are not recommended, as they can cause serious damage to the battery plates through overheating.

12 While charging the battery, note that the temperature of the electrolyte should never exceed 38°C.

Maintenance-free battery

13 This battery type takes considerably longer to fully recharge than the standard type, the time taken being dependent on the extent of discharge, but it can take anything up to three days.

14 A constant voltage type charger is required to be set, when connected, to 13.9 to 14.9 volts with a charger current below 25 amps. Using this method, the battery should be usable within three hours, giving a voltage reading of 12.5 volts, but this is for a partially-discharged battery and, as mentioned, full charging can take considerably longer.

15 If the battery is to be charged from a fully-discharged state (condition reading less than 12.2 volts), have it recharged by your Peugeot dealer or local automotive electrician, as the charge rate is higher and constant supervision during charging is necessary.

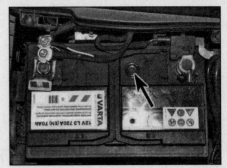

3.5 Charge condition indicator (arrowed)

4 Battery – removal and refitting

Note: *The radio/cassette/CD player/autochanger unit fitted as standard equipment by Peugeot is equipped with an anti-theft system, to deter thieves. If the power source is disconnected, the unit will automatically recode itself as long as it is still fitted to the correct vehicle. If the unit is removed it will not operate in another vehicle.*

Note: *Prior to disconnecting the battery, wait 15 minutes after switching off the ignition to allow the vehicle's ECMs to store all learnt values in their memories.*

Removal

1 Prior to disconnecting the battery, close all windows and the sunroof, and ensure that the vehicle alarm system is deactivated (see Owner's Handbook or Chapter 12, Section 20).

2 The battery is located on the left-hand side front of the engine compartment.

3 Lift off the battery plastic cover, and then disconnect the negative terminal lead from the battery (see illustration).

4 Lift up the quick-release lever (coloured red) and remove the positive battery lead from the battery (see illustration).

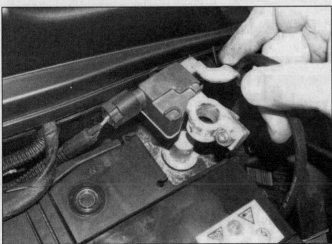
4.3 Disconnect the negative earth connection

4.4 Lift up the quick-release lever and disconnect the positive lead

4.5 Use a half-inch extension bar to undo the battery securing clamp (arrowed)

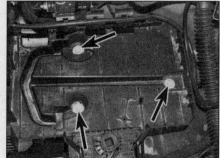

4.7a Undo the battery tray bolts (arrowed) . . .

4.7b . . . release the wiring loom securing clips . . .

4.7c . . . unclip the battery cable . . .

4.7d . . and then remove the battery tray

5 Turn the battery retaining clamp locking ring anti-clockwise a quarter of a turn, using a half-inch extension bar, to release the battery from the tray **(see illustration)**.
6 Lift the battery out of the engine compartment.
7 To remove the battery tray, slacken the three retaining bolts in the top of the battery tray, and then release the wiring loom and cables from the side of the tray, then withdraw it from the engine compartment **(see illustrations)**. Note the fitted position of the wiring loom and cables for refitting.

Refitting

8 Refitting is a reversal of removal, but smear petroleum jelly on the terminals after reconnecting the leads.
9 With the battery reconnected, switch on the ignition and wait at least 1 minute before

starting the engine. This will allow the vehicle electronic systems and control modules to stabilise. Also refer to Chapter 12, Section 20, on models with the anti-theft alarm system.

5 Charging system – testing

Note: *Refer to the warnings given in 'Safety first!' and in Section 1 of this Chapter before starting work.*
1 If the ignition warning light fails to illuminate when the ignition is switched on, first check the alternator wiring connections for security. If satisfactory, check that the warning light has not blown, and that the LED is secure in its location in the instrument panel. If the light still fails to illuminate, check the continuity of the warning light feed wire from the alternator to

the instrument panel. If all is satisfactory, the alternator is at fault and should be renewed or taken to an auto-electrician for testing and repair.
2 If the ignition warning light illuminates when the engine is running, stop the engine and check that the drivebelt is correctly fitted and tensioned (see Section 6) and that the alternator connections are secure. If all is so far satisfactory, have the alternator checked by an auto-electrician for testing and repair.
3 If the alternator output is suspect even though the warning light functions correctly, the regulated voltage may be checked as follows.
4 Connect a voltmeter across the battery terminals and start the engine.
5 Increase the engine speed until the voltmeter reading remains steady; the reading should be approximately 12 to 13 volts, and no more than 14 volts.
6 Switch on as many electrical accessories (eg, the headlights, heated rear window and heater blower) as possible, and check that the alternator maintains the regulated voltage of around 13 to 14 volts.
7 If the regulated voltage is not as stated, the fault may be due to worn brushes, weak brush springs, a faulty voltage regulator, a faulty diode, a severed phase winding or worn or damaged slip-rings. The alternator should be renewed or taken to an auto-electrician for testing and repair.

6 Auxiliary (alternator) drivebelt – removal, refitting and tensioning

1 Chock the rear wheels, raise the front of the vehicle and support it securely on axle stands (see *Jacking and vehicle support*). Remove the right-hand front roadwheel.
2 Undo the fasteners and remove the right-hand front wheel arch liner. Note the rear of the liner is retained by an expanding plastic rivet, accessible once the mudflap (where fitted) has been removed.
3 If the belt is to be refitted, mark its direction of normal rotation with a pen.
4 Using a spanner on the centre bolt, rotate the tensioner pulley, and slacken the belt **(see illustrations)**.

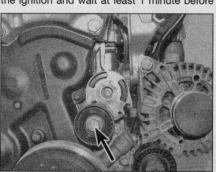

6.4a Rotate the tensioner clockwise with a spanner on the bolt (arrowed) – 1.6 litre engine

6.4b Use a spanner (arrowed) on the bolt to rotate the tensioner anti-clockwise – 2.0 litre engine

6.5a Insert a 4.0 mm drill bit/rod through the holes in the tensioner (arrowed) – 1.6 litre engine

6.5a Insert a 4.0 mm drill bit/rod through the holes in the tensioner (arrowed) – 2.0 litre engine

6.7a Belt routing – 1.6 litre engines with air-conditioning

1 Tensioner pulley bolt
2 Crankshaft pulley
3 Air conditioning compressor pulley
4 Idler pulley
5 Alternator pulley
6 Power steering pump pulley

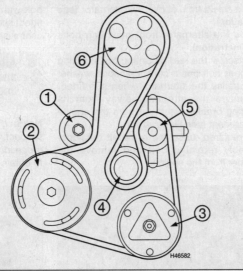

6.7b View of the auxiliary belt routing – 1.6 litre engines with air conditioning

5 Lock the tensioner in this position using a 4.0 mm drill bit through the holes in the tensioner **(see illustrations)**.
6 Manoeuvre the belt from the pulleys. Take the opportunity to check the tensioner and idler pulleys spin freely, with no signs of roughness or slack.
7 Begin refitting by placing the belt on the pulleys, ensuring it's correctly located in grooves of the pulleys **(see illustrations)**.
8 Hold the tensioner in place with the spanner, remove the locking drill bit, and slowly allow the tensioner pulley to rotate anti-clockwise and act against the belt. The belt is automatically tensioned by the spring-loaded tensioner.
9 Refit the wheel arch liner and roadwheel, and then lower the vehicle to the ground.

7 Alternator –
removal and refitting

Removal

1 Disconnect the battery (see Section 4).
2 Remove the auxiliary drivebelt as described in the previous Section.
3 Remove the rubber cover from the alternator

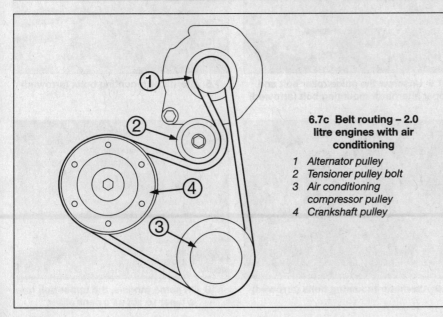

6.7c Belt routing – 2.0 litre engines with air conditioning

1 Alternator pulley
2 Tensioner pulley bolt
3 Air conditioning compressor pulley
4 Crankshaft pulley

7.3a Prise out the rubber cover, then disconnect the alternator wiring connector (arrowed)

7.3b Disconnect the wiring plug connector . . .

7.3c . . . and release the wiring clip (arrowed) from the rear of the alternator

terminal(s), then unscrew the retaining nut(s) and disconnect the wiring from the rear of the alternator **(see illustrations)**. Prise out the retaining clip to release the wiring harness routed around the left-hand end of the alternator.

1.6 litre models

4 Undo the retaining clips and remove the air inlet hoses from the front of the engine compartment **(see illustration)**.
5 Undo the alternator front lower mounting bolt **(see illustration)**, which also secures the idler roller, and remove the idler roller from the mounting bracket.
6 Unscrew the remaining mounting bolts and manoeuvre the alternator away from its mounting brackets and out from the engine compartment **(see illustration)**.
7 If required, undo the drivebelt tensioner

assembly retaining bolt and remove the tensioner from the engine.

2.0 litre models

8 Undo the three retaining screws, unclip the filter drain tube and remove the plastic fuel spillage shield from above the alternator **(see illustration)**.
9 Undo the alternator front mounting bolts **(see illustration)**.
10 Unscrew the rear mounting bolts; noting the upper bolt has a conical-shaped washer to centralise the alternator when it is fitted. Manoeuvre the alternator away from its mounting brackets and out from the engine compartment **(see illustration)**.
11 If required, undo the drivebelt tensioner assembly retaining bolt and remove the tensioner from the engine.

Refitting

12 Refitting is a reversal of removal, tensioning the auxiliary drivebelt as described in the previous Section. Ensure that the alternator mountings are securely tightened and the rear bolt with the conical-shaped washer (where fitted) should be tightened first, as it acts as a centraliser.

8 Alternator brushes, regulator and drive pulley – inspection and renewal

Note: *If the alternator is thought to be suspect, check on the cost of repairs before proceeding, as it may prove more economical to obtain a new or exchange alternator.*

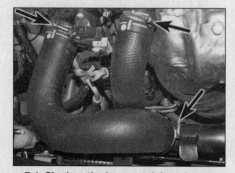

7.4 Slacken the hose retaining clamps (arrowed)

7.5 Unscrew the guide roller bolt and upper alternator mounting bolt (arrowed)

7.6 Alternator mounting bolts (arrowed)

7.8 Remove the plastic shield from above the alternator

7.9 Alternator mounting bolts (arrowed)

7.10 On some models, the upper bolt has a taper to act as a centraliser

8.2 Undo the screws/nuts (arrowed) and remove the cover from the alternator

8.4 Undo the bolts (arrowed) and remove the regulator/brush holder

Brushes and regulator

1 Remove the alternator as described in Section 7.

2 Unscrew the nuts/screws securing the cover to the rear of the alternator **(see illustration)**.

3 Using a screwdriver, lever off the cover, and remove it from the rear of the alternator.

4 Unscrew and remove the three retaining screws, and remove the regulator/brush holder from the rear of the alternator **(see illustration)**.

5 Check the brushes for excessive wear and damage. No specifications for brush length are given by Peugeot. If the brushes are suspect, renew them along with the regulator as a complete assembly.

6 If the brushes are in good condition, clean them and check that they move freely in their holders.

7 Wipe clean the alternator slip-rings, and check them for signs of scoring or burning **(see illustration)**. It may be possible to have the slip-rings renovated by an electrical specialist.

8 Use a paper clip to restrain the brushes, then refit the regulator/brush holder assembly and securely tighten the retaining screws **(see illustration)**.

8.7 Check the condition of the alternator slip-rings

9 Refit the cover, then insert and tighten the retaining screws/nuts.

10 Refit the alternator with reference to Section 7.

Drive pulley

11 The alternator drive pulley is fitted with a one-way clutch to reduce wear and stress on the auxiliary drivebelt. In order to remove the pulley, a special tool will be required to hold the alternator shaft whilst unscrewing the pulley. This tool should be available from

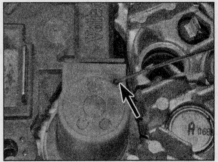

8.8 Use a screwdriver to push back the brushes against the springs, then insert a thin rod (arrowed) as shown to hold them in place

auto electrical specialists/automotive tool specialists.

12 Prise the plastic cap from the pulley.

13 Insert the special tool into the splines of the pulley, engaging the central Torx bit with the alternator shaft **(see illustrations)**. Unscrew the pulley anti-clockwise whilst holding the shaft with the Torx bit, and remove the pulley.

14 Fit the pulley to the alternator shaft, and tighten it securely using the special tool.

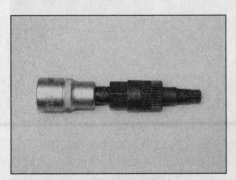

8.13a A special tool is required to remove the alternator pulley

8.13b Insert the central Torx bit into the end of the alternator shaft, unscrew the pulley . . .

8.13c . . . and remove it from the shaft

9.3 Check the earth strap bolt (arrowed) on the top of the transmission

9 Starting system – testing

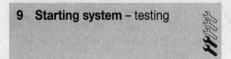

Note: *Refer to the precautions given in 'Safety first!' and in Section 1 of this Chapter before starting work.*

1 If the starter motor fails to operate when the ignition key is turned to the appropriate position, the following possible causes may be to blame.

a) *The engine immobiliser is faulty.*
b) *The battery is faulty.*
c) *The electrical connections between the switch, solenoid, battery and starter motor are somewhere failing to pass the necessary current from the battery through the starter to earth.*
d) *The solenoid is faulty.*
e) *The starter motor is mechanically or electrically defective.*

2 To check the battery, switch on the headlights. If they dim after a few seconds, this indicates that the battery is discharged – recharge (see Section 3) or renew the battery. If the headlights glow brightly, operate the ignition switch and observe the lights. If they

dim, then this indicates that current is reaching the starter motor; therefore the fault must lie in the starter motor. If the lights continue to glow brightly (and no clicking sound can be heard from the starter motor solenoid), this indicates that there is a fault in the circuit or solenoid – see following paragraphs. If the starter motor turns slowly when operated, but the battery is in good condition, then this indicates that either the starter motor is faulty, or there is considerable resistance somewhere in the circuit.

3 If a fault in the circuit is suspected, disconnect the battery leads (including the earth connection to the body), the starter/solenoid wiring and the engine/transmission earth strap – located on the top of the transmission housing **(see illustration)**. Thoroughly clean the connections and reconnect the leads and wiring, then use a voltmeter or test lamp to check that full battery voltage is available at the battery positive lead connection to the solenoid, and that the earth is sound. Smear petroleum jelly around the battery terminals after connection to prevent corrosion – corroded connections are amongst the most frequent causes of electrical system faults.

4 If the battery and all connections are in good condition, check the circuit by disconnecting the wire from the solenoid blade terminal. Connect a voltmeter or test lamp between the wire end and a good earth (such as the battery negative terminal), and check that the wire is live when the ignition switch is turned to the 'start' position. If it is, then the circuit is sound – if not the circuit wiring can be checked as described in Chapter 12.

5 The solenoid contacts can be checked by connecting a voltmeter or test lamp between the battery positive feed connection on the starter side of the solenoid, and earth. When

the ignition switch is turned to the 'start' position, there should be a reading or lighted bulb, as applicable. If there is no reading or lighted bulb, the solenoid is faulty and should be renewed.

6 If the circuit and solenoid are proved sound, the fault must lie in the starter motor. In this event, it may be possible to have the starter motor overhauled by a specialist, but check on the cost of spares before proceeding, as it may prove more economical to obtain a new or exchange motor.

10 Starter motor – removal and refitting

Removal

1 Disconnect the battery (see Section 4).

1.6 litre models

2 So that access to the motor can be gained both from above and below, apply the handbrake then jack up the front of the vehicle and support it on axle stands (see *Jacking and vehicle support*). Release the screws and remove the engine undershield (where fitted).

3 Remove the air cleaner housing and inlet hoses as described in Chapter 4A.

4 Undo the retaining bolt and remove the vacuum reservoir from below the starter motor, on the rear of the engine **(see illustration)**.

5 Slacken and remove the two retaining nuts and disconnect the wiring from the starter motor solenoid. Recover the washers under the nuts **(see illustration)**.

6 Where applicable, to allow for more movement of the starter motor cables, undo the bolt securing the wiring loom support plate above the starter motor **(see illustration)**.

10.4 Vacuum reservoir retaining bolt (arrowed) – 1.6 litre engines

10.5 Disconnect the starter motor wiring (arrowed)

10.6 Undo the bolt (arrowed) securing the wiring loom support bracket

10.7 Starter motor mounting bolts (arrowed)

10.10 Disconnect the starter motor wiring (arrowed)

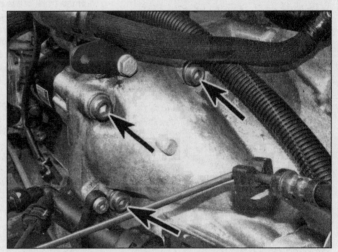

10.11 Undo the starter motor mounting bolts (arrowed) . . .

7 Undo the three mounting bolts (two at the rear of the motor, and one which comes through from the top of the transmission housing) supporting the motor as the bolts are withdrawn. Recover the washers from under the bolt heads and note the locations of any wiring or hose brackets secured by the bolts **(see illustration)**.

8 Manoeuvre the starter motor out from underneath the engine, if required recover the locating dowel(s) from the motor/transmission.

2.0 litre models

9 Remove the air cleaner housing and inlet hoses as described in Chapter 4A.

10 Slacken and remove the two retaining nuts and disconnect the wiring from the starter motor solenoid. Recover the washers under the nuts **(see illustration)**.

11 Undo the three mounting bolts, supporting the motor as the bolts are withdrawn. Recover the washers from under the bolt heads as they are removed **(see illustration)**.

12 Manoeuvre the starter motor out from

bellhousing, if required recover the locating dowel(s) from the motor/transmission **(see illustration)**.

Refitting

13 Refitting is a reversal of removal, ensuring that the locating dowel(s) are correctly positioned. Also make sure that any wiring or hose brackets are in place as noted prior to removal.

11 Starter motor – testing and overhaul

If the starter motor is thought to be suspect, it should be removed from the vehicle and taken to an auto-electrician for testing. Most auto-electricians will be able to supply and fit brushes at a reasonable cost. However, check on the cost of repairs before proceeding, as it may prove more economical to obtain a new or exchange motor.

12 Ignition switch – removal and refitting

The ignition switch is integral with the steering column lock, and can be removed as described in Chapter 10.

10.12 . . . and withdraw the starter motor from the bellhousing

13.1a The oil pressure switch location (arrowed) – 2.0 litre engines . . .

13.1b . . . or at the front, right-hand end of the cylinder block – 1.6 litre engine

13.3 Unscrew the pressure switch from the housing

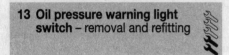

13 Oil pressure warning light switch – removal and refitting

Removal

1 The switch is fitted at the front of the cylinder block, in the following locations (see illustrations):

14.2 Oil level sensor – 2.0 litre engine

1.6 litre engines
Adjacent to the oil dipstick guide tube at the front right-hand side of the engine.
2.0 litre engines
Screwed into the base of the oil filter housing at the front of the engine.

Note that on some models access to the switch may be improved if the vehicle is jacked up and supported on axle stands, and the engine undershield removed, so that the switch can be reached from underneath the vehicle (see *Jacking and vehicle support*).
2 Remove the protective sleeve from the wiring plug (where applicable), and then disconnect the wiring from the switch.
3 Unscrew the switch from the cylinder block/filter housing, and recover the sealing washer (see illustration). Be prepared for oil spillage, and if the switch is to be left removed from the engine for any length of time, plug the hole in the cylinder block.

Refitting

4 Examine the sealing washer for signs of damage or deterioration and if necessary renew.
5 Refit the switch, complete with washer, and tighten it securely. Reconnect the wiring connector.
6 Lower the vehicle to the ground, and then check, and if necessary, top-up the engine oil as described in *Weekly checks*.

14 Oil level sensor – removal and refitting

1 The sensor is fitted in the following locations:
1.6 litre engines
Rear side of the cylinder block, between cylinders 2 and 3.
2.0 litre engines
Front side of the upper edge of the sump, below the starter motor.

2 The removal and refitting procedure is as described for the oil pressure switch in Section 13. Access is most easily obtained from underneath the vehicle (see illustration).

Chapter 5 Part B:
Pre/post-heating system

Contents

Degrees of difficulty

Easy, suitable for novice with little experience	Fairly easy, suitable for beginner with some experience	Fairly difficult, suitable for competent DIY mechanic	Difficult, suitable for experienced DIY mechanic	Very difficult, suitable for expert DIY or professional

Specifications

Preheating system

Preheating period at ambient temperatures of (approximate values):

-30° C	20 seconds
-10° C	5 seconds
0° C	0.5 seconds
18° C	0 seconds

Post-heating system

Post-heating period at ambient temperatures of (approximate values):

-30° C	3 minutes
-10° C	3 minutes
0° C	1 minutes
18° C	30 seconds
40° C	0 seconds

Torque wrench settings

	Nm	lbf ft
Glow plugs:		
1.6 litre engines	10	7
2.0 litre engines	22	16

1 Pre/post-heating system – description and testing

Description

1 To assist cold starting, diesel engines are fitted with a preheating system, which consists of four of glow plugs (one per cylinder), a glow plug relay unit, a facia-mounted warning lamp, the engine management ECM, and the associated electrical wiring.

2 The glow plugs are miniature electric heating elements, encapsulated in a metal case with a probe at one end and electrical connection at the other. Each combustion chamber has one glow plug threaded into it, with the tip of the glow plug probe positioned directly in line with incoming spray of fuel from the injectors. When the glow plug is energised, it heats up rapidly, causing the fuel passing over the glow plug probe to be heated to its optimum temperature, ready for combustion. In addition, some of the fuel passing over the glow plugs is ignited and this helps to trigger the combustion process.

3 The preheating system begins to operate as soon as the ignition key is switched to the second position, but only if the engine coolant temperature is below 20° C and the engine is turned at more than 70 rpm for 0.2 seconds. A facia-mounted warning lamp informs the driver that preheating is taking place. The lamp extinguishes when sufficient preheating has taken place to allow the engine to be started, but power will still be supplied to the glow plugs for a further period until the engine is started. If no attempt is made to start the engine, the power supply to the glow plugs is switched off after 10 seconds, to prevent battery drain and glow plug burn-out.

4 With the electronically-controlled diesel injection systems fitted to models in this manual, the glow plug relay unit is controlled by the engine management system ECM, which determines the necessary preheating time based on inputs from the various system sensors. The system monitors the temperature of the inlet air, and then alters the preheating time (the length for which the glow plugs are supplied with current) to suit the conditions.

5 Post-heating takes place after the ignition key has been released from the 'start' position, but only if the engine coolant temperature is below 20° C, the injected fuel flow is less than a certain rate, and the engine speed is less than 2000 rpm. The glow plugs continue to operate for a maximum of 60 seconds, helping to improve fuel combustion whilst the engine is warming-up, resulting in quieter, smoother running and reduced exhaust emissions.

Testing

6 If the system malfunctions, testing is ultimately by substitution of known good units, but some preliminary checks may be made as follows.

7 Connect a voltmeter or 12 volt test lamp between the glow plug supply cable and earth (engine or vehicle metal). Make sure that the live connection is kept clear of the engine and bodywork.

8 Have an assistant switch on the ignition, and check that voltage is applied to the glow plugs. Note the time for which the warning light is lit, and the total time for which voltage is applied before the system cuts out. Switch off the ignition.

9 Compare the results with the information given in the Specifications. Warning light time will increase with lower temperatures and decrease with higher temperatures.

10 If there is no supply at all, the control module or associated wiring is at fault.

11 To gain access to the glow plugs for further testing, remove the following components, according to model:

1.6 litre engine
Remove the cylinder head cover/manifold assembly as described in Chapter 2A.

2.0 litre engine
Working as described in Chapter 4B, undo the bolts and move the EGR heat exchanger and valve assembly to one side.

12 Disconnect the main supply cable and the interconnecting wire or strap from the top of the glow plugs. Be careful not to drop the nuts and washers.

13 Use a continuity tester, or a 12 volt test lamp connected to the battery positive terminal, to check for continuity between each glow plug terminal and earth. The resistance of a glow plug in good condition is very low

(less than 1 ohm), so if the test lamp does not light or the continuity tester shows a high resistance, the glow plug is certainly defective.

14 If an ammeter is available, the current draw of each glow plug can be checked. After an initial surge of 15 to 20 amps, each plug should draw 12 amps. Any plug which draws much more or less than this is probably defective.

15 As a final check, the glow plugs can be removed and inspected as described in the following Section. On completion, refit any components removed for access.

2 Glow plugs – removal, inspection and refitting

Caution: If the preheating system has just been energised, or if the engine has been running, the glow plugs will be very hot.

Removal

1 Ensure the ignition is turned off. To gain access to the glow plugs, remove the components described in Section 1, paragraph 11, according to engine.

2 Unscrew the nuts from the glow plug terminals, and recover the washers **(see illustration)**.

3 Where applicable, carefully move any obstructing pipes or wires to one side to enable access to the relevant glow plug(s).

4 Unscrew the glow plug(s) and remove from the cylinder head **(see illustrations)**.

Inspection

5 Inspect each glow plug for physical damage. Burnt or eroded glow plug tips can be caused by a bad injector spray pattern. Have the injectors checked if this sort of damage is found.

6 If the glow plugs are in good physical condition, check them electrically using a 12 volt test lamp or continuity tester as described in the previous Section.

7 The glow plugs can be energised by applying 12 volts to them to verify that they heat up evenly and in the required time. Observe the following precautions.

a) Support the glow plug by clamping it

2.2 Undo the nuts (arrowed) securing the glow plug connections

2.4a Unscrew the glow plugs (arrowed) from the cylinder head – 1.6 litre engine

2.4b Unscrew the glow plugs from the cylinder head – 2.0 litre engine

3.3 Remove the electronic control module (ECM)

3.4 Undo the retaining screw (arrowed)

carefully in a vice or self-locking pliers. Remember it will become red-hot.
b) Make sure that the power supply or test lead incorporates a fuse or overload trip to protect against damage from a short circuit.
c) After testing, allow the glow plug to cool for several minutes before attempting to handle it.

8 A glow plug in good condition will start to glow red at the tip after drawing current for 5 seconds or so. Any plug that takes much longer to start glowing, or which starts glowing in the middle instead of at the tip is defective.

Refitting

9 Refit by reversing the removal operations. Apply a smear of copper-based anti-seize compound to the plug threads and tighten the glow plugs to the specified torque. Do not overtighten, as this can damage the glow plug element.

10 Refit any components removed for access.

3 Pre/post-heating system relay unit – removal and refitting

Removal

1 The relay unit is located in the electrical box on the left-hand side of the engine compartment. Undo the fasteners and remove the electrical box lid.
2 Disconnect the battery (see Chapter 5A).
3 Undo the 2 Torx bolts and remove the ECM to one side (see illustration). Note there is no need to disconnect the ECM wiring plugs. See Chapter 4A, Section 12, for removal refitting procedure of the ECM.
4 Unscrew the retaining Torx bolt securing the unit to the bottom of the electrical box (see illustration).

5 Lift out the unit, release the wiring connector locking clip and disconnect the wiring plug from the relay (see illustration).

Refitting

6 Refitting is a reversal of removal, ensuring that the wiring connectors are correctly connected.

3.5 Release the locking clip and disconnect the wiring plug

Chapter 6
Clutch

Contents

Degrees of difficulty

Easy, suitable for novice with little experience	Fairly easy, suitable for beginner with some experience	Fairly difficult, suitable for competent DIY mechanic	Difficult, suitable for experienced DIY mechanic	Very difficult, suitable for expert DIY or professional

Specifications

Engine identification

1.6 litre:
    Designation. DV6TED4
    Engine codes . . . . 9HY or 9HZ
2.0 litre:
    Designation. . . . . DW10BTED4 or DW10CTED4
    Engine codes:
      DW10BTED4. . . . . RHF, RHL or RHR
      DW10CTED4. . . . . RHH

Type

All models. . . . . Single dry disc with diaphragm spring, hydraulic operation

Clutch operation

All models. . . . . Hydraulic
Type:
    1.6 litre engines . . . . Push type clutch
    2.0 litre engines . . . . Push type clutch with wear compensation

Flywheel

Type . . . . Double 'damping' flywheel

Friction disc diameter

1.0 litre engines . . . . 228 mm
2.0 litre engines:
    DW10BTED4. . . . . 235 mm
    DW10CTED4 . . . . 242 mm

Torque wrench settings

	Nm	lbf ft
Clutch slave cylinder bolts	20	15
Pressure plate retaining bolts.	20	15

1 General information

The clutch consists of a friction disc, a pressure plate assembly, a release bearing and release fork; all of these components are contained in the large cast-aluminium alloy bellhousing, sandwiched between the engine and the transmission. The release mechanism is hydraulic on all models.

The friction disc is fitted between the engine flywheel and the clutch pressure plate, and is allowed to slide on the transmission input shaft splines.

The pressure plate assembly is bolted to the engine flywheel. When the engine is running, drive is transmitted from the crankshaft, via the flywheel, to the friction disc (these components being clamped securely together by the pressure plate assembly) and from the friction disc to the transmission input shaft.

To interrupt the drive, the spring pressure must be relaxed. This is done by means of the clutch release bearing, fitted concentrically around the transmission input shaft. The bearing is pushed onto the pressure plate assembly by means of the release fork actuated by clutch slave cylinder pushrod.

The clutch pedal is connected to the clutch master cylinder by a short pushrod. The master cylinder is mounted on the engine side of the bulkhead in front of the driver and receives its hydraulic fluid supply from the brake master cylinder reservoir. Depressing the clutch pedal moves the piston in the master cylinder forwards, so forcing hydraulic fluid through the hydraulic pipe to the slave cylinder. The piston in the slave cylinder moves forward on the entry of the fluid and actuates the clutch release fork by means of a short pushrod. The release fork pivots on its mounting stud, and the other end of

the fork then presses the release bearing against the pressure plate spring fingers. This causes the springs to deform and releases the clamping force on the pressure plate.

Adjustment of the clutch to compensate for wear of the friction disc linings is automatically taken up by the self-adjusting hydraulic clutch components. On some models, a self-adjusting clutch (SAC) is fitted, where an adjustment ring rotates in the pressure plate assembly, adjusting the diaphragm spring fingers pivot points as the friction disc wears. This maintains the clutch pedal 'bite point'.

2 Clutch hydraulic system – bleeding

⚠️ **Warning: Hydraulic fluid is poisonous; wash off immediately and thoroughly in the case of skin contact, and seek immediate medical advice if any fluid is swallowed or gets into the eyes. Certain types of hydraulic fluid are inflammable, and may ignite when allowed into contact with hot components; when servicing any hydraulic system, it is safest to assume that the fluid IS inflammable, and to take precautions against the risk of fire as though it is petrol that is being handled. Hydraulic fluid is also an effective paint stripper, and will attack plastics. If any is spilt, it should be washed off immediately, using copious quantities of clean water. When topping-up or renewing the fluid, always use the recommended type, and ensure that it comes from a freshly-opened sealed container.**

1 Obtain a clean jar, a suitable length of rubber or clear plastic tubing, which is a tight fit over the bleed screw on the clutch slave cylinder, and a tin of the specified hydraulic fluid. The help of an assistant will also be

required. (If a one-man do-it-yourself bleeding kit for bleeding the brake hydraulic system is available, this can be used quite satisfactorily for the clutch also. Full information on the use of these kits may be found in Chapter 9.)

2 On 2.0 litre models, remove the air cleaner housing as described in Chapter 4A. On 1.6 litre models, undo the securing clips and remove the air inlet pipe from the front of the engine compartment **(see illustration)**.

3 Remove the filler cap from the brake master cylinder reservoir, and if necessary top-up the fluid. Keep the reservoir topped-up during subsequent operations.

4 Remove the dust cap from the slave cylinder bleed screw, located on the lower front facing side of the transmission **(see illustration)**.

5 Connect one end of the bleed tube to the bleed screw, and insert the other end of the tube in the jar containing sufficient clean hydraulic fluid to keep the end of the tube submerged.

6 Open the bleed screw half a turn and have your assistant depress the clutch pedal and then slowly release it. Continue this procedure until clean hydraulic fluid, free from air bubbles, emerges from the tube. Now tighten the bleed screw at the end of a down stroke. Make sure that the brake master cylinder reservoir is checked frequently to ensure that the level does not drop too far, allowing air into the system.

7 Check the operation of the clutch pedal. After a few strokes it should feel normal. Any sponginess would indicate air still present in the system.

8 On completion remove the bleed tube and refit the dust cover. Top-up the master cylinder reservoir if necessary and refit the cap. Fluid expelled from the hydraulic system should now be discarded, as it will be contaminated with moisture, air and dirt, making it unsuitable for further use.

2.2 Remove the air ducting from the engine compartment

2.4 Remove the dust cap from the bleed screw

3.1 Unclip the trim panel from under the facia

3.2 Prise the end of the pushrod (arrowed) from the pedal pin

3 Clutch master cylinder – removal and refitting

Note: *Before starting work, refer to the note at the beginning of Section 2 concerning the dangers of hydraulic fluid.*

Removal

1 Release the securing clips and remove the trim panel from above the pedals **(see illustration)**.
2 Release the securing clips, and then using a flat-bladed screwdriver, prise the master cylinder pushrod end from the pedal pin **(see illustration)**.
3 Working in the engine compartment, remove the brake master cylinder reservoir filler cap then tighten it down onto a piece of polythene to obtain an airtight seal. This will minimise hydraulic fluid loss from the supply pipe as it is removed from the master cylinder.

4 Place absorbent rags under the clutch master cylinder pipe connections in the engine compartment and be prepared for hydraulic fluid loss.
5 Release the master cylinder hydraulic pressure pipe from its retaining clips on the engine compartment bulkhead, then prise out the retaining wire clip and disconnect the pipe from the master cylinder **(see illustration)**. Suitably plug or cap the pipe end to prevent further fluid loss and dirt entry.
6 Disconnect the hydraulic fluid supply hose from the top of the clutch master cylinder, suitably plug or cap the hose end.
7 Rotate the master cylinder 45° clockwise, and withdraw it from the bulkhead **(see illustration)**.

Refitting

8 Refitting the master cylinder is the reverse sequence to removal, bearing in mind the following points.
  a) *Ensure all retaining clips are correctly refitted.*

  b) *Remove the piece of polythene from the top of the reservoir.*
  c) *Bleed the clutch hydraulic system as described in Section 2 on completion.*

4 Clutch slave cylinder – removal and refitting

Note: *Before starting work, refer to the note at the beginning of Section 2 concerning the dangers of hydraulic fluid.*

Removal

1 Remove the brake master cylinder reservoir filler cap then tighten it down onto a piece of polythene to obtain an airtight seal. This will minimise hydraulic fluid loss from the supply pipe as it is removed from the slave cylinder.
2 On 2.0 litre models, remove the air cleaner housing as described in Chapter 4A. On 1.6 litre models, undo the securing clips and

3.5 Prise out the securing clip (arrowed)

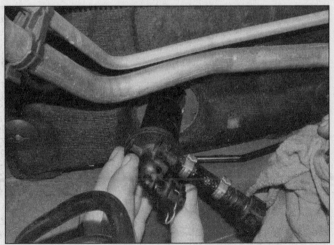

3.7 Turn the master cylinder 90° clockwise, and remove it from the bulkhead

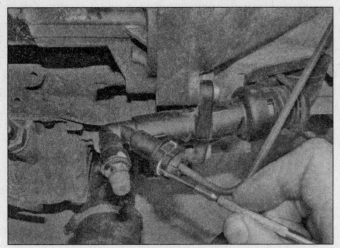

4.5 Lever out the hydraulic pipe retaining clip

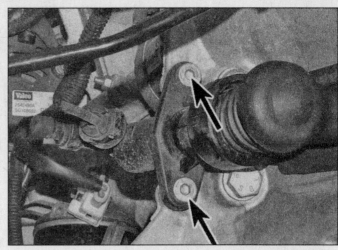

4.6 Undo the two bolts (arrowed) and remove the clutch slave cylinder

5.4 Use a cable-tie (arrowed) to secure the spring assembly together

5.5 Withdraw the spring assembly out from the pedal

remove the air inlet pipe from the front of the engine compartment (see illustration 2.2).

3 Place absorbent rags under the clutch slave cylinder located on the lower front facing side of the transmission. Be prepared for hydraulic fluid loss.

4 Where necessary for better access, release the wiring harness from the retaining clips and move the harness clear of the slave cylinder.

5 Lever out the retaining clip a little, and then disconnect the hydraulic pipe from the side of the slave cylinder (see illustration). Suitably plug or cap the pipe end to prevent further fluid loss and dirt entry.

6 Undo the two retaining bolts and remove the cylinder from the transmission housing (see illustration).

Refitting

7 Refitting the slave cylinder is the reverse sequence to removal, bearing in mind the following points.

a) Apply a little Molykote BR2 Plus grease to the end of the slave cylinder pushrod.
b) Bleed the clutch hydraulic system as described in Section 2 on completion.

5 Clutch pedal – removal and refitting

Removal

1 Release the securing clips and remove the trim panel from above the pedals (see illustration 3.1).

2 Release the securing clips, and then using a flat-bladed screwdriver, prise the master cylinder pushrod end from the pedal pin (see illustration 3.2).

3 Remove the brake pedal upper pivot bolt and move the brake pedal to one side to access the clutch pedal pivot bolt. Refer to Chapter 9 for further information on brake pedal removal.

4 Fasten a cable-tie around the clutch pedal return spring to prevent it coming apart when removed (see illustration).

5 Move the clutch pedal and remove the clutch return spring from the locating pegs (see illustration).

6 Undo the nut from the clutch pedal pivot bolt and withdraw the bolt (see illustration).

5.6 Clutch pedal pivot bolt retaining nut (arrowed)

7 Remove the clutch pedal from the pedal bracket and recover the bush (where applicable) from the pedal pivot.

8 Check the condition of the pedal, pivot bush and return spring assembly and renew any components as necessary.

Refitting

9 Lubricate the pedal pivot bolt with multipurpose grease, then locate the pedal in the bracket and insert the pivot bolt. Refit the pivot bolt nut and tighten it securely.

10 Reconnect the return spring to the pedal and pedal bracket, making sure it locates correctly **(see illustration)**. Cut the cable-tie from around the spring, once it is in its fitted position.

11 Reconnect the clutch master cylinder pushrod to the clutch pedal.

12 Refit the brake pedal pivot bolt, with reference to Chapter 9.

13 Depress the pedal two or three times and check the operation of the clutch release mechanism.

14 Refit the facia lower trim panel and secure with the plastic clips.

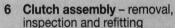

6	Clutch assembly – removal, inspection and refitting

⚠️ *Warning: Dust created by clutch wear and deposited on the clutch components may contain asbestos, which is a health hazard. DO NOT blow it out with compressed air, nor inhale any of it. DO NOT use petrol or petroleum-based solvents to clean off the dust. Brake system cleaner or methylated spirit should be used to flush the dust into a suitable receptacle. After the clutch components are wiped clean with rags, dispose of the contaminated rags and cleaner in a sealed, marked container.*

5.10 Spring locating pegs (arrowed) on the pedal bracket

Note: *Although most friction materials no longer contain asbestos, it is safest to assume that some still do, and to take precautions accordingly.*

Removal

1 Unless the complete engine/transmission unit is to be removed from the car and separated for major overhaul (see Chapter 2C), the clutch can be reached by removing the transmission as described in Chapter 7A.

2 Before disturbing the clutch, use chalk or a marker pen to mark the relationship of the pressure plate assembly to the flywheel **(see illustration)**.

3 Working in a diagonal sequence, slacken the pressure plate bolts by half a turn at a time, until spring pressure is released and the bolts can be unscrewed by hand **(see illustration)**.

4 Prise the pressure plate assembly off its locating dowels, and collect the friction disc, noting which way round the disc is fitted.

Inspection

Note: *Due to the amount of work necessary to remove and refit clutch components, it is considered good practice to renew the clutch friction disc, pressure plate assembly*

and release bearing as a matched set, even if only one of these is worn enough to require renewal. It is worth considering the renewal of the clutch components on a preventative basis if the engine and/or transmission have been removed for some other reason.

5 When cleaning clutch components, read first the warning at the beginning of this Section; remove dust using a clean, dry cloth, and working in a well-ventilated atmosphere.

6 Check the friction disc facings for signs of wear, damage or oil contamination. If the friction material is cracked, burnt, scored or damaged, or if it is contaminated with oil or grease (shown by shiny black patches), the friction disc must be renewed.

7 If the friction material is still serviceable, check that the centre boss splines are unworn, that the torsion springs are in good condition and securely fastened, and that all the rivets are tight. If any wear or damage is found, the friction disc must be renewed.

8 If the friction material is fouled with oil, this must be due to an oil leak from the crankshaft left-hand oil seal, from the sump-to-cylinder block joint, or from the transmission input shaft. Renew the seal or repair the joint, as appropriate, as described in the relevant Part of Chapter 2 or 7, before installing the new friction disc.

9 Check the pressure plate assembly for obvious signs of wear or damage; shake it to check for loose rivets or worn or damaged fulcrum rings, and check that the drive straps securing the pressure plate to the cover do not show signs of overheating (such as a deep yellow or blue discoloration). If the diaphragm spring is worn or damaged, or if its pressure is in any way suspect, the pressure plate assembly should be renewed.

10 Examine the machined bearing surfaces of the pressure plate and of the flywheel; they should be clean, completely flat, and free from scratches or scoring. If either is discoloured from excessive heat, or shows signs of

6.2 Mark the position of the pressure plate on the flywheel

6.3 Undo the pressure plate bolts (arrowed)

6.13a Fit the disc so the spring hub assembly faces away from the flywheel . . .

6.13b . . . or the protruding hub away from the flywheel

cracks, it should be renewed – although minor damage of this nature can sometimes be polished away using emery paper.

11 Check that the release bearing contact surface rotates smoothly and easily, with no sign of noise or roughness. Also check that the surface itself is smooth and unworn, with no signs of cracks, pitting or scoring. If there is any doubt about its condition, the bearing must be renewed.

Refitting

12 On reassembly, ensure that the bearing surfaces of the flywheel and pressure plate are completely clean, smooth, and free from oil or grease. Use solvent to remove any protective grease from new components.

13 Fit the friction disc so that its spring hub assembly faces away from the flywheel; there may be a marking showing which way round the disc is to be refitted **(see illustrations)**.

Models with self-adjusting clutch

14 On these models, the clutch pressure plate is unusual, as there is a pre-adjustment mechanism to compensate for wear in the

friction disc (this is termed by Peugeot as a self-adjusting clutch (SAC), which is slightly ambiguous as all clutches fitted to these models are essentially self-adjusting). However, this mechanism must be reset before refitting the pressure plate. A new plate may be supplied preset, in which case this procedure can be ignored.

15 A large diameter bolt (M14 at least) long enough to pass through the pressure plate, a matching nut, and several large diameter washers, will be needed for this procedure. Mount the bolt head in the jaws of a sturdy bench vice, with one large washer fitted.

16 Offer the plate over the bolt, friction disc surface facing down, and locate it centrally over the bolt and washer – the washer should bear on the centre hub **(see illustration)**.

17 Fit several further large washers over the bolt, so that they bear on the ends of the spring fingers, then add the nut and tighten by hand to locate the washers.

18 The purpose of the procedure is to turn the plate's internal adjuster disc so that the three

small coil springs visible on the plate's outer surface are fully compressed. Tighten the nut just fitted until the adjuster disc is free to turn. Using a pair of thin-nosed, or circlip, pliers in one of the two windows in the top surface, open the jaws of the pliers to turn the adjuster disc anti-clockwise, so that the springs are fully compressed **(see illustration)**.

19 Hold the pliers in this position, and then unscrew the centre nut. Once the nut is released, the adjuster disc will be gripped in position, and the pliers can be removed. Take the pressure plate from the vice, and it is ready to fit.

All models

20 Refit the pressure plate assembly, aligning the marks made on dismantling (if the original pressure plate is re-used), and locating the pressure plate on its three locating dowels. Fit the pressure plate bolts, but tighten them only finger-tight, so that the friction disc can still be moved.

21 The friction disc must now be centralised, so that when the transmission is refitted, its

6.16 Using some threaded rod, washers and 2 nuts, compress the spring and the pressure plate together . . .

6.18 . . . then move the adjusting ring (arrowed) anti-clockwise to the stop

6.22 Centralise the friction plate on the flywheel using a clutch aligning tool

7.2 Slide the release bearing from the input shaft

input shaft will pass through the splines at the centre of the friction disc.

22 Centralisation can be achieved by passing a screwdriver or other long bar through the friction disc and into the hole in the crankshaft; the friction disc can then be moved around until it is centred on the crankshaft hole. Alternatively, a clutch-aligning tool can be used to eliminate the guesswork; these can be obtained from most accessory shops **(see illustration)**.

23 When the friction disc is centralised, tighten the pressure plate bolts evenly and in a diagonal sequence to the specified torque setting.

24 Apply a **thin** smear of molybdenum disulphide grease (Peugeot recommend the use of Molykote BR2 Plus – available from your dealer) to the splines of the friction disc and the transmission input shaft, and also to the release bearing bore and release fork shaft.

25 Refit the transmission as described in Chapter 7A.

---

7 Clutch release mechanism – removal, inspection and refitting

Note: *Refer to the warning concerning the* *dangers of asbestos dust at the beginning of Section 7.*

Removal

1 Unless the complete engine/transmission unit is to be removed from the car and separated for major overhaul (see Chapter 2C), the clutch release mechanism can be reached by removing the transmission only, as described in Chapter 7A.

2 Unhook the release bearing from the fork, and slide it off the input shaft **(see illustration)**.

3 Squeeze together the tabs of the retaining clip and pull the release fork off the pivot ball-stud. Recover the shim where fitted. The mounting stud unscrews from the transmission housing **(see illustrations)**.

Inspection

4 Check that the release bearing contact surface rotates smoothly and easily, with no sign of noise or roughness, and that the surface itself is smooth and unworn, with no signs of cracks, pitting or scoring. If there is any doubt about its condition, the bearing must be renewed.

5 Check the bearing surfaces and points of contact on the release fork and pivot ball-stud, renewing any component that is worn or damaged.

Refitting

6 Apply a smear of molybdenum disulphide grease to the pivot ball-stud.

7 Insert the outer end of the release fork through the rubber boot in the side of the transmission bellhousing.

8 Engage the arms of the release fork with the release-bearing collar, then slide the release bearing onto the guide tube.

9 Position the shim over the tabs of the pivot ball-stud clip, then push the fork over the stud, ensuring the tabs of the retaining clip engage correctly with the fork **(see illustration)**.

10 Refit the transmission as described in Chapter 7A.

7.3a Squeeze the tabs of the retaining clip together and remove the release fork . . .

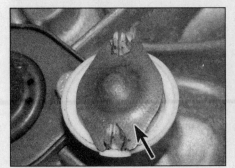

7.3b . . . recover the shim (arrowed) . . .

7.3c . . . then unscrew the pivot ball-stud

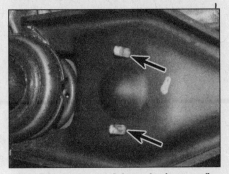

7.9 Ensure the retaining tabs (arrowed) engage correctly with the release fork

Chapter 7 Part A:
Manual transmission

Contents

Degrees of difficulty

Easy, suitable for novice with little experience	Fairly easy, suitable for beginner with some experience	Fairly difficult, suitable for competent DIY mechanic	Difficult, suitable for experienced DIY mechanic	Very difficult, suitable for expert DIY or professional

Specifications

General

Type .... Manual, five or six forward speeds and reverse. Synchromesh on all forward speeds

Designation:
  1.6 litre models BE4R
  2.0 litre models ML6C

Lubrication

Recommended oil type .... See *Lubricants and fluids*
Capacity .... See Chapter 1

Torque wrench settings

	Nm	lbf ft
BE4R transmission		
Clutch release bearing guide sleeve bolts	12	9
Engine-to-transmission fixing bolts	55	41
Front subframe retaining bolts	65	48
Gearchange lever mounting nuts	8	6
Left-hand engine/transmission mounting:		
Mounting bracket to transmission	55	41
Mounting to bracket	60	44
Oil drain plug	35	26
Oil filler/level plug	20	15
Rear engine/transmission mounting:		
Connecting link to mounting assembly	60	44
Connecting link-to-subframe nut/bolt	60	44
Mounting to engine.	60	44
Reversing light switch	25	18
Roadwheel bolts.	90	66
Subframe strengthening bar retaining bolts.	125	92
Speedometer drive housing bolts	15	11
ML6C transmission		
Clutch release bearing guide sleeve bolts	10	7
Driveshaft seal thrust plate (left-hand side)	20	15
Engine movement limiter to subframe	65	48
Engine-to-transmission fixing bolts	60	44
Front subframe retaining bolts	65	48
Gearchange lever housing bolts.	7	5
Left-hand engine/transmission mounting:		
Bracket-to-transmission bolts	60	44
Bracket-to-transmission nut.	55	41
Mounting to body/bracket	60	44
Oil drain plug	30	22
Reversing light switch	25	18
Roadwheel bolts.	90	66
Subframe strengthening bar retaining bolts.	125	92

1 General information

1 The transmission is contained in a cast-aluminium alloy casing bolted to the engine's left-hand end, and consists of the gearbox and final drive differential – often called a transaxle.
2 Two transmission types are fitted according to model, the types being BE4R and ML6C. The transmissions have 5 or 6 forward gears and 1 reverse gear, and are similar in operation. The ML6C transmission was specially developed to cope with the high torque output of the 2.0 litre diesel engines. With 6 forward speeds and capable of handling 350 Nm of torque, the transmission is 'filled for life' with fluid – there's no recommended interval for changing the fluid or checking the level, although it may be prudent to do so at some stage in the vehicle's life.
3 Drive is transmitted from the crankshaft via the clutch to the input shaft, which has a splined extension to accept the clutch friction disc, and rotates in sealed ball-bearings. From the input shaft, drive is transmitted to the output shaft, which rotates in a roller bearing at its right-hand end, and a sealed ball-bearing at its left-hand end. From the output shaft, the drive is transmitted to the differential crownwheel, which rotates with the differential case and planetary gears, thus driving the sun gears and driveshafts. The rotation of the planetary gears on their shaft allows the inner roadwheel to rotate at a slower speed than the outer roadwheel when the car is cornering.
4 The input and output shafts are arranged side-by-side, parallel to the crankshaft and driveshafts, so that their gear pinion teeth are in constant mesh. In the neutral position, the output shaft gear pinions rotate freely, so that drive cannot be transmitted to the crownwheel.
5 Gear selection is via a floor-mounted lever and cable mechanism **(see illustration)**. The selector/gearchange cables causes the appropriate selector fork to move its respective synchro-sleeve along the shaft,

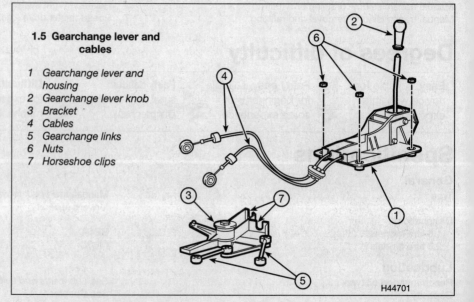

1.5 Gearchange lever and cables

1   Gearchange lever and housing
2   Gearchange lever knob
3   Bracket
4   Cables
5   Gearchange links
6   Nuts
7   Horseshoe clips

H44701

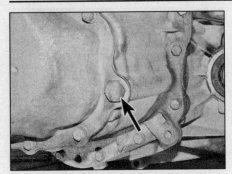

2.4 Oil filler/level plug (arrowed) – BE4R transmission

2.5a Oil drain plug (arrowed) – BE4R transmission

2.5b Oil drain plug (arrowed) – ML6C transmission

to lock the gear pinion to the synchro-hub. Since the synchro-hubs are splined to the output shaft, this locks the pinion to the shaft, so that drive can be transmitted. To ensure that gearchanging can be made quickly and quietly, a synchromesh system is fitted to all forward gears, consisting of baulk rings and spring-loaded fingers, as well as the gear pinions and synchro-hubs. The synchromesh cones are formed on the mating faces of the baulk rings and gear pinions.

2 Manual transmission – draining and refilling

Note: *A suitable square section wrench may be required to undo the transmission filler/ level and drain plugs on some models. These wrenches can be obtained from most motor factors or your Peugeot dealer.*

1 This operation is much quicker and more efficient if the car is first taken on a journey of sufficient length to warm the engine/transmission up to normal operating temperature.
2 Park the car on level ground, switch off the ignition and apply the handbrake firmly. For improved access, jack up the front of the car and support it securely on axle stands (see *Jacking and vehicle support*). Note that the car must be level to ensure accuracy when refilling and checking the oil level. Undo the screws and remove the engine undershield (where fitted).
3 To improve access to the filler/level plug, remove the plastic rivets (push in the centre pin

a little then remove the complete plastic rivet) and remove the left-hand wheel arch liner.
4 Wipe clean the area around the filler/level plug. On the BE4R transmission, the filler/level plug is the largest bolt among those securing the end cover to the transmission. Remove the filler/level plug from the transmission and recover the sealing washer **(see illustration)**. On the ML6C transmission, fluid is added through the breather valve on the top face of the transmission.
5 Position a suitable container under the drain plug (situated on the final drive casing at the rear of the transmission) and unscrew the plug **(see illustrations)**
6 Allow the oil to drain completely into the container. If the oil is hot, take precautions against scalding. Clean both the filler/level and the drain plugs, being especially careful to wipe any metallic particles off the magnetic inserts. Discard the original sealing washers; they should be renewed whenever they are disturbed.
7 When the oil has finished draining, clean the drain plug threads and those of the transmission casing, fit a new sealing washer and refit the drain plug, tightening it to the specified torque wrench setting. Refit the undercover (where fitted) then lower the vehicle to the ground.
8 Refilling the transmission is an extremely awkward operation. Above all, allow plenty of time for the oil level to settle properly before checking it. Note that the car must be parked on flat level ground when checking the oil level.

BE4R transmissions

9 Refill the transmission with the exact amount of the specified type of oil **(see illustration)**, and then check the oil level as described in the relevant part of Chapter 1; if the correct amount was poured into the transmission and a large amount flows out on checking the level, refit the filler/level plug and take the car on a short journey so that the new oil is distributed fully around the transmission components, then check the level again on your return. Once the oil level is correct, securely refit the inner cover/wheel arch liner (as applicable).

ML6C transmissions

10 Remove the air cleaner assembly as described in Chapter 4A.
11 Carefully prise off the breather from the top of the transmission casing, and add the exact amount of oil specified **(see illustrations)**.
12 Refit the breather cap.
13 Refit the air cleaner assembly, and the engine/transmission undershield, and lower the vehicle to the ground.

3 Gearchange lever and cables – removal, refitting and adjustment

Removal

1 Chock the rear wheels then jack up the front of the vehicle and support it on axle stands (see *Jacking and vehicle support*). Remove the engine/transmission undershield.

2.9 On BE4R transmissions, top-up the oil through the wheel arch

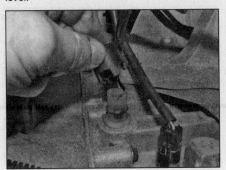

2.11a Prise off the breather cap . . .

2.11b . . . and add the exact amount of fluid specified using a funnel

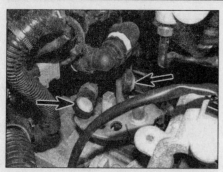

3.3 Detach the selector cables (arrowed) from the balljoints

3.4a Unclip the outer cables from the mounting bracket . . .

3.4b . . . they may be held in the bracket with cable-ties (arrowed)

2 Remove the air cleaner assembly and air inlet ducts as described in Chapter 4A.
3 Note their fitted positions, and then detach the ends of the selector cables from the lever balljoints at the transmission end **(see illustration)**. On some models it may be necessary to press down the centre buttons on the ends of the cables to release the balljoints.
4 Release the outer cables from the bracket on the transmission. Note that the cables may be secured in place with cable-ties, to prevent them from coming out of the bracket **(see illustrations)**.
5 Remove the front section of the exhaust pipe as described in Chapter 4A, and then remove the heat shield **(see illustrations)** beneath the gearchange lever location. Note that in order to remove the heat shield, the edges of the underbody panels must be released.

ML6C transmissions

6 Remove the left-hand front roadwheel, then remove the wheel arch liner.
7 Undo the bolt and remove the reverse gear unlocking device from the left-hand rear upper edge of the transmission housing **(see illustrations)**. Unclip the cable from the support bracket. Discard the O-ring seal; as a new one must be fitted.

All transmissions

8 Remove the centre console (see Chapter 11). Release the securing clip and remove the heater ducting from around the gear lever assembly **(see illustration)**
9 Remove the rubber trim piece around the top of the gearchange lever housing, then undo the 4 nuts, release the clip, and remove the lever housing and gearchange cables as an assembly from under the car **(see illustrations)**.

3.5a Unclip the plastic undershields . . .

3.5b . . . and remove the exhaust heat shields

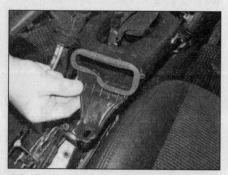

3.7a Working through the wheel arch aperture, undo the Torx bolt . . .

3.7b . . . and remove the reverse gear locking device from the transmission

3.8 Unclip the heater ducting from around the gear lever

3.9a Remove the rubber cover . . .

3.9b . . . and undo the 4 mounting nuts (arrowed)

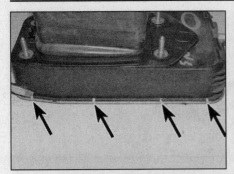

3.10 Fold back the baseplate clips (arrowed)

3.11a Pull out the retaining clip . . .

3.11b . . . and pull the cable and bush from the lever

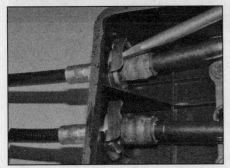

3.11c Prise out the clips securing the outer cable

3.12a Prise the inner cable fitting from the collar . . .

3.12b . . . and pull the outer cable from the bracket

10 Cut through/fold back the clips securing the baseplate to the lever housing, and prise the plate from place (see illustration).

11 Note their fitted positions, then carefully prise the end of the gear engagement control cables from the lever, then on BE4R gearboxes, pull out the pin, remove the bush and detach the end of the gear selection cable from its lever. On ML6C gearboxes, prise both cables from the levers. Prise out the retaining clip and pull the cables from the housing (see illustrations).

ML6C transmissions

12 To remove the reverse gear unlocking cable, disengage the inner cable end fitting from the lifting collar, and pull the outer cable from the bracket on the lever (see illustrations).

13 Release the retaining clip and pull the outer cable grommet from the lever housing, then withdraw the cable from the housing (see illustration).

Refitting

14 Refitting is a reversal of the removal procedure, noting the following points:

a) Ensure that the sound-proofing foam is correctly positioned when refitting the lever housing.

b) Ensure that the cables are fitted to the correct selector levers on the transmission.

c) Apply a bead of silicone sealant to the base of the lever housing, and refit the plate (see illustration).

d) On ML6C transmissions, renew the reverse gear unlocking device O-ring.

e) If required, adjust the cables as described later in this Section.

f) Refit the heat shields, exhaust components, air cleaner assembly, and the centre console.

Adjustment

15 Remove the air cleaner assembly as described in Chapter 4A, to access the gearchange cables at the top of the transmission.

16 If not already done so, remove the centre console as described in Chapter 11.

17 Ensure the transmission is in neutral.

18 Disconnect the ends of the gearchange cables from the levers on the transmission as described previously in this Section.

19 The gearchange lever must be secured in the neutral position. Peugeot tool (No 0216.M) may be available for this task, or it is possible to fabricate a homemade equivalent (see illustration).

3.13 Squeeze together the sides of the clip to release the outer cable

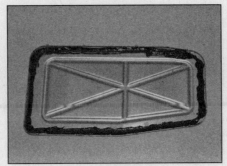

3.14 Apply a bead of silicone sealant to the baseplate

3.19 Peugeot gear lever setting tool – dimensions shown

3.20 Insert the tool through the left-hand side of the housing to hold the lever in the neutral position

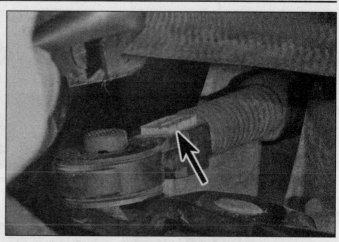

3.21 Prise up the yellow locking catch (arrowed)

3.22 Depress the security pawl (arrowed) and rotate the plastic collar clockwise

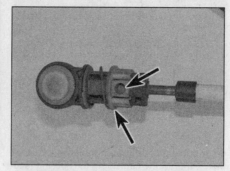

3.25 Pull the collar forwards and prise up the locking catch (arrowed)

All transmissions

28 Check the operation of the gearchange lever. If all is satisfactory, refit the centre console and air cleaner assembly.

4 Oil seals – renewal

Driveshaft oil seals

1 Remove the appropriate driveshaft as described in Chapter 8.

All except left-hand side seal on ML6C transmissions

2 Carefully prise the oil seal out of the transmission, using a large flat-bladed screwdriver **(see illustration)**.
3 Remove all traces of dirt from the area around the oil seal aperture, then apply a smear of grease to the outer lip of the new oil seal. Fit the new seal into its aperture, and drive it squarely into position using a suitable tubular drift (such as a socket), which bears only on the hard outer edge of the seal, until it abuts its locating shoulder. If the seal was supplied with a plastic protector sleeve, leave this in position until the driveshaft has been refitted **(see illustrations)**.

20 Insert the tool into the side of the gearchange lever housing to lock the lever in neutral **(see illustration)**
BE4R transmissions
21 Carefully prise out the yellow catch to release the end fitting locking sleeve on the gearchange cable **(see illustration)**.
22 Using 2 small screwdrivers, depress the security pawls, and rotate the selector cable outer sleeve in the opposite direction to the arrow on the sleeve body **(see illustration)**.
23 Check the gearchange lever is still in the neutral position, and then press the ends of the cables on the balljoints at the transmission.

24 Press the yellow locking catch into place, and secure the gearchange cable, then rotate the sleeve in the direction of the arrow and secure the gear selector cable.
ML6C transmissions
25 On these transmissions, only the gear selection control cable can be adjusted. Pull the locking sleeve on the transmission end of the cable, towards the end, and prise up the locking catch **(see illustration)**.
26 Check the gearchange lever is still in the neutral position, and then press the ends of the cables on the balljoints at the transmission.
27 Press down the locking catch to secure the cables locking sleeve.

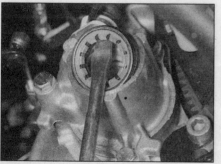

4.2 Prise the driveshaft oil seal from place

4.3a Fit the new seal to the transmission, noting the plastic seal protector . . .

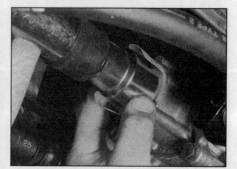

4.3b . . . and tap it into position using a tubular drift/socket

4.4 Thrust plate (arrowed) on left-hand side of transmission

4.5a Remove the thrust plate from the transmission . . .

Left-hand side seal on ML6C transmissions

4 On the ML6C transmission, the passenger side oil seal is fitted to a thrust plate, bolted to the differential casing **(see illustration)**.

5 Undo the four retaining bolts and remove the thrust plate, noting the fitted position of the oil seal. Remove the seal from the thrust plate **(see illustrations)**.

6 Remove all traces of dirt from around the thrust plate, then apply a smear of grease to the outer lip of the new oil seal. Fit the new seal into its aperture, and drive it squarely into position using a suitable tubular drift, which bears only on the hard outer edge of the seal, until it's located in the thrust plate to the position noted on removal **(see illustrations)**.

7 Apply a bead of sealant around the outer edge of the thrust plate, and then refit to the casing **(see illustration)**. Tighten the oil seal thrust plate bolts to the specified torque setting.

All oil seals

8 Apply a film of grease to the inside of the oil seal lip **(see illustration)**.

9 Refit the driveshaft as described in Chapter 8.

Input shaft oil seal

10 Remove the transmission as described in Section 7, and the clutch release mechanism as described in Chapter 6.

4.5b . . . and drift out the oil seal

4.6b . . . using a drift; make sure it is fitted squarely

11 Undo the bolts securing the clutch release bearing guide sleeve in position, and slide the guide off the input shaft, along

4.6a Fit the new seal to the thrust plate . . .

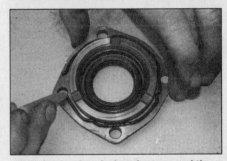

4.7 Apply a bead of sealant around the thrust plate

with its sealing ring or gasket (as applicable) **(see illustrations)**. Recover any shims or thrustwashers which have stuck to the rear of

4.8 Apply a small amount of grease to the seal inner lips

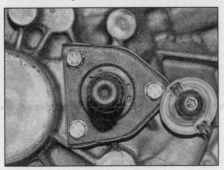

4.11a Undo the bolts and remove the guide sleeve . . .

4.11b . . . and note any shims

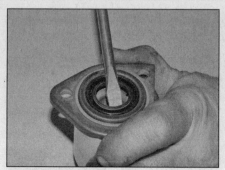

4.12 Lever the old oil seal from the sleeve

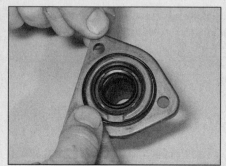

4.15 Fit a new O-ring/gasket (as applicable) to the guide sleeve

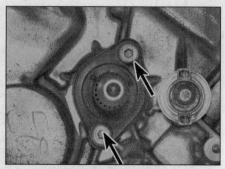

4.16 Guide sleeve Torx bolts (arrowed) – ML6C transmission

the guide sleeve, and refit them to the input shaft. Note that on the ML6C transmission, the oil seal appears to be integral with the guide sleeve. Check with your Peugeot parts specialist.

BE4R transmissions

12 Carefully lever the oil seal out of the guide using a suitable flat-bladed screwdriver **(see illustration)**.

13 Before fitting a new seal, check the input shaft's seal rubbing surface for signs of burrs, scratches or other damage, which may have caused the seal to fail in the first place. It may be possible to polish away minor faults of this sort using fine abrasive paper; however, more serious defects will require the renewal of the input shaft. Ensure that the input shaft is clean and greased, to protect the seal lips on refitting.

14 Dip the new seal in clean oil, and fit it to the guide sleeve.

15 Fit a new sealing ring or gasket (as applicable) to the rear of the guide sleeve, then carefully slide the sleeve into position over the input shaft. Refit the retaining bolts and tighten them to the specified torque setting **(see illustration)**.

ML6C transmissions

16 Lubricate the lips of the new seal within the guide tube, then position the tube over the input shaft, and tighten the retaining bolts securely **(see illustration)**.

All transmissions

17 Take the opportunity to inspect the clutch components if not already done and

then refit (refer to Chapter 6). Finally, refit the transmission as described in Section 7.

Selector shaft oil seal

BE4R transmissions

18 Park the car on level ground, apply the handbrake, slacken the left-hand front roadwheel bolts, then jack up the front of the vehicle and support it on axle stands (see *Jacking and vehicle support*). Remove the left-hand front roadwheel.

19 Using a large flat-bladed screwdriver, lever the link rod balljoint off the transmission selector shaft, and disconnect the link rod.

20 Using a large flat-bladed screwdriver, carefully prise the selector shaft seal out of the housing, and slide it off the end of the shaft.

21 Before fitting a new seal, check the selector shaft's seal rubbing surface for signs of burrs, scratches or other damage, which may have caused the seal to fail in the first place. It may be possible to polish away minor faults of this sort using fine abrasive paper; however, more serious defects will require the renewal of the selector shaft.

22 Apply a smear of grease to the new seal's outer edge and sealing lip, then carefully slide the seal along the selector rod. Press the seal fully into position in the transmission housing.

23 Refit the link rod to the selector shaft, ensuring that its balljoint is pressed firmly onto the shaft. Lower the car to the ground.

ML6C transmissions

24 On these transmissions, part of the transmission housing must be dismantled

to be able to renew the selector shaft seal. This task should therefore be entrusted to a Peugeot dealer or transmission specialist.

---

5 Reversing light switch – testing, removal and refitting

Testing

1 The reversing light circuit is controlled by a plunger-type switch screwed into the top of the transmission casing. If a fault develops, first ensure that the circuit fuse has not blown.

2 To test the switch, disconnect the wiring connector **(see illustration)**, and use a multimeter (set to the resistance function) or a battery-and-bulb test circuit to check that there is continuity between the switch terminals only when reverse gear is selected. If this is not the case, and there are no obvious breaks or other damage to the wires, the switch is faulty, and must be renewed.

Removal

3 Where necessary, to improve access to the switch, remove the air cleaner housing inlet duct assembly (as applicable – see Chapter 4A).

4 Disconnect the wiring connector, and then unscrew the switch from the transmission casing along with its sealing washer **(see illustrations)**.

5.2 Disconnect the reversing light wiring connector – ML6C transmission

5.4a Unscrew the switch (arrowed) from the front of the housing – BE4R transmission

5.4b Unscrew the switch (arrowed) from the top of the housing – ML6C transmission

7.8a Undo the mounting bolts (arrowed) . . .

7.8b . . . and remove the lower bumper bar

7.9 Strengthener bar securing bolts (arrowed)

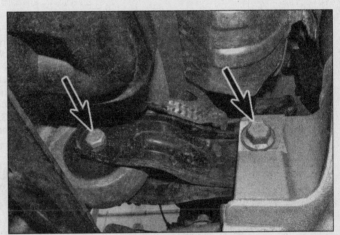

7.10a Undo the two mounting bolts (arrowed) . . .

Refitting

5 Fit a new sealing washer to the switch, then screw it back into position in the top of the transmission housing and tighten it to the specified torque setting. Refit the wiring plug, and test the operation of the circuit. Refit any components removed for access.

7.10b . . . and remove the rear mounting link bar

6 Speedometer drive – general information

The transmissions fitted to the engines in this workshop manual do not have a speedometer drive pinion fitted. The speedometer receives vehicle speed data from the engine management ECM, which is supplied by the wheel speed sensors and the ABS ECM.

7 Manual transmission – removal and refitting

Removal

1 Chock the rear wheels, then firmly apply the handbrake. Slacken both front roadwheel bolts. Jack up the front of the vehicle, and securely support it on axle stands (see *Jacking and vehicle support*). Remove both front roadwheels and the engine undershield.

2 Drain the transmission oil as described in Section 2, and then refit the drain and filler plugs (where applicable). Fit a new sealing washer and then tighten the drain plug to the specified torque setting.
3 Remove both driveshafts as described in Chapter 8.
4 In order to prevent any damage, remove the exhaust front section, as described in Chapter 4A.
5 Remove the battery and battery box (see Chapter 5A).
6 Remove the air cleaner housing and inlet ducting as described in Chapter 4A.
7 Remove the front bumper as described in Chapter 11.
8 Undo the retaining bolts and remove the lower crossbeam from the front of the vehicle **(see illustrations)**.
9 Undo the retaining bolts and remove the strengthener bar from across the front of the main subframe **(see illustration)**.
10 Undo the nuts and bolts and remove the mounting link securing the rear engine/ transmission mounting to the subframe **(see illustrations)**.

7.11a Undo the power steering pipe securing bracket bolt (arrowed) . . .

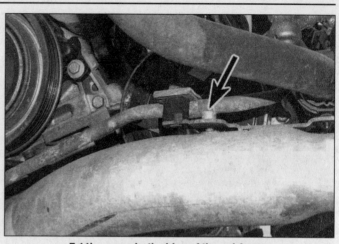

7.11b . . . on both sides of the subframe

11 Undo the retaining bolts and disconnect the power steering pipe brackets from the front subframe **(see illustrations)**.
12 Undo the four bolts (two each side) securing the front subframe to the main subframe **(see illustration)**.
13 Undo the two bolts on the front securing brackets, and then remove the front subframe from the front of the vehicle **(see illustrations)**.

14 On ML6C transmissions, undo the three retaining nuts and remove the alloy impact absorber from the rear of the differential casing **(see illustration)**.
15 Undo the three retaining nuts and disconnect the gearchange cable mounting bracket from the transmission housing **(see illustration)**, or disconnect the cables as described in Section 3.
16 Remove the starter motor (Chapter 5A).

17 Detach the clutch slave cylinder from the transmission as described in Chapter 6. Note there is no need to disconnect the fluid pipe from the cylinder.
18 Note their fitted positions, and then disconnect any wiring plugs/connectors from the transmission. Note the harness routing and move the harness to one side **(see illustration)**.
19 On ML6C transmissions, disconnect

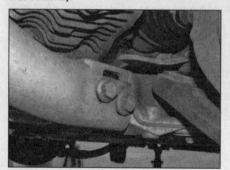

7.12 Undo the front subframe mounting bolts (one side shown)

7.13a Undo the front mounting bolts . . .

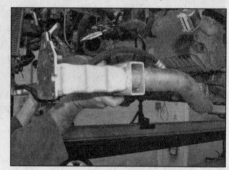

7.13b . . . and withdraw the front subframe from under the vehicle

7.14 Undo the impact absorber retaining nuts (arrowed)

7.15 Undo the gear selector cable mounting bracket retaining nuts (arrowed)

7.18 Disconnect the earth cable from the transmission (arrowed)

7.24 Remove the mounting stud and washer from the transmission casing

7.25 On 1.6 litre engines, remove the mounting stud (arrowed) which obscures the transmission-to-engine bolt

the reverse gear unlocking device from the left-hand rear upper edge of the transmission housing, as described in Section 3 **(see illustrations 3.7a and 3.7b)**.

20 Depending on model, there may be a lower cover plate fitted to the transmission. Where fitted, undo the retaining bolts, and remove the cover plate from the transmission.

21 Place a jack with a block of wood beneath the engine, to take the weight of the engine. Alternatively, attach a couple of lifting eyes to the engine, and fit a hoist or support bar to take the engine weight.

22 Place a jack and block of wood beneath the transmission, and raise the jack to take the weight of the transmission.

23 Slacken and remove the mounting bolts/nuts from the left-hand transmission mounting and remove it from the top of the transmission. Refer to Chapter 2A or 2B for further information on engine/transmission mountings.

24 On BE4R transmissions, slide the spacer off the mounting stud (where fitted), then unscrew the stud from the top of the transmission housing and remove it, along with its washer **(see illustration)**.

25 With the jack positioned beneath the transmission taking the weight, slacken and remove the remaining bolts securing the transmission housing to the engine. Note the correct fitted positions of each bolt and the necessary brackets, as they are removed, to use as a reference on refitting. On 1.6 litre engines, unscrew the left-hand catalytic converter mounting stud, to allow access to the front transmission-to-engine bolt **(see illustration)**.

26 Make a final check that all components have been disconnected, and are positioned clear of the transmission so that they will not hinder the removal procedure.

Caution: As the engine is lowered, make sure no wiring, hoses or cables are being stretched or damaged in any way.

27 With the bolts removed, move the trolley jack and transmission to the left, to free it from its locating dowels. Lower the engine slightly to enable the transmission to be freed.

Caution: Take great care not to damage the radiator if the engine is moved – place a sheet of thick cardboard over the rear face of the radiator. On models equipped with air conditioning, care must also be taken to ensure the auxiliary drivebelt pulleys do not damage the air conditioning pipes on the right-hand side of the engine compartment.

28 Once the transmission is free, lower the jack and manoeuvre the unit out from under the car. Remove the locating dowels from the transmission or engine if they are loose, and keep them in a safe place.

Refitting

29 The transmission is refitted by a reversal of the removal procedure, bearing in mind the following points:

a) *Prior to refitting, check the clutch assembly and release mechanism components (see Chapter 6). Lubricate the release bearing guide with a little high melting-point grease (Peugeot recommend the use of Molykote BR2 Plus). Do not apply too much grease, otherwise there is a possibility of the grease contaminating the clutch friction disc, and ensure no grease is applied to the input shaft/friction disc splines.*

b) *Ensure that the locating dowels are correctly positioned prior to installation.*

c) *On BE4R transmissions, apply thread-locking fluid to the left-hand engine/ transmission mounting stud threads, prior to refitting it to the transmission. Tighten the stud to the specified torque.*

d) *Tighten all nuts and bolts to the specified torque (where given).*

e) *Renew the driveshaft oil seals, then refit the driveshafts (see Chapter 8).*

f) *Refit the slave cylinder (see Chapter 6).*

g) *On completion, refill the transmission with the specified type and quantity of lubricant, as described in Section 2.*

8 Manual transmission overhaul – general information

1 Overhauling a manual transmission is a difficult and involved job for the DIY home mechanic. In addition to dismantling and reassembling many small parts, clearances must be precisely measured and, if necessary, changed by selecting shims and spacers. Internal transmission components are also often difficult to obtain, and in many instances, extremely expensive. Because of this, if the transmission develops a fault or becomes noisy, the best course of action is to have the unit overhauled by a specialist repairer, or to obtain an exchange reconditioned unit.

2 Nevertheless, it is not impossible for the more experienced mechanic to overhaul the transmission, provided the special tools are available, and the job is done in a deliberate step-by-step manner, so that nothing is overlooked.

3 The tools necessary for an overhaul include internal and external circlip pliers, bearing pullers, a slide hammer, a set of pin punches, a dial test indicator, and possibly a hydraulic press. In addition, a large, sturdy workbench and a vice will be required.

4 During dismantling of the transmission, make careful notes of how each component is fitted, to make reassembly easier and more accurate.

5 Before dismantling the transmission, it will help if you have some idea what area is malfunctioning. Certain problems can be closely related to specific areas in the transmission, which can make component examination and renewal easier. Refer to the *Fault finding* Section for more information.

Chapter 7 Part B:
Automatic transmission

Contents

Degrees of difficulty

Easy, suitable for novice with little experience	Fairly easy, suitable for beginner with some experience	Fairly difficult, suitable for competent DIY mechanic	Difficult, suitable for experienced DIY mechanic	Very difficult, suitable for expert DIY or professional

Specifications

General
Type:
AL4 . . . . Automatic, four forward speeds and reverse
AM6 . . . . Automatic, six forward speeds and reverse

Lubrication
Recommended fluid . . . . Refer to *Lubricants and fluids*
Capacity . . . . Refer to Chapter 1

Torque wrench settings

	Nm	lbf ft
AL4 transmission		
Engine-to-transmission securing bolts.	52	38
Fluid cooler centre bolt.	50	37
Fluid drain plug.	33	24
Fluid filler plug	24	18
Fluid level plug:		
To RPO 9855 (hexagonal).	24	18
From RPO 9856 (socket key)	9	7
Fluid pressure sensor	8	6
Input shaft speed sensor	10	7
Left-hand engine/transmission mounting.	Refer to Chapter 2A or 2B	
Output speed sensor	10	7
Rear mounting link	Refer to Chapter 2A or 2B	
Multifunction switch bolts	15	11
Torque converter-to-driveplate bolts:*		
Stage 1	10	7
Stage 2	30	22
Transmission selector shaft lever clamp bolt and nut	15	11
AM6 transmission		
Electronic control module selector rod nut	20	15
Electronic control module-to-transmission bolts	24	18
Engine/transmission left-hand mounting:		
Mounting to transmission.	55	41
Engine-to-transmission bolts	60	44
Fluid drain plug.	48	35
Fluid filler plug	40	30
Fluid level plug	7	5
Fluid cooler centre bolt.	42	31
Torque converter bolts:*		
Stage 1	20	15
Stage 2	Slacken 100°	
Stage 3	60	44

Do not re-use

1 General information

AL4 transmission

The AL4 transmission has four forward gears and a reverse, and incorporates electronic control; the automatic gearchanges are electronically-controlled, rather than hydraulically. The advantage of electronic management is to provide a faster gearchange response. A kickdown facility is also provided, to enable a faster acceleration response when required.

The torque converter incorporates an automatic lock-up feature, which eliminates any possibility of converter slip in the top two gears; this aids performance and economy. In addition to the normal alternative of manual change, the three-position mode switch on the centre console (adjacent to the selector lever) provides Normal, Sport or Snow settings, as required. In Sport mode, upshifts are delayed longer, to make full use of engine power. In Snow mode, either 2nd or 3rd gear is used to pull away from rest, maximising traction in slippery conditions.

Another feature of this transmission is the Park Lock, which is partly a safety and partly a security feature. Moving the lever out of the P position requires the ignition to be on, and the brake pedal must also be depressed.

The gear selector cable has an automatic adjuster mechanism, meaning that cable adjustment should not be required. The AL4 transmission is also regarded as being 'lubricated for life', with routine fluid changes not featuring in the manufacturer's maintenance schedule.

In the event of a problem developing with the transmission, the transmission ECM may select one of two emergency back-up modes, to enable the car to continue being driven. When operating in this back-up mode, shifting out of N or R will become more jerky, or the transmission will only select 3rd gear (no gearchanges). If a fault is suspected, your Peugeot dealer will be able to download fault codes from the transmission ECM memory, to speed-up diagnosis.

AM6 transmission

The AM6 transmission is available on 2.0 litre engine models. The transmission is electronically-controlled, with an ECM mounted on the upper face of the transmission casing. This transmission offers 6 forward speeds, with manual or automatic gear selection, and three driving modes: Normal, Sport, and Snow. In function, the transmission is very similar to the AL4 unit, with the transmission ECM communicating with the engine management ECM to provide smooth gearchanges, with minimum fuel consumption and exhaust emissions. Peugeot insist that the transmission is 'lubricated for life', with no requirement for routine changes.

If a fault occurs with the transmission, have the ECM's self-diagnosis facility interrogated by a Peugeot dealer or suitably-equipped specialist, before considering any removal or investigative procedures.

All transmission types

Due to the complexity of the automatic transmission, any repair or overhaul work must be left to a Peugeot dealer or specialist with the necessary special equipment for fault diagnosis and repair. The contents of the following Sections are therefore confined to supplying general information, and any service information and instructions that can be used by the owner.

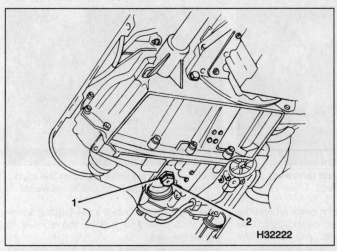

2.3 Transmission fluid drain plug (1) and oil level plug (2), inside the drain plug

2.4 Unscrew the transmission drain plug (arrowed)

2 Automatic transmission fluid – draining and refilling

Note: *Transmission fluid renewal is not a service requirement and the following operations will normally only be necessary to allow transmission repair work to be carried out.*

Note: *A suitable square section wrench may be required to undo the transmission filler plug. These wrenches can be obtained from most motor factors or your Peugeot dealer.*

1 Take the vehicle on a short run, to warm the transmission up to normal operating temperature.

2 Park the vehicle on level ground, switch off the ignition and apply the handbrake firmly. For improved access, chock the rear wheels then jack up the front of the vehicle and support it on axle stands (see *Jacking and vehicle support*). Remove the engine undershield if

fitted. Note that the vehicle must be lowered to the ground and be level to ensure accuracy when refilling and checking the fluid level.

3 Position a suitable container under the drain plug, situated on the base of the transmission **(see illustration).**

⚠ *Warning: If the fluid is hot, take precautions against scalding.*

4 Unscrew the drain plug and allow the fluid to drain completely into the container. Note that the inner oil level plug is screwed into the outer drain plug, and both must be removed to drain the fluid **(see illustration).** Also note that it is not possible to completely drain the torque converter. If the fluid is hot, take precautions against scalding. Clean the drain plug, being especially careful to wipe any metallic particles off the magnetic insert. Discard the original sealing washer which should be renewed whenever it is disturbed.

5 When the fluid has finished draining, clean the drain plug threads and those of the transmission casing, fit a new sealing washer

to the drain plug and refit it to the transmission, tightening securely. Only fit the drain plug and do not fit the centre level plug. If the vehicle was raised for the draining operation, lower it to the ground.

6 Refilling the transmission with fluid is through the fluid filler plug **(see illustrations).**

7 To improve access to the filler plug, remove air cleaner housing as described in Chapter 4A. Wipe clean the area around the filler plug, before removing.

8 Position a container beneath the level plug, and then add the specified type of fluid through the filler plug aperture until it starts to flow from the level plug. Note that the vehicle must be parked on flat level ground when checking the fluid level.

9 Fit a new sealing washer to the filler plug, and then refit and tighten the filler and level plugs.

10 Refit the air cleaner, then start the engine and allow it to idle for a few minutes. Switch the engine off and recheck the level, topping-up if necessary.

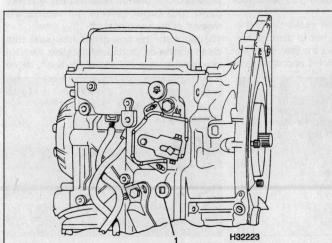

2.6a Fluid filler plug (1) as viewed from above – AL4 transmission

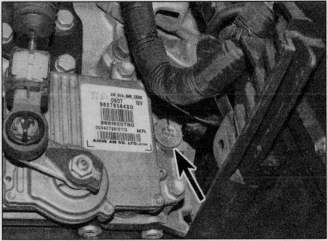

2.6a Fluid filler plug (arrowed) as viewed from above – AM6 transmission

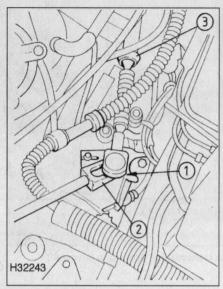

3.5 Prise off the selector cable balljoint (1) using a forked tool (2), then remove the cable from the bracket (3)

11 Take the vehicle on a short run to fully distribute the new fluid around the transmission, and then recheck the fluid level again with reference to the relevant Part of Chapter 1.

3 Selector cable – removal, refitting and adjustment

Removal

1 Apply the handbrake, switch on the ignition, depress the brake pedal and place the selector lever in position N. Switch off the ignition.
2 Remove the air cleaner assembly as described in Chapter 4A.
3 Remove the battery cover.
4 Working in the engine compartment, carefully prise the selector cable balljoint from the selector lever on the transmission lever arm.
5 On AL4 transmissions, pull back the outer cable sleeve and pull the cable upwards from the bracket (see illustration).
6 On AM6 transmissions press out the catch, squeeze together the clips and pull the cable from the bracket (see illustrations).
7 Chock the rear wheels, then jack up the front of the car and support it on axle stands.
8 Refer to Chapter 4A and remove the exhaust system and heat shields, as necessary, for access to the cable and gear selector lever housing under the vehicle.
9 Work back along the selector cable, releasing it from any relevant retaining clips, and noting its correct routing.
10 Working inside the vehicle, remove the centre console (see Chapter 11). Release the securing clip and remove the heater ducting from around the gear lever assembly.

3.6a Push the catch (arrowed) rearwards . . .

11 Remove the rubber trim piece around the top of the gearchange lever housing, then undo the 4 nuts, release the clip, and remove the lever housing and gearchange cables as an assembly from under the car.

Refitting

12 Refitting is the reverse of removal, ensuring that the selector cable is correctly routed and retained with any relevant clips and ties. To adjust the cable, pull out the locking catch, ensure the selector lever and transmission levers are in position N, and then press the locking catch down (see illustrations).

4 Oil seals – renewal

Driveshaft oil seals

1 Refer to Chapter 7A.

Selector shaft oil seal

AL4 transmission

2 To gain access to the transmission selector shaft, remove the air cleaner assembly as described in Chapter 4A.
3 Remove the multifunction switch from the top of the transmission housing as described in Section 6.
4 Carefully remove the oil seal from of the transmission, taking care not to damage the shaft or housing. To remove the seal, carefully punch or drill two small holes opposite each

3.12a Prise up the cable locking catch (arrowed)

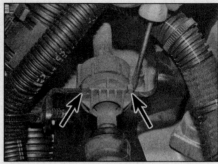

3.6b . . . then squeeze together the clips (arrowed) and pull the cables upwards

other into the seal. Screw a self-tapping screw into each hole and pull on the screws to extract the seal.
5 Remove all traces of dirt from the area around the oil seal aperture, then apply a smear of grease to the outer edge and sealing lip of the new oil seal. Ease the new seal onto the shaft, taking care not to damage its lip, and press it squarely into its aperture.
6 Refit the multifunction switch to the top of the transmission housing as described in Section 6.
7 Secure the selector cable in position with the retaining clip then adjust the cable as described in Section 3.
8 Refit the air cleaner assembly as described in Chapter 4A.

AM6 transmission

9 Remove the air cleaner assembly as described in Chapter 4A.
10 Remove the electronic control module as described in Section 6.
11 Punch or drill two small holes opposite each other in the seal. Screw a self-tapping screw into each, and pull on the screws with pliers to extract the seal.
12 Clean the seal housing, and polish off any burrs or raised edges, which may have caused the seal to fail in the first place. Small imperfections can be removed using emery paper, but larger defects will require the renewal of the selector shaft.
13 Lubricate the lips of the new seal with clean engine oil, and carefully ease the seal into position over the end of the shaft, taking

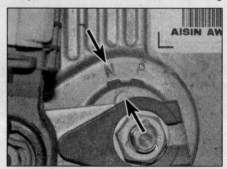

3.12b Ensure the transmission lever shaft lug is aligned with the N on the casing (arrowed)

5.6a Fluid cooler hose clips (arrowed) –
AL4 transmission

5.6b Fluid cooler hose clips (arrowed) –
AM6 transmission

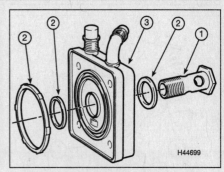

5.7 Fluid cooler – AL4 transmission
1 Bolt   2 Seals   3 Fluid cooler

great care not to damage its sealing lip. Tap
the seal into position until it is flush with the
transmission casing, using a suitable tubular
drift (such as a socket), which bears only on
the hard outer edge of the seal. Note that the
seal lips should face inwards.
14 Refit the electronic control module as
described in Section 6.
15 Refit the air cleaner assembly as described
in Chapter 4A.

Torque converter seal

16 Remove the transmission unit as described
in Section 7.
17 Carefully slide the torque converter off
the transmission shaft whilst being prepared
for fluid spillage. Although the transmission
oil has been drained, the torque converter will
contain a large amount of fluid.
18 Note the correct fitted position of the seal in
the housing then carefully lever it out of position,
taking care not to mark the housing or shaft.
19 Remove all traces of dirt from the area
around the oil seal aperture. Ease the new seal
into its aperture, ensuring its sealing lip is facing
inwards, then press it squarely into position.
20 Engage the torque converter with the
transmission shaft splines and slide it into
position, taking care not to damage the oil seal.
21 Refit the transmission unit as described in
Section 7.

5 Fluid cooler – removal and refitting

*Caution: Be careful not to allow dirt into the
transmission unit during this procedure.*

Removal

1 The fluid cooler is mounted on the
transmission housing. On AL4 transmissions
it is on the rear of the transmission housing.
On AM6 transmissions it is on the front of the
transmission housing.
2 To gain access to the fluid cooler, chock the
rear wheels jack up the front of the vehicle and
support it on axle stands (see *Jacking and vehicle
support*). Remove the engine undershield.
3 On models with AL4 transmissions, it may
also be necessary to remove the left-hand front
wheel, to access the rear of the transmission.

4 On AM6 transmissions, it will be necessary
to drain the transmission oil as the fluid cooler
is fitted to the lower part of the transmission
housing.
5 Using hose clamps or similar, clamp both
of the fluid cooler coolant hoses to minimise
coolant loss during subsequent operations.
6 Disconnect both coolant hoses from the
fluid cooler, being prepared for some coolant
spillage **(see illustrations)**. Wash off any spilt
coolant immediately with cold water, and dry
the surrounding area before proceeding further.
7 Slacken and remove the fluid cooler
mounting bolt, and remove the cooler from
the transmission. Remove the mounting bolt
seal(s), and the two seals fitted to the base of
the cooler, and discard them; new ones must
be used on refitting **(see illustration)**.

Refitting

8 Lubricate the new seals with clean
automatic transmission fluid, then fit the two
new seals to the base of the fluid cooler, and a
new seal to the mounting bolt.
9 Locate the fluid cooler on the transmission
housing, then refit the mounting bolt, and
tighten to the specified torque setting. Note
that on AM6 transmission, the tab at the top
of the fluid cooler must align between the two
notches on the transmission casing.
10 Reconnect the coolant hoses to the fluid
cooler and remove the hose clamps.
11 Refit the inlet duct/air cleaner or support
bracket components, engine undershield/
roadwheel as applicable.
12 On AM6 transmissions, refill the automatic
transmission fluid as described in Section 2.
13 On completion, top-up the cooling system
and check the automatic transmission fluid
level as described in Chapter 1.

6 Transmission control system components – removal and refitting

Note: *The automatic transmission
electronic control system relies on accurate
communication between the engine
management ECM and the automatic
transmission control module. If either electronic
control module is renewed, then both must*

be 'initialised'. The initialisation procedure
requires access to specialised electronic test
equipment and so it is recommended that this
operation be entrusted to a suitably-equipped
Peugeot dealer or specialist.

Multifunction switch – AL4 transmissions

Note: *The multifunction switch is slotted to
allow for adjustment. Accurate adjustment
requires the use an accurate multimeter – see
the text later in this Section.*

Removal

1 Remove the air cleaner assembly as
described in Chapter 4A.
2 Fully apply the handbrake, then turn on the
ignition and place the selector lever in position
N. Turn off the ignition and wait 15 mins, then
disconnect the battery negative terminal.
3 Slacken and remove the nut and clamp bolt
securing the selector lever to the transmission
shaft **(see illustration)**. Make alignment marks
between the shaft and lever then free the lever
from the shaft.
4 Remove the retaining clip and free the
selector cable from transmission bracket.
Position the cable clear of the selector shaft.
5 Unscrew the two bolts and free the main
wiring connector from the transmission unit.
Cut the cable-tie securing the wiring to the
connector cover then release the clips and
slide the cover off the connector.
6 Trace the wiring back from the switch to
the main wiring connector, freeing it from all
the relevant retaining clips and ties. Carefully

6.3 Unscrew the nut and clamp bolt
(arrowed) and free the selector lever from
the transmission shaft

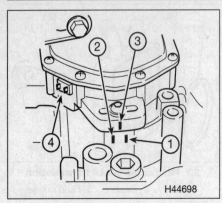

6.19 Multifunction switch adjustment

1 *1st alignment mark*
2 *2nd alignment mark*
3 *Switch body alignment mark*
4 *Switch external contacts*

release the retaining clips then slide the green 12-way connector out from the rear of the main connector, noting which way around it is fitted.

7 Make accurate alignment marks between the multifunction switch and transmission unit then unscrew the retaining bolts and remove the switch.

Refitting

8 If required, fit a new seal to the transmission housing as described in Section 4.

9 Locate the multifunction switch back on the selector shaft. Align the marks made prior to removal then refit the switch bolts, tightening them to the specified torque.

10 Clip the wiring back into the main wiring connector, ensuring it is fitted the right way around. Slide the cover back onto the main connector, ensuring it is clipped securely in position, and secure the wiring to the cover with a new cable-tie. Locate the connector on the transmission unit and securely tighten its retaining bolts.

11 Reconnect the main wiring connector to the transmission unit.

12 Seat the selector cable in the transmission

bracket and engage the selector lever with the transmission shaft. Ensure the marks made on removal are correctly aligned then refit the lever clamp bolt and nut, and tighten securely.

13 Secure the selector cable in position with the retaining clip, and then adjust the cable as described in Section 3, and the multifunction switch as described in the following paragraphs.

Adjustment

14 Slacken the switch mounting bolts and rotate the switch fully anti-clockwise as far as it will go.

15 Set the multimeter to measure ohms, and connect the meter terminals to the external switch contacts.

16 Slowly rotate the switch clockwise until the switch contacts close (the meter should register zero ohms – no resistance).

17 In this position, make an alignment mark between the switch and the transmission casing.

18 Continue to rotate the switch clockwise until the contacts open (the meter should register infinite ohms or similar)

19 Make another alignment mark between the transmission casing and the mark made previously on the switch **(see illustration)**.

20 Rotate the switch until the alignment mark on the switch body is exactly halfway between the two marks made on the transmission casing. Tighten the switch mounting bolts to the specified torque.

21 Refit the air cleaner assembly as described in Chapter 4A.

22 Check that the selector lever operation and road test.

Electronic control module – A6M transmissions

Removal

23 Remove the air cleaner assembly as described in Chapter 4A.

24 Fully apply the handbrake, then turn on the ignition and place the selector lever in position N. Turn off the ignition and wait 15 mins, then disconnect the battery negative terminal.

25 Squeeze together the side of the clip and pull the end of the selector cable from the balljoint on the transmission lever.

Caution: Support the selector rod and lever when slackening or tightening the securing nut, as damage can occur to the slide valve in the hydraulic block.

26 Undo the securing nut and remove the selector lever from the top of the control module selector rod.

27 Disconnect the wiring plug connector from the control module.

28 Undo the 3 retaining bolts, and lift the control module straight upwards and over the end of the selector shaft, disconnecting the control module from the transmission internal connections as it's withdrawn **(see illustration)**.

Refitting

29 If required, fit new selector seal to transmission housing as described in Section 4.

30 Check the condition of the electrical connections in the top of the transmission housing. Make sure the locating tab on the connector is secured in the notch on the transmission casing.

31 When the control module is refitted to the top of the transmission, check the selector rod is in the Neutral position and the dot on the selector shaft is aligned with the arrow on the control module casing.

32 With the control module in the correct position, ensure the locating notch fits over the lug on the casing. Tighten the control module retaining bolts to the specified torque setting.

33 The refitting is a reversal of removal. Note that if a new control module has been fitted, it must be programmed and matched to the engine management control module using Peugeot diagnostic equipment. Entrust this task to a Peugeot dealer or suitably-equipped specialist. Even after reprogramming/matching, the vehicle should be taken on an extensive road test, on a route which will allow numerous gearchanges and full use of the transmission mode settings. Initially,

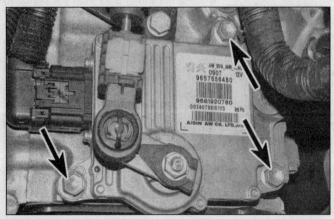

6.28 Transmission ECM mounting bolts (arrowed)

6.39 The fluid pressure sensor is secured to the base of the transmission by two bolts (arrowed)

transmission response and gearchange quality may be less than acceptable, but should improve as the ECM control circuitry adapts to the transmission parameters.

Fluid pressure sensor – AL4 transmissions

Caution: Be careful not to allow dirt into the transmission unit during this procedure.

Removal

34 The fluid pressure sensor is located on the base of the transmission unit.

35 To gain access to the sensor, chock the rear wheels, firmly apply the handbrake then jack up the front of the vehicle and securely support it on axle stands (see *Jacking and vehicle support*).

36 Remove the air cleaner assembly as described in Chapter 4A.

37 Unscrew the two bolts and free the main wiring connector from the transmission unit. Cut the cable-tie securing the wiring to the connector cover then release the clips and slide the cover off the connector.

38 Trace the wiring back from the sensor being removed, freeing it from all the relevant retaining clips and ties, to the main wiring connector. Carefully release the retaining clips then slide the green 3-way sensor connector out from the rear of the main connector, noting which way around it is fitted.

39 Wipe clean the area around the sensor. Slacken and remove the retaining bolts then remove the sensor, along with its sealing ring **(see illustration)**. Discard the sealing ring; a new one must be used on refitting. Be prepared for fluid spillage, and plug the opening to minimise fluid loss.

Refitting

40 Refitting is the reverse of removal, noting the following points.

 a) *Fit a new sealing ring to the sensor and tighten the sensor bolts to the specified torque.*
 b) *Ensure the sensor wiring is correctly routed and retained by all the necessary clips and ties.*

 c) *Clip the sensor wiring back into the main wiring connector, ensuring it is fitted the right way around. Slide the cover back onto the main connector, ensuring it is clipped securely in position, and secure the wiring to the cover with a new cable-tie.*
 d) *On completion, check the transmission fluid level as described in Chapter 1.*

Input shaft speed sensor – AL4 transmissions

Caution: Be careful not to allow dirt into the transmission unit during this procedure.

Removal

41 The input shaft speed sensor is located on the left-hand end of the transmission unit, above the left-hand driveshaft.

42 To gain access to the sensor, chock the rear wheels, firmly apply the handbrake, then jack up the front of the vehicle and securely support it on axle stands (see *Jacking and vehicle support*).

43 To gain access to the main wiring connector, remove the battery and battery box (see Chapter 5A).

44 Lift the retaining clip and disconnect the main wiring connector from the top of the transmission unit.

45 Unscrew the two bolts and free the main wiring connector from the transmission unit. Cut the cable tie securing the wiring to the connector cover then release the clips and slide the cover off the connector.

46 Trace the wiring back to the main wiring connector, freeing it from all the relevant retaining clips and ties,. Carefully release the retaining clips then slide the sensor connector out from the rear of the main connector, noting which way around it is fitted.

47 Wipe clean the area around the sensor. Slacken and remove the retaining bolt then remove the sensor, along with its sealing ring. Discard the sealing ring; a new one must be used on refitting.

Refitting

48 Refitting is the reverse of removal, noting the following points.

 a) *Fit a new sealing ring to the sensor and tighten the sensor bolt to the specified torque.*
 b) *Ensure the sensor wiring is correctly routed and retained by all the necessary clips and ties.*
 c) *Clip the sensor wiring back into the main wiring connector, ensuring it is fitted the right way around. Slide the cover back onto the main connector, ensuring it is clipped securely in position, and secure the wiring to the cover with a new cable-tie. Secure the connector to the transmission unit with the retaining bolts.*
 d) *On completion, check the transmission fluid level as described in Chapter 1.*

7 Automatic transmission – removal and refitting

Removal

1 Chock the rear wheels, then firmly apply the handbrake. Slacken both front roadwheel bolts. Jack up the front of the vehicle, and securely support it on axle stands (see *Jacking and vehicle support*). Remove both front roadwheels and the engine undershield.

2 Drain the transmission fluid as described in Section 2, and then refit the drain and filler plugs (where applicable). Fit a new sealing washer and then tighten the drain plug to the specified torque setting.

3 Remove both driveshafts as described in Chapter 8.

4 In order to prevent any damage, remove the exhaust front section, as described in Chapter 4A.

5 Remove the battery and battery box (see Chapter 5A).

6 Remove the air cleaner housing and inlet ducting as described in Chapter 4A.

7 Remove the front bumper as described in Chapter 11.

8 Undo the retaining bolts and remove the lower crossbeam from the front of the vehicle **(see illustrations)**.

7.8a Undo the mounting bolts (arrowed) . . .

7.8b . . . and remove the lower front crossbeam

7.9 Strengthener bar securing bolts (arrowed)

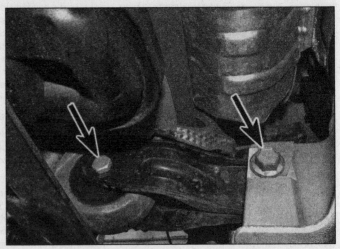

7.10a Undo the two mounting bolts (arrowed) . . .

7.10b . . . and remove the rear mounting link bar

9 Undo the retaining bolts and remove the strengthener bar from across the front of the main subframe (see illustration).
10 Undo the nuts and bolts and remove the mounting link securing the rear engine/transmission mounting to the subframe (see illustrations).
11 Undo the retaining bolts and disconnect the power steering pipe brackets from the front subframe (see illustrations).
12 Undo the four bolts (two each side) securing the front subframe to the main subframe (see illustration).
13 Undo the two bolts on the front securing

brackets, and then remove the subframe from the front of the vehicle (see illustrations).
14 Disconnect the gearchange selector cable as described in Section 3.
15 Remove the starter motor (Chapter 5A).
16 Note their fitted positions, and then disconnect the various wiring connectors from the transmission. Note the harness routing and release from any retaining clips, and then move the harness to one side (see illustration).
17 Using hose clamps or similar, clamp both the fluid cooler coolant hoses to minimise coolant loss and remove the fluid cooler as

7.11a Undo the power steering pipe securing bracket bolt (arrowed) . . .

7.11b . . . on both sides of the subframe

7.12 Undo the front subframe mounting bolts (one side shown)

7.13a Undo the front mounting bolts . . .

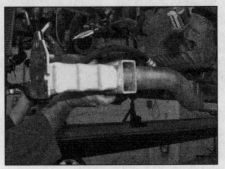

7.13b . . . and withdraw the front subframe from under the vehicle

7.16 Transmission earth lead (arrowed)

7.18 Access to the torque converter nuts is gained via the access hole (arrowed) above the driveshaft

described in Section 5. Plug or cover the openings to prevent contamination.

18 Locate the access hole (remove the driveplate lower cover plate, where fitted) at the lower rear of the cylinder block, then turn the crankshaft, by means of a socket on the crankshaft pulley bolt, until one of the torque converter retaining bolts is accessible through the access hole **(see illustration)**.

19 Undo the accessible torque converter bolt then turn the crankshaft as necessary and undo the remaining two bolts. Discard the bolts, as new ones must be fitted.

20 Place a jack with a block of wood beneath the engine, to take the weight of the engine. Alternatively, attach a couple of lifting eyes to the engine, and fit a hoist or support bar to take the engine weight.

21 Place a jack and block of wood beneath the transmission, and raise the jack to take the weight of the transmission.

22 Slacken and remove the mounting bolts/nuts from the left-hand transmission mounting and remove it from the top of the transmission. Refer to Chapter 2A or 2B for further information on engine/transmission mountings.

23 With the jack positioned beneath the transmission taking the weight, slacken and remove the remaining bolts securing the transmission housing to the engine. Note the correct fitted positions of each bolt and the necessary brackets as they are removed, to use as a reference on refitting.

24 Make a final check that all components have been disconnected, and are positioned clear of the transmission so that they will not hinder the removal procedure.

Caution: As the engine is lowered, make sure no wiring, hoses or cables are being stretched or damaged in any way.

25 With the bolts removed, move the trolley jack and transmission to the left, to free it from its locating dowels. Lower the engine slightly to enable the transmission to be freed. Pull the transmission to the left, to free it from its locating dowels. Ensure the torque converter stays with the transmission, and is not pulled from the input shaft.

26 On AM6 transmissions, once the transmission is free, and sufficient clearance exists, insert a bolt with a suitable washer through the sensor hole in the transmission bellhousing to retain the torque converter on the transmission. It's essential the torque converter stays on the transmission input shaft.

Caution: Take great care not to damage the radiator if the engine is moved – place a sheet of thick cardboard over the rear face of the radiator. On models equipped with air conditioning, care must also be taken to ensure the auxiliary drivebelt pulleys do not damage the air conditioning pipes on the right-hand side of the engine compartment.

27 Once the transmission is free, lower the jack and manoeuvre the unit out from under the car. Remove the locating dowels from the transmission or engine if they are loose, and keep them in a safe place.

28 With the transmission removed, make sure that the torque converter is held securely in place using a bracket across the bellhousing, etc.

Refitting

29 Ensure that the bush fitted to the centre of the crankshaft is in good condition, and apply a little Molykote BR2 grease to the torque converter centering pin.

Caution: Do not apply too much; otherwise there is a possibility of the grease contaminating the torque converter.

30 Ensure that the engine/transmission

locating dowels are correctly positioned then raise the transmission unit into position. Align the torque converter studs with the driveplate holes then engage the transmission unit with the engine.

Caution: Do not allow the weight of the transmission unit to hang on the torque converter as the unit is installed.

31 With the transmission and engine correctly joined, refit the transmission-to-engine unit bolts and tighten them to the specified torque.

32 Screw the new nuts onto the torque converter studs, tightening them lightly only, rotating the crankshaft as necessary. Tighten all three nuts to the specified torque setting.

33 The remainder of refitting is the reverse of removal, noting the following.

a) Apply thread-locking fluid to the left-hand engine/transmission mounting stud threads, prior to refitting it to the transmission. Tighten the stud to the specified torque.

b) Tighten all nuts and bolts to the specified torque (where given).

c) Renew the driveshaft oil seals, then refit the driveshafts (see Chapter 8).

d) Reconnect the selector cable and adjust as described in Section 3.

e) On completion, refill the transmission fluid as described in Section 2.

8 Automatic transmission overhaul – general information

In the event of a fault occurring with the transmission, it is first necessary to determine whether it is of an electrical, mechanical or hydraulic nature, and to do this, special test equipment is required. It is therefore essential to have the work carried out by a Peugeot dealer or suitably-equipped specialist if a transmission fault is suspected.

Do not remove the transmission from the car for possible repair before professional fault diagnosis has been carried out, since most tests require the transmission to be in the vehicle.

Chapter 8
Driveshafts

Contents

Degrees of difficulty

Easy, suitable for novice with little experience	Fairly easy, suitable for beginner with some experience	Fairly difficult, suitable for competent DIY mechanic	Difficult, suitable for experienced DIY mechanic	Very difficult, suitable for expert DIY or professional

Specifications

Lubrication (overhaul only – see text)

Lubricant type/specification .... Use only special grease supplied in sachets with gaiter kits – joints are otherwise pre-packed with grease and sealed

Torque wrench settings	Nm	lbf ft
Driveshaft retaining nut	345	255
Drop link to anti-roll bar retaining nut	55	41
Right-hand driveshaft intermediate bearing retaining bolt nuts	20	15
Roadwheel bolts	90	66
Track rod end retaining nut	45	33
Lower suspension arm to alloy suspension housing	75	55
Lower suspension strut/drop link assembly retaining nut	205	151

1 General information

Drive is transmitted from the differential to the front wheels by means of two solid-steel driveshafts of unequal length.

Both driveshafts are splined at their outer ends, to accept the wheel hubs, and are threaded so that each hub can be fastened by a large nut. The inner end of each driveshaft is splined, to accept the differential sun gear.

Constant velocity (CV) joints are fitted to each end of the driveshafts, to ensure that the smooth and efficient transmission of power at all suspension and steering angles. The outer constant velocity joints are of the ball-and-cage type, and the inner constant velocity joints are of the tripod type.

On the right-hand side, due to the length of the driveshaft, the inner constant velocity joint is situated approximately halfway along the shaft's length, and an intermediate support

bearing is mounted in the engine/transmission rear mounting bracket. The inner end of the driveshaft passes through the bearing (which prevents any lateral movement of the driveshaft inner end) and the inner constant velocity joint outer member.

2 Driveshafts – removal and refitting

Note: Always renew any self-locking nuts when working on the suspension/steering components.

Removal

1 Remove the wheel trim/hub cap (as applicable) then withdraw the R-clip and remove the locking cap from the driveshaft retaining nut (see illustrations). Slacken the driveshaft nut with the vehicle resting on its wheels, do not completely remove at this stage. Also slacken the wheel bolts.
2 Chock the rear wheels of the car, firmly

apply the handbrake, and then jack up the front of the car and support it on axle stands (see Jacking and vehicle support). Remove the appropriate front roadwheel.
3 On manual transmission models drain the transmission oil as described in Chapter 7A. On automatic transmission models there is no need to drain the fluid.
4 To make access easier, remove the brake disc as described in Chapter 9.
5 The driveshaft retaining nut can now be removed. If the nut was not slackened with the wheels on the ground (see paragraph 1), withdraw the R-clip and remove the locking cap. Refit at least two roadwheel bolts to the front hub, tightening them securely, then have an assistant firmly depress the brake pedal to prevent the front hub from rotating, whilst you slacken and remove the driveshaft retaining nut. Alternatively, a tool can be fabricated from two lengths of steel strip (one long, one short) and a nut and bolt, the nut and bolt forming the pivot of a forked tool (see illustrations).
6 Slacken and remove the retaining nut, and

2.1a Withdraw the R-clip . . .

2.1b . . . and remove the locking cap

2.5a Remove the driveshaft retaining nut . . .

2.5b . . . using a fabricated tool to hold the hub stationary, if required

2.6a Undo the retaining nut . . .

2.6b . . . and disconnect the track rod end balljoint

2.7a Undo the retaining nut (arrowed) . . .

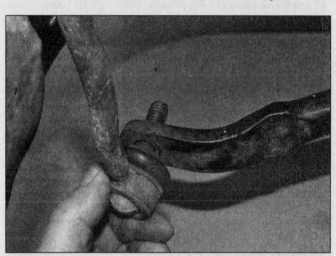

2.7b . . . and disconnect the drop link balljoint from the anti-roll bar

then disconnect the track rod end from the hub carrier **(see illustrations)**.

7 Slacken and remove the retaining nut, and

then disconnect the drop link balljoint from the anti-roll bar **(see illustrations)**.

8 Undo the retaining nut and withdraw the

suspension strut lower mounting bolt/drop link assembly from the alloy suspension housing **(see illustrations)**.

2.8a Undo the retaining nut (arrowed) . . .

2.8b . . . and remove the drop link assembly from the suspension housing

Left-hand driveshaft

9 Slacken and remove the lower suspension arm bolt and carefully lever the lower suspension arm away from the alloy suspension housing **(see illustrations)**.

10 Carefully pull the hub carrier/alloy

2.9a Remove the lower arm securing bolt (arrowed)

suspension housing outwards, and withdraw the driveshaft outer constant velocity joint from the hub assembly **(see illustration)**. If necessary, the shaft can be tapped out of the hub using a soft-faced mallet.

11 Support the driveshaft, and then withdraw the inner constant velocity joint from the transmission, taking care not to damage the driveshaft oil seal. Remove the driveshaft from the vehicle **(see illustration)**.

Caution: Do not allow the vehicle to rest on its wheels with one or both driveshafts removed, as damage to the wheel bearing(s) may result. If moving the vehicle is unavoidable, temporarily insert the outer end of the driveshaft(s) in the hub(s) and tighten the driveshaft nut(s). Support the inner end(s) of the driveshaft(s) to avoid damage.

Right-hand driveshaft

12 Loosen the two intermediate bearing

retaining bolts, then rotate the retaining plate, so that it releases the bearing in the housing **(see illustration)**. **Note:** *it is not necessary to remove the bolts completely, as the upper hole in the retaining plate is elongated to allow the plate to be rotated away from the housing.*

13 Slacken and remove the lower suspension arm bolt and carefully lever the lower suspension arm away from the alloy suspension housing **(see illustrations 2.9a and 2.9b)**.

14 Carefully pull the hub carrier/alloy suspension housing outwards, and withdraw the driveshaft outer constant velocity joint from the hub assembly **(see illustration 2.10)**. If necessary, the shaft can be tapped out of the hub using a soft-faced mallet.

15 Support the outer end of the driveshaft, then pull on the inner end of the shaft to free the intermediate bearing from its mounting bracket.

16 Once the driveshaft end is free from the

2.9b Using a bar and chain to disengage the lower arm from the suspension

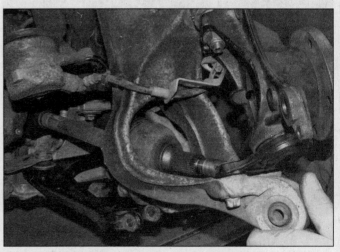

2.10 Pull the suspension housing outwards . . .

2.11 . . . and remove the driveshaft

2.12 Slacken the two intermediate bearing bolts (arrowed)

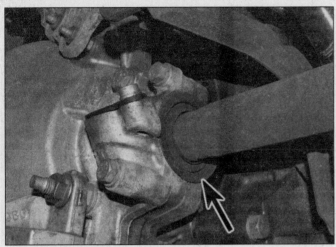

2.16 Note the position of the dust shield (arrowed) – where fitted

2.21 Secure the nut in position with the locking cap and R-clip

transmission, slide the dust seal (where fitted) off the inner end of the shaft, noting which way around it is fitted, and remove the driveshaft from the vehicle **(see illustration)**. Check the condition of the splined shaft O-ring (where fitted).

Caution: Do not allow the vehicle to rest on its wheels with one or both driveshafts removed, as damage to the wheel bearing(s) may result. If moving the vehicle is unavoidable, temporarily insert the outer end of the driveshaft(s) in the hub(s) and tighten the driveshaft nut(s). Support the inner end(s) of the driveshaft(s) to avoid damage.

Refitting

17 Before installing the driveshaft, examine the driveshaft oil seal in the transmission for signs of damage or deterioration and, if necessary, renew it as described in Chapter 7A or 7B. It is highly recommended that the seal be renewed, regardless of its apparent condition.
18 Thoroughly clean the driveshaft splines, and the apertures in the transmission and hub assembly. Apply a thin film of grease to the oil seal lips, and to the driveshaft splines and shoulders. Check that all gaiter clips are securely fastened.

Left-hand driveshaft

19 Offer up the driveshaft, and locate the joint splines with those of the differential sun gear, taking great care not to damage the oil seal. Push the joint fully into position.
20 Locate the outer constant velocity joint splines with those of the swivel hub, and insert the bolt into the lower suspension arm. Do not tighten the retaining bolt at this point, this will need to be tightened when the vehicle is in the ride height position (see Chapter 10).
21 Lubricate the inner face and threads of the driveshaft nut with clean engine oil, and refit it to the end of the driveshaft. Use the method

employed on removal to prevent the hub from rotating (see paragraph 5), and tighten the driveshaft retaining nut to the specified torque. Check that the hub rotates freely then engage the locking cap with the driveshaft nut, so that one of its cut-outs is aligned with the driveshaft hole, and secure the cap in position with the R-clip **(see illustration)**. Alternatively, lightly tighten the nut at this stage, and tighten it to the specified torque once the car is resting on its wheels again.
22 Refit the suspension strut lower mounting bolt/drop link assembly to the alloy suspension housing and tighten the retaining nut.
23 Reconnect the drop link balljoint to the anti-roll bar and tighten the retaining nut.
24 Reconnect the track rod end to the hub carrier and tighten the retaining nut.
25 Refit the brake disc and brake caliper as described in Chapter 9.
26 Refit the roadwheel, then lower the vehicle to the ground and tighten the roadwheel bolts to the specified torque. If not already done, tighten the driveshaft retaining nut to the specified torque then refit the locking cap, aligning its cut-outs with the driveshaft hole, and secure it in position with the R-clip.
27 Refill the transmission with the specified type and amount of oil, and check the level using the information given in Chapter 1.

Right-hand driveshaft

28 Check that the intermediate bearing rotates smoothly, without any sign of roughness or undue free play between its inner and outer races. If necessary, renew the bearing as described in Section 5. Examine the dust seal for signs of damage or deterioration, and renew if necessary. Check the condition of the differential splined shaft O-ring seal and renew if necessary.
29 Apply a smear of grease to the outer race of the intermediate bearing, and to the inner lip of the dust seal (where fitted).
30 Pass the inner end of the shaft through

the bearing mounting bracket then, where necessary, carefully slide the dust seal into position on the driveshaft, ensuring that its flat surface is facing the transmission.
31 On manual transmission models, carefully locate the inner driveshaft splines with those of the differential sun gear, taking care not to damage the oil seal.
32 On automatic transmission models, located the end of the driveshaft over the differential splined shaft.
33 On all models, align the intermediate bearing with its mounting bracket, and push the driveshaft fully into position. If necessary, use a soft-faced mallet to tap the outer race of the bearing into position in the mounting bracket.
34 Locate the outer constant velocity joint splines with those of the swivel hub, and insert the bolt into the lower suspension arm. Do not tighten the retaining bolt at this point, this will need to be tightened when the vehicle is in the ride height position, see Chapter 10.
35 Ensure that the intermediate bearing is correctly seated, and then rotate its retaining plate back into position against the bearing outer race and tighten the retaining bolts to the specified torque. Where necessary, ensure that the dust seal is tight against the driveshaft oil seal.
36 Carry out the operations described above in paragraphs 21 to 27.

3 Driveshaft rubber gaiters – renewal

Outer joint

1 Remove the driveshaft from the vehicle as described in Section 2.
2 Secure the driveshaft in a vice equipped with soft jaws, and release the two outer gaiter retaining clips. If necessary, the gaiter

3.2 If necessary, cut through the gaiter clips

3.4 Use a punch to drive the inner member of the outer joint from the shaft

3.5 Prise the old circlip from the shaft

retaining clips can be cut to release them **(see illustration)**.

3 Slide the rubber gaiter down the shaft, to expose the outer constant velocity joint. Scoop out the excess grease.

4 Using a hammer and suitable soft metal drift, sharply strike the inner member of the outer joint to drive it off the end of the shaft **(see illustration)**. The joint is retained on the driveshaft by a circlip, and striking the joint in this manner forces the circlip into its groove, so allowing the joint to slide off.

5 Once the joint assembly has been removed, remove the circlip from the groove in the driveshaft splines, and discard it **(see illustration)**. A new circlip must be fitted on reassembly.

6 Withdraw the rubber gaiter from the driveshaft. Depending on type of gaiter fitted, there may be a plastic bush fitted to the driveshaft. Where necessary, slide off the inner end plastic bush **(see illustration)**.

7 With the constant velocity joint removed from the driveshaft, thoroughly clean the joint using paraffin, or a suitable solvent, and dry it thoroughly. Carry out a visual inspection of the joint.

8 Move the inner splined driving member from side-to-side, to expose each ball in turn at the top of its track. Examine the balls for cracks, flat spots, or signs of surface pitting.

9 Inspect the ball tracks on the inner and outer members. If the tracks have widened, the balls will no longer be a tight fit. At the same time, check the ball cage windows for wear or cracking between the windows.

10 If, on inspection, any of the constant velocity joint components are found to be worn or damaged in any way, it will be necessary to renew the complete joint assembly (where available), or even the complete driveshaft if no joint components are available separately. Refer to your Peugeot dealer for further information on parts availability. If the joint is in satisfactory condition, obtain a repair kit consisting of a new gaiter, circlip, retaining clips, and the correct type and quantity of grease. Note that some types of gaiters have hard plastic rings and plastic bushes fitted **(see illustration)**.

11 To install the new gaiter, perform the

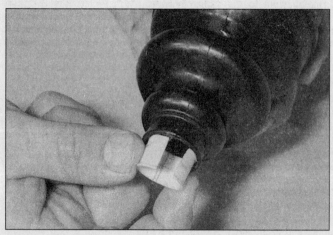

3.6 Where applicable, remove the plastic bush

3.10 Where applicable, fit the hard plastic rings to the outer CV joint gaiter

3.11a Fit the small diameter clip to the new gaiter, and slide it over the end of the driveshaft . . .

3.11b . . . fit a new circlip into the groove on the end of the shaft . . .

3.11c . . . align the outer joint inner member with the splines on the shaft . . .

3.11d . . . and tap the outer joint into place with a soft-faced hammer. Ensure the joint is securely retained by the circlip . . .

3.11e . . . pack the joint with the contents of the grease sachet supplied with the kit. Work the grease well into the joint . . .

operations shown **(see illustrations)**. Be sure to stay in order, and follow the captions carefully. Note the gaiter retaining clips supplied with the repair kit may be different to those shown in the sequence.

12 Check that the constant velocity joint moves freely in all directions, and then refit the driveshaft to the vehicle as described in Section 2.

Inner joint

13 Remove the driveshaft from the vehicle as described in Section 2.

14 Remove the outer constant velocity joint as described above in paragraphs 1 to 5.

15 Tape over the splines on the driveshaft, and carefully remove the outer constant velocity joint rubber gaiter, and (where fitted) the gaiter inner end plastic bush. It is recommended that the outer joint gaiter is also renewed, regardless of its apparent condition.

16 Release the retaining clips, then slide the inner gaiter off the shaft and (where fitted) remove its plastic bush **(see illustration 3.6)**.

17 As the gaiter is released, the joint outer member will also be freed from the end of the shaft **(see illustrations)**.

18 Thoroughly clean the joint using paraffin, or a suitable solvent, and dry it thoroughly. Check the tripod joint bearings and joint outer member for signs of wear, pitting or scuffing on

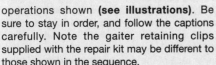
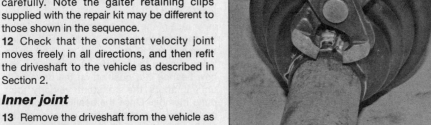

3.11f . . . locate the small diameter of the gaiter in the groove on the shaft, and crimp the retaining clip . . .

3.11g . . . with the large diameter of the gaiter located on the outside of the outer joint, crimp the retaining clip

3.17a Release the inner gaiter retaining clips, and remove the joint outer member

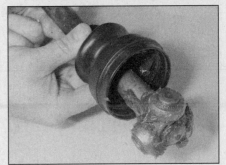

3.17b Slide the gaiter off the end of the driveshaft

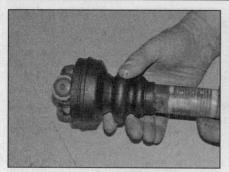

3.21 Locate the new gaiter in the groove on the shaft

3.22 Fit the new clips and crimp them into place

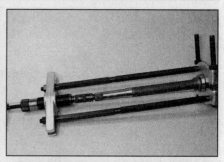

5.3 Use a long-reach bearing puller to remove the intermediate bearing from the right-hand driveshaft

their bearing surfaces. Check that the bearing rollers rotate smoothly and easily around the tripod joint, with no traces of roughness.

19 If, on inspection, the tripod joint or outer member reveal signs of wear or damage, it will be necessary to renew the complete driveshaft assembly, since the joint is not available separately. If the joint is in satisfactory condition, obtain a repair kit consisting of a new gaiter, retaining clips, and the correct type and quantity of grease.

20 On reassembly, pack the inner joint with the grease supplied in the gaiter kit. Work the grease well into the bearing tracks and rollers, while twisting the joint.

21 Clean the shaft, using emery cloth to remove any rust or sharp edges which may damage the gaiter, then slide the plastic bush (where fitted) and inner joint gaiter along the driveshaft. Locate the plastic bush in its recess on the shaft, and seat the inner end of the gaiter on top of the bush; where no bush is fitted, seat the inner end of the driveshaft gaiter in the recess on the shaft **(see illustration)**.

22 Fit the outer member over the end of the shaft, and locate the gaiter in the groove on the joint outer member. Push the outer member onto the joint, so that its spring-loaded plunger is compressed, then lift the outer edge of the gaiter to equalise air pressure in the gaiter. Fit both the inner and outer retaining clips, securing them in position using the information given in paragraph 11. Ensure that the gaiter retaining clips are securely tightened, and

then check that the joint moves freely in all directions **(see illustration)**.

23 Refit the outer constant velocity joint components as described previously in the Section.

4 Driveshaft overhaul – general information

1 If any of the checks described in Chapter 1 reveal wear in any driveshaft joint, first remove the roadwheel trim or centre cap (as appropriate).

2 If the R-clip is still in position, the driveshaft nut should be correctly tightened; if in doubt, remove the R-clip and locking cap, and use a torque wrench to check that the nut is securely fastened. Once tightened, refit the locking cap and R-clip, and then refit the centre cap or trim. Repeat this check on the remaining driveshaft nut.

3 Road test the vehicle, and listen for a metallic clicking from the front as the vehicle is driven slowly in a circle on full-lock. If a clicking noise is heard, this indicates wear in the outer constant velocity joint. This means that the joint must be renewed; reconditioning is not possible.

4 If vibration, consistent with roadspeed, is felt through the car when accelerating, there is a possibility of wear in the inner joints.

5 To check the joints for wear, remove the driveshafts, and then dismantle them as described in Section 3; if any wear or free play is found, the affected joint must be renewed. In the case of the inner joints (and on some models,

the outer joints), this means that the complete driveshaft assembly must be renewed, as the joints are not available separately. Refer to your Peugeot dealer for latest information on the availability of driveshaft components.

5 Right-hand driveshaft intermediate bearing – renewal

Note: *A suitable bearing puller will be required, to draw the bearing and collar off the driveshaft end.*

1 Remove the right-hand driveshaft as described in Section 2 of this Chapter.

2 Check that the bearing outer race rotates smoothly and easily, without any signs of roughness or undue free play between the inner and outer races. If necessary, renew the bearing as follows.

3 Using a long-reach universal bearing puller, carefully draw the collar and intermediate bearing off the driveshaft inner end **(see illustration)**. Apply a smear of grease to the inner race of the new bearing, and then fit the bearing over the end of the driveshaft. Using a hammer and suitable piece of tubing which bears only on the bearing inner race, tap the new bearing into position on the driveshaft, until it abuts the constant velocity joint outer member. Once the bearing is correctly positioned, tap the bearing collar onto the shaft until it contacts the bearing inner race.

4 Check that the bearing rotates freely, then refit the driveshaft as described in Section 2.

Chapter 9
Braking system

Contents

Degrees of difficulty

Easy, suitable for novice with little experience	Fairly easy, suitable for beginner with some experience	Fairly difficult, suitable for competent DIY mechanic	Difficult, suitable for experienced DIY mechanic	Very difficult, suitable for expert DIY or professional

Specifications

Engine identification
1.6 litre:
  Designation. DV6TED4
  Engine codes . . . . 9HY or 9HZ
2.0 litre:
  Designation. . . . . DW10BTED4 or DW10CTED4
  Engine codes:
    DW10BTED4. . . . . RHF, RHL or RHR
    DW10CTED4. . . . . RHH

Front brakes
Type . . . . Vented discs, with single-piston sliding caliper on all models except coupe. Coupe has twin-piston sliding caliper
Disc diameter:
  DV6TED4 . . . . 283 mm
  DW10BTED4:
    Except coupe . . . . 283 mm
    Coupe. . . . . 330 mm
  DW10CTED4 . . . . 304 mm
Disc thickness:
  New:
    DV6TED4 . . . . 26 mm
    DW10BTED4:
      Except coupe . . . . 26 mm
      Coupe. . . . . 30 mm
    DW10CTED4 . . . . 28 mm
  Minimum:
    DV6TED4 . . . . 24 mm
    DW10BTED4:
      Except coupe . . . . 24 mm
      Coupe. . . . . 28 mm
    DW10CTED4 . . . . 26 mm

Front brakes (continued)
Maximum disc run-out . . . . 0.07 mm
Brake caliper:
  Make:
    DV6TED4 . . . . TRW
    DW10BTED4 . . . . TRW
    DW10CTED4 . . . . TEVES
  Piston diameter:
    DV6TED4 . . . . 57 mm
    DW10BTED4:
      Except coupe . . . . 57 mm
      Coupe (twin piston caliper) . . . . 40 mm and 45 mm
    DW10CTED4 . . . . 60 mm
Brake pad friction material thickness (minimum) . . . . 2.0 mm

Rear disc brakes
Type . . . . Solid disc, with single-piston sliding caliper
Disc diameter . . . . 290 mm
Disc thickness:
  New . . . . 12.0 mm
  Minimum thickness . . . . 10.0 mm
Maximum disc run-out . . . . 0.07 mm
Brake caliper make . . . . TRW
Brake caliper piston diameter . . . . 38 mm
Brake pad friction material thickness (minimum) . . . . 2.0 mm

Brake servo
Type . . . . TEVES
Diameter:
  Up to RPO No 12057 . . . . 250 mm
  From RPO No 12058 . . . . 255 mm

Brake master cylinder
Make . . . . TEVES
Diameter:
  DV6TED4 . . . . 22.2 mm
  DW10BTED4 . . . . 22.2 mm
  DW10CTED4 . . . . 23.8 mm

Torque wrench settings

	Nm	lbf ft
ABS system components:		
Regulator unit nuts	8	6
Wheel sensor retaining bolts*	8	6
Crossover linkage housing nuts and bolts (right-hand drive models)	25	18
Disc retaining screws	10	7
Front brake caliper:		
Guide pin bolts (TWR):*	29	21
Guide pins (TEVES)	27	20
Mounting bracket bolts*	115	85
Handbrake lever nuts	15	11
Hydraulic hose/pipe union nuts	15	11
Hydraulic hose-to-caliper union bolt	40	30
Master cylinder retaining nuts	20	15
Rear brake caliper:		
Guide pin bolts*	30	22
Mounting bracket bolts*	108	80
Roadwheel bolts	90	66
Vacuum pump (brakes):		
DV6TED4:		
Stage 1	5	4
Stage 2	18	13
Stage 3	Angle-tighten a further 5°	
DW10BTED4	9	7
DW10CTED4	10	7
Vacuum servo unit to bracket/bulkhead mounting nuts	25	18

* Do not re-use.

1 General information

The braking system is of the servo-assisted, dual-circuit hydraulic type. The arrangement of the hydraulic system is such that each circuit operates one front and one rear brake from a tandem master cylinder. Under normal circumstances, both circuits operate in unison. However, in the event of hydraulic failure in one circuit, full braking force will still be available at two wheels.

All models are equipped with disc brakes on all wheels. ABS is fitted as standard (refer to Section 18 for further information on ABS operation).

The disc brakes are actuated by single-piston sliding type calipers (on all models except 2.0 litre coupe models, which have 2 pistons), which ensure that equal pressure is applied to each disc pad.

On all models, the handbrake provides an independent mechanical means of rear brake application. The handbrake cable operates a lever on the caliper, which forces the piston to press the pad against the disc surface. A self-adjust mechanism is incorporated, to automatically compensate for brake pad wear.

A vacuum pump is fitted to the engine, to provide sufficient vacuum to operate the servo unit. The vacuum pump is mounted on the end of the cylinder head, and is driven directly off the end of the camshaft.

Note: *When servicing any of the system, work carefully and methodically; also observe scrupulous cleanliness when overhauling any of the hydraulic system. Always renew components (in axle sets, where applicable) if in doubt about their condition, and use only genuine Peugeot parts, or at least those of known good quality. Note the warnings given in 'Safety first!' and at relevant points in this Chapter concerning the dangers of asbestos dust and hydraulic fluid.*

2 Hydraulic system – bleeding

⚠️ **Warning: Hydraulic fluid is poisonous; wash off immediately and thoroughly in the case of skin contact, and seek immediate medical advice if any fluid is swallowed or gets into the eyes. Certain types of hydraulic fluid are inflammable, and may ignite when allowed into contact with hot components; when servicing any hydraulic system, it is safest to assume that the fluid is inflammable, and to take precautions against the risk of fire as though it is petrol that is being handled. Hydraulic fluid is also an effective paint**

stripper, and will attack plastics. If any is spilt, it should be washed off immediately, using copious quantities of fresh water. Finally, it is hygroscopic (it absorbs moisture from the air) – old fluid may be contaminated and unfit for further use. When topping-up or renewing the fluid, always use the recommended type, and ensure that it comes from a freshly-opened sealed container.

Caution: *Ensure the ignition is switched off before starting the bleeding procedure, to avoid any possibility of voltage being applied to the hydraulic modulator before the bleeding procedure is complete. Ideally, the battery should be disconnected. If voltage is applied to the modulator before the bleeding procedure is complete, this will effectively drain the hydraulic fluid in the modulator, rendering the unit unserviceable. Do not, therefore, attempt to 'run' the modulator in order to bleed the brakes.*

Note: *If difficulty is experienced in bleeding the braking circuit, this maybe due to air being trapped in the ABS regulator unit. If this is the case then the vehicle should be taken to a Peugeot dealer or suitably-equipped specialist so that the system can be bled using special electronic test equipment.*

Note: *A hydraulic clutch shares its fluid reservoir with the braking system, and may also need to be bled (see Chapter 6).*

General

1 The correct operation of any hydraulic system is only possible after removing all air from the components and circuit; this is achieved by bleeding the system.

2 During the bleeding procedure, add only clean, unused hydraulic fluid of the recommended type; never re-use fluid that has already been bled from the system. Ensure that sufficient fluid is available before starting work.

3 If there is any possibility of incorrect fluid being already in the system, the brake components and circuit must be flushed completely with uncontaminated, correct fluid, and new seals should be fitted to the various components.

4 If hydraulic fluid has been lost from the system, or air has entered because of a leak, ensure that the fault is cured before proceeding further.

5 Park the vehicle on level ground, switch off the engine and select first or reverse gear, then chock the wheels and release the handbrake.

6 Check that all pipes and hoses are secure, unions tight and bleed screws closed. Clean any dirt from around the bleed screws.

7 Unscrew the master cylinder reservoir cap, and top the master cylinder reservoir up to the MAX level line; refit the cap loosely, and remember to maintain the fluid level at least above the MIN/DANGER level line throughout

the procedure, or there is a risk of further air entering the system.

8 There is a number of one-man, do-it-yourself brake bleeding kits currently available from motor accessory shops. It is recommended that one of these kits is used whenever possible, as they greatly simplify the bleeding operation, and also reduce the risk of expelled air and fluid being drawn back into the system. If such a kit is not available, the basic (two-man) method must be used, which is described in detail below.

9 If a kit is to be used, prepare the vehicle as described previously, and follow the kit manufacturer's instructions, as the procedure may vary slightly according to the type being used; generally, they are as outlined below in the relevant sub-section.

10 Whichever method is used, the same sequence must be followed (paragraphs 11 and 12) to ensure that the removal of all air from the system.

Bleeding

Sequence

11 If the system has been only partially disconnected, and suitable precautions were taken to minimise fluid loss, it should be necessary only to bleed that of the system (ie, the primary or secondary circuit).

12 If the complete system is to be bled, then it should be done working in the following sequence:

 a) Left-hand front brake.
 b) Right-hand front brake.
 c) Left-hand rear brake.
 d) Right-hand rear brake.

Basic (two-man) method

13 Collect a clean glass jar, a suitable length of plastic or rubber tubing which is a tight fit over the bleed screw, and a ring spanner to fit the screw. The help of an assistant will also be required.

14 Remove the dust cap from the first screw in the sequence. Fit the spanner and tube to the screw, place the other end of the tube in the jar, and pour in sufficient fluid to cover the end of the tube **(see illustration)**.

15 Ensure that the master cylinder reservoir fluid level is maintained at least above the

2.14 Bleeding a rear brake caliper

MIN/DANGER level line throughout the procedure **(see illustration).**

16 Have the assistant fully depress the brake pedal several times to build-up pressure, and then maintain it on the final downstroke.

17 While pedal pressure is maintained, unscrew the bleed screw (approximately one turn) and allow the compressed fluid and air to flow into the jar. The assistant should maintain pedal pressure, following it down to the floor if necessary, and should not release it until instructed to do so. When the flow stops, tighten the bleed screw again, have the assistant release the pedal slowly, and recheck the reservoir fluid level.

18 Repeat the steps given in paragraphs 16 and 17 until the fluid emerging from the bleed screw is free from air bubbles. If the master cylinder has been drained and refilled, and air is being bled from the first screw in the sequence, allow approximately five seconds between cycles for the master cylinder passages to refill.

19 When no more air bubbles appear, tighten the bleed screw securely, remove the tube and spanner, and refit the dust cap. Do not overtighten the bleed screw.

20 Repeat the procedure on the remaining screws in the sequence, until all air is removed from the system and the brake pedal feels firm again.

Using a one-way valve kit

21 As their name implies, these kits consist of a length of tubing with a one-way valve fitted, to prevent expelled air and fluid being drawn back into the system; some kits include a translucent container, which can be positioned so that the air bubbles can be more easily seen flowing from the end of the tube.

22 The kit is connected to the bleed screw, which is then opened. The user returns to the driver's seat, depresses the brake pedal with a smooth, steady stroke, and slowly releases it; this is repeated until the expelled fluid is clear of air bubbles.

23 Note that these kits simplify work so much that it is easy to forget the master cylinder reservoir fluid level; ensure that this is maintained at least above the MIN/DANGER level line at all times.

Using a pressure-bleeding kit

24 These kits are usually operated by the reservoir of pressurised air contained in the spare tyre. However, note that it will probably be necessary to reduce the pressure to a lower level than normal; refer to the instructions supplied with the kit.

25 By connecting a pressurised, fluid-filled container to the master cylinder reservoir, bleeding can be carried out simply by opening each screw in turn (in the specified sequence), and allowing the fluid to flow out until no more air bubbles can be seen in the expelled fluid.

26 This method has the advantage that the large reservoir of fluid provides an additional safeguard against air being drawn into the system during bleeding.

2.15 Brake fluid reservoir upper and lower levels (arrowed)

27 Pressure-bleeding is particularly effective when bleeding 'difficult' systems, or when bleeding the complete system at the time of routine fluid renewal.

All methods

28 When bleeding is complete, and firm pedal feel is restored, wash off any spilt fluid, tighten the bleed screws securely, and refit their dust caps.

29 Check the hydraulic fluid level in the master cylinder reservoir, and top-up if necessary (see *Weekly checks*).

30 Discard any hydraulic fluid that has been bled from the system; it will not be fit for re-use.

31 Check the feel of the brake pedal. If it feels at all spongy, air must still be present in the system, and further bleeding is required. Failure to bleed satisfactorily after a reasonable repetition of the bleeding procedure may be due to worn master cylinder seals.

---

3 Hydraulic pipes and hoses – renewal

Caution: Ensure the ignition is switched off before disconnecting any braking system hydraulic union and do not switch it on until after the hydraulic system has been bled. Failure to do this could lead to air entering the regulator unit requiring the unit to be bled using special Peugeot test equipment (see Section 2).

Note: *Before starting work, refer to the note at the beginning of Section 2 concerning the dangers of hydraulic fluid.*

1 If any pipe or hose is to be renewed, minimise fluid loss by first removing the master cylinder reservoir cap, then tightening it down onto a piece of polythene to obtain an airtight seal. Alternatively, flexible hoses can be sealed, if required, using a proprietary brake hose clamp; metal brake pipe unions can be plugged (if care is taken not to allow dirt into the system) or capped immediately they are disconnected. Place a wad of rag under any union that is to be disconnected, to catch any spilt fluid.

2 If a flexible hose is to be disconnected, unscrew the brake pipe union nut before

3.2 Slacken the union nut (arrowed) and then remove the spring clip

removing the spring clip which secures the hose to its mounting bracket **(see illustration).**

3 To unscrew the union nuts, it is preferable to obtain a brake pipe spanner of the correct size; these are available from most large motor accessory shops. Failing this, a close-fitting open-ended spanner will be required, though if the nuts are tight or corroded, their flats may be rounded-off if the spanner slips. In such a case, a self-locking wrench is often the only way to unscrew a stubborn union, but it follows that the pipe and the damaged nuts must be renewed on reassembly. Always clean a union and surrounding area before disconnecting it. If disconnecting a component with more than one union, make a careful note of the connections before disturbing any of them.

4 If a brake pipe is to be renewed, it can be obtained, cut to length and with the union nuts and end flares in place, from Peugeot dealers. All that is then necessary is to bend it to shape, following the line of the original, before fitting it to the car. Alternatively, most motor accessory shops can make up brake pipes from kits, but this requires very careful measurement of the original, to ensure that the new one is of the correct length. The safest answer is usually to take the original to the shop as a pattern.

5 On refitting, do not overtighten the union nuts. It is not necessary to exercise brute force to obtain a sound joint.

6 Ensure that the pipes and hoses are correctly routed, with no kinks, and that they are secured in the clips or brackets provided. After fitting, remove the polythene from the reservoir, and bleed the hydraulic system as described in Section 2. Wash off any spilt fluid, and check carefully for fluid leaks.

---

4 Front brake pads – renewal

⚠ *Warning: Renew both sets of front brake pads at the same time – never renew the pads on only one wheel, as uneven braking may result. Note that the dust created by wear of the pads may contain asbestos, which is a health hazard.*

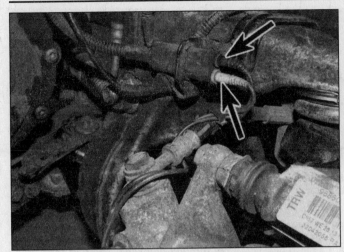

4.3a Disconnect the brake pad wear sensors wiring plugs (arrowed) . . .

4.3b . . . and unclip the wiring from the dust cap retaining clip

Never blow it out with compressed air, and don't inhale any of it. An approved filtering mask should be worn when working on the brakes. DO NOT use petrol or petroleum-based solvents to clean brake parts; use brake cleaner or methylated spirit only.
Note: *New guide pin bolts/guide pins must be used on refitting.*

Removal

1 Apply the handbrake, slacken the front roadwheel bolts, then jack up the front of the vehicle and support it on axle stands. Remove the front roadwheels.

2 The piston can be pushed back into its bore, by pulling the caliper outwards. Check the level of the brake fluid in the reservoir before pushing the piston back, as there could be some spillage.
3 Disconnect the brake warning light wiring connectors (where fitted), and then release the wiring from the securing clips **(see illustrations)**.
4 To allow for more movement of the brake caliper, undo the retaining bolts/nut and disconnect the flexible hose brackets from the hub carrier and alloy housing **(see illustrations)**.

TRW calipers

5 Slacken and remove the upper and lower caliper guide pin bolts **(see illustrations)**. Use an open-ended spanner to hold the guide, while the securing bolt is removed. Discard the guide pin bolts – new ones must be used on refitting.
6 With the bolts removed, withdraw the caliper away from the brake pads and mounting bracket. Fasten the caliper to the inner wing or suspension strut, using a suitable piece of wire **(see illustrations)**.
7 Withdraw the two brake pads from the

4.4a Undo the nut and bolt (arrowed) . . .

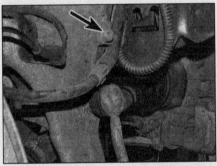

4.4b . . . and the bracket securing bolt (arrowed) on the suspension

4.5a Use an open-ended spanner to hold the guide . . .

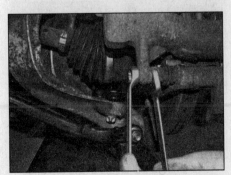

4.5b . . . while removing the upper and lower retaining bolts

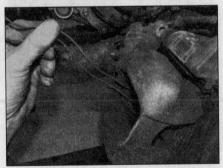

4.6a Withdraw the caliper from the brake pads . . .

4.6b . . . and secure it safely to one side

4.7a Remove the outer . . .

4.7b . . . and inner brake pads from the mounting bracket

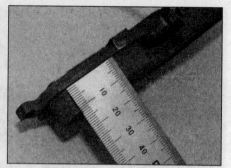

4.12 Measure the thickness of the pads friction material

caliper mounting bracket; the shims (where fitted) should be bonded to the pad, but may have come unstuck in use (see illustrations).

TEVES calipers

8 Release the legs of the retaining spring from the outside of the caliper body, and then unclip the spring from the caliper mounting bracket.

9 Remove the dust caps at the rear of the caliper from the upper and lower caliper guide pins.

10 Unscrew the guide pins from the rear of the caliper and withdraw the caliper away from the brake pads and mounting bracket. Fasten the caliper to the inner wing or suspension strut, using a suitable piece of wire to prevent the hose getting damaged.

11 Remove the two brake pads; the shims (where fitted) should be bonded to the pad, but may have come unstuck in use.

All calipers

12 First measure the thickness of each brake pad's friction material (see illustration). If either pad is worn at any point to the specified minimum thickness or less, all four pads must be renewed. Also, the pads should be renewed if any are fouled with oil or grease; there is no satisfactory way of degreasing friction material, once contaminated. If any of the brake pads are worn unevenly, or are fouled with oil or grease, trace and rectify the cause before reassembly.

13 If the brake pads are still serviceable,

carefully clean them using a clean, fine wire brush or similar, paying particular attention to the sides and back of the metal backing. Clean out the grooves in the friction material, and pick out any large embedded particles of dirt or debris. Carefully clean the pad locations in the caliper mounting bracket.

14 Prior to fitting the pads, check that the guide pins are free to slide easily in the caliper mounting bracket, and check that the rubber guide pin gaiters are undamaged (see illustration). Brush the dust and dirt from the caliper and piston, but do not inhale it, as it is a health hazard. Inspect the dust seal around the piston for damage, and the piston for evidence of fluid leaks, corrosion or damage. If attention to any of these components is necessary, refer to Section 8.

15 If new brake pads are to be fitted, the caliper piston(s) must be pushed back into the cylinder to make room for them. Either use a G-clamp or similar tool, or use suitable pieces of wood as levers. Clamp off the flexible brake hose leading to the caliper then connect a brake bleeding kit to the caliper bleed nipple. Open the bleed nipple as the piston is retracted, the surplus brake fluid will then be collected in the bleed kit vessel (see illustration). Close the bleed nipple just before the caliper piston is pushed fully into the caliper. This should ensure no air enters the hydraulic system.

Caution: The ABS unit contains hydraulic components that are very sensitive to

impurities in the brake fluid. Even the smallest particles can cause the system to fail through blockage. The pad retraction method described here prevents any debris in the brake fluid expelled from the caliper from being passed back to the ABS hydraulic unit, as well as preventing any chance of damage to the master cylinder seals.

Refitting

TRW calipers

16 Check to make sure the shims at the top and bottom of the caliper bracket are correctly fitted (see illustration).

17 Ensuring that the friction material of each pad is against the brake disc, fit the pads to the caliper mounting bracket. If the shims (where fitted) have become detached, ensure that they are correctly positioned on each pads backing plate. If the pads have a chamfer at one edge, fit the pads so that the chamfer is at the top.

18 Refit the caliper into position over the pads; making sure that any warning light wiring is passed up through the caliper. If the threads of the new guide pin bolt are not already precoated with locking compound, apply a suitable thread-locking compound to them (Peugeot recommend Loctite Frenetanch – available from your Peugeot dealer). Press the caliper into position, then install the guide pin

4.14 Check the condition of the guide pin rubbers

4.15 Open the bleed nipple and push the piston back (piston retraction tool shown)

4.16 Ensure the shims at the top and bottom of the caliper mounting bracket are correctly fitted

4.18 Apply thread-locking compound to the guide pin bolts

5.2 Disengage the handbrake cable from the caliper lever

5.3 Release the brake hose from the retaining clip

bolts, tightening them to the specified torque setting (see illustration).

TEVES calipers

19 Apply a small amount of high-melting point copper brake grease to the pad contact areas of the caliper mounting bracket.

20 Ensuring that the friction material of each pad is against the brake disc, fit the pads to the caliper mounting bracket. If the shims (where fitted) have become detached, ensure that they are correctly positioned on each pads backing plate. If the pads have a chamfer at one edge, fit the pads so that the chamfer is at the top.

21 Refit the caliper into position over the pads; making sure that any warning light wiring (where fitted) is passed up through the caliper. If the threads of the new guide pins are not already precoated with locking compound, apply a suitable thread-locking compound to them (Peugeot recommend Loctite Frenetanch – available from your Peugeot dealer). Press the caliper into position, then install the guide pins, tightening them to the specified torque setting.

22 Refit the dust caps at the rear of the caliper to the upper and lower caliper guide pins.

23 Locate the retaining spring legs into the holes in the caliper, and then hold the legs in place and locate the spring behind the lugs on the mounting bracket.

All calipers

24 Refit the flexible hose bracket to the hub

carrier and tighten the retaining bolts and nut. Make sure the hose is routed correctly and not twisted.

25 Reconnect the brake warning light wiring connectors and secure the wiring in the securing clips.

26 Depress the brake pedal repeatedly, until the pads are pressed into firm contact with the brake disc, and normal (non-assisted) pedal pressure is restored.

27 Repeat the above procedure on the remaining front brake caliper.

28 Refit the roadwheels, then lower the vehicle to the ground and tighten the roadwheel bolts to the specified torque.

29 Check the hydraulic fluid level as described in Weekly checks.

Caution: New pads will not give full braking efficiency until they have bedded-in. Be prepared for this, and avoid hard braking as far as possible for the first hundred miles or so after pad renewal.

5 Rear brake pads – renewal

⚠ *Warning: Renew both sets of rear brake pads at the same time – never renew the pads on only one wheel, as uneven braking may result. Note that the dust created by wear of the pads may contain asbestos, which is a health hazard.*

Never blow it out with compressed air, and don't inhale any of it. An approved filtering mask should be worn when working on the brakes. DO NOT use petrol or petroleum-based solvents to clean brake parts; use brake cleaner or methylated spirit only.

Note: *New guide pin bolts must be fitted on reassembly.*

1 Chock the front wheels, slacken the rear roadwheel bolts, and then jack up the rear of the vehicle and support it on axle stands (see *Jacking and vehicle support*). Remove the rear roadwheels and leave the handbrake in the off position.

2 Using a pair of pliers, release the handbrake cable from the caliper lever and pull the cable from the support bracket (see illustration).

3 Unclip the flexible brake hose from the mounting brackets at the rear of the hub carrier (see illustration).

4 Slacken and remove the upper and lower caliper guide pin bolts (see illustrations). Use an open-ended spanner to hold the guide, while the securing bolt is removed. Discard the guide pin bolts – new ones must be used on refitting.

5 With the bolts removed, withdraw the caliper away from the brake pads and mounting bracket. Fasten the caliper to the inner wing or suspension strut, using a suitable piece of wire (see illustration).

6 Withdraw the two brake pads from the caliper mounting bracket; the shims (where fitted) should be bonded to the pad, but may

5.4a Use an open-ended spanner to hold the guide . . .

5.4b . . . while removing the upper and lower guide pin bolts

5.5 Withdraw the caliper from the brake pads and secure it safely to one side

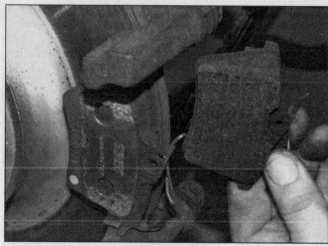

5.6a Remove the inner . . .

5.6b . . . and outer brake pads from the mounting bracket

have come unstuck in use **(see illustrations)**.

7 First measure the thickness of the friction material of each brake pad. If either pad is worn at any point to the specified minimum thickness or less, all four pads must be renewed. Also, the pads should be renewed if any are fouled with oil or grease; there is no satisfactory way of degreasing friction material, once contaminated. If any of the brake pads are worn unevenly, or fouled with oil or grease, trace and rectify the cause before reassembly. Examine the retaining pins for signs of wear and renew if necessary. New brake pads and retaining pin kits are available from Peugeot dealers.

8 If the brake pads are still serviceable, carefully clean them using a clean, fine wire brush or similar, paying particular attention to the sides and back of the metal backing. Clean out the grooves in the friction material, and pick out any large embedded particles of dirt or debris. Carefully clean the pad locations in the caliper body/mounting bracket.

9 Prior to fitting the pads, check that the guide sleeves are free to slide easily in the caliper body, and check that the rubber guide sleeve gaiters are undamaged. Brush the dust and dirt from the caliper and piston, but **do not** inhale it, as it is a health hazard. Inspect the dust seal around the piston for

damage, and the piston for evidence of fluid leaks, corrosion or damage. If attention to any of these components is necessary, refer to Section 9.

10 If new brake pads are to be fitted, the caliper piston must be pushed back into the cylinder to make room for them. In order to retract the piston, the piston must be turned clockwise as it is pushed into the caliper. Peugeot tool No 0805-JZ is available to retract the pistons, as are several available from good accessory/parts retailers **(see illustration)**. Clamp off the flexible brake hose leading to the caliper then connect a brake bleeding kit to the caliper bleed nipple. Open the bleed nipple as the piston is retracted, the surplus brake fluid will then be collected in the bleed kit vessel. Close the bleed nipple just before the caliper piston is pushed fully into the caliper. This should ensure no air enters the hydraulic system.

Caution: The ABS unit contains hydraulic components that are very sensitive to impurities in the brake fluid. Even the smallest particles can cause the system to fail through blockage. The pad retraction method described here prevents any debris in the brake fluid expelled from the caliper from being passed back to the ABS hydraulic unit, as well as preventing any

chance of damage to the master cylinder seals.

11 Check to make sure the shims at the top and bottom of the caliper bracket are correctly fitted **(see illustration)**.

12 Slide the brake pads into position in the caliper; ensuring each pad's friction material is facing the brake disc. If the shims (where fitted) have become detached, ensure that they are correctly positioned.

13 Refit the caliper into position over the pads, if the threads of the new guide pin bolts are not already precoated with locking compound, apply a suitable thread-locking compound to them (Peugeot recommend Loctite Frenetanch – available from your Peugeot dealer). Press the caliper into position, then install the guide pin bolts, tightening them to the specified torque setting **(see illustration)**.

14 Slide the handbrake cable into the support bracket and reconnect the cable end fitting.

15 Refit the flexible brake hose to the mounting brackets at the rear of the hub carrier. Make sure the hose is routed correctly and not twisted.

16 Depress the brake pedal repeatedly until the pads are pressed into firm contact with the brake disc, and normal (non-assisted) pedal pressure is restored.

5.10 Use a retraction tool to rotate the piston whilst pushing it back in at the same time

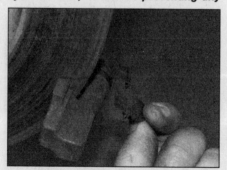

5.11 Ensure the shims at the top and bottom of the caliper mounting bracket are correctly fitted

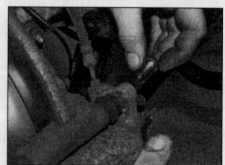

5.13 Apply thread-locking compound to the guide pin bolts

17 Repeat the above procedure on the remaining rear brake caliper.

18 Check the operation of the handbrake, and if necessary, carry out the adjustment procedure as described in Section 14.

19 Refit the roadwheels, and then lower the vehicle to the ground. Tighten the roadwheel bolts to the specified torque setting.

20 Check the hydraulic fluid level as described in *Weekly checks*.

Caution: New pads will not give full braking efficiency until they have bedded-in. Be prepared for this, and avoid hard braking as far as possible for the first hundred miles or so after pad renewal.

6.3 Use a micrometer to measure the disc thickness

6.4 Check the disc run-out using a dial gauge

6 Front brake disc – inspection, removal and refitting

Note: *Before starting work, refer to the note at the beginning of Section 4 concerning the dangers of asbestos dust.*

Inspection

Note: *If either disc requires renewal, BOTH should be renewed at the same time, to ensure even and consistent braking. New brake pads should also be fitted.*

1 Apply the handbrake, slacken the front roadwheel bolts, then jack up the front of the car and support it on axle stands (see *Jacking and vehicle support*). Remove the appropriate front roadwheel.

2 Slowly rotate the brake disc so that the full area of both sides can be checked; remove the brake pads if better access is required to the inboard surface. Light scoring is normal in the area swept by the brake pads, but if heavy scoring or cracks are found, the disc must be renewed.

3 It is normal to find a lip of rust and brake dust around the disc's perimeter; this can be scraped off if required. If, however, a lip has formed due to excessive wear of the brake pad swept area, then the disc's thickness must be measured using a micrometer. Take measurements at several places around the disc, at the inside and outside of the pad swept area; if the disc has worn at any point to the specified minimum thickness or less, the disc must be renewed **(see illustration)**.

4 If the disc is thought to be warped, it can be checked for run-out. Either use a dial gauge mounted on any convenient fixed point, while the disc is slowly rotated, or use feeler blades to measure (at several points all around the disc) the clearance between the disc and a fixed point, such as the caliper mounting bracket **(see illustration)**. If the measurements obtained are at the specified maximum or beyond, the disc is excessively warped, and must be renewed; however, it is worth checking first that the hub bearing is in good condition (Chapter 1). Also try the effect of removing the

disc and turning it through 180°, to reposition it on the hub; if the run-out is still excessive, the disc must be renewed.

5 Check the disc for cracks, especially around the wheel bolt holes, and any other wear or damage, and renew if necessary.

Removal

6 Remove the front brake pads as described in Section 4.

7 Slacken and remove the two bolts securing the brake caliper mounting bracket to the hub carrier, and then remove the mounting bracket from the hub **(see illustrations)**.

8 Use chalk or paint to mark the relationship of the disc to the hub, then remove the screws securing the brake disc to the hub, and remove the disc **(see illustrations)**. If it is tight,

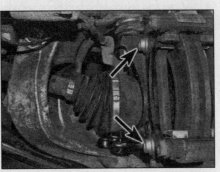
6.7a Undo the two Torx bolts (arrowed) . . .

6.7b . . . and remove the caliper mounting bracket

lightly tap its rear face with a hide or plastic mallet.

Refitting

9 Refitting is the reverse of the removal procedure, noting the following points:

a) Ensure that the mating surfaces of the disc and hub are clean and flat.

b) Align (if applicable) the marks made on removal, and tighten the disc retaining screws to the specified torque setting.

c) If a new disc has been fitted, use a suitable solvent to wipe any preservative coating from the disc, before refitting the caliper.

d) Refit the caliper mounting bracket into position, if the threads of the new bolts are not already precoated with locking

6.8a Undo the Torx screws . . .

6.8b . . . and remove the brake disc

6.9 Fit new bolts, with thread-locking compound

7.4a Undo the two Torx bolts (arrowed) . . .

7.4b . . . and remove the caliper mounting bracket

compound **(see illustration),** apply a suitable thread-locking compound to them (Peugeot recommend Loctite Frenetanch – available from your Peugeot dealer).
e) Refit the brake pads as described in Section 4.
f) Refit the roadwheel then lower the vehicle to the ground and tighten the wheel bolts to the specified torque. Apply the footbrake several times to force the pads back into contact with the disc before driving the vehicle.

7 Rear brake disc – inspection, removal and refitting

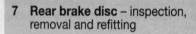

Note: Before starting work, refer to the note at the beginning of Section 5 concerning the dangers of asbestos dust.

Inspection

Note: If either disc requires renewal, BOTH should be renewed at the same time, to ensure even and consistent braking. New brake pads should also be fitted.
1 Firmly chock the front wheels, slacken the appropriate rear roadwheel bolts, and then jack up the rear of the car and support it on axle stands (see Jacking and vehicle support). Remove the relevant rear roadwheel.
2 Inspect the disc as described in Section 6.

Removal

3 Remove the rear brake pads as described in Section 5.

4 Slacken and remove the two bolts securing the brake caliper mounting bracket to the hub carrier, and then remove the mounting bracket from the hub **(see illustrations).**
5 Use chalk or paint to mark the relationship of the disc to the hub, and then undo the screws securing the disc to the hub. If necessary, gently tap the disc from behind and release it from the hub **(see illustrations).**

Refitting

6 Refitting is the reverse of the removal procedure, noting the following points:
a) Ensure that the mating surfaces of the disc and hub are clean and flat.
b) Align (if applicable) the marks made on removal, and tighten the disc retaining screws to the specified torque.
c) If a new disc has been fitted, use a suitable solvent to wipe any preservative coating from the disc, before refitting the caliper.
d) Refit the caliper mounting bracket into position, if the threads of the new bolts are not already precoated with locking compound, apply a suitable thread-locking compound to them (Peugeot recommend Loctite Frenetanch – available from your Peugeot dealer).
e) Refit the brake pads as described in Section 5.
f) Refit the roadwheel, then lower the vehicle to the ground and tighten the roadwheel bolts to the specified torque. Depress the brake pedal several times to force the pads back into contact with the disc.

8 Front brake caliper – removal, overhaul and refitting

Caution: Ensure the ignition is switched off before disconnecting any braking system hydraulic union and do not switch it on until after the hydraulic system has been bled. Failure to do this could lead to air entering the regulator unit requiring the unit to be bled using special Peugeot test equipment (see Section 2).
Note: Before starting work, refer to the note at the beginning of Section 2 concerning the dangers of hydraulic fluid, and to the warning at the beginning of Section 4 concerning the dangers of asbestos dust.
Note: New caliper guide pin bolts or guide pins and caliper mounting bracket bolts will be required on reassembly.

Removal

1 Apply the handbrake, slacken the relevant front roadwheel bolts, then jack up the front of the vehicle and support it on axle stands (see Jacking and vehicle support). Remove the appropriate roadwheel.
2 Minimise fluid loss by first removing the master cylinder reservoir cap, and then tightening it down onto a piece of polythene, to obtain an airtight seal. Alternatively, use a brake hose clamp, a G-clamp or a similar tool to clamp the flexible hose **(see illustration).**
3 Clean the area around the caliper hose union, then slacken and remove the union

7.5a Undo the Torx screws . . .

7.5b . . . and remove the brake disc

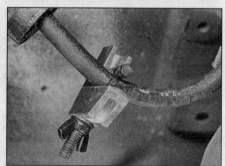

8.2 To minimise fluid loss, fit a brake hose clamp to the flexible hose

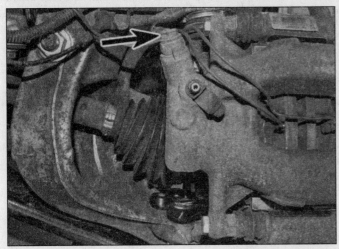

8.3 Remove the brake union bolt (arrowed) from the caliper

8.4 Remove the brake caliper guide pin bolts (arrowed)

bolt from the caliper (see illustration). Place absorbent rags beneath the pipe union, to catch any spilt fluid.

4 Slacken and remove the upper and lower caliper guide pin bolts/guide pins (see illustration), with reference to Section 4. Discard the bolts; new ones must be used on refitting. Where fitted disconnect the brake warning light wiring and lift the caliper away from the brake pads. Note that the brake pads need not be disturbed, and can be left in position in the caliper mounting bracket.

5 If required, the caliper mounting bracket can be unbolted from the hub carrier (see illustrations 6.7a and 6.7b). Discard the bolts, as new ones must be fitted on re-assembly.

Overhaul

Note: Check the availability of repair kits for the caliper before dismantling.

6 With the caliper on the bench, wipe away all traces of dust and dirt, but avoid inhaling the dust, as it is a health hazard.

7 Withdraw the partially ejected piston(s) from the caliper body, and remove the dust seal.

8 Using a small screwdriver, extract the piston hydraulic seal, taking great care not to damage the caliper bore.

9 Thoroughly clean all components, using only methylated spirit, isopropyl alcohol or clean hydraulic fluid as a cleaning medium. Never use mineral-based solvents such as petrol or paraffin, as they will attack the hydraulic system's rubber components. Dry the components immediately, using compressed air or a clean, lint-free cloth. Use compressed air to blow clear the fluid passages.

10 Check all components, and renew any that are worn or damaged. Check particularly the cylinder bore and piston; these should be renewed (note that this means the renewal of the complete body assembly) if they are scratched, worn or corroded in any way. Similarly check the condition of the guide pins and their gaiters; both pins should be undamaged and (when cleaned) a reasonably

tight sliding fit in the caliper bracket. If there is any doubt about the condition of any component, renew it.

11 If the assembly is fit for further use, obtain the appropriate repair kit; the components should be available from Peugeot dealers in various combinations. All rubber seals should be renewed as a matter of course; these should never be re-used.

12 On reassembly, ensure that all components are clean and dry.

13 Soak the piston and the new piston (fluid) seal in clean brake fluid. Smear clean fluid on the cylinder bore surface.

14 Fit the new piston (fluid) seal, using only your fingers (no tools) to manipulate it into the cylinder bore groove.

15 Fit the new dust seal to the rear of the piston and seat the outer lip of the seal in the caliper body groove. Carefully ease the piston squarely into the cylinder bore using a twisting motion. Press the piston fully into position, and seat the inner lip of the dust seal in the piston groove.

16 If the guide pins are being renewed, lubricate the pin shafts with the special grease supplied in the repair kit, and fit the gaiters to the pin grooves. Insert the pins into the caliper bracket and seat the gaiters correctly in the bracket grooves.

Refitting

17 If previously removed, refit the caliper mounting bracket to the hub carrier, and tighten the new bolts to the specified torque.

18 Ensure that the brake pads are correctly fitted in the caliper mounting bracket and refit the caliper (see Section 4).

19 If the threads of the new guide pin bolts/ guide pins are not already precoated with locking compound, apply a suitable locking compound to them (Peugeot recommend Loctite Frenetanch – available from your Peugeot dealer). Fit the new lower guide pin bolt, then press the caliper into position and fit the new upper guide pin bolt. Tighten both

guide pin bolts/guide pins to the specified torque.

20 Tighten the brake hose union bolt to the specified torque, then remove the brake hose clamp or polythene (where fitted).

21 Bleed the hydraulic system as described in Section 2. Note that, providing the precautions described were taken to minimise brake fluid loss, it should only be necessary to bleed the relevant front brake.

22 Refit the roadwheel, then lower the vehicle to the ground and tighten the roadwheel bolts to the specified torque.

9 Rear brake caliper – removal, overhaul and refitting

Caution: Ensure the ignition is switched off before disconnecting any braking system hydraulic union and do not switch it back on until after the hydraulic system has been bled. Failure to do this could lead to air entering the regulator unit requiring the unit to be bled using special Peugeot test equipment (see Section 2).

Note: Before starting work, refer to the note at the beginning of Section 2 concerning the dangers of hydraulic fluid, and to the warning at the beginning of Section 5 concerning the dangers of asbestos dust.

Note: New caliper mounting bracket bolts and guide pin bolts when be required on reassembly.

Removal

1 Chock the front wheels, slacken the relevant rear roadwheel bolts, then jack up the rear of the vehicle and support on axle stands (see Jacking and vehicle support). Remove the rear roadwheels and leave the handbrake in the off position.

2 Minimise fluid loss by first removing the master cylinder reservoir cap, and then tightening it down onto a piece of polythene, to obtain an airtight seal. Alternatively, use

9.3 Slacken the brake union nut (arrowed) from the top of the caliper

9.4 Remove the brake caliper guide pin bolts (arrowed)

10.3 Disconnect the fluid level wiring connector

a brake hose clamp, a G-clamp or a similar tool to clamp the flexible hose at the nearest convenient point to the brake caliper (see illustration 8.2).

3 Wipe away all traces of dirt around the brake hose union on the caliper. Unscrew the union nut and disconnect the brake pipe from the caliper (see illustration). Plug the pipe and caliper unions to minimise fluid loss and prevent dirt entry.

4 Slacken and remove the upper and lower caliper guide pin bolts (see illustration), with reference to Section 5. Discard the bolts; new ones must be used on refitting. Disconnect the handbrake cable and lift the caliper away from the brake pads. Note that the brake pads need not be disturbed, and can be left in position in the caliper mounting bracket.

5 If required, the caliper mounting bracket can be unbolted from the hub carrier (see illustrations 7.4a and 7.4b). Discard the bolts, as new ones must be fitted on re-assembly.

Overhaul

6 At the time of writing, no parts were available to recondition the rear caliper assembly, with the excepting of the guide pin bolts, guide pins and guide pin gaiters. Check the condition of the guide pins and their gaiters; both pins should be undamaged and (when cleaned) a reasonably tight sliding fit in the caliper bracket. If there is any doubt about the condition of any component, renew it.

Refitting

7 If previously removed, refit the caliper

mounting bracket to the hub carrier, and tighten the new bolts to the specified torque.

8 Refit the brakes pads/caliper with reference to Section 5; insert the new guide pin bolts, tightening them to the specified torque settings.

9 Reconnect the brake pipe to the caliper, and tighten the brake hose union nut to the specified torque. Remove the brake hose clamp or polythene (where fitted).

10 Bleed the hydraulic system as described in Section 2. Note that, providing the precautions described were taken to minimise brake fluid loss, it should only be necessary to bleed the relevant rear brake.

11 Refit the roadwheel, then lower the vehicle to the ground and tighten the roadwheel bolts to the specified torque.

10 Master cylinder – removal, overhaul and refitting

Caution: Ensure the ignition is switched off before disconnecting any braking system hydraulic union and do not switch it back on until after the hydraulic system has been bled. Failure to do this could lead to air entering the regulator unit requiring the unit to be bled using special Peugeot test equipment (see Section 2).
Note: Before starting work, refer to the warning at the beginning of Section 2 concerning the dangers of hydraulic fluid.

Removal

1 Remove the air cleaner assembly and inlet hoses as described in Chapter 4A. Also to make access easier, remove the cover from the engine fusebox, at the left-hand rear of the engine compartment.

2 Remove the master cylinder reservoir cap and filter, and siphon the hydraulic fluid from the reservoir. Note: Do not siphon the fluid by mouth, as it is poisonous; use a syringe or an old antifreeze tester. Alternatively, open any convenient bleed screw in the system, and gently pump the brake pedal to expel the fluid through a plastic tube connected to the screw until the reservoir is emptied (see Section 2).

3 Disconnect the wiring connector from the brake fluid level sender unit (see illustration).

4 Disconnect the clutch master cylinder fluid supply pipe from the side of the reservoir (see illustration). Plug the pipe opening to prevent dirt ingress.

5 Remove the locking clip and withdraw the securing pin from the bottom of the reservoir (see illustration).

6 With the securing pin removed, pull the reservoir upwards to release it from the top of the master cylinder. Be prepared for fluid spillage, place absorbent rags beneath the reservoir to catch any surplus fluid.

7 Wipe clean the area around the brake pipe unions on the underside of the master cylinder (see illustration), and place absorbent rags beneath the pipe unions to catch any surplus fluid. Make a note of the correct fitted positions of the unions, then unscrew the union nuts and

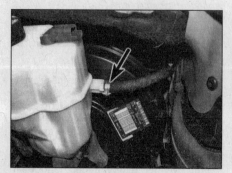

10.4 Disconnect the clutch fluid supply hose (arrowed)

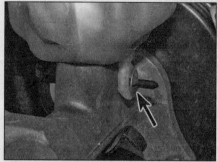

10.5 Release the reservoir retaining clip (arrowed)

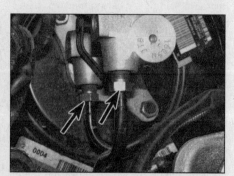

10.7 Slacken the brake fluid pipes (arrowed) from under the master cylinder

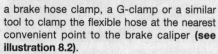

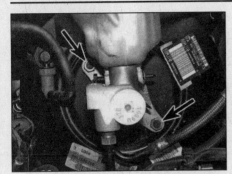

10.8 Master cylinder mounting nuts (arrowed)

11.4 Disconnect the switch wiring connector

11.5 Release the pushrod retaining clip/ pin

carefully withdraw the pipes. Plug or tape over the pipe ends and master cylinder orifices, to minimise the loss of brake fluid, and to prevent the entry of dirt into the system. Wash off any spilt fluid immediately with cold water.

8 Slacken and remove the two nuts securing the master cylinder to the vacuum servo unit **(see illustration)**, then withdraw the unit from the engine compartment. If the sealing ring fitted to the rear of the master cylinder shows signs of damage or deterioration, it must be renewed.

Overhaul

9 At the time of writing, no overhaul parts were available for the master cylinder, with the exception of the reservoir mounting rubber grommets. If the cylinder is faulty, it may have to be renewed as a complete unit – check with a Peugeot dealer or parts specialist.

Refitting

10 Remove all traces of dirt from the master cylinder and servo unit mating surfaces and ensure that the sealing ring is correctly fitted to the rear of the master cylinder.

11 Fit the master cylinder to the servo unit. Refit the master cylinder mounting nuts, and tighten them to the specified torque.

12 Wipe clean the brake pipe unions and refit them to the master cylinder ports, tightening them to the specified torque.

13 Make sure the rubber grommet seals are fitted fully into the top of master cylinder ports, and then carefully ease the fluid reservoir into position. Slide the reservoir securing pin into position, making sure the locking clip is correctly fitted on the securing pin.

14 Reconnect the clutch master cylinder supply pipe, and level sensor wiring plug.

15 Refit any components removed to improve access, and then refill the master cylinder reservoir with new fluid. Bleed the complete hydraulic system as described in Section 2. **Note:** *The hydraulic clutch shares its fluid reservoir with the braking system, and may also need to be bled (see Chapter 6).*

11 Brake pedal assembly – removal and refitting

Note: *The brake pedal is a complete part of the pedal mounting bracket which is bolted to the bulkhead. The brake servo is fitted on the left-hand side of the engine compartment, so the pedal mounting bracket is fitted behind*

the heater housing from the driver's side to the passenger's side.

Removal

1 Remove the heater housing assembly, as described in Chapter 3.

2 Remove the clutch pedal, as described in Chapter 6.

3 Remove the accelerator pedal, as described in Chapter 4A.

4 Disconnect the wiring connector from the brake light switch on the pedal mounting bracket **(see illustration)**.

5 Working on the passenger side of the pedal assembly, release the retaining clip and pull out the pin to disconnect the servo actuating rod from the pedal assembly **(see illustration)**.

6 Slacken and remove the left-hand side mounting bracket retaining nuts, and then unclip the wiring loom from the pedal mounting bracket **(see illustration)**.

7 Slacken and remove the right-hand side mounting bracket retaining nuts, and then withdraw the pedal mounting bracket assembly from inside the vehicle **(see illustration)**. Examine all components for signs of wear or damage, renewing them as necessary.

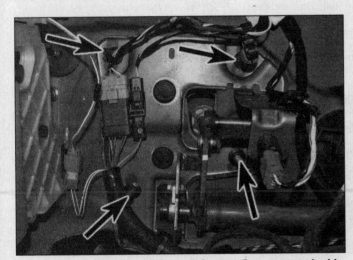

11.6 Pedal assembly mounting nuts (arrowed) – passenger's side

11.7 Pedal assembly mounting nuts (arrowed) – driver's side

12.5 Disconnect the vacuum pipe from the check valve

Refitting

8 Apply a smear of multipurpose grease to all the moving components and manoeuvre the pedal mounting bracket into position, making sure it is correctly engaged with the servo actuating rod.

9 Refit the mounting bracket retaining nuts and tighten securely.

10 Insert the clevis pin into the end of the servo actuating rod and lock it in position.

11 Refit the brake light switch wiring connector and secure the wiring loom into position on the mounting bracket.

12 Refit the accelerator pedal, as described in Chapter 4A.

13 Refit the clutch pedal, as described in Chapter 6.

14 Refit the heater housing assembly, as described in Chapter 3.

12 Vacuum servo unit – testing, removal and refitting

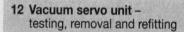

Testing

1 To test the operation of the servo unit, depress the footbrake several times to exhaust the vacuum, then start the engine whilst keeping the pedal firmly depressed. As the engine starts, there should be a noticeable 'give' in the brake pedal as the vacuum builds-up. Allow the engine to run for at least

12.8 Servo mounting nuts (arrowed) – 2 are behind the rubber grommets

two minutes, and then switch it off. If the brake pedal is now depressed it should feel normal, but further applications should result in the pedal feeling firmer, with the pedal stroke decreasing with each application.

2 If the servo does not operate as described, first inspect the servo unit check valve as described in Section 13. Also check the operation of the vacuum pump as described in Section 21.

3 If the servo unit still fails to operate satisfactorily, the fault lies within the unit itself. Repairs to the unit are not possible – if faulty, the servo unit must be renewed.

Removal

4 Remove the master cylinder as described in Section 10.

5 Slacken or release the retaining clip (depending on type of securing clip), then disconnect the vacuum pipe from the servo unit check valve **(see illustration)**.

6 Working in the passenger's footwell, release the securing clips and remove the trim beneath the passenger's glovebox.

7 Rotate the crossover shaft-to-servo pushrod clevis pin and remove it from the linkage **(see illustration 11.5)**. Discard the clevis pin; a new one must be fitted.

8 Slacken and remove the four nuts securing the servo to the mounting bracket **(see illustration)**.

9 Working inside the engine compartment, make sure any wiring harness, cables or hoses do not foul the servo as it is being removed, making a note of there fitted position.

10 Manoeuvre the servo unit out of position, along with its gasket, which is fitted between the servo and mounting bracket. Renew the gasket if it shows signs of damage.

Refitting

11 Refitting is the reverse of removal, noting the following points.

a) Lubricate all crossover linkage pivot points with multipurpose grease.

b) Tighten the servo unit and mounting bracket nuts and bolts to their specified torque settings.

c) Refit the master cylinder as described in Section 10 and bleed the complete hydraulic system as described in Section 2.

d) Always renew the servo actuating rod clevis pin.

13 Vacuum servo unit check valve – removal, testing and refitting

Note: *The check valve is fitted directly into the servo unit, although on models from RPO No 11193, there is also a valve fitted in the pipe to the vacuum pump* **(see illustration)**.

Removal

1 Slacken or release the retaining clip (depending on type of securing clip), then disconnect the vacuum hose from the servo unit check valve **(see illustration)**.

2 Release the plastic securing clip from around the valve and then withdraw the valve from its rubber sealing grommet, using a pulling and twisting motion. Remove the grommet from the servo.

3 If required, remove the other end of the brake vacuum pipe from the vacuum pump **(see illustration)**, release the connection and disconnect the vacuum hoses from the connection.

Testing

4 Examine the check valve for signs of damage, and renew if necessary. The valve may be tested by blowing through it in both directions. Air should flow through the valve in one direction only – when blown through

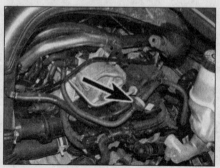

13.0 In-line check valve (arrowed) – fitted to some models

13.1 Disconnect vacuum pipe from check valve fitted to servo

13.3 Depress the buttons (arrowed) to release the vacuum pipe

from the servo unit end of the valve. Renew the valve if this is not the case.

5 Examine the rubber sealing grommet and flexible vacuum hose for signs of damage or deterioration, and renew as necessary.

Refitting

6 Fit the sealing grommet into position in the servo unit.

7 Carefully ease the check valve into position, taking great care not to displace or damage the grommet. Reconnect the vacuum hose to the valve and vacuum pump, making sure that the connections are secure.

8 On completion, start the engine and check for air leaks at each connection on the vacuum pipe.

14 Handbrake – adjustment

1 To check the handbrakes adjustment, apply normal moderate pressure and pull the handbrake lever to the fully applied position, counting the number of clicks emitted from the handbrake ratchet mechanism. If adjustment is correct, there should be 1 notch before the brakes begin to apply, and no more than 4 notches before the handbrake is fully applied. If this is not the case, adjust as follows.

2 Chock the front wheels, then jack up the rear of the vehicle and support it on axle stands (see *Jacking and vehicle support*).

3 Working inside the vehicle, unclip the trim from around the handbrake in the centre console (see illustration).

4 Release the handbrake, leaving it in the lowered position and press the automatic adjustment unlocking button at the base of the handbrake mounting bracket (see illustration).

5 Pull the handbrake lever on and check it does not exceed 4 notches.

6 Release the lever and check by hand that the rear wheels rotate freely.

7 Switch the ignition on and then pull the handbrake lever on 1 notch, and check if the warning light comes on the instrument panel.

8 Refit the handbrake trim panel to the centre console, and then lower the vehicle to the floor.

14.3 Unclip the handbrake lever gaiter trim

15 Handbrake lever – removal and refitting

Removal

1 Chock the front wheels then jack up the rear of the vehicle and support it on axle stands (see *Jacking and vehicle support*).

2 Remove the centre console as described in Chapter 11.

3 Release the handbrake, leaving it in the lowered position and press the automatic adjustment unlocking button at the base of the handbrake mounting bracket (see illustration 14.4).

4 Press on the automatic adjustment unlocking button and the end of the ratchet

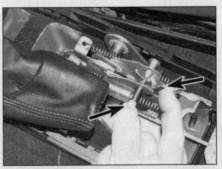
15.4 Press in the positions shown (arrowed)

14.4 Press the automatic adjustment button (arrowed)

mechanism (see illustration), and then lift the handbrake lever to the first notch. Then release the unlocking button and ratchet, and lower the handbrake lever to the lowered position.

5 Detach the handbrake cables from the equaliser at the rear of the handbrake (see illustration).

6 Disconnect the wiring connector from the handbrake warning light switch, and then unclip the switch from the mounting bracket (see illustrations).

7 Slacken and remove the mounting bracket retaining nuts, and remove the assembly from the vehicle (see illustration).

Refitting

8 Refitting is a reversal of removal. Tighten the lever retaining nuts to the specified torque, and adjust the handbrake (see Section 14).

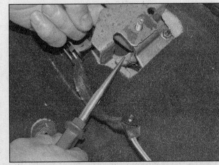
15.5 Release the inner cables from the equaliser plate

15.6a Disconnect the wiring connector . . .

15.6b . . . and unclip the switch from the mounting bracket

15.7 Handbrake mounting bracket bolt/ nuts (arrowed)

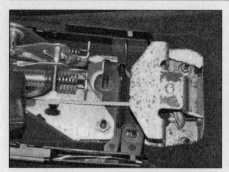

16.1 Single cable from lever to equaliser plate

16.8 Unclip the plastic undershield to access the cable

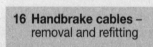

16 Handbrake cables –
removal and refitting

Removal

1 The handbrake cable consists of a left-hand section and a right-hand section connecting the rear brakes to the equaliser linkage at the rear of the handbrake, and a short cable attached to the handbrake lever **(see illustration)**. The two rear cables can be removed separately.

16.5 Undo two retaining nuts (arrowed) to access equaliser plate

16.9 Handbrake cable securing bracket – one side shown

2 Firmly chock the front wheels, slacken the relevant rear roadwheel bolts, and then jack up the rear of the vehicle and support it on axle stands (see *Jacking and vehicle support*).
3 Remove the centre console as described in Chapter 11.
4 Press on the automatic adjustment unlocking button and the end of the ratchet mechanism **(see illustration 15.4)**, and then lift the handbrake lever to the first notch. Then release the unlocking button and ratchet and lower the handbrake lever to the lowered position.
5 Undo the two retaining nuts and remove the

mounting bracket from above the equaliser linkage **(see illustration)**.
6 The relevant cable end fitting can now be disengaged from the equaliser plate **(see illustration 15.5)**.
7 Working under the vehicle, release the cable end fitting from the lever on the brake caliper, and remove the cable from the support bracket **(see illustration 5.2)**.
8 Release the retaining clips and remove the plastic undershields from under the rear of the vehicle **(see illustration)**.
9 Note the cable's fitted location, and then free the cable from the various retaining clips/brackets along its route **(see illustration)**, and pull the front end of the cable from the opening in the floor. Withdraw the cable from underneath the vehicle.

Refitting

10 Refitting is a reversal of the removal procedure, adjusting the handbrake as described in Section 14.

17 Brake light switch – removal, refitting and adjustment

1 The brake light switch is located on the pedal crossover shaft bracket behind the passenger side of the facia. On models with automatic transmission or cruise control there may be two switches fitted to the mounting bracket.

Removal

2 Working in the passenger's footwell, release the retaining clips and remove the trim beneath the passenger's glovebox.
3 Disconnect the wiring, then rotate the switch 90° anti-clockwise and remove it from the bracket **(see illustrations)**.

17.3a Disconnect the wiring connector . . .

17.3b . . . and rotate the switch 90° anti-clockwise and pull it from the bracket

17.4 Align the red locking catch (arrowed) with the centring lug

17.6 Make sure the plunger (arrowed) is up against the pedal bracket

monitors the vehicles cornering forces and steering wheel angle, then applies the braking force to the appropriate roadwheel to enhance the stability of the vehicle.

If a fault does develop in the any of these systems, the vehicle must be taken to a Peugeot dealer or suitably-equipped specialist for fault diagnosis and repair.

Refitting and adjustment

4 Check that the red locking latch is in line with the locating lug on the side of the switch **(see illustration)**.

5 Refit the switch back into position in the mounting bracket, and turn it 90° clockwise, to lock it in position.

6 Reconnect the wiring connector, and check that the switch plunger is up against the brake pedal lever bracket **(see illustration)**.

7 Check the operation of the brake lights and refit the trim below the glovebox.

18 Anti-lock Braking System (ABS) – general information

ABS is fitted to all models as standard; the system comprises a hydraulic regulator unit and the four roadwheel sensors. The regulator unit contains the electronic control module (ECM), the hydraulic solenoid valves and the electrically driven return pump. The purpose of the system is to prevent the wheel(s) locking during heavy braking. This is achieved by automatic release of the brake on the relevant wheel, followed by re-application of the brake.

The solenoid valves are controlled by the ECM, which itself receives signals from the four wheel sensors (front sensors are fitted to the hubs, and the rear sensors are fitted to the caliper mounting brackets), which monitor the speed of rotation of each wheel. By comparing these signals, the ECM can determine the speed at which the vehicle is traveling. It can then use this speed to determine when a wheel is decelerating at an abnormal rate, compared to the speed of the vehicle, and therefore predicts when a wheel is about to lock. During normal operation, the system functions in the same way as a non-ABS braking system.

If the ECM senses that a wheel is about to lock, it closes the relevant outlet solenoid valves in the hydraulic unit, which then isolates the relevant brake(s) on the wheel(s) which is/ are about to lock from the master cylinder, effectively sealing-in the hydraulic pressure.

If the speed of rotation of the wheel continues to decrease at an abnormal rate, the ECM

opens the inlet solenoid valves on the relevant brake(s), and operates the electrically-driven return pump which pumps the hydraulic fluid back into the master cylinder, releasing the brake. Once the speed of rotation of the wheel returns to an acceptable rate, the pump stops; the solenoid valves switch again, allowing the hydraulic master cylinder pressure to return to the caliper, which then re-applies the brake. This cycle can be carried out many times a second.

The action of the solenoid valves and return pump creates pulses in the hydraulic circuit. When the ABS system is functioning, these pulses can be felt through the brake pedal.

The operation of the ABS system is entirely dependent on electrical signals. To prevent the system responding to any inaccurate signals, a built-in safety circuit monitors all signals received by the ECM. If an inaccurate signal or low battery voltage is detected, the ABS system is automatically shutdown, and the warning light on the instrument panel is illuminated, to inform the driver that the ABS system is not operational. Normal braking should still be available, however.

The Peugeot 407 is also equipped with additional safety features built around the ABS system. These systems are EBFD (Electronic Brake Force Distribution), which automatically apportions braking effort between the front and rear wheels, EBA (Emergency Brake Assist) which guarantees full braking effort in the event of an emergency stop by monitoring the rate at which the brake pedal is depressed, and ESP (Electronic Stability Program) which

19 Anti-lock Braking System (ABS) components – removal and refitting

Hydraulic valve block/ modulator and ECM

Caution: Disconnect the battery (see Chapter 5A) before disconnecting the hydraulic unions, and do not reconnect the battery until after the hydraulic system has been bled. Also ensure that the unit is stored upright (in the same position as it is fitted to the vehicle) and is not tipped onto its side or upside down. Failure to do this could lead to air entering the regulator unit, requiring the unit to be bled using special Peugeot test equipment on refitting (see Section 2).

Note: *Before starting work, refer to the warning at the beginning of Section 2 concerning the dangers of hydraulic fluid.*

Removal

1 Disconnect the battery negative lead as described in Chapter 5A.

2 Remove the engine management ECM and fusebox lower housing, as described in the relevant part of Chapter 4 and Chapter 12.

3 Use a brake pedal depressor tool, or length of wood jammed between the steering wheel and the pedal to firmly depress the brake pedal. This will minimise the amount of fluid loss.

4 Disconnect the wiring plug from the ABS ECM **(see illustration)**.

5 Note their fitted positions, then loosen the unions, and disconnect the fluid pipes from the valve block **(see illustration)**. Be prepared for fluid spillage, and plug the open ends of the pipes and valve block to avoid further fluid spillage and dirt ingress.

19.4 Lift the locking catch and disconnect the wiring plug

19.5 Disconnect the pipes from the valve block, noting their position

19.6 Brake hydraulic unit mounting nuts (arrowed)

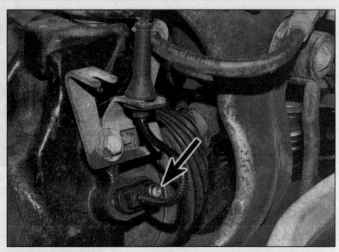

19.11 ABS front wheel speed sensor retaining bolt (arrowed)

6 Slacken the two securing nuts (see illustration), then lift the hydraulic unit, complete with the electronic control module, from the rubber grommets in the mounting bracket. No further dismantling of the modulator assembly is recommended.

Refitting

7 Refitting is a reversal of removal, bearing in mind the following points:

a) New valve blocks/modulator are supplied pre-filled with fluid – remove the plugs prior to connecting the fluid pipes.

b) New ECMs must be initialised and programmed using Peugeot dedicated diagnostic equipment. Entrust this task to a Peugeot dealer or suitably-equipped specialist.

c) On completion, bleed the brake hydraulic system as described in Section 2.

Electronic control module (ECM)

8 The ECM is integral with the hydraulic valve block/modulator (see paragraphs 1 to 7), and is not available separately.

Front wheel sensor

Removal

9 Ensure the ignition is turned off.

19.12 Carefully withdraw the sensor from the hub

10 Apply the handbrake, slacken the appropriate front roadwheel bolts, then jack up the front of the vehicle and support securely on axle stands (see Jacking and vehicle support).

11 Slacken and remove the sensor retaining bolt from the rear of the hub carrier (see illustration).

12 Carefully rotate the sensor using an open-ended spanner and withdraw the sensor from the hub carrier (see illustration). Take care, as the sensors are fragile – avoid contact with the tip of the sensor to prevent any damage.

13 Trace the wiring back from the sensor

19.13 Release the wiring from the retaining brackets (arrowed)

up through the inner wing panel, unclipping the wiring from the securing brackets as it is removed (see illustration).

14 Working inside the engine compartment, releasing it from all the relevant clips and ties whilst noting its correct routing, disconnect the wiring connector (see illustrations).

Refitting

15 Ensure that the mating faces of the sensor and the swivel hub are clean, and apply a little anti-seize grease (Peugeot recommend Total N4128) to the swivel hub bore before refitting (see illustration).

19.14a Disconnect the wiring plug connector under the ECM housing – left-hand side

19.14b Disconnect the wiring plug connector (arrowed) on the inner wing panel – right-hand side

19.15 Apply a small amount of grease on refitting – NOT on the tip of the sensor

19.21a Unclip the fuel sender unit plastic cover . . .

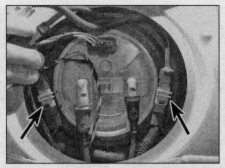

19.21b . . . to access the rear ABS sensor wiring plug connectors (arrowed)

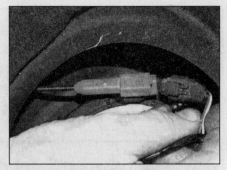

19.23 Disconnecting the sensor wiring plug connector

16 Make sure the sensor tip is clean and ease it into position in the swivel hub.

17 Clean the threads of the sensor bolt and apply a few drops of thread-locking compound (Peugeot recommend Loctite Frenetanch – available from your Peugeot dealer). Refit the retaining bolt and tighten it to the specified torque.

18 Work along the sensor wiring, making sure it is correctly routed, securing it in position with all the relevant clips and ties. Reconnect the wiring connector.

19 Lower the vehicle and tighten the wheel bolts to the specified torque.

Rear wheel sensor

Removal

20 Ensure the ignition is turned off.

21 Lift the rear seat cushion and remove the fuel tank sender unit cover from the rear floor panel **(see illustrations)**. Refer to Chapter 4A for further information.

22 Working as described in the relevant part of Chapter 4A, lower the fuel tank sufficiently to gain access to the ABS sensor wiring harness clips on the top of the fuel tank, and the clips on the rear suspension arm.

23 Disconnect the sensor wiring connector, and then tie a length of string to the connector on the end of the wiring harness **(see illustration)**.

24 Apply the handbrake, slacken the appropriate rear roadwheel bolts, then chock the front wheels and jack up the rear of the vehicle, support securely on axle stands (see *Jacking and vehicle support*).

25 Slacken and remove the sensor retaining bolt from the rear of the hub carrier **(see illustration)**.

26 Carefully rotate the sensor using an open-ended spanner and withdraw the sensor from the hub carrier **(see illustration)**. Take care, as the sensors are fragile – avoid contact with the tip of the sensor to prevent any damage.

27 Make sure the sensor wiring clips are all released and withdraw the sensor wiring, complete with string attached, from above the fuel tank. Note, leave the

19.25 ABS rear wheel speed sensor retaining bolt (arrowed)

string in position over the fuel tank to pull the sensor wiring back into position on refitting.

Refitting

28 Ensure that the mating faces of the sensor and the swivel hub are clean, and apply a little anti-seize grease (Peugeot recommend Total N4128) to the swivel hub bore before refitting **(see illustration 19.15)**.

29 Make sure the sensor tip is clean and ease it into position in the hub carrier **(see illustration)**.

30 Clean the threads of the sensor bolt and apply a few drops of thread-locking compound (Peugeot recommend Loctite Frenetanch – available from your Peugeot dealer). Refit the retaining bolt and tighten it to the specified torque.

31 Tie a length of string to the connector on

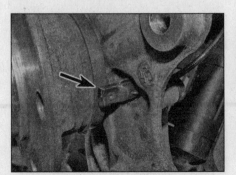

19.29 Make sure the tip of the sensor (arrowed) is free from dirt and grease

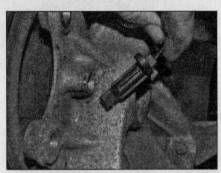

19.26 Carefully withdraw the sensor from the rear housing

the end of the wiring harness and pull it back into position over the fuel tank.

32 Work along the sensor wiring, making sure it is correctly routed, securing it in position with all the relevant clips and ties. Reconnect the wiring connector.

33 Refit the fuel tank as described in Chapter 4A.

34 Lower the vehicle and tighten the wheel bolts to the specified torque.

Yaw rate sensors

Note: *Two yaw rate sensors are fitted, one on each side of the car.*

35 Remove the front seat as described in Chapter 11.

36 Remove the lower trim panel and pull back the carpet from the base of the B-pillar **(see illustration)**.

19.36 Pull back the carpet to access the sensor . . .

19.37 . . . and disconnect the wiring plug (arrowed)

20.1 Remove the turbo air inlet hose

20.2 Disconnect the vacuum pipe (arrowed)

20.3a Vacuum pump retaining bolt (arrowed)

37 Release the clip then disconnect the wiring plug (see illustration).
38 Drill out the rivets and remove the sensor complete with mounting bracket.
39 Refitting is a reversal of removal, ensuring the arrow on the top of the sensor points to the front of the vehicle.

20 Vacuum pump – removal and refitting

Removal

1.6 litre models

1 The pump is located at the left-hand end of the cylinder head. To improve access to the vacuum pump, remove the air cleaner duct and turbo inlet hose (see illustration). Refer to Chapter 4A for further information.
2 Depress the retaining clip button and disconnect the vacuum hose from the pump (see illustration).
3 Slacken and remove the retaining bolts securing the pump to the left-hand end of the cylinder head, then remove the pump (see illustrations). Discard the sealing rings – new ones must be used on refitting.

2.0 litre models

4 The pump is located at the left-hand end of the cylinder head. To improve access to the vacuum pump, remove the air cleaner assembly (see Chapter 4A)
5 Depress the retaining clip button and disconnect the vacuum hose from the pump (see illustration).
6 Unclip the wiring loom retaining clips and remove the bracket from below the vacuum pump (see illustrations).
7 Undo the retaining nut and remove the bracket from the top of the vacuum pump

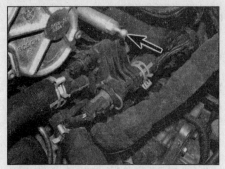

20.3b On some models one of the retaining bolts (arrowed) is used as a locating peg

20.5 Depress the buttons and disconnect the vacuum pipe

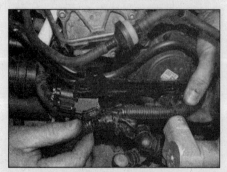

20.6a Unclip the wiring loom . . .

20.6b . . . and unbolt the mounting bracket

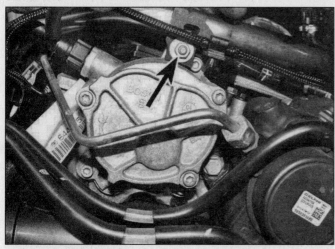

20.7 Undo the upper bracket securing nut (arrowed)

20.8a Vacuum pump retaining bolts (arrowed)

20.8b Renew the pump O-ring seals (arrowed)

20.9 Ensure the drive lugs engage with the slot in the end of the camshaft (arrowed)

(see illustration). Then remove the pillar stud, which the bracket was attached to, from the top of the pump. Move the retaining clip from the pillar stud and move it to one side.

8 Slacken and remove the retaining bolts securing the pump to the left-hand end of the cylinder head, then remove the pump (see illustrations). Discard the sealing rings – new ones must be used on refitting.

Refitting

9 Fit new sealing ring(s) to the pump recess(es), and then align the drive dog with the slot in the end of the camshaft, and refit the pump to the cylinder head, ensuring that the sealing ring(s) remain correctly seated (see illustration).

10 Refit the pump mounting bolts, and then tighten them securely.

11 Reconnect the vacuum hose to the pump, ensuring its retaining clip engages correctly.

12 On 2.0 litre models, refit the mounting brackets and secure the wiring and hoses as noted on removal.

13 Refit the air cleaner assembly, ducting and turbo inlet hose (as applicable), with reference to Chapter 4A.

21 Vacuum pump – testing

1 The operation of the braking system

vacuum pump can be checked using a vacuum gauge.

2 Disconnect the vacuum pipe from the pump, and connect the gauge to the pump union using a suitable length of hose.

3 Start the engine and allow it to idle, and then measure the vacuum created by the pump. As a guide, after one minute, a minimum of approximately 500 mm Hg should be recorded. If the vacuum registered is significantly less than this, it is likely that the pump is faulty. However, seek the advice of a Peugeot dealer before condemning the pump.

4 Overhaul of the vacuum pump is not possible, since no components are available separately for it. If faulty, the complete pump assembly must be renewed.

Chapter 10
Suspension and steering

Contents

Degrees of difficulty

Easy, suitable for novice with little experience 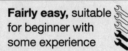	**Fairly easy,** suitable for beginner with some experience	**Fairly difficult,** suitable for competent DIY mechanic	**Difficult,** suitable for experienced DIY mechanic	**Very difficult,** suitable for expert DIY or professional

Specifications

Wheel alignment and steering angles

Front wheel:
  Saloon and estate (SW):
    Tracking at axle . . . . 0° 09' ± 0° 09'
    Camber . . . . 0° 36' ± 0° 30'
    Castor . . . . 5° 24' ± 0° 30'
    Pivot angle . . . . 8° 24' ± 0° 30'
  Coupe:
    Tracking at axle . . . . 0° 09' ± 0° 09'
    Camber . . . . 0° 42' ± 0° 30'
    Castor . . . . 5° 24' ± 0° 30'
    Pivot angle . . . . 8° 35' ± 0° 30'
Rear wheel:
  Saloon and estate (SW):
    Tracking at axle . . . . 0° 34' ± 0° 09'
    Camber . . . . -1° 45' ± 0° 30'
    Thrust angle . . . . 0° ± 0° 30'
  Coupe:
    Tracking at axle . . . . 0° 43' ± 0° 09'
    Camber . . . . -2° 21' ± 0° 30'
    Thrust angle . . . . 0° ± 0° 30'

Ride height settings

Front suspension:
  Saloon and estate (SW) .... 176 mm
  Coupe .... 186 mm
Rear suspension:
  Saloon .... 128 mm
  Estate (SW) .... 124 mm
  Coupe .... 151 mm

Roadwheels

Type .... Pressed-steel or aluminium alloy (depending on model)
Tyre sizes .... 205/60 R16, 215/55 R17 or 235/45 R18
Tyre pressures .... See end of *Weekly checks* on page 0•18

Torque wrench settings

	Nm	lbf ft
Steering		
Column-to-steering rack pinch-bolt	20	15
Power steering pump mounting bolts (1.6 litre models)	22	16
Hydraulic pipe unions:		
To rack	20	15
To pump (1.6 litre models)	33	24
Steering column mounting nuts	20	15
Steering rack mounting bolts	150	111
Steering rack pinion securing bolts	20	15
Steering wheel bolt	33	24
Track rod:		
Balljoint-to-hub carrier nut*	45	33
Balljoint locknut	53	39
Inner balljoint to steering rack	90	66
Front suspension		
Anti-roll bar:		
Mounting clamp bolts	45	33
Drop link:		
Lower balljoint nut*	85	63
Upper balljoint/ lower strut mounting bolt retaining nut	200	148
Driveshaft retaining nut	345	255
Lower arm-to-pivot support bolt	75	55
Lower arm to subframe:		
Front mounting bolt	123	91
Rear mounting bolts:		
M12 x 175	65	48
M14 x 200	110	81
Lower balljoint to pivot support:		
M10 x 150	65	48
M14 x 150	170	126
Front subframe:		
Mounting bolts to main subframe	65	48
Mounting bolts to front brackets	65	48
Over-rider to body bolts	50	37
Lower arm support bracket bolts	80	59
Main subframe:		
Mounting bolts to body (M14 x 200)	140	103
Rear bracket bolts to body (M12 x 175)	100	74
Subframe strengthener bar bolts	125	92
Suspension assembly:		
Upper mounting plate-to-body nuts	30	22
Upper mounting plate-to-strut bearing nuts	15	11
Upper arm front pivot support bolt	85	63
Upper arm rear bearing support bolts	45	33
Suspension strut:		
Lower mounting bolt retaining nut	200	148
Upper spring seat nut*	30	22
Upper balljoint:		
Securing nut	60	44
Threaded into pivot support (Peugeot tool required)	200	148

Torque wrench settings (continued)

	Nm	lbf ft
Rear suspension		
Anti-roll bar:		
Models up to RPO No 10942:		
Mounting clamp bolts..................................	18	13
Mounting plate-to-body bolt............................	70	52
Drop link nuts*	40	30
Models from RPO No 10943:		
Mounting clamp bolts.................................	35	26
Bracket securing nut................................	20	15
Mounting plate-to-body bolt...........................	75	55
Drop link nuts*	40	30
Axle mounting bolts	75	55
Hub nut	250	185
Lower longitudinal suspension arm:		
To rear hub carrier	70	52
To body:		
Stage 1...	33	24
Stage 2...	Angle-tighten a further 150°	
Lower suspension arm:		
To subframe	70	52
To rear axle	70	52
Shock absorber:		
Lower mounting bolt/nut	70	52
Upper mounting bolt/nut	70	52
Upper eye on strut	60	44
Suspension upper wishbone:		
To axle bolts/nuts.....................................	70	52
To hub carrier bolt/nut	70	52
Track adjusting arm bolts..................................	70	52
Roadwheels		
Wheel bolts..	90	66

* Do not re-use

1 General information

The independent suspension on the 407 is an all-new type, which has not been used on previous Peugeots.

The front is fitted with double wishbones, with a drop linked alloy support for the hub carrier, which rotates on upper and lower balljoints. There is a strut, incorporating a coil spring and integral telescopic shock absorber; this is bolted to the upper mounting plate and the lower end to the alloy support housing. The front hub carriers, which carry the wheel bearings, brake calipers and the hub/disc assemblies, are connected to the alloy support housing by upper and lower balljoints. A front anti-roll bar is fitted to all models; it is rubber-mounted onto the subframe, and is connected to the front suspension struts by drop link rods.

The rear suspension is a 5-point multilink suspension with shock absorbers, which are angled to enhance stability. The shock absorbers also incorporate the coil springs; these are fitted between the hub carrier and the axle housing. The rear axle has an anti-roll bar, which is mounted on brackets at the rear of the axle assembly. It is rubber-mounted onto the brackets, and is connected to the rear hub carrier by drop link rods.

The steering column has a universal joint fitted to its lower end, which is connected to the steering rack pinion by means of a clamp bolt.

The steering rack is mounted onto the front subframe, and is connected by two track rods, with balljoints at their outer ends, to the steering arms projecting rearwards from the hub carriers. The track rod ends are threaded, to facilitate adjustment.

Power assisted steering is fitted to all models, although two different systems maybe encountered. The first, used on 1.6 litre engines, is a traditional system where fluid pressure is supplied from a pump driven by the auxiliary drivebelt – the same belt that drives the alternator. Fluid for the pump is supplied from the reservoir on the driver's side inner wing panel. The second type, fitted to 2.0 litre engines, is an electro-hydraulic system where a combined electric motor/pump/ECM unit is fitted on the right-hand front inner wing, with fluid provided inside the attached fluid reservoir. The advantages of the electro-hydraulic system is that assistance, and therefore fluid pressure, is only provided when needed, and can be varied in relation to vehicle speed, steering wheel angle rate-of-change, etc, resulting in reduced fuel consumption and exhaust emissions.

2 Front hub carrier assembly – removal and refitting

Note: A new track rod balljoint nut, upper balljoint nut and brake caliper mounting bracket bolts will be required on refitting.

Removal

1 Remove the wheel trim/hub cap (as applicable) then withdraw the R-clip and remove the locking cap from the driveshaft

2.1a Withdraw the R-clip . . .

2.1b . . . and remove the locking cap

2.3 Using a fabricated tool to hold the hub stationary

retaining nut **(see illustrations)**. Slacken the driveshaft nut with the vehicle resting on its wheels. Also slacken the wheel bolts.

2 Chock the rear wheels of the car, firmly apply the handbrake, and then jack up the front of the car and support it on axle stands (see *Jacking and vehicle support*). Remove the appropriate front roadwheel.

3 Slacken and remove the driveshaft retaining nut. If the nut was not slackened with the wheels on the ground (see paragraph 1), withdraw the R-clip and remove the locking cap. Refit at least two roadwheel bolts to the front hub, tightening them securely, then have an assistant firmly depress the brake pedal to prevent the front hub from rotating whilst you slacken and remove the driveshaft retaining nut. Alternatively, a tool can be fabricated

to hold the hub stationary **(see illustration)**.

4 Unbolt the wheel speed sensor and position it clear of the hub assembly (see Chapter 9, Section 19). Note that there is no need to disconnect the wiring.

5 Remove the front brake disc as described in Chapter 9.

6 Undo the retaining bolts and remove the brake disc shield from the hub carrier **(see illustration)**.

7 Slacken and remove the nut securing the steering rack track rod end to the hub carrier then free the balljoint from the hub **(see illustration)**. If the balljoint is tight, use a universal balljoint separator to free it. Discard the nut, as a new one should be used on refitting.

8 Undo the retaining nuts and remove the anti-roll bar drop link as described in Section 9.

9 Undo the retaining nut and remove the lower suspension arm-to-alloy hub support securing bolt. With the bolt removed, lever the lower arm downwards to release it from the hub support housing **(see illustrations)**.

10 Undo the three retaining bolts and disconnect the lower balljoint housing from the hub support housing **(see illustrations)**.

11 Pull the hub support housing outwards, releasing the driveshaft splines from the centre of the hub. Suspend the driveshaft by string to the underside of the vehicle body to prevent and damage to the constant velocity joints, making sure that the inner driveshaft joint does not pull out of the transmission.

2.6 Remove the brake disc shield

2.7 Undo the retaining nut and disconnect the track rod end balljoint

2.9a Remove the lower arm securing bolt (arrowed) . . .

2.9b . . . and use a bar and chain to disengage the lower arm from the suspension

2.10a Lower balljoint securing bolts

2.10b Removing one of the securing bolts

2.12a Undo the retaining nut (arrowed) . . .

2.12b . . . and release the hub carrier from the balljoint

12 Undo the upper balljoint retaining nut and remove the hub carrier from the alloy hub support **(see illustrations)**. If the balljoint is tight, use a universal balljoint separator to free it. Discard the nut, as a new one should be used on refitting.

Refitting

13 Fit the hub carrier to the upper balljoint and tighten the securing nut to the specified torque setting.
14 Ensure that the driveshaft outer constant velocity joint and hub splines are clean, and then slide the hub onto the driveshaft splines.
15 Refit the three retaining bolts to the lower balljoint housing and tighten them to the specified torque setting.
16 Refit the lower suspension arm to the alloy hub support, and fit the retaining bolt/nut. Do not fully tighten at this stage, as the ride height setting will need to set. Lever the lower arm downwards **(see illustration 2.9b)**, to aid refitting.
17 Refit the anti-roll bar drop link as described in Section 9.
18 Refit the steering rack track rod to the hub carrier and tighten the new retaining nut to the specified torque setting.
19 Fit the brake disc shield to the hub carrier and tighten the securing bolts.
20 Refit the front brake disc as described in Chapter 9, Section 6.
21 Refit the wheel speed sensor to the hub assembly; refer to Chapter 9, Section 19, for further information, if required.
22 Lubricate the inner face and threads of the driveshaft retaining nut with clean engine oil, and refit it to the end of the driveshaft. Use the method employed on removal to prevent the hub from rotating **(see illustration 2.3)**, and tighten the driveshaft retaining nut to the specified torque. Alternatively, lightly tighten the nut at this stage and tighten it to the specified torque once the vehicle is resting on its wheels again.
23 Check that the hub rotates freely then engage the locking cap with the driveshaft nut, so that one of its cut-outs is aligned with the driveshaft hole, and secure the cap in position with the R-clip.

24 Before refitting the roadwheel, set the suspension to the ride height position, as described in Section 28 and tighten the suspension nuts/bolts to their specified torque setting.
25 Refit the roadwheel, then lower the vehicle to the ground and tighten the roadwheel bolts to the specified torque. If not already having done so, tighten the driveshaft retaining nut to the specified torque then refit the locking cap, aligning its cut-outs with the driveshaft hole, and secure it in position with the R-clip **(see illustrations 2.1a and 2.1b)**.

3 Front hub bearings – renewal

Note: *The bearing is a sealed, pre-adjusted and pre-lubricated, double-row roller type, and is intended to last the car's entire service life without maintenance or attention. Never overtighten the driveshaft nut beyond the specified torque wrench setting in an attempt to 'adjust' the bearing.*
Note: *A press will be required to dismantle and rebuild the assembly; if such a tool is not available, a large bench vice and spacers (such as large sockets) will serve as an adequate substitute. The bearing's inner races are an interference fit on the hub; if the inner race remains on the hub when it is pressed out of*

the hub carrier, a knife-edged bearing puller will be required to remove it. A new bearing retaining circlip must be used on refitting.
1 Remove the hub carrier assembly as described in Section 2.
2 Extract the bearing retaining circlip from the inner end of the hub carrier assembly **(see illustration)**.
3 Support the hub carrier securely on blocks or in a vice. Using a tubular spacer, which bears only on the inner end of the hub flange, press the hub flange out of the bearing **(see illustration)**. Alternatively the bearing can be drifted out, using a spacer and nut and bolt.
4 If the bearing's outboard inner race remains on the hub, remove it using a bearing puller **(see illustration)**.

3.2 Extract the circlip from the inner side of the hub carrier

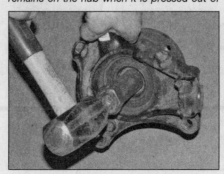

3.3 Using a hammer and drift to remove the inner hub flange

3.4 Using a puller to remove the inner bearing race from the inner hub flange

3.5a Use a threaded rod and spacers to . . .

3.5b . . . withdraw the bearing from the hub . . .

3.5c . . . or use a hammer and drift to remove bearing

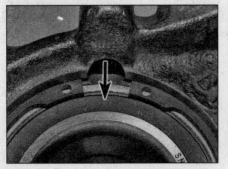

3.8 The inner race of the bearing (arrowed) is fitted with a decoder for the wheel speed sensor

3.9 Using a threaded rod and spacers/old bearing to press the new bearing into place

inboard face. Take care not to damage this encoder, or place it adjacent to a magnetic source. Ensure the encoder face is clean. The bearing will need to be pressed into position, as using a hammer to knock it in will damage the encoder.

9 Securely support the hub carrier, and locate the bearing in the hub. Press the bearing fully into position, ensuring that it enters the hub squarely, using a tubular spacer (old bearing), which bears only on the bearing outer race **(see illustration)**.

10 Once the bearing is correctly seated, secure the bearing in position with the new circlip, ensuring that it is correctly located in the groove in the hub carrier **(see illustration)**. **Note:** *Align the gap between the ends of the circlip with the gap for the ABS wheel speed sensor.*

11 Securely support the outer face of the hub flange, and locate the hub carrier bearing inner race over the end of the hub flange **(see illustration)**. Press the bearing onto the hub, using a tubular spacer that bears only on the inner race of the hub bearing until it seats against the hub shoulder. Check that the hub flange rotates freely, and wipe off any excess oil or grease.

12 Refit the hub carrier assembly as described in Section 2.

5 Where necessary, refit the outboard inner race back into position in the bearing. Using a tubular spacer, which bears only on the inner race, press the complete bearing assembly out of the hub carrier. If a press is not available, use a vice, threaded rod, spacers, large washers and nuts, to withdraw the bearing from the hub carrier **(see illustrations)**. Alternatively the bearing can be drifted out, using a spacer and nut and bolt.

6 Thoroughly clean the hub and hub carrier, removing all traces of dirt and grease, and polish away any burrs or raised edges that might hinder reassembly. Check both for cracks or any other signs of wear or damage, and renew them if necessary. Renew the circlip, regardless of its apparent condition.

7 On reassembly, apply a light film of oil (Peugeot recommend Molykote 321R – available from your Peugeot dealer) to the bearing outer race and hub flange shaft, to aid installation of the bearing.

8 When fitting the bearing, ensure this face is inboard adjacent to the ABS wheel speed sensor **(see illustration)**, as the bearing is equipped with a magnetic encoder on its

3.10 Fit the new circlip correctly, allowing the opening for the sensor to be clear

3.11 Using a threaded rod and spacers to press the hub flange back into the bearing/hub carrier

4 Front suspension strut – removal and refitting

Note: *Always renew any self-locking nuts when working on the suspension/steering components.*

Removal

1 Open the bonnet and unclip the scuttle trim panel from the front of the windscreen, and then unbolt the plastic cover from the top of the strut **(see illustrations)**.

2 Remove the wheel trim/hub cap (as applicable) then withdraw the R-clip and remove the locking cap from the driveshaft retaining nut **(see illustrations 2.1a and 2.1b)**. Slacken the driveshaft nut with the vehicle resting on its wheels. Also slacken the wheel bolts.

3 Chock the rear wheels of the car, firmly apply the handbrake, and then jack up the front of the car and support it on axle stands (see *Jacking and vehicle support*). Remove the appropriate front roadwheel.

4 Slacken and remove the driveshaft retaining nut. If the nut was not slackened with the wheels on the ground (see paragraph 1), withdraw the R-clip and remove the locking cap. Refit at least two roadwheel bolts to the front hub, tightening them securely, then have an assistant firmly depress the brake pedal to prevent the front hub from rotating whilst you slacken and remove the driveshaft retaining nut. Alternatively, a tool can be fabricated to hold the hub stationary **(see illustration 2.3)**.

5 Slacken and remove the nut securing the steering rack track rod end to the hub carrier then free the balljoint from the hub **(see illustration 2.7)**. If the balljoint is tight, use a universal balljoint separator to free it. Discard the nut, as a new one should be used on refitting.

6 Undo the retaining nuts and remove the anti-roll bar drop link as described in Section 9.

7 Undo the retaining nut and remove the lower suspension arm-to-alloy hub support securing bolt. With the bolt removed, lever the lower arm downwards to release it from the hub support housing **(see illustrations 2.9a and 2.9b)**.

8 Pull the hub support housing outwards, releasing the driveshaft splines from the centre of the hub. Suspend the driveshaft by string from the suspension strut to prevent and damage to the constant velocity joints, making sure that the inner driveshaft joint does not pull out of the transmission.

9 Release the bottom of the strut from the alloy hub support housing, and then undo the three upper retaining nuts and withdraw the strut from under the wheel arch **(see illustrations)**.

4.1a Unclip the scuttle trim . . .

4.1b . . . and remove the strut plastic cover

4.9a Undo the three upper retaining nuts . . .

4.9b . . . and withdraw the strut from under the front wing

Caution: *As soon as the upper mounting nuts are removed, the strut will be unsupported.*

Refitting

10 Refitting is the reverse of removal, using new nuts where required. Before refitting the roadwheel, set the suspension to the ride height position, as described in Section 28 and tighten the suspension nuts/bolts to their specified torque setting.

5 Front suspension strut – overhaul

  Warning: *Before attempting to dismantle the front suspension strut, a suitable tool to hold the coil*

spring in compression must be obtained. *Adjustable coil spring compressors are readily available, and are recommended for this operation. Any attempt to dismantle the strut without such a tool is likely to result in damage or personal injury.*

Note: *Always renew any self-locking nuts when working on the suspension/steering components.*

1 With the strut removed from the car (as described in Section 4), clean away all external dirt, and then mark the position of the upper mounting plate to the lower mount bush **(see illustration)**.

2 Fit the spring compressor and compress the coil spring until tension is relieved from the spring seats **(see illustration)**.

3 Slacken and remove the upper spring seat

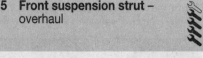

5.1 Make alignment marks between the upper and lower mountings

5.2 Fit the coil compressor to the spring

5.3 Slacken the top nut whilst retaining the rod with a small spanner

5.4a Remove the retaining nut . . .

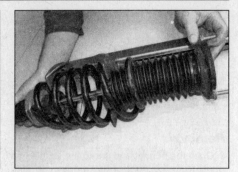

5.4b . . . and withdraw the upper mounting assembly

5.5a Remove the dust gaiter . . .

5.5b . . . followed by the rubber spring seat . . .

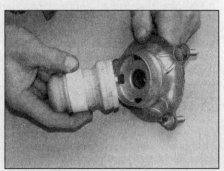

5.5c . . . and the bump stop

5.6a Mark the position of the end of the spring against the lower seat . . .

housing nut whilst retaining the shock absorber piston with a spanner (see illustration).

4 Remove the nut then lift off the spring seat housing, rubber bump stop and dust gaiter (see illustrations).

5 Check the condition of the gaiter, rubber spring seat (noting its fitted position) and bump stop (see illustrations).

6 Mark the position of the end of the spring on the lower seat on the damper, and then withdraw the damper from the coil spring (see illustrations).

7 Examine the shock absorber for signs of fluid leakage. Check the piston for signs of pitting along its entire length, and check the shock body for signs of damage. While holding it in an upright position, test the operation of the shock absorber by moving the piston through a full stroke, and then through short strokes of 50 to 100 mm. In both cases, the resistance felt should be smooth and continuous. If the resistance is jerky, or uneven, or if there is any visible sign of wear or damage to the shock absorber, renewal is necessary.

8 Inspect all other components for signs of damage or deterioration, and renew any that are suspect (see illustration).

9 Refit the damper to the coil spring; making sure

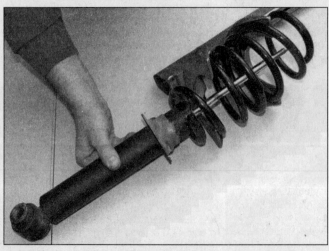

5.6b . . . and then withdraw the strut from the coil spring

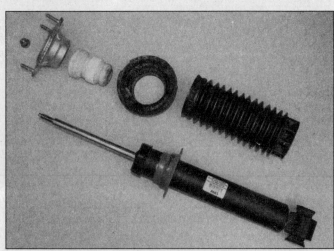

5.8 Check the suspension strut components for wear

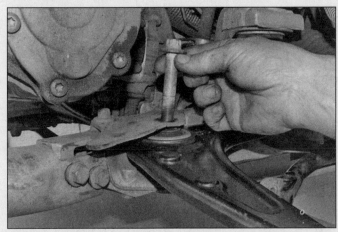

6.6 Remove the lower arm front mounting bolt

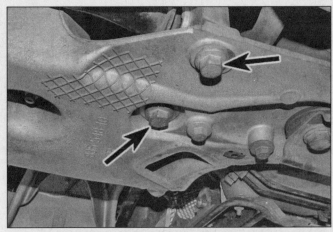

6.7 Lower arm rear mounting bolts (arrowed)

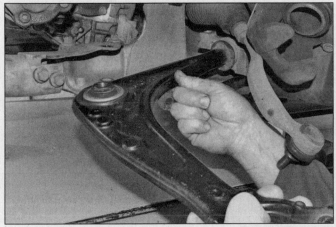

6.8 Withdraw the lower arm from the subframe

6.9 Rear bush (arrowed) is part of the lower arm

the lower end of the spring is correctly seated against the spring seat as marked on removal.

10 Reassemble the bump stop, spring rubber seat and the gaiter to the upper spring seat housing and slide it into position over the damper piston.

11 Fit the new retaining nut to the top of the upper spring seat housing and tighten, making sure the upper spring seat is aligned correctly as noted on removal. Release the spring compressor and remove the strut.

12 Retain the shock absorber piston with a spanner, and then tighten the upper spring seat nut to the specified torque.

13 Refit the front suspension strut to the vehicle, as described in previous Section.

6 Front suspension arms – removal, overhaul and refitting

Note: *Always renew any self-locking nuts when working on the suspension/steering components.*

Lower suspension arm

Removal

1 Remove the wheel trim/hub cap (as applicable) then withdraw the R-clip and remove the locking cap from the driveshaft retaining nut **(see illustrations 2.1a and 2.1b)**. Slacken the driveshaft nut with the vehicle resting on its wheels. Also slacken the wheel bolts.

2 Chock the rear wheels of the car, firmly apply the handbrake, and then jack up the front of the car and support it on axle stands (see *Jacking and vehicle support*). Remove the appropriate front roadwheel.

3 Slacken and remove the driveshaft retaining nut. If the nut was not slackened with the wheels on the ground (see paragraph 1), withdraw the R-clip and remove the locking cap. Refit at least two roadwheel bolts to the front hub, tightening them securely, then have an assistant firmly depress the brake pedal to prevent the front hub from rotating whilst you slacken and remove the driveshaft retaining nut. Alternatively, a tool can be fabricated to hold the hub stationary **(see illustration 2.3)**.

4 Undo the retaining nut and remove the lower suspension arm-to-alloy hub support securing bolt. With the bolt removed, lever the lower arm downwards to release it from the hub support housing **(see illustrations 2.9a and 2.9b)**.

5 Pull the hub support housing outwards, releasing the driveshaft splines from the centre of the hub. Suspend the driveshaft by string from the suspension strut to prevent and damage to the constant velocity joints, making sure that the inner driveshaft joint does not pull out of the transmission.

6 Move the driveshaft to one side and remove the lower arm front mounting bolt from the top of the subframe **(see illustration)**.

7 Slacken and remove the two rear pivot bolts from under the rear of the subframe **(see illustration)**.

8 Manoeuvre the lower arm out from underneath the vehicle **(see illustration)**.

Overhaul

9 Thoroughly clean the lower arm and the area around the arm mountings, removing all traces of dirt and underseal if necessary, then check carefully for cracks, distortion or any other signs of wear or damage, paying particular attention to the bushes, and renew components as necessary. The only bush available separately is the front bush, if there is any sign of wear in the rear bush **(see illustration)**, the lower arm will need to be renewed.

10 Renewal of the front pivot bush will

6.11a Using spacers and a threaded rod . . .

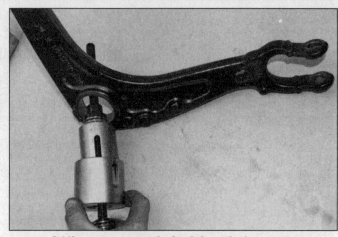

6.11b . . . to remove the bush from the lower arm

required the use of a hydraulic press, or a selection of different size tubular spacers, a threaded bar, washers and retaining nuts.

11 Using a tubular spacer, which bears on the lower arm (big enough to receive the bush), and another smaller tubular spacer, that fits against the outer part of the bush, press the bush out of the lower arm **(see illustrations)**.

12 Using the same method, with tubular spacers, press the new bush into the lower arm **(see illustrations)**.

Refitting

13 Manoeuvre the lower arm assembly into position, and refit the front pivot bolt, and then tighten to the specified torque.

14 Refit the rear pivot bolts, and then tighten to the specified torque.

15 Ensure that the driveshaft outer constant velocity joint and hub splines are clean, and then slide the hub onto the driveshaft splines.

16 Refit the lower suspension arm to the alloy hub support, and tighten the retaining bolt/nut. Do not fully tighten at this stage, as the ride height setting will need to set. Lever the lower arm downwards **(see illustration 2.9b)**, to aid refitting.

17 Lubricate the inner face and threads of the driveshaft retaining nut with clean engine oil, and refit it to the end of the driveshaft. Use the method employed on removal to prevent the hub from rotating **(see illustration 2.3)**,

and tighten the driveshaft retaining nut to the specified torque. Alternatively, lightly tighten the nut at this stage and tighten it to the specified torque once the vehicle is resting on its wheels again.

18 Check that the hub rotates freely then engage the locking cap with the driveshaft nut, so that one of its cut-outs is aligned with the driveshaft hole, and secure the cap in position with the R-clip.

19 Before refitting the roadwheel, set the suspension to the ride height position, as described in Section 28 and tighten the suspension nuts/bolts to their specified torque setting. Check and, if necessary, adjust the front wheel alignment as described in Section 29.

20 Refit the roadwheel, then lower the vehicle to the ground and tighten the roadwheel bolts to the specified torque. If not already having done so, tighten the driveshaft retaining nut to the specified torque then refit the locking cap, aligning its cut-outs with the driveshaft hole, and secure it in position with the R-clip **(see illustrations 2.1a and 2.1b)**.

Upper suspension arm

Removal

21 Carry out the procedures as described in paragraphs 1 to 4 of this Section.

22 Open the bonnet and unclip the scuttle trim panel from the front of the windscreen, and then unbolt the plastic cover from the top of the strut **(see illustrations 4.1a and 4.1b)**.

23 Unbolt the wheel speed sensor and position it clear of the hub assembly (see Chapter 9, Section 19). Note that there is no need to disconnect the wiring.

24 Remove the front brake pads and position the brake caliper to one side as described in Chapter 9. Undo the retaining bolts/nut and remove the brake hose mounting bracket from the hub carrier **(see illustrations)**.

25 Slacken and remove the nut securing the steering rack track rod to the hub carrier then free the balljoint from the hub as described in Section 25.

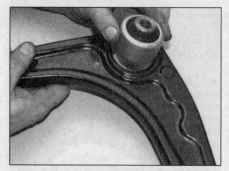

6.12a Make sure the bush sits square in the lower arm . . .

6.12b . . . and press it in using spacers and threaded rod

6.24a Remove the hose mounting bracket from the hub . . .

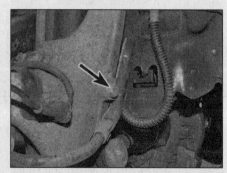

6.24b . . . and then undo the hose bracket securing bolt (arrowed)

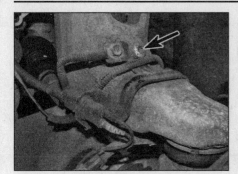

6.27a Undo the wiring bracket securing bolt (arrowed) . . .

6.27b . . . and then remove the bracket from the suspension housing

6.29 Remove the suspension housing assembly from the vehicle

26 Undo the retaining nuts and remove the anti-roll bar drop link as described in Section 9.
27 Undo the retaining bolt and remove the wiring bracket from the alloy hub support housing **(see illustrations)**.
28 Pull the hub support housing outwards, releasing the driveshaft splines from the centre of the hub. Suspend the driveshaft by string to the underside of the vehicle body to prevent and damage to the constant velocity joints, making sure that the inner driveshaft joint does not pull out of the transmission.
29 Support the weight of the suspension assembly, and then undo the three upper retaining nuts and withdraw the suspension assembly from under the wheel arch **(see illustration)**.
30 Undo the retaining bolts and remove the

upper suspension arms from the top of the alloy hub support housing **(see illustrations)**.
Caution: As soon as the upper mounting nuts are removed, the suspension assembly will be unsupported.

Overhaul

31 Thoroughly clean the upper arms and the area around the arm mountings, removing all traces of dirt and underseal if necessary, then check carefully for cracks, distortion or any other signs of wear or damage, paying particular attention to the bushes, and renew components as necessary.
32 Renewal of the bushes will required the use of a selection of different size tubular spacers, a threaded bar, washers and retaining nuts.
33 To remove the bushes from the alloy

support housing, first cut the inner section of the bush away **(see illustration)**.
34 Using a tubular spacer (socket), which bears on the alloy housing (big enough to receive the bush), and a nut and washer that fits against the bush, press the bush out of the lower arm **(see illustrations)**.
35 Using the same method, remove the bush from the other side of the alloy hub support housing.
36 To refit the bushes, insert them into the support housing and then using a threaded bar, washer and nuts, press them into the housing **(see illustration)**. Make sure the bushes are pressed into the housing squarely.
37 To remove the bushes from the alloy upper housing, use a tubular spacer (socket), which bears on the alloy housing (big enough to receive the bush), and a nut, washer and

6.30a Remove the upper suspension arm front . . .

6.30b . . . and rear pivot bolts

6.33 Cut a section out of one of the bushes

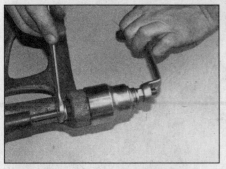

6.34a Using a threaded rod and spacers/ socket . . .

6.34b . . . to press the old bush out of the housing

6.36 Using the threaded rod, washers and nuts to draw the new bushes into place

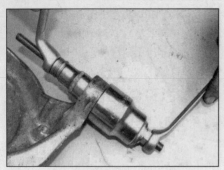

6.37a Using a threaded rod and spacers/ socket . . .

6.37b . . . to press the old bush out of the upper mounting

6.38 Make sure the bush sits squarely in the upper mounting plate

tubular spacer (socket) that fits against the bush, press the bush out of the housing **(see illustrations)**.

38 To refit the bushes, insert them into the housing, making sure the bushes are seated squarely in the housing **(see illustrations)**. Note the fitted position of any plastic washers on the bushes, for refitting.

39 Using a tubular spacer (socket), which bears on the alloy housing, and a tubular spacer (socket), nut and washer that fits against the bush, press the bush into the housing **(see illustration)**.

Refitting

40 Refit the upper suspension arms to the top

of the alloy hub support housing and tighten the retaining bolts. Do not fully tighten at this stage, as the ride height setting will need to set, as described in Section 28.

41 Manoeuvre the suspension assembly into position, and refit the upper mounting nuts on the inner wing panel, and then tighten to the specified torque.

42 Ensure that the driveshaft outer constant velocity joint and hub splines are clean, and then slide the hub onto the driveshaft splines.

43 Refit the wiring bracket back to the alloy hub support housing and tighten the retaining bolt.

44 Refit the anti-roll bar drop link as described in Section 9.

45 Refit the steering rack track rod end to the hub carrier as described in Section 25.

46 Refit the front brake pads as described in Chapter 9. Make sure the brake hose is routed and secured correctly.

47 Refit the wheel speed sensor as described in Chapter 9, Section 19.

48 Refit the plastic cover to the top of the strut mount on the inner wing panel, and then refit the scuttle trim panel to the front of the windscreen.

49 Carry out the procedures as described in paragraphs 17 to 20 of this Section.

7 Front suspension balljoints – removal and refitting

Lower balljoint

Removal

1 Remove the hub carrier assembly as described in Section 2.

2 Unclip the seal from the balljoint using a thin screwdriver **(see illustration)**.

3 Twist the balljoint and extract some of the roller bearings from the balljoint, and then remove the balljoint from the hub carrier **(see illustrations)**.

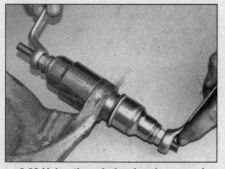

6.39 Using threaded rod and spacers/ sockets to press the new bush into place

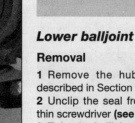

7.2 Unclip the seal from the balljoint

7.3a Pull and twist the balljoint . . .

7.3b . . . and remove some of the rollers from the bearing

7.4a Remove the seal from the pivot . . .

7.4b . . . then using a puller . . .

7.4c . . . withdraw the inner bearing race . . .

4 Unclip the seal and then using a puller, withdraw the bearing inner race from the pivot shaft on the base of the hub carrier. Also remove the bearing upper shield from the pivot shaft **(see illustrations)**.

Refitting

5 Thoroughly clean the pivot shaft at the base of the hub carrier, removing all traces of dirt and grease, and polish away any burrs or raised edges that might hinder reassembly.
6 Fit the new upper shield to the hub pivot **(see illustration)**.
7 Apply some grease to the seal on the top of the bearing (Peugeot recommend Total N4128), and then press the balljoint onto the pivot shaft of the hub carrier **(see illustrations)**.
8 Refit the hub carrier assembly as described in Section 2.

7.4d . . . and the upper shield

Upper balljoint
Removal

9 Remove the hub carrier assembly as described in Section 2.
10 Fit the special castellated socket (Peugeot

7.6 Fit a new shield to the hub pivot

tool No 0627) to the upper balljoint, and then fit the securing nut to the balljoint to keep the socket firmly in place **(see illustrations)**.
11 Using a long bar and socket, slacken the upper balljoint and unscrew it from the alloy hub support housing **(see illustrations)**.

7.7a Apply grease to the bearing and seal . . .

7.7b . . . and press the balljoint on to the hub pivot

7.10a Fit the Peugeot tool to the balljoint . . .

7.10b . . . and secure it in place with the balljoint retaining nut

7.11a Using a long bar, slacken the balljoint . . .

7.11b . . . and remove it from the suspension housing

7.14 Using a drift to stake the balljoint in position

8.2a Use a Torx bit to counterhold the balljoint . . .

8.2b . . . and then disconnect it from the anti-roll bar

Refitting

12 Check the condition of the threads in the alloy support housing, and then thread the new balljoint into the housing, taking care not to damage the rubber gaiter on the balljoint as it is being fitted.

13 With the socket firmly fitted in place over the balljoint as described on removal, tighten the balljoint to the specified torque setting.

14 Once the balljoint has been tightened, use a drift to peen the edge of the balljoint into the notch(es) on the alloy housing **(see illustration)**.

15 Refit the hub carrier assembly as described in Section 2.

8 Front anti-roll bar – removal and refitting

Note: *Always renew any self-locking nuts when working on the suspension/steering components.*

Removal

1 Chock the rear wheels, firmly apply the handbrake, slacken the front roadwheel bolts, then jack up the front of the vehicle and support on axle stands (see *Jacking and vehicle support*). Remove both front roadwheels.

2 Slacken and remove the nuts securing the left- and right-hand drop links to the anti-roll bar, and position the links clear of the bar; if necessary, retain the balljoint shank with a

Torx bit to prevent rotation whilst the nut is slackened **(see illustrations)**. Discard the nuts; new ones should be used on refitting.

3 Slacken the two anti-roll bar mounting clamp retaining bolts, and remove both clamps from the top of the subframe **(see illustrations)**.

4 At this point the rubber bushes can be removed from the anti-roll bar, noting their fitted position **(see illustration)**. Note the anti-roll bar has flats at each side of the bar to accommodate the rubber bushes.

5 If the complete anti-roll bar needs to be removed it will be necessary to lower the front alloy main subframe, with reference to Section 10 of this Chapter. Manoeuvre the anti-roll bar out from between the subframe and the body as required.

Refitting

6 Carefully examine the anti-roll bar components for signs of wear, damage or deterioration, paying particular attention to the mounting bushes, and drop link balljoints. Renew worn components as necessary.

7 Fit the rubber mounting bushes to the anti-roll bar. Position each bush so that its flat surface is at the bottom, and its internal flats are correctly engaged with the flats on the anti-roll bar.

8 Offer up the anti-roll bar, and manoeuvre it into position on the subframe. Where applicable refit the subframe with reference to Section 10.

9 Refit the mounting clamps, ensuring that

they are fitted over the rubbers correctly on the subframe, and then refit the retaining bolts. Engage the drop links with the ends of the bar then tighten the mounting clamp retaining bolts to the specified torque.

10 Fit the new retaining nuts to the drop links and tighten them to the specified torque setting.

11 Refit the roadwheels then lower the vehicle to the ground and tighten the wheel bolts to the specified torque.

9 Front anti-roll bar drop link – removal and refitting

Note: *New drop link nuts will be required on refitting.*

Removal

1 Chock the rear wheels, firmly apply the handbrake, slacken the relevant roadwheel bolts, then jack up the front of the vehicle and support on axle stands (see *Jacking and vehicle support*). Remove the relevant roadwheel.

2 Slacken and remove the nuts securing the drop link lower balljoint to the anti-roll bar **(see illustrations 8.2a and 8.2b)**. Discard the nuts; new ones should be used on refitting.

3 Slacken and remove the nuts securing the drop link upper balljoint to the lower strut mounting on the alloy support housing **(see**

8.3a Undo the mounting bolts (arrowed) . . .

8.3b . . . and then remove the upper clamp from the anti-roll bar

8.4 Note the fitted position of the rubber bushes

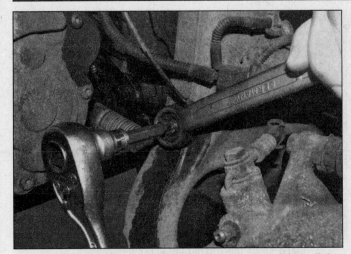

9.3 Use a Torx bit to counterhold the lower strut bolt/drop link

9.4 Withdraw the lower strut bolt/drop link from the suspension

illustration). If necessary, retain the balljoint shanks with a Torx bit to prevent rotation whilst each nut is slackened.

4 With the nut removed withdraw the drop link upper balljoint/bolt from the suspension support housing (see illustration).

5 Inspect the link for signs of wear or damage and renew if necessary.

Refitting

6 Refitting is the reverse of removal, using new securing nuts. Before refitting the road wheel, set the suspension to the ride height position, as described in Section 28 and tighten the drop link upper nuts/bolts to the specified torque setting.

10 Front subframe – removal, overhaul and refitting

Note: Always renew any self-locking nuts when working on the suspension/steering components.

Removal

1 Chock the rear wheels, firmly apply the handbrake, slacken the front roadwheel bolts, and then jack up the front of the vehicle

and support it on axle stands (see *Jacking and vehicle support*). Remove both front roadwheels.

2 Remove the front bumper as described in Chapter 11.

3 Undo the retaining bolts and remove the lower crossbeam from the front of the vehicle (see illustrations).

4 Slacken and remove the nuts securing the drop link lower balljoint to the anti-roll bar (see illustration 8.2a and 8.2b). Discard the nuts; new ones should be used on refitting. The anti-roll bar can stay bolted to the top of the subframe.

5 Slacken and remove the steering rack mounting nuts and washers (see illustration). Discard the nuts, as new ones must be fitted. Lift the steering rack slightly to disengage it from the top of the subframe, as the steering rack will stay in place as the subframe is lowered. Use cable-ties (or similar) to support the steering rack, once the subframe has been removed.

6 Undo the retaining bolts and disconnect the power steering pipe brackets from the subframe (see illustrations).

7 Undo the retaining bolts and remove the

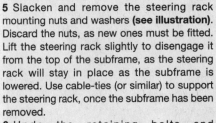

10.3a Undo the mounting bolts (arrowed) . . .

10.3b . . . and remove the lower bumper bar

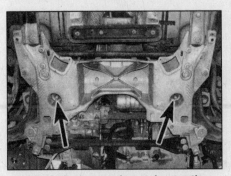

10.5 Undo the steering rack mounting nuts/studs (arrowed)

10.6a Undo the power steering pipe securing bracket bolt (arrowed) . . .

10.6b . . . on both sides of the subframe

10.7 Strengthener bar securing bolts (arrowed)

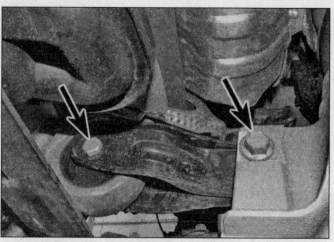

10.8a Undo the two mounting bolts (arrowed) . . .

10.8b . . . and remove the rear mounting link bar

strengthener bar from across the front of the main subframe (see illustration).

8 Undo the nuts and bolts, and remove the mounting link securing the rear engine/transmission mounting to the subframe (see illustrations).

9 Undo the four bolts (two each side) securing the front subframe to the main subframe (see illustration).

10 Undo the two bolts on the front securing brackets, and then remove the front subframe from the front of the vehicle (see illustrations).

11 Undo the retaining nuts and remove the lower suspension arm to alloy hub support securing bolts. With the bolts removed, lever the lower arms downwards to release

them from the hub support housing (see illustrations 2.9a and 2.9b).

12 Make a final check that all control cables/hoses that are attached to the subframe have been released and positioned clear so that they will not hinder the removal procedure.

13 Place a jack and a suitable block of wood under the main subframe to support the subframe as it is lowered.

14 Slacken and remove the main subframe rear mounting bolts and remove the retaining plates from each side (see illustrations).

15 Mark the position of the main subframe to the body to aid refitting, and then slacken and remove the mounting bolts at each side of the subframe (see illustration).

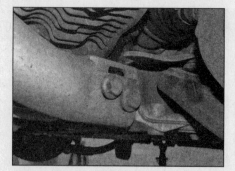

10.9 Undo the front subframe mounting bolts (one side shown)

10.10a Undo the front mounting bolts . . .

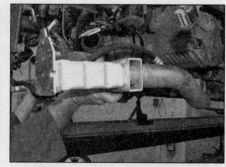

10.10b . . . and withdraw the front subframe from under the vehicle

10.14a Undo the rear subframe bolts (arrowed) . . .

10.14b . . . and remove the mounting bracket plates

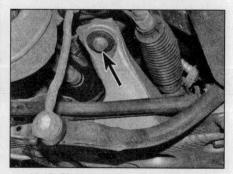

10.15 Slacken and remove the front mounting bolts (arrowed) – one side shown

10.16 Note the locating peg (arrowed) on the body to align subframe

10.17 Prise out the rubber bush

10.18 Mark the position of the bush in the subframe

10.19a Using a threaded rod and spacers . . .

10.19b . . . to press the old bush out of the subframe

10.20 Using threaded rod and spacers to press the new bush into place

16 Carefully lower the subframe assembly out from underneath the vehicle, taking great care to ensure that the subframe assembly does not catch the power steering pipes as it is lowered out of position. Note the left-hand rear mounting has a locating dowel on the body for refitting **(see illustration)**.

Overhaul

17 Thoroughly clean the area around the mountings, removing all traces of dirt and underseal if necessary, then check carefully for cracks, distortion or any other signs of wear or damage, paying particular attention to the bushes, and renew components as necessary. If there is any sign of wear in the bushes they will need to be renewed. Use a screwdriver to remove the lower rubber sealing cup **(see illustration)**.

18 Mark the position of the bush in the subframe **(see illustration)**, as the new bush will need to be fitted in the same position.

19 Using a tubular spacer, which bears on the upper part of the subframe (big enough to receive the bush), and another smaller tubular spacer, that fits against the outer part of the bush, use a threaded bar with nuts and washers to press the bush out of the subframe **(see illustrations)**.

20 Using the same method, with tubular spacers, press the new bush into the lower arm **(see illustration)**.

Refitting

21 Refitting is a reversal of the removal procedure, noting the following points:

a) Use new drop link and lower arm retaining nuts, and steering rack nuts.
b) Tighten all nuts and bolts to the specified torque settings (where given).
c) Before refitting the roadwheel, set the suspension to the ride height position, as described in Section 28 and tighten the suspension nuts/bolts to their specified torque setting.
d) On completion check and, if necessary, adjust the front wheel alignment as described in Section 29.

---

11 Rear hub assembly –
removal and refitting

Note: *Do not remove the hub assembly unless it is absolutely necessary. A puller will be* required to draw the hub assembly off the stub axle, and the hub bearing will almost certainly be damaged by the removal procedure, necessitating renewal of the hub assembly. A new hub nut and centre cap must be used on refitting.

Removal

1 Remove the rear brake disc as described in Chapter 9.

2 Prise out the cap from the centre of the hub and discard; a new cap should be used on refitting **(see illustration)**.

3 Using a hammer and punch, tap up the staking securing the hub retaining nut to the groove in the stub axle **(see illustration)**.

4 Using a socket and long bar, unscrew the rear hub nut and discard it; a new hub nut should be used on refitting.

5 Using a puller, draw the hub assembly off

11.2 Prise the cap from the centre of the hub

11.3 Unstake the retaining nut

11.5 Use a puller to remove the hub

11.10a Stake the new nut . . .

11.10b . . . then fit a new hub cap

the stub axle, along with the outer bearing race **(see illustration)**. If necessary, with the hub removed, use the puller to draw the inner bearing race off the stub axle.

6 Check the hub bearing for signs of roughness. It is recommended that the hub bearing should be renewed as a matter of course, as it is likely to have been damaged during removal. This means that the complete hub assembly must be renewed, since it is not possible to obtain the bearing separately.

7 With the hub removed, examine the stub axle shaft for signs of wear or damage, and if necessary renew it (see Section 15).

Refitting

8 Ensure that the bearing is packed with grease and lubricate the stub axle shaft with clean engine oil.

9 Fit the new bearing assembly, tapping it fully onto the stub axle using a hammer and a tubular drift that bears only on the flat inside edge of the bearing inner race.

10 Fit the new hub nut and tighten it to the specified torque. Stake the nut firmly into the groove on the stub axle to secure it in position, and then tap the new hub cap into place in the centre of the hub **(see illustrations)**.

11 Refit the rear brake disc as described in Chapter 9.

12 Rear hub bearings – renewal

The hub bearing is an integral part of the hub assembly and is not available

separately. If the bearing is worn, renew the complete hub assembly as described in Section 11.

13 Rear suspension strut – removal and refitting

Note: *Always renew any self-locking nuts when working on the suspension/steering components.*

Removal

1 Chock the front wheels, slacken the relevant rear roadwheel bolts, and then jack up the rear of the vehicle and support it on axle stands (see *Jacking and vehicle support*). Remove the relevant rear roadwheel.

2 Unclip the plastic shield from the lower part of the shock absorber **(see illustration)**.

3 Slacken and remove the lower shock absorber mounting bolt **(see illustration)**.

4 Slacken and remove the upper mounting bolt and withdraw the shock absorber out from under the vehicle **(see illustrations)**. For the right-hand shock absorber, open the boot/tailgate, lift up the luggage compartment carpet, and unclip the rubber grommet to access the upper mounting bolt.

Refitting

5 Examine the suspension bump stop for

13.2 Unclip the plastic shield from the shock absorber

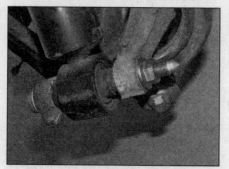

13.3 Undo the shock absorber lower mounting bolt

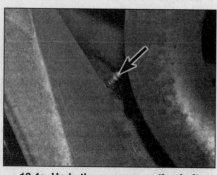

13.4a Undo the upper mounting bolt (arrowed) . . .

13.4b . . . and withdraw the shock absorber out from under the vehicle

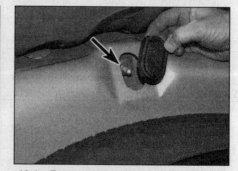

13.4c Remove the rubber grommet in the boot, to access the right-hand side upper mounting bolt

13.5 Check the condition of the rear suspension bump stop

14.2 Fit the coil compressor to the spring

14.3 Unscrew the upper mounting

signs of damage or deterioration, renew worn bump stop as necessary **(see illustration)**.

6 Apply a smear of multipurpose grease to the mounting bolts and contact face of the new nuts (Peugeot recommend Molykote G Rapide Plus – available from your Peugeot dealer).

7 Refit the upper mounting bolts, and tighten them lightly only at this stage.

8 Align the shock absorber lower mounting with the lower arm and refit the mounting bolt. Fit the new nut, also tightening it lightly at this stage.

9 Before refitting the roadwheel, set the suspension to the ride height position, as described in Section 28 and tighten the mounting bolts/nuts to the specified torque setting.

10 Refit the rear roadwheel then lower the vehicle to the ground and tighten the wheel bolts to the specified torque.

14 Rear suspension strut –
overhaul

> ⚠ *Warning: Before attempting to dismantle the rear suspension strut, a suitable tool to hold the coil spring in compression must be obtained. Adjustable coil spring compressors are readily available, and are recommended for this operation. Any*

14.10 Fit a new washer (arrowed) when reassembling

attempt to dismantle the strut without such a tool is likely to result in damage or personal injury.
Note: *Always renew any self-locking nuts when working on the suspension/steering components.*

1 With the strut removed from the car (as described in Section 13), clean away all external dirt, and then mark the position of the upper eye/bush to the lower mount bush.

2 Fit the spring compressor and compress the coil spring until tension is relieved from the spring seats **(see illustration)**.

3 Slacken and remove the upper eye nut whilst retaining the shock absorber piston with a spanner **(see illustration)**.

4 With the upper eye/bush removed, lift off the upper spring seat housing, rubber bump stop and dust gaiter. Check the condition of the gaiter, rubber spring seat (noting its fitted position) and bump stop.

5 Note the position of the end of the spring on the lower seat on the damper, and then withdraw the damper from the coil spring.

6 Examine the shock absorber for signs of fluid leakage. Check the piston for signs of pitting along its entire length, and check the shock body for signs of damage. While holding it in an upright position, test the operation of the shock absorber by moving the piston through a full stroke, and then through short strokes of 50 to 100 mm. In both cases, the resistance felt should be smooth and continuous. If the resistance is jerky, or uneven, or if there is any

15.2 Disconnect the drop link from the hub carrier

visible sign of wear or damage to the shock absorber, renewal is necessary.

7 Inspect all other components for signs of damage or deterioration, and renew any that are suspect.

8 Refit the damper to the coil spring; making sure the lower end of the spring is correctly seated against the spring seat as marked on removal.

9 Reassemble the bump stop, spring rubber seat, gaiter and upper spring seat housing and slide it into position over the damper piston.

10 Fit a new washer to the top of the piston rod **(see illustration)**, and then fit the upper eye/bush and tighten. Make sure the upper spring seat is aligned correctly as noted on removal. Release the spring compressor and remove the strut.

11 Retain the shock absorber piston with a spanner, and then tighten the upper eye/bush nut to the specified torque.

12 Refit the rear suspension strut to the vehicle, as described in previous Section.

15 Rear hub carrier – removal, overhaul and refitting

Note: *Always renew any self-locking nuts when working on the suspension/steering components.*

Removal

1 Chock the front wheels, slacken the relevant rear roadwheel bolts, and then jack up the rear of the vehicle and support it on axle stands (see *Jacking and vehicle support*). Remove the relevant roadwheel.

2 Undo the retaining nut and disconnect the anti-roll bar drop link from the hub carrier **(see illustration)**.

3 Remove the rear brake disc as described in Chapter 9.

4 Unbolt the wheel speed sensor and position it clear of the hub assembly (see Chapter 9, Section 19). Note that there is no need to disconnect the wiring.

5 Undo the retaining bolts and remove the

15.5 Remove the brake disc shield

15.8 Undo the lower arm mounting bolt (arrowed)

15.9 Undo the adjusting arm mounting bolt (arrowed)

brake disc shield from the hub carrier (see illustration).

6 If required the hub assembly can be removed, as described in Section 11. **Note:** *If the hub carrier is to be renewed, there is no need to remove the hub assembly, as the act of removal destroys the bearing necessitating its renewal.*

7 Slacken and remove the lower shock absorber mounting bolt.

8 Remove the lower arm-to-hub carrier mounting bolt (see illustration).

9 Remove the adjusting arm-to-hub carrier mounting bolt (see illustration).

10 Slacken and remove the longitudinal arm-to-hub carrier mounting bolt, and pull it downwards to disengage it from the hub carrier (see illustration).

11 Undo the upper mounting nut and bolt securing the hub carrier to the upper suspension wishbone and remove it from the rear axle (see illustration).

12 Inspect the hub carrier for signs of wear or damage. If the stub axle shaft is worn or damaged then the assembly must be renewed.

Refitting

13 Obtain all the new nuts required and lubricate the shanks of the pivot bolts

and contact faces of the new nuts with multipurpose grease (Peugeot recommend Molykote G Rapide Plus – available from your Peugeot dealer).

14 Offer up the hub carrier, and then insert the upper wishbone bolt and tighten, do not fully-tighten at this stage, as the ride height setting will need to set.

15 Refit the longitudinal arm-to-hub carrier mounting bolt, the adjusting arm-to-hub carrier mounting bolt, the lower arm-to-hub carrier mounting bolt, and the lower shock absorber mounting bolt and tighten. Do not fully-tighten at this stage, as the ride height setting will need to set.

16 If removed, fit the new hub assembly as described in Section 11.

17 Refit the wheel speed sensor to the hub assembly; refer to Chapter 9, Section 19, for further information, if required.

18 Fit the brake disc shield to the hub carrier and tighten the securing bolts.

19 Refit the rear brake disc as described in Chapter 9.

20 Refit the anti-roll bar drop link to the hub carrier and tighten the new retaining nut to the specified torque setting.

21 Before refitting the roadwheel, set the suspension to the ride height position, as

described in Section 28 and tighten the suspension nuts/bolts to their specified torque setting.

22 Refit the rear roadwheel then lower the vehicle to the ground and tighten the wheel bolts to the specified torque.

16 Rear axle assembly – removal, overhaul and refitting

Note 1: *Always renew any self-locking nuts when working on the suspension/steering components.*

Note 2: *Peugeot use special locating pegs (Tool No 0546-Z), to centralise the rear axle when refitting.*

Removal

1 Chock the front wheels, slacken the relevant rear roadwheel bolts, and then jack up the rear of the vehicle and support it on axle stands (see *Jacking and vehicle support*). Remove the relevant roadwheel.

2 Slacken the securing clamps and remove the rear section of the exhaust system.

3 Unbolt the wheel speed sensor and position it clear of the hub assembly (see Chapter 9,

15.10 Remove the longitudinal arm-to-hub carrier mounting bolt (arrowed)

15.11 Hub carrier upper mounting bolt (arrowed)

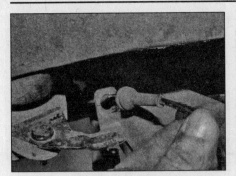

16.3 Unclip the ABS wiring from the retaining bracket

16.6 Remove the longitudinal arm-to-body mounting bolt (arrowed)

16.7 Undo the anti-roll bar mounting bracket securing bolt (arrowed)

Section 19). Note that there is no need to disconnect the wiring. Free the sensor harness from any retaining clips on the rear axle assembly (see illustration).

4 Disconnect the handbrake cables from the rear calipers and move them to one side. Free them from any retaining clips, referring to Chapter 9, Section 16, for further information.

5 Remove the rear brake pads, as described in Chapter 9. Move the caliper to one side, and free the brake hose from any retaining clips on the rear hub assembly.

6 Slacken and remove the longitudinal arm-to-body mounting bolt, and pull it downwards to disengage it from the underside of the body (see illustration).

7 Slacken and remove the anti-roll bar mounting bracket upper bolts from the underside of the vehicle (see illustration).

8 Support the rear axle with two trolley jacks, one at each side. DO NOT put one jack under the centre of the rear axle, as this may damage it.

9 With the axle supported, check around the axle for cables, hoses and wiring to make sure they are free from the axle. Make alignment marks between the axle mounting brackets and the vehicle body to aid refitment.

10 Undo the four subframe mounting bolts and lower the axle to the ground, then withdraw it from under the vehicle (see illustrations). If the axle is to be renewed, remove the suspension components as described in this Chapter.

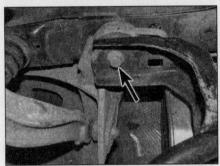

16.10a Undo the subframe rear mounting bolt (arrowed) . . .

16.10b . . . and front mounting bolt (arrowed) – one side shown

Overhaul

11 Thoroughly clean the axle and the area around the axle mountings, removing all traces of dirt and underseal if necessary, then check carefully for cracks, distortion or any other signs of wear or damage, paying particular attention to the pivot bushes.

12 Renewal of the rear axle mounting bushes are the same as the front subframe, see Section 10 of this Chapter, for the procedure for removing the bushes.

Refitting

13 Lubricate the shanks of the rear axle mounting bolts with multipurpose grease (Peugeot recommend Molykote G Rapide Plus – available from your Peugeot dealer).

14 Offer up the axle (making sure it is NOT jacked up in the centre of the axle) aligning the previously-made marks, and insert the

mounting bolts. Insert the Peugeot locating pegs (Tool No 0546-Z) through the mounting bracket into the body, and lock in position with the retaining clip (see illustrations). Once in place tighten the mounting bolts to the specified torque.

15 Refit the anti-roll bar mounting bracket retaining bolts and tighten.

16 Refit the longitudinal arm-to-body mounting bolt, and tighten to the specified torque setting.

17 Refit the rear brake pads, as described in Chapter 9. Refit the brake hose to the retaining clips on the rear hub assembly.

18 Reconnect the handbrake cables to the rear calipers and adjust, secure them in the retaining clips, referring to Chapter 9, Section 16.

19 Refit the wheel speed sensor to the hub assembly; refer to Chapter 9, Section 19, for further information, if required.

20 Refit the rear section of the exhaust system and tighten the securing clamps.

21 Refit the rear roadwheels and then lower the vehicle to the ground, tighten the wheel bolts to the specified torque.

17 Rear suspension arms –
removal, overhaul and refitting

Note: Always renew any self-locking nuts when working on the suspension/steering components.

1 Chock the front wheels, slacken the relevant rear roadwheel bolts, and then jack up the rear

16.14a Insert the subframe alignment tool . . .

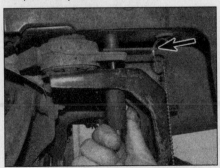

16.14b . . . and secure in place with the retaining clip

17.2 Lower arm mounting bolts (arrowed)

17.6a Undo the mounting bolts . . .

17.6b . . . and remove the longitudinal arm from the base of the hub carrier

of the vehicle and support it on axle stands (see *Jacking and vehicle support*). Remove the relevant roadwheel.

Lower suspension arm

Removal

2 Slacken and remove the two lower arm mounting bolts and remove the arm from under the vehicle **(see illustration)**.

Overhaul

3 Thoroughly clean the lower arm and the area around the arm mountings, removing all traces of dirt and underseal if necessary, then check carefully for cracks, distortion or any other signs of wear or damage, paying particular attention to the bushes. Renew the suspension arm as necessary.

Refitting

4 Refitting is the reverse of removal. Before

fully-tightening the mounting bolts, set the suspension to the ride height position, as described in Section 28 and then tighten the lower arm mounting bolts to the specified torque setting.
5 Refit the roadwheel, then lower the vehicle to the ground and tighten the roadwheel bolts to the specified torque.

Lower longitudinal suspension arm

Removal

6 Slacken and remove the suspension arm-to-body mounting bolt, and then the mounting bolt to the rear hub carrier. Pull the arm downwards to disengage it from the rear hub carrier **(see illustrations)**.

Overhaul

7 Thoroughly clean the lower arm and the

area around the arm mountings, removing all traces of dirt and underseal if necessary, then check carefully for cracks, distortion or any other signs of wear or damage, paying particular attention to the bushes, and renew components as necessary.
8 Renewal of the bushes will required the use of a hydraulic press, or a selection of different size tubular spacers, a threaded bar, washers and retaining nuts.
9 Before removing the bushes, note their fitted position, as the new bushes will need to be fitted in the same position **(see illustrations)**.
10 Using a tubular spacer, which bears on the lower arm (big enough to receive the bush), and another smaller tubular spacer, that fits against the outer part of the bush, press the bush out of the lower arm **(see illustrations)**.
11 Using the same method, with tubular spacers, press the new bushes into the lower arm. Making sure they are fitted correctly as noted on removal **(see illustrations 17.9a and 17.9b)**.

Refitting

12 Refitting is the reverse of removal. Before fitting the suspension arm to the hub carrier, make sure that the metal sleeve protrudes through the bush by 10 mm **(see illustration)**. This metal sleeve locates in the bottom of the hub carrier. Tighten the lower arm mounting bolts to the specified torque setting.
13 Refit the roadwheel, then lower the vehicle to the ground and tighten the roadwheel bolts to the specified torque.

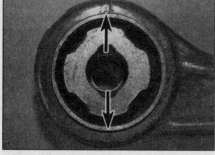

17.9a Make a note of the position of the bushes . . .

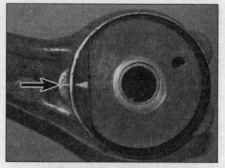

17.9b . . . in both ends of the longitudinal arm

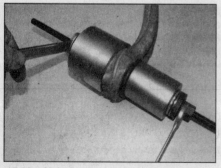

17.10a Using a threaded rod and spacers, press the old bush out of the arm

17.10b . . . noting the marks made (arrowed) for refitting

17.12 The sleeve must protrude by 10 mm at the top of the arm

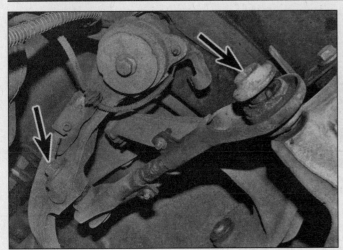

17.14 Adjusting arm mounting bolts (arrowed)

17.18 Wishbone upper mounting bolts (arrowed)

Track adjusting arm

Removal

14 Remove the adjusting arm mounting bolts, and remove the arm from under the vehicle (see illustration).

Overhaul

15 Thoroughly clean the adjusting arm and the area around the arm mountings, removing all traces of dirt and underseal if necessary, then check carefully for cracks, distortion or any other signs of wear or damage, paying particular attention to the bushes. Renew the adjusting arm as necessary.

Refitting

16 Refitting is the reverse of removal. Before fully-tightening the mounting bolts, set the suspension to the ride height position, as described in Section 28.

17 Refit the roadwheel, then lower the vehicle to the ground and tighten the roadwheel bolts to the specified torque. On completion check and, if necessary, adjust the wheel alignment as described in Section 29.

Suspension upper wishbone

Removal

18 Undo the upper mounting bolt securing the hub carrier to the suspension upper

wishbone (see illustration). Note the fitted position of the brake hose retaining bracket, for refitting.

19 Undo the retaining bolts and remove the suspension upper wishbone from the rear axle. If required, carefully pull the hub carrier outwards at the top to allow for the removal of the wishbone.

Overhaul

20 Thoroughly clean the upper arms and the area around the arm mountings, removing all traces of dirt and underseal if necessary, then check carefully for cracks, distortion or any other signs of wear or damage, paying particular attention to the bushes, and renew components as necessary.

21 Renewal of the bushes will required the use of a selection of different size tubular spacers, a threaded bar, washers and retaining nuts.

22 Renewal of the rear suspension wishbone bushes are the same as the front suspension upper arm, see Section 6 of this Chapter for the procedure for removing the bushes.

Refitting

23 Refitting is the reverse of removal. Before fully-tightening the mounting bolts, set the suspension to the ride height position, as described in Section 28.

24 Refit the roadwheel, then lower the vehicle

to the ground and tighten the roadwheel bolts to the specified torque. On completion check and, if necessary, adjust the wheel alignment as described in Section 29.

18 Rear anti-roll bar – removal and refitting

Note: *Always renew any self-locking nuts when working on the suspension/steering components.*

Removal

1 Chock the front wheels, slacken the relevant rear roadwheel bolts, and then jack up the rear of the vehicle and support it on axle stands (see *Jacking and vehicle support*). Remove the relevant roadwheel.

2 Slacken and remove the nuts securing the left- and right-hand drop links to the anti-roll bar, and position the links clear of the bar; if necessary, retain the balljoint shank with a Torx bit to prevent rotation whilst the nut is slackened (see illustration). Discard the nuts; new ones should be used on refitting.

3 On models from RPO No 10943, slacken and remove the bracket securing nut (see illustration).

4 Slacken the two anti-roll bar mounting

18.2 Disconnect the drop link from the anti-roll bar

18.3 Undo the bracket locating nut (arrowed)

18.4 Remove the anti-roll bar mounting bracket bolts (arrowed) . . .

18.5 ... and withdraw the mounting brackets from the anti-roll bar

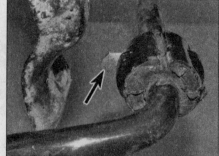

18.6 Note the locating peg (arrowed) is part of the rubber bush

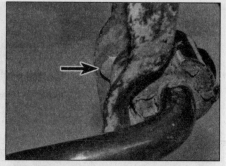

18.11 Make sure the peg (arrowed) locates in the mounting bracket correctly

clamp retaining bolts, and the bolt securing the bracket to the body (see illustration).

5 Withdraw the mounting brackets from the anti-roll bar mounting rubbers, and then remove the anti-roll bar from under the vehicle (see illustration).

6 On models from RPO No 10943 there is a locating peg in the rubber mounting that locates in a slot in the mounting bracket (see illustration). The rubber mounting is part of the anti-roll bar and cannot be renewed separately.

7 On models up to RPO No 10942 remove the rubber mountings from the anti-roll bar and renew if required. Note their position on the anti-roll bar for refitting.

Refitting

8 Carefully examine the anti-roll bar components for signs of wear, damage or deterioration, paying particular attention to the mounting bushes, and drop link balljoints. Renew worn components as necessary.

9 On models up to RPO No 10942, fit the rubber mounting bushes to the anti-roll bar, in their correct position as noted on removal.

10 Offer up the anti-roll bar, and manoeuvre it into position on the mounting brackets.

11 On models from RPO No 10943, make sure the locating pegs in the rubber mounting are positioned in the bracket correctly (see illustration).

12 Refit the mounting clamps, ensuring that they are fitted over the rubbers correctly, and

then refit the retaining bolts/nuts and tighten them to the specified torque setting.

13 Engage the drop links with the ends of the bar then fit the new retaining nuts and tighten them to the specified torque setting.

14 Refit the roadwheels then lower the vehicle to the ground and tighten the wheel bolts to the specified torque.

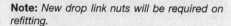

19 Rear anti-roll bar drop link – removal and refitting

Note: New drop link nuts will be required on refitting.

Removal

1 Chock the front wheels, slacken the relevant rear roadwheel bolts, and then jack up the rear of the vehicle and support it on axle stands (see Jacking and vehicle support). Remove the relevant roadwheel.

2 Slacken and remove the nuts securing the drop link lower balljoint to the anti-roll bar (see illustration 18.2). If necessary, retain the balljoint shanks with a Torx bit to prevent rotation whilst each nut is slackened. Discard the nuts; new ones should be used on refitting.

3 Slacken and remove the nuts securing the drop link upper balljoint to the rear hub carrier (see illustration). If necessary, retain the balljoint shanks with a Torx bit to

prevent rotation whilst each nut is slackened. Discard the nuts; new ones should be used on refitting.

4 With the nuts removed, disconnect the balljoints and remove the drop link from the vehicle.

5 Inspect the link for signs of wear or damage and renew if necessary.

Refitting

6 Refitting is the reverse of removal, using new securing nuts. Tighten the drop link retaining nuts to the specified torque setting.

20 Steering wheel – removal and refitting

Note: All models are equipped with a driver's airbag.

⚠️ **Warning: Refer to the precautions given in Chapter 12 before proceeding.**

Removal

1 Remove the airbag unit as described in Chapter 12.

2 Position the front wheels in the straight-ahead position and engage the steering lock.

3 Slacken and remove the steering wheel retaining bolt, note the markings of the steering wheel and steering column shaft in relation to each other (see illustrations).

19.3 Disconnect the drop link from the hub carrier

20.3a Undo the steering wheel securing bolt (arrowed) ...

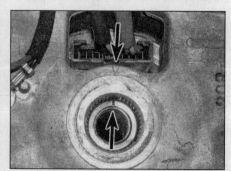

20.3b ... noting the alignment marks (arrowed) for refitting

20.4 Feed the wiring through the steering wheel on removal

4 Lift the steering wheel off the column splines, feeding the airbag wires through the aperture in the steering wheel as it is withdrawn (see illustration).

Refitting

5 Prior to refitting the steering wheel, ensure that the front wheels are still in the straight-ahead position.
6 Refitting is a reversal of removal, noting the following points:
  a) *Prior to refitting, ensure that the column switches have not been moved from their central position.*
  b) *On refitting, align the marks noted on removal, taking great care not to damage the airbag unit wiring as it is fed back through the steering wheel.*
  c) *Make sure the steering wheel bolt is coated with threadlock, and then tightened to the specified torque.*

  d) *On completion, refit the airbag unit as described in Chapter 12.*

21 Steering column – removal, inspection and refitting

Note: *As all models are equipped with a driver's airbag, refer to the precautions given in Chapter 12 before proceeding.*
Note: *A new pinch-bolt nut will be needed on refitting.*

Removal

1 Remove the steering wheel as described in Section 20.
2 Move the driver's seat as far back as possible and remove the trim panel from above the pedals (see illustration).
3 Working in the driver's footwell, make alignment marks between the universal joint and the steering rack pinion, release the retaining clip, then undo and remove the pinch-bolt/nut from the joint at the base of the column (see illustration).
4 Remove the combination switches from the top of the steering column as described in Chapter 12.
5 Remove the driver's knee airbag (where fitted), as described in Chapter 12. On models not equipped with driver's knee airbag, release the retaining clips and remove the lower facia panel on the driver's side.
6 Disconnect the wiring connector from the ignition switch (see illustration).
7 Check along the steering column and

free the wiring loom from the retaining clips along the column. Note its fitted position, and position it clear so that it does not hinder column removal.
8 Slacken and remove the four mounting nuts from the top of the column (see illustrations). Slide the column assembly upwards, and free the lower joint from the steering rack pinion. Then carefully withdraw the steering column from inside the vehicle.

Inspection

9 Before refitting the steering column, examine the column and mountings for signs of damage and deformation, and renew as necessary. Check the steering shaft for signs of free play in the column bushes, and check the universal joints for signs of damage or roughness in the joint bearings. If any damage or wear is found on the steering column universal joint or shaft bushes, the column must be renewed as an assembly.

Refitting

10 Align the marks made prior to removal and engage the column universal joint with the steering rack pinion.
11 Slide the column assembly into position making sure its mounting bracket is correctly engaged with the facia bracket. Refit the column mounting nuts and tighten them to the specified torque setting.
12 Refit the universal joint pinch-bolt and nut, tighten them to the specified torque setting, and then refit the retaining clip (see illustration).

21.2 Unclip the lower trim panel

21.3 Release the retaining clip then remove the pinch-bolt/nut (arrowed)

21.6 Disconnect the wiring connector

21.8a Undo the steering column mounting nuts (arrowed) . . .

21.8b . . . and withdraw the steering column from the facia

21.12 Position of the securing clip on the bottom of the column

22.2 Undo the lower shroud retaining screws (arrowed)

22.3 Disconnect the transponder wiring plug (arrowed) from the rear of the switch assembly

22.4 Lift the transponder ring securing clips and slide it from the ignition switch

13 The remainder of refitting is a reversal of the removal procedure, noting the following.
 a) Ensure that all wiring is correctly routed and retained by all the necessary clips and ties.
 b) Refit the steering column switches, as described in Chapter 12.
 c) Refit the driver's knee airbag, as described in Chapter 12.
 d) Refit the steering wheel, as described in Section 20.

22 Ignition switch/lock cylinder/ steering lock – removal and refitting

Ignition switch/steering lock
Removal

1 Disconnect the battery (see Chapter 5A).

2 Undo the retaining screws securing the steering column lower shroud in position, then unclip the upper shroud, and release it from the retaining clips at its front edge (see illustration).
3 Trace the wiring back from the transponder and release the connector from the rear of the steering column combination switches (see illustration).
4 Lift the two retaining clips and carefully pull the transponder immobiliser unit to release it from the ignition switch housing (see illustration). Take care not to damage the transponder assembly.
5 Disconnect the wiring connector from the rear of the ignition switch (see illustration).
6 Use a centre punch to mark the centre of the lock housing retaining screw then, using a drill and an extractor, remove the screw (see illustrations). Obviously, a new screw will be required for refitting.

7 Insert the key into the steering lock and turn it to the first position, and then using a small screwdriver, depress the locating peg and slide the ignition switch from the steering column housing (see illustrations).

Refitting

8 Refitting is a reversal of removal, noting the following points:
 a) Ensure all wiring is correctly routed, and securely clipped back into its original positions.
 b) Refit the steering lock housing with a new retaining/shear bolt (see illustration). Tighten the bolt until the head shears off, leaving the threaded part securing the lock.

Lock cylinder

9 At the time of writing, the lock cylinder was not available separately from the ignition switch assembly.

22.5 Disconnect the ignition switch wiring connector

22.6a Drill out the centre of the shear bolt . . .

22.6b . . . and use an extractor to remove the bolt

22.7a Depress the locating peg with a thin screwdriver . . .

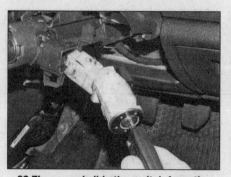

22.7b . . . and slide the switch from the steering column

22.8 Fit the new shear bolt – tighten until the head shears off

23.2 Clamp the fluid supply hose to the power steering pump

23.4a Remove the lower pinch-bolt/nut (arrowed), from the steering column

23.4b Remove the rubber seal/bearing . . .

23 Steering rack assembly – removal, overhaul and refitting

Note: *A balljoint separator tool will be required for this operation. New track rod balljoint nuts, and a new intermediate shaft-to-steering rack pinion pinch-bolt will be required on refitting. Also new hydraulic fluid pipe seals will be required.*

Removal

1 Disconnect the battery negative lead as described in Chapter 5A.

2 Use a hose clamp to pinch the fluid supply hose to the power steering pump **(see illustration)**. Note this only applies to non-electropump steering.

3 Ensure the front wheels are in the 'straight-ahead' position, then chock the rear wheels, raise the front of the vehicle and support it securely on axle stands (see *Jacking and vehicle support*). Remove the front roadwheels.

4 Working inside the driver's footwell, remove the trim panel above the pedals, and then undo the nut and withdrawn the steering column universal joint pinch-bolt. Move the security clip and slide the joint up from the

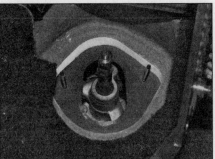

23.4c . . . to access the pinion shaft

steering rack pinion. Undo the retaining nuts and remove the rubber seal/bearing from the floor panel to access the pinion shaft **(see illustrations)**.

5 Detach both the track rod ends from the hub carriers as described in Section 25.

6 Undo the nuts/bolts securing the various power steering pipes to their support brackets **(see illustration)**.

7 The front subframe will need to be lowered, to allow the steering rack to be completely removed from the vehicle. Refer to Section 10 of this Chapter for the subframe removal and refitting procedure.

8 Clean the area around the rack pinion

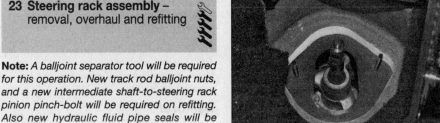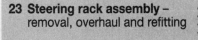

housing, then undo the nuts securing the fluid pipes to the rack pinion housing, release the pipes from the retaining clamp, and drain the fluid into a container **(see illustration)**. Turn the steering wheel from lock-to-lock to assist the draining process, remembering to recentre the steering wheel afterwards. Discard the pipes' O-ring seals, new ones must be fitted. Plug the ends of the pipes to prevent dirt ingress.

9 If not already done, undo and remove the rack mounting nuts **(see illustration)**. Recover the spacers/washers (where fitted) between the rack and the subframe, noting their fitted positions. Discard the rack mounting nuts, as new ones must be fitted.

23.6 Undo the pipe bracket securing nut (arrowed)

23.8 Undo the fluid pipe retaining plate screw (arrowed)

23.9 Steering rack mounting nuts (arrowed)

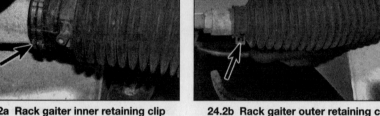

24.2a Rack gaiter inner retaining clip (arrowed)

24.2b Rack gaiter outer retaining clip (arrowed)

25.2 Track rod end locknut (arrowed) for adjustment

10 Lower the subframe a little, and manoeuvre the steering rack out through the wheel arch.

Overhaul

11 Examine the steering rack assembly for signs of wear or damage, and check that the rack moves freely throughout the full length of its travel, with no signs of roughness or excessive free play between the steering rack pinion and rack. Inspect all the steering rack fluid unions for signs of leakage, and check that all union nuts are securely tightened.

12 It is possible to overhaul the steering rack assembly, but this task should be entrusted to a Peugeot dealer. The only components that can be renewed easily by the home mechanic are the rubber gaiters (see Section 24), and the track rod ends (see Section 25).

Refitting

13 Refitting is a reversal of removal, bearing in mind the following points:

a) Centralise the rack so that the steering is effectively in the straight-ahead position before refitting the steering rack.

b) Use new nuts when reconnecting the track rod balljoints, and use a new nut when refitting the steering universal joint pinch-bolt.

c) Use new seals when reconnecting the fluid pipes to the steering rack.

d) Ensure that the steering wheel is in the straight-ahead position, and that the steering rack is centralised before

reconnecting the intermediate shaft to the steering rack.

e) Bleed the hydraulic system as described in Section 26.

f) On completion, check and if necessary adjust the ride height settings and front wheel alignment as described in Sections 28 and 29.

24 Steering rack rubber gaiters – renewal

1 Remove the track rod end as described in Section 25.

2 Mark the correct fitted position of the gaiter on the track rod, then release the retaining clips and slide the gaiter off the steering rack housing and track rod arm **(see illustrations)**.

3 Thoroughly clean the track rod and the steering rack housing, using fine abrasive paper to polish off any corrosion, burrs or sharp edges which might damage the new gaiter's sealing lips on installation. Scrape off any grease from inside the old gaiter, and apply new grease as required.

4 Carefully slide the new gaiter over the end of the rack, and locate it on the steering rack housing. Align the outer edge of the gaiter with the mark made on the track rod prior to removal, and then secure it in position with new retaining clips.

5 Refit the track rod end as described in Section 25.

25 Track rod end – removal and refitting

Note: A new balljoint retaining nut will be required on refitting.

Removal

1 Apply the handbrake, slacken the appropriate front roadwheel bolts, then jack up the front of the vehicle and support it on axle stands (see Jacking and vehicle support). Remove the appropriate front roadwheel.

2 Clean the threads and then slacken the track rod end locknut by a quarter of a turn **(see illustration)**. Do not move the locknut from this position, as it will serve as a handy reference mark on refitting. Make reference marks as required, on the end of the rack.

3 Slacken and remove the nut securing the track rod end balljoint to the hub carrier; discard the nut; a new one will be needed on refitting. Release the balljoint tapered shank using a universal balljoint separator **(see illustrations)**.

4 Counting the **exact** number of turns necessary to do so, unscrew the track rod end from the rack.

5 Count the number of exposed threads between the end of the track rod and locknut, and record this figure. If a new balljoint is to be fitted, unscrew the locknut from the old balljoint.

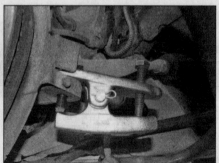

25.3a Undo the balljoint retaining nut . . .

25.3b . . . then use a balljoint separator . . .

25.3c . . . to release the tapered shank

6 Carefully clean the track rod and the threads. Renew the track rod end if the balljoint's movement is sloppy or too stiff, if excessively worn, or if damaged in any way; carefully check the stud taper and threads. If the balljoint gaiter is damaged, the complete track rod end assembly must be renewed; it is not possible to obtain the gaiter separately.

Refitting

7 If a new track rod end is to be fitted, screw the locknut onto its threads, and position it so that the same number of exposed threads are visible, as was noted prior to removal.
8 Screw the track rod end into the end of the rack by the number of turns noted on removal. This should bring the balljoint locknut to within a quarter of a turn of the alignment marks that were made on removal (if applicable).
9 Where applicable, ensure that the protector plate is in position, and then locate the balljoint shank in the hub carrier. Fit a new retaining nut and tighten it to the specified torque.
10 Refit the roadwheel, then lower the vehicle to the ground and tighten the roadwheel bolts to the specified torque.
11 Check and, if necessary, adjust the front wheel alignment as described in Section 29, then securely tighten the track rod end locknut.

26 Power steering system – bleeding

1 This procedure will only be necessary when any of the hydraulic system has been disconnected.
2 Referring to *Weekly checks*, remove the fluid reservoir filler cap, and top-up with the new specified fluid to the upper level mark.
3 Start the engine and allow it to idle for 3 minutes without moving the steering wheel. Check the fluid level frequently during this period and top it up if necessary.
4 Slowly move the steering from lock-to-lock several times to purge out the trapped air, then top-up the level in the fluid reservoir. Repeat this procedure until the fluid level in the reservoir does not drop any further.
5 Turn the engine off and allow the system to cool. Once cool, check that fluid level is up to the upper mark on the power steering fluid reservoir, topping-up if necessary.

27 Power steering pump – removal and refitting

Removal

1 Note that 2 types of power steering pumps maybe fitted. The first type is the traditional mechanical pump driven by the auxiliary drivebelt (1.6 litre engines); the second type is an electropump assembly, fitted in front of the right-hand roadwheel, behind the wing

27.3 Slacken the hose securing clamps (arrowed)

(2.0 litre engines). Proceed as described under the relevant heading.

Auxiliary drivebelt driven pump

2 Remove the auxiliary drivebelt as described in Chapter 5A.
3 Remove the plastic cover on the top of the engine, and then undo the securing clips and remove the air inlet hose from above the pump **(see illustration)**.
4 Use hose clamps to pinch the fluid supply and return hoses, to prevent the reservoir from draining **(see illustration)**.
5 Slacken the clip on the hose to the pump and disconnect, be prepared for some fluid spillage. Undo the union and disconnect the pressure pipe from the pump, also remove the pipe securing bracket from the top of the pump **(see illustration)**. Plug the openings to prevent contamination.

27.5 Disconnect the fluid pipes and pipe bracket securing bolt (arrowed)

27.8 Disconnect the low-pressure hose (arrowed)

27.4 Clamp the hoses (arrowed) to help prevent some fluid loss

6 Undo the mounting bolts/nuts and remove the pump **(see illustration)**.

Electropump

7 Chock the rear wheels, raise the front of the vehicle and support it securely on axle stands (see *Jacking and vehicle support*).
8 Have a container ready and disconnect the low-pressure return pipe from the power steering fluid reservoir **(see illustration)**. Drain the fluid into the container, if required; lock the steering from side to side to drain the system.
9 Disconnect the battery negative lead as described in Chapter 5A.
10 Release the securing clips and disconnect the wiring plugs from the electropump **(see illustration)**.
Caution: Make sure that the power steering fluid does not contaminate the wiring connectors.

27.6 Pump mounting bolts (arrowed) – mechanical pump

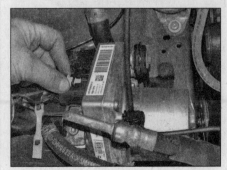
27.10 Disconnect the wiring connectors

27.11 Undo the high-pressure pipe securing bolt (arrowed)

11 Undo the Torx retaining bolt, and disconnect the pressure pipe from the assembly **(see illustration)**. Be prepared for fluid spillage, and plug the openings to prevent contamination. Discard the O-ring seal; a new one must be fitted.
12 Undo the 2 mounting bracket bolts and manoeuvre the electropump assembly from position **(see illustration)**.
13 No further dismantling of the electropump assembly is recommended. At the time of writing, the electropump was only available as a complete assembly – consult a Peugeot dealer or parts specialist.

Refitting

14 Refitting is a reversal of removal, noting the following points:
a) Renew the pressure pipe O-ring seals.

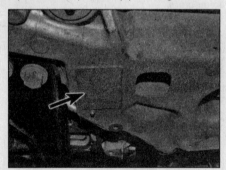

28.2a Flat area (arrowed) on front subframe as reference point when checking ride height

28.3 Using a scissor jack to secure a straight bar to the reference point

27.12 Pump mounting bolts (arrowed) – electropump

b) Tighten the fasteners to the specified torque, where given.
c) Bleed the hydraulic system as described in Section 26.
d) Ensure the steering system functions correctly before taking the vehicle onto the road.

28 Ride height settings – information, checking and adjustment

Information

1 Before the suspension securing bolts/nuts can be fully-tightened, the suspension must set to its ride height position (see Specifications). If the suspension bolts/nuts

28.2b Flat area (arrowed) on rear subframe as reference point when checking ride height

28.4a Take a measurement from the straight bar to the centre of the hub

are tightened while the vehicle is on a jack or on a wheel-free ramp, the suspension will be set too high. This will cause the vehicle to be unsafe, as it will have an effect on the handling and stability of the vehicle.

Checking and adjustment

2 There is a square flat area under the front subframe and rear axle to use as a reference point for the ride height setting **(see illustrations)**.
3 Using a scissor jack or G-clamp, secure a straight-edge (length of bar) up against the square flat area under the subframe **(see illustration and illustration 28.4b)**.
4 Using a trolley jack under the lower suspension arm outer mounting point, jack the suspension up until the centre of the hub nut is set to the correct distance to the top of the straight-edge **(see illustrations)**. See Specifications at the beginning of this Chapter for ride height settings.
5 When the correct ride height setting is achieved, all the suspension bolts/nuts can be tightened to their specified torque setting.

29 Wheel alignment and steering angles – information, checking and adjustment

Definitions

1 A car's steering and suspension geometry is defined in four basic settings – all angles are expressed in degrees (toe settings are also expressed as a measurement); the steering axis is defined as an imaginary line drawn through the axis of the suspension strut, extended where necessary to contact the ground.
2 Camber is the angle between each roadwheel and a vertical line drawn through its centre and tyre contact patch, when viewed from the front or rear of the car. Positive camber is when the roadwheels are tilted outwards from the vertical at the top; negative camber is when they are tilted inwards. The camber angle is not adjustable.
3 Castor is the angle between the steering axis and a vertical line drawn through each roadwheel's centre and tyre contact patch,

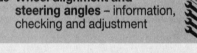

28.4b Checking the measurement on the rear of the vehicle – using a G-clamp to secure the straight bar

when viewed from the side of the car. Positive castor is when the steering axis is tilted so that it contacts the ground ahead of the vertical; negative castor is when it contacts the ground behind the vertical. The castor angle is not adjustable.

4 Toe is the difference, viewed from above, between lines drawn through the roadwheel centres and the car's centre-line. 'Toe-in' is when the roadwheels point inwards, towards each other at the front, while 'toe-out' is when they splay outwards from each other at the front.

5 The front wheel toe setting is adjusted by screwing the track rod in or out of its balljoints, to alter the effective length of the track rod assembly.

6 Rear wheel toe setting is not adjustable.

Checking and adjustment

7 Due to the special measuring equipment necessary to check the wheel alignment and steering angles, and the skill required to use it properly, the checking and adjustment of these settings is best left to a Peugeot dealer or similar expert. Note that most tyre-fitting shops now possess sophisticated checking equipment. The following is provided as a guide, should the owner decide to carry out a DIY check.

Front wheel toe setting

8 The front wheel toe setting is checked by measuring the angle of the wheels in relation to the longitudinal axis of the vehicle. Proprietary toe measurement gauges are available from motor accessory shops. Adjustment is made by screwing the track rod ends in or out of the end of the steering rack, to alter the effective length of the track rod assemblies.

9 Before starting work, check first that the tyre sizes and types are as specified, then check the tyre pressures and tread wear, the roadwheel run-out, the condition of the hub bearings, the steering wheel free play, and the condition of the front suspension components (see *Weekly checks* and the relevant Part of Chapter 1). Correct any faults found.

10 Park the vehicle on level ground, check that the front roadwheels are in the straight-ahead position, then rock the rear and front ends to settle the suspension. Release the handbrake, and roll the vehicle backwards 1 metre, then forwards again, to relieve any stresses in the steering and suspension components. If possible, set the reference height of the vehicle as described in Paragraph 9.

11 Follow the tracking gauge manufacturer's instructions and measure the toe setting.

12 If adjustment is necessary, apply the handbrake, then jack up the front of the vehicle and support it securely on axle stands. Turn the steering wheel onto full-left lock, and record the number of exposed threads on the right-hand track rod end. Now turn the steering onto full-right lock, and record the number of threads on the left-hand side. If there is the same number of threads visible on both sides, then subsequent adjustment should be made equally on both sides. If there are more threads visible on one side than the other, it will be necessary to compensate for this during adjustment. **Note:** *It is most important that after adjustment, the same number of threads is visible on each track rod end.*

13 First clean the track rod threads; if they are corroded, apply penetrating fluid before starting adjustment.

14 Disconnect the track rod end from the hub carrier as described in Section 25.

15 Alter the length of the track rod ends by screwing them into or out of the end of the steering rack. Shortening the track rods (screwing them into the end of the rack) will reduce toe-in/increase toe-out.

16 When the setting is correct, hold the track rods and tighten the locknuts to the specified torque setting. Check that the balljoints are seated correctly in their sockets, and count the exposed threads to check the length of both track rods. If they are not the same, then the adjustment has not been made equally, and problems will be encountered with tyre scrubbing in turns; also, the steering wheel spokes will no longer be horizontal when the wheels are in the straight-ahead position.

17 If the track rod lengths are the same, lower the vehicle to the ground and recheck the toe setting; re-adjust if necessary. When the setting is correct, tighten the track rod balljoint locknuts to the specified torque. Ensure that the rubber gaiters are seated correctly, and are not twisted or strained, and secure them in position with new retaining clips (where necessary).

Chapter 11
Bodywork and fittings

Contents

Degrees of difficulty

Easy, suitable for novice with little experience	Fairly easy, suitable for beginner with some experience	Fairly difficult, suitable for competent DIY mechanic	Difficult, suitable for experienced DIY mechanic	Very difficult, suitable for expert DIY or professional

Specifications

Torque wrench setting	Nm	lbf ft
Seat belt mountings	30	22

1 General information

The bodyshell is made of pressed-steel sections, and is available in a saloon, coupe or estate (SW) versions. Most components are welded together, but some use is made of structural adhesives. The front wings are bolted on.

A number of structural components and body panels are made of galvanised steel to provide a high level of protection against corrosion. Also some panels are further protected by being coated with an anti-chip primer prior to being sprayed.

Extensive use is made of plastic materials, mainly in the interior, but also in some exterior components. The front and rear bumpers and the front grille are injection-moulded from a synthetic material, which is very strong, yet light. Plastic components such as wheel arch liners are fitted to the underside of the vehicle, to improve the body's resistance to corrosion.

2 Maintenance – bodywork and underframe

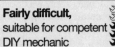

The general condition of a vehicle's bodywork is the one thing that significantly affects its value. Maintenance is easy, but needs to be regular. Neglect, particularly after minor damage, can lead quickly to further deterioration and costly repair bills. It is important also to keep watch on those parts of the vehicle not immediately visible, for instance the underside, inside all the wheel arches, and the lower part of the engine compartment.

The basic maintenance routine for the bodywork is washing – preferably with a lot of water, from a hose. This will remove all the loose solids, which may have stuck to the vehicle. It is important to flush these off in such a way as to prevent grit from scratching the finish. The wheel arches and underframe need washing in the same way, to remove any accumulated mud that will retain moisture and tend to encourage rust. Paradoxically enough, the best time to clean the underframe and wheel arches is in wet weather, when the mud is thoroughly wet and soft. In very wet weather, the underframe is usually cleaned of large accumulations automatically, and this is a good time for inspection.

Periodically, except on vehicles with a wax-based underbody protective coating, it is a good idea to have the whole of the underframe of the vehicle steam-cleaned, engine compartment included, so that a thorough inspection can be carried out to see what minor repairs and renovations are necessary. Steam cleaning is available at many garages, and is necessary for the removal of the accumulation of oily grime, which sometimes is allowed to become thick in certain areas. If steam-cleaning facilities are not available, there are one or two excellent grease solvents available, which can be brush-applied; the dirt can then be simply hosed off. Note that these methods should not be used on vehicles with wax-based underbody protective coating, or the coating will be removed. Such vehicles should be inspected annually, preferably just prior to winter, when the underbody should be washed down, and any damage to the wax coating repaired using underseal. Ideally, a completely fresh coat should be applied. It would also be worth considering the use of wax-based protection for injection into door panels, sills, box sections, etc, as an additional safeguard against rust damage, where such protection is not provided by the vehicle manufacturer.

After washing paintwork, wipe off with a chamois leather to give an unspotted clear finish. A coat of clear protective wax polish will give added protection against chemical pollutants in the air. If the paintwork sheen has dulled or oxidised, use a cleaner/ polisher combination to restore the brilliance of the shine. This requires a little effort, but such dulling is usually caused because regular washing has been neglected. Care needs to be taken with metallic paintwork, as a special non-abrasive cleaner/polisher is required to avoid damage to the finish. Always check that the door and ventilator opening drain holes and pipes are completely clear, so that water can be drained out. Brightwork should be treated in the same way as paintwork. Windscreens and windows can be kept clear of the smeary film that often appears, by the use of proprietary glass cleaner. Never use any form of wax or other body or chromium polish on glass.

3 Maintenance – upholstery and carpets

Mats and carpets should be brushed or vacuum-cleaned regularly, to keep them free of grit. If they are badly stained, remove them from the vehicle for scrubbing or sponging, and make quite sure they are dry before refitting. Seats and interior trim panels can be kept clean by wiping with a damp cloth and proprietary upholstery cleaner. If they do become stained (which can be more apparent on light-coloured upholstery), use a little liquid detergent and a soft nail brush to scour the grime out of the grain of the material. Do not forget to keep the headlining clean in the same way as the upholstery. When using liquid cleaners inside the vehicle, do not over-wet the surfaces being cleaned. Excessive damp could get into the seams and padded interior, causing stains, offensive odours or even rot. If the inside of the vehicle gets wet accidentally, it is worthwhile taking some trouble to dry it out properly, particularly where carpets are involved.

Caution: Do not leave oil or electric heaters inside the vehicle for this purpose.

4 Minor body damage – repair

Scratches

If the scratch is very superficial, and does not penetrate to the metal of the bodywork, repair is very simple. Lightly rub the area of the scratch with a paintwork renovator, or a very fine cutting paste, to remove loose paint from the scratch, and to clear the surrounding bodywork of wax polish. Rinse the area with clean water.

Apply touch-up paint to the scratch using a fine paintbrush; continue to apply fine layers of paint until the surface of the paint in the scratch is level with the surrounding paintwork. Allow the new paint at least two weeks to harden, and then blend it into the surrounding paintwork by rubbing the scratch area with a paintwork renovator or a very fine cutting paste. Finally apply wax polish.

Where the scratch has penetrated right through to the metal of the bodywork, causing the metal to rust, a different repair technique is required. Remove any loose rust from the bottom of the scratch with a penknife, and then apply rust-inhibiting paint, to prevent the formation of rust in the future. Using a rubber or nylon applicator, fill the scratch with bodystopper paste. If required, this paste can be mixed with cellulose thinners, to provide a very thin paste, which is ideal for filling narrow scratches. Before the stopper-paste in the scratch hardens, wrap a piece of smooth cotton rag around the top of a finger. Dip the finger in cellulose thinners, and quickly sweep it across the surface of the stopper-paste in the scratch; this will ensure that the surface of the stopper-paste is slightly hollowed. The scratch can now be painted over as described earlier in this Section.

Dents

When deep denting of the vehicle's bodywork has taken place, the first task is to pull the dent out, until the affected bodywork almost attains its original shape. There is little point in trying to restore the original shape completely, as the metal in the damaged area will have stretched on impact, and cannot be reshaped fully to its original contour. It is better to bring the level of the dent up to a point, which is about 3 mm below the level of the surrounding bodywork. In cases where the dent is very shallow anyway, it is not worth trying to pull it out at all. If the underside of the dent is accessible, it can be hammered out gently from behind, using a mallet with a wooden or plastic head. Whilst doing this, hold a suitable block of wood firmly against the outside of the panel, to absorb the impact from the hammer blows and thus prevent a large area of the bodywork from being 'belled-out'.

Should the dent be in a section of the bodywork that has a double skin, or some other factor making it inaccessible from behind, a different technique is called for. Drill several small holes through the metal inside the area – particularly in the deeper section. Then screw long self-tapping screws into the holes, just sufficiently for them to gain a good purchase in the metal. Now the dent can be pulled out by pulling on the protruding heads of the screws with a pair of pliers.

The next stage of the repair is the removal of the paint from the damaged area, and from an inch or so of the surrounding 'sound' bodywork. This is accomplished most easily by using a wire brush or abrasive pad on a power drill, although it can be done just as effectively by hand, using sheets of abrasive paper. To complete the preparation for filling, score the surface of the bare metal with a screwdriver or the tang of a file, or alternatively, drill small holes in the affected area. This will provide a really good 'key' for the filler paste.

To complete the repair, see the Section on filling and re-spraying.

Rust holes or gashes

Remove all paint from the affected area, and from an inch or so of the surrounding 'sound' bodywork, using an abrasive pad or a wire brush on a power drill. If these are not available, a few sheets of abrasive paper will do the job most effectively. With the paint removed, you will be able to judge the severity of the corrosion, and therefore decide whether to renew the whole panel (if this is possible) or to repair the affected area. New body panels are not as expensive as most people think, and it is often quicker and more satisfactory to fit a new panel than to attempt to repair large areas of corrosion.

Remove all fittings from the affected area, except those, which will act as a guide to the original shape of the damaged bodywork (e.g. headlight shells etc). Then, using tin snips or a hacksaw blade, remove all loose metal and any other metal badly affected by corrosion. Hammer the edges of the hole inwards, in order to create a slight depression for the filler paste.

Wire-brush the affected area to remove the powdery rust from the surface of the remaining metal. Paint the affected area with rust-inhibiting paint; if the back of the rusted area is accessible, treat this also.

Before filling can take place, it will be

necessary to block the hole in some way. This can be achieved by the use of aluminium or plastic mesh, or aluminium tape.

Aluminium or plastic mesh, or glassfibre matting, is probably the best material to use for a large hole. Cut a piece to the approximate size and shape of the hole to be filled, then position it in the hole so that its edges are below the level of the surrounding bodywork. It can be retained in position by several blobs of filler paste around its periphery.

Aluminium tape should be used for small or very narrow holes. Pull a piece off the roll, trim it to the approximate size and shape required, then pull off the backing paper (if used) and stick the tape over the hole; it can be overlapped if the thickness of one piece is insufficient. Burnish down the edges of the tape with the handle of a screwdriver or similar, to ensure that the tape is securely attached to the metal underneath.

Filling and respraying

Before using this Section, see the Sections on dent, minor scratch, rust holes and gash repairs.

Many types of bodyfiller are available, but generally speaking, those proprietary kits, which contain a tin of filler paste and a tube of resin hardener, are best for this type of repair; some can be used directly from the tube. A wide, flexible plastic or nylon applicator will be found invaluable for imparting a smooth and well-contoured finish to the surface of the filler.

Mix up a little filler on a clean piece of card or board – measure the hardener carefully (follow the maker's instructions on the pack), otherwise the filler will set too rapidly or too slowly. Using the applicator, apply the filler paste to the prepared area; draw the applicator across the surface of the filler to achieve the correct contour and to level the surface. As soon as a contour that approximates to the correct one is achieved, stop working the paste – if you carry on too long, the paste will become sticky and begin to 'pick-up' on the applicator. Continue to add thin layers of filler paste at 20-minute intervals, until the level of the filler is just proud of the surrounding bodywork.

Once the filler has hardened, the excess can be removed using a metal plane or file. From then on, progressively finer grades of abrasive paper should be used, starting with a 40-grade production paper, and finishing with a 400-grade wet-and-dry paper. Always wrap the abrasive paper around a flat rubber, cork, or wooden block – otherwise the surface of the filler will not be completely flat. During the smoothing of the filler surface, the wet-and-dry paper should be periodically rinsed in water. This will ensure that a very smooth finish is imparted to the filler at the final stage.

At this stage, the 'dent' should be surrounded by a ring of bare metal, which in turn should be encircled by the finely 'feathered' edge of the good paintwork. Rinse the repair area with clean water, until all of the dust produced by the rubbing-down operation has gone.

Spray the whole area with a light coat of primer – this will show up any imperfections in the surface of the filler. Repair these imperfections with fresh filler paste or bodystopper, and once more smooth the surface with abrasive paper. If bodystopper is used, it can be mixed with cellulose thinners, to form a really thin paste that is ideal for filling small holes. Repeat this spray-and-repair procedure until you are satisfied that the surface of the filler, and the feathered edge of the paintwork, are perfect. Clean the repair area with clean water, and allow to dry fully.

The repair area is now ready for final spraying. Paint spraying must be carried out in a warm, dry, windless and dust-free atmosphere. This condition can be created artificially if you have access to a large indoor working area, but if you are forced to work in the open, you will have to pick your day very carefully. If you are working indoors, dousing the floor in the work area with water will help to settle the dust, which would otherwise be in the atmosphere. If the repair area is confined to one body panel, mask off the surrounding panels; this will help to minimise the effects of a slight mismatch in paint colours. Bodywork fittings (e.g. chrome strips, door handles etc) will also need to be masked off. Use genuine masking tape, and several thicknesses of newspaper, for the masking operations.

Before commencing to spray, agitate the aerosol can thoroughly, and then spray a test area (an old tin, or similar) until the technique is mastered. Cover the repair area with a thick coat of primer; the thickness should be built up using several thin layers of paint, rather than one thick one. Using 400-grade wet-and-dry paper, rub down the surface of the primer until it is really smooth. While doing this, the work area should be thoroughly doused with water, and the wet-and-dry paper periodically rinsed in water. Allow to dry before spraying on more paint.

Spray on the top coat, again building up the thickness by using several thin layers of paint. Start spraying at the top of the repair area, and then, using a side-to-side motion, work downwards until the whole repair area and about 2 inches of the surrounding original paintwork is covered. Remove all masking material 10 to 15 minutes after spraying on the final coat of paint.

Allow the new paint at least two weeks to harden, then, using a paintwork renovator or a very fine cutting paste, blend the edges of the paint into the existing paintwork. Finally, apply wax polish.

Plastic components

With the use of more and more plastic body components by the vehicle manufacturers (e.g. bumpers. spoilers, and in some cases major body panels), rectification of more serious damage to such items has become a matter of either entrusting repair work to a specialist in this field, or renewing complete components. Repair of such damage by the DIY owner is not really feasible, owing to the cost of the equipment and materials required for effecting such repairs. The basic technique involves making a groove along the line of the crack in the plastic, using a rotary burr in a power drill. The damaged part is then welded back together, using a hot air gun to heat up and fuse a plastic filler rod into the groove. Any excess plastic is then removed, and the area rubbed down to a smooth finish. It is important that a filler rod of the correct plastic is used, as body components can be made of a variety of different types (e.g. polycarbonate, ABS, polypropylene).

Damage of a less serious nature (abrasions, minor cracks etc) can be repaired by the DIY owner using a two-part epoxy filler repair material. Once mixed in equal proportions, this is used in similar fashion to the bodywork filler used on metal panels. The filler is usually cured in twenty to thirty minutes, ready for sanding and painting.

If the owner is renewing a complete component himself, or if he has repaired it with epoxy filler, he will be left with the problem of finding a suitable paint for finishing which is compatible with the type of plastic used. At one time, the use of a universal paint was not possible, owing to the complex range of plastics encountered in body component applications. Standard paints, generally speaking, will not bond to plastic or rubber satisfactorily. However, it is now possible to obtain a plastic body parts finishing kit, which consists of a pre-primer treatment, a primer and coloured topcoat. Full instructions are normally supplied with a kit, but basically, the method of use is to first apply the pre-primer to the component concerned, and allow it to dry for up to 30 minutes. Then the primer is applied, and left to dry for about an hour before finally applying the special-coloured topcoat. The result is a correctly coloured component, where the paint will flex with the plastic or rubber, a property that standard paint does not normally posses.

5 Major body damage – repair

Where serious damage has occurred, or large areas need renewal due to neglect, it means that complete new panels will need welding-in, and this is best left to professionals. If the damage is due to impact, it will also be necessary to check the alignment of the bodyshell, and this can only be carried out accurately by a Peugeot dealer, or accident repair specialist, using special jigs. If the body is left misaligned, it is primarily dangerous, as the car will not handle properly, and secondly, uneven stresses will be imposed on the steering, suspension and possibly transmission, causing abnormal wear, or complete failure, particularly to such items as the tyres.

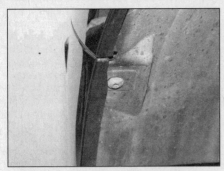

6.2a Undo the retaining screw . . .

6.2b . . . release the securing clips . . .

6.2c . . . then undo the lower screws . . .

6.2d . . . and remove the undershield

6.3 Bumper upper securing screws (arrowed)

6.4 Undo the securing bolt (arrowed) from behind the number plate

6 Front bumper – removal and refitting

Note: *The help of an assistant is useful to support the bumper during the removal and refitting procedure.*

Removal

1 Firmly apply the handbrake, slacken the front wheel and then jack up the front of the vehicle and support it securely on axle stands (see *Jacking and vehicle support*).

2 Remove both front roadwheels and undo the retaining screws and remove the front part of the inner wheel arch liners from both sides of the vehicle **(see illustrations)**.

3 Open the bonnet, and then undo the retaining screws and clips securing the upper part of the bumper to the upper crossmember **(see illustration)**.

4 Remove the front number plate and undo the retaining bolt in the centre of the bumper **(see illustration)**.

5 Working under the front edge of the bumper, undo the two lower retaining screws **(see illustration)**.

6 Working inside the front wheel arch, undo the three bolts securing the bumper to the inner wing panel at each side of the vehicle **(see illustration)**. Note some models only have two bolts at each side.

7 Disconnect the wiring connector from the

6.5 Bumper lower securing screws (arrowed)

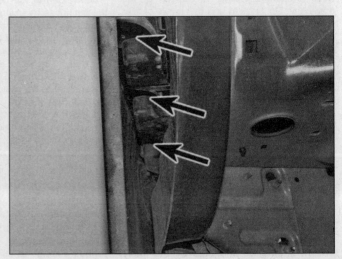

6.6 Undo the bumper-to-wing retaining bolts (arrowed)

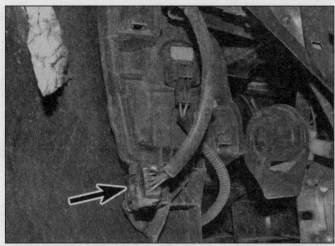

6.7 Disconnect the wiring plug (arrowed)

6.9a Insert the rod into the gap inside the wing . . .

rear of the front foglight on the left-hand side of the bumper (see illustration).

8 Where applicable, disconnect the headlamp washer pipe from the washer reservoir on the right-hand side of the front bumper. Plug the end of the washer pipe to prevent fluid leaking.

9 Using a length of rod with a 10.00 mm 90° bend at the end, release the two clips (one each side) securing the bumper to the front of the wing (see illustrations). Insert the rod above the location of the securing bolts at each side, and then twist the rod 90° anti-clockwise to release the bumper.

10 With the help of an assistant, carefully pull the bumper forward slightly and unclip the sides of the bumper from the securing clips (see illustration). Take care no to damage the bumper as it is withdrawn from the front of the vehicle.

11 If required, the bumper inserts and grilles

6.9b . . . then twist the clip (arrowed) to release the bumper

can be carefully removed from the bumper using a plastic spatula to release the retaining clips.

12 To remove the bumper bars, undo the bolts at each side and then remove the bumper bar (see illustrations).

6.10 Unclip the bumper from the wing panel

Refitting

13 Refitting is a reversal of removal, ensuring that the bumper correctly engages with the retaining clips each side as it is located in position.

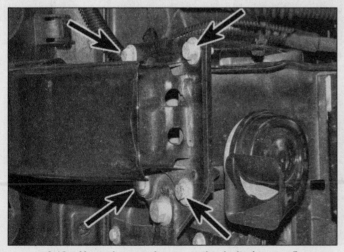

6.12a Upper bumper bar mounting bolts (arrowed)

6.12b Lower bumper bar mounting bolts (arrowed)

7 Rear bumper –
removal and refitting

Note: *The help of an assistant is useful to support the bumper during the removal and refitting procedure.*

Removal

1 Chock the front wheels, then jack up the rear of the vehicle and support securely on axle stands (see *Jacking and vehicle support*).
2 Remove the rear light cluster on both sides as described in Chapter 12.
3 Undo the securing nut from inside the rear light aperture on both sides of the vehicle **(see illustrations)**. On estate models, also release the retaining clip in the top of the bumper trim panel.
4 At each end of the underside of the bumper, undo the two retaining screws (left-hand side) and three retaining screws (right-hand side) **(see illustrations)**.
5 Working under the rear edge of the bumper, undo the lower retaining nut at the centre of the bumper and release the plastic trim from the stud **(see illustrations)**.
6 At the front upper edge of the bumper undo the retaining screw at each side of the vehicle **(see illustration)**. Release the inner wheel arch liner from the edge of the bumper.
7 Working inside the luggage compartment, undo the four retaining screws (two at each side) securing the upper sides of the bumper to the rear body panel **(see illustration)**.
8 Depending on model it may be necessary

7.3a Undo the securing nut (arrowed) – saloon/coupe models

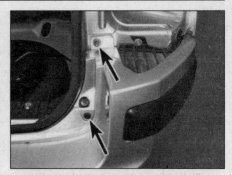

7.3b Undo the securing nut and clip (arrowed) – estate (SW) models

7.4a Bumper lower securing screws (arrowed) – left-hand side

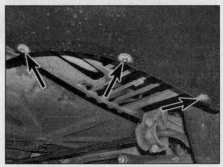

7.4b Bumper lower securing screws (arrowed) – right-hand side

to disconnect the wiring for the number plate lights or parking sensors as the bumper is withdrawn. Lift up the luggage compartment carpet to access the wiring grommet in the rear body panel **(see illustration)**.

9 With the help of an assistant, carefully unclip the sides of the bumper from the securing clips at each side **(see illustration)**. Take care not to damage the bumper as it is withdrawn from the rear of the vehicle.

7.5a Undo the centre lower securing nut . . .

7.5b . . . and unclip the bumper from the stud

7.6 Undo the retaining screw from the edge of the bumper

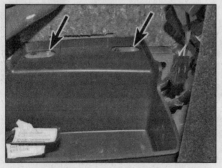

7.6 Undo the securing bolts (arrowed) – inside the luggage compartment

7.8 Release the wiring grommet (arrowed)

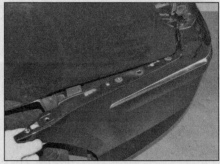

7.9 Unclip the bumper from the wing panel

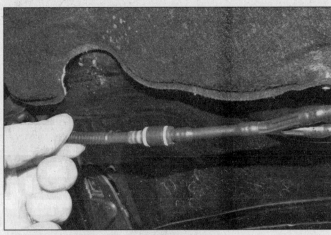

8.3a Disconnect the washer hose . . .

8.3b . . . and undo the trim retaining screw (arrowed)

10 To remove the bumper bar, undo the mounting bolts on both sides, and withdraw the bar from the rear of the vehicle.
11 If required, the rubber bumper inserts can be prised from place using a plastic spatula after the bumper cover has been removed.

Refitting

12 Refitting is a reversal of removal.

8 Bonnet – removal, refitting and adjustment

Removal

1 Open the bonnet and have an assistant support it, then using a pencil or felt tip pen, mark the outline of each bonnet hinge relative to the bonnet, to use as a guide on refitting.
2 The bonnet insulation panel is secured by plastic expanding rivets. If required, prise up the centre pins, lever out the rivets, and remove the insulation panel.
3 Disconnect the washer jet tubing, and jet heater wiring (where fitted). Undo the retaining screw and remove the plastic trim from the hinge. Release the tubing and wiring from any retaining clips **(see illustrations)**.

4 Unscrew the bonnet-to-hinge retaining bolts each side **(see illustration)**. With the help of the assistant, carefully lift the bonnet from the vehicle. Store the bonnet out of the way in a safe place.
5 Inspect the bonnet hinges for signs of wear and free play at the pivots, and if necessary renew.

Refitting and adjustment

6 With the aid of an assistant, offer up the bonnet, and engage the retaining bolts. Align the hinges with the marks made on removal, and then tighten the retaining bolts securely.
7 Close the bonnet, and check for alignment with the adjacent panels. If necessary, slacken the hinge bolts and re-align the bonnet to suit. When correctly aligned, tighten the hinge bolts securely.
8 Once the bonnet is correctly aligned, check that the bonnet fastens and releases in a satisfactory manner. If adjustment is necessary, slacken the bonnet lock retaining bolts, and adjust the position of the lock to suit. Once the lock is operating correctly, securely tighten its retaining bolts.
9 Reconnect the washer jet tuning and wiring (where applicable), and refit the bonnet insulation panel.

8.4 Undo the two bonnet hinge bolts each side

9 Bonnet release cable – removal and refitting

Removal

1 Remove the front bumper as described in Section 6.
2 Working in the engine compartment, undo the two retaining nuts and the retaining screw, then remove the plastic shield from bonnet lock assembly **(see illustrations)**.
3 Using a small ring spanner to release the securing clip, disconnect the end of the cable from the lock lever **(see illustration)**. Work

9.2a Undo the fasteners (arrowed) . . .

9.2b . . . and remove the plastic cover

9.3 Unclip the cable from the lever

9.5a Undo the securing nuts (arrowed) . . .

9.5b . . . and withdraw the bonnet release handle

9.6 Bonnet release cable grommet (arrowed) in bulkhead

along the length of the cable in the engine compartment, note their fitted locations, and release the cable retaining clips. It may be necessary to remove the battery (see Chapter 5A), and engine compartment fusebox (see Chapter 12) to make removal of the cable possible.

4 Remove the passenger side glove compartment, as described in Section 27.

5 Working under the facia on the left-hand side, unscrew the release lever retaining nuts, and withdraw the lever assembly from its location (see illustrations).

6 Use a screwdriver to carefully withdraw the cable bulkhead grommet into the passenger compartment (see illustration). The cable is located around the rear of the facia fusebox. If required slacken the fusebox retaining nuts and pull it away from the bulkhead, to allow the cable to be withdrawn.

7 Tie a length of string to the end of the cable in the engine compartment, note its routing, and then carefully pull the cable through into the passenger compartment. Untie the string from the end of the cable, and leave it in position to aid refitting.

Refitting

8 Locate the cable in position in the passenger compartment.

9 Tie the end of the new cable to the string, and pull it through into the engine compartment.

10 Check that the bulkhead grommet is securely seated, then remove the string and connect the cable to the bonnet lock lever.

Refit the plastic cover over the cable and lock assembly.

11 Secure the release lever in place, tightening its retaining bolt securely. Secure the cable in place with its retaining clips and check the lock operates satisfactorily before proceeding.

12 Refit the glove compartment as described in Section 27.

13 If removed refit the fusebox and battery as required.

14 Refit the front bumper as described in Section 6.

10 Bonnet lock – removal and refitting

Removal

1 Remove the front bumper as described in Section 6.

2 Undo the two retaining nuts and the retaining screw, then remove the plastic shield from bonnet lock assembly (see illustrations 9.2a and 9.2b).

3 Disconnect the bonnet release cable from the lock lever (see illustrations 9.3).

4 Unscrew the two securing nuts and withdraw the lock assembly from the body upper crossmember (see illustration).

Refitting

5 Refitting is a reversal of removal. On completion, check the operation of the lock and, if necessary, adjust the position of the

10.4 Bonnet lock retaining nuts (arrowed)

lock within the elongated bolt holes to achieve satisfactory operation prior to closing the bonnet.

11 Door – removal, refitting and adjustment

Removal

1 With the door in the open position, use a small screwdriver to carefully prise up the locking catch, and then disconnect the door wiring connector (see illustrations).

2 Unscrew the securing bolt, and disconnect the door check strap from the door pillar (see illustration).

3 With the help of an assistant, ensure that the door is adequately supported.

4 Slide out the hinge pin retaining clips, and then remove the upper and lower hinge pins

11.1a Lever up the locking catch . . .

11.1b . . . and disconnect the wiring plug

11.2 Undo the door check strap bolt (arrowed)

11.4a Withdraw the retaining clip . . .

11.4b . . . and tap the pin out from the hinge

11.5 Door striker securing bolts

(see illustrations). Carefully lift the door from the vehicle.

Refitting

5 Refitting is a reversal of removal. Once the door is fitted, adjust the striker plate so that the door opens and closes easily but firmly. With the door handle pulled out, shut the door and check that the lock slides over the striker plate without scraping (see illustration).

12 Door inner trim panel – removal and refitting

Front door

Removal

1 Unclip the trim cover, undo the door handle switch retaining screw, and carefully prise up the switch/panel assembly. Disconnect the wiring plug connectors as the switch is removed (see illustrations).
2 Unclip the courtesy light from the bottom of the door panel and disconnect the wiring plug connector (see illustration).
3 Using a suitable lever, work around the front edge of the handle trim panel, and release the securing clips (see illustrations). Slide the trim forwards to release it from the door inner trim panel.
4 Undo the two screws located at the rear edge of the door inner trim panel (see illustration).

12.1a Lift out the trim cover . . .

12.1b . . . and undo the screw . . .

12.1c . . . then lever up the switch/panel assembly

12.2 Unclip the courtesy light unit

12.3a Carefully unclip the trim . . .

12.3b . . . and slide it forwards to remove

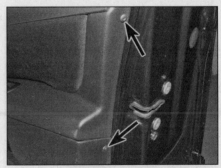

12.4 Undo the two screws (arrowed) at the rear edge of the door trim

12.7 Undo the lower handle securing screw

12.8 Unclip the courtesy light unit

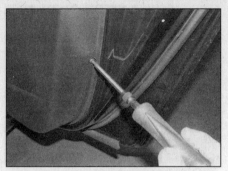

12.9 Undo the screw at the rear edge of the door trim

5 Using a suitable forked tool, work around the lower and side edges of the trim panel, then release the securing clips. Pull the panel outwards, lift it up and remove it from the door.

Refitting

6 Before refitting, check whether any of the

12.10a Carefully unclip the trim . . .

12.10b . . . and disconnect the wiring connector – where fitted

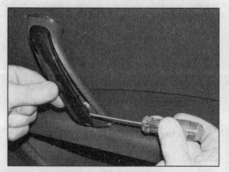

12.12a Unclip the trim . . .

trim panel retaining studs were broken on removal. Renew the panel retaining studs as necessary, and then refit the panel using a reversal of removal.

Rear door

Removal

7 Open the door, remove the screw trim cover (where fitted), and then undo the retaining screw from below the door grab handle **(see illustration)**.

8 Unclip the courtesy light from the bottom of the door panel and disconnect the wiring plug connector **(see illustration)**.

9 Undo the retaining screw located at the rear edge of the door inner trim panel **(see illustration)**.

10 Using a suitable lever, work around the front edge of the handle trim panel, and release the securing clips **(see illustrations)**. Slide the trim

12.11a Pull the winder handle from the spindle . . .

12.12b . . . and undo the upper handle securing screw

forwards to release it from the door inner trim panel, and then disconnect the wiring connector from the switch (electric window models).

11 On models with manual windows, pull the window winder handle to release it from the window regulator spindle **(see illustrations)**.

12 Carefully prise the grab handle insert trim, and then undo the upper retaining screw **(see illustrations)**

13 Using a suitable forked tool, work around the lower and side edges of the trim panel, then release the securing clips. Pull the panel outwards, lift it up and remove it from the door **(see illustration)**.

Refitting

14 Before refitting, check whether any of the trim panel retaining studs were broken on removal. Renew the panel retaining studs as necessary, and then refit the panel using a reversal of removal.

12.11b . . . and remove the plastic sleeve

12.13 Remove the door trim panel

13.2 Slide the door release lever out from the door panel

13.3a Release the securing clip . . .

13.3b . . . and disconnect the cable from the lever

13 Door handle and lock components – removal and refitting

Interior door release lever

Removal

1 Remove the door inner trim panel, as described in Section 12.

2 Release the inner release lever, by sliding the housing towards the rear of the door, and then unclip it from its locating slots in the door panel **(see illustration)**.

3 Unclip the retaining clip and disconnect the operating cable from the lever **(see illustrations)**.

Refitting

4 Refitting is a reversal of removal, but ensure that the operating cable is correctly reconnected, and refit the inner trim panel (see Section 12).

Exterior door handle

Removal

5 Open the door and then peel back the blanking cover seal, at the rear edge of the door. Slacken the retaining screw; this does not need to be completely removed **(see illustrations)**.

6 Carefully prise the push button/lock cylinder out from the door handle assembly **(see illustration)**. Take care not to damage the paintwork as it is removed.

7 Detach the handle by sliding it to the rear of the door, and then pulling it out from the handle recess **(see illustrations)**.

Refitting

8 Refitting is a reversal of removal, but ensure that the seal is fitted to the door correctly **(see illustration)**, and the handle locates securely inside the door lock housing.

13.5a Peel back the cover . . .

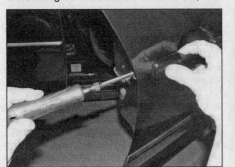

13.5b . . . and slacken the retaining screw

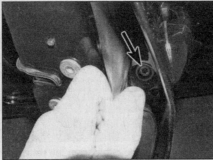

13.5c On rear doors, pull back the rubber door seal to access screw (arrowed)

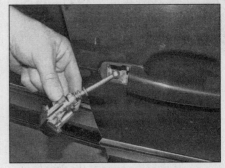

13.6 Withdraw the push button/lock cylinder

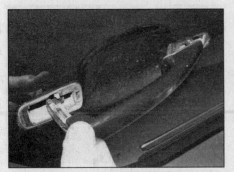

13.7a Pull out the rear of the handle . . .

13.7b . . . and disengage from the pin at the front

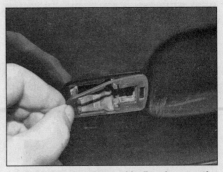

13.8 Make sure the seal is fitted correctly

13.10 Using a knife to release the inner sealing sheet

13.11 Undo the outer retaining screw

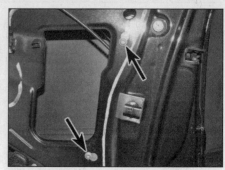

13.12a Slacken the retaining screws (arrowed) . . .

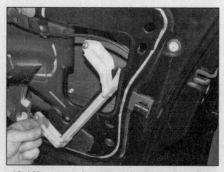

13.12b . . . and remove the lower window guide – front door

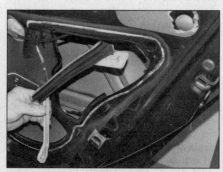

13.12c Remove the lower window guide – rear door

Door lock assembly

Note: *A new door sealing sheet may be required on refitting.*

Removal

9 Make sure the window glass is in the fully-closed position, and then remove the interior door handle as described previously in this Section.

10 Using a sharp knife, carefully release the sealing sheet from the adhesive bead and remove the sheet from the area to access the door lock **(see illustration)**. If care is taken, it may just be possible to remove the sheet in one piece and re-use it when refitting.

11 Remove the exterior door handle as described previously in this Section, and then undo the retaining screw for the door handle housing on the outside of the door **(see illustration)**.

12 Slacken the two retaining screws and remove the lower window glass guide from the rear of the door frame **(see illustrations)**.

13 Undo the two screws securing the lock assembly to the rear edge of the door **(see illustration)**.

14 Release the interior handle operating cable from the guide clips on the door, then lower the lock assembly and manipulate it out through the door aperture **(see illustrations)**.

15 Disconnect the locking motor wiring plug and remove the lock assembly **(see illustration)**.

13.13 Two screws (arrowed) secure the lock to the edge of the door

13.14a Unclip the cable from the retaining clip . . .

13.14b . . . and withdraw the lock assembly – front door

13.14c Withdraw the lock assembly – rear door

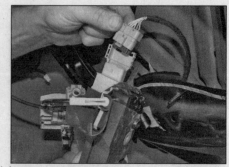

13.15 Disconnect the wiring plug as the lock is removed

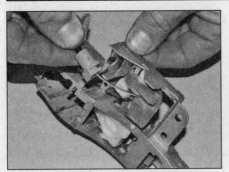

13.16 Unclip the cable from the lock assembly

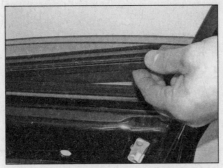

14.2 Carefully prise up the door waist seals

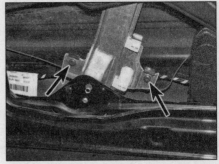

14.4a Undo the two window clamp screws (arrowed) . . .

16 If required, unclip the door lock operating cable from the lever on the exterior handle and door lock housing (**see illustration**).

Refitting

17 Refitting is a reversal of removal. Fit a new sealing sheet to the door if the original was damaged in any way during removal. On completion, refit the door inner trim panel as described in Section 12.

14 Door window glass, regulator and quarter light – removal and refitting

Note: *A new door sealing sheet may be required on refitting.*

Front door window glass

1 Lower the door window glass, and then remove the door inner trim panel as described in Section 12.
2 Carefully remove the interior and exterior waist seal from the window aperture (**see illustration**).
3 Using a sharp knife, carefully release the sealing sheet from the adhesive bead and remove the sheet from the inside of the door. If care is taken, it may just be possible to remove the sheet in one piece and re-use it when refitting.
4 Undo the two window clamp screws, and slide the window glass upwards and unclip

14.4b . . . and remove the retaining clips from the glass

the plastic retaining clips from the bottom of the glass (**see illustrations**).
5 Tilt the glass up at the rear and withdraw it up through the aperture, and out of the door (**see illustration**). Take care not to damage the paintwork on the door as the glass is withdrawn.
6 Refitting is a reversal of removal, but fit a new sealing sheet to the inside of the door if the original was damaged in any way during removal. On completion, refit the inner trim panel as described in Section 12.

Front door window regulator

7 Lower the door window glass, and then remove the door inner trim panel as described in Section 12.

14.5 Lift up the rear end and manoeuvre the window from the door

8 Using a sharp knife, carefully release the sealing sheet from the adhesive bead and remove the sheet from the inside of the door. If care is taken, it may just be possible to remove the sheet in one piece and re-use it when refitting.
9 Undo the two window clamp screws (**see illustration 14.4a**), and then slide the window up to the fully-closed position and secure it in this position with masking tape over the top of the door frame.
10 Undo the three Torx screws, disconnect the wiring plugs and remove the electric motor from the window regulator (**see illustrations**).
11 Using a sharp knife, carefully release the sealing sheet from behind the motor on the door panel (**see illustration**).

14.10a Undo the three retaining screws . . .

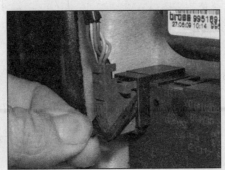

14.10b . . . and disconnect the wiring plug connectors

14.11 Use a knife to release the sealing sheet

14.12 Drill out the regulator assembly rivets (arrowed)

14.13 Release the regulator retaining clips

14.20a Drill out the front window lower guide rivets (arrowed) . . .

14.20b . . . and the upper guide rivet (arrowed)

12 Drill out the two rivets securing the regulator assembly to the door frame (**see illustration**).

13 Release the three clips securing the regulator assembly to the door panel (**see illustration**).

14 Lower the regulator assembly, and manoeuvre it out from inside the door.

15 Make sure that the bottom of the door has been cleaned out of bits of metal from the rivets that have been drilled out.

16 Refitting is a reversal of removal. Use new rivets to secure the window regulator assembly in place and fit a new sealing sheet to the inside of the door if the original was damaged in any way during removal.

Front door quarter light

17 Completely remove the front door window

glass, as described in paragraphs 1 to 5 of this Section.

18 Remove the front door window regulator, as described in paragraphs 10 to 14 of this Section.

19 Prise the window guide rubber from around the window aperture adjacent to the quarter light pillar.

20 Drill out the rivets securing the front window guide to the door frame (**see illustrations**).

21 Pull the top of the quarter light guide to the rear, and manoeuvre the quarter light from the door.

22 Make sure that the bottom of the door has been cleaned out of bits of metal from the rivets that have been drilled out.

23 Refitting is a reversal of removal. Use new rivets to secure the window regulator

assembly and window guide in place and fit a new sealing sheet to the inside of the door if the original was damaged in any way during removal.

Rear door window glass

24 Lower the door window glass, and then remove the door inner trim panel as described in Section 12.

25 Carefully remove the interior and exterior waist seal from the window aperture (**see illustration**).

26 Using a sharp knife, carefully release the sealing sheet from the adhesive bead and remove the sheet from the inside of the door. If care is taken, it may just be possible to remove the sheet in one piece and re-use it when refitting.

27 Undo the two window clamp screws, and slide the window glass upwards (**see illustration**). If required, unclip the plastic retaining clips from the bottom of the glass.

28 Tilt the glass and withdraw it up through the aperture, and out of the door (**see illustration**). Take care not to damage the paintwork on the door as the glass is withdrawn.

29 Refitting is a reversal of removal, but fit a new sealing sheet to the inside of the door if the original was damaged in any way during removal. On completion, refit the inner trim panel as described in Section 12.

Rear door window regulator

30 Lower the door window glass, and then remove the door inner trim panel as described in Section 12.

31 Using a sharp knife, carefully release the sealing sheet from the adhesive bead and remove the sheet from the inside of the door. If care is taken, it may just be possible to remove the sheet in one piece and re-use it when refitting.

32 Undo the two window clamp screws (**see illustration 14.27**), and then slide the window up to the fully closed position and secure it in this position with masking tape over the top of the doorframe.

33 On electric window models, disconnect the wiring plug, undo the three Torx screws

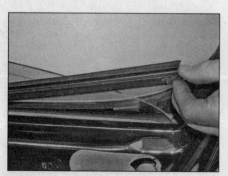

14.25 Carefully prise up the door waist seals

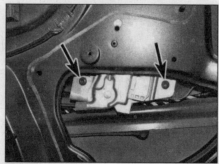

14.27 Undo the two window clamp screws (arrowed)

14.28 Lift up and manoeuvre the window from the door

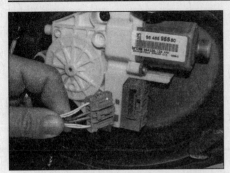

14.33a Disconnect the wiring plug connector . . .

14.33b . . . undo the retaining screws . . .

14.33c . . . and remove the regulator from the door panel

14.34 Manual window retaining screws

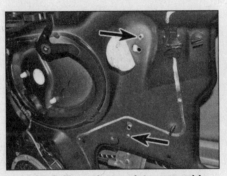

14.35 Drill out the regulator assembly rivets (arrowed) . . .

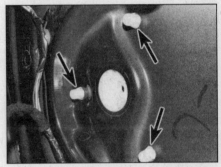

14.36 . . . and release the regulator retaining clips (arrowed)

and remove the electric motor from the window regulator (see illustrations).

34 On manual window models, undo the three Torx screws and remove the window regulator mechanism (see illustration).

35 Drill out the two rivets securing the regulator assembly to the door frame (see illustration).

36 Release the three clips securing the regulator assembly to the door panel (see illustration).

37 Lower the regulator assembly, and manoeuvre it out from inside the door.

38 Make sure that the bottom of the door has been cleaned out of bits of metal from the rivets that have been drilled out.

39 Refitting is a reversal of removal. Use new rivets to secure the window regulator assembly in place and fit a new sealing sheet to the inside of the door if the original was damaged in any way during removal.

15 Tailgate/boot lid and support struts – removal and refitting

Tailgate

Removal

1 Remove the tailgate trim panels as described in Section 25.

2 Disconnect the wiring harness connectors at the tailgate internal components, referring to the relevant procedures contained in Chap-

ter 12. Release the grommet from the tailgate and withdraw the wiring harness.

3 With the aid of an assistant, suitably support the tailgate, and then remove the support struts, as described in paragraphs 15 to 17 of this Section.

4 Let the tailgate down, without it closing on the lock mechanism, and then open the upper glass hatch part of the tailgate. Using a pencil or felt tip pen, mark the outline of each hinge relative to the tailgate, to use as a guide on refitting.

5 Slacken and remove the tailgate upper hinge mounting bolts – one at each side (see illustration). Remove the tailgate from the rear of the vehicle, taking care not to damage the paintwork.

Caution: An assistant will be required, as the tailgate is heavy and will need to be carefully removed from the vehicle.

6 If required, remove the tailgate upper glass hatch as described in Section 19.

Refitting

7 If a new tailgate is to be fitted, transfer all serviceable components (lock mechanism, wiper motor, etc) to it, with reference to the relevant procedures in this Chapter, and in Chapter 12.

8 Refitting is a reversal of removal, bearing in mind the following points:

a) If necessary, adjust the rubber buffers to obtain a good fit when the tailgate is shut (see illustration).

b) If necessary, adjust the position of the tailgate lock and/or hinge bolts within their elongated holes to achieve satisfactory lock operation.

15.5 Tailgate upper hinge securing bolts (arrowed)

15.8 Adjust the rubber buffer (arrowed)

15.10 Unclip the wiring grommet from the boot lid

15.11 Release the strut retaining clip

15.12 Boot hinge mounting bolts (arrowed)

15.14 Adjust the rubber buffer – if required

15.16 Release the strut upper retaining clip . . .

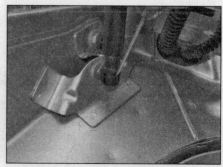

15.17 . . . and lower retaining clip

Boot lid

Removal

9 Remove the boot trim interior panel as described in Section 25. Using a pencil or felt tip pen, mark the outline of each hinge relative to the boot, to use as a guide on refitting.

10 Disconnect the wiring harness connectors at the boot internal components, referring to the relevant procedures contained in Chapter 12. Release the grommet from the boot lid and withdraw the wiring harness **(see illustration)**.

11 With the aid of an assistant, suitably support the boot lid, and then prise out the support strut spring clips, and pull the struts from the balljoints **(see illustration)**.

12 Unscrew the two Torx bolts each side securing the hinges to the boot lid **(see illustration)**, and carefully lift the boot lid from the vehicle.

Refitting

13 If a new boot is to be fitted, transfer all serviceable components (lock mechanism, etc) to it, with reference to the relevant procedures in this Chapter, and in Chapter 12.

14 Refitting is a reversal of removal, bearing in mind the following points:

a) If necessary, adjust the rubber buffers to obtain a good fit when the boot lid is shut **(see illustration)**.

b) If necessary, adjust the position of the boot lock and/or hinge bolts within their elongated holes to achieve satisfactory lock operation.

Support struts

Removal

15 Support the tailgate/boot lid in the open position, with the help of an assistant, or using a stout piece of wood.

16 Using a small screwdriver, release the spring clip, and pull the support strut from its balljoint on the body **(see illustration)**.

17 Similarly, release the strut from the balljoint on the tailgate/boot lid, and withdraw the strut from the vehicle **(see illustration)**.

Refitting

18 Refitting is a reversal of removal, but ensure the spring clips are correctly engaged.

16 Tailgate/boot lid lock components – removal and refitting

Tailgate lock

1 Remove the tailgate lower trim panel as described in Section 25.

2 Disconnect the wiring connector **(see illustration)**.

3 Undo the two lock retaining screws and withdraw the lock **(see illustration)**.

4 Refitting is a reversal of removal, but adjust the tailgate lock striker as necessary to obtain satisfactory closure.

Tailgate lock striker

5 Undo the screws and remove the tailgate

16.2 Disconnect the wiring plug . . .

16.3 . . . and undo the two lock retaining screws

16.5 Remove the lower chrome trim panel

16.6 Undo the two lock striker retaining screws (arrowed)

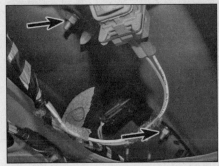

16.9 Rear trim securing nuts (two arrowed)

aperture lower chrome panel **(see illustration)** for access to the striker plate retaining bolts.
Caution: The edges of this metal trim panel are sharp, take care when removing.
6 Mark the position of the striker on the body, for use when refitting. Unscrew the two securing bolts, and remove the striker from the body **(see illustration)**.
7 Refitting is a reversal of removal. Before tightening the securing bolts, the position of the striker should be altered (the securing bolt holes are elongated) until satisfactory lock operation is obtained. Use the marks made prior to removal, if appropriate.

Tailgate exterior switch/handle

8 Remove the tailgate lower trim panel as described in Section 25.
9 Working inside the tailgate, slacken and

remove the six retaining nuts along the rear of the exterior handle trim panel **(see illustration)**.
10 Release the two securing clips and then withdraw the trim panel from the outside of the tailgate **(see illustration)**.
11 Disconnect the wiring connector from the switch/handle as the trim panel is removed **(see illustration)**.
12 If required, unclip the tailgate switch/handle from the rear trim panel **(see illustration)**.
13 Refitting is a reversal of removal.

Glass hatch lock

14 Remove the tailgate upper plastic trim as described in Section 25.
15 Disconnect the wiring connector from the lock **(see illustration)**.

16 Undo the two lock retaining screws and withdraw the lock from the tailgate.
17 Refitting is a reversal of removal,

Glass hatch lock striker

18 Open the glass hatch and unclip the trim panel from the striker plate bracket **(see illustration)**.
19 Remove the glass hatch exterior switch/handle, as described in paragraphs 22 to 25.
20 Note the position of the striker bracket on the tailgate glass and also the wiper drive arm position, for use when refitting. Disconnect the wiring connector and then unscrew the securing nut, and remove the striker bracket from the glass **(see illustration)**.
21 Refitting is a reversal of removal. Before tightening the securing nut, check the position of the striker and wiper drive as noted on removal.

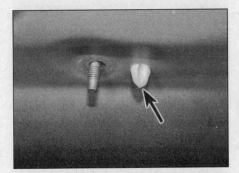

16.10 Release the securing clips (arrowed)

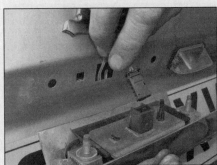

16.11 Disconnect the wiring connector . . .

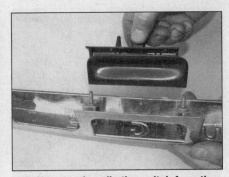

16.12 . . . and unclip the switch from the trim panel

16.15 Disconnect the wiring plug (arrowed) and undo the two retaining screws

16.18 Unclip the plastic trim cover

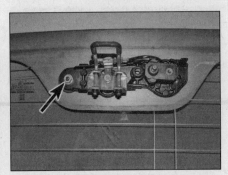

16.20 Undo the bracket securing nut (arrowed)

16.24 Release the wiring connector from the clip (arrowed)

16.25 Unclip the plastic cover and remove the securing nut

16.28 Undo the two lock securing screws . . .

Glass hatch exterior switch/handle

22 Remove the rear wiper blade as described in Chapter 12.

23 Open the glass hatch and unclip the trim panel from the striker plate bracket (see illustration 16.18).

24 Release the wiring from the retaining clip on the mounting bracket and disconnect the wiring connector (see illustration).

25 Remove the plastic cover from the wiper arm spindle, undo the retaining nut (see illustration), and then remove the switch from the glass hatch.

26 Refitting is a reversal of removal.

Boot lock

27 Remove the boot lid inner trim panel, as described in Section 25.

28 Undo the two lock retaining screws and withdraw the lock (see illustration).

29 Disconnect the wiring connector as the lock is removed (see illustration).

30 Refitting is a reversal of removal, but adjust the tailgate lock striker as necessary to obtain satisfactory closure.

Boot lock striker

31 Undo the lower securing nuts, release the retaining clips and remove the luggage compartment lower trim panel (see illustration), for access to the striker plate retaining bolts.

32 Mark the position of the striker on the body, for use when refitting. Unscrew the two securing nuts, and remove the striker from the rear body panel (see illustration).

33 Refitting is a reversal of removal. Before tightening the securing nuts, the position of the striker should be altered (the securing bolt holes are elongated) until satisfactory lock operation is obtained. Use the marks made prior to removal, if appropriate.

Boot exterior switch

34 Remove the boot lid inner trim panel, as described in Section 25.

35 Press the boot opening button in, while releasing the securing clips inside the rear of the boot lid (see illustrations).

36 Disconnect the wiring connector from the switch when it is withdrawn from inside the boot lid (see illustration).

37 Refitting is a reversal of removal.

16.29 . . . and disconnect the wiring plug as the lock is removed

16.31 Remove the luggage compartment rear plastic trim panel

16.32 Undo the two lock striker retaining nuts

16.35a Press the boot release button . . .

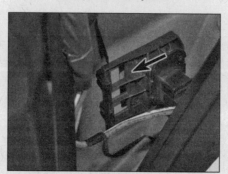

16.35b . . . and slide the switch in the direction of the arrow

16.36 Disconnect the wiring plug from the switch

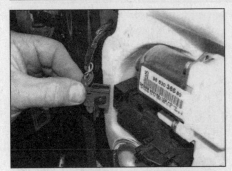

18.3 Disconnect the mirror wiring connector

18.4a Use a deep socket and undo the retaining nut . . .

18.4b . . . and remove the mirror from the door panel

17 Central locking components – removal and refitting

Control module

1 The central locking system is controlled by the Built-in Systems Interface (BSI) which is the vehicle central computer controlling the main body electrical system functions. The unit is located behind the glove compartment on the left-hand side of the facia. Refer to Chapter 12 for further information.

2 Should any problems be experienced with the operation of the central locking system or any of the other functions controlled by the BSI, the vehicle should be taken to a Peugeot dealer for diagnostic investigation.

Door lock motor

3 The motor is integral with the door lock assembly. Removal and refitting of the lock assembly is described in Section 13.

Tailgate lock motor

4 Removal of the tailgate lock motor is described as part of the tailgate lock removal and refitting procedure described in Section 16.

Remote control transmitter

Battery renewal

5 When the remote control transmitter battery is nearing the end of its life, an audible signal will be emitted from within the vehicle, accompanied by a message on the instrument panel multifunction screen. The battery should then be renewed with a type CR 1620 (3 volt) battery.

6 Using a small screwdriver or coin, carefully prise the two halves of the transmitter apart, and remove the battery.

7 Fit the new battery and reassemble the transmitter. If required, initialise the remote control as described in the next paragraph.

Initialisation

8 To initialise the unit after renewing the battery, switch off the ignition, then switch on the ignition and immediately press the locking button for a few seconds. Switch off the ignition and remove the key from the ignition lock. The remote control should now operate correctly.

18 Mirrors and mirror glass – removal and refitting

Exterior mirror assembly

1 Ensure the ignition is turned off.

2 Remove the door inner trim panel as described in Section 12.

3 Disconnect the mirror wiring plug connector from the window motor/relay unit (see illustration).

4 Using a deep socket, undo the retaining nut and remove the mirror from the outside of the door (see illustrations).

5 As the mirror is removed, withdraw the wiring out through the door aperture (see illustration).

6 Refitting is a reversal of removal.

Exterior mirror glass

7 Working through the gap between the mirror glass and the housing, using a flat lever, release the clips that secure the mirror glass to the mirror body (see illustration).

8 Withdraw the glass, and disconnect the

18.5 Withdraw the wiring loom from the door panel

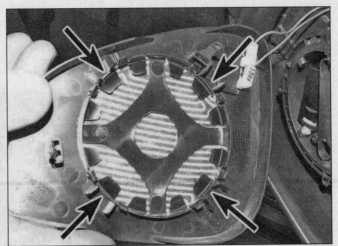

18.7 Insert a flat lever at the outer edge of the mirror glass to release the retaining clips (arrowed)

18.8 Disconnect the wiring connectors from the mirror glass

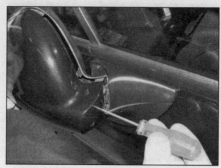

18.10a Carefully lever the trim cover . . .

18.10b . . . and remove it from the rear of the mirror

18.12 Unclip the plastic trim cover . . .

18.13 . . . and disconnect the wiring plug connector

18.14 Pull the mirror from the mounting base

heating element wiring connectors **(see illustration)**.
9 To refit, carefully push the mirror glass onto the mirror body until the securing clips lock into position.

 Warning: It is advisable to wear gloves to protect your hands, even if the glass is not broken, due to the risk of glass breakage.

Exterior mirror shell

10 Fold the mirror back against the door and then, working through the gap between the mirror shell, release the clips that secure the mirror shell to the mirror body **(see illustrations)**.
11 To refit, carefully push the mirror shell onto the mirror body until the securing clips lock into position.

Interior mirror

12 Using a small flat-bladed screwdriver carefully prise apart the two plastic covers over the mirror base housing **(see illustration)**.
13 Disconnect the wiring plug connector at the rear of the mirror **(see illustration)**.
14 The mirror can now be pulled sharply downwards, to release it from the mounting base on the windscreen **(see illustration)**.
15 To refit the interior mirror to the base, offer it up to the mounting base at about 60° degrees offset from its final position and then twist it, to secure it in the correct place. Reconnect the wiring connector and refit the plastic trim covers.

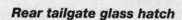

19 Windscreen, tailgate and fixed/hinged side window glass – general information

These areas of glass are secured by the tight fit of the weatherstrip in the body aperture, and are bonded in position with a special adhesive. Renewal of such fixed glass is a difficult, messy and time-consuming task, which is considered beyond the scope of the home mechanic. It is difficult, unless one has plenty of practice, to obtain a secure, waterproof fit. Furthermore, the task carries a high risk of breakage; this applies especially to the laminated glass windscreen. In view of this, owners are strongly advised

to have this sort of work carried out by one of the many specialist windscreen fitters.

Rear tailgate glass hatch
Estate (SW) models

1 Open the tailgate hatch, and then unclip the trim panel from the top of the tailgate hatch **(see illustration)**.
2 Remove the high-level brake light unit as described in Chapter 12.
3 Disconnect the washer pipe connection at the right-hand side of the tailgate **(see illustration)**.
4 Disconnect the wiring connectors from the glass hatch and release the wiring

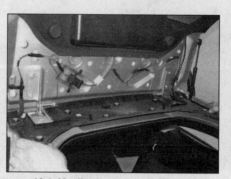

19.1 Unclip the upper plastic trim

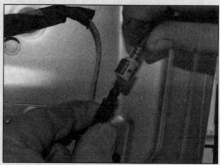

19.3 Disconnect the washer hose connection

19.4 Disconnect the wiring connector and retaining clips (arrowed)

19.5 Release the strut upper retaining clip

19.6 Glass hatch hinge securing bolts (arrowed)

loom from the retaining clips **(see illustration)**.

5 With the aid of an assistant, suitably support the glass hatch, and then prise out the support strut spring clips, and pull the struts from the balljoints **(see illustration)**.

6 Using a pencil or felt tip pen, mark the outline of each hinge relative to the glass hatch, to use as a guide on refitting. Unscrew the two bolts each side securing the hinges to the glass hatch **(see illustration)**, and carefully lift the glass hatch from the vehicle.

7 Refitting is a reversal of removal.

20 Sunroof – general information

Due to the complexity of the sunroof mechanism, considerable expertise is required to repair, renew or adjust the sunroof components successfully. Removal of the roof first requires the headlining to be removed, which is a tedious operation, and not a task to be undertaken lightly. Any problems with the sunroof should be referred to a Peugeot dealer.

If the sunroof action becomes sluggish, the slides and/or cables may need lubricating – consult a Peugeot dealer or specialist for advice on a suitable product to use. Further checks in the event of non-operation are limited to checking the fuse and wiring, with reference to the wiring diagrams at the end of Chapter 12.

21 Body exterior fittings – removal and refitting

Wheel arch liners/mud shields

1 The wheel arch liners are secured by various fasteners such as nuts, screws and expanding plastic rivets **(see illustration)**. To remove the plastic rivets, pull out the centre pins a little, and then prise the complete rivet from place.

2 With all the fasteners removed, manoeuvre the liner from the wheel arch **(see illustration)**

Body trim strips and badges

3 The various body trim strips and badges are held in position with a special adhesive membrane. Removal requires the trim/badge to be heated, to soften the adhesive, and then cut away from the surface. Due to the high risk of damage to the vehicle paintwork during this operation, it is recommended that this task should be entrusted to a Peugeot dealer.

22 Scuttle grille panel – removal and refitting

Removal

1 Open the bonnet and support it in the highest position.

2 Remove the windscreen wiper arms as described in Chapter 12.

3 Pull the scuttle grille panel up at each end to release it from the retaining clips, and then release it from the lower part of the windscreen **(see illustration)**.

Refitting

4 Refitting is a reversal of removal.

23 Seats – removal and refitting

Front seats

 Warning: The front seats are equipped with side airbags built into the outer sides of the seats. Refer to Chapter 12 for the precautions which should be observed when dealing with an airbag system. Do not tamper with the airbag unit in any way, and do not attempt to test any airbag system components. Note that the airbag is triggered if the mechanism is supplied with an electrical current (including via an ohmmeter), or if the assembly is subjected to a temperature of greater than 100°C.

1 De-activate the airbag system (see Chapter 12) before attempting to remove the seat.

2 Move the seat fully forwards, and then remove the bolts (one on each side) securing

21.1 Release the securing clips . . .

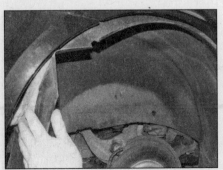

21.2 . . . and remove the inner wheel arch liner

22.3 Unclip the trim panel from the windscreen

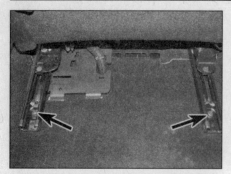

23.2 Undo the seat rear mounting bolts (arrowed) . . .

23.3 . . . and front mounting bolts (arrowed)

23.4a Release the plastic cover . . .

the rear of the seat rails to the vehicle floor (see illustration).

3 Move the seat fully rearwards, and then remove the bolts (one bolt on each side) securing the front of the seat frame to the floor (see illustration).

4 Tilt the seat backwards slightly and unclip the plastic cover from the floor panel. Disconnect the wiring seat connectors from under the plastic cover (see illustrations).

5 With all the wiring disconnected the seat can now be removed from the passenger compartment.

6 Refitting is a reversal of removal, but observe the following precautions before reconnecting the battery.

a) Ensure that there are no occupants in the vehicle, and that there are no loose objects around the vicinity of the seats.

b) Ensure that the ignition is switched off then reconnect the airbag ECM and the battery.

c) Open the driver's door and switch on the ignition, without sitting inside the vehicle. Check that the airbag warning light illuminates briefly then extinguishes.

d) Switch off the ignition.

e) If the airbag warning light does not operate as described in paragraph c), consult a Peugeot dealer before driving the vehicle.

Rear seats

Seat cushion

7 Lift the front edge first, followed by the rear edge, then push the stays to the side and remove the seat from the vehicle (see illustration).

Seat backs

8 With the seat cushions folded forward, remove the plastic cap and undo the hinge bolt in the centre (see illustration).

9 Undo the retaining bolt and disconnect the centre seat belt anchorage point from the floor panel (see illustration).

10 Fold the seat backs forward and lift up the luggage compartment carpet.

11 Undo the bolts securing the seats outer hinges to the vehicle floor, and the nut holding the centre hinge to the floor panel (see illustrations).

12 Refitting is a reversal of removal, tightening the hinge bolts securely.

Seat centre armrest

13 Remove the rear seat backs as described in paragraphs 8 to 11.

23.4b . . . and disconnect the wiring connectors

23.7 Pull the mounting bracket stays to one side to disengage

23.8 Undo the rear seat centre bolt (arrowed)

23.9 Centre seat belt anchorage bolt

23.11a Undo the rear seat outer mounting bolts . . .

23.11b . . . and centre bracket mounting nut

23.14 Undo the retaining screw from the centre armrest

23.15 Withdraw the pivot pin . . .

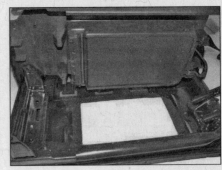

23.16 . . . then unclip the plastic trim panel

14 Undo the retaining screw **(see illustration)**, and remove the centre armrest cushion.
15 Release the plastic securing clip and then withdraw the pivot pin from the seat frame **(see illustration)**.
16 If required, unclip the plastic hatch cover from the seat frame **(see illustration)**.
17 Refitting is a reversal of removal.

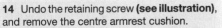

24 Seat belt components – removal and refitting

Note: *Record the positions of the washers and spacers on the seat belt anchors, and ensure they are refitted in their original positions.*

Front seat belt

⚠ **Warning: The front seat belt inertia reels are equipped with a pyrotechnic pretensioner mechanism. Refer to the airbag system precautions contained in Chapter 12, which apply equally to the seat belt pretensioners. Do not tamper with the inertia reel pretensioner unit in any way, and do not attempt to test the unit. Note that the unit is triggered if the mechanism is supplied with an electrical current (including via an ohmmeter), or if the assembly is subjected to a temperature of greater than 100°C.**

1 De-activate the airbag system (which will also de-activate the pyrotechnic pretensioner mechanism) as described in Chapter 12 before attempting to remove the seat belt.
2 If desired, to improve access, remove the relevant front seat as described in Section 23.

3 Remove the B-pillar trim panels as described in Section 25.
4 Release the locking clip and disconnect the wiring connector from the top of the inertia reel unit **(see illustration)**.
5 Remove the plastic cover and undo the seat belt lower anchor bolt and the inertia reel anchor bolt, and recover the washers **(see illustration)**.
6 Undo the seat belt upper anchor bolt and release the belt from its guide clip on the door pillar **(see illustrations)**. Withdraw the inertia reel from the door pillar and remove it from the vehicle.
7 Refitting is a reversal of removal, but observe the following precautions before reconnecting the battery.
a) Ensure that there are no occupants in the vehicle, and that there are no loose objects around the vicinity of the seats.
b) Ensure that the ignition is switched off then reconnect the battery.

c) Open the driver's door and switch on the ignition, without sitting inside the vehicle. Check that the airbag warning light illuminates briefly then extinguishes.
d) Switch off the ignition.
e) If the airbag warning light does not operate as described in paragraph c), consult a Peugeot dealer before driving the vehicle.
f) Tighten the seat belt mountings to the specified torque.

Rear seat belts

8 Tilt the rear seat backs forwards to access the rear trim panels. If required, remove the rear seat backs as described in Section 23.

Saloon and coupe models

9 Remove the plastic cover and undo the bolt securing the seat belt anchor to the vehicle body **(see illustration)**.

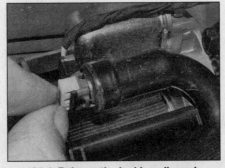

24.4 Release the locking clip and disconnect the wiring plug

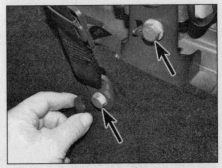

24.5 Undo the inertia reel and seat belt anchorage bolts (arrowed)

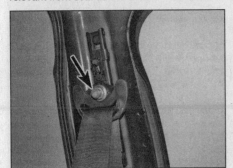

24.6a Undo the upper seat belt anchorage bolt . . .

24.6b . . . and release the seat belt retaining clip from the pillar

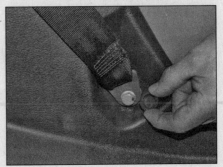

24.9 Prise off the rubber cap and undo the lower seat belt anchorage bolt

24.11 Remove the insulating cover . . .

24.12 . . . and undo the inertia reel mounting nut (arrowed)

24.13 Seat belt stalk anchor bolt

24.17 Remove the insulated cover and undo the inertia reel mounting nut (arrowed)

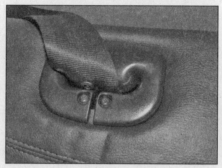

24.21 Undo the trim retaining screws

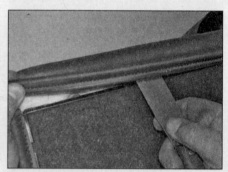

24.22a Unclip the seat cover . . .

10 Remove the C-pillar trim panels and parcel shelf trim as described in Section 25.
11 Lift the insulating cover from the inertia reel seat belt (see illustration).
12 Undo the nut securing the seat belt inertia reel to the vehicle body (see illustration).
13 To remove the seat belt stalk, fold the rear seat backs up, and undo the bolt securing the seat belt stalk to the vehicle body (see illustration).
14 Refitting is a reversal of removal. Tighten the mounting bolts to the specified torque.

Estate (SW) models
15 Remove the plastic cover and undo the

bolt securing the seat belt anchor to the vehicle body (see illustration 24.9).
16 Remove the luggage compartment side trim panels, as described in Section 25.
17 Lift the insulating cover and undo the nut securing the seat belt inertia reel to the vehicle body (see illustration).
18 To remove the seat belt stalk, fold the rear seat backs up, and undo the bolt securing the seat belt stalk to the vehicle body (see illustration 24.13).
19 Refitting is a reversal of removal. Tighten the mounting bolts to the specified torque.

Rear centre seat belts
20 To remove the centre seat belt inertia reel, the seat back cover must be partially removed. Remove the seat back as described in Section 23.
21 Undo the two retaining screws and remove the plastic trim from around the seat belt (see illustration).
22 Working your way around the seat, unclip the cover from the seat frame (see illustrations).
23 Reach up inside the back of the seat and release the headrest guides from the top of the seat frame (see illustration).

24.22b . . . and remove it from the seat frame

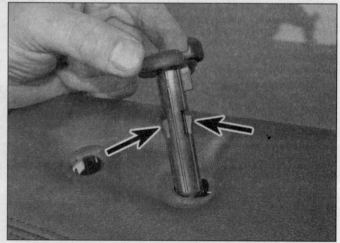

24.23 Press in the two clips to release the headrest guides

24 Release the seat catch plastic trim cover from the top of the seat frame (**see illustration**).

25 Lift off the seat cover and withdraw the seat belt through the top of the cover (**see illustration**).

26 Undo the nut securing the seat belt inertia reel to the seat frame (**see illustration**).

27 If required, undo the two retaining screws to remove the seat catch from the top of the seat frame (**see illustration**).

28 Refitting is a reversal of removal. Tighten the mounting bolts to the specified torque.

24.24 Unclip the plastic trim from the seat catch

24.25 Withdraw the belt through the seat cover

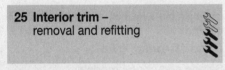

25 Interior trim –
removal and refitting

Door inner trim

1 Refer to Section 12.

A-pillar trim

2 Prise the weatherstrip from the front door aperture adjacent to the pillar trim.

3 Carefully prise the trim away from the pillar starting at the middle, and then pull the top edge from behind the headlining.

4 Lift the trim up to disengage the lower locating lugs and remove it from the vehicle.

5 Refitting is a reversal of removal, but ensure that all retaining clips are fully engaged and that the weatherstrip is fully seated.

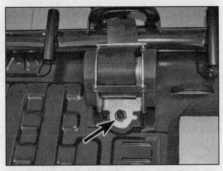

24.26 Undo the inertia reel mounting nut (arrowed)

Lower B-pillar trim

6 Carefully release the front sill trim panel from below the facia, and then pull it upwards

24.27 Undo the seat catch retaining screws (arrowed)

to release its retaining clips along its length (**see illustration**).

7 Release the front edge of the rear sill/C-pillar trim from its retaining clips in the rear edge of the lower B-pillar trim (**see illustration 25.15**).

8 Carefully unclip the upper end of the trim from its retaining clips, and then lift the trim upwards to disengage the trim lower locating lugs in the sill body panel (**see illustrations**).

9 Refitting is a reversal of removal, but ensure that all retaining clips are fully engaged.

Upper B-pillar trim

10 Remove the lower B-pillar trim panel, as previously described.

11 Undo the retaining screw, then release the securing clip and pull the lower end of the trim from the pillar (**see illustrations**).

25.6 Unclip the trim panel from along the front sill

25.8a Unclip the upper part of the B-pillar . . .

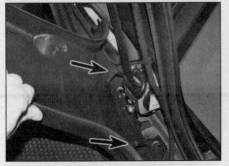

25.8b . . . and lift the lower locating lugs (arrowed) out from the sill

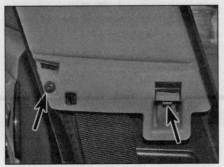

25.11a Undo the retaining screw and release the retaining clip (arrowed) . . .

25.11b . . . from the B-pillar

25.12a Pull the upper trim outwards . . .

25.12b . . . and withdraw it from under the headlining

25.15 Unclip the lower end of the trim panel from along the rear sill . . .

12 Pull the upper part of the trim panel away from the pillar to release the locating pegs, then down and out from under the headlining **(see illustrations)**.

13 Refitting is a reversal of removal, but ensure that all retaining clips are fully engaged and that the seat belt height adjuster is located correctly.

Lower C-pillar trim

Saloon and coupe models

14 Tilt the seat cushion forwards and undo the rear seat belt lower anchorage bolt **(see illustration 24.9)**. Note the fitted position of the spacers and washers on the seat belt anchorage bolt for refitting.

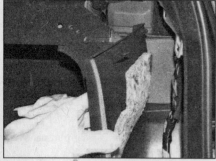

25.16 . . . and the upper edge from the C-pillar upper trim panel

15 Pull the lower part of the trim panel upwards to release it from the floor panel, and disconnect it from the rear edge of the lower B-pillar trim panel **(see illustration)**.

16 Tilt the seat back forwards (or completely remove the seat back as described in Section 23), and pull the upper part of the trim panel away from the pillar to release the locating clips in the lower edge of the upper trim panel **(see illustration)**.

17 Refitting is a reversal of removal, but ensure that all retaining clips are fully engaged and that the seat belt anchorage point is secure.

Estate (SW) models

18 Tilt the seat cushion forwards and undo the rear seat belt lower anchorage bolt **(see illustration 24.9)**. Note the fitted position of the spacers and washers on the seat belt anchorage bolt for refitting.

19 Tilt the seat back forwards (or completely remove the seat back as described in Section 23), and remove the plastic securing clip from by the seat catch bracket **(see illustration)**.

20 Pull the lower part of the trim panel upwards to release it from the floor panel, and disconnect it from the rear edge of the lower B-pillar trim panel.

21 Pull the upper part of the trim panel away from the pillar to release the locating clips, and remove the trim panel.

22 Refitting is a reversal of removal, but ensure that all retaining clips are fully engaged

and that the seat belt anchorage point is secure.

Upper C-pillar trim

Saloon and coupe models

23 Remove the lower C-pillar trim panel, as previously described.

24 Pull the trim panel away from the body panel to release the locating clips in the upper trim panel **(see illustration)**.

25 Refitting is a reversal of removal, but ensure that all retaining clips are fully engaged

Estate (SW) models

26 Remove the parcel shelf support panel, as described later in this Section.

27 Remove the D-pillar upper trim panel, as described later in this Section.

28 Carefully pull the trim panel away from the pillar to release the securing clips.

29 Refitting is a reversal of removal, but ensure that all retaining clips are fully engaged

D-pillar trim

Estate (SW) models

30 Pull away the rubber weatherstrip from the tailgate aperture adjacent to the D-pillar trim **(see illustration)**.

31 Carefully pull the rear trim panel at the rear of the headlining downwards to release

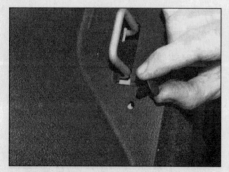

25.19 Release the trim securing clip

25.24 Unclip the C-pillar upper trim panel

25.30 Peel back the tailgate aperture seal . . .

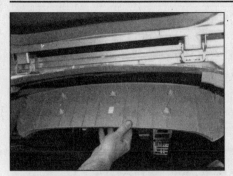

25.31 . . . and unclip the trim panel from along the roof panel

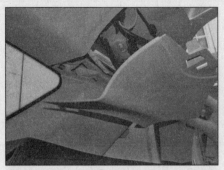

25.32 Unclip the D-pillar upper trim panel

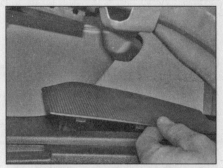

25.36a Unclip the grille panel . . .

the securing clips, disengaging it from the upper part of the D-pillar trim at each side **(see illustration)**.

32 Carefully pull the D-pillar trim away, releasing the retaining clips as it is removed, disengaging it from the upper part of the C-pillar trim at each side **(see illustration)**.

33 Refitting is a reversal of removal.

Parcel shelf support panel

Estate (SW) models

34 Tilt the seat cushion forwards and undo the rear seat belt lower anchorage bolt **(see illustration 24.9)**. Note the fitted position of the spacers and washers on the seat belt anchorage bolt for refitting.

35 Tilt the seat back forwards (or completely remove the seat back as described in Section 23), and remove the plastic securing clip from by the seat catch bracket **(see illustration 25.19)**.

36 Unclip the grille cover from the top of the shelf support panel, and release the fastener to the body panel **(see illustrations)**.

37 Undo the two retaining screws securing the lower edge of the parcel shelf support to the inner panel **(see illustration)**.

38 Lift the trim panel upwards to release the retaining clips along the upper edge of the panel, and then remove the support panel from the luggage compartment **(see illustration)**. As the parcel shelf support is being withdrawn, guide the seat belt through the front of the panel to release it. **Note:** *Depending on model*

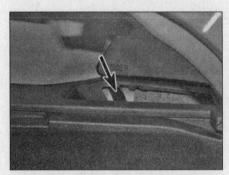

25.36b . . . and release the fastener (arrowed) – where fitted

25.37 Undo the side trim retaining screws (arrowed)

or which side of the vehicle is being worked on, disconnect the wiring connectors from the luggage compartment light and/or accessory socket as the panel is withdrawn.

39 Refitting is a reversal of removal, but ensure that all retaining clips are fully engaged and that the seat belt anchorage point is secure.

Luggage compartment side trim

Estate (SW) models

40 Remove the parcel shelf support panel as described previously in this Section.

41 Remove the luggage compartment floor panel/carpet, and then release the securing clips and remove the carpet side trim panels from the luggage compartment **(see illustration)**

42 Refitting is a reversal of removal.

Saloon and coupe models

43 Open the boot lid and remove the luggage compartment floor panel/carpet.

44 Release the securing clips and remove the carpet side trim panels from the luggage compartment **(see illustration)**. **Note:** *Depending on model or which side of the vehicle is being worked on, disconnect the wiring connectors from the luggage compartment light and/or accessory socket as the side trim panel is withdrawn.*

45 Refitting is a reversal of removal.

Parcel shelf trim panel

Saloon and coupe models

46 Tilt the seat cushion forwards and undo

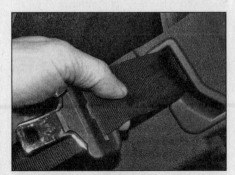

25.38 Withdraw the belt through the trim panel

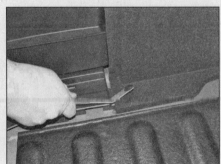

25.41 Unclip the lower plastic securing clips

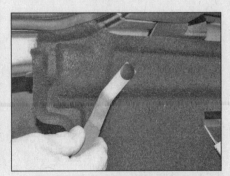

25.44 Unclip the side carpet upper securing clips

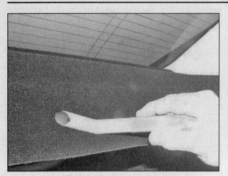

25.47 Unclip the securing clips from along the rear parcel shelf

25.48 Withdraw the belt through the parcel shelf

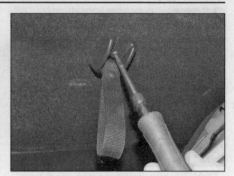

25.50 Undo the retaining screw from the grab handle

the rear seat belt lower anchorage bolt **(see illustration 24.9)**. Note the fitted position of the spacers and washers on the seat belt anchorage bolt for refitting.
47 Tilt the seat back forwards and then release

the securing clips along the front edge of the parcel shelf trim panel **(see illustration)**.
48 Lift the shelf trim panel upwards to release it from below the rear screen, and then remove the trim panel from the rear of the passenger

compartment. As the parcel shelf trim is being withdrawn, unclip the plastic guide and withdraw the seat belt through the front of the shelf trim panel **(see illustration)**.
49 Refitting is a reversal of removal.

Tailgate trim
Lower carpet trim panel
50 Undo the retaining screw and remove the pull strap from the tailgate **(see illustration)**.
51 Unclip the luggage compartment light from the trim panel, and disconnect the wiring connector **(see illustration)**.
52 Release the plastic securing clips from the sides and the lower edge of the trim panel **(see illustration)**.
53 Carefully pull the panel away from the tailgate, releasing it from the upper plastic trim panel as it is removed **(see illustration)**.
54 Refitting is a reversal of removal.

Upper plastic trim panel
55 Remove the lower carpet trim panel as described previously in this Section.
56 Close the tailgate and open the upper glass hatch. Pull away the rubber weatherstrip from the tailgate aperture adjacent to the trim panel **(see illustration)**.
57 Release the plastic securing clip from the top of the plastic trim panel **(see illustration)**.
58 Pull the trim panel away from the tailgate to release the securing clips **(see illustrations)**. As the trim is removed, take care not to damage the rear wiper motor drive. **Note:** *The outer rivets/washers are just locating pegs for the trim panel to slide behind.*
59 Refitting is a reversal of removal.

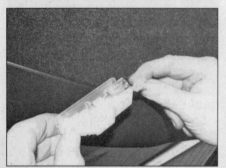

25.51 Unclip the courtesy light and disconnect the wiring plug

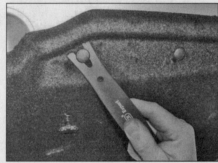

25.52 Release the securing clips . . .

25.53 . . . and remove the trim panel from the tailgate

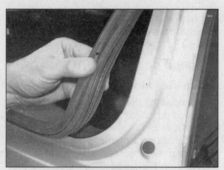

25.56 Peel back the glass hatch aperture seal

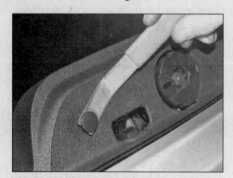

25.57 Unclip the trim upper securing clip

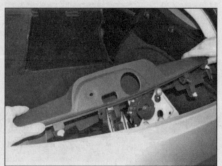

25.58a Release the plastic trim from the tailgate . . .

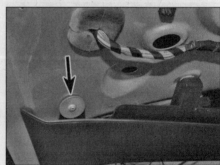

25.58b . . . pulling it upwards from behind the locating pegs/washers (arrowed)

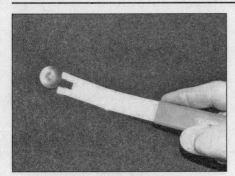

25.60 Release the securing clips . . .

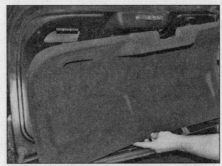

25.61 . . . and remove the trim panel from the boot lid

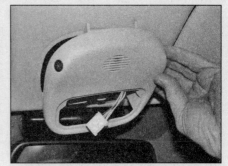

25.68a Unclip the upper light console . . .

Boot lid trim

60 Open the boot lid and release the plastic securing clips from around the edges of the trim panel (see illustration).
61 Carefully pull the trim panel away from the boot lid (see illustration).
62 Refitting is a reversal of removal.

Inner sill trim

Front

63 See the removal procedure for the lower B-pillar trim panel earlier in this Section (see illustration 25.6).

Rear

64 The rear sill trim is part of the lower C-pillar trim panel; remove as described earlier in this Section (see illustration 25.15).

Headlining

Note: Headlining removal requires considerable skill and experience if it is to be carried out without damage, and is therefore best entrusted to a Peugeot dealer or bodywork specialist. A general overview of the procedure is given below for those with the expertise to attempt the operation on a DIY basis.
65 The headlining is clipped and glued to the roof, and can be withdrawn only once all fittings such as the grab handles, courtesy lights, sunvisors, sunroof (if fitted), pillar trim panels, and associated additional panels have been removed. The door, tailgate and sunroof aperture weatherstrips will also have to be prised clear and any additional screws and clips removed. Once the headlining attachments are released, the adhesive bonding in the centre panels must be broken using a hot air gun and spatula, starting at the front and working rearwards.
66 When refitting, a coat of neoprene adhesive (available from Peugeot dealers) must be applied to the centre panels in the locations noted during removal. Position the headlining carefully and refit all components disturbed during removal. Clean the headlining with soap and water, or white spirit, on completion.

Overhead console

67 Prise the lens from the interior light unit, then lever backwards the two retaining clips

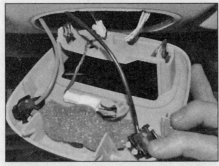

25.68b . . . and disconnect the wiring

and remove the light unit from the console. Disconnect the wiring plug as the unit is withdrawn, refer to Chapter 12 for further information.
68 Release the two retaining clips and pull the front of the console down, then pull it forward to disengage the locating lugs at the rear (see illustrations). Disconnect any wiring plugs as the console is removed.
69 Refitting is a reversal of removal.

Sunvisor

70 Prior to removing the sunvisor, remove the overhead console as described in paragraphs 67 and 68, and disconnect the wiring plugs.
71 The sunvisor is retained by a retaining clip, using a small screwdriver withdraw the retaining clip from the sunvisor outer mounting bracket (see illustration). The sunvisor can then be unclipped from the inner

25.73a Release the outer securing clip . . .

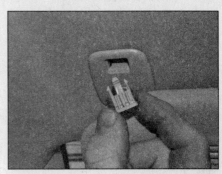

25.71 Release the plastic securing clip

locating mounting bracket and removed from the roof panel. Where applicable, identify the sunvisor vanity light wiring plug at the overhead console, and tie a length of string to it. Withdraw the sunvisor, pulling the string through the interior light aperture. When the string emerges at the sunvisor mount aperture, untie it from the wiring plug and leave it in place in the roof panel for refitting.
72 When refitting the sunvisor, tie the length of string to the visor wiring, and pull it back through to the interior light aperture. Reconnect the wiring plug.
73 To remove the inner locating mounting bracket, withdraw the retaining clip and then unclip the mounting from the roof panel (see illustrations).
74 Refitting is a reversal of removal.

Grab handle

75 Carefully prise the retaining clips from

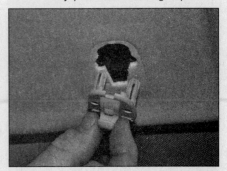

25.73b . . . and remove the visor mounting bracket

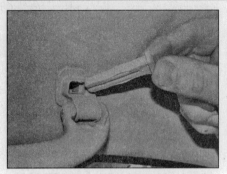

25.75 Withdraw the plastic securing clip from the grab handle

26.1a Undo the retaining screw (arrowed) . . .

26.1b . . . and remove the front trim panel

each end of the grab handle, and then pull the handle to release it from the roof panel **(see illustration)**.
76 Refitting is a reversal of removal.

26 Centre console – removal and refitting

Removal

1 Move the two front seats fully rearwards, then undo the retaining screws and remove the trim panels from each side of the console **(see illustrations)**.
2 On manual transmission models, unclip the gaiter from the top of the console **(see illustration)**.

3 On automatic transmission models, remove the gear lever knob and unclip the selector gate trim from the top of the console. Disconnect the wiring connectors from the gear selector buttons (depending on model), as the trim is removed.
4 Unclip the handbrake lever gaiter from the top of the console and pull it back up the handbrake lever **(see illustration)**.
5 Open the armrest/storage compartment and remove the rubber base **(see illustration)**.
6 Undo the three retaining screws and lift out the storage compartment from the centre console. Release the securing clip and disconnect the diagnostic plug connector from the storage compartment **(see illustrations)**.
7 Carefully release the upper trim cover from the top of the console, taking care not to break the securing clips **(see illustration)**.

26.2 Unclip the gear lever gaiter from the console

8 Undo the two retaining screws from the front upper edge of the console **(see illustration)**.
9 Remove the ashtray from the rear of the

26.4 Unclip the handbrake lever gaiter from the console

26.5 Remove the storage compartment inner tray . . .

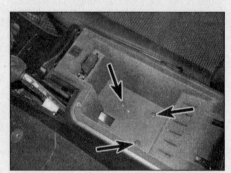

26.6a . . . undo the retaining screws (arrowed) . . .

26.6b . . . and release the diagnostic plug

26.7 Carefully unclip the trim panel from the top of the console

26.8 Undo the retaining screws (arrowed) from the front of the console

26.9a Unclip the ashtray from the rear of the console . . .

26.9b . . . and then unclip the ashtray outer trim panel

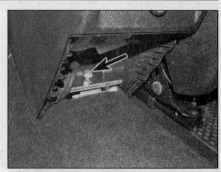
26.10a Undo the retaining nut (arrowed) from inside the rear of the console . . .

26.10b . . . and disconnect the wiring connector from the auxiliary 12V socket

26.11 Withdraw the console upwards and out from the vehicle

27.2a Release the glove compartment hinges/arms . . .

console, and then unclip the rear panel from the console **(see illustrations)**.
10 Undo the mounting bolt from inside the rear of the console, and then disconnect the wiring connector from the accessory socket in the rear of the console **(see illustrations)**.
11 Withdraw the console away from the facia, check for any wiring still connected to the console, and then lift it over the handbrake lever, and rearwards out of the passenger compartment **(see illustration)**.

Refitting

12 Refitting is a reversal of removal.

27 Facia panel components – removal and refitting

Glovebox

Removal

1 Release the retaining clips and remove the trim cover from below the glove compartment, under the facia panel.
2 Open the glove compartment and release the hinges/arms from the back of the glove compartment. On the right-hand side hinge/arm, reach up behind the facia to release the hinge/arm from the pivot **(see illustrations)**.
3 Working under the facia undo the four retaining screws from along the lower edge of the glove compartment door and remove it from the facia **(see illustration)**.
4 Unclip the light unit from inside the glove compartment and disconnect the wiring connector **(see illustration)**.
5 Undo the screws securing the glove compartment to the facia and withdraw it.

27.2b . . . disconnecting the right hinge/ arm from the pivot (arrowed) behind the facia

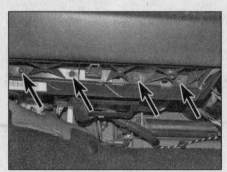
27.3 Undo the lower retaining screws (arrowed)

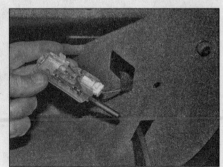
27.4 Unclip the glove compartment light and disconnect

27.5a Undo the retaining screws . . .

27.5b . . . remove the glove compartment from the facia . . .

27.5c . . . and disconnect any wiring connectors

27.12 Remove the centre air vent panel

27.13 Remove the upper grille panel from the facia

27.14 Undo the securing bolts (arrowed) from the centre of the facia

Disconnect any wiring plug connectors as the glovebox is withdrawn (see illustrations).

Refitting

6 Refitting is a reversal of removal.

Complete facia assembly

Note: *This is an involved operation entailing the removal of numerous components and assemblies, and the disconnection of a multitude of wiring connectors. Make notes of the location of all disconnected wiring, or attach labels to the connectors, to avoid confusion when refitting.*

Removal

7 Disconnect the battery, as described in Chapter 5A.

8 Remove the passenger side glove compartment as described previously in this Section.

9 Remove the centre console as described in Section 26.

10 Remove the radio/cassette/CD player and multifunction display unit, as described in Chapter 12.

11 Remove the heater/climate controls, as described in Chapter 3.

12 Undo the two retaining screws and remove the upper air vents from the centre of the facia panel (see illustration).

13 Undo the two retaining screws and remove the upper grille panel from the centre of the facia panel (see illustration). Disconnect the wiring connector from the sunlight sensor as the grille is removed. .

14 Undo the two retaining bolts that secure the centre of the facia panel to the lower part of the heater housing (see illustration).

15 Remove the speakers from the top of the facia, at each end, as described in Chapter 12.

16 Unscrew the two lower steering column

27.15a Remove the upper . . .

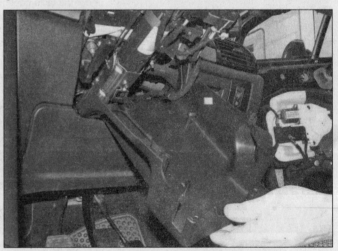

27.15b . . . and lower steering column shrouds

27.18a Withdraw the soundproofing . . .

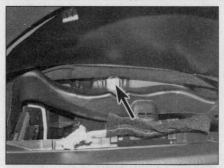

27.18b . . . and undo the facia securing bolt (arrowed)

27.19 Unclip the lower trim panel

27.22a Unclip the left-hand trim panel . . .

27.22b . . . and right-hand trim panel from the ends of the facia

27.23 Remove the light switch from the facia

shroud securing screws. Unclip and lift off the upper shroud, then remove the lower shroud **(see illustrations)**.

17 Remove the instrument panel, as described in Chapter 12.

18 Withdraw the foam soundproofing from inside the instrument panel aperture and then undo the retaining bolt from the bulkhead **(see illustrations)**.

19 Release the two retaining clips and remove the trim cover from below the driver's side facia, above the pedal assembly **(see illustration)**.

20 Remove the driver's airbag and knee airbag, as described in Chapter 12.

21 Remove the steering column, as described in Chapter 10.

22 Unclip the trim covers from each end of the facia panel **(see illustrations)**.

23 Reach inside the right-hand side of the facia panel and disconnect the wiring connector(s) from the switch(es) in the facia **(see illustration)**.

24 Undo the retaining bolts/nut and remove the mounting bracket from the right-hand side of the heater housing **(see illustration)**.

25 Undo the retaining bolt and disconnect the earth cable at the left-hand side of the heater housing **(see illustration)**.

27.24 Remove the mounting bracket from the right-hand side of the heater housing

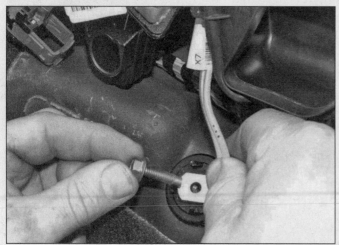

27.25 Disconnect the earth wire from the left-hand side of the heater housing

27.26 Undo the securing bolts (arrowed) from the centre of the facia

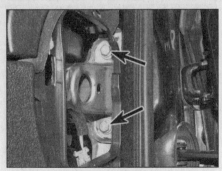

27.27a Undo the mounting bolts (arrowed) from inside the right-hand . . .

27.22b . . . and left-hand ends of the facia

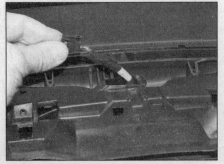

27.28 Tie a piece of string to the wiring and pass it down through the facia

27.30 With the aid of an assistant remove the complete facia from inside the vehicle

26 Undo the two retaining bolts from inside the centre of the facia panel **(see illustration)**.

27 Working inside the each end of the facia panel, slacken and remove the crossmember mounting bolts (two each side) **(see illustrations)**.

28 Withdraw the wiring to the sunlight sensor down through the ducting in the top of the facia panel **(see illustration)**.

29 With the help of an assistant, lift the facia from place, and check for any wiring plugs that may still be connected to the rear of the facia. Take note of the location of the various wiring harness retaining clips, to aid refitment.

30 With everything clear remove the complete facia panel out from the passenger compartment **(see illustration)**. Note this will be heavy as the crossmember will remain connected to the facia panel as it is removed.

Refitting

31 Refitting is a reversal of removal ensuring that all wiring is correctly reconnected and all mountings securely tightened.

Chapter 12
Body electrical systems

Contents

Degrees of difficulty

Easy, suitable for novice with little experience	**Fairly easy,** suitable for beginner with some experience	**Fairly difficult,** suitable for competent DIY mechanic	**Difficult,** suitable for experienced DIY mechanic	**Very difficult,** suitable for expert DIY or professional

Specifications

General

System type	12 volt negative earth

Bulbs

	Type	Wattage
Brake light	Bayonet	21
Direction indicator light	Bayonet	21
Direction indicator side repeater	Push-fit	5
Front ashtray light	Push-fit	1.2
Front foglight	H1	55
Glovebox light	Push-fit	5
Headlights:		
Main beam bulbs	H1	55
Dip beam bulbs	H7	55
High-level brake light	Push-fit	5
Interior/courtesy lights	Push-fit	5
Luggage compartment light	Push-fit	5
Number plate light	Push-fit	5
Rear foglight	Bayonet	21
Reversing light	Bayonet	21
Sidelights	Push-fit	5
Tail light	Bayonet	5

Torque wrench setting

	Nm	lbf ft
Airbag control module retaining nuts	8	6

1 General information

⚠️ **Warning: Before carrying out any work on the electrical system, read through the precautions given in 'Safety first!' at the beginning of this manual, and in Chapter 5A.**

The electrical system is of 12 volt negative earth type. Power for the lights and all electrical accessories is supplied by a lead-acid type battery, which is charged by the alternator.

Many of the body electrical systems are controlled by individual electronic control modules (ECMs) and these are in turn controlled by a main ECM known as a built-in systems interface (BSI). The various ECMs and the BSI exchange data with each other via a multiplex network. The multiplex network is a two-wire system linking the BSI with the system ECMs and is termed by Peugeot as CAN (controlled area network) and VAN (vehicle area network). Essentially this means that the BSI and the ECMs controlling the 'comfort' systems, safety systems, security systems, and entertainment systems in the vehicle, are all inter-connected via vehicle area networks.

An ECM connected to the multiplex network only receives some of the data needed for it to operate directly, with the remaining data being supplied by the other ECMs on the network. Because the ECMs share information via the network, several ECMs can control the operation of the same system. Also, one ECM can control several systems in an autonomous manner. The BSI is the manager of this information interchange as well as also being responsible for the control of certain vehicle systems itself. The BSI has a full diagnostic capability whereby any fault in any of the ECMs on the multiplex network can be traced using diagnostic equipment connected to the vehicle diagnostic connector. Should any fault develop with a system on the network, have the self-diagnosis facility interrogated by a Peugeot dealer or suitably-equipped specialist.

This Chapter covers repair and service procedures for the various electrical components not associated with the engine. Information on the battery, alternator and starter motor can be found in Chapter 5A.

It should be noted that, prior to working on any component in the electrical system, the battery should first be disconnected; to prevent the possibility of electrical short-circuits (see Chapter 5A).

Caution: The Peugeot 407 electrical system is extremely complex. The ECMs/ECUs are connected via a 'Databus' (multiplex) system, where they are able to share information from the various sensors, and communicate with each other. Many of the electrical components are operated via a multiplex system, identified by 2 wires twisted together. Due to the design of the Databus/Multiplex system, it is not advisable to backprobe the ECMs with a multimeter in the traditional manner. Instead, the electrical systems are equipped with a sophisticated self-diagnosis system, which can interrogate the various ECMs to reveal stored fault codes, and help pinpoint faults. In order to access the self-diagnosis system, specialist test equipment (fault code reader/scanner) is required.

2 Electrical fault finding – general information

Note: *Refer to the precautions given in 'Safety first!' and in Chapter 5A before starting work. The following tests relate to testing of the main electrical circuits, and should not be used to test delicate electronic circuits (such as anti-lock braking systems), particularly where an electronic control module (ECM) or multiplexing is used (see Section 1).*

General

1 A typical electrical circuit consists of an electrical component; any switches, relays, motors, fuses, fusible links or circuit breakers related to that component, and the wiring and connectors which link the component to both the battery and the chassis. To help to pinpoint a problem in an electrical circuit, wiring diagrams are included at the end of this Chapter.

2 Before attempting to diagnose an electrical fault, first study the appropriate wiring diagram, to obtain a more complete understanding of the components included in the particular circuit concerned. The possible sources of a fault can be narrowed down by noting whether other components related to the circuit are operating properly. If several components or circuits fail at one time, the problem is likely to be related to a shared fuse or earth connection.

3 Electrical problems usually stem from simple causes, such as loose or corroded connections, a faulty earth connection, a blown fuse, a melted fusible link, or a faulty relay (refer to Section 3 for details of testing relays). Visually inspect the condition of all fuses, wires and connections in a problem circuit before testing the components. Use the wiring diagrams to determine which terminal connections will need to be checked, in order to pinpoint the trouble spot.

4 The basic tools required for electrical fault finding include a circuit tester or voltmeter; an ohmmeter (to measure resistance); a battery and set of test leads; and a jumper wire, preferably with a circuit breaker or fuse incorporated, which can be used to bypass suspect wires or electrical components. Before attempting to locate a problem with test instruments, use the wiring diagram to determine where to make the connections.

5 To find the source of an intermittent wiring fault (usually due to a poor or dirty connection, or damaged wiring insulation), a 'wiggle' test can be performed on the wiring. This involves wiggling the wiring by hand, to see if the fault occurs as the wiring is moved. It should be possible to narrow down the source of the fault to a particular section of wiring. This method of testing can be used in conjunction with any of the tests described in the following sub-Sections.

6 Apart from problems due to poor connections, two basic types of fault can occur in an electrical circuit – open-circuit, or short-circuit.

7 Open-circuit faults are caused by a break somewhere in the circuit, which prevents current from flowing. An open-circuit fault will prevent a component from working, but will not cause the relevant circuit fuse to blow.

8 Short-circuit faults are caused by a 'short' somewhere in the circuit, which allows the current flowing in the circuit to 'escape' along an alternative route, usually to earth. Short-circuit faults are normally caused by a breakdown in wiring insulation, which allows a feed wire to touch either another wire, or an earthed component such as the bodyshell. A short-circuit fault will normally cause the relevant circuit fuse to blow. **Note:** *As an aid to economy and to prevent battery discharge, certain functions of the electrical system can only be used for 30 minutes after the engine has been stopped. Bear this in mind when tracing power supply faults on these systems.*

Functions affected

- *Windscreen wipers.*
- *Electric windows.*
- *Sunroof.*
- *Courtesy lights.*
- *Audio equipment.*

After this period the BSI (Built-in Systems Interface) cuts the power to these circuits. To restore power, start the engine. It is also possible for the BSI to turn off certain functions (heater blower, heated rear window) depending on the state of charge of the battery. When tracing a fault, ensure the battery is in a good state of charge.

Finding an open-circuit

9 To check for an open-circuit, connect one lead of a voltmeter to either the negative battery terminal or a known good earth.

10 Connect the other lead to a connector in the circuit being tested, preferably nearest to the battery or fuse.

11 Switch on the circuit, bearing in mind that some circuits are live only when the ignition switch is moved to a particular position.

12 If voltage is present (indicated either by the tester bulb lighting or a voltmeter reading, as applicable), this means that the section of the circuit between the relevant connector and the battery is problem-free.

13 Continue to check the remainder of the circuit in the same fashion.

14 When a point is reached at which no

2.20a Earth connection on top of the transmission . . .

2.20b . . . in front of the engine compartment fuse/relay box . . .

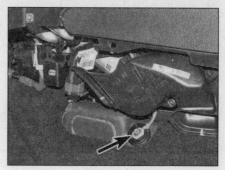

2.20c . . . and inside the passenger compartment (arrowed)

voltage is present, the problem must lie between that point and the previous test point with voltage. Most problems can be traced to a broken, corroded or loose connection.

 Warning: Under no circumstances may live measuring instruments such as ohmmeters, voltmeters or a bulb and test leads be used to test any of the airbag circuitry. Any testing of these components must be left to a Peugeot dealer or specialist, as there is a danger of activating the system if the correct procedures are not followed.

Finding a short-circuit

15 To check for a short-circuit; first disconnect the load(s) from the circuit (loads are the components which draw current from a circuit, such as bulbs, motors, heating elements, etc).
16 Remove the relevant fuse from the circuit, and connect a circuit tester or voltmeter to the fuse connections.
17 Switch on the circuit, bearing in mind that some circuits are live only when the ignition switch is moved to a particular position.
18 If voltage is present (indicated either by the tester bulb lighting or a voltmeter reading, as applicable), this means that there is a short-circuit.
19 If no voltage is present, but the fuse still blows with the load(s) connected, this indicates an internal fault in the load(s).

Finding an earth fault

20 The battery negative terminal is connected to 'earth' – the metal of the engine/transmission

and the car body – and most systems are wired so that they only receive a positive feed, the current returning via the metal of the car body. This means that the component mounting and the body form part of that circuit. Loose or corroded mountings can therefore cause a range of electrical faults, ranging from total failure of a circuit, to a puzzling partial fault. In particular, lights may shine dimly (especially when another circuit sharing the same earth point is in operation), motors (eg, wiper motors or the radiator cooling fan motor) may run slowly, and the operation of one circuit may have an apparently unrelated effect on another. Note that on many vehicles, earth straps are used between certain components, such as the engine/transmission and the body, usually where there is no metal-to-metal contact between components, due to flexible rubber mountings, etc **(see illustrations)**.
21 To check whether a component is properly earthed, disconnect the battery, and connect one lead of an ohmmeter to a known good earth point. Connect the other lead to the wire or earth connection being tested. The resistance reading should be zero; if not, check the connection as follows.
22 If an earth connection is thought to be faulty, dismantle the connection, and clean back to bare metal both the bodyshell and the wire terminal or the component earth connection mating surface. Be careful to remove all traces of dirt and corrosion, and then use a knife to trim away any paint, so that a clean metal-to-metal joint is made. On reassembly, tighten the joint fasteners

securely; if a wire terminal is being refitted, use serrated washers between the terminal and the bodyshell, to ensure a clean and secure connection. When the connection is remade, prevent the onset of corrosion in the future by applying a coat of petroleum jelly or silicone-based grease, or by spraying on (at regular intervals) a proprietary ignition sealer or water-dispersant lubricant.

3 Fuses and relays – general information

Fuses

1 Fuses are designed to break a circuit when a predetermined current is reached, in order to protect the components and wiring, which could be damaged by excessive current flow. Any excessive current flow will be due to a fault in the circuit, usually a short-circuit (see Section 2).
2 The majority of fuses are located behind the glove compartment lid on the passenger's side of the facia. Additional fuses (including the larger, higher-rated fuses) are located under the fuse/relay box on the left-hand side of the engine compartment **(see illustration)**.
3 To gain access to the facia fuses, open the glove compartment, release the upper securing clips and hinge the cover downwards **(see illustrations)**. To gain access to the fuses in the engine compartment, release the four securing clips and lift off the cover from the fuse/relay box.

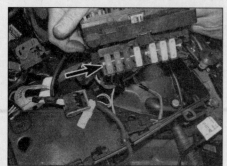

3.2 More fuses are located under the engine compartment fuseboard

3.3a Pull down the cover to access the facia fusebox

3.3b Undo the securing screws to access the engine compartment fusebox

3.5 Use the plastic pliers supplied to pull the fuse from its socket

3.8 Cooling fan relay (arrowed)

4.4 Remove the steering column shrouds

4 A list of circuits each fuse protects is given in the Peugeot vehicle handbook and later in this Manual with the wiring diagrams.

5 To remove a fuse, first switch off the circuit concerned (or the ignition), and then pull the fuse out of its terminals using the small plastic pliers supplied **(see illustration)**. The wire within the fuse should be visible; if the fuse has blown it will be broken or melted.

6 Always renew a fuse with one of the correct rating; never use a fuse with a different rating from that specified. The fuse rating is stamped on the top of the fuse; the fuses are also colour-coded as follows. Refer to the wiring diagrams for details of the fuse ratings and the circuits protected.

Colour	Rating
Orange	5A
Red	10A
Blue	15A
Yellow	20A
Clear or white	25A
Green	30A

7 Never renew a fuse more than once without tracing the source of the trouble. If the new fuse blows immediately, find the cause before renewing it again; a short to earth as a result of faulty insulation is most likely. Where a fuse protects more than one circuit, try to isolate the fault by switching on each circuit in turn (where possible) until the fuse blows again. Always carry a supply of spare fuses of each relevant rating on the vehicle; a spare of each rating should be clipped into the fusebox.

Relays

8 The majority of relay functions are incorporated into the built-in system interface (BSI) unit (see Section 23). Other relays are located in the fuse/relay box in the engine compartment and the cooling fan relay(s) is/are located in front panel **(see illustration)**.

9 If a circuit or system controlled by a relay develops a fault and the relay is suspect, operate the system. If the relay is functioning, it should be possible to hear it 'click' as it is energised. If this is the case, the fault lies with the components or wiring of the system. If the relay is not being energised, then either the relay is not receiving a main supply or a switching voltage, or the relay itself is faulty. Testing is by the substitution of a known good unit, but be careful – while some relays are identical in appearance and in operation, others look similar but perform different functions.

10 To remove a relay, first ensure that the relevant circuit is switched off. The relay can then simply be pulled out from the socket, and pushed back into position.

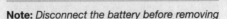

4 Switches – removal and refitting

Note: *Disconnect the battery before removing*

any switch, and reconnect the lead after refitting the switch (see Chapter 5A).

Ignition switch

1 Refer to Chapter 10.

Steering column switches

2 Remove the driver's airbag as described in Section 22.

3 Remove the steering wheel as described in Chapter 10.

4 Unscrew the two lower steering column shroud securing screws. Unclip and lift off the upper shroud, then remove the lower shroud **(see illustration)**.

5 Disconnect the wiring connectors from the rear of the switch assembly **(see illustration)**.

Caution: Take great care not to damage the switch assembly retaining catches.

6 If required, the cruise control switch (left-hand side) and remote radio/audio control switch (right-hand side) can be unclipped from the combination switch assembly **(see illustrations)**.

7 If the switch assembly is to be refitted, immobilise the airbag rotary contact disc with adhesive tape. Note that as long as the wheels are in the straight-ahead position, the contact disc should lock in position. Slacken the switch assembly retaining clamp, then using a small screwdriver, carefully prise the retaining catches away from the column

4.5 Wiring connections on the rear of the switch assembly

4.6a Unclip the cruise control switch . . .

4.6b . . . and radio/audio control switch

4.7a Slacken the clamp retaining bolt (arrowed) . . .

4.7b . . . then release the upper (arrowed) . . .

and lift the switch assembly from place **(see illustrations)**.

8 Although refitting is a reversal of removal, the airbag contact unit built into the switch assembly must be set in the correct position as follows:

9 Ensure the wheels are in the straight-ahead position.

10 If refitting the existing switch assembly, simply remove the adhesive tape applied during removal.

11 If the new switch assemblies are manufactured by Delphi or Valeo a setting-up procedure must be carried out. Units supplied by other manufacturers are supplied with the contact ring immobilised in the correct position by a self-adhesive label, which should be removed just prior to steering wheel refitment.

12 The following procedure applies to new or used Delphi or Valeo units. Press in the centre collar of the rotary contact unit, then gently rotate the collar clockwise until it comes to a stop. Turn the collar 2.5 revolutions anti-clockwise until the three triangles are in line, and the contact needle is in the third groove **(see illustration)**. If the steering wheel is not to be fitted immediately, immobilise the contact in this position with adhesive tape. **Note:** *If*

a new switch assembly if fitted to a vehicle with ESP (electronic stability programme) the unit must be initialised using dedicated test equipment. Entrust this task to a Peugeot dealer or suitably-equipped specialist.
Caution: Do not turn the collar anti-clockwise until the 'stop' has been reached – the unit will be irreparably damaged.

Audio unit control stalk and cruise control switch

13 Undo the two screws securing the steering column lower shroud in place, then lift the rear edge of the upper shroud and disengage the lugs at the front edge **(see illustration 4.4)**.

14 Release the clips and slide the switch from position, disconnecting the wiring plug(s) as the unit is withdrawn **(see illustration 4.6a and 4.6b)**.

15 Refitting is the reversal of removal.

Central locking, alarm and ESP switches

16 The facia-mounted switches for the central locking, alarm and ESP are located in the heater/ventilation control panel, and cannot be renewed separately. If any switch is faulty, the complete control panel must be renewed – refer to Chapter 3 for details.

4.7c . . . and lower securing clips (arrowed)

Heating/ventilation control

17 The switches are an integral part of the heater/ventilation control panel, and cannot be renewed separately. If any switch is faulty, the complete control panel must be renewed – refer to Chapter 3 for details.

Headlight height adjustment

18 Unclip the trim cover from the right-hand side of the facia panel **(see illustration)**.

19 Reach inside the right-hand side of the facia panel, and release the retaining clips at the rear of the switch and remove it from the

4.12 Align the marks on the rotary contact unit

4.18 Unclip the trim cover from the facia

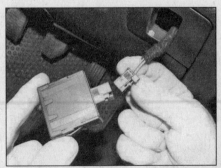

4.19 Disconnect the wiring plug from the switch

4.20 Disconnect the wiring plug connector . . .

4.21a . . . release the securing clips . . .

4.21b . . . and withdraw the switch from the trim panel

facia. Disconnect the wiring connector from the switch (see illustration).

Passenger airbag on/off switch

20 Unclip the trim cover from the right-hand side of the facia panel and disconnect the wiring connector from the rear of the switch (see illustration).
21 Release the retaining clips at the rear of the switch and remove it from the panel (see illustrations).

Courtesy light switch

22 The courtesy light switches are an integral part of the door lock assemblies. Refer to Chapter 11 for door lock removal and refitting details.

Luggage area light switch

23 The luggage compartment light switch

function is integral with the tailgate/boot lock assembly. For tailgate/boot lock removal, refer to Chapter 11.

Glovebox illumination switch

24 The switch is integral with the light. Remove the light as described in Section 6.

Brake light switch

25 Refer to Chapter 9.

Handbrake warning light switch

26 Remove the centre console as described in Chapter 11.
27 Disconnect the switch wiring connector, then unclip the switch from the handbrake mounting bracket (see illustrations).
28 Refitting is the reverse of removal.

Sunlight sensor

29 Remove the facia centre air vents and upper grille panel as described in Chapter 11, Section 27.
30 Disconnect the wiring connector and release the retaining clips at the rear of the switch, and remove it from the grille panel (see illustration).
31 Refitting is the reverse of removal.

Windscreen rain sensor

32 Ensure the ignition is switch off, and then unclip the trim cover from the sensor on the top of the windscreen (see illustration).
33 Disconnect the wiring connector then carefully release the side retaining clips and remove the rain sensor from the windscreen (see illustration).
Caution: Do not touch the rain sensor lens or the windscreen glass in the area of the sensor. These areas must be kept spotlessly clean if the sensor is to function correctly.
34 Refitting is the reverse of removal, ensuring the sensor is securely retained by its securing the clips in the windscreen. Note: *If a new sensor is being fitted, it will be necessary to remove the protective film from the sensor prior to installation.*
35 On completion, check the sensor operation by spraying the screen with water (wiper stalk in the auto position).

4.27a Disconnect the wiring plug connector . . .

4.27b . . . and release the switch from the mounting bracket

4.30 Disconnect the wiring connector from the sensor

4.32 Unclip the trim cover . . .

4.33 . . . and disconnect the wiring connector from the sensor

5.4 Unclip the protective cover from the rear of the light unit

5.5 Disconnect the headlight bulb wiring plug

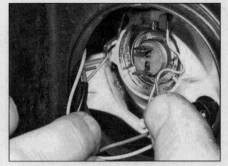

5.6a Release the retaining clip . . .

5 Bulbs (exterior lights) – renewal

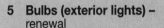

General

1 Whenever a bulb is renewed, note the following points:
 a) *Remember that, if the light has just been in use, the bulb may be extremely hot.*
 b) *Always check the bulb contacts and holder, ensuring that there is clean metal-to-metal contact between the bulb and its live(s) and earth. Clean off any corrosion or dirt before fitting a new bulb.*
 c) *Wherever bayonet-type bulbs are fitted (see Specifications), ensure that the live contact(s) bear firmly against the bulb contact.*
 d) *Always ensure that the new bulb is of the correct rating, and that it is completely clean before fitting it; this applies particularly to headlight/foglight bulbs (see below).*

Headlight

2 Where fitted, remove the plastic cover from above the rear of the headlight unit. The cover is secured by expanding plastic rivets. Push in the centre pins a little, then prise the complete rivets from place and release the side clip.
3 When handling the new bulb, use a tissue or clean cloth to avoid touching the glass with the fingers; moisture and grease from the skin can cause blackening and rapid failure of

5.6b . . . and remove the bulb

this type of bulb. If the glass is accidentally touched, wipe it clean using methylated spirit.

Dipped beam

Note: *Some vehicles are fitted with Xenon bulbs (D2S-35W); it is recommended that a Peugeot dealer or specialist renew these.*
4 Reach behind the headlamp, and unclip the dipped beam's protective cover and remove it **(see illustration)**.
5 Disconnect the wiring plug from the bulb **(see illustration)**.
6 Release the bulb retaining clip, and withdraw the bulb **(see illustrations)**.
7 Install the new bulb, ensuring that its locating tabs are correctly seated in the light cut-outs, and secure it in position with the retaining clip.
8 Reconnect the wiring plug, and refit the protective cover.

5.9 Unclip the protective cover from the rear of the light unit

Main beam

9 Reach behind the headlamp, and unclip the main beam's protective cover and remove it **(see illustration)**.
10 Disconnect the wiring plug from the bulb **(see illustration)**.
11 Release the bulb retaining clip, and withdraw the bulb **(see illustrations)**.
12 Install the new bulb, ensuring that it's located correctly in the light unit cut-out, and secure it in position with the retaining clip.
13 Reconnect the wiring plug, and refit the protective cover.

Sidelight

14 Where fitted, remove the plastic cover from above the rear of the headlight unit. The cover is secured by expanding plastic rivets. Push in the centre pins a little, then prise the

5.10 Disconnect the headlight bulb wiring connector

5.11a Release the retaining clip . . .

5.11b . . . and remove the bulb

5.16a Pull the bulbholder from the rear of the light unit . . .

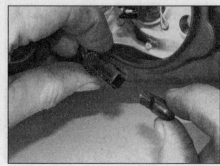

5.16b . . . and then pull the bulb from the holder

5.19a Rotate the bulbholder anti-clockwise . . .

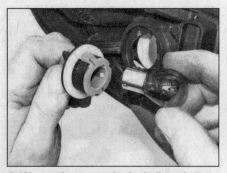

5.19b . . . then press in the bulb and rotate it anti-clockwise to remove it

5.21a Push the side repeater to one side . . .

5.21b . . . and ease it out of the wing panel

complete rivets from place and release the side clip.
15 Reach behind the headlight and unclip the dipped beam protective cover and remove it **(see illustration 5.4)**.
16 Squeeze together the retaining clips and pull the bulbholder from the rear of the headlight unit. The bulb is of the capless (push-fit) type, and can be removed by simply pulling it out of the holder **(see illustrations)**.
17 Refitting is the reverse of the removal procedure, ensuring that the bulbholder seal is in good condition.

Front direction indicator

18 Where fitted, remove the plastic cover from above the rear of the headlight unit. The

cover is secured by expanding plastic rivets. Push in the centre pins a little, then prise the complete rivets from place and release the side clip.
19 Rotate the bulbholder anti-clockwise, and free it from the rear of the headlight unit. The bulb is a bayonet-fit in the holder, and can be removed by pressing it in and rotating it anti-clockwise **(see illustrations)**.
20 Refitting is the reverse of the removal procedure, ensuring that the bulbholder seal is in good condition.

Side repeater

21 Push the light unit to the front or rear to free its retaining clip, and then ease it out from the front wing **(see illustrations)**.
22 Disconnect the wiring connector from the

light unit **(see illustration)**. The bulb is part of the light unit; the side repeater will need to be renewed as a complete unit.
23 Refitting is a reversal of the removal procedure.

Front foglight

24 The front foglights are located in the front bumper. Chock the rear wheels then jack up the front of the vehicle and support it on axle stands (see *Jacking and vehicle support*). Release the liner from the front of the wheel arch by removing the fasteners **(see illustration)**.
25 Reach up under the front bumper and disconnect the wiring connector from the foglight bulbholder **(see illustration)**.
26 Turn the bulbholder 90° anti-clockwise

5.22 Disconnect the wiring connector from the light unit

5.24 Remove the undershield from under the bumper

5.25 Disconnect the wiring plug connector . . .

5.26 . . . and then rotate the bulbholder anti-clockwise to remove

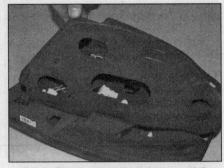

5.30 Unclip the seal from the rear of the light unit

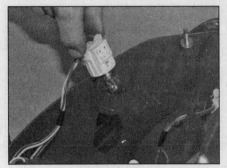

5.31 Squeeze together the tabs and remove the bulbholder . . .

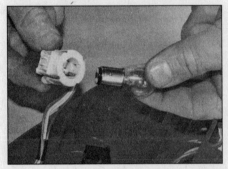

5.32 . . . then press in the bulb and rotate it anti-clockwise to remove it

5.35 Unclip the bulbholder from the rear of the light unit . . .

5.36 . . . then press in the bulb and rotate it anti-clockwise to remove it

and withdraw it from the rear of the foglight, then remove the bulb (see illustration).

27 When handling the new bulb, use a tissue or clean cloth to avoid touching the glass with the fingers; moisture and grease from the skin can cause blackening and rapid failure of this type of bulb. If the glass is accidentally touched, wipe it clean using methylated spirit.
28 Fit the new bulb using a reversal of the removal procedure.

Rear light cluster

Saloon models

29 Remove the relevant rear light unit as described in Section 7.
30 Unclip the foam seal from the rear of the light unit (see illustration).
31 Squeeze together the retaining tabs

and remove the bulbholder assembly (see illustration).
32 All the bulbs have bayonet fittings. The relevant bulb can be removed by pressing it inwards, and then rotating it anti-clockwise before withdrawing (see illustration).
33 Refitting is the reverse of removal, ensuring the light unit and bulbholder seals are in good condition.

Estate (SW) models

34 Remove the relevant rear light unit as described in Section 7.
35 Unclip the plastic bulbholder from the rear of the light unit (see illustration).
36 All the bulbs have bayonet fittings. The relevant bulb can be removed by pressing it inwards, and then rotating it anti-clockwise before withdrawing (see illustration).

37 Refitting is the reverse of removal, ensuring the light unit and bulbholder seals are in good condition.

Rear foglight

Estate (SW) models

38 The rear foglights on estate models are located in the rear tailgate. Remove the tailgate inner trim panel as described in Chapter 11.
39 Disconnect the wiring connector from the foglight bulbholder (see illustration).
40 Turn the bulbholder through 90° and withdraw it from the rear of the foglight (see illustration).
41 The bulbs have bayonet fittings, remove by carefully pressing the bulb inwards, and then rotating it anti-clockwise before withdrawing (see illustration).

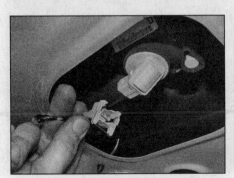

5.39 Disconnect the wiring plug connector . . .

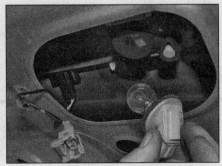

5.40 . . . and then rotate the bulbholder anti-clockwise to remove

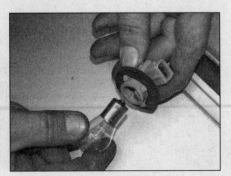

5.41 Press in the bulb and rotate it anti-clockwise to remove it

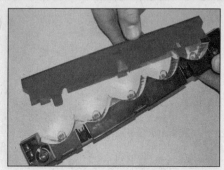

5.44 Unclip the red lens . . .

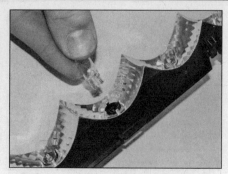

5.45 . . . and then pull the capless bulb from the light unit

5.50a Carefully prise the light lens from place

5.50b . . . and then pull the capless bulb from the light unit

42 Fit the new bulb using a reversal of the removal procedure.

High-level brake light

Saloon models

43 Remove the high-level brake light unit as described in Section 7.
44 Unclip the red light lens from the light unit base **(see illustration)**.
45 Each bulb is of the capless (push-fit) type, and can be removed by simply pulling it out of the bulbholder **(see illustration)**.

46 Fit the new bulb using a reversal of the removal procedure.

Estate (SW) models

47 Remove the high-level brake light unit as described in Section 7.
48 The bulbs fitted to the high-level brake light on estate models are light emitting diodes (LEDs). The light unit will need to be renewed as a complete item, or may be able to be repaired by an electrical specialist.
49 Refitting is the reverse of removal.

Number plate light

Saloon models

50 Using a small flat-bladed screwdriver, carefully prise the end of the lens downwards, and remove it. The bulb is of the capless (push-fit) type, and can be removed by simply pulling it out of the light unit **(see illustrations)**.
51 Refitting is the reverse of the removal procedure, ensuring that the lens is securely clipped in position.

Estate (SW) models

52 Using a small flat-bladed screwdriver, carefully prise the end of the lens downwards, and remove it. The bulb is of the capless (push-fit) type, and can be removed by simply pulling it out of the light unit.
53 Refitting is the reverse of the removal procedure, ensuring that the lens is securely clipped in position.

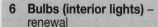

6 Bulbs (interior lights) – renewal

General

1 Refer to Section 5, paragraph 1.

Front console light

2 Using a flat bladed-screwdriver, carefully ease the light unit lens from the light base **(see illustration)**.
3 The bulb is of the capless (push-fit) type, and can be removed by simply pulling it out of the bulbholder **(see illustration)**.
4 Refitting is the reverse of the removal procedure

Passenger compartment lights

5 Using a flat bladed-screwdriver, carefully ease the light unit out of position and

6.2 Prise the lens from the light unit . . .

6.3 . . . and pull the bulb from the holder

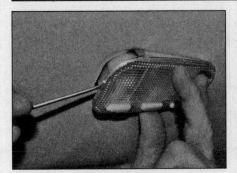

6.5 Prise the light unit from place in the headlining

6.6a Prise the lens from the light unit . . .

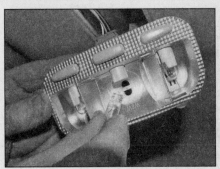

6.6b . . . and pull the bulb from the holder

disconnect it from the wiring connector **(see illustration)**.

6 Carefully prise the lens from the light. The bulb is of the capless (push-fit) type, and can be removed by simply pulling it out of the bulbholder **(see illustrations)**.

7 Refitting is the reverse of the removal procedure.

Instrument panel lights

8 The instrument panel and warning lights are illuminated by integral LEDs. It is not possible to renew them independently of the panel. Instrument panel renewal is described in Section 9.

Heating/ventilation control illumination

9 The heating control panel and switches are illuminated by integral LEDs. It is not possible to renew them independently of the panel. Heater control panel can be removed as described in Chapter 3.

Multifunction display illumination

10 The multifunction control panel is illuminated by integral LEDs. It is not possible to renew them independently of the panel. Remove the multifunction display as described in Section 10.

Ashtray illumination

11 Unclip the ashtray and remove it from the front of the centre console.

6.15 Unclip the light unit from inside the glove compartment . . .

12 Disconnect the wiring connector and free the bulbholder from the rear of the ashtray and pull the bulb out from its holder.

13 Securely fit the new bulb to its holder then clip the holder back into position on the console. Refit the ashtray.

Switch illumination

14 All of the switches that are illuminated are done so by LEDs. These LEDs are an integral part of the switch and cannot be renewed separately. Renewal will therefore require renewal of the complete switch assembly (see Section 4).

Glovebox illumination

15 Open the glovebox, and carefully prise the front end of the light from place. Remove the

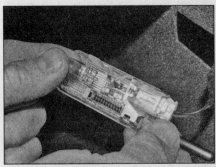

6.16 . . . and pull the bulb from the holder

light unit, and disconnect the wiring plug as it is withdrawn **(see illustration)**. Note that the switch is integral with the light.

16 The capless bulb simply pulls from the bulbholder **(see illustration)**.

Luggage compartment lights

17 Using a flat bladed-screwdriver, carefully ease the light unit out of position and disconnect it from the wiring connector **(see illustration)**.

18 Release the retaining clips and carefully prise open the cover from the rear of the light unit. The bulb is of the capless (push-fit) type, and can be removed by simply pulling it out of the bulbholder **(see illustrations)**.

19 Refitting is the reverse of the removal procedure.

6.17 Unclip the light unit from inside the luggage compartment

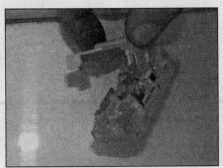

6.18a Unclip the rear of the light unit . . .

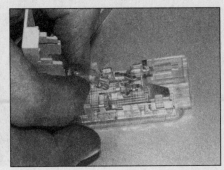

6.18b . . . and pull the bulb from the holder

7.2 Slide up the locking latch and disconnect the wiring plug

7.3 Undo the three headlamp mounting bolts (arrowed)

7.11 Remove the luggage compartment side cover

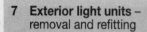

7 Exterior light units – removal and refitting

Headlight

1 Remove the front bumper (see Chapter 11).
2 Reach behind the headlight, slide down the locking latch and disconnect the wiring connector from the rear of the headlight unit **(see illustration)**.
3 Slacken and remove the three mounting bolts and free the headlight unit from its mounting, then manoeuvre the unit out of position **(see illustration)**.
4 When refitting, offer up the headlight unit and securely reconnect its wiring connectors.
5 Position the headlight in its aperture, and then refit and tighten the headlight mounting bolts.
6 Check the operation of the headlight, then refit the front bumper.
7 Check the headlight beam alignment using the information given in Section 8.

Front indicator side repeater

8 Push the light unit to the front or rear to free its retaining clip, and then ease it out from the front wing **(see illustrations 5.21a and 5.21b)**.
9 Disconnect the wiring connector from the

7.12 Disconnect the wiring plug from the rear of the light unit

light unit **(see illustration 5.22)**. The bulb is part of the light unit; the side repeater will need to be renewed as a complete unit.
10 Refitting is a reversal of the removal procedure.

Rear light unit

Saloon models

11 Turn the securing clips and move the luggage compartment side trim panel to one side to access the rear of the light unit **(see illustration)**.
12 Reach inside the rear panel and disconnect the wiring connector from the rear of the light

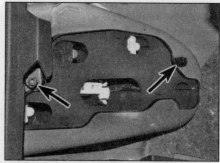

7.13a Undo the two securing nuts (arrowed) . . .

unit **(see illustration)**. Unclip the wiring loom retaining clip from the rear of the light unit.
13 Undo the two securing nuts and withdraw the light unit from the rear of the vehicle **(see illustrations)**.
14 Refitting is the reverse of removal, ensuring the light unit seal is in good condition.

Estate (SW) models

15 Turn the securing clips and move the luggage compartment side trim panel to one side to access the rear of the light unit **(see illustration)**.
16 Undo the securing nut and withdraw the light unit from the rear of the vehicle. Using a

7.13b . . . and remove the rear light unit

7.15 Remove the luggage compartment side cover

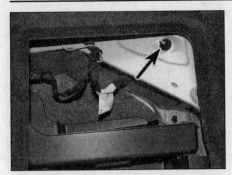

7.16a Undo the securing nut (arrowed) . . .

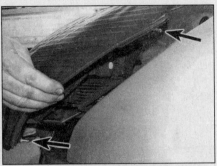

7.16b . . . then pull the light unit to release the locating pegs (arrowed) . . .

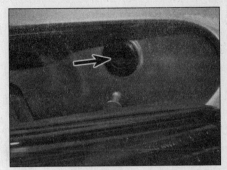

7.16c . . . from the grommets (arrowed) in the inner wing panel

flat lever (spatula), carefully lever the side of the light unit outwards, away from the rear wing panel, to release the upper and lower locating pegs **(see illustrations)**.

17 Disconnect the wiring connector from the rear of the light unit, as it is withdrawn from the vehicle **(see illustration)**.

18 Refitting is the reverse of removal, ensuring the light unit seal is in good condition.

High-level brake light

Saloon models

19 Carefully unclip the trim cover from the high-level brake light, on the top of the rear screen **(see illustration)**.

20 Undo the two securing screws and withdraw the light unit from the rear screen **(see illustration)**.

21 Disconnect the wiring connector from the light unit, as it is withdrawn from the rear screen **(see illustration)**.

22 Refitting is the reverse of removal.

Estate (SW) models

23 Open the upper glass hatch and carefully unclip the trim cover from the high-level brake light, on the top of the rear screen **(see illustration)**.

24 Undo the two securing screws and withdraw the light unit from the rear screen **(see illustration)**.

25 Disconnect the wiring connector from the light unit, as it is withdrawn from the rear screen **(see illustration)**.

26 Refitting is the reverse of removal.

7.17 Disconnect the wiring plug from the rear of the light unit

7.19 Unclip the plastic trim cover . . .

7.20 . . . undo the two retaining screws . . .

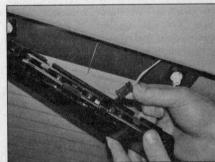

7.21 . . . and disconnect the wiring plug

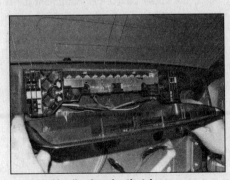

7.23 Unclip the plastic trim cover . . .

7.24 . . . undo the two retaining screws (arrowed) . . .

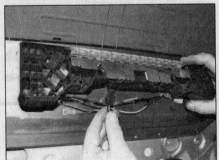

7.25 . . . and disconnect the wiring plug

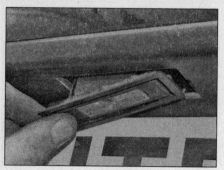

7.27 Unclip the light unit . . .

7.28 . . . and disconnect the wiring plug

7.31 Number plate lights (arrowed) –
estate (SW) models

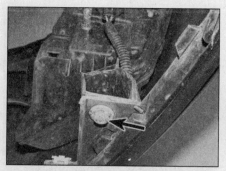

7.35 Front foglight mounting bolt
(arrowed)

7.39a Release the retaining clips
(arrowed) . . .

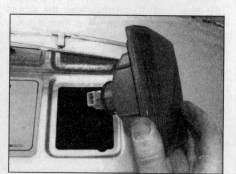

7.39b . . . and unclip the light unit from the
tailgate

Number plate light

Saloon models

27 Using a small flat-bladed screwdriver, carefully prise the end of the light unit downwards, and remove it from the bumper **(see illustration)**.
28 Disconnect the wiring connector from the light unit, as it is withdrawn **(see illustration)**.
29 Refitting is the reverse of the removal procedure.

Estate (SW) models

30 Using a small flat-bladed screwdriver, carefully prise the end of the light unit downwards, and remove it from the tailgate trim panel. Disconnect the wiring connector from the light unit, as it is withdrawn.
31 To make removal of the light units easier, it may be necessary to remove the rear tailgate handle trim **(see illustration)**, as described in Chapter 11.
32 Refitting is the reverse of the removal procedure.

Front foglights

33 The front foglights are located in the front bumper. Chock the rear wheels then jack up the front of the vehicle and support it on axle stands (see *Jacking and vehicle support*). Release the liner from the front of the wheel arch by removing the fasteners **(see illustration 5.24)**.
34 Reach up under the front bumper and disconnect the wiring connector from the rear of the foglight.

35 Undo the lower mounting bolt and withdraw the foglight unit from behind the front bumper **(see illustration)**.
36 Refitting is a reversal of removal.

Rear foglights

Estate (SW) models

37 The rear foglights on estate models are located in the rear tailgate. Remove the tailgate inner trim panel as described in Chapter 11.
38 Disconnect the wiring connector from the foglight bulbholder **(see illustration 5.39)**.
39 Release the securing clips on the inside of the tailgate, and then withdraw the light unit from the outside of the tailgate **(see illustrations)**.
40 Refitting is a reversal of removal.

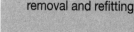

8 Headlight beam alignment – general information

1 Accurate adjustment of the headlight beam is only possible using optical beam-setting equipment, and this work should therefore be carried out by a Peugeot dealer or suitably-equipped workshop.
2 For reference, the vertical and horizontal alignment of the headlights can be adjusted by rotating the adjuster assemblies, which are accessible at the rear of the headlight casing **(see illustration)**.

3 On models equipped with headlight leveling, ensure the adjuster switch inside the vehicle, is set to position 0 before the headlights are adjusted.

9 Instrument panel – removal and refitting

Removal

1 Disconnect the battery as described in Chapter 5A.
2 Sit in the driver's seat and lower the steering column to its lowest position, this will make removal of the instrument panel easier.
3 Using a thin screwdriver or flat lever, carefully unclip the upper part of the instrument panel

8.2 Headlight adjusters (arrowed) on the
rear of the light unit

from the upper trim cover, to release the upper locating pegs **(see illustrations)**.

4 Release the locking lever and then disconnect the wiring connector, as the instrument panel is withdrawn **(see illustration)**. Should the instrument panel develop a fault, have the vehicle's self-diagnosis facility interrogated by a Peugeot dealer or suitably-equipped specialist. With the exception of the panel 'glass', no parts are available separately for the instrument panel, if faulty; the complete assembly must be renewed.

Refitting

5 Refitting is a reversal of removal, ensuring that the upper locating lugs of the panel engage correctly inside the facia housing.

10 Clock/multifunction unit – removal and refitting

Removal

1 Ensure the ignition is switched off, and then remove the audio unit as described in Section 17.

2 Undo the two retaining screws and remove the trim panel, from around the multifunction display unit **(see illustration)**.

3 Undo the four retaining screws (two each side) and remove the multifunction display unit from the facia **(see illustration)**.

4 Disconnect the wiring plug connectors, as the unit is withdrawn **(see illustration)**.

Refitting

5 Refitting is a reversal of removal.

11 Cigarette lighter/accessory socket – removal and refitting

Removal

1 Remove the ashtray from the front of the centre console for the front accessory socket. Remove the ashtray from the rear of the centre console to access the rear accessory socket. Remove the left-hand trim panel in the

9.3a Unclip the upper part of the instrument panel . . .

9.3b . . . in the three positions (arrowed) . . .

9.3c . . . and withdraw the instrument panel

9.4 Release the locking clip and disconnect the wiring plug

luggage compartment for the rear accessory socket.

2 Carefully release the retaining clips and slide the illumination light assembly off the base of the accessory socket, taking great care not to break its electrical contacts.

3 Open the accessory socket cover then release the tangs and push out the metal insert/accessory socket. The plastic outer section can then be removed from the console.

Refitting

4 Align the plastic outer sections tab with the cut-out, and then insert it into the ashtray/ console.

5 Align the bulbholder contact on the metal insert with the holder tangs on the plastic outer then clip the insert into position.

6 Slide the illumination light assembly onto the metal insert and clip it securely onto the plastic outer.

7 Ensure the accessory socket is correctly assembled, and then refit the ashtray(s) or rear trim panel.

12 Horn – removal and refitting

Removal

1 The horns are located behind the front bumper, on the left-hand side, below the headlamp.

2 Remove the front bumper as described in Chapter 11.

10.2 Remove the trim from around the display unit

10.3 Remove the multifunction display unit from the facia . . .

10.4 . . . and disconnect the wiring plug connectors

12.3 Horn mounting bracket securing bolts (arrowed)

13.1 Alignment marks on windscreen for wiper blade

13.2 Undo the wiper arm retaining nut

3 Disconnect the wiring connector(s) then slacken the mounting bracket bolts and remove the horns from the vehicle **(see illustration)**.

Refitting

4 Refitting is a reversal of removal.

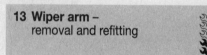

13 Wiper arm – removal and refitting

Note: *The wiper arms are a very tight fit on their spindles and it is likely that a puller will be needed to remove them safely and without damage.*

Front wiper

Removal

1 Operate the wiper motor, then switch it off so that the wiper arm returns to the at-rest position. Check the alignment mark on the glass or stick tape to the screen alongside the wiper blade to ensure correct fitment.
2 Lift up the wiper arm spindle nut cover (where fitted) then slacken and remove the spindle nut.
3 Lift the blade off the glass, and pull the wiper arm off its spindle. If the arm is very tight, free it from the spindle using a suitable puller.

Refitting

4 Ensure that the wiper arm and spindle splines are clean and dry, then refit the arm to the spindle, aligning the wiper blade with the tape fitted on removal, or the alignment marks provided.
5 Refit the spindle nut, tightening it securely, and clip the nut cover (where fitted) back into position.

Rear wiper

Removal

6 Operate the wiper motor, then switch it off so that the wiper arm returns to the at-rest position. Stick tape to the screen alongside the wiper blade to ensure the correct position for fitment.

13.3a If required, use a small puller to remove ...

7 Insert a small screwdriver, release the retaining clips and remove the plastic cover from the tailgate glass hatch switch/handle **(see illustration)**.
8 Remove the wiper arm spindle nut, lift the blade off the glass, and pull the wiper arm off its spindle. If the arm is very tight, free it from the spindle using a suitable puller **(see illustration)**.

Refitting

9 Ensure that the wiper arm and spindle splines are clean and dry, then refit the arm to the spindle, aligning the wiper blade with the tape fitted on removal, or the alignment marks provided.
10 Refit the spindle nut, tightening it securely, and clip switch/handle cover back into position.

14.2a Unclip the scuttle panel trim ...

13.3b ... the wiper arm from the wiper motor spindle

14 Windscreen wiper motor and linkage – removal and refitting

Note: *There are two windscreen wiper motors fitted, each wiper arm has an individual motor fitted to the corner of the scuttle panel.*

Removal

1 Remove the relevant wiper arm, as described in Section 13.
2 Unclip the trim panel from the lower part of the windscreen, and remove it from the scuttle panel. To make access easier, unbolt the plastic cover from the top of the suspension strut **(see illustrations)**.

14.2b ... and remove the plastic cover from the top strut mounting

14.3 Unclip the wiring loom from the mounting bracket

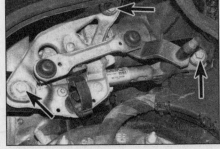

14.4a Undo the wiper motor mounting bracket bolts (arrowed) . . .

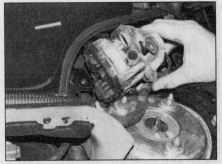

14.4b . . . and withdraw it from inside the scuttle panel

3 Unclip the wiring loom from the retaining clip on the wiper motor bracket **(see illustration)**.
4 Each wiper motor assembly is secured by three mounting bolts. Undo the bolts; lift the assembly and manoeuvre it out from the scuttle panel **(see illustrations)**.
5 Disconnect the wiring plug from the wiper motor as it is removed **(see illustration)**.
6 Unclip the linkage from the drive on the motor, and then undo the three retaining bolts to remove the motor from the mounting bracket **(see illustration)**.

Refitting

7 Refitting is a reversal of removal, ensuring all fasteners are securely tightened. Note that before tightening the three mounting bolts, ensure the assembly is correctly fitted inside the scuttle panel and the wiring plug is connected securely.

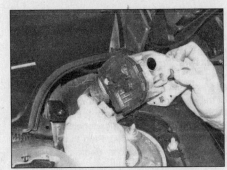

14.5 Disconnect the wiring connector as the motor is removed

3 Disconnect the wiring connector from wiper motor **(see illustration)**.
4 The wiper motor assembly is secured by three mounting bolts, undo the bolts and remove the motor from the tailgate **(see illustration)**.
5 If required, undo the retaining nut and withdraw the plastic drive wheel from the end of the motor drive spindle **(see illustration)**. Take care when removing as this can be a tight fit on the wiper spindle, note its fitted position on the spindle for refitting.

Refitting

6 Manoeuvre the wiper motor into position and secure with the mounting bolts.
7 Reconnect the wiring connector to the motor, and then refit the trim panel to the tailgate.

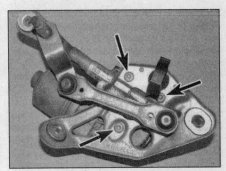

14.6 Wiper motor-to-mounting bracket retaining bolts (arrowed)

8 Close the glass hatch, turn on the ignition, and then check the operation of the wiper.

---

16 Washer system components – removal and refitting

1 The washer reservoir is located behind the right-hand side of the front bumper and supplies both the windscreen and tailgate washers via the same pump. On models equipped with headlight washers, the reservoir also supplies the headlight washer jets via an additional pump.

Washer fluid reservoir

2 Remove the front bumper as described in Chapter 11.

---

15 Tailgate window wiper motor – removal and refitting

Removal

1 Ensure the ignition is turned off and open the upper glass hatch part of the tailgate.
2 Remove the tailgate upper plastic trim as described in Chapter 11, Section 25.

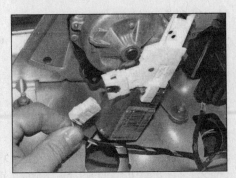

15.3 Disconnect the wiring connector . . .

15.4 . . . and undo the wiper motor retaining bolts (arrowed) . . .

15.5 Undo the retaining nut and remove the drive wheel

16.4 Disconnect the wiring plug from the top of the pump

16.5a Undo the reservoir front mounting bolt (arrowed) . . .

16.5b . . . and release the fastener (arrowed) at the side

3 Note the correct fitted location of the washer hose, and then disconnect the hose(s) from the washer pump(s). Plug the end of the hoses to prevent fluid loss, or drain the washer reservoir before removal.
4 Disconnect the wiring connector from the top of the washer pump **(see illustration)**.
5 Slacken and remove the retaining bolt at the front of the reservoir and then release the fastener at the side of the reservoir and remove it from the inner wing panel **(see illustrations)**.
6 Refitting is the reverse of removal, ensuring that the hoses are securely reconnected. Refill the reservoir and check for leaks.

Washer pump

7 Remove the front right-hand wheel arch

16.8 Washer pump fitted to base of reservoir

16.16 Unclip the upper trim panel from the tailgate

liner. The liner is secured by various fasteners, including screws and plastic rivets. Pull out the centre pins, and then prise the plastic rivets from place, and manoeuvre the front section of the liner out from underneath the wing.
8 The washer pump is on the lower rear edge of the reservoir **(see illustration)**.
9 Note the correct fitted location of the washer hose, and then disconnect the hose(s) from the washer pump(s). Plug the end of the hoses to prevent fluid loss, or drain the washer reservoir before removal.
10 Disconnect the wiring connector from the top of the washer pump **(see illustration 16.4)**.
11 Position a container beneath the reservoir to catch the washer fluid (if not already drained), as the pump is removed.

16.14 Unclip the washer jet from the bonnet

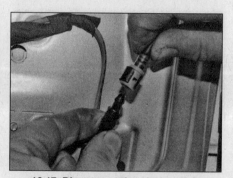

16.17 Disconnect the washer pipe connection

12 Carefully ease the pump out from the reservoir, and recover its sealing grommet. Wash off any spilt fluid with cold water.
13 Refitting is the reverse of removal, using a new sealing grommet if the original shows signs of damage or deterioration. Refill the reservoir and check the pump grommet for leaks on completion.

Windscreen washer jet

14 Open the bonnet and pull back the bonnet insulation panel to gain access to the base of the windscreen washer jets. Depress the retaining clips and ease the jet out of position, disconnect the washer hose from the jet as it is removed **(see illustration)**.
15 On refitting, clip the jet into the bonnet and reconnect the hose. Check the operation of the washer jet.

Tailgate washer jet

16 Open the tailgate glass hatch and unclip the upper plastic trim panel **(see illustration)**.
17 Disconnect the washer hose on the right-hand side of the tailgate **(see illustration)**, and then free the jet from the upper part of the tailgate, taking care not to damage the paintwork.
18 Refitting is the reverse of removal. Make sure the washer hose is connected securely and check operation of the washer jet.

Headlight washer jet

19 Carefully prise the jet cover from the bumper, and pull the assembly out to its full extent. To prevent any damage to the paintwork around the washer jet, use masking tape on the front bumper.
20 Have an assistant grip the washer jet tube with a pair or grips, then depress the two retaining clips and pull the jet from the tube.
21 To remove the washer cylinders, remove the front bumper as described in Chapter 11, then disconnect the washer tubing, and unclip the cylinders.
22 Refitting is the reverse of removal.

17.2 Insert two pins (one each side) of the unit, to release the securing clips . . .

17.3a . . . pull the audio unit from place . . .

17.3b . . . then disconnect the aerial and wiring connectors

17 Audio unit – removal and refitting

Note: *The following procedure is for the range of equipment fitted by Peugeot.*

Removal

1 Ensure the audio unit and ignition is switched off.
2 If fitted, remove Torx screws or insert a small screwdriver/punch into the hole on each side of the unit and pushing it in until the clip releases **(see illustration)**.
3 Once both retaining clips have been released, slide the audio unit out of position. Disconnect the wiring connections and aerial lead **(see illustrations)** and remove the unit from the vehicle.

Refitting

4 Prior to refitting, reset the unit retaining clips.
5 Securely reconnect the aerial lead and wiring connectors then slide the unit back into position, taking care not to trap the wiring.

18 Loudspeakers – removal and refitting

Removal

Door speakers

1 Remove the door inner trim panel as described in Chapter 11.
2 Slacken and remove the retaining screws then remove the speaker from the door,

disconnecting the wiring connector as it becomes accessible **(see illustrations)**.

Front tweeter

3 Carefully prise the tweeter cover from the top corner of the facia and remove it along with the tweeter **(see illustrations)**. Disconnect the wiring plug as it is withdrawn.
4 Rotate the tweeter speaker to release it from the retaining clips in the cover, if required.

Refitting

5 Refitting is a reversal of removal. Ensure the trim panels are clipped securely in position and are correctly located behind the edges of the sealing strips.

19 Radio aerial – removal and refitting

Note: *Saloon and coupe models have the aerials incorporated in the rear screen.*

Removal

Roof aerial

1 On estate models, the aerial mast is a screw-fit in its base and is easily removed **(see illustration)**.
2 To remove the complete aerial on estate models where the aerial is mounted on the rear of the roof, open the tailgate then free the sealing strip from the top of its aperture. Unclip

18.2a Undo the retaining screws (arrowed) . . .

18.2b . . . and remove the speaker from the door

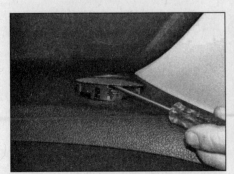

18.3a Carefully prise the tweeter cover from the facia . . .

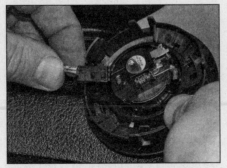

18.3b . . . and disconnect the wiring connector

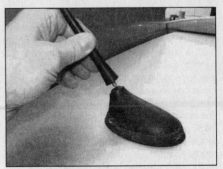

19.1 Unscrew the aerial mast from the base

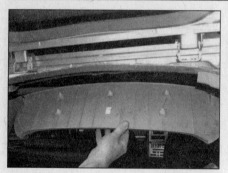

19.2 Unclip the trim panel from the rear of the headlining

19.4 Aerial booster – saloon/coupe models

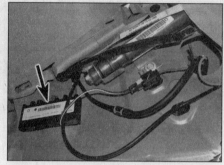

19.5 Aerial booster (arrowed) – estate (SW) models

the rear trim panel **(see illustration)**, and then carefully lower the rear of the headlining to gain access to the aerial retaining nut.
3 Disconnect the wiring plug, undo the nut and remove the aerial base from the roof panel.

Aerial booster

4 On saloon and coupe models, remove the rear parcel shelf carpet as described in Chapter 11. Disconnect the wiring connectors, undo the retaining bolt and remove the booster from the right-hand rear of the parcel shelf **(see illustration)**.
5 On estate (SW) models, remove the right-hand rear D-pillar trim panel as described in Chapter 11. Disconnect the wiring connector(s), undo the retaining bolt and remove the booster from the right-hand rear body pillar **(see illustration)**.

Refitting

6 Refitting is the reverse of removal.

20 Engine immobiliser and anti-theft alarm system – general information

Note: *This information is applicable only to the systems fitted by Peugeot as standard equipment.*

Engine immobiliser

1 An engine immobiliser system is fitted as standard to all models and the system is operated automatically every time the ignition key is inserted/removed.
2 The immobiliser system ensures the vehicle can only be started using the original Peugeot ignition key. The key contains an electronic chip (transponder), which is programmed with a code. When the key is inserted into the ignition switch it uses the current present in the sensor ring (which is fitted to the ignition switch housing) to send a signal to the immobiliser electronic control module (ECM). The ECM is incorporated into the built-in systems interface (BSI) unit (see Section 23). The ECM checks this code every time the ignition is switched on. If the key code does not match the ECM code, the ECM will disable the starter, fuel and ignition (as applicable) to prevent the engine being started.
3 When the vehicle is new, a confidential

security card is supplied along with the other vehicle documentation. This card contains the security code, which your Peugeot dealer requires when carrying out any work on the immobiliser system. Keep this card in a safe place at home; never store it in the vehicle. If the ignition key is lost, a new one can be obtained from a Peugeot dealer. Take the confidential security card and all the existing keys along to your Peugeot dealer who will supply a new key and reprogramme all the keys with a new security code; this will render the lost key useless.
Caution: Without the confidential security card, it will not be possible to have the keys and immobiliser system reprogrammed.
4 Any problems with the engine immobiliser system should be referred to a Peugeot dealer.

Anti-theft alarm system

5 Most models covered in this were also equipped with an anti-theft alarm system as standard equipment. The system was available as a option on all other models. The alarm is automatically armed when the deadlocking is set using the remote central locking transmitter and is disarmed when the doors are unlocked using the remote transmitter. The alarm system has switches on the bonnet, tailgate and each of the doors and also has ultrasonic sensing, which detects movement inside the vehicle, via sensors mounted on either side of the vehicle interior.
6 When the system is activated, the direction indicators will flash continuously for two seconds and the indicator light on the alarm switch, fitted to the rear section of the centre console, will flash continuously. **Note:** *If the bonnet, tailgate or one of the doors are not properly closed when the alarm is set, the siren will sound briefly. If the bonnet/tailgate/door (as applicable) is properly closed within 45 seconds the alarm will be armed. If not the alarm will remain disarmed.*
7 If for some reason the remote central locking transmitter fails whilst the alarm is armed, the alarm can be disarmed using the key. To do this, open the door with the key, and then enter the vehicle, noting that the alarm will sound as the door is opened. Insert the key and switch on the ignition, the immobiliser will recognise the key and will switch off the alarm.

8 If required, the ultrasonic sensing facility of the alarm can be switched off, whilst retaining the switched side of the system. To switch off the ultrasonic sensing, with the ignition switched off, depress the alarm switch (mounted on the facia above the centre air vents) until the alarm indicator light on the switch is continuously lit. Get out of the vehicle and operate the deadlocking function using the remote transmitter to arm the alarm. The direction indicators will flash as normal but only the switched (door, tailgate and bonnet) side of the alarm system will be operational. This facility is useful, as it allows you to leave the windows/sunroof open, and still arm the alarm. If the windows/sunroof are left open with the ultrasonic sensing not switched off, the alarm may be falsely triggered by a gust of wind.
9 Prior to disconnecting the battery, the alarm system should be disabled; this will prevent the alarm sounding when the battery is disconnected/reconnected. To do this, switch on the ignition then immediately depress and hold the alarm switch for two seconds; the indicator light on the switch should then flash rapidly for approximately three seconds indicating the alarm has been disabled. Switch off the ignition and disconnect the battery.
10 Once the battery has been reconnected, operate the deadlocking with the remote transmitter then unlock the vehicle. The alarm will be set as normal the next time the deadlocking is set.
11 Should the alarm system become faulty, the vehicle should be taken to a Peugeot dealer for examination.

21 Airbag system – general information and precautions

Warning: Before carrying out any operations on the airbag system, disconnect the battery (see Chapter 5A) and wait at least two minutes. Remove the centre console (see Chapter 11), and then release the retaining clip and disconnect the wiring connector(s) from the airbag control module. When the operations are complete, securely reconnect the control module then refit the centre

console (see Chapter 11). Make sure no one is inside the vehicle when the battery is reconnected, and then with the driver's door open, switch the ignition on from outside vehicle and check the operation of the airbag warning light.

1 All models in the range are fitted with a driver's airbag, passenger's airbag, side front airbags, and side curtain airbags.

2 The airbag system is triggered in the event of a heavy frontal impact above a predetermined force, depending on the point of impact. The airbag is then inflated within milliseconds, and forms a safety cushion between the cabin occupants and the vehicle interior. This prevents contact between the upper body and vehicle interior, and therefore greatly reduces the risk of injury. The airbag then deflates almost immediately. The control module also operates the front seat belt tensioner mechanisms at the same time (see Chapter 11).

3 The side airbags are fitted to the seat back of each front seat. Each airbag unit has its own lateral acceleration sensor, which is mounted onto the vehicle body on the outside of each front seat. The side airbags are not linked in any way and operate individually.

4 The curtain airbags are fitted behind the windscreen pillars and headlining on each side of the passenger cabin.

5 Every time the ignition is switched on, the airbag control module performs a self-test. The self-test takes approximately six seconds and during this time the warning light in the instrument panel will be illuminated. After the self-test is complete, the warning light will go out (unless the passenger airbag unit has been deactivated – see paragraph 6). If the warning light fails to come on, remains illuminated after the self-test period, or comes on at any time when the vehicle is being driven, there is a fault in the airbag system. The vehicle should be taken to a Peugeot dealer for examination at the earliest possible opportunity.

6 Most vehicles with a passenger airbag are equipped with a disabling switch fitted to the right-hand side of the facial panel. The switch is operated using the ignition key and switches off the passenger airbag (it is not possible to disable the driver's or side/curtain airbags) to enable a rear-facing child seat to be installed in the passenger seat. Whilst the passenger airbag is disabled, the airbag warning light on the instrument panel will remain illuminated all the time.

⚠ *Warning: Do not subject the area of the body around the control module to any form of shock, which could trigger the system.*

• Note that the airbags must not be subjected to temperatures in excess of 100°C. When the airbag is removed, ensure that it is stored the correct way up to prevent possible inflation.
• Do not allow any solvents or cleaning agents to contact the airbag assemblies. They must be cleaned using only a damp cloth.
• The airbags and control module are both sensitive to impact. If either is dropped or damaged they should be renewed.
• Disconnect the airbag control module wiring connector prior to using arc-welding equipment on the vehicle.

• Never fit a rear-facing child seat to the front passenger seat unless the passenger airbag has been disabled (paragraph 6).
• Peugeot recommend that the airbag units be renewed every ten years.

22 Airbag system components – removal and refitting

⚠ *Warning: Refer to the precautions given in Section 21 before carrying out the following operations.*

Driver's airbag

Removal

1 Disconnect the battery (see Chapter 5A) and wait at least two minutes. Remove the centre console (see Chapter 11), and then release the retaining clips and disconnect the wiring connectors from the airbag control module in front of the gear lever/selector **(see illustration)**.

2 With the wheel in the straight-ahead position and the steering lock engaged, insert thin flat-bladed screwdriver into the hole in the underside rear of the steering wheel boss, and release the retaining clips **(see illustrations)**.

3 Carefully lift the airbag unit away from the steering wheel, release the locking clips, and disconnect the wiring connectors from each side of the airbag and the earth wire on the rear as they become accessible **(see illustrations)**.

22.1 Airbag control module (arrowed)

22.2a Insert a long screwdriver into the rear of the steering wheel . . .

22.2b . . . to release the airbag retaining spring (arrowed)

22.3a Withdraw the airbag from the steering wheel . . .

22.3b . . . and release the locking clips to disconnect the wiring plugs

22.3c Earth connection (arrowed) on the rear of the airbag unit

22.12 Undo the airbag securing nuts from around the outside of the unit

22.13 Undo the airbag mounting bracket retaining screw (arrowed)

22.14a Release the locking clips . . .

 Warning: Do not knock or drop the airbag unit and store it with its padded surface uppermost.

Refitting

4 Securely reconnect the wiring connectors then seat the airbag unit in the steering wheel, ensuring the wiring does not become trapped. Note that the main connectors are colour-coded to correspond with their respective sockets.
5 Fit the airbag unit in to place on the steering wheel; press it into place until the retaining clips engage.
6 Securely reconnect the airbag control module wiring connectors. Refit the centre console (see Chapter 11). Make sure no one is inside the vehicle then reconnect the battery. With the driver's door open, switch the ignition on from outside vehicle and check the operation of the warning light.

Driver's knee airbag

7 Disconnect the battery and wait at least two minutes.
8 Using a thin spatula, release the knee airbag panel from its mountings under the steering column.
9 Refitting is the reverse of removal.

Passenger airbag

Removal

10 Disconnect the battery and wait at least two minutes. Remove the centre console (see Chapter 11), and then release the retaining clip and disconnect the wiring connectors from the airbag control module in front of the gear lever/selector **(see illustration 22.1)**.

11 The passenger airbag is bolted to the underside of the facia panel. Remove the facia as described in Chapter 11, Section 27.
12 Working your way around the airbag unit, slacken and remove the nuts securing the airbag to the underside of the facia panel **(see illustration)**.
13 Undo the retaining screw, securing the airbag unit to the facia crossmember **(see illustration)**.
14 Release the securing clips and disconnect the wiring plug connectors from each end of the airbag unit **(see illustrations)**. Release the wiring harness from any retaining clips, noting their fitted position and harness routing.
15 Release the airbag from the locating studs and remove it from the facia.

Refitting

16 Fit the airbag unit to the underside of the facia trim, ensuring the wiring is correctly routed, and the nuts are securely tightened.
17 The remainder of refitting is the reverse of removal. On completion, securely reconnect the airbag control module wiring connectors. Refit the centre console (see Chapter 11). Make sure no one is inside the vehicle then reconnect the battery. With the driver's door open, switch the ignition on from outside vehicle and check the operation of the warning light.

Airbag control module

Removal

18 Disconnect the battery and wait at least two minutes. Remove the centre console (see Chapter 11), and then release the retaining

clip and disconnect the wiring connectors from the airbag control module in front of the gear lever/selector **(see illustration 22.1)**.
19 Unscrew the retaining nuts then remove the control module from the vehicle **(see illustration)**.

Refitting

20 Refit the control module, making sure the arrow on the top of the unit is pointing towards the front of the vehicle. Refit the control module retaining nuts and tighten them to the specified torque.
21 Securely reconnect the airbag control module wiring connectors.
22 Refit the centre console (see Chapter 11). Make sure no one is inside the vehicle then reconnect the battery. With the driver's door open, switch the ignition on from outside vehicle and check the operation of the warning light.

Side airbag

23 Removal and refitting of the side airbag units should be entrusted to a Peugeot dealer. The seat must be dismantled to enable the airbag unit to removed/refitted.

Side airbag acceleration sensor

Removal

24 Remove the relevant front seat as described in Chapter 11.
25 Referring to Section 25 of Chapter 11, remove the B-pillar lower trim panels.
26 Peel back the carpet to gain access to the side airbag control module **(see illustration)**.

22.14b . . . and disconnect the wiring plugs from each side

22.19 Airbag control module mounting nuts (arrowed)

22.26 Airbag acceleration sensor location (arrowed)

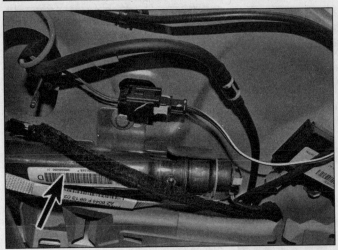

22.30 Rear curtain airbag unit (arrowed) located behind headlining

23.1 Built-in system interface (BSI) unit location

27 Disconnect the wiring connector then undo the retaining bolt (or drill out the rivet) and remove the control module from the vehicle.

Refitting

28 Refitting is the reverse of removal, tightening the acceleration sensor bolt securely.

Curtain airbag

29 Removal and refitting of the curtain airbag units should be entrusted to a Peugeot dealer.
30 The inner trim panels (see Chapter 11, Section 25) and the headlining must be partially removed to enable the airbag units to be removed (see illustration).

---

23 Built-in systems interface (BSI) unit and fusebox – general, removal and refitting

General information

1 The built-in systems interface (BSI) unit is an electronic control module, which controls a variety of functions, normally controlled by individual control modules and relays. The BSI unit is located behind the glove compartment on the passenger's side of the facia, where it is the rear part of the passenger compartment fusebox (see illustration). The BSI unit controls the following functions (not all functions are fitted to all models).

- *Direction indicator/hazard warning lights.*
- *Windscreen/tailgate wiper motors.*
- *Rear screen heating element.*
- *Immobiliser system.*
- *Anti-theft alarm system.*
- *Lights-on/ignition key warning buzzer.*
- *Central locking/deadlocking, including the remote central locking receiver.*
- *Door open indicator.*
- *Courtesy light delay timer.*
- *Automatic transmission audible warning system.*

2 Should any of the above functions become faulty, first check the condition of the fuses. If this fails to locate the problem, take the vehicle to a Peugeot dealer for testing. The only satisfactory way to test the BSI unit is by substitution with another unit that is known to be functioning correctly.

Removal

BSI/fusebox

3 Disconnect the battery (see Chapter 5A).
4 Remove the passenger side glovebox as described in Section 27 of Chapter 11, to access the BSI unit. It may be necessary to partially withdraw the facia from the front of the vehicle to completely remove the BSI unit.
5 Release the two lower retaining clips at the front, and then lift the cover upwards to release the upper locating pegs (see illustrations).
6 Lift up the front edge of the unit and slide it from place (see illustration).
7 Note their fitted positions, release the retaining clips then disconnect all the wiring connectors and remove the BSI unit from the vehicle. Note that there are several different designs of locking catches for the various connectors. Take your time to study the wiring connectors, and release them without using excessive force as they are easily damaged.

Engine compartment fusebox

8 Disconnect the battery (see Chapter 5A).
9 Remove the electronic control module from the engine compartment electrical box, as described in Section 12 of Chapter 4A.
10 Before disconnecting any of the wiring to the fusebox make a note of the wiring connections and the routing of the wiring loom.
11 Undo the retaining nut and disconnect

23.5a Release the front securing clips (arrowed) . . .

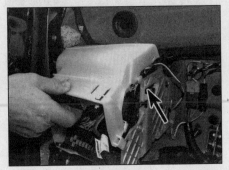

23.5b . . . and unclip the rear locating pegs (arrowed)

23.6 Withdraw the built-in system interface (BSI) unit from the housing

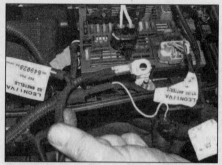

23.11 Disconnect the battery cable from the fusebox

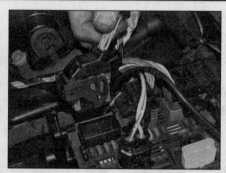

23.12a Release the locking clips . . .

23.12b . . . and disconnect the wiring plugs

23.13a Release the locking clips (arrowed) . . .

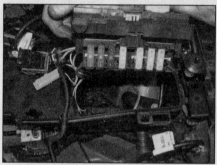

23.13b . . . and withdraw the fusebox from the housing

the battery cable from the front of the fusebox **(see illustration)**.

12 Note their fitted positions, release the retaining clips then disconnect all the wiring connectors from the top of the fusebox **(see illustrations)**. Note that there are several different designs of locking catches for the various connectors. Take your time to study the wiring connectors, and release them without using excessive force as they are easily damaged.

13 Release the two retaining clips, and then lift the fusebox upwards to release the locating pegs from the housing **(see illustrations)**. Note there are more fuses under the engine compartment fusebox.

14 If the fusebox needs to be completely removed from the vehicle, trace the wiring connectors from under the fusebox and disconnect them at their connectors. Note the position of the connectors and the routing of the wiring loom and then release the wiring retaining clips.

15 To remove the lower part of the fusebox housing, unclip the vent pipe from the front of the housing, and then undo the two retaining bolts and lift out the lower housing **(see illustrations)**. Unclip any wiring retaining clips from the housing as it is removed, noting their fitted position.

Refitting

16 Refitting is the reverse of removal, ensuring the wiring connectors are all securely reconnected.

23.15a Unclip the air vent pipe . . .

23.15b . . . undo the retaining bolts . . .

23.15c . . . and remove the lower housing

Peugeot 407 wiring diagrams

Diagram 1

At the time of writing, certain wiring diagram technical information was unavailable. As a result these diagrams are intended as a representative set covering most major electrical systems typically encountered on this model range.

WARNING: This vehicle is fitted with a supplemental restraint system (SRS) consisting of a combination of driver (and passenger) airbag(s), side impact protection airbags and seatbelt pre-tensioners. The use of electrical test equipment on any SRS wiring systems may cause the seatbelt pre-tensioners to abruptly retract and airbags to explosively deploy, resulting in potentially severe personal injury. Extreme care should be taken to correctly identify any circuits to be tested to avoid choosing any of the SRS wiring in error.

For further information see airbag system precautions in body electrical systems chapter.

Note: The SRS wiring harness can normally be identified by yellow and/or orange harness or harness connectors.

The prime method of wire identification is by the number code printed on each wire. Additionally, the wires can be identified by using the terminal pin numbers (moulded into each component or connector and shown in the diagrams).

To relate each diagram to the vehicle wiring, locate the relevant component or connector illustrated and find the wire(s) connected to the terminal pin(s) as shown in the diagram.

Caution: Whilst a number (indicating the function of that wire) may be printed on each wire, this is not always the case, and in such instances, this is reflected by the absence of such wire numbering on our diagrams. Similarly, numbering of the connector/component terminal pins is not always available from the manufacturers' source information and may also be missing from our diagrams.

Key to symbols

Solenoid actuator		Bulb		Wire splice, soldered joint, or unspecified connector	
Earth point	E7	Switch			
		Fuse	F26	Diode	
Wire identification	MC50A	Maxifuse fusible link	MF1	Light-emitting diode	
Connecting wires		Resistor		Item number	12
Dashed outline denotes part of a larger item, containing in this case an electronic or solid state device.	16GR 5 9 K	Variable resistor		Motor/pump	M
16GR - 16 pin grey connector, pins 5 & 9		Variable resistor		Heating element	

Engine fusebox ④

Fuse	Rating	Circuit protected
F1	20A	Engine management, engine cooling fan
F2	15A	Horn
F3	10A	Front/rear screen washer pump
F4	20A	Headlight washer pump
F5	15A	Fuel gauge, fuel pump, EGR
F6	10A	Auto. transmission
F7	10A	Power steering, coolant level switch, ESP
F8	15A	Starter
F9	10A	LH & RH headlights
F10	30A	Engine management
F11	40A	Blower motor relay
F12	30A	Front wiper
F13	40A	Built-in systems interface
F14	30A	Secondary air pump
MF1	50A	Engine cooling fan
MF2	40A	ESP
MF3	70A	Powersteering
MF4	80A	Built-in systems interface
MF5	80A	Luggage compartment fusebox
MF6	80A	Built-in systems interface
MF7	60A	Passenger compartment fusebox
MF8	20A	Suspension control unit

Built-in systems interface ⑥

Fuse	Rating	Circuit protected
F1	15A	Diagnostic connector, rear fusebox
F4	20A	Auto. transmission selector lever, memory seats, alarm, multifunction screen, audio/phone
F5	15A	Tyre pressure monitor, alarm
F6	10A	Diagnostic connector, auto. transmission, photochromic rear view mirror, stop light switch, vanity mirror lights, overhead console, SRS, ESP
F7	15A	Seatbelt control unit
F9	30A	Rear electric windows
F10	20A	Glove box light, front cigar lighter, 12v socket
F11	15A	Central locking
F12	30A	Electric windows, sunroof
F14	10A	Front wiper motor, memory seats, steering column adjustment switch, engine fusebox, luggage compartment fusebox
F15	15A	Instrument cluster, light sensor, seat adjustment, SRS, air conditioning
F16	30A	Central locking
F20	-	Spare
F21	-	Spare
F22	-	Spare

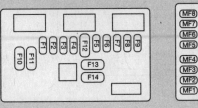

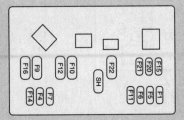

H47387

Peugeot 407 wiring diagrams

Diagram 2

Luggage compartment fusebox

Fuse	Rating	Circuit protected
F1	15A	Rear wiper
F2	15A	Fuel filler flap motor
F3	15A	Rear 12v accessory socket
F4	15A	Fuel additive control unit
F5	40A	Heated rear window

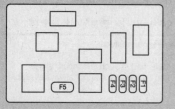

Engine fusebox (alternative) 4

Fuse	Rating	Circuit protected
F1	20A	Engine management
F2	15A	Horn
F3	10A	Front/rear screen washer pump
F4	20A	Headlight washer pump
F5	15A	Fuel gauge, fuel pump
F6	10A	ESP
F7	10A	Auto. transmission, stop light switch, photochromic rear view mirror
F8	25A	Starter
F9	10A	LH & RH headlights, stop light switch, power steering
F10	30A	Engine management
F11	40A	Air conditioning
F12	30A	Front wiper
F13	40A	Built-in systems interface
F14	-	Spare
F15	-	Spare
F16	-	Spare
F17	-	Spare
F18	-	Spare
F19	15A	Fuel additive pump, auto. transmission control unit
F20	10A	Engine management, fuel pump
F21	5A	Engine cooling fan
MF1	60A	ESP
MF2	20A	ESP
MF3	-	Spare
MF4	80A	Built-in systems interface
MF5	80A	Built-in systems interface
MF6	-	Spare
MF7	80A	Passenger fusebox
MF8	20A	Suspension, power steeering

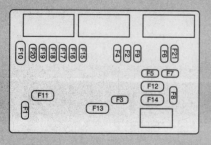

Built-in systems interface (alternative) 6

Fuse	Rating	Circuit protected
F1	15A	Windsreen wiper relay
F2	30A	Central locking
F3	5A	SRS
F4	20A	Diagnostic connector, sunroof, steering angle sensor, ESP
F5	30A	Electric windows
F6	30A	Electric windows, sunroof motor
F7	5A	Vanity mirror lights, overhead console, glovebox light
F8	20A	Alarm, multifunction screen, audio/phone
F9	30A	Front 12vsocket, front cigar lighter, passenger fusebox
F10	20A	Tyre pressure monitor
F11	15A	Central locking
F12	30A	Trailer, hands-free kit, parking aid
F13	5A	Engine fusebox
F14	15A	Air cnditioning, memory seats
F15	30A	Central locking
F17	40A	Heated rear window

Passenger fusebox (alternative) 26

Fuse	Rating	Circuit protected
F30	-	Spare
F31	-	Spare
F33	-	Spare
F34	-	Spare
F35	-	Spare
F36	25A	Audio amplifier
F37	15A	Auto. transmission
F38	20A	Heated seats, memory seats
F39	30A	Heared seats
F40	30A	Memory seats

Luggage compartment fusebox (alternative)

Fuse	Rating	Circuit protected
F1	15A	Trailer socket

Earth locations

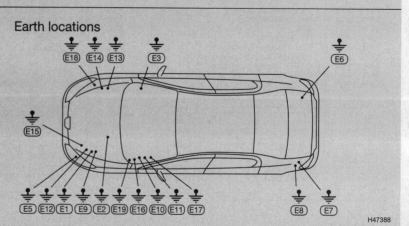

H47388

Colour codes

BA	White	OR	Orange
BE	Blue	RG	Red
BG	Beige	RS	Pink
GR	Grey	VE	Green
JN	Yellow	VI	Mauve
MR	Brown	VJ	Green/
NR	Black		Yellow

Key to items

1 Battery
2 Starter motor
3 Alternator
4 Engine fusebox
5 Ignition switch
6 Built-in systems interface
7 Instrument cluster
8 Engine management control unit
9 Engine coolant temperature sensor
10 Air conditioning pressostat
11 Engine cooling fan
12 Active thermostat
13 Coolant outlet solenoid
14 Coolant degassing solenoid
15 Glow plug control unit
16 Glow plugs

Diagram 3

H47389

Typical starting & charging

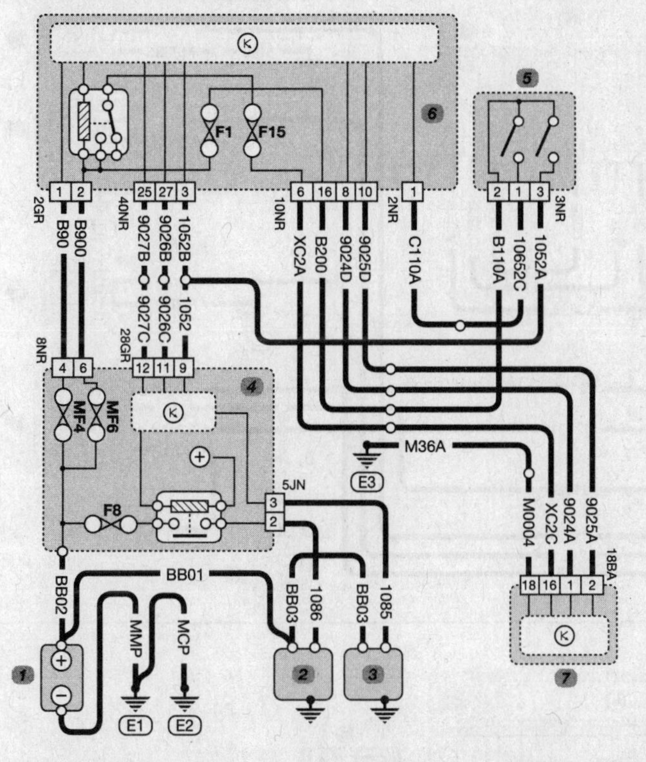

Typical pre/post heating

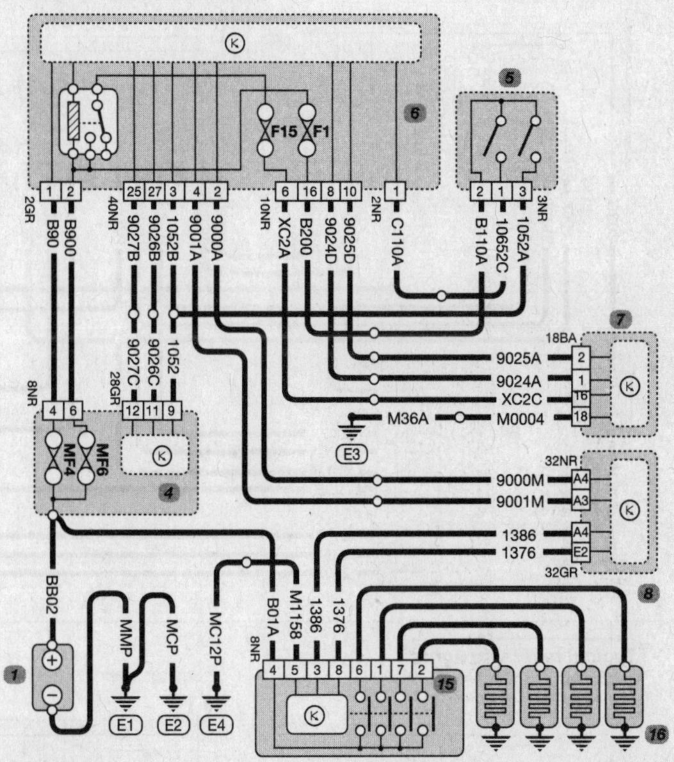

Typical engine cooling fan

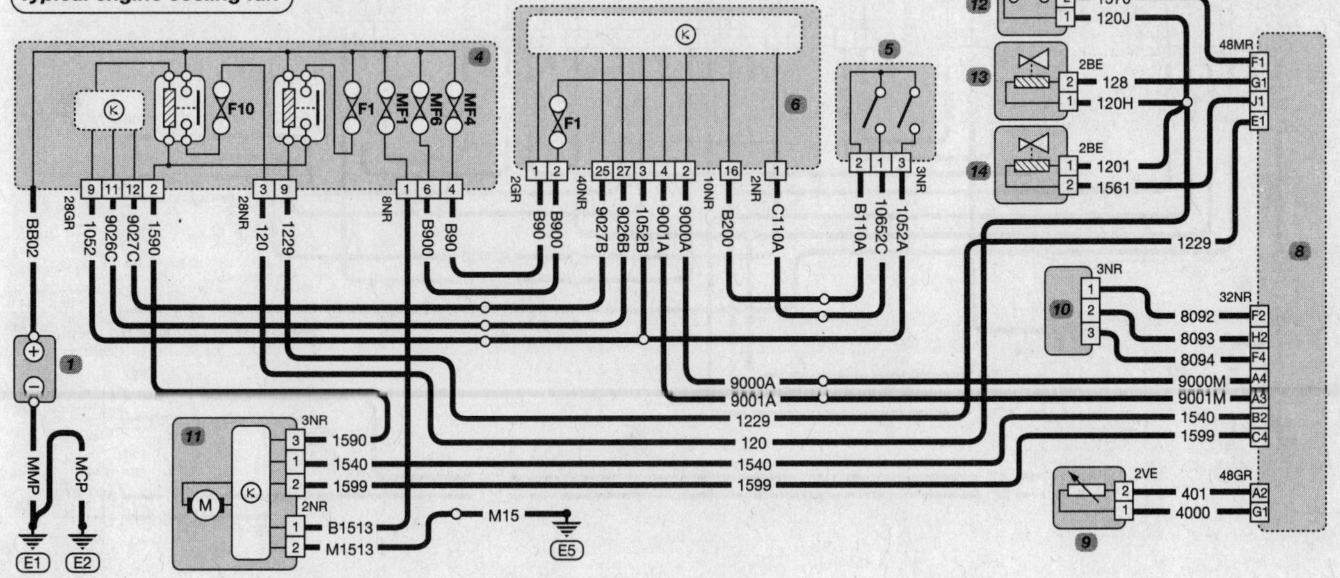

Colour codes

BA	White	**OR**	Orange
BE	Blue	**RG**	Red
BG	Beige	**RS**	Pink
GR	Grey	**VE**	Green
JN	Yellow	**VI**	Mauve
MR	Brown	**VJ**	Green/
NR	Black		Yellow

Key to items

1 Battery
4 Engine fusebox
5 Ignition switch
6 Built-in systems interface
8 Engine management control unit
20 High level brake light
21 Stop light switch
22 Reversing light switch
23 LH rear light unit
  a = reversing light
  b = stop light
24 RH rear light unit
  (as above)
25 ESP control unit
26 Passenger fusebox
27 Steering column control unit

Diagram 4

H47390

Typical stop lights

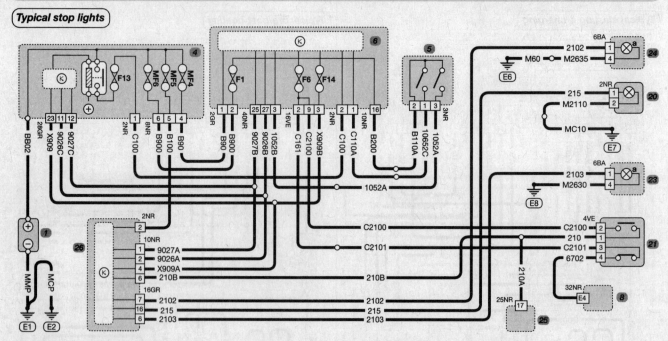

Typical reversing lights

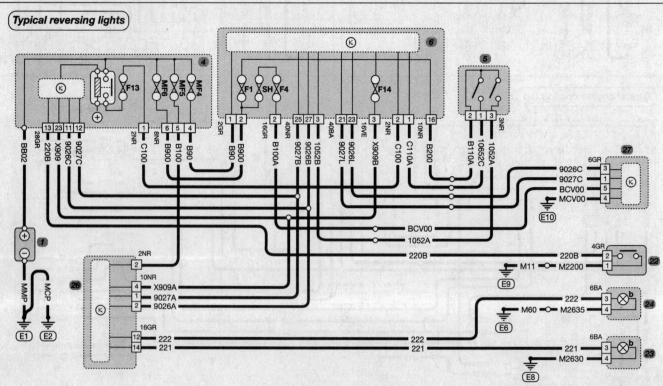

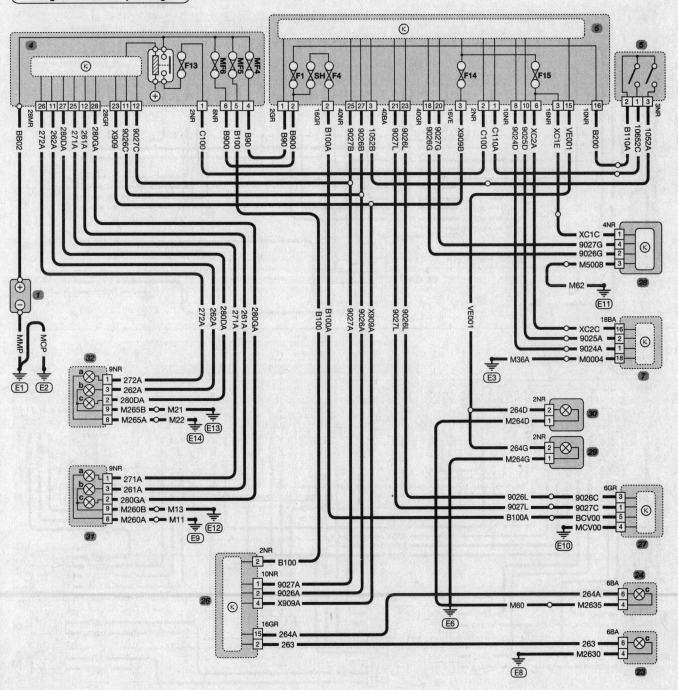

H47391

Colour codes

BA	White	OR	Orange
BE	Blue	RG	Red
BG	Beige	RS	Pink
GR	Grey	VE	Green
JN	Yellow	VI	Mauve
MR	Brown	VJ	Green/
NR	Black		Yellow

Key to items

1 Battery
4 Engine fusebox
5 Ignition switch
6 Built-in systems interface
7 Instrument cluster
23 LH rear light unit
  d = fog light
  e = direction indicator

24 RH rear light unit
  (as above)
26 Passenger fusebox
27 Steering column control unit
31 LH headlight unit
  d = direction indicator
32 RH headlight unit
  (as above)

35 LH front fog light
36 RH front fog light
37 LH indicator side repeater
38 RH indicator side repeater
39 Hazard warning light switch

Diagram 6

H47392

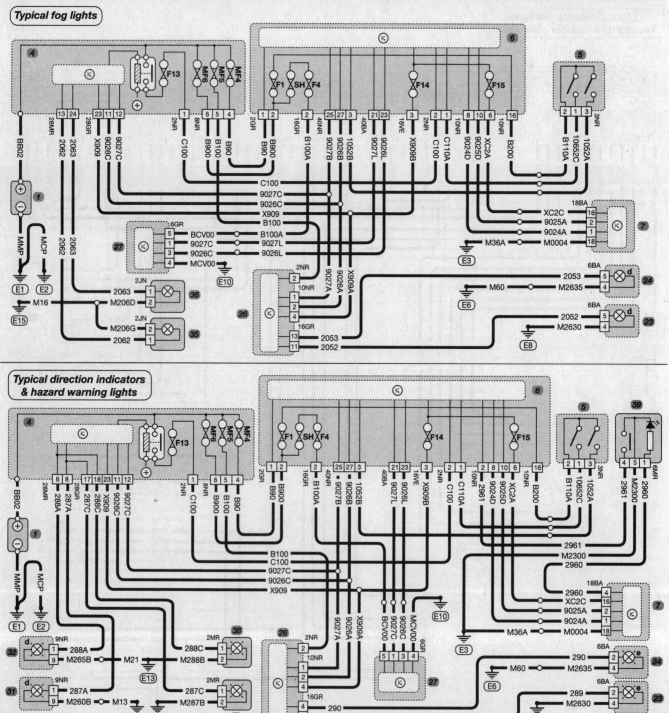

Typical fog lights

Typical direction indicators & hazard warning lights

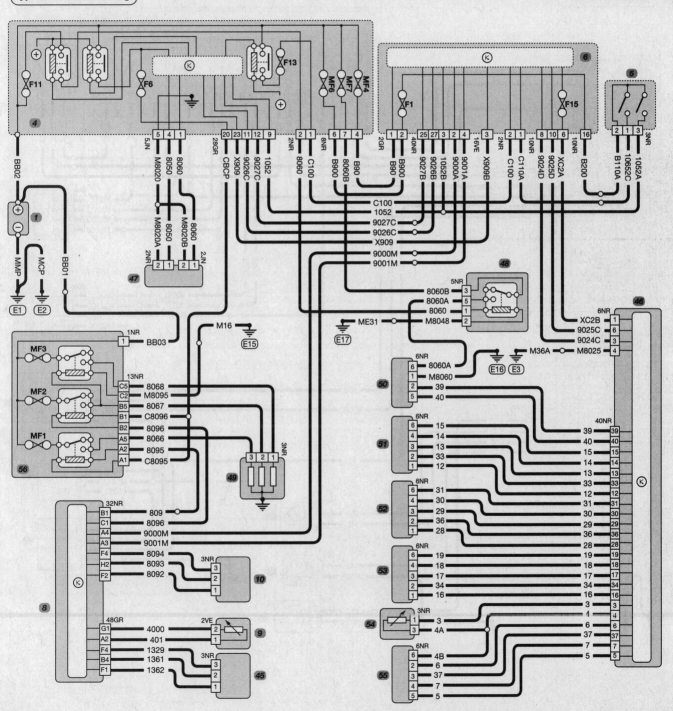

H47393

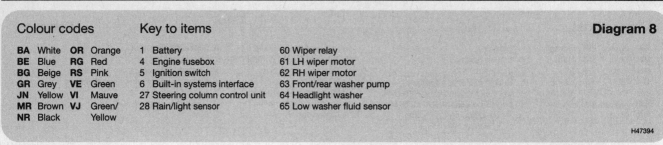

Colour codes

BA	White	**OR**	Orange
BE	Blue	**RG**	Red
BG	Beige	**RS**	Pink
GR	Grey	**VE**	Green
JN	Yellow	**VI**	Mauve
MR	Brown	**VJ**	Green/
NR	Black		Yellow

Key to items

1 Battery
4 Engine fusebox
5 Ignition switch
6 Built-in systems interface
27 Steering column control unit
28 Rain/light sensor
60 Wiper relay
61 LH wiper motor
62 RH wiper motor
63 Front/rear washer pump
64 Headlight washer
65 Low washer fluid sensor

Diagram 8

H47394

Typical wash/wipe

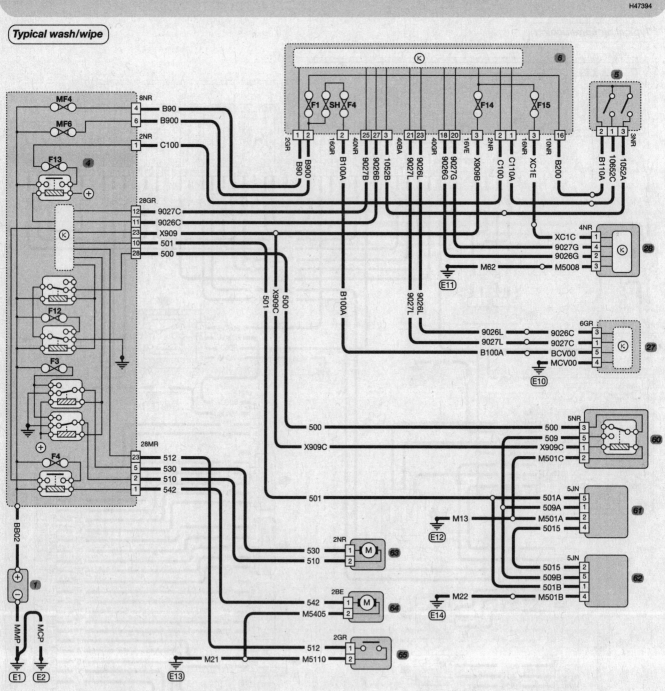

Colour codes

BA	White	OR	Orange
BE	Blue	RG	Red
BG	Beige	RS	Pink
GR	Grey	VE	Green
JN	Yellow	VI	Mauve
MR	Brown	VJ	Green/
NR	Black		Yellow

Key to items

1 Battery
4 Engine fusebox
5 Ignition switch
6 Built-in systems interface
8 Engine management control unit
21 Stop light switch
25 ESP control unit

70 Power steering pump
71 Steering angle sensor
72 LH front wheel sensor
73 RH front wheel sensor
74 LH rear wheel sensor
75 RH rear wheel sensor
76 Diagnostic connector

77 LH front pad wear sensor
78 RH front pad wear sensor
79 Low brake fluid switch
80 Yaw sensor

Diagram 9

H47395

Typical power steering

Typical ABS/ESP

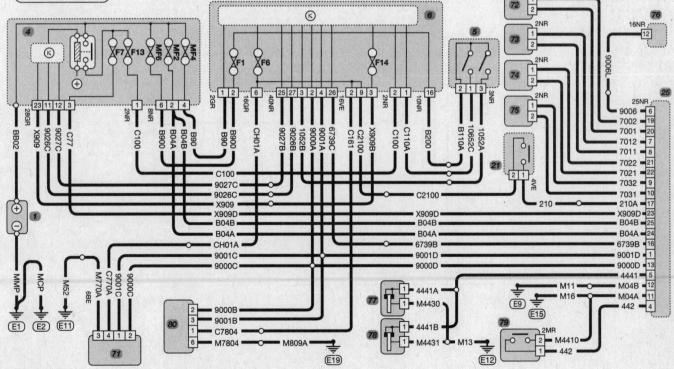

Dimensions and weights

Note: *All figures are approximate, and may vary according to model. Refer to manufacturer's data for exact figures.*

Dimensions

	Saloon/coupe	Estate (SW)
Overall length	4676 mm	4763 mm
Overall width:		
Excluding mirrors	1811 mm	1811 mm
Including mirrors.	2105 mm	2105 mm
Overall height (unladen)	1455 mm	1494 mm
Wheelbase	2725 mm	2725 mm

Weights

Kerb weight:
  1.6 litre engine . . . . 1659 kg
  2.0 litre engine:
    Manual transmission. . . . . 1735 kg
    Automatic transmission:
      DW10BTED4 engine . . . . 1797 kg
      DW10CTED4 engine . . . . 1815 kg
Maximum gross vehicle weight:*
  1.6 litre engine . . . . 2127 kg
  2.0 litre engine:
    Manual transmission. . . . . 2195 kg
    Automatic transmission:
      DW10BTED4 engine . . . . 2215 kg
      DW10CTED4 engine . . . . 2230 kg
Maximum gross train (vehicle and trailer) weight:*
  1.6 litre engine . . . . 3127 kg
  2.0 litre engine:
    Manual transmission. . . . . 3795 kg
    Automatic transmission:
      DW10BTED4 engine . . . . 3215 kg
      DW10CTED4 engine . . . . 3320 kg
Maximum towing weight:**
  Unbraked trailer:
    1.6 litre engine . . . . 750 kg
    2.0 litre engine . . . . 750 kg
  Braked trailer:
    1.6 litre engine . . . . 1000 kg
    2.0 litre engine:
      Manual transmission. . . . . 1600 kg
      Automatic transmission . . . . 1000 kg

* *Refer to the Vehicle Identification Plate for the exact figures for your vehicle – see 'Vehicle identification numbers' later in this Section.*
** *Ensure the combined weight of the trailer and vehicle never exceeds the gross train weight when towing.*

Fuel economy

Although depreciation is still the biggest part of the cost of motoring for most car owners, the cost of fuel is more immediately noticeable. These pages give some tips on how to get the best fuel economy.

Working it out

Manufacturer's figures

Car manufacturers are required by law to provide fuel consumption information on all new vehicles sold. These 'official' figures are obtained by simulating various driving conditions on a rolling road or a test track. Real life conditions are different, so the fuel consumption actually achieved may not bear much resemblance to the quoted figures.

How to calculate it

Many cars now have trip computers which will

display fuel consumption, both instantaneous and average. Refer to the owner's handbook for details of how to use these.

To calculate consumption yourself (and maybe to check that the trip computer is accurate), proceed as follows.

1. Fill up with fuel and note the mileage, or zero the trip recorder.
2. Drive as usual until you need to fill up again.
3. Note the amount of fuel required to refill the tank, and the mileage covered since the previous fill-up.
4. Divide the mileage by the amount of fuel used to obtain the consumption figure.

For example:

Mileage at first fill-up (a) = 27,903
Mileage at second fill-up (b) = 28,346
Mileage covered (b - a) = 443
Fuel required at second fill-up = 48.6 litres

The half-completed changeover to metric units in the UK means that we buy our fuel in litres, measure distances in miles and talk about fuel consumption in miles per gallon. There are two ways round this: the first is to convert the litres to gallons before doing the calculation (by dividing by 4.546, or see Table 1). So in the example:

48.6 litres ÷ 4.546 = 10.69 gallons
443 miles ÷ 10.69 gallons = 41.4 mpg

The second way is to calculate the consumption in miles per litre, then multiply that figure by 4.546 (or see Table 2).

So in the example, fuel consumption is:

443 miles ÷ 48.6 litres = 9.1 mpl
9.1 mpl x 4.546 = 41.4 mpg

The rest of Europe expresses fuel consumption in litres of fuel required to travel 100 km (l/100 km). For interest, the conversions are given in Table 3. In practice it doesn't matter what units you use, provided you know what your normal consumption is and can spot if it's getting better or worse.

Table 1: conversion of litres to Imperial gallons

litres	1	2	3	4	5	10	20	30	40	50	60	70
gallons	0.22	0.44	0.66	0.88	1.10	2.24	4.49	6.73	8.98	11.22	13.47	15.71

Table 2: conversion of miles per litre to miles per gallon

miles per litre	5	6	7	8	9	10	11	12	13	14
miles per gallon	23	27	32	36	41	46	50	55	59	64

Table 3: conversion of litres per 100 km to miles per gallon

litres per 100 km	4	4.5	5	5.5	6	6.5	7	8	9	10
miles per gallon	71	63	56	51	47	43	40	35	31	28

Maintenance

A well-maintained car uses less fuel and creates less pollution. In particular:

Filters

Change air and fuel filters at the specified intervals.

Oil

Use a good quality oil of the lowest viscosity specified by the vehicle manufacturer (see *Lubricants and fluids*). Check the level often and be careful not to overfill.

Spark plugs

When applicable, renew at the specified intervals.

Tyres

Check tyre pressures regularly. Under-inflated tyres have an increased rolling resistance. It is generally safe to use the higher pressures specified for full load conditions even when not fully laden, but keep an eye on the centre band of tread for signs of wear due to over-inflation.

When buying new tyres, consider the 'fuel saving' models which most manufacturers include in their ranges.

Driving style

Acceleration

Acceleration uses more fuel than driving at a steady speed. The best technique with modern cars is to accelerate reasonably briskly to the desired speed, changing up through the gears as soon as possible without making the engine labour.

Air conditioning

Air conditioning absorbs quite a bit of energy from the engine – typically 3 kW (4 hp) or so. The effect on fuel consumption is at its worst in slow traffic. Switch it off when not required.

Anticipation

Drive smoothly and try to read the traffic flow so as to avoid unnecessary acceleration and braking.

Automatic transmission

When accelerating in an automatic, avoid depressing the throttle so far as to make the transmission hold onto lower gears at higher speeds. Don't use the 'Sport' setting, if applicable.

When stationary with the engine running, select 'N' or 'P'. When moving, keep your left foot away from the brake.

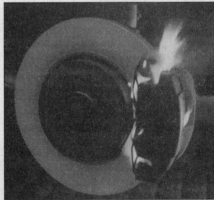

Braking

Braking converts the car's energy of motion into heat – essentially, it is wasted. Obviously some braking is always going to be necessary, but with good anticipation it is surprising how much can be avoided, especially on routes that you know well.

Carshare

Consider sharing lifts to work or to the shops. Even once a week will make a difference.

Electrical loads

Electricity is 'fuel' too; the alternator which charges the battery does so by converting some of the engine's energy of motion into electrical energy. The more electrical accessories are in use, the greater the load on the alternator. Switch off big consumers like the heated rear window when not required.

Freewheeling

Freewheeling (coasting) in neutral with the engine switched off is dangerous. The effort required to operate power-assisted brakes and steering increases when the engine is not running, with a potential lack of control in emergency situations.

In any case, modern fuel injection systems automatically cut off the engine's fuel supply on the overrun (moving and in gear, but with the accelerator pedal released).

Gadgets

Bolt-on devices claiming to save fuel have been around for nearly as long as the motor car itself. Those which worked were rapidly adopted as standard equipment by the vehicle manufacturers. Others worked only in certain situations, or saved fuel only at the expense of unacceptable effects on performance, driveability or the life of engine components.

The most effective fuel saving gadget is the driver's right foot.

Journey planning

Combine (eg) a trip to the supermarket with a visit to the recycling centre and the DIY store, rather than making separate journeys.

When possible choose a travelling time outside rush hours.

Load

The more heavily a car is laden, the greater the energy required to accelerate it to a given speed. Remove heavy items which you don't need to carry.

One load which is often overlooked is the contents of the fuel tank. A tankful of fuel (55 litres / 12 gallons) weighs 45 kg (100 lb) or so. Just half filling it may be worthwhile.

Lost?

At the risk of stating the obvious, if you're going somewhere new, have details of the route to hand. There's not much point in

achieving record mpg if you also go miles out of your way.

Parking

If possible, carry out any reversing or turning manoeuvres when you arrive at a parking space so that you can drive straight out when you leave. Manoeuvering when the engine is cold uses a lot more fuel.

Driving around looking for free on-street parking may cost more in fuel than buying a car park ticket.

Premium fuel

Most major oil companies (and some supermarkets) have premium grades of fuel which are several pence a litre dearer than the standard grades. Reports vary, but the consensus seems to be that if these fuels improve economy at all, they do not do so by enough to justify their extra cost.

Roof rack

When loading a roof rack, try to produce a wedge shape with the narrow end at the front. Any cover should be securely fastened – if it flaps it's creating turbulence and absorbing energy.

Remove roof racks and boxes when not in use – they increase air resistance and can create a surprising amount of noise.

Short journeys

The engine is at its least efficient, and wear is highest, during the first few miles after a cold start. Consider walking, cycling or using public transport.

Speed

The engine is at its most efficient when running at a steady speed and load at the rpm where it develops maximum torque. (You can find this figure in the car's handbook.) For most cars this corresponds to between 55 and 65 mph in top gear.

Above the optimum cruising speed, fuel consumption starts to rise quite sharply. A car travelling at 80 mph will typically be using 30% more fuel than at 60 mph.

Supermarket fuel

It may be cheap but is it any good? In the UK all supermarket fuel must meet the relevant British Standard. The major oil companies will say that their branded fuels have better additive packages which may stop carbon and other deposits building up. A reasonable compromise might be to use one tank of branded fuel to three or four from the supermarket.

Switch off when stationary

Switch off the engine if you look like being stationary for more than 30 seconds or so. This is good for the environment as well as for your pocket. Be aware though that frequent restarts are hard on the battery and the starter motor.

Windows

Driving with the windows open increases air turbulence around the vehicle. Closing the windows promotes smooth airflow and

reduced resistance. The faster you go, the more significant this is.

And finally . . .

Driving techniques associated with good fuel economy tend to involve moderate acceleration and low top speeds. Be considerate to the needs of other road users who may need to make brisker progress; even if you do not agree with them this is not an excuse to be obstructive.

Safety must always take precedence over economy, whether it is a question of accelerating hard to complete an overtaking manoeuvre, killing your speed when confronted with a potential hazard or switching the lights on when it starts to get dark.

Conversion factors

Length (distance)

Inches (in)	x 25.4	= Millimetres (mm)	x 0.0394	= Inches (in)
Feet (ft)	x 0.305	= Metres (m)	x 3.281	= Feet (ft)
Miles	x 1.609	= Kilometres (km)	x 0.621	= Miles

Volume (capacity)

Cubic inches (cu in; in³)	x 16.387	= Cubic centimetres (cc; cm³)	x 0.061	= Cubic inches (cu in; in³)
Imperial pints (Imp pt)	x 0.568	= Litres (l)	x 1.76	= Imperial pints (Imp pt)
Imperial quarts (Imp qt)	x 1.137	= Litres (l)	x 0.88	= Imperial quarts (Imp qt)
Imperial quarts (Imp qt)	x 1.201	= US quarts (US qt)	x 0.833	= Imperial quarts (Imp qt)
US quarts (US qt)	x 0.946	= Litres (l)	x 1.057	= US quarts (US qt)
Imperial gallons (Imp gal)	x 4.546	= Litres (l)	x 0.22	= Imperial gallons (Imp gal)
Imperial gallons (Imp gal)	x 1.201	= US gallons (US gal)	x 0.833	= Imperial gallons (Imp gal)
US gallons (US gal)	x 3.785	= Litres (l)	x 0.264	= US gallons (US gal)

Mass (weight)

Ounces (oz)	x 28.35	= Grams (g)	x 0.035	= Ounces (oz)
Pounds (lb)	x 0.454	= Kilograms (kg)	x 2.205	= Pounds (lb)

Force

Ounces-force (ozf; oz)	x 0.278	= Newtons (N)	x 3.6	= Ounces-force (ozf; oz)
Pounds-force (lbf; lb)	x 4.448	= Newtons (N)	x 0.225	= Pounds-force (lbf; lb)
Newtons (N)	x 0.1	= Kilograms-force (kgf; kg)	x 9.81	= Newtons (N)

Pressure

Pounds-force per square inch (psi; lbf/in²; lb/in²)	x 0.070	= Kilograms-force per square centimetre (kgf/cm²; kg/cm²)	x 14.223	= Pounds-force per square inch (psi; lbf/in²; lb/in²)
Pounds-force per square inch (psi; lbf/in²; lb/in²)	x 0.068	= Atmospheres (atm)	x 14.696	= Pounds-force per square inch (psi; lbf/in²; lb/in²)
Pounds-force per square inch (psi; lbf/in²; lb/in²)	x 0.069	= Bars	x 14.5	= Pounds-force per square inch (psi; lbf/in²; lb/in²)
Pounds-force per square inch (psi; lbf/in²; lb/in²)	x 6.895	= Kilopascals (kPa)	x 0.145	= Pounds-force per square inch (psi; lbf/in²; lb/in²)
Kilopascals (kPa)	x 0.01	= Kilograms-force per square centimetre (kgf/cm²; kg/cm²)	x 98.1	= Kilopascals (kPa)
Millibar (mbar)	x 100	= Pascals (Pa)	x 0.01	= Millibar (mbar)
Millibar (mbar)	x 0.0145	= Pounds-force per square inch (psi; lbf/in²; lb/in²)	x 68.947	= Millibar (mbar)
Millibar (mbar)	x 0.75	= Millimetres of mercury (mmHg)	x 1.333	= Millibar (mbar)
Millibar (mbar)	x 0.401	= Inches of water (inH₂O)	x 2.491	= Millibar (mbar)
Millimetres of mercury (mmHg)	x 0.535	= Inches of water (inH₂O)	x 1.868	= Millimetres of mercury (mmHg)
Inches of water (inH₂O)	x 0.036	= Pounds-force per square inch (psi; lbf/in²; lb/in²)	x 27.68	= Inches of water (inH₂O)

Torque (moment of force)

Pounds-force inches (lbf in; lb in)	x 1.152	= Kilograms-force centimetre (kgf cm; kg cm)	x 0.868	= Pounds-force inches (lbf in; lb in)
Pounds-force inches (lbf in; lb in)	x 0.113	= Newton metres (Nm)	x 8.85	= Pounds-force inches (lbf in; lb in)
Pounds-force inches (lbf in; lb in)	x 0.083	= Pounds-force feet (lbf ft; lb ft)	x 12	= Pounds-force inches (lbf in; lb in)
Pounds-force feet (lbf ft; lb ft)	x 0.138	= Kilograms-force metres (kgf m; kg m)	x 7.233	= Pounds-force feet (lbf ft; lb ft)
Pounds-force feet (lbf ft; lb ft)	x 1.356	= Newton metres (Nm)	x 0.738	= Pounds-force feet (lbf ft; lb ft)
Newton metres (Nm)	x 0.102	= Kilograms-force metres (kgf m; kg m)	x 9.804	= Newton metres (Nm)

Power

Horsepower (hp)	x 745.7	= Watts (W)	x 0.0013	= Horsepower (hp)

Velocity (speed)

Miles per hour (miles/hr; mph)	x 1.609	= Kilometres per hour (km/hr; kph)	x 0.621	= Miles per hour (miles/hr; mph)

Fuel consumption*

Miles per gallon, Imperial (mpg)	x 0.354	= Kilometres per litre (km/l)	x 2.825	= Miles per gallon, Imperial (mpg)
Miles per gallon, US (mpg)	x 0.425	= Kilometres per litre (km/l)	x 2.352	= Miles per gallon, US (mpg)

Temperature

Degrees Fahrenheit = (°C x 1.8) + 32   Degrees Celsius (Degrees Centigrade; °C) = (°F - 32) x 0.56

*It is common practice to convert from miles per gallon (mpg) to litres/100 kilometres (l/100km), where mpg x l/100 km = 282

Spare parts are available from many sources, including maker's appointed garages, accessory shops, and motor factors. To be sure of obtaining the correct parts, it will sometimes be necessary to quote the vehicle identification number. If possible, it can also be useful to take the old parts along for positive identification. Items such as starter motors and alternators may be available under a service exchange scheme – any parts returned should be clean.

Our advice regarding spare parts is as follows.

Officially appointed garages

This is the best source of parts which are peculiar to your car, and which are not otherwise generally available (eg, badges, interior trim, certain body panels, etc). It is also the only place at which you should buy parts if the car is still under warranty.

Accessory shops

These are very good places to buy materials and components needed for the maintenance of your car (oil, air and fuel filters, light bulbs, drivebelts, greases, brake pads, touch-up paint, etc). Components of this nature sold by a reputable shop are usually of the same standard as those used by the car manufacturer.

Besides components, these shops also sell tools and general accessories, usually have convenient opening hours, charge lower prices, and can often be found close to home. Some accessory shops have parts counters where components needed for almost any repair job can be purchased or ordered.

Motor factors

Good factors will stock all the more important components which wear out comparatively quickly, and can sometimes supply individual components needed for the overhaul of a larger assembly (eg, brake seals and hydraulic parts, bearing shells, pistons, valves). They may also handle work such as cylinder block reboring, crankshaft regrinding, etc.

Engine reconditioners

These specialise in engine overhaul and can also supply components. It is recommended that the establishment is a member of the Federation of Engine Re-Manufacturers, or a similar society.

Tyre and exhaust specialists

These outlets may be independent, or members of a local or national chain. They frequently offer competitive prices when compared with a main dealer or local garage, but it will pay to obtain several quotes before making a decision. When researching prices, also ask what extras may be added – for instance fitting a new valve, balancing the wheel and tyre disposal all both commonly charged on top of the price of a new tyre.

Other sources

Beware of parts or materials obtained from market stalls, car boot sales, on-line auctions or similar outlets. Such items are not invariably sub-standard, but there is little chance of compensation if they do prove unsatisfactory. In the case of safety-critical components such as brake pads, there is the risk not only of financial loss, but also of an accident causing injury or death.

Second-hand components or assemblies obtained from a car breaker can be a good buy in some circumstances, but this sort of purchase is best made by the experienced DIY mechanic.

Whenever servicing, repair or overhaul work is carried out on the car or its components, observe the following procedures and instructions. This will assist in carrying out the operation efficiently and to a professional standard of workmanship.

Joint mating faces and gaskets

When separating components at their mating faces, never insert screwdrivers or similar implements into the joint between the faces in order to prise them apart. This can cause severe damage which results in oil leaks, coolant leaks, etc upon reassembly. Separation is usually achieved by tapping along the joint with a soft-faced hammer in order to break the seal. However, note that this method may not be suitable where dowels are used for component location.

Where a gasket is used between the mating faces of two components, a new one must be fitted on reassembly; fit it dry unless otherwise stated in the repair procedure. Make sure that the mating faces are clean and dry, with all traces of old gasket removed. When cleaning a joint face, use a tool which is unlikely to score or damage the face, and remove any burrs or nicks with an oilstone or fine file.

Make sure that tapped holes are cleaned with a pipe cleaner, and keep them free of jointing compound, if this is being used, unless specifically instructed otherwise.

Ensure that all orifices, channels or pipes are clear, and blow through them, preferably using compressed air.

Oil seals

Oil seals can be removed by levering them out with a wide flat-bladed screwdriver or similar implement. Alternatively, a number of self-tapping screws may be screwed into the seal, and these used as a purchase for pliers or some similar device in order to pull the seal free.

Whenever an oil seal is removed from its working location, either individually or as part of an assembly, it should be renewed.

The very fine sealing lip of the seal is easily damaged, and will not seal if the surface it contacts is not completely clean and free from scratches, nicks or grooves. If the original sealing surface of the component cannot be restored, and the manufacturer has not made provision for slight relocation of the seal relative to the sealing surface, the component should be renewed.

Protect the lips of the seal from any surface which may damage them in the course of fitting. Use tape or a conical sleeve where possible. Where indicated, lubricate the seal lips with oil before fitting and, on dual-lipped seals, fill the space between the lips with grease.

Unless otherwise stated, oil seals must be fitted with their sealing lips toward the lubricant to be sealed.

Use a tubular drift or block of wood of the appropriate size to install the seal and, if the seal housing is shouldered, drive the seal down to the shoulder. If the seal housing is unshouldered, the seal should be fitted with its face flush with the housing top face (unless otherwise instructed).

Screw threads and fastenings

Seized nuts, bolts and screws are quite a common occurrence where corrosion has set in, and the use of penetrating oil or releasing fluid will often overcome this problem if the offending item is soaked for a while before attempting to release it. The use of an impact driver may also provide a means of releasing such stubborn fastening devices, when used in conjunction with the appropriate screwdriver bit or socket. If none of these methods works, it may be necessary to resort to the careful application of heat, or the use of a hacksaw or nut splitter device. Before resorting to extreme methods, check that you are not dealing with a left-hand thread!

Studs are usually removed by locking two nuts together on the threaded part, and then using a spanner on the lower nut to unscrew the stud. Studs or bolts which have broken off below the surface of the component in which they are mounted can sometimes be removed using a stud extractor.

Always ensure that a blind tapped hole is completely free from oil, grease, water or other fluid before installing the bolt or stud. Failure to do this could cause the housing to crack due to the hydraulic action of the bolt or stud as it is screwed in.

For some screw fastenings, notably cylinder head bolts or nuts, torque wrench settings are no longer specified for the latter stages of tightening, "angle-tightening" being called up instead. Typically, a fairly low torque wrench setting will be applied to the bolts/nuts in the correct sequence, followed by one or more stages of tightening through specified angles.

When checking or retightening a nut or bolt to a specified torque setting, slacken the nut or bolt by a quarter of a turn, and then retighten to the specified setting. However, this should not be attempted where angular tightening has been used.

Locknuts, locktabs and washers

Any fastening which will rotate against a component or housing during tightening should always have a washer between it and the relevant component or housing.

Spring or split washers should always be renewed when they are used to lock a critical component such as a big-end bearing retaining bolt or nut. Locktabs which are folded over to retain a nut or bolt should always be renewed.

Self-locking nuts can be re-used in non-critical areas, providing resistance can be felt when the locking portion passes over the bolt or stud thread. However, it should be noted that self-locking stiffnuts tend to lose their effectiveness after long periods of use, and should then be renewed as a matter of course.

Split pins must always be replaced with new ones of the correct size for the hole.

When thread-locking compound is found on the threads of a fastener which is to be re-used, it should be cleaned off with a wire brush and solvent, and fresh compound applied on reassembly.

Special tools

Some repair procedures in this manual entail the use of special tools such as a press, two or three-legged pullers, spring compressors, etc. Wherever possible, suitable readily-available alternatives to the manufacturer's special tools are described, and are shown in use. In some instances, where no alternative is possible, it has been necessary to resort to the use of a manufacturer's tool, and this has been done for reasons of safety as well as the efficient completion of the repair operation. Unless you are highly-skilled and have a thorough understanding of the procedures described, never attempt to bypass the use of any special tool when the procedure described specifies its use. Not only is there a very great risk of personal injury, but expensive damage could be caused to the components involved.

Environmental considerations

When disposing of used engine oil, brake fluid, antifreeze, etc, give due consideration to any detrimental environmental effects. Do not, for instance, pour any of the above liquids down drains into the general sewage system, or onto the ground to soak away. Many local council refuse tips provide a facility for waste oil disposal, as do some garages. You can find your nearest disposal point by calling the Environment Agency on 08708 506 506 or by visiting www.oilbankline.org.uk.

Note: It is illegal and anti-social to dump oil down the drain. To find the location of your local oil recycling bank, call 08708 506 506 or visit www.oilbankline.org.uk.

The jack supplied with the vehicle should only be used for changing the roadwheels – see *Wheel changing* at the front of this manual. When carrying out any other kind of work, raise the vehicle using a hydraulic (or 'trolley') jack, and always supplement the jack with axle stands at the vehicle jacking points.

When using a hydraulic jack or axle stands, always position the jack head or axle stand head under one of the relevant jacking points; the jacking point is the area in below the cut-out on the sill. Use a block of wood between the jack or axle stand and the sill – the block of wood should have a groove cut into it, into which the welded flange of the sill will locate.

Do not attempt to jack the vehicle under the front or rear crossmember, the sump, or any of the suspension components.

The jack supplied with the vehicle locates in the jacking points on the underside of the sills **(see illustration)** – see *Wheel changing*. Ensure that the jack head is correctly engaged before attempting to raise the vehicle.

Never work under, around, or near a raised vehicle, unless it is adequately supported in at least two places.

The jacking point is below the cut-out in the sill

Vehicle identification numbers

Modifications are a continuing and unpublicised process in vehicle manufacture, quite apart from major model changes. Spare parts manuals and lists are compiled upon a numerical basis, the individual vehicle identification numbers being essential for correct identification of the part concerned.

When ordering spare parts, always give as much information as possible. Quote the car model, year of manufacture, body and engine numbers, but most importantly, the production code (sometimes referred to as the 'spares number').

The *vehicle production code* is on a label located on the driver's door A-pillar, adjacent to the door hinges **(see illustration)**. The code provides Peugeot dealers with details of the exact build date and model. The vehicle paint code and tyre pressures are also given here.

The *vehicle identification number (VIN)* is stamped onto right-hand inner wing panel, on the upper section at the rear of the engine compartment **(see illustration)**.

The *vehicle identification number (VIN)* is also on a label at the bottom of the driver's side B-pillar, and on a plate visible through the base of the windscreen **(see illustrations)**.

The engine number is situated on the front face of the cylinder block on the flat surface located on the left- (2.0 litre engines) or right-hand (1.6 litre engines) side of the oil filter/cooler. **Note:** *The first part of the engine number gives the engine code, eg, RHF.*

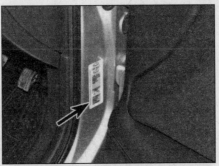

The vehicle production code is on a label located on the driver's door A-pillar

The vehicle identification number (VIN) is stamped onto right-hand inner wing panel

The vehicle identification number (VIN) is also on a label at the bottom of the driver's side B-pillar . . .

. . . and on a plate visible through the base of the windscreen

Introduction

A selection of good tools is a fundamental requirement for anyone contemplating the maintenance and repair of a motor vehicle. For the owner who does not possess any, their purchase will prove a considerable expense, offsetting some of the savings made by doing-it-yourself. However, provided that the tools purchased meet the relevant national safety standards and are of good quality, they will last for many years and prove an extremely worthwhile investment.

To help the average owner to decide which tools are needed to carry out the various tasks detailed in this manual, we have compiled three lists of tools under the following headings: *Maintenance and minor repair*, *Repair and overhaul*, and *Special*. Newcomers to practical mechanics should start off with the *Maintenance and minor repair* tool kit, and confine themselves to the simpler jobs around the vehicle. Then, as confidence and experience grow, more difficult tasks can be undertaken, with extra tools being purchased as, and when, they are needed. In this way, a *Maintenance and minor repair* tool kit can be built up into a *Repair and overhaul* tool kit over a considerable period of time, without any major cash outlays. The experienced do-it-yourselfer will have a tool kit good enough for most repair and overhaul procedures, and will add tools from the *Special* category when it is felt that the expense is justified by the amount of use to which these tools will be put.

Maintenance and minor repair tool kit

The tools given in this list should be considered as a minimum requirement if routine maintenance, servicing and minor repair operations are to be undertaken. We recommend the purchase of combination spanners (ring one end, open-ended the other); although more expensive than open-ended ones, they do give the advantages of both types of spanner.

☐ *Combination spanners:*
   Metric - 8 to 19 mm inclusive
☐ *Adjustable spanner - 35 mm jaw (approx.)*
☐ *Spark plug spanner (with rubber insert) - petrol models*
☐ *Spark plug gap adjustment tool - petrol models*
☐ *Set of feeler gauges*
☐ *Brake bleed nipple spanner*
☐ *Screwdrivers:*
   Flat blade - 100 mm long x 6 mm dia
   Cross blade - 100 mm long x 6 mm dia
   Torx - various sizes (not all vehicles)
☐ *Combination pliers*
☐ *Hacksaw (junior)*
☐ *Tyre pump*
☐ *Tyre pressure gauge*
☐ *Oil can*
☐ *Oil filter removal tool (if applicable)*
☐ *Fine emery cloth*
☐ *Wire brush (small)*
☐ *Funnel (medium size)*
☐ *Sump drain plug key (not all vehicles)*

Repair and overhaul tool kit

These tools are virtually essential for anyone undertaking any major repairs to a motor vehicle, and are additional to those given in the *Maintenance and minor repair* list. Included in this list is a comprehensive set of sockets. Although these are expensive, they will be found invaluable as they are so versatile - particularly if various drives are included in the set. We recommend the half-inch square-drive type, as this can be used with most proprietary torque wrenches.

The tools in this list will sometimes need to be supplemented by tools from the *Special* list:

☐ *Sockets to cover range in previous list (including Torx sockets)*
☐ *Reversible ratchet drive (for use with sockets)*
☐ *Extension piece, 250 mm (for use with sockets)*
☐ *Universal joint (for use with sockets)*
☐ *Flexible handle or sliding T "breaker bar" (for use with sockets)*
☐ *Torque wrench (for use with sockets)*
☐ *Self-locking grips*
☐ *Ball pein hammer*
☐ *Soft-faced mallet (plastic or rubber)*
☐ *Screwdrivers:*
   Flat blade - long & sturdy, short (chubby), and narrow (electrician's) types
   Cross blade – long & sturdy, and short (chubby) types
☐ *Pliers:*
   Long-nosed
   Side cutters (electrician's)
   Circlip (internal and external)
☐ *Cold chisel - 25 mm*
☐ *Scriber*
☐ *Scraper*
☐ *Centre-punch*
☐ *Pin punch*
☐ *Hacksaw*
☐ *Brake hose clamp*
☐ *Brake/clutch bleeding kit*
☐ *Selection of twist drills*
☐ *Steel rule/straight-edge*
☐ *Allen keys (inc. splined/Torx type)*
☐ *Selection of files*
☐ *Wire brush*
☐ *Axle stands*
☐ *Jack (strong trolley or hydraulic type)*
☐ *Light with extension lead*
☐ *Universal electrical multi-meter*

Sockets and reversible ratchet drive

Brake bleeding kit

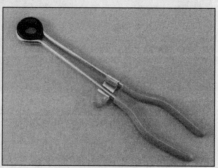

Torx key, socket and bit

Hose clamp

Angular-tightening gauge

Special tools

The tools in this list are those which are not used regularly, are expensive to buy, or which need to be used in accordance with their manufacturers' instructions. Unless relatively difficult mechanical jobs are undertaken frequently, it will not be economic to buy many of these tools. Where this is the case, you could consider clubbing together with friends (or joining a motorists' club) to make a joint purchase, or borrowing the tools against a deposit from a local garage or tool hire specialist.

The following list contains only those tools and instruments freely available to the public, and not those special tools produced by the vehicle manufacturer specifically for its dealer network. You will find occasional references to these manufacturers' special tools in the text of this manual. Generally, an alternative method of doing the job without the vehicle manufacturers' special tool is given. However, sometimes there is no alternative to using them. Where this is the case and the relevant tool cannot be bought or borrowed, you will have to entrust the work to a dealer.

- ☐ *Angular-tightening gauge*
- ☐ *Valve spring compressor*
- ☐ *Valve grinding tool*
- ☐ *Piston ring compressor*
- ☐ *Piston ring removal/installation tool*
- ☐ *Cylinder bore hone*
- ☐ *Balljoint separator*
- ☐ *Coil spring compressors (where applicable)*
- ☐ *Two/three-legged hub and bearing puller*
- ☐ *Impact screwdriver*
- ☐ *Micrometer and/or vernier calipers*
- ☐ *Dial gauge*
- ☐ *Tachometer*
- ☐ *Fault code reader*
- ☐ *Cylinder compression gauge*
- ☐ *Hand-operated vacuum pump and gauge*
- ☐ *Clutch plate alignment set*
- ☐ *Brake shoe steady spring cup removal tool*
- ☐ *Bush and bearing removal/installation set*
- ☐ *Stud extractors*
- ☐ *Tap and die set*
- ☐ *Lifting tackle*

Buying tools

Reputable motor accessory shops and superstores often offer excellent quality tools at discount prices, so it pays to shop around.

Remember, you don't have to buy the most expensive items on the shelf, but it is always advisable to steer clear of the very cheap tools. Beware of 'bargains' offered on market stalls, on-line or at car boot sales. There are plenty of good tools around at reasonable prices, but always aim to purchase items which meet the relevant national safety standards. If in doubt, ask the proprietor or manager of the shop for advice before making a purchase.

Care and maintenance of tools

Having purchased a reasonable tool kit, it is necessary to keep the tools in a clean and serviceable condition. After use, always wipe off any dirt, grease and metal particles using a clean, dry cloth, before putting the tools away. Never leave them lying around after they have been used. A simple tool rack on the garage or workshop wall for items such as screwdrivers and pliers is a good idea. Store all normal spanners and sockets in a metal box. Any measuring instruments, gauges, meters, etc, must be carefully stored where they cannot be damaged or become rusty.

Take a little care when tools are used. Hammer heads inevitably become marked, and screwdrivers lose the keen edge on their blades from time to time. A little timely attention with emery cloth or a file will soon restore items like this to a good finish.

Working facilities

Not to be forgotten when discussing tools is the workshop itself. If anything more than routine maintenance is to be carried out, a suitable working area becomes essential.

It is appreciated that many an owner-mechanic is forced by circumstances to remove an engine or similar item without the benefit of a garage or workshop. Having done this, any repairs should always be done under the cover of a roof.

Wherever possible, any dismantling should be done on a clean, flat workbench or table at a suitable working height.

Any workbench needs a vice; one with a jaw opening of 100 mm is suitable for most jobs. As mentioned previously, some clean dry storage space is also required for tools, as well as for any lubricants, cleaning fluids, touch-up paints etc, which become necessary.

Another item which may be required, and which has a much more general usage, is an electric drill with a chuck capacity of at least 8 mm. This, together with a good range of twist drills, is virtually essential for fitting accessories.

Last, but not least, always keep a supply of old newspapers and clean, lint-free rags available, and try to keep any working area as clean as possible.

Micrometers

Dial test indicator ("dial gauge")

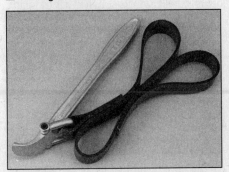

Oil filter removal tool (strap wrench type)

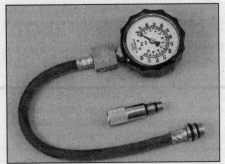

Compression tester

Bearing puller

This is a guide to getting your vehicle through the MOT test. Obviously it will not be possible to examine the vehicle to the same standard as the professional MOT tester. However, working through the following checks will enable you to identify any problem areas before submitting the vehicle for the test.

It has only been possible to summarise the test requirements here, based on the regulations in force at the time of printing. Test standards are becoming increasingly stringent, although there are some exemptions for older vehicles.

An assistant will be needed to help carry out some of these checks.

The checks have been sub-divided into four categories, as follows:

1 Checks carried out **FROM THE DRIVER'S SEAT**

2 Checks carried out **WITH THE VEHICLE ON THE GROUND**

3 Checks carried out **WITH THE VEHICLE RAISED AND THE WHEELS FREE TO TURN**

4 Checks carried out on **YOUR VEHICLE'S EXHAUST EMISSION SYSTEM**

---

1 Checks carried out **FROM THE DRIVER'S SEAT**

Handbrake (parking brake)

☐ Test the operation of the handbrake. Excessive travel (too many clicks) indicates incorrect brake or cable adjustment.
☐ Check that the handbrake cannot be released by tapping the lever sideways. Check the security of the lever mountings.

☐ If the parking brake is foot-operated, check that the pedal is secure and without excessive travel, and that the release mechanism operates correctly.
☐ Where applicable, test the operation of the electronic handbrake. The brake should engage and disengage without excessive delay. If the warning light does not extinguish when the brake is disengaged, this could indicate a fault which will need further investigation.

Footbrake

☐ Depress the brake pedal and check that it does not creep down to the floor, indicating a master cylinder fault. Release the pedal,

wait a few seconds, then depress it again. If the pedal travels nearly to the floor before firm resistance is felt, brake adjustment or repair is necessary. If the pedal feels spongy, there is air in the hydraulic system which must be removed by bleeding.

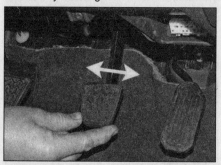

☐ Check that the brake pedal is secure and in good condition. Check also for signs of fluid leaks on the pedal, floor or carpets, which would indicate failed seals in the brake master cylinder.
☐ Check the servo unit (when applicable) by operating the brake pedal several times, then keeping the pedal depressed and starting the engine. As the engine starts, the pedal will move down slightly. If not, the vacuum hose or the servo itself may be faulty.

Steering wheel and column

☐ Examine the steering wheel for fractures or looseness of the hub, spokes or rim.
☐ Move the steering wheel from side to side and then up and down. Check that the steering wheel is not loose on the column, indicating wear or a loose retaining nut. Continue moving the steering wheel as before, but also turn it slightly from left to right.

☐ Check that the steering wheel is not loose on the column, and that there is no abnormal movement of the steering wheel, indicating wear in the column support bearings or couplings.
☐ Check that the ignition lock (where fitted) engages and disengages correctly.
☐ Steering column adjustment mechanisms (where fitted) must be able to lock the column securely in place with no play evident.

Windscreen, mirrors and sunvisor

☐ The windscreen must be free of cracks or other significant damage within the driver's field of view. (Small stone chips are acceptable.) Rear view mirrors must be secure, intact, and capable of being adjusted.

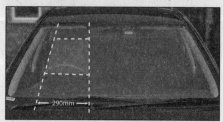

☐ The driver's sunvisor must be capable of being stored in the "up" position.

Seat belts and seats

Note: *The following checks are applicable to all seat belts, front and rear.*

☐ Examine the webbing of all the belts (including rear belts if fitted) for cuts, serious fraying or deterioration. Fasten and unfasten each belt to check the buckles. If applicable, check the retracting mechanism. Check the security of all seat belt mountings accessible from inside the vehicle, ensuring any height adjustable mountings lock securely in place.

☐ Seat belts with pre-tensioners, once activated, have a "flag" or similar showing on the seat belt stalk. This, in itself, is not a reason for test failure.

☐ The front seats themselves must be securely attached and the backrests must lock in the upright position.

Doors

☐ Both front doors must be able to be opened and closed from outside and inside, and must latch securely when closed.

Bonnet and boot/tailgate

☐ The bonnet and boot/tailgate must latch securely when closed.

2 Checks carried out WITH THE VEHICLE ON THE GROUND

Vehicle identification

☐ Number plates must be in good condition, secure and legible, with letters and numbers correctly spaced – spacing at (A) should be 33 mm and at (B) 11 mm. At the front, digits must be black on a white background and at the rear black on a yellow background. Other background designs (such as honeycomb) are not permitted.

☐ The VIN plate and/or homologation plate must be permanently displayed and legible.

Electrical equipment

☐ Switch on the ignition and check the operation of the horn.

☐ Check the windscreen washers and wipers, examining the wiper blades; renew damaged or perished blades. Also check the operation of the stop-lights.

☐ Check the operation of the sidelights and number plate lights. The lenses and reflectors must be secure, clean and undamaged.

☐ Check the operation and alignment of the headlights. The headlight reflectors must not be tarnished and the lenses must be undamaged.

☐ Switch on the ignition and check the operation of the direction indicators (including the instrument panel tell-tale) and the hazard warning lights. Operation of the sidelights and stop-lights must not affect the indicators - if it does, the cause is usually a bad earth at the rear light cluster. Indicators should flash at a rate of between 60 and 120 times per minute – faster or slower than this could indicate a fault with the flasher unit or a bad earth at one of the light units.

☐ Check the operation of the rear foglight(s), including the warning light on the instrument panel or in the switch.

☐ The warning lights must illuminate in accordance with the manufacturer's design. For most vehicles, the ABS and other warning lights should illuminate when the ignition is switched on, and (if the system is operating properly) extinguish after a few seconds. Refer to the owner's handbook.

Footbrake

☐ Examine the master cylinder, brake pipes and servo unit for leaks, loose mountings, corrosion or other damage. If ABS is fitted, this unit should also be examined for signs of leaks or corrosion.

☐ The fluid reservoir must be secure and the fluid level must be between the upper (A) and lower (B) markings.

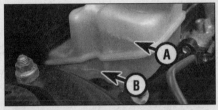

☐ Inspect both front brake flexible hoses for cracks or deterioration of the rubber. Turn the steering from lock to lock, and ensure that the hoses do not contact the wheel, tyre, or any part of the steering or suspension mechanism. With the brake pedal firmly depressed, check the hoses for bulges or leaks under pressure.

Steering and suspension

☐ Have your assistant turn the steering wheel from side to side slightly, up to the point where the steering gear just begins to transmit this movement to the roadwheels. Check for excessive free play between the steering wheel and the steering gear, indicating wear or insecurity of the steering column joints, the column-to-steering gear coupling, or the steering gear itself.

☐ Have your assistant turn the steering wheel more vigorously in each direction, so that the roadwheels just begin to turn. As this is done, examine all the steering joints, linkages, fittings and attachments. Renew any component that shows signs of wear or damage. On vehicles with power steering, check the security and condition of the steering pump, drivebelt and hoses.

☐ Check that the vehicle is standing level, and at approximately the correct ride height.

Shock absorbers

☐ Depress each corner of the vehicle in turn, then release it. The vehicle should rise and then settle in its normal position. If the vehicle continues to rise and fall, the shock absorber is defective. A shock absorber which has seized will also cause the vehicle to fail.

Exhaust system

☐ Start the engine. With your assistant holding a rag over the tailpipe, check the entire system for leaks. Repair or renew leaking sections.

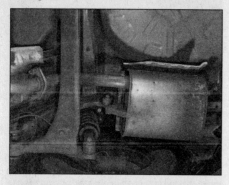

3 Checks carried out
WITH THE VEHICLE RAISED AND THE WHEELS FREE TO TURN

Jack up the front and rear of the vehicle, and securely support it on axle stands. Position the stands clear of the suspension assemblies. Ensure that the wheels are clear of the ground and that the steering can be turned from lock to lock.

Steering mechanism

☐ Have your assistant turn the steering from lock to lock. Check that the steering turns smoothly, and that no part of the steering mechanism, including a wheel or tyre, fouls any brake hose or pipe or any part of the body structure.
☐ Examine the steering rack rubber gaiters for damage or insecurity of the retaining clips. If power steering is fitted, check for signs of damage or leakage of the fluid hoses, pipes or connections. Also check for excessive stiffness or binding of the steering, a missing split pin or locking device, or severe corrosion of the body structure within 30 cm of any steering component attachment point.

Front and rear suspension and wheel bearings

☐ Starting at the front right-hand side, grasp the roadwheel at the 3 o'clock and 9 o'clock positions and rock gently but firmly. Check for free play or insecurity at the wheel bearings, suspension balljoints, or suspension mount-ings, pivots and attachments.
☐ Now grasp the wheel at the 12 o'clock and 6 o'clock positions and repeat the previous inspection. Spin the wheel, and check for roughness or tightness of the front wheel bearing.

☐ If excess free play is suspected at a component pivot point, this can be confirmed by using a large screwdriver or similar tool and levering between the mounting and the component attachment. This will confirm whether the wear is in the pivot bush, its retaining bolt, or in the mounting itself (the bolt holes can often become elongated).

☐ Carry out all the above checks at the other front wheel, and then at both rear wheels.

Springs and shock absorbers

☐ Examine the suspension struts (when applicable) for serious fluid leakage, corrosion, or damage to the casing. Also check the security of the mounting points.
☐ If coil springs are fitted, check that the spring ends locate in their seats, and that the spring is not corroded, cracked or broken.
☐ If leaf springs are fitted, check that all leaves are intact, that the axle is securely attached to each spring, and that there is no deterioration of the spring eye mountings, bushes, and shackles.

☐ The same general checks apply to vehicles fitted with other suspension types, such as torsion bars, hydraulic displacer units, etc. Ensure that all mountings and attachments are secure, that there are no signs of excessive wear, corrosion or damage, and (on hydraulic types) that there are no fluid leaks or damaged pipes.
☐ Inspect the shock absorbers for signs of serious fluid leakage. Check for wear of the mounting bushes or attachments, or damage to the body of the unit.

Driveshafts (fwd vehicles only)

☐ Rotate each front wheel in turn and inspect the constant velocity joint gaiters for splits or damage. Also check that each driveshaft is straight and undamaged.

Braking system

☐ If possible without dismantling, check brake pad wear and disc condition. Ensure that the friction lining material has not worn excessively, (A) and that the discs are not fractured, pitted, scored or badly worn (B).

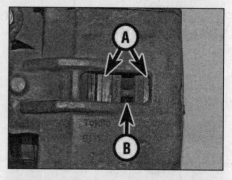

☐ Examine all the rigid brake pipes underneath the vehicle, and the flexible hose(s) at the rear. Look for corrosion, chafing or insecurity of the pipes, and for signs of bulging under pressure, chafing, splits or deterioration of the flexible hoses.
☐ Look for signs of fluid leaks at the brake calipers or on the brake backplates. Repair or renew leaking components.
☐ Slowly spin each wheel, while your assistant depresses and releases the footbrake. Ensure that each brake is operating and does not bind when the pedal is released.

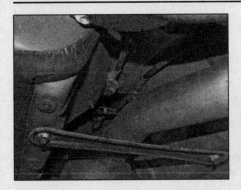

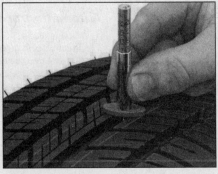

□ Examine the handbrake mechanism, checking for frayed or broken cables, excessive corrosion, or wear or insecurity of the linkage. Check that the mechanism works on each relevant wheel, and releases fully, without binding.

□ It is not possible to test brake efficiency without special equipment, but a road test can be carried out later to check that the vehicle pulls up in a straight line.

Fuel and exhaust systems

□ Inspect the fuel tank (including the filler cap), fuel pipes, hoses and unions. All components must be secure and free from leaks. Locking fuel caps must lock securely and the key must be provided for the MOT test.

□ Examine the exhaust system over its entire length, checking for any damaged, broken or missing mountings, security of the retaining clamps and rust or corrosion.

Wheels and tyres

□ Examine the sidewalls and tread area of each tyre in turn. Check for cuts, tears, lumps, bulges, separation of the tread, and exposure of the ply or cord due to wear or damage. Check that the tyre bead is correctly seated on the wheel rim, that the valve is sound and properly seated, and that the wheel is not distorted or damaged.

□ Check that the tyres are of the correct size for the vehicle, that they are of the same size and type on each axle, and that the pressures are correct.

□ Check the tyre tread depth. The legal minimum at the time of writing is 1.6 mm over the central three-quarters of the tread width. Abnormal tread wear may indicate incorrect front wheel alignment or wear in steering or suspension components.

□ If the spare wheel is fitted externally or in a separate carrier beneath the vehicle, check that mountings are secure and free of excessive corrosion.

Body corrosion

□ Check the condition of the entire vehicle structure for signs of corrosion in load-bearing areas. (These include chassis box sections, side sills, cross-members, pillars, and all suspension, steering, braking system and seat belt mountings and anchorages.) Any corrosion which has seriously reduced the thickness of a load-bearing area (or is within 30 cm of safety-related components such as steering or suspension) is likely to cause the vehicle to fail. In this case professional repairs are likely to be needed.

□ Damage or corrosion which causes sharp or otherwise dangerous edges to be exposed will also cause the vehicle to fail.

Towbars

□ Check the condition of mounting points (both beneath the vehicle and within boot/hatchback areas) for signs of corrosion, ensuring that all fixings are secure and not worn or damaged. There must be no excessive play in detachable tow ball arms or quick-release mechanisms.

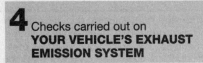

4 Checks carried out on **YOUR VEHICLE'S EXHAUST EMISSION SYSTEM**

Petrol models

□ The engine should be warmed up, and running well (ignition system in good order, air filter element clean, etc).

□ Before testing, run the engine at around 2500 rpm for 20 seconds. Let the engine drop to idle, and watch for smoke from the exhaust. If the idle speed is too high, or if dense blue or black smoke emerges for more than 5 seconds, the vehicle will fail. Typically, blue smoke signifies oil burning (engine wear);

black smoke means unburnt fuel (dirty air cleaner element, or other fuel system fault).

□ An exhaust gas analyser for measuring carbon monoxide (CO) and hydrocarbons (HC) is now needed. If one cannot be hired or borrowed, have a local garage perform the check.

CO emissions (mixture)

□ The MOT tester has access to the CO limits for all vehicles. The CO level is measured at idle speed, and at 'fast idle' (2500 to 3000 rpm). The following limits are given as a general guide:

At idle speed – Less than 0.5% CO
At 'fast idle' – Less than 0.3% CO
Lambda reading – 0.97 to 1.03

□ If the CO level is too high, this may point to poor maintenance, a fuel injection system problem, faulty lambda (oxygen) sensor or catalytic converter. Try an injector cleaning treatment, and check the vehicle's ECU for fault codes.

HC emissions

□ The MOT tester has access to HC limits for all vehicles. The HC level is measured at 'fast idle' (2500 to 3000 rpm). The following limits are given as a general guide:

At 'fast idle' – Less then 200 ppm

□ Excessive HC emissions are typically caused by oil being burnt (worn engine), or by a blocked crankcase ventilation system ('breather'). If the engine oil is old and thin, an oil change may help. If the engine is running badly, check the vehicle's ECU for fault codes.

Diesel models

□ The only emission test for diesel engines is measuring exhaust smoke density, using a calibrated smoke meter. The test involves accelerating the engine at least 3 times to its maximum unloaded speed.

Note: *On engines with a timing belt, it is VITAL that the belt is in good condition before the test is carried out.*

□ With the engine warmed up, it is first purged by running at around 2500 rpm for 20 seconds. A governor check is then carried out, by slowly accelerating the engine to its maximum speed. After this, the smoke meter is connected, and the engine is accelerated quickly to maximum speed three times. If the smoke density is less than the limits given below, the vehicle will pass:

Non-turbo vehicles: 2.5m-1
Turbocharged vehicles: 3.0m-1

□ If excess smoke is produced, try fitting a new air cleaner element, or using an injector cleaning treatment. If the engine is running badly, where applicable, check the vehicle's ECU for fault codes. Also check the vehicle's EGR system, where applicable. At high mileages, the injectors may require professional attention.

Fault finding

Engine

- ☐ Engine fails to rotate when attempting to start
- ☐ Engine rotates, but will not start
- ☐ Engine difficult to start when cold
- ☐ Engine difficult to start when hot
- ☐ Starter motor noisy or excessively-rough in engagement
- ☐ Engine starts, but stops immediately
- ☐ Engine idles erratically
- ☐ Engine misfires at idle speed
- ☐ Engine misfires throughout the driving speed range
- ☐ Engine hesitates on acceleration
- ☐ Engine stalls
- ☐ Engine lacks power
- ☐ Engine backfires
- ☐ Oil pressure warning light on with engine running
- ☐ Engine runs-on after switching off
- ☐ Engine noises

Cooling system

- ☐ Overheating
- ☐ Overcooling
- ☐ External coolant leakage
- ☐ Internal coolant leakage
- ☐ Corrosion

Fuel and exhaust systems

- ☐ Excessive fuel consumption
- ☐ Fuel leakage and/or fuel odour
- ☐ Excessive noise or fumes from exhaust system

Clutch

- ☐ Pedal travels to floor – no pressure or very little resistance
- ☐ Clutch fails to disengage (unable to select gears)
- ☐ Clutch slips (engine speed rises, with no increase in vehicle speed)
- ☐ Judder as clutch is engaged
- ☐ Noise when depressing or releasing clutch pedal

Manual transmission

- ☐ Noisy in neutral with engine running
- ☐ Noisy in one particular gear
- ☐ Difficulty engaging gears
- ☐ Jumps out of gear
- ☐ Vibration
- ☐ Lubricant leaks

Automatic transmission

- ☐ Fluid leakage
- ☐ Transmission fluid brown, or has burned smell
- ☐ General gear selection problems
- ☐ Transmission will not downshift (kickdown) on full throttle
- ☐ Engine won't start in any gear, or starts in gears other than P or N
- ☐ Transmission slips, shifts roughly, is noisy, or has no drive in forward or reverse gears

Driveshafts

- ☐ Clicking or knocking noise on turns (at slow speed on full-lock)
- ☐ Vibration when accelerating or decelerating

Braking system

- ☐ Vehicle pulls to one side under braking
- ☐ Noise (grinding or high-pitched squeal) when brakes applied
- ☐ Excessive brake pedal travel
- ☐ Brake pedal feels spongy when depressed
- ☐ Excessive brake pedal effort required to stop vehicle
- ☐ Judder felt through brake pedal or steering wheel when braking
- ☐ Brakes binding
- ☐ Rear wheels locking under normal braking

Suspension and steering systems

- ☐ Vehicle pulls to one side
- ☐ Wheel wobble and vibration
- ☐ Excessive pitching and/or rolling around corners, or during braking
- ☐ Wandering or general instability
- ☐ Excessively-stiff steering
- ☐ Excessive play in steering
- ☐ Lack of power assistance
- ☐ Tyre wear excessive

Electrical system

- ☐ Battery will not hold a charge for more than a few days
- ☐ Ignition/no-charge warning light stays on with engine running
- ☐ Ignition/no-charge warning light fails to come on
- ☐ Lights inoperative
- ☐ Instrument readings inaccurate or erratic
- ☐ Horn inoperative, or unsatisfactory in operation
- ☐ Windscreen/tailgate wipers failed, or unsatisfactory in operation
- ☐ Windscreen/tailgate washers failed, or unsatisfactory in operation
- ☐ Electric windows inoperative, or unsatisfactory in operation
- ☐ Central locking system inoperative, or unsatisfactory in operation

Introduction

The vehicle owner who does his or her own maintenance according to the recommended service schedules should not have to use this section of the manual very often. Modern component reliability is such that, provided those items subject to wear or deterioration are inspected or renewed at the specified intervals, sudden failure is comparatively rare. Faults do not usually just happen as a result of sudden failure, but develop over a period of time. Major mechanical failures in particular are usually preceded by characteristic symptoms over hundreds or even thousands of miles. Those components that do occasionally fail without warning are often small and easily carried in the vehicle.

With any fault-finding, the first step is to decide where to begin investigations. Sometimes this is obvious, but on other occasions, a little detective work will be necessary. The owner who makes half a dozen haphazard adjustments or replacements may be successful in curing a fault (or its symptoms), but will be none the wiser if the fault recurs, and ultimately may have spent more time and money than was necessary. A calm and logical approach will be found to be more satisfactory in the long run. Always take into account any warning signs or abnormalities that may have been noticed in the period preceding the fault – power loss, high or low gauge readings, unusual smells,

etc – and remember that failure of components such as fuses or spark plugs may only be pointers to some underlying fault.

The pages that follow provide an easy-reference guide to the more common problems, which may occur during the operation of the vehicle. These problems and their possible causes are grouped under headings denoting various components or systems, such as Engine, Cooling system, etc. The general Chapter that deals with the problem is also shown in brackets; refer to the relevant part of that Chapter for system-specific information. Whatever the fault, certain basic principles apply. These are as follows:

Verify the fault. This is simply a matter of

being sure that you know what the symptoms are before starting work. This is particularly important if you are investigating a fault for someone else, who may not have described it very accurately.

Don't overlook the obvious. For example, if the vehicle won't start, is there fuel in the tank? (Don't take anyone else's word on this particular point, and don't trust the fuel gauge either!) If an electrical fault is indicated, look for loose or broken wires before digging out the test gear.

Cure the disease, not the symptom. Substituting a flat battery with a fully charged one will get you off the hard shoulder, but if the underlying cause is not attended to, the new battery will go the same way.

Don't take anything for granted. Particularly, don't forget that a 'new' component may itself be defective (especially if it's been rattling around in the boot for months), and don't leave components out of a fault diagnosis sequence just because they are new or recently fitted. When you do finally diagnose a difficult fault, you'll probably realise that all the evidence was there from the start.

Diesel fault diagnosis

The majority of starting problems on small diesel engines are electrical in origin. The mechanic who is familiar with petrol engines but less so with diesel may be inclined to view the diesel's injectors and pump in the same light as the spark plugs and distributor, but this is generally a mistake.

When investigating complaints of difficult starting for someone else, make sure that the correct starting procedure is understood and is being followed. Some drivers are unaware of the significance of the preheating warning light – many modern engines are sufficiently forgiving for this not to matter in mild weather, but with the onset of winter, problems begin. Glow plugs in particular are often neglected – just one faulty plug will make cold-weather starting very difficult.

As a rule of thumb, if the engine is difficult to start but runs well when it has finally got going, the problem is electrical (battery, starter motor or preheating system). If poor performance is combined with difficult starting, the problem is likely to be in the fuel system. The low-pressure (supply) side of the fuel system should be checked before suspecting the injectors and high-pressure pump. The most common fuel supply problem is air getting into the system, and any pipe from the fuel tank forwards must be scrutinised if air leakage is suspected.

Engine

Engine fails to rotate when attempting to start

☐ Battery terminal connections loose or corroded (*Weekly checks*).
☐ Battery discharged or faulty (Chapter 5A).
☐ Broken, loose or disconnected wiring in the starting circuit (Chapter 5A).
☐ Defective starter motor (Chapter 5A).
☐ Starter pinion or flywheel/driveplate ring gear teeth loose or broken (Chapter 2A , 2B or 2C and 5A).
☐ Engine earth strap broken or disconnected (Chapter 5A).

Engine rotates, but will not start

☐ Fuel tank empty.
☐ Battery discharged (engine rotates slowly) (Chapter 5A).
☐ Battery terminal connections loose or corroded (*Weekly checks*).
☐ Preheating system faulty (Chapter 5B).
☐ Air in fuel system (Chapter 4A).
☐ Fuel injector/injection pump fault (Chapter 4AB).
☐ Low cylinder compressions (Chapter 2A, 2B or 2C).
☐ Major mechanical failure (e.g. camshaft drive) (Chapter 2A, 2B or 2C).

Engine difficult to start when cold

☐ Battery discharged (Chapter 5A).
☐ Battery terminal connections loose or corroded (*Weekly checks*).
☐ Preheating system faulty (Chapter 5B).
☐ Fuel injector/injection pump fault (Chapter 4A.

Engine difficult to start when hot

☐ Fuel injector/injection pump fault (Chapter 4A.
☐ Low cylinder compressions (Chapter 2A, 2B or 2C).

Starter motor noisy or excessively-rough in engagement

☐ Starter pinion or flywheel/driveplate ring gear teeth loose or broken (Chapters 2A, 2B or 2C and 5A).
☐ Starter motor mounting bolts loose or missing (Chapter 5A).
☐ Defective starter motor (Chapter 5A).

Engine starts, but stops immediately

☐ Air in fuel system (Chapter 4A).
☐ Fuel injector/injection pump fault (Chapter 4A).

Engine idles erratically

☐ Air in fuel system (Chapter 4A).
☐ Fuel injector/injection pump fault (Chapter 4A).
☐ Uneven or low cylinder compressions (Chapter 2A, 2B or 2C).
☐ Camshaft lobes worn (Chapter 2A, 2B or 2C).
☐ Timing belt incorrectly fitted (Chapter 2A, 2B or 2C).

Engine misfires at idle speed

☐ Faulty injector(s) (Chapter 4A).
☐ Uneven or low cylinder compressions (Chapter 2A, 2B or 2C).
☐ Disconnected, leaking, or perished crankcase ventilation hoses (Chapter 4B).

Engine misfires throughout the driving speed range

☐ Fuel filter blocked (Chapter 1).
☐ Fuel pump faulty (Chapter 4A).
☐ Fuel tank vent blocked, or fuel pipes restricted (Chapter 4A).
☐ Fuel injector/injection pump fault (Chapter 4A).
☐ Uneven or low cylinder compressions (Chapter 2A, 2B or 2C).

Engine hesitates on acceleration

☐ Fuel injector/injection pump fault (Chapter 4A).

Engine stalls

☐ Fuel filter blocked (Chapter 1).
☐ Fuel pump faulty (Chapter 4A).
☐ Fuel tank vent blocked, or fuel pipes restricted (Chapter 4A).
☐ Fuel injector/injection pump fault (Chapter 4A).

Engine (continued)

Engine lacks power

- [ ] Timing belt incorrectly fitted (Chapter 2A, 2B or 2C).
- [ ] Fuel filter blocked (Chapter 1).
- [ ] Fuel pump faulty (Chapter 4A).
- [ ] Uneven or low cylinder compressions (Chapter 2A, 2B or 2C).
- [ ] Fuel injector/injection pump fault (Chapter 4A).
- [ ] Brakes binding (Chapters 1 and 9).
- [ ] Clutch slipping (Chapter 6).

Engine backfires

- [ ] Timing belt incorrectly fitted (Chapter 2A, 2B or 2C).

Oil pressure warning light on with engine running

- [ ] Low oil level, or incorrect oil grade (*Weekly checks*).
- [ ] Faulty oil pressure warning light switch (Chapter 5A).
- [ ] Worn engine bearings and/or oil pump (Chapter 2C).
- [ ] High engine operating temperature (Chapter 3).
- [ ] Oil pressure relief valve defective (Chapter 2A, 2B or 2C).
- [ ] Oil pick-up strainer clogged (Chapter 2A, 2B or 2C).

Engine runs-on after switching off

- [ ] Excessive carbon build-up in engine (Chapter 2C).
- [ ] High engine operating temperature (Chapter 3).
- [ ] Fuel injection pump fault (Chapter 4A).

Engine noises

Pre-ignition (pinking) or knocking during acceleration or under load

- [ ] Excessive carbon build-up in engine (Chapter 2C).

Whistling or wheezing noises

- [ ] Leaking vacuum hose (Chapters 4A and 9).
- [ ] Blowing cylinder head gasket (Chapter 2A, 2B or 2C).

Tapping or rattling noises

- [ ] Worn valve gear or camshaft (Chapter 2A, 2B or 2C).
- [ ] Ancillary component fault (coolant pump, alternator, etc) – (Chapters 3, 5A, etc).

Knocking or thumping noises

- [ ] Worn big-end bearings (regular heavy knocking, perhaps less under load) (Chapter 2C).
- [ ] Worn main bearings (rumbling and knocking, perhaps worsening under load) (Chapter 2C).
- [ ] Piston slap (most noticeable when cold) (Chapter 2C).
- [ ] Ancillary component fault (coolant pump, alternator, etc) – (Chapters 3, 5A, etc).

Cooling system

Overheating

- [ ] Insufficient coolant in system (*Weekly checks*).
- [ ] Thermostat faulty (stuck closed) (Chapter 3).
- [ ] Radiator core blocked, or grille restricted (Chapter 3).
- [ ] Electric cooling fan or sensor faulty (Chapter 3).
- [ ] Pressure cap faulty (Chapter 3).
- [ ] Inaccurate temperature gauge/sensor (Chapter 3).
- [ ] Airlock in cooling system (Chapter 1).
- [ ] Engine management system fault (Chapter 4).

Overcooling

- [ ] Thermostat faulty (stuck open) (Chapter 3).
- [ ] Inaccurate temperature gauge/sensor (Chapter 3).

External coolant leakage

- [ ] Deteriorated or damaged hoses or hose clips (Chapter 1).
- [ ] Radiator core or heater matrix leaking (Chapter 3).
- [ ] Pressure cap faulty (Chapter 3).
- [ ] Coolant pump leaking (Chapter 3).
- [ ] Boiling due to overheating (Chapter 3).
- [ ] Core plug leaking (Chapter 2C).

Internal coolant leakage

- [ ] Leaking cylinder head gasket (Chapter 2A, 2B or 2C).
- [ ] Cracked cylinder head or cylinder bore (Chapter 2A, 2B or 2C).

Corrosion

- [ ] Infrequent draining and flushing (Chapter 1).
- [ ] Incorrect coolant mixture or inappropriate coolant type (Chapter 1).

Fuel and exhaust systems

Excessive fuel consumption

- [ ] Air filter element dirty or clogged (Chapter 1).
- [ ] Engine management system fault (Chapter 4).
- [ ] Faulty injector(s) (Chapter 4).
- [ ] Tyres under-inflated (*Weekly checks*).
- [ ] Brakes binding (Chapters 1 and 9).

Fuel leakage and/or fuel odour

- [ ] Damaged or corroded fuel tank, pipes or connections (Chapter 4A).

Excessive noise or fumes from exhaust system

- [ ] Leaking exhaust system or manifold joints (Chapters 1 and 4A).
- [ ] Leaking, corroded or damaged silencers or pipe (Chapters 1 and 4A).
- [ ] Broken mountings causing body or suspension contact (Chapters 1 and 4A).

Clutch

Pedal travels to floor – no pressure or very little resistance

☐ Air in hydraulic system/faulty master or slave cylinder (Chapter 6).
☐ Broken clutch release bearing or fork (Chapter 6).
☐ Broken diaphragm spring in clutch pressure plate (Chapter 6).

Clutch fails to disengage (unable to select gears)

☐ Air in hydraulic system/faulty master or slave cylinder (Chapter 6).
☐ Clutch disc sticking on gearbox input shaft splines (Chapter 6).
☐ Clutch disc sticking to flywheel or pressure plate (Chapter 6).
☐ Faulty pressure plate assembly (Chapter 6).
☐ Clutch release mechanism worn or incorrectly assembled (Chapter 6).

Clutch slips (engine speed rises, with no increase in vehicle speed)

☐ Faulty hydraulic release system (Chapter 6).

☐ Clutch disc linings excessively worn (Chapter 6).
☐ Clutch disc linings contaminated with oil or grease (Chapter 6).
☐ Faulty pressure plate or weak diaphragm spring (Chapter 6).

Judder as clutch is engaged

☐ Clutch disc linings contaminated with oil or grease (Chapter 6).
☐ Clutch disc linings excessively worn (Chapter 6).
☐ Faulty or distorted pressure plate or diaphragm spring (Chapter 6).
☐ Worn or loose engine or gearbox mountings (Chapter 2A or 2B).
☐ Clutch disc hub or gearbox input shaft splines worn (Chapter 6).

Noise when depressing or releasing clutch pedal

☐ Worn clutch release bearing (Chapter 6).
☐ Worn or dry clutch pedal bushes (Chapter 6).
☐ Faulty pressure plate assembly (Chapter 6).
☐ Pressure plate diaphragm spring broken (Chapter 6).
☐ Broken clutch disc cushioning springs (Chapter 6).

Manual transmission

Noisy in neutral with engine running

☐ Input shaft bearings worn (noise apparent with clutch pedal released, but not when depressed) (Chapter 7A).*
☐ Clutch release bearing worn (noise apparent with clutch pedal depressed, possibly less when released) (Chapter 6).

Noisy in one particular gear

☐ Worn, damaged or chipped gear teeth (Chapter 7A).*

Difficulty engaging gears

☐ Clutch fault (Chapter 6).
☐ Worn or damaged gear selection cables (Chapter 7A).
☐ Worn synchroniser units (Chapter 7A).*

Jumps out of gear

☐ Worn or damaged gear selection cables (Chapter 7A).
☐ Worn synchroniser units (Chapter 7A).*
☐ Worn selector forks (Chapter 7A).*

Vibration

☐ Lack of oil (Chapters 1 and 7A).
☐ Worn bearings (Chapter 7A).*

Lubricant leaks

☐ Leaking differential output oil seal (Chapter 7A).
☐ Leaking housing joint (Chapter 7A).*
☐ Leaking input shaft oil seal (Chapter 7A).

Although the corrective action necessary to remedy the symptoms described is beyond the scope of the home mechanic, the above information should be helpful in isolating the cause of the condition, so that the owner can communicate clearly with a professional mechanic.

Automatic transmission

Note: *Due to the complexity of the automatic transmission, it is difficult for the home mechanic to properly diagnose and service this unit. For problems other than the following, the vehicle should be taken to a Peugeot dealer service department or suitably-equipped specialist.*

Fluid leakage

☐ Automatic transmission fluid is usually dark in colour. Fluid leaks should not be confused with engine oil, which can easily be blown onto the transmission by airflow.

☐ To determine the source of a leak, first remove all built-up dirt and grime from the transmission housing and surrounding areas using a degreasing agent, or by steam-cleaning. Drive the vehicle at low speed, so airflow will not blow the leak far from its source. Raise and support the vehicle, and determine where the leak is coming from.

Transmission fluid brown, or has burned smell

☐ Transmission fluid level low, or fluid in need of renewal (Chapter 1 and 7B).

General gear selection problems

☐ Chapter 7B deals with checking and adjusting the selector cable on automatic transmissions. The following are common problems, which may be caused by a poorly adjusted cable:

a) Engine starting in gears other than Park or Neutral.
b) Indicator panel showing a gear other than that being used.
c) Vehicle moves when in Park or Neutral.
d) Poor gear shift quality or erratic gear changes.
☐ Refer to Chapter 7B for the selector cable adjustment procedure.

Transmission will not downshift (kickdown) at full throttle

☐ Low transmission fluid level (Chapter 1).
☐ Incorrect selector cable adjustment (Chapter 7B).

Engine won't start in any gear, or starts in gears other than Park or Neutral

☐ Incorrect multi-function switch adjustment (Chapter 7B).
☐ Incorrect selector cable adjustment (Chapter 7B).

Transmission slips, shifts roughly, is noisy, or has no drive in forward or reverse gears

☐ There are many probable causes for the above problems, but the home mechanic should be concerned with only one possibility – fluid level. Before taking the vehicle to a dealer or transmission specialist, check the fluid level as described in Chapter 1. Correct the fluid level as necessary, or change the fluid. If the problem persists, professional help will be necessary.

Driveshafts

Clicking or knocking noise on turns (at slow speed on full-lock)

☐ Lack of constant velocity joint lubricant, possibly due to damaged gaiter (Chapter 8).
☐ Worn outer constant velocity joint (Chapter 8).

Vibration when accelerating or decelerating

☐ Worn inner constant velocity joint (Chapter 8).
☐ Bent or distorted driveshaft (Chapter 8).
☐ Worn intermediate bearing (Chapter 8).

Braking system

Note: *Before assuming that a brake problem exists, make sure that the tyres are in good condition and correctly inflated, that the front wheel alignment is correct, and that the vehicle is not loaded with weight in an unequal manner. Apart from checking the condition of all pipe and hose connections, any faults occurring on the anti-lock braking system should be referred to a Peugeot dealer for diagnosis.*

Vehicle pulls to one side under braking

☐ Worn, defective, damaged or contaminated brake pads on one side (Chapter 9).
☐ Seized or partially-seized front brake caliper (Chapter 9).
☐ A mixture of brake pad materials fitted between sides (Chapter 9).
☐ Brake caliper mounting bolts loose (Chapter 9).
☐ Worn or damaged steering or suspension components (Chapters 1 and 10).

Noise (grinding or high-pitched squeal) when brakes applied

☐ Brake pad material worn down to metal backing (Chapters 1 and 9).
☐ Excessive corrosion of brake disc. May be apparent after the vehicle has been standing for some time (Chapter 9).
☐ Foreign object (stone chipping, etc) trapped between brake disc and shield (Chapter 9).

Excessive brake pedal travel

☐ Faulty master cylinder (Chapter 9).
☐ Air in hydraulic system (Chapter 9).
☐ Faulty vacuum servo unit (Chapter 9).

Brake pedal feels spongy when depressed

☐ Air in hydraulic system (Chapter 9).

☐ Deteriorated flexible rubber brake hoses (Chapters 1 and 9).
☐ Master cylinder mounting nuts loose (Chapter 9).
☐ Faulty master cylinder (Chapter 9).

Excessive brake pedal effort required to stop vehicle

☐ Faulty vacuum servo unit (Chapter 9).
☐ Disconnected, damaged or insecure brake servo vacuum hose (Chapter 9).
☐ Primary or secondary hydraulic circuit failure (Chapter 9).
☐ Seized brake caliper (Chapter 9).
☐ Brake pads incorrectly fitted (Chapter 9).
☐ Incorrect grade of brake pads fitted (Chapter 9).
☐ Brake pads contaminated (Chapter 9).

Judder felt through brake pedal or steering wheel when braking

☐ Excessive run-out or distortion of discs (Chapters 9).
☐ Brake pads worn (Chapters 1 and 9).
☐ Brake caliper mounting bolts loose (Chapter 9).
☐ Wear in suspension or steering components or mountings (Chapters 1 and 10).

Brakes binding

☐ Seized brake caliper (Chapter 9).
☐ Incorrectly-adjusted handbrake mechanism (Chapter 9).
☐ Faulty master cylinder (Chapter 9).

Rear wheels locking under normal braking

☐ Rear brake pads contaminated (Chapters 1 and 9).
☐ ABS system fault (Chapter 9).

uspension and steering

Note: *Before diagnosing suspension or steering faults, be sure that the trouble is not due to incorrect tyre pressures, mixtures of tyre types, or binding brakes.*

Vehicle pulls to one side

- ☐ Defective tyre (*Weekly checks*).
- ☐ Excessive wear in suspension or steering components (Chapters 1 and 10).
- ☐ Incorrect front wheel alignment (Chapter 10).
- ☐ Damage to steering or suspension components (Chapter 1).

Wheel wobble and vibration

- ☐ Front roadwheels out of balance (vibration felt mainly through the steering wheel) (Chapters 1 and 10).
- ☐ Rear roadwheels out of balance (vibration felt throughout the vehicle) (Chapters 1 and 10).
- ☐ Roadwheels damaged or distorted (Chapters 1 and 10).
- ☐ Faulty or damaged tyre (*Weekly checks*).
- ☐ Worn steering or suspension joints, bushes or components (Chapters 1 and 10).
- ☐ Wheel bolts loose (Chapters 1 and 10).

Excessive pitching and/or rolling around corners, or during braking

- ☐ Defective shock absorbers (Chapters 1 and 10).
- ☐ Broken or weak spring and/or suspension part (Chapters 1 and 10).
- ☐ Worn or damaged anti-roll bar or mountings (Chapter 10).

Wandering or general instability

- ☐ Incorrect front wheel alignment (Chapter 10).
- ☐ Worn steering or suspension joints, bushes or components (Chapters 1 and 10).
- ☐ Roadwheels out of balance (Chapters 1 and 10).
- ☐ Faulty or damaged tyre (*Weekly checks*).
- ☐ Wheel bolts loose (Chapters 1 and 10).
- ☐ Defective shock absorbers (Chapters 1 and 10).

Excessively-stiff steering

- ☐ Lack of power steering fluid (Chapter 10).

- ☐ Seized track rod end balljoint or suspension balljoint (Chapters 1 and 10).
- ☐ Incorrect front wheel alignment (Chapter 10).
- ☐ Steering rack or column bent or damaged (Chapter 10).
- ☐ Power steering pump fault (Chapter 10).

Excessive play in steering

- ☐ Worn steering column universal joint (Chapter 10).
- ☐ Worn steering track rod end balljoints (Chapters 1 and 10).
- ☐ Worn steering rack (Chapter 10).
- ☐ Worn steering or suspension joints, bushes or components (Chapters 1 and 10).

Lack of power assistance

- ☐ Incorrect power steering fluid level (*Weekly checks*).
- ☐ Restriction in power steering fluid hoses (Chapter 1).
- ☐ Faulty power steering pump (Chapter 10).
- ☐ Faulty steering rack (Chapter 10).

Tyre wear excessive

Tyre treads exhibit feathered edges
- ☐ Incorrect toe setting (Chapter 10).

Tyres worn in centre of tread
- ☐ Tyres over-inflated (*Weekly checks*).

Tyres worn on inside and outside edges
- ☐ Tyres under-inflated (*Weekly checks*).

Tyres worn on inside or outside edges
- ☐ Incorrect camber/castor angles (wear on one edge only) – (Chapter 10).
- ☐ Worn steering or suspension joints, bushes or components (Chapters 1 and 10).
- ☐ Excessively-hard cornering.
- ☐ Accident damage.

Tyres worn unevenly
- ☐ Tyres/wheels out of balance (*Weekly checks*).
- ☐ Excessive wheel or tyre run-out (Chapter 1).
- ☐ Worn shock absorbers (Chapters 1 and 10).
- ☐ Faulty tyre (*Weekly checks*).

Electrical system

Note: *For problems associated with the starting system, refer to the faults listed under 'Engine' earlier in this Section.*

Battery won't hold a charge for more than a few days

- ☐ Battery defective internally (Chapter 5A).
- ☐ Battery terminal connections loose or corroded (*Weekly checks*).
- ☐ Auxiliary drivebelt broken, worn or incorrectly adjusted (Chapter 1).
- ☐ Alternator not charging at correct output (Chapter 5A).
- ☐ Alternator or voltage regulator faulty (Chapter 5A).
- ☐ Short-circuit causing continual battery drain (Chapters 5A and 12).

Ignition/no-charge warning light stays on with engine running

- ☐ Auxiliary drivebelt broken, worn, or incorrectly adjusted (Chapter 1).
- ☐ Internal fault in alternator or voltage regulator (Chapter 5A).
- ☐ Broken, disconnected, or loose wiring in charging circuit (Chapter 5A).

Ignition/no-charge warning light fails to come on

- ☐ Warning light bulb blown (Chapter 12).
- ☐ Broken, disconnected, or loose wiring in warning light circuit (Chapter 12).
- ☐ Alternator faulty (Chapter 5A).

Lights inoperative

- ☐ Bulb blown (Chapter 12).
- ☐ Corrosion of bulb or bulbholder contacts (Chapter 12).
- ☐ Blown fuse (Chapter 12).
- ☐ Faulty relay (Chapter 12).
- ☐ Broken, loose, or disconnected wiring (Chapter 12).
- ☐ Faulty switch (Chapter 12).

Instrument readings inaccurate or erratic

Fuel or temperature gauges give no reading

- ☐ Faulty gauge sensor unit (Chapter 3 or 4).
- ☐ Wiring open-circuit (Chapter 12).
- ☐ Faulty gauge (Chapter 12).

Fuel or temperature gauges give continuous maximum reading

- ☐ Faulty gauge sensor unit (Chapter 3 or 4).
- ☐ Wiring short-circuit (Chapter 12).
- ☐ Faulty gauge (Chapter 12).

Horn inoperative, or unsatisfactory in operation

Horn operates all the time

- ☐ Horn push either earthed or stuck down (Chapter 12).
- ☐ Horn cable-to-horn push earthed (Chapter 12).

Horn fails to operate

- ☐ Blown fuse (Chapter 12).
- ☐ Cable or cable connections loose, broken or disconnected (Chapter 12).
- ☐ Faulty horn (Chapter 12).

Horn emits intermittent or unsatisfactory sound

- ☐ Cable connections loose (Chapter 12).
- ☐ Horn mountings loose (Chapter 12).
- ☐ Faulty horn (Chapter 12).

Windscreen/tailgate wipers failed, or unsatisfactory in operation

Wipers fail to operate, or operate very slowly

- ☐ Wiper blades stuck to screen, or linkage seized or binding (Chapters 1 and 12).

- ☐ Blown fuse (Chapter 12).
- ☐ Cable or cable connections loose, broken or disconnected (Chapter 12).
- ☐ Faulty built-in system interface (BSI) unit (Chapter 12).
- ☐ Faulty wiper motor (Chapter 12).

Wiper blades sweep over too large or too small an area of the glass

- ☐ Wiper arms incorrectly positioned on spindles (Chapter 12).
- ☐ Excessive wear of wiper linkage (Chapter 12).
- ☐ Wiper motor or linkage mountings loose or insecure (Chapter 12).

Wiper blades fail to clean the glass effectively

- ☐ Wiper blade rubbers worn or perished (*Weekly checks*).
- ☐ Wiper arm tension springs broken, or arm pivots seized (Chapter 12).
- ☐ Insufficient windscreen washer additive to adequately remove road film (*Weekly checks*).

Windscreen/tailgate washers failed, or unsatisfactory in operation

One or more washer jets inoperative

- ☐ Blocked washer jet (*Weekly checks*).
- ☐ Disconnected, kinked or restricted fluid hose (Chapter 12).
- ☐ Insufficient fluid in washer reservoir (*Weekly checks*).

Washer pump fails to operate

- ☐ Broken or disconnected wiring or connections (Chapter 12).
- ☐ Blown fuse (Chapter 12).
- ☐ Faulty washer switch (Chapter 12).
- ☐ Faulty washer pump (Chapter 12).

Electric windows inoperative, or unsatisfactory in operation

Window glass will only move in one direction

- ☐ Faulty switch (Chapter 12).

Window glass slow to move

- ☐ Regulator seized or damaged, or in need of lubricant (Chapter 11).
- ☐ Door internal components or trim fouling regulator (Chapter 11).
- ☐ Faulty motor (Chapter 11).

Window glass fails to move

- ☐ Blown fuse (Chapter 12).
- ☐ Broken or disconnected wiring or connections (Chapter 12).
- ☐ Faulty motor (Chapter 11).
- ☐ Faulty built-in systems interface (BSI) unit (Chapter 12).

Central locking system inoperative, or unsatisfactory in operation

Complete system failure

- ☐ Blown fuse (Chapter 12).
- ☐ Broken or disconnected wiring or connections (Chapter 12).
- ☐ Faulty built-in system interface (BSI) unit (Chapter 12).

Door/tailgate locks but will not unlock, or unlocks but will not lock

- ☐ Broken or disconnected link rod(s) (Chapter 11).
- ☐ Faulty lock motor (Chapter 11).

One lock fails to operate

- ☐ Broken or disconnected wiring or connections (Chapter 12).
- ☐ Faulty lock motor (Chapter 11).
- ☐ Broken, binding or disconnected link rod(s) (Chapter 11).

A

ABS (Anti-lock brake system) A system, usually electronically controlled, that senses incipient wheel lockup during braking and relieves hydraulic pressure at wheels that are about to skid.

Air bag An inflatable bag hidden in the steering wheel (driver's side) or the dash or glovebox (passenger side). In a head-on collision, the bags inflate, preventing the driver and front passenger from being thrown forward into the steering wheel or windscreen.

Air cleaner A metal or plastic housing, containing a filter element, which removes dust and dirt from the air being drawn into the engine.

Air filter element The actual filter in an air cleaner system, usually manufactured from pleated paper and requiring renewal at regular intervals.

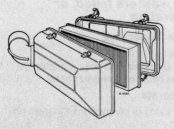

Air filter

Allen key A hexagonal wrench which fits into a recessed hexagonal hole.

Alligator clip A long-nosed spring-loaded metal clip with meshing teeth. Used to make temporary electrical connections.

Alternator A component in the electrical system which converts mechanical energy from a drivebelt into electrical energy to charge the battery and to operate the starting system, ignition system and electrical accessories.

Ampere (amp) A unit of measurement for the flow of electric current. One amp is the amount of current produced by one volt acting through a resistance of one ohm.

Anaerobic sealer A substance used to prevent bolts and screws from loosening. Anaerobic means that it does not require oxygen for activation. The Loctite brand is widely used.

Antifreeze A substance (usually ethylene glycol) mixed with water, and added to a vehicle's cooling system, to prevent freezing of the coolant in winter. Antifreeze also contains chemicals to inhibit corrosion and the formation of rust and other deposits that would tend to clog the radiator and coolant passages and reduce cooling efficiency.

Anti-seize compound A coating that reduces the risk of seizing on fasteners that are subjected to high temperatures, such as exhaust manifold bolts and nuts.

Asbestos A natural fibrous mineral with great heat resistance, commonly used in the composition of brake friction materials.

Asbestos is a health hazard and the dust created by brake systems should never be inhaled or ingested.

Axle A shaft on which a wheel revolves, or which revolves with a wheel. Also, a solid beam that connects the two wheels at one end of the vehicle. An axle which also transmits power to the wheels is known as a live axle.

Axleshaft A single rotating shaft, on either side of the differential, which delivers power from the final drive assembly to the drive wheels. Also called a driveshaft or a halfshaft.

B

Ball bearing An anti-friction bearing consisting of a hardened inner and outer race with hardened steel balls between two races.

Bearing The curved surface on a shaft or in a bore, or the part assembled into either, that permits relative motion between them with minimum wear and friction.

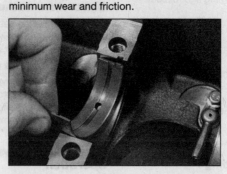

Bearing

Big-end bearing The bearing in the end of the connecting rod that's attached to the crankshaft.

Bleed nipple A valve on a brake wheel cylinder, caliper or other hydraulic component that is opened to purge the hydraulic system of air. Also called a bleed screw.

Brake bleeding Procedure for removing air from lines of a hydraulic brake system.

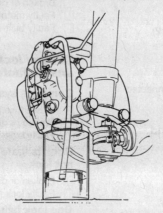

Brake bleeding

Brake disc The component of a disc brake that rotates with the wheels.

Brake drum The component of a drum brake that rotates with the wheels.

Brake linings The friction material which contacts the brake disc or drum to retard the vehicle's speed. The linings are bonded or riveted to the brake pads or shoes.

Brake pads The replaceable friction pads that pinch the brake disc when the brakes are applied. Brake pads consist of a friction material bonded or riveted to a rigid backing plate.

Brake shoe The crescent-shaped carrier to which the brake linings are mounted and which forces the lining against the rotating drum during braking.

Braking systems For more information on braking systems, consult the *Haynes Automotive Brake Manual*.

Breaker bar A long socket wrench handle providing greater leverage.

Bulkhead The insulated partition between the engine and the passenger compartment.

C

Caliper The non-rotating part of a disc-brake assembly that straddles the disc and carries the brake pads. The caliper also contains the hydraulic components that cause the pads to pinch the disc when the brakes are applied. A caliper is also a measuring tool that can be set to measure inside or outside dimensions of an object.

Camshaft A rotating shaft on which a series of cam lobes operate the valve mechanisms. The camshaft may be driven by gears, by sprockets and chain or by sprockets and a belt.

Canister A container in an evaporative emission control system; contains activated charcoal granules to trap vapours from the fuel system.

Canister

Carburettor A device which mixes fuel with air in the proper proportions to provide a desired power output from a spark ignition internal combustion engine.

Castellated Resembling the parapets along the top of a castle wall. For example, a castellated balljoint stud nut.

Castor In wheel alignment, the backward or forward tilt of the steering axis. Castor is positive when the steering axis is inclined rearward at the top.

Catalytic converter A silencer-like device in the exhaust system which converts certain pollutants in the exhaust gases into less harmful substances.

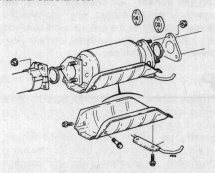

Catalytic converter

Circlip A ring-shaped clip used to prevent endwise movement of cylindrical parts and shafts. An internal circlip is installed in a groove in a housing; an external circlip fits into a groove on the outside of a cylindrical piece such as a shaft.

Clearance The amount of space between two parts. For example, between a piston and a cylinder, between a bearing and a journal, etc.

Coil spring A spiral of elastic steel found in various sizes throughout a vehicle, for example as a springing medium in the suspension and in the valve train.

Compression Reduction in volume, and increase in pressure and temperature, of a gas, caused by squeezing it into a smaller space.

Compression ratio The relationship between cylinder volume when the piston is at top dead centre and cylinder volume when the piston is at bottom dead centre.

Constant velocity (CV) joint A type of universal joint that cancels out vibrations caused by driving power being transmitted through an angle.

Core plug A disc or cup-shaped metal device inserted in a hole in a casting through which core was removed when the casting was formed. Also known as a freeze plug or expansion plug.

Crankcase The lower part of the engine block in which the crankshaft rotates.

Crankshaft The main rotating member, or shaft, running the length of the crankcase, with offset "throws" to which the connecting rods are attached.

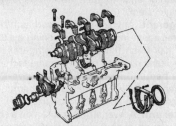

Crankshaft assembly

Crocodile clip See Alligator clip

D

Diagnostic code Code numbers obtained by accessing the diagnostic mode of an engine management computer. This code can be used to determine the area in the system where a malfunction may be located.

Disc brake A brake design incorporating a rotating disc onto which brake pads are squeezed. The resulting friction converts the energy of a moving vehicle into heat.

Double-overhead cam (DOHC) An engine that uses two overhead camshafts, usually one for the intake valves and one for the exhaust valves.

Drivebelt(s) The belt(s) used to drive accessories such as the alternator, water pump, power steering pump, air conditioning compressor, etc. off the crankshaft pulley.

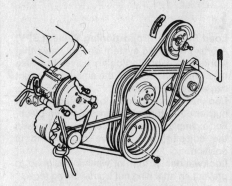

Accessory drivebelts

Driveshaft Any shaft used to transmit motion. Commonly used when referring to the axleshafts on a front wheel drive vehicle.

Drum brake A type of brake using a drum-shaped metal cylinder attached to the inner surface of the wheel. When the brake pedal is pressed, curved brake shoes with friction linings press against the inside of the drum to slow or stop the vehicle.

E

EGR valve A valve used to introduce exhaust gases into the intake air stream.

Electronic control unit (ECU) A computer which controls (for instance) ignition and fuel injection systems, or an anti-lock braking system. For more information refer to the *Haynes Automotive Electrical and Electronic Systems Manual.*

Electronic Fuel Injection (EFI) A computer controlled fuel system that distributes fuel through an injector located in each intake port of the engine.

Emergency brake A braking system, independent of the main hydraulic system, that can be used to slow or stop the vehicle if the primary brakes fail, or to hold the vehicle stationary even though the brake pedal isn't depressed. It usually consists of a hand lever that actuates either front or rear brakes mechanically through a series of cables and linkages. Also known as a handbrake or parking brake.

Endfloat The amount of lengthwise movement between two parts. As applied to a crankshaft, the distance that the crankshaft can move forward and back in the cylinder block.

Engine management system (EMS) A computer controlled system which manages the fuel injection and the ignition systems in an integrated fashion.

Exhaust manifold A part with several passages through which exhaust gases leave the engine combustion chambers and enter the exhaust pipe.

F

Fan clutch A viscous (fluid) drive coupling device which permits variable engine fan speeds in relation to engine speeds.

Feeler blade A thin strip or blade of hardened steel, ground to an exact thickness, used to check or measure clearances between parts.

Feeler blade

Firing order The order in which the engine cylinders fire, or deliver their power strokes, beginning with the number one cylinder.

Flywheel A heavy spinning wheel in which energy is absorbed and stored by means of momentum. On cars, the flywheel is attached to the crankshaft to smooth out firing impulses.

Free play The amount of travel before any action takes place. The "looseness" in a linkage, or an assembly of parts, between the initial application of force and actual movement. For example, the distance the brake pedal moves before the pistons in the master cylinder are actuated.

Fuse An electrical device which protects a circuit against accidental overload. The typical fuse contains a soft piece of metal which is calibrated to melt at a predetermined current flow (expressed as amps) and break the circuit.

Fusible link A circuit protection device consisting of a conductor surrounded by heat-resistant insulation. The conductor is smaller than the wire it protects, so it acts as the weakest link in the circuit. Unlike a blown fuse, a failed fusible link must frequently be cut from the wire for replacement.

G

Gap The distance the spark must travel in jumping from the centre electrode to the side electrode in a spark plug. Also refers to the spacing between the points in a contact breaker assembly in a conventional points-type ignition, or to the distance between the reluctor or rotor and the pickup coil in an electronic ignition.

Adjusting spark plug gap

Gasket Any thin, soft material - usually cork, cardboard, asbestos or soft metal - installed between two metal surfaces to ensure a good seal. For instance, the cylinder head gasket seals the joint between the block and the cylinder head.

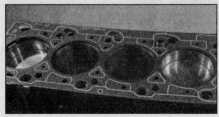
Gasket

Gauge An instrument panel display used to monitor engine conditions. A gauge with a movable pointer on a dial or a fixed scale is an analogue gauge. A gauge with a numerical readout is called a digital gauge.

H

Halfshaft A rotating shaft that transmits power from the final drive unit to a drive wheel, usually when referring to a live rear axle.

Harmonic balancer A device designed to reduce torsion or twisting vibration in the crankshaft. May be incorporated in the crankshaft pulley. Also known as a vibration damper.

Hone An abrasive tool for correcting small irregularities or differences in diameter in an engine cylinder, brake cylinder, etc.

Hydraulic tappet A tappet that utilises hydraulic pressure from the engine's lubrication system to maintain zero clearance (constant contact with both camshaft and valve stem). Automatically adjusts to variation in valve stem length. Hydraulic tappets also reduce valve noise.

I

Ignition timing The moment at which the spark plug fires, usually expressed in the number of crankshaft degrees before the piston reaches the top of its stroke.

Inlet manifold A tube or housing with passages through which flows the air-fuel mixture (carburettor vehicles and vehicles with throttle body injection) or air only (port fuel-injected vehicles) to the port openings in the cylinder head.

J

Jump start Starting the engine of a vehicle with a discharged or weak battery by attaching jump leads from the weak battery to a charged or helper battery.

L

Load Sensing Proportioning Valve (LSPV) A brake hydraulic system control valve that works like a proportioning valve, but also takes into consideration the amount of weight carried by the rear axle.

Locknut A nut used to lock an adjustment nut, or other threaded component, in place. For example, a locknut is employed to keep the adjusting nut on the rocker arm in position.

Lockwasher A form of washer designed to prevent an attaching nut from working loose.

M

MacPherson strut A type of front suspension system devised by Earle MacPherson at Ford of England. In its original form, a simple lateral link with the anti-roll bar creates the lower control arm. A long strut - an integral coil spring and shock absorber - is mounted between the body and the steering knuckle. Many modern so-called MacPherson strut systems use a conventional lower A-arm and don't rely on the anti-roll bar for location.

Multimeter An electrical test instrument with the capability to measure voltage, current and resistance.

N

NOx Oxides of Nitrogen. A common toxic pollutant emitted by petrol and diesel engines at higher temperatures.

O

Ohm The unit of electrical resistance. One volt applied to a resistance of one ohm will produce a current of one amp.

Ohmmeter An instrument for measuring electrical resistance.

O-ring A type of sealing ring made of a special rubber-like material; in use, the O-ring is compressed into a groove to provide the sealing action.

Overhead cam (ohc) engine An engine with the camshaft(s) located on top of the cylinder head(s).

Overhead valve (ohv) engine An engine with the valves located in the cylinder head, but with the camshaft located in the engine block.

Oxygen sensor A device installed in the engine exhaust manifold, which senses the oxygen content in the exhaust and converts this information into an electric current. Also called a Lambda sensor.

P

Phillips screw A type of screw head having a cross instead of a slot for a corresponding type of screwdriver.

Plastigage A thin strip of plastic thread, available in different sizes, used for measuring clearances. For example, a strip of Plastigage is laid across a bearing journal. The parts are assembled and dismantled; the width of the crushed strip indicates the clearance between journal and bearing.

Plastigage

Propeller shaft The long hollow tube with universal joints at both ends that carries power from the transmission to the differential on front-engined rear wheel drive vehicles.

Proportioning valve A hydraulic control valve which limits the amount of pressure to the rear brakes during panic stops to prevent wheel lock-up.

R

Rack-and-pinion steering A steering system with a pinion gear on the end of the steering shaft that mates with a rack (think of a geared wheel opened up and laid flat). When the steering wheel is turned, the pinion turns, moving the rack to the left or right. This movement is transmitted through the track rods to the steering arms at the wheels.

Radiator A liquid-to-air heat transfer device designed to reduce the temperature of the coolant in an internal combustion engine cooling system.

Refrigerant Any substance used as a heat transfer agent in an air-conditioning system. R-12 has been the principle refrigerant for many years; recently, however, manufacturers have begun using R-134a, a non-CFC substance that is considered less harmful to the ozone in the upper atmosphere.

Rocker arm A lever arm that rocks on a shaft or pivots on a stud. In an overhead valve engine, the rocker arm converts the upward movement of the pushrod into a downward movement to open a valve.

Rotor In a distributor, the rotating device inside the cap that connects the centre electrode and the outer terminals as it turns, distributing the high voltage from the coil secondary winding to the proper spark plug. Also, that part of an alternator which rotates inside the stator. Also, the rotating assembly of a turbocharger, including the compressor wheel, shaft and turbine wheel.

Runout The amount of wobble (in-and-out movement) of a gear or wheel as it's rotated. The amount a shaft rotates "out-of-true." The out-of-round condition of a rotating part.

S

Sealant A liquid or paste used to prevent leakage at a joint. Sometimes used in conjunction with a gasket.

Sealed beam lamp An older headlight design which integrates the reflector, lens and filaments into a hermetically-sealed one-piece unit. When a filament burns out or the lens cracks, the entire unit is simply replaced.

Serpentine drivebelt A single, long, wide accessory drivebelt that's used on some newer vehicles to drive all the accessories, instead of a series of smaller, shorter belts. Serpentine drivebelts are usually tensioned by an automatic tensioner.

Serpentine drivebelt

Shim Thin spacer, commonly used to adjust the clearance or relative positions between two parts. For example, shims inserted into or under bucket tappets control valve clearances. Clearance is adjusted by changing the thickness of the shim.

Slide hammer A special puller that screws into or hooks onto a component such as a shaft or bearing; a heavy sliding handle on the shaft bottoms against the end of the shaft to knock the component free.

Sprocket A tooth or projection on the periphery of a wheel, shaped to engage with a chain or drivebelt. Commonly used to refer to the sprocket wheel itself.

Starter inhibitor switch On vehicles with an automatic transmission, a switch that prevents starting if the vehicle is not in Neutral or Park.

Strut See MacPherson strut.

T

Tappet A cylindrical component which transmits motion from the cam to the valve stem, either directly or via a pushrod and rocker arm. Also called a cam follower.

Thermostat A heat-controlled valve that regulates the flow of coolant between the cylinder block and the radiator, so maintaining optimum engine operating temperature. A thermostat is also used in some air cleaners in which the temperature is regulated.

Thrust bearing The bearing in the clutch assembly that is moved in to the release levers by clutch pedal action to disengage the clutch. Also referred to as a release bearing.

Timing belt A toothed belt which drives the camshaft. Serious engine damage may result if it breaks in service.

Timing chain A chain which drives the camshaft.

Toe-in The amount the front wheels are closer together at the front than at the rear. On rear wheel drive vehicles, a slight amount of toe-in is usually specified to keep the front wheels running parallel on the road by offsetting other forces that tend to spread the wheels apart.

Toe-out The amount the front wheels are closer together at the rear than at the front. On front wheel drive vehicles, a slight amount of toe-out is usually specified.

Tools For full information on choosing and using tools, refer to the *Haynes Automotive Tools Manual*.

Tracer A stripe of a second colour applied to a wire insulator to distinguish that wire from another one with the same colour insulator.

Tune-up A process of accurate and careful adjustments and parts replacement to obtain the best possible engine performance.

Turbocharger A centrifugal device, driven by exhaust gases, that pressurises the intake air. Normally used to increase the power output from a given engine displacement, but can also be used primarily to reduce exhaust emissions (as on VW's "Umwelt" Diesel engine).

U

Universal joint or U-joint A double-pivoted connection for transmitting power from a driving to a driven shaft through an angle. A U-joint consists of two Y-shaped yokes and a cross-shaped member called the spider.

V

Valve A device through which the flow of liquid, gas, vacuum, or loose material in bulk may be started, stopped, or regulated by a movable part that opens, shuts, or partially obstructs one or more ports or passageways. A valve is also the movable part of such a device.

Valve clearance The clearance between the valve tip (the end of the valve stem) and the rocker arm or tappet. The valve clearance is measured when the valve is closed.

Vernier caliper A precision measuring instrument that measures inside and outside dimensions. Not quite as accurate as a micrometer, but more convenient.

Viscosity The thickness of a liquid or its resistance to flow.

Volt A unit for expressing electrical "pressure" in a circuit. One volt that will produce a current of one ampere through a resistance of one ohm.

W

Welding Various processes used to join metal items by heating the areas to be joined to a molten state and fusing them together. For more information refer to the *Haynes Automotive Welding Manual*.

Wiring diagram A drawing portraying the components and wires in a vehicle's electrical system, using standardised symbols. For more information refer to the *Haynes Automotive Electrical and Electronic Systems Manual*.

Note: *References throughout this index are in the form* "**Chapter number**" • "**Page number**". *So, for example, 2C•15 refers to page 15 of Chapter 2C.*

Note: *References throughout this index are in the form "Chapter number" • "Page number". So, for example, 2C•15 refers to page 15 of Chapter 2C.*

Note: *References throughout this index are in the form "Chapter number" • "Page number". So, for example, 2C•15 refers to page 15 of Chapter 2C.*

Note: *References throughout this index are in the form* **"Chapter number"** • **"Page number"**. *So, for example, 2C•15 refers to page 15 of Chapter 2C.*

Haynes Manuals – The Complete UK Car List

Title	Book No.
ALFA ROMEO Alfasud/Sprint (74 - 88) up to F *	0292
Alfa Romeo Alfetta (73 – 87) up to E *	0531
AUDI 80, 90 & Coupe Petrol (79 – Nov 88) up to F	0605
Audi 80, 90 & Coupe Petrol (Oct 86 – 90) D to H	1491
Audi 100 & A6 Petrol & Diesel (May 91 – May 97) H to P	3504
Audi A3 Petrol & Diesel (96 – May 03) P to 03	4253
Audi A3 Petrol & Diesel (June 03 – Mar 08) 03 to 08	4884
Audi A4 Petrol & Diesel (95 – 00) M to X	3575
Audi A4 Petrol & Diesel (01 – 04) X to 54	4609
Audi A4 Petrol & Diesel (Jan 05 – Feb 08) 54 to 57	4885
AUSTIN A35 & A40 (56 – 67) up to F *	0118
Mini (59 – 69) up to H *	0527
Mini (69 – 01) up to X	0646
Austin Healey 100/6 & 3000 (56 – 68) up to G *	0049
BEDFORD/Vauxhall Rascal & Suzuki Supercarry (86 – Oct 94) C to M	3015
BMW 1-Series 4-cyl Petrol & Diesel (04 – Aug 11) 54 to 11	4918
BMW 316, 320 & 320i (4-cyl)(75 – Feb 83) up to Y *	0276
BMW 3- & 5- Series Petrol (81 – 91) up to J	1948
BMW 3-Series Petrol (Apr 91 – 99) H to V	3210
BMW 3-Series Petrol (Sept 98 – 06) S to 56	4067
BMW 3-Series Petrol & Diesel (05 – Sept 08) 54 to 58	4782
BMW 5-Series 6-cyl Petrol (April 96 – Aug 03) N to 03	4151
BMW 5-Series Diesel (Sept 03 – 10) 53 to 10	4901
BMW 1500, 1502, 1600, 1602, 2000 & 2002 (59 – 77) up to S *	0240
CHRYSLER PT Cruiser Petrol (00-09) W to 09	4058
CITROEN 2CV, Ami & Dyane (67 – 90) up to H	0196
Citroen AX Petrol & Diesel (87- 97) D to P	3014
Citroen Berlingo & Peugeot Partner Petrol & Diesel (96 – 10) P to 60	4281
Citroen C1 Petrol (05 – 11) 05 to 11	4922
Citroen C3 Petrol & Diesel (02 – 09) 51 to 59	4890
Citroen C4 Petrol & Diesel (04 – 10) 54 to 60	5576
Citroen C5 Petrol & Diesel (01 – 08) Y to 08	4745
Citroen C15 Van Petrol & Diesel (89 – Oct 98) F to S	3509
Citroen CX Petrol (75 – 88) up to F	0528
Citroen Saxo Petrol & Diesel (96 – 04) N to 54	3506
Citroen Visa Petrol (79 – 88) up to F	0620
Citroen Xantia Petrol & Diesel (93 – 01) K to Y	3082
Citroen XM Petrol & Diesel (89 – 00) G to X	3451
Citroen Xsara Petrol & Diesel (97 – Sept 00) R to W	3751
Citroen Xsara Picasso Petrol & Diesel (00 – 02) W to 52	3944
Citroen Xsara Picasso (Mar 04 – 08) 04 to 58	4784
Citroen ZX Diesel (91 – 98) J to S	1922
Citroen ZX Petrol (91 – 98) H to S	1881
FIAT 126 (73 – 87) up to E *	0305
Fiat 500 (57 – 73) up to M *	0090
Fiat 500 & Panda (04 – 12) 53 to 61	5558
Fiat Bravo & Brava Petrol (95 – 00) N to W	3572
Fiat Cinquecento (93 – 98) K to R	3501
Fiat Panda (81 – 95) up to M	0793
Fiat Punto Petrol & Diesel (94 – Oct 99) L to V	3251
Fiat Punto Petrol (Oct 99 – July 03) V to 03	4066
Fiat Punto Petrol (03 – 07) 03 to 07	4746

Title	Book No.
Fiat Punto Petrol (Oct 99 – 07) V to 07	5634
Fiat X1/9 (74 – 89) up to G *	0273
FORD Anglia (59 – 68) up to G *	0001
Ford Capri II (& III) 1.6 & 2.0 (74 – 87) up to E *	0283
Ford Capri II (& III) 2.8 & 3.0 V6 (74 – 87) up to E	1309
Ford C-Max Petrol & Diesel (03 – 10) 53 to 60	4900
Ford Escort Mk I 1100 & 1300 (68 – 74) up to N *	0171
Ford Escort Mk I Mexico, RS 1600 & RS 2000 (70 – 74) up to N *	0139
Ford Escort Mk II Mexico, RS 1800 & RS 2000 (75 – 80) up to W *	0735
Ford Escort (75 – Aug 80) up to V *	0280
Ford Escort Petrol (Sept 80 – Sept 90) up to H	0686
Ford Escort & Orion Petrol (Sept 90 – 00) H to X	1737
Ford Escort & Orion Diesel (Sept 90 – 00) H to X	4081
Ford Fiesta Petrol (Feb 89 – Oct 95) F to N	1595
Ford Fiesta Petrol & Diesel (Oct 95 – Mar 02) N to 02	3397
Ford Fiesta Petrol & Diesel (Apr 02 – 08) 02 to 58	4170
Ford Fiesta Petrol & Diesel (08 – 11) 58 to 11	4907
Ford Focus Petrol & Diesel (98 – 01) S to Y	3759
Ford Focus Petrol & Diesel (Oct 01 – 05) 51 to 05	4167
Ford Focus Petrol (05 – 09) 54 to 09	4785
Ford Focus Diesel (05 – 09) 54 to 09	4807
Ford Fusion Petrol & Diesel (02 – 11) 02 to 61	5566
Ford Galaxy Petrol & Diesel (95 – Aug 00) M to W	3984
Ford Galaxy Petrol & Diesel (00 – 06) X to 06	5556
Ford Granada Petrol (Sept 77 – Feb 85) up to B *	0481
Ford Ka (96 – 08) P to 58	5567
Ford Mondeo Petrol (93 – Sept 00) K to X	1923
Ford Mondeo Petrol & Diesel (Oct 00 – Jul 03) X to 03	3990
Ford Mondeo Petrol & Diesel (July 03 – 07) 03 to 56	4619
Ford Mondeo Petrol & Diesel (Apr 07 – 12) 07 to 61	5548
Ford Mondeo Diesel (93 – Sept 00) L to X	3465
Ford Sierra V6 Petrol (82 – 91) up to J	0904
Ford Transit Connect Diesel (02 – 11) 02 to 11	4903
Ford Transit Diesel (Feb 86 – 99) C to T	3019
Ford Transit Diesel (00 – Oct 06) X to 56	4775
Ford 1.6 & 1.8 litre Diesel Engine (84 – 96) A to N	1172
HILLMAN Imp (63 – 76) up to R *	0022
HONDA Civic (Feb 84 – Oct 87) A to E	1226
Honda Civic (Nov 91 – 96) J to N	3199
Honda Civic Petrol (Mar 95 – 00) M to X	4050
Honda Civic Petrol & Diesel (01 – 05) X to 55	4611
Honda CR-V Petrol & Diesel (02 – 06) 51 to 56	4747
Honda Jazz (02 to 08) 51 to 58	4735
JAGUAR E-Type (61 – 72) up to L *	0140
Jaguar Mk I & II, 240 & 340 (55 – 69) up to H *	0098
Jaguar XJ6, XJ & Sovereign, Daimler Sovereign (68 – Oct 86) up to D	0242
Jaguar XJ6 & Sovereign (Oct 86 – Sept 94) D to M	3261
Jaguar XJ12, XJS & Sovereign, Daimler Double Six (72 – 88) up to F	0478
JEEP Cherokee Petrol (93 – 96) K to N	1943
LAND ROVER 90, 110 & Defender Diesel (83 – 07) up to 56	3017
Land Rover Discovery Petrol & Diesel (89 – 98) G to S	3016

Title	Book No.
Land Rover Discovery Diesel (Nov 98 – Jul 04) S to 04	4606
Land Rover Discovery Diesel (Aug 04 – Apr 09) 04 to 09	5562
Land Rover Freelander Petrol & Diesel (97 – Sept 03) R to 53	3929
Land Rover Freelander (97 – Oct 06) R to 56	5571
Land Rover Series II, IIA & III 4-cyl Petrol (58 – 85) up to C	0314
Land Rover Series II, IIA & III Petrol & Diesel (58 – 85) up to C	5568
MAZDA 323 (Mar 81 – Oct 89) up to G	1608
Mazda 323 (Oct 89 – 98) G to R	3455
Mazda B1600, B1800 & B2000 Pick-up Petrol (72 – 88) up to F	0267
Mazda MX-5 (89 – 05) G to 05	5565
Mazda RX-7 (79 – 85) up to C *	0460
MERCEDES-BENZ 190, 190E & 190D Petrol & Diesel (83 – 93) A to L	3450
Mercedes-Benz 200D, 240D, 240TD, 300D & 300TD 123 Series Diesel (Oct 76 – 85) up to C	1114
Mercedes-Benz 250 & 280 (68 – 72) up to L *	0346
Mercedes-Benz 250 & 280 123 Series Petrol (Oct 76 – 84) up to B *	0677
Mercedes-Benz 124 Series Petrol & Diesel (85 – Aug 93) C to K	3253
Mercedes-Benz A-Class Petrol & Diesel (98 – 04) S to 54	4748
Mercedes-Benz C-Class Petrol & Diesel (93 – Aug 00) L to W	3511
Mercedes-Benz C-Class (00 – 07) X to 07	4780
Mercedes-Benz Sprinter Diesel (95 – Apr 06) M to 06	4902
MGA (55 – 62)	0475
MGB (62 – 80) up to W	0111
MGB 1962 to 1980 (special edition) *	4894
MG Midget & Austin-Healey Sprite (58 – 80) up to W *	0265
MINI Petrol (July 01 – 06) Y to 56	4273
MINI Petrol & Diesel (Nov 06 – 13) 56 to 13	4904
MITSUBISHI Shogun & L200 Pick-ups Petrol (83 – 94) up to M	1944
MORRIS Minor 1000 (56 – 71) up to K	0024
NISSAN Almera Petrol (95 – Feb 00) N to V	4053
Nissan Almera & Tino Petrol (Feb 00 – 07) V to 56	4612
Nissan Micra (83 – Jan 93) up to K	0931
Nissan Micra (93 – 02) K to 52	3254
Nissan Micra Petrol (03 – Oct 10) 52 to 60	4734
Nissan Primera Petrol (90 – Aug 99) H to T	1851
Nissan Qashqai Petrol & Diesel (07 – 12) 56 to 62	5610
OPEL Ascona & Manta (B-Series) (Sept 75 – 88) up to F *	0316
Opel Ascona Petrol (81 – 88)	3215
Opel Ascona Petrol (Oct 91 – Feb 98)	3156
Opel Corsa Petrol (83 – Mar 93)	3160
Opel Corsa Petrol (Mar 93 – 97)	3159
Opel Kadett Petrol (Oct 84 – Oct 91)	3196
Opel Omega & Senator Petrol (Nov 86 – 94)	3157
Opel Vectra Petrol (Oct 88 – Oct 95)	3158
PEUGEOT 106 Petrol & Diesel (91 – 04) J to 53	1882
Peugeot 107 Petrol (05 – 11) 05 to 11	4923
Peugeot 205 Petrol (83 – 97) A to P	0932
Peugeot 206 Petrol & Diesel (98 – 01) S to X	3757

* Classic reprint

Title	Book No.
Peugeot 206 Petrol & Diesel (02 – 06) 51 to 06	4613
Peugeot 207 Petrol & Diesel (06 – July 09) 06 to 09	4787
Peugeot 306 Petrol & Diesel (93 – 02) K to 02	3073
Peugeot 307 Petrol & Diesel (01 – 08) Y to 58	4147
Peugeot 308 Petrol & Diesel (07 – 12) 07 to 12	5561
Peugeot 405 Diesel (88 – 97) E to P	3198
Peugeot 406 Petrol & Diesel (96 – Mar 99) N to T	3394
Peugeot 406 Petrol & Diesel (Mar 99 – 02) T to 52	3982
Peugeot 407 Diesel (04 -11) 53 to 11	5550
PORSCHE 911 (65 – 85) up to C	0264
Porsche 924 & 924 Turbo (76 – 85) up to C	0397
RANGE ROVER V8 Petrol (70 – Oct 92) up to K	0606
RELIANT Robin & Kitten (73 – 83) up to A *	0436
RENAULT 4 (61 – 86) up to D *	0072
Renault 5 Petrol (Feb 85 – 96) B to N	1219
Renault 19 Petrol (89 – 96) F to N	1646
Renault Clio Petrol (91 – May 98) H to R	1853
Renault Clio Petrol & Diesel (May 98 – May 01) R to Y	3906
Renault Clio Petrol & Diesel (June 01 – 05) Y to 55	4168
Renault Clio Petrol & Diesel (Oct 05 – May 09) 55 to 09	4788
Renault Espace Petrol & Diesel (85 – 96) C to N	3197
Renault Laguna Petrol & Diesel (94 – 00) L to W	3252
Renault Laguna Petrol & Diesel (Feb 01 – May 07) X to 07	4283
Renault Megane & Scenic Petrol & Diesel (96 – 99) N to T	3395
Renault Megane & Scenic Petrol & Diesel (Apr 99 – 02) T to 52	3916
Renault Megane Petrol & Diesel (Oct 02 – 08) 52 to 58	4284
Renault Scenic Petrol & Diesel (Sept 03 – 06) 53 to 06	4297
Renault Trafic Diesel (01 – 11) Y to 11	5551
ROVER 216 & 416 Petrol (89 – 96) G to N	1830
Rover 211, 214, 216, 218 & 220 Petrol & Diesel (Dec 95 – 99) N to V	3399
Rover 25 & MG ZR Petrol & Diesel (Oct 99 – 06) V to 06	4145
Rover 414, 416 & 420 Petrol & Diesel (May 95 – 99) M to V	3453
Rover 45 / MG ZS Petrol & Diesel (99 – 05) V to 55	4384
Rover 618, 620 & 623 Petrol (93 – 97) K to P	3257
Rover 75 / MG ZT Petrol & Diesel (99 – 06) S to 06	4292
Rover 820, 825 & 827 Petrol (86 – 95) D to N	1380
Rover 3500 (76 – 87) up to E *	0365
Rover Metro, 111 & 114 Petrol (May 90 – 98) G to S	1711
SAAB 95 & 96 (66 – 76) up to R *	0198
Saab 90, 99 & 900 (79 – Oct 93) up to L	0765
Saab 900 (Oct 93 – 98) L to R	3512
Saab 9000 4-cyl (85 – 98) C to S	1686
Saab 9-3 Petrol & Diesel (98 – Aug 02) R to 02	4614
Saab 9-3 Petrol & Diesel (92 – 07) 52 to 57	4749
Saab 9-3 Petrol & Diesel (07-on) 57 on	5569
Saab 9-5 4-cyl Petrol (97 – 05) R to 55	4156
Saab 9-5 (Sep 05 – Jun 10) 55 to 10	4891
SEAT Ibiza & Cordoba Petrol & Diesel (Oct 93 – Oct 99) L to V	3571
Seat Ibiza & Malaga Petrol (85 – 92) B to K	1609
Seat Ibiza Petrol & Diesel (May 02 – Apr 08) 02 to 08	4889

Title	Book No.
SKODA Fabia Petrol & Diesel (00 – 06) W to 06	4376
Skoda Felicia Petrol & Diesel (95 – 01) M to X	3505
Skoda Octavia Petrol (98 – April 04) R to 04	4285
Skoda Octavia Diesel (May 04 – 12) 04 to 61	5549
SUBARU 1600 & 1800 (Nov 79 – 90) up to H *	0995
SUNBEAM Alpine, Rapier & H120 (68 – 74) up to N *	0051
SUZUKI SJ Series, Samurai & Vitara 4-cyl Petrol (82 – 97) up to P	1942
Suzuki Supercarry & Bedford/Vauxhall Rascal (86 – Oct 94) C to M	3015
TOYOTA Avensis Petrol (98 – Jan 03) R to 52	4264
Toyota Aygo Petrol (05 – 11) 05 to 11	4921
Toyota Carina E Petrol (May 92 – 97) J to P	3256
Toyota Corolla (80 – 85) up to C	0683
Toyota Corolla (Sept 83 – Sept 87) A to E	1024
Toyota Corolla (Sept 87 – Aug 92) E to K	1683
Toyota Corolla Petrol (Aug 92 – 97) K to P	3259
Toyota Corolla Petrol (July 97 0 Feb 02) P to 51	4286
Toyota Corolla Petrol & Diesel (02 – Jan 07) 51 to 56	4791
Toyota Hi-Ace & Hi-Lux Petrol (69 – Oct 83) up to A	0304
Toyota RAV4 Petrol & Diesel (94 – 06) L to 55	4750
Toyota Yaris Petrol (99 – 05) T to 05	4265
TRIUMPH GT6 & Vitesse (62 0 74) up to N *	0112
Triumph Herald (59 – 71) up to K *	0010
Triumph Spitfire (62 – 81) up to X	0113
Triumph Stag (70 – 78) up to T *	0441
Triumph TR2, TR3, TR3A, TR4 & TR4A (52 – 67) up to F *	0028
Triumph TR5 & TR6 (67 – 75) up to P *	0031
Triumph TR7 (75 – 82) up to Y *	0322
VAUXHALL Astra Petrol (Oct 91 – Feb 98) J to R	1832
Vauxhall/Opel Astra & Zafira Petrol (Feb 98 – Apr 04) R to 04	3758
Vauxhall/Opel Astra & Zafira Diesel (Feb 98 – Apr 04) R to 04	3797
Vauxhall/Opel Astra Petrol (04 – 08)	4732
Vauxhall/Opel Astra Diesel (04 – 08)	4733
Vauxhall/Opel Astra Petrol & Diesel (Dec 09 – 13) 59 to 13	5578
Vauxhall/Opel Calibra (90 – 98) G to S	3502
Vauxhall Cavalier Petrol (Oct 88 0 95) F to N	1570
Vauxhall/Opel Corsa Diesel (Mar 93 – Oct 00) K to X	4087
Vauxhall Corsa Petrol (Mar 93 – 97) K to R	1985
Vauxhall/Opel Corsa Petrol (Apr 97 – Oct 00) P to X	3921
Vauxhall/Opel Corsa Petrol & Diesel (Oct 03 – Aug 06) 53 to 06	4617
Vauxhall/Opel Corsa Petrol & Diesel (Sept 06 – 10) 56 to 10	4886
Vauxhall/Opel Corsa Petrol & Diesel (00 – Aug 06) X to 06	5577
Vauxhall/Opel Frontera Petrol & Diesel (91 – Sept 98) J to S	3454
Vauxhall/Opel Insignia Petrol & Diesel (08 – 12) 08 to 61	5563
Vauxhall/Opel Meriva Petrol & Diesel (03 – May 10) 03 to 10	4893
Vauxhall/Opel Omega Petrol (94 – 99) L to T	3510
Vauxhall/Opel Vectra Petrol & Diesel (95 – Feb 99) N to S	3396

Title	Book No.
Vauxhall/Opel Vectra Petrol & Diesel (Mar 99 – May 02) T to 02	3930
Vauxhall/Opel Vectra Petrol & Diesel (June 02 – Sept 05) 02 to 55	4618
Vauxhall/Opel Vectra Petrol & Diesel (Oct 05 – Oct 08) 55 to 58	4887
Vauxhall/Opel Vivaro Diesel (01 – 11) Y to 11	5552
Vauxhall/Opel Zafira Petrol & Diesel (05 -09) 05 to 09	4792
Vauxhall/Opel 1.5, 1.6 & 1.7 litre Diesel Engine (82 – 96) up to N	1222
VW Beetle 1200 (54 – 77) up to S	0036
VW Beetle 1300 & 1500 (65 – 75) up to P	0039
VW 1302 & 1302S (70 – 72) up to L *	0110
VW Beetle 1303, 1303S & GT (72 – 75) up to P	0159
VW Beetle Petrol & Diesel (Apr 99 – 07) T to 57	3798
VW Golf & Jetta Mk 1 Petrol 1.1 & 1.3 (74 – 84) up to A	0716
VW Golf, Jetta & Scirocco Mk 1 Petrol 1.5, 1.6 & 1.8 (74 – 84) up to A	0726
VW Golf & Jetta Mk 1 Diesel (78 – 84) up to A	0451
VW Golf & Jetta Mk 2 Petrol (Mar 84 – Feb 92) A to J	1081
VW Golf & Vento Petrol & Diesel (Feb 92 – Mar 98) J to R	3097
VW Golf & Bora Petrol & Diesel (Apr 98 – 00) R to X	3727
VW Golf & Bora 4-cyl Petrol & Diesel (01 – 03) X to 53	4169
VW Golf & Jetta Petrol & Diesel (04 – 09) 53 to 09	4610
VW LT Petrol Vans & Light Trucks (76 – 87) up to E	0637
VW Passat 4-cyl Petrol & Diesel (May 88 – 96) E to P	3498
VW Passat 4-cyl Petrol & Diesel (Dec 96 – Nov 00) P to X	3917
VW Passat Petrol & Diesel (Dec 00 – May 05) X to 05	4279
VW Passat Diesel (June 05 – 10) 05 to 60	4888
VW Polo Petrol (Nov 90 – Aug 94) H to.L	3245
VW Polo Hatchback Petrol & Diesel (94 – 99) M to S	3500
VW Polo Hatchback Petrol (00 – Jan 02) V to 51	4150
VW Polo Petrol & Diesel (02 – May 05) 51 to 05	4608
VW Transporter 1600 (68 – 79) up to V	0082
VW Transporter 1700, 1800 & 2000 (72 – 79) up to V *	0226
VW Transporter (air cooled) Petrol (79 – 82) up to Y *	0638
VW Transporter (water cooled) Petrol (82 – 90) up to H	3452
VW Type 3 (63 – 73) up to M *	0084
VOLVO 120 & 130 Series (& P1800) (61 – 73) up to M *	0203
Volvo 142, 144 & 145 (66 – 74) up to N *	0129
Volvo 240 Series Petrol (74 – 93) up to K	0270
Volvo 440, 460 & 480 Petrol (87 – 97) D to P	1691
Volvo 740 & 760 Petrol (82 – 91) up to J	1258
Volvo 850 Petrol (92 – 96) J to P	3260
Volvo 940 Petrol (90 – 98) H to R	3249
Volvo S40 & V40 Petrol (96 – Mar 04) N to 04	3569
Volvo S40 & V50 Petrol & Diesel (Mar 04 – Jun 07) 04 to 07	4731
Volvo S60 Petrol & Diesel (01 – 08) X to 09	4793
Volvo S70, V70 & C70 Petrol (96 – 99) P to V	3573
Volvo V70 / S80 Petrol & Diesel (98 – 07) S to 07	4263
Volvo V70 Diesel (June 07 – 12) 07 to 61	5557
Volvo XV60 / 90 Diesel (03 – 12) 52 to 62	5630

* Classic reprint

All the products featured on this page are available through most motor accessory shops, cycle shops and book stores. Our policy of continuous updating and development means that titles are being constantly added to the range. For up-to-date information on our complete list of titles, please telephone: (UK) **+44 1963 442030** • (USA) **+1 805 498 6703** • (Sweden) **+46 18 124016** • (Australia) **+61 9763 8100**

CL 27.08.13

Preserving Our Motoring Heritage

< The Model J Duesenberg Derham Tourster. Only eight of these magnificent cars were ever built – this is the only example to be found outside the United States of America

Almost every car you've ever loved, loathed or desired is gathered under one roof at the Haynes Motor Museum. Over 300 immaculately presented cars and motorbikes represent every aspect of our motoring heritage, from elegant reminders of bygone days, such as the superb Model J Duesenberg to curiosities like the bug-eyed BMW Isetta. There are also many old friends and flames. Perhaps you remember the 1959 Ford Popular that you did your courting in? The magnificent 'Red Collection' is a spectacle of classic sports cars including AC, Alfa Romeo, Austin Healey, Ferrari, Lamborghini, Maserati, MG, Riley, Porsche and Triumph.

A Perfect Day Out

Each and every vehicle at the Haynes Motor Museum has played its part in the history and culture of Motoring. Today, they make a wonderful spectacle and a great day out for all the family. Bring the kids, bring Mum and Dad, but above all bring your camera to capture those golden memories for ever. You will also find an impressive array of motoring memorabilia, a comfortable 70 seat video cinema and one of the most extensive transport book shops in Britain. The Pit Stop Cafe serves everything from a cup of tea to wholesome, home-made meals or, if you prefer, you can enjoy the large picnic area nestled in the beautiful rural surroundings of Somerset.

> John Haynes O.B.E., Founder and Chairman of the museum at the wheel of a Haynes Light 12.

< Graham Hill's Lola Cosworth Formula 1 car next to a 1934 Riley Sports.

The Museum is situated on the A359 Yeovil to Frome road at Sparkford, just off the A303 in Somerset. It is about 40 miles south of Bristol, and 25 minutes drive from the M5 intersection at Taunton.
Open 9.30am - 5.30pm (10.00am - 4.00pm Winter) 7 days a week, *except Christmas Day, Boxing Day and New Years Day*
Special rates available for schools, coach parties and outings Charitable Trust No. 292048